10-95.

KU-510-485

N 0014331 6

Programming for
Staff Development:
Fanning the Flame

MIS 92/1

Programming for Staff Development: Fanning the Flame

Edited by
Peter Burke, Robert Heideman
and Carroll Heideman

NEWMAN COLLEGE
BARTLEY GREEN
BIRMINGHAM, 32.

CLASS	371.1
ACCESSION	93896
AUTHOR	BUR

 The Falmer Press

(A member of the Taylor & Francis Group)
London · New York · Philadelphia

UK   The Falmer Press, Rankine Road, Basingstoke, Hampshire, RG24 0PR

USA   The Falmer Press, Taylor & Francis Inc., 1900 Frost Road, Suite 101, Bristol, PA 19007

© Selection and editorial copyright P. Burke, R. Heideman and C. Heideman, 1990

All rights reserved. No part of this publication may be repro-duced, stored in a retrieval system, or transmitted in any form or by any means, electronic, mechanical, photocopying, recording or otherwise, without permission in writing from the Publisher.

First published in 1990

British Library Cataloguing in Publication Data
Fanning the flame: programming for staff development.
  1. Educational institutions. Staff development
  I. Burke, Peter II. Heideman, Robert III. Heideman, Carroll
  371.1
  ISBN 1-85000-751-9
  ISBN 1-85000-752-7 pbk

Library of Congress Cataloging-in-Publication Data
is available on request

Jacket design by Caroline Archer

Typeset in 10.5/12pt Caledonia
by Graphicraft Typesetters Ltd., Hong Kong

Printed and bound in Great Britain by Burgess Science Press, Basingstoke

Contents

Contents

Preface

Public schools are entering a time when 'business as usual' no longer applies. Cosmetic changes and platitudes will no longer suffice if our educational systems are to keep pace with national and global shifts and if we are to produce educators with the competence and background to enable them to respond to change. It is true that we have employed demographic data in educational planning for a considerable period of time. However until recently, we have made little serious attempt to integrate the often confusing and overlapping pieces of information into integrated patterns, to say nothing of shaping some kind of long-term and productive response. For example, it is only recently that educators have begun to respond to descriptions and forecasts of a deterioration of US economic competitiveness in the world; it is only recently that educators have begun to realize that the decreased quality of education in the US population has a significant correlation with that deterioration.

What can careful reading of demographic data tell us? What insights into the nature of the world and its changes can we glean, and what use will either information or insights be to us as we teach, as we train future teachers, or as we encourage professionals to renew themselves?

I believe four significant points should be made. First, we need to accept the inevitability of adjusting to exponential rates of change as opposed to arithmetic rates. The pace of change in our world has already shifted from a comfortable, understandable arithmetic rate of increase to exponential, almost headlong, rates of speed.

We have only to look at population statistics to become painfully aware of this. Various projections indicate that without checks, world population will increase from five billion now to ten billion in forty years and could double to twenty billion in eighty years. Most of the growth will be in developing countries with high poverty, illiteracy, and low gross national products. Ironically, in the so-termed developed countries — Western democracies and some Pacific Rim countries — populations are either stabilizing or declining, those populations with lower poverty, more literacy, and high gross national products. Accompanying changes are not far behind: environmental degradation, economic interdependency, burgeoning technology, political upheaval, all with their interrelated impacts on the social and psychological well-being — or lack of it — in societies around the world. In school populations we see alarming increases of at-risk students, of homeless children, of drug-users, all sub-populations with profound influences on what and how we teach.

A second and concomitant point is that given this almost dizzying rate of change in so many aspects of the world and our lives, our responses are shifting and will continue to shift from *preventive* to *adaptive*. In the future, we will not be able to prevent as much as adapt to changing circumstances.

Third, we need to understand that solutions can never be simple because problems are not; there may even be no 'solutions'. A many-layered, multi-faceted approach is our best bet, changing and adapting to fit changing situations, as long as we understand that even our most careful predictions are mere approximations of what will be.

Yet this approach must not become a grab-bag of fads and hand-outs from the latest band-wagon. Implicit in any 'solution', in any adaptation, must be the development of a coherent vision. There must be a conceptual framework that shapes, and in turn is shaped by, long-range planning, or in other terms, strategic planning.

Finally, let us not forget the so-called 'butterfly effect' (Gleick, 1987); small efforts, small changes may/can have significant and unexpected effects reaching far into the future. I believe that each of us must set our efforts to being 'butterflies'.

No one doubts that the ultimate test of any educational adaptation to change must be found in improved student behaviors and improved student achievement, but perhaps not so widely accepted is an understanding that the means to this desired end must be the changed beliefs and the redirected practices of teachers and administrators, from elementary schools through colleges and universities. Institutions that prepare teachers have their own unique responsibilities: to prepare teachers who are competent in their fields, to prepare teachers who seek growth and are trained to accommodate change. The public schools, for their much larger part, must promote vigorous professional growth of all staff through staff development programming that is well-planned, that is a permanent part of the schools' structure, that is sensitive to the needs of both the widest definable community as well as to those of the individual teachers.

For the benefit of the educators, the students, and ultimately our society, it is essential that the adaptive changes — through the vehicle of staff development — will need to involve:

- An understanding and incorporation of the concepts of participatory decision-making. If education is to be effective, indeed if governments are to be effective, the principles of participatory decision-making embodied in concepts such as site-based decision-making in schools must be implemented.

- A modification of curriculum to reflect not only current change but flexibility to anticipate future change. This needs to be an *issue-oriented* curriculum which will embody the elements of informational data-basing, strategic planning, critical thinking and problem-solving. It will be a curriculum that incorporates a significant body of concepts and information needed to promote cultural literacy. Of necessity it will need to emphasize the development of skills related to employment, that is, education for employment and effective living in a democratic society.
- Creative and informed staff development programming with the potential for enhancing staff attitudes and beliefs combined with the capacity to meet both personal and professional needs. Coordinated efforts need to be incorporated at many levels — district, regional, state and national.
- The increased use of realistic and pragmatic programs involving joint efforts of the community, schools and universities.

This text offers a range of staff development models, each incorporating these adaptations in varying degrees. All of the chapters indicate ways in which the concept of participatory decision-making, an element of teacher empowerment, is used as a means to gain acceptance and support for planned change. Each of the chapters has implicit in it the understanding that modification and improvement of curriculum must be the direct route to improved student achievement. Explicit are methods and models for developing sensitivity to professional and personal needs of staff, for modifying attitudes and beliefs, while coordinating efforts and levels of authority which may be conflicting in nature. Finally, the chapters in this book will offer suggestions and ideas to help draw groups in the larger society into the process of planning for the future, for school problems and concerns do not belong to the school alone but to the community and to the larger society beyond.

Robert Heideman
April 1990

Reference

GLEICK, JAMES (1987) *Chaos: Making a New Science*, New York, Viking.

Part 1
The Wide Perspective

1 Introduction to Staff Development

Carroll Heideman

The literature in education concerning staff development reflects divergent opinion. For instance, Ron Edmonds (1982) argued for staff development which is geared directly to the improvement of student test scores. Critics of this idea counter the argument by calling attention to the affective development of the whole child. For them staff development would include a balance of cognitive and affective objectives. Focusing on a different aspect, Thomas Guskey (1986) postulated that practices in the classroom must be changed before attitudes and beliefs will change. His concept of staff development is one of changing teacher classroom practices which in turn will change student learning outcomes leading ultimately to changes in teachers' attitudes and beliefs. Alan Tom (1986) in a response to Guskey, argued for the opposite approach to teacher attitudes. Tom argued that positive attitudes must first exist if meaningful change in practice is to occur. Staff developers, for Tom, become support personnel for teachers who play the major role in professional development.

An additional category of staff development programming, that is, meeting staff needs, has been posited by Kenneth Howey (1981) as an instrumental first step in planning. Other authors, however, question the ability of teachers to assess their own needs realistically. These critics call for highly structured planning of specific programs by staff development specialists rather than implementing a variety of unrelated program elements based on the results of needs assessments.

These ideas and others are examined critically in this book. Readers will find that varying concepts may not indeed be mutually exclusive but complementary, lending themselves to varieties of permutations and combinations, lending themselves to adaptation and modification in a multiplicity of school systems and classrooms.

Definition of Staff Development

Staff development offers a process for growth to all professional educators. It is designed to influence their knowledge, attitudes or skills thus enabling them to create educational concepts and design instructional programs to improve student learning. These programs should be based on needs identified at the local, state, national or global level — often the result of societal changes. The concept of strategic planning, involving both a scan of the internal educational environment as well as the external one, is a part of successful staff development.

Inservice education is not synonymous with staff development. Inservice education is only one part of staff development, being almost exclusively informational in nature. In contrast, staff development goes beyond the informational stage; it involves adaptations to change with the purpose of modifying instructional activities, of changing teacher attitudes and improving student achievement. Staff development is concerned with personal as well as professional and organizational needs.

The process for staff development as described in this book includes five program elements. These are (1) assessment of needs, (2) long-range and strategic planning, (3) implementation of programs, (4) evaluation of outcomes and (5) participant empowerment. These program elements serve as organizing factors for a number of the chapters in this book, particularly those that present working models (Chapters 6–11). Even if not specifically detailed, however, these program elements can nevertheless be found embedded in the thinking and writing of each of the authors; they provide an underlying structure throughout the book.

Goals of the Text

The primary and fundamental goal of this book is to bring to the attention of all educators, whether teachers or administrators, the *need* to develop and implement comprehensive, integrated staff development programs. By simply detailing the variety of possible program designs, the editors hope that readers and students, educators of all kinds, will become newly aware of their professional and organizational needs. The editors further hope that educators will newly appreciate the power and flexibility of the tool of staff development to enhance both teaching and learning.

A second goal is to provide essential *perspectives* for staff development whatever the level of involvement — local, regional, state, even national. This book provides philosophical bases for staff development, both explicit and implicit; even beyond the chapter giving a philosophical foundation to the text, each following chapter has its own philosophical underpinnings. This book also provides perpectives on both human and organizational factors, being always mindful of the needs, competencies and achievements of individual educators. Frequent references to significant research by all the authors as well as the research study described in Chapter 5 by Herzog and Koll bring to our attention the paramount importance of personal and psychological factors in any staff development programming. One can begin to glimpse the complexity of interactions between people, within organizations, and can begin to appreciate the necessity for increased sensitivity to these elements.

Third — and most practically — this book provides specific and realistic *models* for use in school settings. Educators at any level will find potent and usable programming designs, models which can be successfully applied and modified to accommodate a great variety of needs and situations.

Finally, this book offers a *vision* of what can be accomplished. Some of the many existing and successful programs are outlined and described, from designs suitable for a single teacher to those applicable to large groups of educators state-wide, from designs suitable for teachers of kindergartens to those for professors at universities. In this book there appears a panoramic and inspiring view of staff development possibilities — and realities.

Parts of the Book

Programming for Staff Development is divided into four parts of varying lengths. These include discussions of philosophical and organizational considerations, followed by a part which focuses more specifically on staff development from the perspective of the practitioners, be they administrators, teachers, or staff development personnel. The third and largest section of the book is devoted to descriptions of six different staff development models written by practicing professionals who have either developed the models, assisted in their implementation, or both. The final chapter then discusses future directions of staff development based on the need to prepare staff development practitioners.

The Wide Perspective

Chapter 2 gives a philosophical and, by implication, a psychological grounding to all the following discussions and models. St. Maurice develops a unique argument through which he explores and analyzes personal and institutional interactions in terms of a theory of rhetoric: how communication is given and received profoundly influences and in turn is influenced by the communicator, the circumstances of communication, and the purposes for communicating. Too often well-meaning staff development efforts are subverted through inattention to the significance of these interacting elements.

In Chapter 3 Reyes discusses theories of human motivation based on Maslow's ideas and modifications of his work. He continues by describing a variety of factors influencing organizations in general and schools in particular, each with important implications for the restructuring of schools. Attributes of organizations such as size, complexity and the degree of centralization, to mention a few, must be kept in mind in any programming for successful staff development.

Focusing the Perspective

The teacher-as-leader is becoming an increasingly potent concept, not only in its enhancement of the perception and reality of professionalism, but as it enables schools and administrators to tap the enormous resource of teacher knowledge and expertise. In Chapter 4 Fessler argues for teacher leadership as an imperative in school improvement initiatives through the use of key strategies and role options.

Chapter 5 is a discussion of a field-based research project. It details a study surveying teachers who were nominated as teacher of the year and principals nominated as principal of the year regarding their attitudes toward staff development; it compares their responses to those of a random sample of teachers and principals. Herzog and Koll draw implications for principals and staff developers as they program for staff development and make suggestions to teacher educators in their own critical roles.

Staff Development in Action

In this first of the 'model chapters' Parker gives a prototypic design for staff development. It is comprehensive in its attention to and development of the five program elements previously mentioned: (1) needs assessment, (2) long-range planning, (3) implementation of programs, (4) evaluation of outcomes, (5) participant empowerment. Throughout Chapter 6 there is continuing awareness of the human components of motivation, attitude, empowerment; it is indeed a human resource model.

Chapter 7 presents a model which is powerful in its flexibility and its adaptability to individual circumstances. The Career Lattice as developed by McDonnell and Christensen offers a vehicle for both the empowerment and the career enhancement of any staff member using it. It meets the needs of the mature educator seeking renewal as well as the needs of the new professional.

Every school district looks both for a long-range plan for staff development and a useful and usable model to implement that plan. Blair and Lange present such a design in Chapter 8 with a detailed and logical sequence of phases carefully structured to take into account the needs and desires of the local professionals as well as the necessity to adapt to the needs and pressures of the larger community from town or city to the world itself. It offers a 'pull-out' plan adaptable to a wide variety of school systems.

Given the fact that there are many more small districts in the nation than large urban centers, it is no surprise that small districts are continually searching for methods to broaden programs through cooperatives or consortial efforts. Letven and Klobuchar present an innovative approach to staff development: a regional center which coordinates activities of educators from school districts in two counties in collaboration with educators from the University of Wisconsin-Parkside. Chapter 9 describes a linkage between public schools and post-secondary education that is exemplary.

In today's changing world it is essential that new information and new perspectives should be infused into the teaching/learning process. In Chapter 10 Conzemius presents a statewide staff development design that uses the idea of exponential expansion, cadres of teachers training teachers who then train other teachers. This model provides both professional empowerment and the opportunity to spread significant knowledge to hundreds of classrooms.

The model presented in Chapter 11 addresses a shamefully neglected area, teaching techniques and strategies used in post-secondary institutions. A staff development plan tailored for and successfully used in the University of Wisconsin Medical School is outlined by Stone in this chapter. Without question, this model is one of very few in operation in any college or university.

Looking Ahead

There is a growing need to prepare professionally trained staff development specialists. The future of program growth and improvement relies heavily upon dynamic and reflective professionals who will assume leadership in an adaptive and flexible way. Chapter 12 stands alone in the last part of the book as Burke outlines future directions for schools and universities in staff development programming.

A Final Word

It seems appropriate to end this introductory chapter with some concluding thoughts. Permeating this book is the now-popular concept of teacher empowerment; it could be called the newest catchword in the lexicon of education. Key elements of empowerment include decentralizing decision-making, bringing it to the level closest to program impact, and delegating authority to allocate the necessary resources. Educators are given a voice in their own professional development and a rationale for their actions. However, it is of the utmost importance to recognize that for true empowerment even to exist and for that empowerment to flourish, it must be collegial. Teacher empowerment at the expense of other colleagues or at the expense of administrators will become ineffective at best and adversarial at worst. *Collegial empowerment* should be the watchword.

Equally as important must be the concept of *coherent vision*. How frequently do efforts at school improvement change from year to year; each new idea, each new technique seems helpful, useful, maybe even 'the answer'. Yet without a coherent vision of what schools and schooling should be, educators find themselves grappling with fragments of programs, with overlays of the latest notions, with confusion, with frustrating lack of integration, leading ultimately to disinterest or cynicism.

But how can a coherent vision be developed? What should be the sources for its evolution and growth? If we are convinced that our only realistic response to the world around us is adaptation to change, then we must seek out the nature of those changes in order to shape the essential coherent vision. We must involve ourselves in a constant and continuous practice of both internal and external environmental scanning. Not only must there be continuous monitoring of the internal environment of the educational organization, including budgeting, local demographics, staff needs, as well as program strengths and weaknesses, there must be continuous external environmental scanning as well. This means not only watching for and reading about important trends in educational research and innovative practices, but just as importantly it means watching for and reading about changes and developments both nationally and globally. Educators must become familiar with a wide range of trends, social, economic, political, demographic, technological. No planning for staff development, whether short-range and immediate or long-range and strategic, can begin to be adequate without a broad base of information and ideas gathered from many and varied sources.

And finally a word about *continuity*. None of our efforts, however visionary, however collegial, however well-planned, will be fruitful and effective if persistence, long-term implementation, i.e., continuity, are not woven into the fabric of school improvement through staff development. Implementation can never be finished. Staff development must be a dynamic occurrence, never a static one. It must continually adapt, continually evolve if it is to fulfill its highest potential.

References

EDMONDS, RONALD R. (1982) 'Programs of school improvement: an overview', *Educational Leadership*, December, 40, 3, pp. 4–11.

GUSKEY, THOMAS R. (1986) 'Staff development and the process of teacher change', *Educational Researcher*, May, pp. 5–12.

HOWEY, KENNETH., *et al.* (1981) *School-Focused Inservice: Descriptions and Discussions*, Reston, VA, Association of Teacher Educators.

TOM, ALAN (1986) 'Response to Guskey', *Educational Researcher*, December, pp. 12–16.

2　A Philosophical Basis for Staff Development: A Rhetorical Approach

Henry St. Maurice

In this chapter theories and methods from the field of rhetoric will be employed in taking a philosophical approach to the concepts, discourses and practices of contemporary staff development in America. The purpose of this chapter is to direct attention toward the central role played by communication in philosophical inquiry and educational practice. Many recent philosophical studies have made a so-called 'linguistic turn', giving primacy to systems of communication as complex human constructions that inform and guide knowledge and action. Communicative actions are not merely neutral transmissions of knowledge, but are frameworks that define the possibilities and limits of knowledge (Nelson *et al.*, 1987; Rorty, 1979). Philosophical approaches that emphasize communication are especially pertinent to the study of social organizations, particularly educational ones. After all, language is the stock in trade of education, whether its explicit purposes are schooling for citizenship and economic productivity or, more generally, for cultural transmission and psychological growth.

A Theory of Rhetoric

The field of rhetoric is ancient and complex; most cultures have rhetorical traditions that antedate written language. Aristotle defined rhetoric as an art 'not concerned with any special or definite class of subjects', and 'the faculty of observing in any given case the means of persuasion' (McKeon, 1941, p. 1329). The study of rhetorical forms has long been enshrined as the second of the seven liberal arts that have dominated European culture; for centuries, as Vickers (1970) says, rhetoric *was* education *was* culture ... It is difficult to grasp this equation today, but it is essential if we are to understand that when writers from Quintillian to Dante to Puttenham say that eloquence is the most important of human disciplines, they mean it literally. (p. 23)

Classical and medieval rhetoricians developed detailed technical manuals for public and private persuasion, most notably the legal or political address epitomized in Ciceronian orations and dramatically rendered in such familiar parts of the school curriculum as Marc Antony's speech in Shakespeare's *Julius Caesar* or Lincoln's 'Gettysburg Address'.

As modern science won dominance over traditional humanism, rhetoric fell into disrepute. It has since been caricatured as imprecise, deceptive, and bombastic misuse of language, epitomized in the epithet, 'mere rhetoric'. Despite occasional attempts to present principles of effective communication scientifically, rhetoricians have occupied increasingly marginal positions in academic and public circles.

During the few past decades, however, a new generation of rhetorical theorists has emerged, led by legal scholars in Europe and literary theorists in America (Bitzer and Black, 1971; Nelson *et al.*, 1987; Perelman and Olbrechts-Tyteca, 1969). In the tradition of pragmatist philosophers such as William James or John Dewey, rhetorical theorists began asserting that language as a form of action was complex and dynamic, requiring cautious interpretation, since all forms of linguistic analysis are themselves linguistic systems made up of ambiguous and symbolic parts. Language, in other words, could not be treated as a natural phenomenon subject to experimental control whose outcomes could thus be predicted, especially in its practical applications.

Yet the realm of rhetoric studies, much like those of qualitative researchers, is pragmatic, specific and detailed; according to Lloyd Bitzer (1971), 'Rhetorical works belong to the class of things which obtain their character from the circumstances of the historical context in which they occur' (Johannsen, 1971, p. 384). Persuasive discourse must be treated as a series of linked actions; as Bitzer further says, 'Rhetoric is a mode of altering reality, not by direct application of energy to objects, but the creation of discourse which changes reality through the mediation of thought and action' (ibid.).

One of the most influential rhetorical scholars of this century is Kenneth Burke, who has been called 'an American sage' because of his varied contributions to literature, social theory, and philosophy. In the shadow of World War II, Burke (1945/69) produced a multi-volume work seeking to understand the role of language in creating and avoiding disastrous conflicts. One of the most famous parts of this work is his 'dramatist' conception of human motives, interrelated parts functioning in terms of a dramatic stage. His 'pentad' of motives was first stated as follows:

> In a rounded statement about motives, you must have some word that names the *act* (names what took place in thought and deed), and another that names the *scene* (the background of the act, the situation in which it occurred); also you must indicate what person or kind of person (*agent*) performed the act, what means or instruments he used (*agency*), and the *purpose*. (p. xv)

In this scheme, both purposeful human actions and their analysis are explicitly interrelated. Human communications cannot be abstracted into variables or general rules, since each 'rounded statement' must show the linkages among varied participants and their circumstances. A photograph of a stage play cannot describe the entire plot, nor can relations among the characters be abstracted without some accompanying sense of the entire narrative. And, most importantly, relations among characters must be examined in terms of the audience's reactions if the purposes of the entire drama are to be investigated.

To a rhetorician such as Burke, the study of human actions therefore is the study of relations among words and deeds, speakers and respondents. For example, a Burkean analysis of school desegregation policies and effects would emphasize the power of modern news media to make local controversies into national issues; it would contrast the public statements and non-violent strategies of African-American organizers with the statements and strategies of the adherents of segregation. The struggle for civil rights in the American South was an intricate web joining many actors and means of action into relations with their audiences both immediate and global. Today's public statements of social change through education are no less complex and require especially subtle and wide-ranging analyses.

In approaching a philosophical basis for planning staff development in educational institutions, the major theoretical framework will be built upon three of Burke's pentad of motives. The entire pentad deserves full attention which cannot be given here; actually, Burke is still in the process of modifying his theories, having recently announced that his famous scheme should now have a sixth part, that of 'attitude', making a hexad (Simons and Melia, 1989). Most rhetorical traditions are hospitable to both emending and amending works of communication, for linguistic acts are demonstrably neither precise nor predictable. Emending Burke's scheme for the sake of conciseness is therefore squarely in Burke's own theoretical tradition. As Burke (1950/69) says, a theory of rhetoric

> . . . must lead through the scramble, the Wrangle of the Market Place, the flurries and flare-ups of the Human Barnyard, the Give

and Take, the wavering line of counterpressure, the logomachy, the onus of ownership, the Wars of Nerves, the War. . . . Rhetoric is concerned with the state of Babel after the Fall. (p. 23)

Education, which takes place within loosely-coupled social systems using open-ended communications, is a manifestly hospitable domain for Burkean rhetoric.

In brief, therefore, recent rhetorical theories stress the practical circumstances under which language is produced, and assess the effectiveness of language by the strength and nature of its impact upon those settings, not according to *a priori* general principles.

Staff Development — A Rhetorical Review

Programs for continuing teacher education following licensure and employment have been known by such names as 'inservice training', 'professional development', or 'staff development'. These terms encompass a wide range of possible activities, depending on the purposes, agents, and structures involved. During the past half-century, staff development activities have increasingly been linked to school change, and thereby to social change. Historical studies of staff development in the United States indicate that progressive-era reforms supplanted disparate local teacher institutes with regional and national in-service initiatives following increased public attention focused by such work as the privately-sponsored journalism of Joseph Rice (1893). Further, staff development was placed in national frames of reference in large research projects sponsored by the US Office of Education (Howey and Vaughn, 1983, pp. 92–4. See also Richey, 1957; Tyack and Hansot, 1982).

Accompanying the growth of mass schooling, competing interest groups have sought to define the shape and content of school curricula and instructional practices. Policies and practices for staff development, along with those of teacher education in general, have taken shape amid controversy and compromise, accommodation and resistance (Burke and Heideman, 1985; Popkewitz, 1987). In concert with the growing authority of secular scientific expertise located in research centers and universities, staff development became increasingly professionalized and technical, encountering more tensions than have been admitted in the theories and practices of scientific progressivism (Clark and Marker, 1975; Ducharme, 1985; Lanier and Little, 1986; Schneider, 1987; Yarger, 1987). Under the reigning philosophy of empiricism, teacher educators during this period assigned essential importance to scientific pursuits in individual and social life. This philosophical approach implicitly recognized divisions even as teacher educators explicitly assured that science could homogenize the interests of administrators, teachers, and students; as David Snedden (1921) claimed,

> Education, like medicine and the other ['applied'] fields ... is also an ancient area of organized practical effort. It, too, can and should draw upon the sciences for guidance especially upon psychology for method and sociology for objectives, but also upon biology and physiology, architecture and statistics, for help in particular needs. (p. 36)

Despite enthusiastic leadership by administrators and policymakers like Snedden, after nearly eight decades of scientific guidance for staff development it is still portrayed by many of its consumers as 'ineffective and a waste of time' (McLaughlin and Marsh, 1978, p. 70), and also by some reseachers as activities whose 'relatively private, eclectic and diffuse character ... thwarts attempts to understand' its contributions and effects (Lanier and Little, 1986, p. 548). Aspects of staff development are frequently described as conflictual: e.g., 'theory' versus 'practice', government versus district, universities versus schools, administrators versus teachers (Griffin and Rehage, 1983; Feiman-Nemser and Floden, 1986; Howey, Matthes and Zimpher, 1986; Romberg and Price, 1983).

These apparent dichotomies, like 'qualitative' versus 'quantitative', exemplify an ancient rhetorical device: the line of argument defined by Aristotle as 'refutative, by the conjunction of incompatible propositions' (McKeon, 1941, p. 1419). For persuasive purposes, conjoined propositions are placed in opposition, and deciding whether such oppositions are wholly or partly artificial is the work of rhetorical analysis. However it is assumed here that, although divisions among aspects of staff development are genuinely experienced by educators, these tensions may not be evidence of permanent and universal conditions.

Tensions and divisions in staff development take many forms. In the following sections, three areas of continuing controversy will be examined. To use terms from Burke's 'pentad of motives', they are: *scene*, i.e., the circumstances, especially as reflected in tensions among researchers and practitioners, but also involving sources of authority within schools; *agent*, i.e., the actors involved, be they individual teachers, formal groups or informal ones; and *purpose*, or the explicit and implicit goals. The three areas will serve to organize a large and diverse body of research literature from which specific examples will be presented, portraying complex relations among interest groups in staff development activities, including the following: federal, state and local statutory educational agencies, academic researchers, educational administrators, individual teachers, both official and unofficial professional organizations, community groups, parent groups, and, by no means least, students. As a rhetorical study of the philosophical bases of staff development, this chapter differentiates the various speakers, audiences, and settings that simultaneously interact in multiple combinations.

Scene

Staff Development on a Split-Level Stage

Staff development activities take place in various settings, ranging from informal teachers' working groups, to mandated school- and district-wide workshops, as well as to course-work at non-school sites such as colleges, universities or proprietary educational organizations. Scholarly literature on staff development is voluminous, including historical studies of the teachers' institutes of the nineteenth and early twentieth centuries (e.g., Antczak, 1985; Richey, 1957; Mattingly, 1975), and descriptions of recent staff development programs in reports of all kinds, from quantitative tabulations to narrative social histories (e.g., McLaughlin and Marsh, 1978; Cuban, 1984). Studies analyzing the discourse of teachers and administrators in staff development are not frequent, but are available in literature on specific implementations such as clinical supervision, action research, teachers' centers, or writing projects (e.g., Carr and Kemmis, 1986; Elliott, 1976; Gomez, 1987; Gray, n.d.; Hovey, 1986; Smyth, 1989; Zigarmi, 1979).

From this heterogeneous literature emerges a composite image of current staff development programs that portrays the interests of teachers, parents, and students ('consumers' of professional knowledge) subordinated to the interests of agencies, researchers and administrators ('producers'). The scene for staff development has been repeatedly described as an incoherent one, uneasily nestled among home, school and workplace communities, in which teachers are disconnected from each other and distant from the priorities of administrators and policymakers (Feiman-Nemser, 1983; Fenstermacher and Berliner, 1985; Joyce *et al.*, 1987; McCloskey *et al.*, 1987; Lanier and Little, 1986; Lortie, 1975; Smylie, 1988; Waller, 1932).

Beginning with widely-heralded work by John Dewey in the University of Chicago Laboratory School at the turn of the century, and continuing through the work of such leaders as Snedden and William Kilpatrick at Teachers College, and Franklin Bobbitt at the University of Chicago, staff development has been conceptualized as divided between 'theory', or the work of university-based teacher educators, and 'practice', or the work of school-based administrators and teachers (Dewey, 1904; Snedden, 1921; Kilpatrick, 1918; Bobbitt, 1918). Although theoretical formulations and practical norms abound within and among both groups of educators, the theory-practice divisions appear to be deep and durable, even insurmountable, to many scholars. For instance, Lieberman and

Miller (1984a) say that, 'Between two worlds there is a chasm! ... School improvement studies alert us to the enormous gap between those who study schools and those who do the work of schools' (p. 87). Lawrence Cremin (1988) traces these distinguishing categories of discourse to a distinct hierarchy separating teacher education from the preparation of administrators and researchers (p. 498).

Tensions between these two interests are apparently compounded by patterns of authority at the educational workplace, as many researchers point out (Blumberg, 1980; Feiman-Nemser, 1983; Lortie, 1975; Mattingly, 1987; Metz, 1978; Sarason, 1982; Tyack and Hansot, 1982). As Douglas Mitchell and Charles Kerchner (1983) state, school labor-management relations more resemble industrial ones than they do those associated with professions, crafts or arts:

> Most school districts now contain two distinct social organizations — each competing for the loyalty and cooperation of teachers. The administrative organization, led by the superintendent, wants teachers to adopt district goals as their own and to pursue those goals diligently. The teacher organization, led by the union president or staff executive, needs teachers to be willing to challenge the legitimacy of management directives and perhaps even withdraw services if a suitable accommodation to their demands is not forthcoming. (p. 225)

Indeed, hierarchical divisions seem to be implicit in most descriptions of staff development with principals assigned predominance over teachers; as Madeline Hunter (1984) puts it,

> Even though someone else may do inservice or work with teachers in classrooms, unless that person is consistently available when needed, a request for help as well as the validation of subsequent effective performance must be met by the principal. ... The principal controls the 'reward' system of the school. Correctly or incorrectly, the principal is perceived as the dispenser of 'good' assignments, supplies, yard duty, committee responsibilities, students, classes, and, most importantly, 'the boss's approval'.

In this passage, Hunter concedes that hierarchical relations defined by a cult of efficiency frame relations among teachers, administrators and policymakers (see Apple, 1987, Chapter 3; Popkewitz, 1987). As Hunter indicates in general, most staff development programs overtly address administrators' needs, accepting as given longstanding race, class and gender inequalities in workplaces.

As an indication of the long-established nature of hierarchical relations, note the deployment of class and gender distinctions as well as industrial and military metaphors in the seventy-year-old passage by Snedden (1921) arguing for differentiated preparation for teachers and administrators:

> Can we require somehow that educators will go to sociology chiefly for those contributions that can actually assist them in solving problems peculiar to education? The idealist, of course, holds that all problems belong to education; but that is not a view that can prevail with the man who effectively plans or executes a day's work. Surely we shall waste valuable time and effort if we repeat for all our pedagogical builders the educational mistakes made in medicine, engineering, and other similar areas where even the prospective soldier of average ability has been forced to attempt to build the same foundation as the man quite certainly destined to be a general or field marshal.
>
> And what shall we say to the study of educational sociology by those thousands of bright, wholesome girls, who throng the classrooms of normal schools, and who will give from three to six years to the vocation of teaching ere they embark on the long voyage of matrimony and homemaking? Must they, too, be expected to build on broad foundations? Not least, certainly, among the problems confronting educators, is that of determining the desirable and practicable objectives of vocational training for the various teaching callings. Here, certainly, we have need of all the leadership the professor of pedagogy can give us. (pp. 36–37)

By invoking supposedly inborn status distinctions between 'soldiers' and 'generals' Snedden implies that leadership is defined by specific class levels, and ascribes to their members exclusive franchises to manage schools efficiently as well as military campaigns, factories, or construction projects. The scene for contemporary staff development inherits a continuing struggle between this 'practical' elite of leaders and theorists, and those 'idealist' intellectuals, teachers, and community members who have sought to define education in different terms.

Facing the Divided Scene

A long shelf of works has been published by researchers and practitioners claiming to explain, explicate, or unify staff development's divided scene (e.g., Gage, 1963; Griffin and Rehage, 1983; Shulman and Sykes, 1983; Travers, 1973; Wittrock, 1986). Gary Griffin (1983), introducing a contemporary collection of studies on staff development, refers to an 'ideological tension' between forces favoring school change and forces preferring stability (p. 5). In the same volume, Judith Lanier (1983) describes 'tragic tension' in a school-university collaboration for staff development (p. 150). Numerous researchers have proposed to investigate such tensions: calling for improved relations among universities and schools, Kenneth Howey and Joseph Vaughn (1983) lay blame on both parties as they conclude, 'Schools presently have limited expertise [in investigating and understanding staff development], while institutions of higher education, especially those with more capacity for research and development, are nonetheless known to be less than prodigious in their production of knowledge' (p. 112). Bruce Joyce and associates (1987) assert that the stability of teachers' practices can be changed only upon the impetus of research-based staff development: 'Most teachers use a narrow range of practices; ... they expand that repertoire only when they are provided substantial and carefully designed training' (p. 22).

One teacher educator who claims to 'translate theory into practice', Madeline Hunter (1984), assures educators that a research-based body of knowledge will ensure a 'common language' if supervisors and teachers devote themselves to acquiring and mastering its principles. By frequently using linguistic metaphors instead of physical ones preferred by such advocates as Spencer and Snedden, Hunter seems to grant importance to communicative interactions among educators. Studies of Hunter's staff development programs are still inconclusive (Slavin, 1987; Stallings *et al.*, 1986), but reports of teachers' testimonies to heightened efficacy and administrators' evaluations of improved instruction could imply that these results may be side-effects of her persuasiveness in motivating community action as well as the direct effects of practices enacting theories of teaching and learning.

In describing an improved setting for staff development, Griffin (1983) takes a position calling for systematic unification of theory and practice, advocating the application of what he calls 'funded knowledge' to staff development programs, interactive application with 'craft knowledge, perceptions of participants, and the history, policies, and practices of the organization' (p. 249). Such a process is described in a study of school change through staff development Griffin conducted with Susan Barnes (1984). Acting as project directors and researchers, they say that an attempt was made to develop a 'link between research findings and the potential users of those findings' (p. 103). After piloting a classic quasi-experimental design with ten teachers and administrators, this study claimed eventual application to over 3,000 educators. The program established a quantitatively-based operational definition: 'The effective teacher is the teacher whose classes regularly score higher on standardized achievement tests than do classes of other teachers after entering differences among the classes are statistically controlled' (p. 106). A treatment of intensive workshops prior to the opening of school was given to one group of teachers and administrators. Then, using observation measures, the researchers found that treatment-group staff-developers and teachers showed significant changes in behavior, although student groups did not. The conclusions of this report employ an exclusively quantitative logic evidently aimed at convincing administrators foremost: claiming that the study was a 'powerful demonstration of the appeal for school people of research knowledge when it is conceptually and practically related to doing the business of schools', and asserting that 'the commonsense approach to doing leadership and doing teaching was compelling to district officials'. Financial cost-effectiveness was also said to be 'undoubtedly attractive' (p. 120). Division between theory and practice was said to be closed through judicious application of theory and careful monitoring of practice.

According to its own assumptions, this program did show immediate success, aiming quantitative data at a receptive audience. Yet, as in most such studies, the daily lives of teachers and students may have been less successfully affected in the long term, as student data seem to suggest. Such shortcomings may be attributable to the researchers' communicative strategy appealing as it does to the needs and interests of administrators and staff developers.

Their approach — or any approach — could not control all 'extraneous variables' convincingly for all parties to the project, verifying a truism of rhetoric that no speaker can persuade all audiences at all times. In rhetoric, even the most logically-expressed practical reason cannot be proven universal truth: any vocabulary is an attempt to make a *reflection* of reality, but may only be a *selection* of reality, as Burke (1945/69) puts it, and 'any selection of reality must, in certain circumstances, function as a *deflection* of reality' (p. 59).

To minimize deflections and reductions of 'reality' in studying staff development in context, multi-pronged approaches are often recommended. For example, in the previous study, entirely different measures of classroom performance might have 'triangulated' the findings. Judith Warren Little (1988) calls for such an approach in reporting on a recent study of California's local initiatives for school reform through staff development. This report noted that, of over 800 activities surveyed, 'the consequences [were] almost never tested at the classroom level. Program evaluations are dominated by participation rates and other process measures; summative measures of classroom effectiveness are fewer and methodologically weaker' (p. 6). Numerous researchers have joined Little in calling for multi-dimensional research strategies incorporating diverse methodologies with divergent conceptions of methodological strength (Hopkins and Wideen, 1984, p. 19; Mathison, 1988; McLaughlin, 1987, p. 177; Sander and Wiggins, 1985).

Such strategies, however, are far from being risk-free; in addition to complexities that might further divide researchers from teachers, multiple methods are susceptible to accusations of methodological and political relativism: apparently unable to choose a 'one best' method, researchers and policymakers would seem to be trying them all. Adding different kinds of researchers to the scene will not bridge longstanding gaps between them and practitioners, any more than adding different kinds of producers reassures already estranged consumers.

The dangers of pluralism are commonly debated in the pragmatist philosophical tradition. The stakes in school reform are high; should programs fail, demoralized teachers and alienated students would encounter serious social problems in both short and long terms. The congruence of words calling for reform and consequent actions presupposes shared convictions that conclusions are morally right and that their consequences are desirable.

Linkages by Rhetoric

A rhetorical approach is particularly suited for bridging a scene as divided as that of contemporary educational staff development. From the pragmatist philosophical perspective, rhetorical analyses of communication provide links among the dialects of theory and practice, administration and instruction. As Stephen Toulmim (1988) says, rhetoric consists of 'arguments that apply theoretical ideas to practical situations, or which seek to criticize those theories, judging their consequences and so becoming "practical"' (p. 348).

Whether qualitative or quantitative, the discourses of research and implementation through staff development must take into account intricate relations among speakers and audiences, or, put more simply, how scenes are set. Little (1984) concludes a report on staff development for educational change entitled 'seductive images and organizational realities', with a speculation that, 'there's no such thing as an "ineffective" or neutral piece of staff development. Every exposure to staff development will either build commitment to professional improvement or will erode that commitment' (p. 99). Rhetorical analyses of 'seductive' imagery and value-laden practices provide researchers, practitioners, administrators and others involved in the educational enterprise methods for understanding how commitment is built. As research and implementation strategies grow more complex, attention to communicative interactions becomes more important.

Studies of staff development that focus on teachers' values, practices, and communicative transactions have emerged from 'action research' projects in America, Australia and Britain (Carr and Kemmis, 1986; Corey, 1957; Elliott, 1976). Jean Rudduck and David Hopkins (1985) distinguish this set of approaches as follows:

Much educational research, because of its allegiance to the psycho-statistical paradigm, expresses its findings as generalizations that cannot claim to offer guidance for action in particular settings. More supportive of teacher practice is research that either issues in hypotheses that can be tested in classrooms or that illuminates particular cases that can be judged against experience. (p. 7)

Numerous examples of such studies have produced abundant analyses of teacher discourse during staff development activities (Brennan and Noffke, 1988; Oja and Pine, 1988). In one instance, Patricia Wood (1988) gives a first-person account of two teachers testing ways to incorporate cooperative learning into their classroom. In a first-person narrative Wood recounts how she and a student teacher took a 'teacher-centered approach to staff development', asserting that, 'The teacher is viewed as an experienced professional fully capable of identifying, researching and finding new solutions for the improvement of her own practice' (p. 13). The scenic scope of this and similar studies is inscribed within particular classrooms in specific communities, as small groups of teachers collaborate in conceptualizing, planning, implementing, and evaluating programs for change through staff development.

Scope or circumference is a crucial aspect of scene in Burke's grammar of human actions (1945/69). It connotes a realm of authority, as, for a philosophical example,

If we locate the human agent and his act in terms of a scene whose orbit is broad enough to include the concept of a supernatural creator, we get a different kind of definition than if our definition were confined to a narrower circumstance that eliminated 'supernatural' as a motivating element in the scene, and did not permit the scenic scope to extend beyond the outer limits of 'nature'. (p. 77)

The scope of district-wide staff development planning and administration for hundreds or even thousands of teachers encompasses different modes of discourse, reason, theory and action from that of three or four teachers discussing and implementing specific changes in their practices. In their relations, the two scopes may be complementary, as one circle nests in another, or oppositional, as a large peg cannot be forced into a small hole. In these latter conflicts, relative broadness or narrowness of scope might have moral implications: one version has to be 'right'. In the former instances of congruence, moral implications can be both incorporated and altered: it would be possible that, as Burke (1945/69) points out, 'circumferences are felt to be, not so much wider or narrower than one another, as merely *different* (p. 87).

The scene for staff development, therefore, might include both broad-scale initiatives, such as mandates requiring racial desegregation or mainstreaming students with disabilities, and narrow-scale activities, such as a single-site implementation of cooperative learning methods or multicultural curricula. As plentiful evidence shows, conflicts are likely within both circumferences but they may not be inevitable. Within different scopes, ways that authority is deployed and managed seem to be a crucial consideration. Tensions between broad and narrow scope, like those between theory and practice, are incorporated in the strategies that researchers, administrators and teachers deploy in communicating their purposes.

The Primacy of Communication

To summarize aspects of the scene for staff development, inservice teacher education activities have usually been set among contention and division among producers and consumers, within both broad and narrow scopes. It seems that multi-dimensional approaches are called for in research, planning and practice in this field and that staff developers, be they researchers, administrators, or teachers, should not hope for comprehensive syntheses, but remain prepared to address multiple, divided audiences. However, pluralistic strategies will only foster division unless direct attention is paid to the means of communication by which one faction attempts to communicate with others. *The primacy of communication is derived from its power to bridge divisions without denying their pervasiveness or assuming that they can be readily reunified.*

Research and implementation strategies in staff development pay little or tangential attention to the assumptions and practices of communication. More commonly, specific audiences are addressed by staff developers: the research community, policymakers, administrators, teacher organizations or individual colleagues. In order to encompass the broad and divided scene, the various dialects in use upon it must be addressed. To do so, the various kinds of agents who occupy the field of staff development will be considered in the following sections.

Agent

Agent/Scene Relations

In the foregoing section, a scene for staff development has been set, described as involving contentions among researchers, administrators, and practitioners. Modern disciplined study of organizations founded upon notions of 'objective' knowledge have typically dwelt upon ideas of structures and the functions, factors and variables that are said to affect them. In contrast, many contemporary researchers have approached educational organizations as more problematic mixtures of social structure and individual agency. Such studies aim at investigating, as Kenneth Zeichner (1986) says, relationships between 'individual intent and institutional constraint' (p. 31). Numerous studies of teacher education have been based on organizational theories arguing that structuralist and functionalist perspectives minimize the roles of individual agents within structures (Gitlin, 1983; Hursh, 1988; Smyth, 1989; Tabachnick and Zeichner, 1985; Zeichner and Liston, 1987). Many such studies derive from the British 'New Sociology of Education' movement, which sought to analyze schooling as both macro- and micro-social systems under the assumption, as Ann and Harold Berlak (1981) say, 'that schooling activity cannot be explained, understood, or adequately described without taking into account the subjective experiences of teachers *and* the social, cultural and political forces and structures that are omnipresent in all social situations' (p. 24).

Many recent studies have adduced contradictions in teachers' and students' reactions to reform implementation, citing them as evidence of both resistance to change and persistence of norms at the micro-social level (e.g., Grant and Sleeter, 1986; Liston and Zeichner, 1988). For example, Linda McNeil (1986) has contributed an ethnographic study of curriculum change, arguing that, 'There has been no systematic attempt to trace external pressures on schools through the internal mechanisms by which those pressures have reached students' (p. 14).

In speaking of 'pressures, mechanisms, or linkages', however, such work clearly circumscribes individual agents within scenic boundaries. This is probably due in part to vague distinctions between concepts of 'individual' and 'structure'. Even as they are overdue and necessary, investigations of relations among concepts of structure and agency (in Burke's terms, *scene* and *agent*) can be like walking through halls of mirrors: orienting the argument involves distinguishing overlapping images. In encounters among researchers, staff developers, and teachers, all parties can be construed as individual agents who simultaneously represent structural constraints to each other. Humans as agents construct and maintain the structures that also can be said to constrain them, just as the structures of our languages both permit and restrict discussion of what languages are — or are not. As Giddens (1987) says, 'structure is not as such external to human action, and is not identified solely with constraint. Structure is both the medium and the outcome of the human activities which it recursively organizes' (p. 61).

Put in terms of staff development, the problems of structure and agency would entail asking whether teachers change their instructional practices in order to change the way schools prepare students, or whether schools change their institutional norms in order to change the way teachers and students interact. So expressed, the issue lies within the realm of rhetoric: if either agent or scene can be medium or outcome, then the process of recognizing and naming particular occurrences in practical affairs assumes central importance. It is in this sense that Burke (1945/69) says that science is possible only if we equate agent and scene:

> One usually thinks of a medium as something in which an agent acts (scene) or something which an agent uses (agency). But what if we equated it with *the very nature of agent itself*? ... we can say that people interpret natural sequences in terms of cause and effect not because of something in the natural scene requiring this interpretation, but *because they are the sort of agents that see things in terms of necessary relations.* (p. 187)

Social relations in schooling, from this perspective, can be expressed either as scene or agent, or both, depending on speakers, circumstances, and audiences making the assertions warrantable. Schools therefore can be largely defined in terms of teachers' roles and actions, and, conversely, teachers' status and responsibilities can be defined by schools. These 'ecological' relations grow additionally complex in staff development as teachers take students' roles, and in reform implementation, as schools act — and are acted upon — like communities under external mandates.

Change Agents

Differing conceptions of agents in staff development emerge in discussions of 'teacher change'. Identifying the individual teacher as the agent of staff development for reform implementation, numerous publications call for focusing staff development on individual teachers' 'stages' of personal or professional growth (e.g., Burke, Fessler and Christensen, 1984; Oja and Pine, 1988; Sprinthall and Thies-Sprinthall, 1983).[1] Implicit in these studies is an assumption that the processes of identifying, categorizing and eventually altering individual teachers' beliefs and practices should produce altered school norms and policies. Calling for such a sequence, Phillip Schlechty and Betty Lou Whitford (1983) contrast 'establishing' and 'maintenance' staff development programs which give priority to institutions as agents, to 'enhancement' programs, which focus on individuals as agents. aiming to 'enhance performance capacities, refine existing skills, and expand existing knowledge' (p. 77).

Studies advocating individual teachers as high-priority agents for school change have been rebutted by works arguing that 'pitfalls of experience' await individual teachers prepared to act as change agents (Feiman-Nemser and Buchmann, 1985). For example, Mark Smylie (1988), surveying over fifty teachers before, during, and after a time-management workshop, concluded that teachers voluntarily adopting new methods were evidently influenced by external factors such as class composition and size as much as by personal preference for the topics presented: 'Teacher change seems rooted in individual perceptions of self as influenced by experiences within classrooms and with teaching colleagues' (p. 24). Similarly, Thomas Guskey (1986) argues that the 'dynamics of the teacher change process' seems more tied to individuals' experiences within immediate school contexts rather than to their personal beliefs: 'significant change in teachers' beliefs and attitudes is likely to take place only after changes in student learning outcomes are evidenced' (p. 7).

From another perspective, the conundrum of agency in teacher education has been examined by a group of teacher educators advocating 'inquiry-oriented' policies (Greene, 1987; Giroux and McLaren, 1986; Tom, 1985; Zeichner, 1983; Zeichner and Liston, 1987). Calling for teacher 'empowerment' or for 'reflective' teaching, these policies would seek, in Carl Glickman's (1984–5) words, to 'reshape the work environment of teachers into one that is conducive to reflective and collective dialogue among staff members who are given power to act upon their decisions' (p. 40). These proposals would entail rebuilding a setting riven long and deep by power struggles among researchers, policymakers, and practitioners. Inquiry-oriented approaches make inferences that teachers as agents, once empowered, would develop conceptions of 'reflective and collective dialogue' thus avoiding what has been called 'a false rubric of inquiry'. They would transform 'the skepticism and tentativeness of inquiry' into practices that 'demonstrate the benevolence of ongoing student-teacher relationships and the legitimacy of professionals as definers of reality' (Popkewitz, Tabachnick and Wehlage, 1982, p. 16). Like stages-of-change theories of teacher education, inquiry-oriented approaches must demonstrate how to avoid both pitfalls of personal experience and quagmires of institutional persistence.

Another important distinction among agents in staff development programs is made between formal ones (i.e., groups or individuals identified with prior organizational titles or responsibilities such as departments or specialities), and informal ones (i.e., groups or individuals without previously-assigned titles or roles). In his review of staff development for school improvement, Zeichner (1985) notes that most formal programs consist of 'one-shot activities scattered over a wide range of topics, focused on the development of individual staff and not school improvement, and containing relatively little follow-through in the form of classroom assistance and observation' (pp. 242–4).

Many researchers, here again those associated with movements for action research, teacher centers, or writing projects, claim that informal programs more successfully develop collegiality and engagement among teachers and administrators (e.g., Carr and Kemmis, 1986; Day, 1985;

Devaney, 1979; Holly, 1983; Little, 1984; Schwartz, 1984; Yonemura, 1982). For example, Barbara McEvoy (1985) reports on a comprehensive set of data describing principals' communicative interactions as follows:

> By examining the fleeting conversational exchanges of these principals and teachers, by listening to what teachers say about the influence of these exchanges, by observing the results of those interchanges as evidenced in classroom happenings, we can see that the 'fragmented' nature of the principal's interactions gains new importance. (p. 21)

Similar importance is given to informal communicative interchanges in staff development led by Frederick Erickson and Douglas Campbell (1986). They claim that their project is 'nonintervening in spirit but hopefully will have an intervening effect', evoking a divided image combining traditional theoretical agents' quest for effects, and contemporary qualitative researchers' pose of studied disinterest. Beginning with three teachers and seven researchers, this project assumed that,

> Teachers know a great deal about teaching, and when given time to reflect on their practice, they can bring about positive change in their classrooms and in their districts. Teachers can be empowered by a staff development program that begins at the teacher level rather than at the administrator level. (p. 3)

Like Wood's action research project on cooperative learning described above, this project is centered on small-scope teacher interactions, and goes further in stating that such interactions can make teachers into agents of institutional change. Such claims call for a brief exploration of how idealistic philosophies inform concepts of agent espoused by researchers, policymakers, administrators, and teachers in staff development for implementing reform. Idealism in this context means primacy of ideas and concepts over the concrete. It does not necessarily imply moral value.

The 'Knower' as Agent

To paraphrase Snedden's statement quoted above, some theorists think that education can do everything: change individuals, and so change cultures or societies. Idealistic notions, according to Burke, are crucial features in conceptualizing what an agent is; 'self', 'subject', 'consciousness', 'sensibility', 'innovation' indicate primacy of reason or spirit invested in individuals or in groups. To assign central importance to agent is to give first priority to the knowing self (or selves). In short, questions of scene are about whether something works within the particular circumstances, but questions of agent are about who has knowledge. As Burke (1945/69) states,

> Diversity and unequal rates of change require as social corrective the unifying function of ideas and ideals 'creatively', at odds with conditions as they look when seen without the idealistic exaltation. And a more technical incentive to idealism derives from the fact that technology, as applied science, invites us to put the major stress upon knowledge. And the problem of knowledge is an epistemological problem, a psychologistic emphasis that falls directly under the head of *agent*. (p. 176)

Rhetorical strategies based on agent as a locus of theoretical knowledge appear in 'stage' approaches or 'inquiry' approaches to staff development, as well as in 'teacher-centered' or 'school-centered' approaches to educational change. All these otherwise dissimilar concepts and settings emphasize teachers as agents, individuals or groups pursuing knowledge about teaching. These approaches to staff development therefore incorporate in their rhetoric concepts of inquiry and growth derived from idealistic social and psychological theories.

For example, Gary Fenstermacher and David Berliner (1985) emphasize idealist conceptions of knowledge in their proposed model for planning and evaluating staff development. The model consists of: '(1) a definition; (2) a mapping sequence; (3) a description of participant roles; and (4) an evaluation perspective'. They say that their definition 'limits the range of staff development to those specific activities that enhance knowledge, skills, and understanding in ways that lead to changes in thought and action' (p. 283). Likewise, their proposed map, roles and evaluation schemes are articulated in terms that feature agents empowered to overcome structural constraints past and present.

This model is strikingly theoretical in its self-sufficiency: it does not refer to the prior conditions in school settings; neither do criteria and procedures for evidence refer to institutional constraints. In its extreme application, such a proposal could completely approve an ill-fated staff development plan, by implication blaming practitioners for failure, since success appears to be assured beforehand by research findings and the implementation plan.

Implementation plans undertaken by American educational reformers in recent decades have been permeated with theories emphasizing the importance of agents. Most educational reform programs of the 1960s and

1970s included strongly teacher-oriented staff development components. In reviewing some of these programs, Thomas Timar and David Kirp (1987) conclude,

> The Great Society reforms, as well as the romantic revival of the individual ... made the individual the focus of public policy.... Public institutions became the agents of this reform agenda. At the same time, public institutions, including the schools, were regarded by many reformers with a good deal of suspicion. Institutions were seen (and certainly not without some justification) to represent vested interests that were opposed to change, particularly change that promised a redistribution of public benefits. Strong mistrust of institutions and a romantic faith in the capacity of the individual on the other, contributed to the fragmentation that characterizes schools today. (p. 329)

Failed reforms not only result in fragmentation, but also and more crucially in broken lines of communication among fragments. Not only do teachers fail to 'add to their knowledge base', but there is no agreement on a uniform kind of knowledge with which to build it (Popkewitz, Tabachnick and Wehlage, 1982, Chapter 7; Lilly, 1986; Valli and Tom, 1988).

Summary

During the past decade, federal policies for educational reform have changed from massively-funded mandates to hortatory reports, but conflicts have not diminished among concepts of autonomous agents, whether individuals, groups or institutions, and concepts of resistant structures. As previously mentioned, the circumstances for reform through staff development are already divided among contesting interest groups. Further it must be added that concepts of teachers or schools as agents for change appear to have problematically theoretical tendencies.

To counter those tendencies, approaches based on the study of rhetoric provide practical strategies for defining the terms of communication and improving their delivery. A rhetoric such as Burke's can be of help in understanding the force of symbols used to promote educational reform programs. In particular, the image of an agent empowered to change a structure is a recurrent motif in contemporary arts and sciences, and rhetoric is a tool for asking whether this image in fact suits the needs of the people who inhabit as complex a social system as a school. In the next section, it will be further supposed that statements of purposes for staff development, when their rhetorical strategies are analyzed, are equally forceful and complex.

Purpose

Unity Through Purpose

To this point, current research on staff development has been discussed in terms of two parts of Burke's pentad of motives. The aim of this discussion has been to show that rhetorical analysis can portray the philosophical bases of discourse, reason, theory and action not only in research on organizations in general but also in staff development in particular. This section explicates *purpose*, a vital part of Burke's theory of dramatism. In this scheme, purpose features those motives associated with mysticism, which Burke (1945/69) defines as 'unity with some cosmic or universal purpose' (p. 288). In other words, purposes encompass agents and scenes, describing directions toward which the entire drama moves and would be eventually unified.[2]

In classic and medieval rhetoric, purposes intimated transcendental unification of human motives with divine ends. Modern purposes, on the other hand, set out to unify human purposes with ends in empirical realms; human motives are linked to belief in objective, scientific 'reality' based on theories about the natural world, such as Darwinian evolution or Einsteinian relativity. According to Burke, the scientific tradition is an extension of ancient beliefs that human reasoning could and should attain universal understanding. Belief in such rationality implies faith in the ultimate knowability of the universe as well as faith in the power of technology, in verifiable knowledge, and in concepts of progress.

Purposes, therefore, are generic conceptions that conjoin agents, acts, agencies and scenes. Modern educational theories and practices are unified through purposes defined by scientific theories and research that are aimed at rational explanations. A rhetorical analysis of educators' statements of purpose examines their words and actions for congruences among choices and consequences.

Two Implicit Purposes of Staff Development

Whether written or spoken, statements of purpose contain implicit images of what staff development 'should' be like. Most educational theorists would avoid making any explicit general statements about how teachers should relate in and with schools, although many theoretical works make statements of purpose that imply general goals. The images of purpose emerge in reply to the question: according to available research, toward what general aims should staff development be directed?

Two examples discussing staff development will be shown to embody differing aims, coherent with discrete strategies for communication and theoretical formulations. Reporting a recent survey of literature on staff development programs for implementing educational reforms, Kenneth Howey (1985) identified six general purposes, as follows:

1 continuing pedagogical development,
2 continuing understanding and discovery of self,
3 continuing cognitive development,
4 continuing theoretical development,
5 continuing professional development,
6 continuing career development. (p. 59)

Howey asserts that most staff development activities incorporate some of these purposes, and that typical programs emphasize the purpose of individual teachers' pedagogical development. He concludes that,

> As paradoxical as it may seem, the present preoccupation with pedagogy is not as likely to improve instruction as would changes in teacher role relationships, more attention to grounded theories, a better understanding of the relationship of teacher cognitive development to instructional practices, and helping teachers become more aware of changes in themselves and the relationship of these changes in their life's work of teaching. (p. 62)

Howey does state that institutional restructuring should accompany changes in individual teachers' practices, but both his normative list of purpose and suggestions assign primacy to an individual teacher's· conceptions, or, in Burke's terminology, idealistic agents (see also Griffin and Rehage, 1983; Lieberman and Miller, 1984a; Wade, 1984/5; Wideen and Andrews, 1987). Howey recognizes that, in purposes for staff development programs, the norm is a mystical faith in rationality manifest in pedagogical techniques and individual teachers as technical agents. In the alternative purposes he proposes, a similar faith is evident.

In rhetorical terms, the topic is still that of the 'knowing agent', and the lines of argument are contained within the following syllogism: teachers need knowledge to improve instruction; knowledge consists of grounded theories, cognitive development, and awareness of personal changes as well as pedagogical techniques; therefore teachers as agents need all these kinds of knowledge in order to improve instruction. These statements of purpose, extracted from current literature and amended by the reviewer, share belief in universal idealism, hoping for a common language of knowledge and ideas that would bring teachers together and inform the institutions of schooling.

In contrast to purposes for staff development that feature faith in rational knowledge manifest in teachers as agents, many teacher educators state purposes that feature faith in community, manifest in schools as scenes for political struggle (Apple, 1987; Beyer, 1988; Giroux and McLaren, 1986). For example, drawing upon critical social theory in the traditions of Marxist philosophy and sociology, Michael Apple (1987) appeals for educational policies based on concerted political action, as follows:

> Our first task as educators in these circumstances is to educate ourselves about these [social] conditions. For the institutions of society to be reconstructed around the principles not of privatization and greed but of the common good, people — including educators — need to be convinced that the current and emerging organization of a larger part of our economic, political, and cultural institutions is neither equal nor just. (p. 178)

This statement of purpose implies that individual teachers as knowing agents are not sufficient as sources of change for educational policies, advocating that the first priority of teacher education should be concerted political action aimed at changing large-scale economic structures, or, in Burke's terms, altering the scenic circumstances. For Burke, the philosophical approach featured in such scenic emphasis is faith in economic ends evident in such terms as 'common good', or 'social structures'. The primary topic in this rhetoric is 'social circumstances', and the line of argument runs according to the following syllogism: communities need justice, and justice is served by teachers' political actions as well as their personal and professional knowledge; therefore communities need teachers' political actions. Such purposes aim toward changing material conditions through collective action, in struggle with antagonistic interests and against structural limitations.

Purposes in Conflict

Despite differences in their primary articles of faith, both these statements of purposes would seem alike in emphasizing communicative interaction and the long-term consequences of those interactions in particular situations. Commonality of means does not lead to commensurability, however, since purposes cancel one another as often as they coincide. Staff development programs might articulate purposes such as Howey's or those described by Apple, but compromise may be impossible. In the end, one set of purposes will be met more closely than the other. Complex relations among diverse purposes and actions defy comprehensive analysis, especially in mass public schooling, a gigantic enterprise that is in many ways still in its youth.

The dilemmas of conflicting purposes are not often addressed in studies of staff development; in the past half-century, only a small amount of research has been directed at its long-term effects (Daresh, 1987; Griffin and Rehage, 1983; Lieberman and Miller, 1984a, 1984b). Pertaining to racial desegregation, for instance, over three decades after court decisions began requiring wide-ranging changes in schooling practices based on racial or ability classifications only a few educational researchers have analyzed how teacher education policies were affected (e.g., Cremin, 1988; Little, 1981; Goodlad, 1984). In particular instances of staff development programs, statements of purpose usually portray teachers and schools as autonomous change agents that would carry out not only the letter of legal requirements, but also the spirit of rehabilitating previously excluded students (Gartner and Lipsky, 1987; Kirp and Jensen, 1986; Singer and Butler, 1987). In the public statements of civil-rights movements that initiated federal mandates for social change, case law and policy both assigned important roles to individuals, as in racial quotas, affirmative action programs, and the Individualized Educational Plan that mainstreaming law requires. It appears that these statements of purpose, unlike broader social purposes such as those stated by Apple, eschew large-scale political action for change and aim to spread cooperative social relations through individual agents to classrooms, schools and communities.

Numerous studies have shown that large-scale programs for staff development must address a broad range of purposes that express divergent beliefs (Baldridge and Deal, 1983; Fullan and Pomfret, 1977; McLaughlin and Marsh, 1978; Reid, 1987; Waugh and Punch, 1987). Historical studies have shown that, when individual or group agents endeavor to alter scenic circumstances, unanticipated consequences occur in the cultures of schools and communities (Cuban, 1984; Popkewitz, Tabachnick and Wehlage, 1982; Reese, 1986). Often an unintended consequence of mandated change is continued stability. In summarizing historical and sociological data on teaching practices during the past century, Larry Cuban (1984) states,

> The school and classroom stuctures, I believe, established the boundaries within which individual teacher beliefs and an occupational ethos worked their influence in shaping a practical pedagogy. (p. 250)

This and similar conclusions imply that staff development programs for educational reform must state two sets of purposes that seem to be at odds: one set of beliefs expression what can be changed, as well as a set of beliefs about what must be left alone. Simply put, purposes express differences between what ought to be and what is.

Words and Purposes — A Summary

The purposes of staff development programs qualify as subjects for rhetorical analysis, because rhetorical criticism can be directed at interactions among what is said and what is left unsaid. Quantitative logic and qualitative narrative can both describe what is not being addressed, although critiques of persuasive language can more fully explore the dialectical relations in appeals to 'Do this, but don't do that'. Divergent interests, settings, agents, purposes and beliefs are difficult to determine from tables of numbers or groups of words, but reside in interplays between specific speakers and audiences. Instead of assuming that certainty is possible when symbols or actions are joined to purposes, rhetoric assumes that doubt is more likely and persuasion is necessary for communicating symbols and eliciting actions. According to Burke (1966), language is essentially negative, in that symbols are unlike the things they would represent permitting humans unique ways to talk about what is not present in acts or thoughts: 'The word for the thing is not the thing' (p. 420).

In brief, the purposes of staff development are complex expressions of what teachers, administrators and researchers believe ought to be done, can be done, and cannot be done. Current research and implementation studies aim at specific changes in schooling without investigating their general consequences, as if the positive qualities found in words, actions, and beliefs could be separated from the negative ones. Accusations of excessive abstraction and idealism have become common criticisms of traditional beliefs in scientific progress informing much educational theory, policy, and practice (e.g., Cherryholmes, 1988; Giddens, 1987; Lindblom and Cohen, 1979; Rajchman and West, 1985; Thomas, 1979). Policies such as racial desegregation for purposes of social justice fueled controversies over those very differences they set out to alter (Kirp and Jensen, 1986; Timar and Kirp, 1987; Wise, 1979). Words, actions, and consequences diverge from purposes, and rhetorical analysis offers ways to examine those divergent philosophical approaches.

Conclusion

This chapter set out to explore philosophical bases of staff development, a part of contemporary research on educational organizations. It has been argued that rhetorical analysis provides a means to do so by inspecting different modes of communication, especially when a theoretical pespective is adopted that evaluates words and actions in terms of practical consequences as well as logical consistencies.

Employing three categories extracted from Burke's pentad of motives, research on staff development has been analyzed in the following terms: *scenes*, or situational circumstances and patterns of authority;

agents, or organs of action; and *purposes*, or coherent beliefs. The works of contemporary scholars were cited to show that staff development is a controversial topic about which theory, research, policy and practice are often deeply divided. In reply to calls for further studies deploying multiple methods, it has been suggested that rhetorical analysis might help mediate among various philosophical approaches to staff development.

Systematic study of the means of persuasion is not common in current educational research after a century of adherence to methods of inquiry that approach teaching and learning as quantifiable or qualifiable processes and products. In these methodologies, linguistic transactions are assumed to be transparent, or at least of lesser importance than the facts and judgments they are supposed to transmit. Some philosophers, (along with researchers in fields such as literary studies, communications and law) have retained and developed traditions assigning a central place to rhetoric (Bitzer and Black, 1971; Brown, 1987; Nelson *et al.*, 1987). Recently, many of these scholars have asserted that closer attention is due to communicative action in a world brought closer together by technology's accomplishments, promises, and threats (e.g., Bernstein, 1983, 1985; Foucault, 1982; Rajchman and West, 1985; Rorty, 1982; Toulmin, 1988). The importance of rhetoric emerges as needs for communication increase, because, as Burke (1950/69) claims,

> . . . rhetoric as such is not rooted in any past condition of human society. It is rooted in an essential function of language itself, a function that is wholly realistic, and continually born anew; the use of language as a symbolic means of inducing cooperation in beings that by nature respond to symbols. (p. 43)

The test of rhetoric is whether thoughts, words and actions are congruent with their consequences. For example, rigorously quantitative technical logic is not congruent with highly interpretive practices that, as James Clifford (1986) says, 'see culture as composed of seriously contested codes and representations [that] assume that the poetic and the political are imseparable, that science is in, not above historical and linguistic processes' (p. 2). During the past century, mass public education has been the site for collisions among technical logics and cultural practices. Incongruent words, actions and consequences can be found in arguments once made by Snedden and others urging that techniques used in mass production of material goods could be appropriated to educational transactions. The study of communicative actions in education could help warn educators whether their words and actions are similarly at odds.

Rhetorical analysis — or any combination of philosophical approaches to staff development — does not guarantee coherence in the massive enterprise of education located as it is among complex matrices involving theorists, researchers, policymakers, administrators, teachers, students and their communities in large institutional arrangements. Rhetorical analysis can mediate among various approaches only if it addresses specific issues in particular sites, precisely locating agents and audiences in their social and conceptual contexts. It is such attention to the particular, without attempts to reduce specific instances of action to atomized representations and generalizable norms, that has emerged in action research studies, critical ethnographies, or first-person narratives. It has been suggested above that some narrow-scope efforts at 'professional growth' or 'critical inquiry' directly address particular problems of agents' beliefs, knowledge, discourses and actions. On another scale, however, wide-scope studies and reviews point out the problems of extending such efforts and the elusiveness of defining educational change and promoting ideas of progress.

The subtleties of communicative actions and their consequences can become topics for theory, research and practice in staff development, but studies of communication apparently can suggest only a limited range of possible paths to follow or traps to avoid. The questions that the first philosophers raised, and that have been raised ever since, remain as open and challenging as ever. It is the work of this chapter, along with its companions in this volume, to continue grappling with a host of questions, rephrasing them in present settings, while striving to anticipate future circumstances.

Notes

1   For a discussion of influences of Herbartian stage theories on late nineteenth-century educational theories, see Kliebard 1988.
2   This corresponds to Aristotle's concept of *entelechy*, or fulfillment. See Burke 1945/69, pp. 292ff.

References

ANTCZAK, F. (1985) *Thought and Character: The Rhetoric of Democratic Education*, Ames, IA, Iowa State University Press.

APPLE, M. (1987) *Teachers and Texts*, Boston, Routledge and Kegan Paul.

BALDRIDGE, J. and DEAL, T. (1983) *The Dynamics of Organizational Change in Education*, Berkeley, McCutchan.

BERLAK, A. and BERLAK, H. (1981) *Dilemmas of Schooling: Teaching and Social Change*, New York, Methuen.

BERNSTEIN, R. (Ed.) (1985) *Habermas and Modernity*, Cambridge, MA, MIT Press.

BEYER, L. (1988) *Knowing and Acting: Inquiry, Ideology, and Educational Studies*, Philadelphia, Falmer Press.

BITZER, L. (1971) 'The rhetorical situation', in JOHANNSEN, R. (Ed.) *Contemporary Theories of Rhetoric*, New York, Harper and Row.

BITZER, L. and BLACK, E. (Eds) (1971) *The Prospect of Rhetoric*, Englewood Cliffs, NJ, Prentice-Hall.

BLUMBERG, A. (1980) *Supervisors and Teachers: A Private Cold War* (2nd ed.), Berkeley, CA, McCutchan.

BOBBITT, J.F. (1912) 'The elimination of waste in education', *The Elementary School Teacher*, 12, 6, pp. 259–269.

BOBBITT, J.F. (1918) *The Curriculum*, Boston, Houghton Mifflin.

BRENNAN, M. and NOFFKE, S. (1988) 'Reflection in student teaching: The place of data in action research', paper presented at the Annual Meeting of the American Educational Research Association, New Orleans, April.

BROWN, R. (1987) *Society as Text*, Chicago, University of Chicago Press.

BURKE, K. (1945/69) *A Grammar of Motives*, Berkeley, University of California Press.

BURKE, K. (1950/69) *A Rhetoric of Motives*, Berkeley, University of California Press.

BURKE, K. (1966) *Language as Symbolic Action*, Berkeley, University of California Press.

BURKE, P. and HEIDEMAN, R. (Eds) (1985) *Career-Long Teacher Education* Springfield, IL, Charles Thomas.

BURKE, P., FESSLER, R. and CHRISTENSEN, J. (1984) *Teacher Career Stages: Implications for Staff Development*, Bloomington, IN, Phi Delta Kappa.

CARR, W. and KEMMIS, S. (1986) *Becoming Critical: Knowing Through Action Research*, Philadelphia, Falmer Press.

CHERRYHOLMES, C. (1988) *Power and Criticism: Poststructural Investigations in Education*, New York, Teachers College Press.

CLARK, D. and MARKER, G. (1975) 'The institutionalization of teacher education', in RYAN K. (Ed.) *Teacher Education*, Chicago, University of Chicago Press.

CLIFFORD, J. and MARCUS, G. (Eds) (1986) *Writing Culture: The Poetics and Politics of Ethnography*, Berkeley, University of California Press.

COREY, S. (1957) 'Inservice education of teachers, supervisors, and administrators', in *Fifty-sixth Yearbook, Part I, of the National Society for the Study of Education*, Chicago, University of Chicago Press.

CREMIN, L. (1971/88) *American Education* (3 vols.), New York, Harper and Row.

CUBAN, L. (1984) *How Teachers Taught: Constancy and Change in American Classrooms, 1890–1980*, New York, Longman.

DARESH, J. (1987) 'Recent trends in staff development and inservice education', *Journal of Education for Teaching*, 13, 1, pp. 3–12.

DAY, C. (1985) 'Professional learning and researcher intervention: An action research perspective', *British Educational Research Journal*, 11, 2, pp. 133–151.

DEVANEY, K. (1979) 'Warmth, concreteness, time and thought in teachers' learning', in DEVANEY, K. (Ed.) *Essays on Teacher Centers*, San Francisco, Far West Laboratory for Educational Research and Development.

DEWEY, J. (1904) 'The relation of theory to practice in education', in BOYDSTON, J. (Ed.) *John Dewey, The Middle Works*, Carbondale and Edwardsville, IL, Southern Illinois University Press.

DUCHARME, E. (1985) 'Establishing the place of teacher education in the university', *Journal of Teacher Education*, 36, 4, pp. 8–11.

ELLIOTT, J. (1976) 'Developing hypotheses about classrooms from teachers' practical constructs: An account of the work of the Ford Teaching Project', *Interchange*, 7, 2, pp. 11–21.

ERICKSON, F. and CAMPBELL, D. (1986) 'Teachers as active agents in staff development', *Communication Quarterly*, Lansing, MI, Institute for Research on Teaching (Spring/Summer, 1986), 8, 3, p. 3.

FEIMAN-NEMSER, S. (1983) 'Learning to teach', in SHULMAN, L. and SYKES, G. (Eds) *Handbook of Teaching and Policy*, New York, Longman.

FEIMAN-NEMSER, S. and BUCHMANN, M. (1985) 'Pitfalls of experience in teacher education', *Teachers College Record*, 87, 1, pp. 58–66.

FEIMAN-NEMSER, S. and FLODEN, R. (1986) 'Cultures of teaching', in WITTROCK, M. (Ed.) *Handbook of Research on Teaching* (3d ed.), New York, Macmillan.

FENSTERMACHER, G. and BERLINER, D. (1985) 'Determining the value of staff development', *Elementary School Journal*, 85, 3, pp. 281–314.

FOUCAULT, M. (1982) 'The subject and power', in DREYFUS, H. and RABINOW, P. (Eds) *Michel Foucault*, Chicago, University of Chicago Press.

FULLAN, M. and POMFRET, A. (1977) 'Research on curriculum and instruction implementation', *Review of Educational Research*, 47, 2, pp. 335–397.

GAGE, N. (Ed.) (1963) *Handbook of Research on Teaching* (1st ed.), Chicago, Rand McNally.

GARTNER, A. and LIPSKY, D. (1987) 'Beyond special education: Toward a quality system for all students', *Harvard Educational Review*, 57, 4, pp. 367–395.

GIDDENS, A. (1987) *Social Theory and Modern Sociology*, Stanford, CA, Stanford University Press.

GIROUX, H. and McLAREN, P. (1986) 'Teacher education and the politics of engagement: The case for democratic schooling', *Harvard Educational Review*, 56, 3, pp. 213–238.

GITLIN, A. (1983) 'School structure and teachers' work', in APPLE, M. and WEIS, L. (Eds) *Ideology and Practice in Schooling*, Philadelphia, Temple University Press, pp. 193–212.

GLICKMAN, C. (1984–5) 'The supervisor's challenge: Changing the teacher's work environment', *Educational Leadership*, 42, 4, pp. 38–40.

GOMEZ, M. (1987) *The Wisconsin Writing Project: An Exemplar of Current Efforts at Planned School Change Through Staff Development*, Madison, WI, Unpublished doctoral dissertation.

GOODLAD, J.I. (1984) *A Place Called School: Prospects for the Future*, New York, McGraw-Hill.

GRANT, C. and SLEETER, C. (1986) *After the School Bell Rings*, Philadelphia, Falmer Press.

GRAY, J. (n.d.) 'The Bay Area Writing Project Model of university-school collaboration', unpublished ms., Berkeley, University of California.

GREENE, M. (1987) 'In search of a critical pedagogy', *Harvard Educational Review*, 56, 4, pp. 427–441.

GRIFFIN, G. and BARNES, S. (1984) 'School change: A craft-based and research-derived strategy', *Teachers College Record*, 86, 1, pp. 103–123.

GRIFFIN, G. and REHAGE, K. (Eds) (1983) 'Staff development', in *82nd Yearbook of the National Society for the Study of Education*, Chicago, University of Chicago Press.

GUSKEY, T. (1986) 'Staff development and the process of teacher change', *Educational Researcher*, 15, 5, pp. 5–12.

HOLLY, M. (1983) 'Teachers' reflections on classroom life: Collaboration and professional development', *Australian Administrator*, 4, 4, pp. 1–6.

HOPKINS, D. and WIDEEN, M. (1984) *Alternative Perspectives on School Improvement*, New York, Falmer Press.

HOVEY, S. (1986) 'Teachers at the center', *American Educator*, 10, 3, pp. 26–30.

HOWEY, K. (1985) 'Six major functions of staff development: An expanded imperative', *Journal of Teacher Education*, 36, 1, pp. 58–64.

HOWEY, K., MATTHES, W. and ZIMPHER, N. (1986) 'Issues and problems in professional development', Report of the Professional Development Program of the North Central Regional Educational Laboratory, Elmhurst, IL.

HUNTER, M. (1984) 'Knowing, teaching, and supervising', in HOSFORD, P. (Ed.) *Using What We Know About Teaching*, Alexandria, VA, Association for Supervision and Curriculum Development, pp. 169–192.

HURSH, D. (1988) *Becoming Teachers: Preservice Teachers' Understandings of School and Society*, Madison, WI, Unpublished doctoral dissertation.

JOHANNSEN, R. (Ed.) (1971) *Contemporary Theories of Rhetoric*, New York, Harper and Row.

JOYCE, B., SHOWERS, B. and ROHLHEISER-BENNETT, C. (1987) 'Staff development and students learning: A synthesis of research on models of teaching', *Educational Leadership*, 45, 2, pp. 11–23.

KILPATRICK, W. (1918) 'The project method', *Teachers College Record*, 19, 4, pp. 319–335.

KIRP, D. and JENSEN, D. (1986) *School Days, Rule Days: The Legalization and Regulation of Education*, Philadelphia, Falmer Press.

KLIEBARD, H. (1988) 'Dewey and the Herbartians', in PINAR, W. (Ed.) *Contemporary Curriculum Discourses*, Scottsdale, AZ, Gorsuch, Scarisbrick.

LANIER, J. (1983) 'Tensions in teaching teachers the skills of pedagogy', in GRIFFIN, G. and REHAGE, K. (Eds) *Staff Development*, Chicago, University of Chicago Press.

LANIER, J. and LITTLE, J. (1986) 'Research on teacher education', in WITTROCK, M. (Ed.) *Handbook of Research on Teaching* (3rd ed.), New York, Macmillan.

LIEBERMAN, A. and MILLER, J. (1984a) *Teachers, Their World, and Their Work: Implications for School Improvement*, Alexandria, VA, Association Supervision and Curriculum Development.

LIEBERMAN, A. and MILLER, J. (1984b) 'School improvement: Research, craft, and concept', *Teachers College Record*, 86, 1, pp. 4–19.

LILLY, M. (1986) 'The relationship between general and special education: A new face on an old issue', *Counterpoint*, March, 6, 1, p. 10.

LINDBLOM, C. and COHEN, D. (1979) *Usable Knowledge: Social Science and Social Problem Solving*, New Haven, Yale University Press.

LISTON, D. and ZEICHNER, K. (1988) 'Critical pedagogy and teacher education', paper presented at the Annual Meeting of American Educational Research Association, New Orleans, April.

LITTLE, J. (1981) *School Success and Staff Development: The Role of Staff Development in Urban Desegregated Schools*, Boulder, CO, Center for Action Research.

LITTLE, J. (1984) 'Seductive images and organizational realities in organizational development', *Teachers College Record*, 86, 1, pp. 84–102.

LITTLE, J. (1988) 'District policy choices and teachers' professional development opportunities', paper presented at the Annual Meeting of the American Educational Research Association, New Orleans, April.

LORTIE, D. (1975) *School Teacher: A Sociological Study*, Chicago, University of Chicago Press.

MATHISON, S. (1988) 'Why triangulate?', *Educational Researcher*, 17, 2, pp. 13–17.

MATTINGLY, P. (1975) *The Classless Profession: American Schoolmen in the Nineteenth Century*, New York, New York University Press.

MATTINGLY, P. (1987) 'Workplace autonomy and the reforming of teacher education', in POPKEWITZ, T. (Ed.) *Critical Studies in Teacher Education*, Philadelphia, Falmer Press.

McCloskey, G., Provenzo, E., Cohn, M. and Kottkamp, R. (1987) 'A profession at risk: Legislated learning as a disincentive to teaching', paper presented at the Annual Meeting of American Educational Research Association, Washington, DC, April.

McEvoy, B. (1985) 'Everyday acts: Staff development as continuous and informal routine', *Educational Leadership*, 44, 5, pp. 73–78.

McKeon, R. (Ed.) (1941) *The Basic Works of Aristotle*, New York, Random House.

McLaughlin, M. (1987) 'Learning from experience: Lessons for policy implementation', *Educational Evaluation and Policy Analysis*, 9, 2, pp. 171–78.

McLaughlin, M. and Marsh, D. (1978) 'Staff development and school change', *Teachers College Record*, 80, 1, pp. 69–84.

McNeil, L. (1986) *Contradictions of Control*, Boston, Routledge and Kegan Paul.

Metz, M. (1978) *Classrooms and Corridors: The Crisis of Authority in Desegregated Secondary Schools*, Berkeley, University of California Press.

Mitchell, D. and Kerchner, C. (1983) 'Labor relations and teacher policy', in Shulman, L. and Sykes, G. (Eds) *Handbook of Teaching and Policy*, New York, Longman.

Nelson, J., Megill, A. and McCloskey, D. (Eds) (1987) *Rhetoric of the Human Sciences: Language and Argument in Scholarship and Public Affairs*, Madison, WI, University of Wisconsin Press.

Oja, S. and Pine, G. (1988) 'A two-year study of teachers' stages of development in relation to collaborative action research: Final report', Durham, NH, University of New Hampshire.

Perelman, Ch. and Olbrechts-Tyteca, L. (1969) *The New Rhetoric: A Treatise on Argumentation*, Notre Dame, IN, Notre Dame University Press.

Popkewitz, T. (Ed.) (1987) *Critical Studies in Teacher Education*, Philadelphia, Falmer Press.

Popkewitz, T., Tabachnick, B. and Wehlage, G. (1982) *The Myth of Educational Reform: A Study of School Responses to a Program of Change*, Madison, University of Wisconsin Press.

Rajchman, J. and West, C. (Eds) (1985) *Post-Analytic Philosophy*, New York, Columbia University Press.

Reese, W. (1986) *Power and the Promise of School Reform: Grassroots Movements During the Progressive Era*, Boston, Routledge and Kegan Paul.

Reid, W. (1987) 'Institutions and practices: Professional education reports and the language of reform', *Educational Researcher*, 16, 8, pp. 10–15.

Rice, J. (1983) *The Public School System of the United States*, New York, Century.

Richey, H. (1957) 'Growth of the modern conception of inservice education', in Henry, N. (Ed.) *Inservice Education: 56th Yearbook of the National Society for the Study of Education*, Chicago, University of Chicago Press.

Romberg, T. and Price, G. (1983) 'Curriculum implementation and staff development as cultural change', in Griffin, G. and Rehage, K. (Eds) *Staff Development*, Chicago, University of Chicago Press.

Rorty, R. (1979) *Philosophy and the Mirror of Nature*, Princeton, NJ, Princeton University Press.

Rorty, R. (1982) *Consequences of Pragmatism*, Minneapolis, University of Minnesota Press.

Rudduck, J. and Hopkins, D. (Eds) (1985) *Research as a Basis for Teaching: Readings from the Work of Lawrence Stenhouse*, Portsmouth, NH, Heinemann.

SANDER, B. and WIGGINS, T. (1985) 'Cultural context of administrative theory: In consideration of a multidimensional paradigm', *Educational Administration Quarterly*, 21, 2, pp. 95–117.

SARASON, S. (1982) *The Culture of School and the Problem of Change* (2nd ed.), Boston, MA, Allyn and Bacon.

SCHLECHTY, P. and WHITFORD, B. (1983) 'The organizational context of school systems and the functions of staff development', in GRIFFIN, G. and REHAGE, K. (Eds) *Staff Development*, Chicago, University of Chicago Press.

SCHNEIDER, B. (1987) 'Tracing the provenance of teacher education', in POPKEWITZ, T. (Ed.) *Critical Studies in Teacher Education*, Philadelphia, Falmer Press.

SHULMAN, L. and SYKES, G. (Eds) (1983) *Handbook of Teaching and Policy*, New York, Longman.

SIMONS, H. and MELIA, T. (Eds) (1989) *The Legacy of Kenneth Burke*, Madison, University of Wisconsin Press.

SINGER, J. and BUTLER, J. (1987) 'The Education for All Handicapped Children Act: Schools as agents of social reform', *Harvard Educational Review*, 57, 2, pp. 125–152.

SLAVIN, R. (1987) 'The Hunterization of American schools', *Instructor*, November.

SMYLIE, M. (1988) 'The enhancement function of staff development: Organizational and psychological antecedents to teacher change', *American Educational Research Journal*, Spring 1988, 25, 1, pp. 1–30.

SMYTH, J. (Ed.) (1989) *Critical Perspectives on Educational Leadership*, Philadelphia, Falmer Press.

SNEDDEN, D. (1921) *Sociological Determination of Objectives in Education*, Philadelphia, J.B. Lippincott.

SPRINTHALL, N. and THIES-SPRINTHALL, L. (1983) 'The teacher as adult learner', in GRIFFIN, G. and REHAGE, K. (Eds) *Staff Development*, Chicago, University of Chicago Press, pp. 13–35.

STALLINGS, J., ROBBINS, P., PRESBREY, L. and SCOTT, J. (1986) 'Effects of instruction based on the Madeline Hunter model on students' achievement: Findings from a follow-through project', *Elementary School Journal*, 86, 5, pp. 571–587.

TABACHNICK, B. and ZEICHNER, K. (1985) 'The development of teacher perspectives: Final report', Madison, WI, Wisconsin Center for Education Research.

THOMAS, D. (1979) *Naturalism and Social Science: A Post-Empirical Philosophy of Social Science*, New York, Cambridge University Press.

TIMAR, T. and KIRP, D. (1987) 'Educational reform and institutional competence', *Harvard Educational Review*, 57, 3, pp. 308–330.

TOM, A. (1985) 'Inquiring into inquiry teacher education', *Journal of Teacher Education*, 35, 9, pp. 35–44.

TOULMIN, S. (1988) 'The recovery of practical philosophy', *American Scholar* (Summer, 1988), 57, 3, pp. 337–352.

TRAVERS, R. (1973) *Second Handbook of Research on Teaching*, Chicago, Rand McNally.

TYACK, D. and HANSOT, E. (1982) *Managers of Virtue: Public School Leadership in America, 1820–1980*, New York, Basic Books.

VICKERS, B. (1970) 'A concise history of rhetoric', in VICKERS, B. *Classical Rhetoric and English Poetry*, New York, St. Martin's Press.

WADE, R. (1984/85) 'What makes a difference in inservice teacher education? A meta-analysis of research', *Educational Leadership*, (December 1984/January 1985), 40, 1, pp. 48–54.

WALLER, W. (1932) *Sociology of Teaching*, New York, Wiley.

WAUGH, R. and PUNCH, K. (1987) 'Teacher receptivity to systemwide change in the implementation stage', *Review of Educational Research*, Fall, 57, 3, pp. 237–254.

WIDEEN, M. and ANDREWS, I. (Eds) (1987) *Staff Development for School Improvement*, Philadelphia, Falmer Press.

WISE, A. (1979) *Legislated Learning: The Bureaucratization of American Classrooms*, Berkeley, CA, University of California Press.

WITTROCK, M. (Ed.) (1986) *Handbook of Research on Teaching* (3d ed.), New York, Macmillan.

WOOD, P. (1988) 'Action research: A field perspective', *Journal of Education for Teaching*, 14, 2, pp. 135–150.

YARGER, S. (1987) 'A national study of teacher education: Introduction, methodology and procedures', paper presented at the Annual Meeting of AERA, Washington, DC, April.

YONEMURA, M. (1982) 'Teacher conversations: A potential source of their own professional growth', *Curriculum Inquiry*, 12, 3, pp. 239–56.

ZEICHNER, K. (1983) 'Alternative paradigms of teacher education', *Journal of Teacher Education*, 34, 3, pp. 3–9.

ZEICHNER, K. (1985) 'Staff development and school effectiveness', Madison, WI, Wisconsin Center for Educational Research.

ZEICHNER, K. (1986) 'Individual and institutional influences on the development of teacher perspectives', in KATZ, L. and RATHS, J. (Eds) *Advances in Teacher Education* (Vol. 2), Norwood, NJ. Ablex.

ZEICHNER, K. and LISTON, D. (1987) 'Teaching student teachers to reflect', *Harvard Educational Review*, 57, 1, pp. 23–38.

ZIGARMI, P. (1979) 'Teacher centers: A model for teacher-initiated staff development', in LIEBERMAN, A. and MILLER, L. (Eds) *Staff Development*, New York, Teachers College Press.

3 The Human and Organizational Context of Schools

Pedro Reyes

When we think about schools, we often think about the various ways they can be designed and run. The possibilities seem endless. They can be run in a bureaucratic fashion, with many rules, regulations and standard procedures, or they can be run in a rather loose and informal way. They can be highly centralized, with most decisions made by a few individuals at the top, or they can be decentralized, with important decisions made by many individuals throughout the school. They can be structured in such a way that jobs are narrowly defined, with each person in the organization performing a single task or structured so that everyone performs several tasks. They can be designed competitively so that employees are responsible for and rewarded on the basis of their own individual performance or designed cooperatively so that group performance and teamwork are rewarded. These contrary views ebb and flow; for instance, teacher empowerment and school-based management are now in vogue (Stimson and Applebaum, 1988).

There may be other possibilities of structuring schools that are not yet envisioned. However, it is important to recognize that any approach to organizing and running schools involves both implicit and explicit assumptions about human nature. There are always certain basic assumptions about what motivates people at work, and in turn, these assumptions suggest ways to reward employees, provide leadership and manage performance. The goals of this chapter are to describe the human and organizational context of schools, and to suggest a process to understand both human and organizational needs.

Human Context of Schools

One fundamental question is whether teachers should be viewed negatively, as naturally lazy and self-serving or positively, as hard-working and self-motivated. Proponents of the first position argue that teachers are unmotivated and need to be pushed, controlled, and kept under supervision; they are never to be trusted. Indeed many of the classical approaches to designing and running schools made these assumptions. Economic rewards were the only ones considered, and close, autocratic supervision was suggested.

On the other hand, the human resources theorists have a positive view of human nature. Teachers are seen as healthy human beings striving for personal and social well-being. If left alone, they will work hard for the intrinsic satisfaction of a job well done. It is from this opposing perspective that many theories have developed focusing on the human context of schools, that is, teacher motivation at work.

Maslow's Theory

Teacher motivation has been conceptualized in several forms. For instance, Maslow's (1954) theory of hierarchic needs proposes that people have five different sets of needs and that the basic or most fundamental need has to be satisfied in order for individuals to move on to a higher level need. In other words Maslow's theory suggests that we have a prepotency of needs; some needs are assumed to be more important (potent) than others, and those that are most important must be satisfied before other needs can serve as motivators. There are five needs categories: physiological needs are the most basic biological functions of the human organism; safety and security needs make up the second level; belonging, love, and social needs are placed in the next hierarchical level; the fourth level involves the need for esteem by others, recognition achievement and status; and finally, at the highest level is self-actualization.

Maslow argues that this category system holds true for most normal, healthy human beings though it is not applicable to everyone. Second, while the idea of prepotency is important, it is not entirely rigid. For example, while this theory argues that belonging needs must be generally satisfied before esteem needs begin to operate as motivators, Maslow did not argue that belonging needs must be completely fulfilled. The general idea is that the greater the fulfillment of a particular need, the less it serves as a motivator, and the more the next highest need becomes activated as a motivator.

As we apply Maslow's theory to education we find that for teachers in our society needs at the two lower levels — physiological and safety — play a relatively minor role. The implication then for school administrators is that higher order needs should be better motivators than the lower ones. This fact seems to be supported by surveys of professional educators about what motivates them.

For example, Trusty and Sergiovanni (1966) reported that the most glaring deficiencies for professional educators were fulfillment of esteem, autonomy, and self-actualization needs — data which were later confirmed by Anderson and Iwanicki (1984). However, Chisolm, Washington, and Thibodeaux (1980) found that school administrators exhibited fewer needs-fulfillment deficiencies than teachers, as measured by the needs satisfaction questionnaire. These researchers also reported that the greatest area of deficiency for both teachers and administrators occurred in the satisfaction of the need for autonomy. Thus the research evidence implies the importance of these higher order needs though it does not support a rigid and specific five-category system.

Nonetheless, the impact of this theory in schools should not be dismissed. Two reasons come to mind. First, Maslow's theory was the first clear statement that 'managers' should recognize the importance of higher order needs. Clearly, Maslow's emphasis implies that school administrators must move away from lower-level needs and focus on higher-order needs of teachers. Whether school administrators have used Maslow's theory or not, it has become an important contribution to management thinking. Secondly, Maslow's theory has forced administrators to pay attention to individual differences since teachers will operate at different levels in the hierarchy at different times. Also school managers must be aware of even further individual differences because what motivates one teacher will not motivate another. Different people want different things and school managers must be sensitive to these needs if they wish their teachers to be highly motivated.

McClelland's Theory

Expanding on these ideas, McClelland (1961, 1985) proposed two other individual needs not specifically dealt with in Maslow's theory: the need for achievement and the need for power. McClelland's need-for-achievement theory suggests that managers have either high or low need to achieve. Those who have high-achievement motivation tend to prefer moderate to high risk, immediate feedback and a sense of accomplishment; while those less motivated to achieve take lower risks and are willing to defer both feedback and sense of accomplishment. Because of this interest in accomplishment, the high-achiever frequently becomes deeply involved with a task, tends to find meaning in work, is task-oriented. The managers with low-achievement needs see work as less central and are more secretive and insensitive.

Unfortunately, this research has not been extended into educational organizations. However, though there is little empirical evidence that supports McClelland's theory in educational organizations, its implications should nevertheless be seen as significant by school administrators. Because need for achievement can often be correlated with employee interest in work, school administrators should identify teachers who exhibit low needs for achievement and work to develop in them a high need for achievement. McClelland (1978) says that adults are able to change and can acquire greater need for achievement. Therefore, school administrators may find McClelland's theory useful as they deal with motivated and unmotivated staff. For example, motivated staff should be encouraged to take more risks in their work, and should be given immediate feedback, while staff development programming should be planned with one objective being to foster a greater need to achieve in the unmotivated staff.

McClelland not only theorized about the achievement motive of individuals, but he also proposed that individuals have needs for power. The limited research literature argues that to be successful, one must be both assertive and determined. Also the nonacademic press has advocated the use of power to get ahead in organizations. While these specific prescriptions may not be based on extensive research evidence, they do suggest that people who desire power frequently get it and are successful because of it.

Although most of the research on individual needs for power has been done with managers (McClelland and Burnham, 1976), there are implications for school administrators. For instance, the literature reports that power-oriented managers are characterized by a preference for influencing others over being liked by them, but this need is tempered by social norms and goal commitment. People with a high need for power are successful only if the need is accompanied by a commitment to organizational goals. Consequently, school adminstrators may find this theory useful in dealing with subordinate administrators who have a high need for power, and would be advised to structure activities around those needs to achieve stated goals.

Further Research

Moving on to research in education itself, we find that the literature supports the idea that teachers should be empowered with leadership in schools (Maeroff, 1988; Barth, 1988; and Lieberman, 1988). Researchers have called for shared leadership in articulating the mission of schools. The literature states that many school administrators are not certain of their vision, thus arguing for greater input from teachers (along with administrators) to articulate clearer school goals. Other people have argued that schools should develop a community of leaders in which teachers take part, while others have called for more sweeping reforms that enhance the teacher's role in school. The overall theme, however, is that teachers have needs to experience power within their world of work, and that administrators should be cognizant of those needs and seek to allow their fulfillment. One means to this end is through staff development programming.

Teachers also demonstrate significant needs for success or competence in teaching. The literature indicates that lack of success in teaching contributes to the turnover of high-quality teachers (Ashton and Webb, 1986). Organizational theory suggests that people are motivated to remain in an occupation only as long as they perceive their rewards to be equal to or greater than the effort they are asked to expend. Research on teachers' rewards however indicates that teachers stress the importance of intrinsic rewards as opposed to monetary rewards although money is an important factor (Lortie, 1975). The primary reward teachers hope to derive is the sense of being instrumental to students' academic growth, that is, a belief or a sense of efficacy in their ability to affect student performance positively. Consequently, those teachers who do not experience the intrinsic professional rewards of teaching have the greatest probability of defection (Bredeson, Kasten, and Fruth, 1983).

This perception of professional efficacy can be raised to an even more critical level. We know that teachers with high academic ability set higher expectations for student achievement than their counterparts, higher expectations which are based on their own ability. If subsequent student learning does not meet those relatively higher expectations, these teachers may consider themselves less effective even though absolute student learning has occurred (Ashton and Webb, 1986). This evidence may explain the fact that the most academically able, or those with the greatest likelihood for classroom success, are among those who leave teaching earliest in their professional careers.

Therefore, effective school administrators must be aware of the teachers' feelings of efficacy in order to provide immediate feedback to teachers when necessary. This should be done by constantly monitoring student progress and teachers' sense of efficacy.

In summary, teachers have and experience different drives and motives at work. Maslow's theory indicates that teachers may operate at different stages of a hierarchy, each of which requires a different set of motivators. McClelland's need-for-achievement theory implies also that teachers should be treated according to their levels of need for achievement. Similarly, his theory of need for power indicates a potent stimulator for goal accomplishment. Finally, teachers also have needs for success or competence in teaching suggesting that such needs are linked to teachers' sense of efficacy and thus to high turnover or attrition. However, teachers' needs are just one aspect of schools; schools as organizations have characteristics (e.g., population, size) that affect human behavior and the way such organizations may proceed. Such characteristics are important in order to understand teachers' and school administrators' behavior at work. Consequently, we need to examine the nature of schools as organizations.

Organizational Context of Schools

When we use the term organization – whether applying it to a school or to a non-profit organization – a number of images come to mind. We often think of rules and regulations, standard operating procedures, people occupying positions of power and authority and multiple departments. At some level, all of these images are true. One has only to walk into a school to see them come to life.

Yet, all these images miss the essence of organizations. Organizations are systems of coordinated behavior (Simon, 1958). Rules, regulations, standard operating procedures, and other images that organizations project are simply mechanisms for coordinating behaviors. It is the behavior itself that is the essence of organizations. Therefore when we speak of organizations, we are in fact speaking about the coordinated behaviors of all the members of the organization (Weick, 1979).

Mizruchi (1983) pointed out that, in the process of organizing, people give up some of their individual flexibility and freedom to attain personal and organizational goals. To be organized is to be coordinated, and coordination is achieved by allowing our behavior to be directed by others. If people do not allow their behavior to be directed by others and behave independently, coordination is impossible and the organization will cease to exist.

Schools are no different from other organizations. They have rules, regulations, standard operating procedures, multiple departments, and people occupying positions of power and authority, all of which serve as mechanisms for coordinating teacher behaviors. Schools also exist to facilitate goal attainment, and teachers as well as administrators must relinquish some of their individual flexibility and freedom to achieve personal and organizational goals. Staff development needs flow from stated personal and organizational goals.

Goals and Goal Setting

Schools as organizations facilitate goal attainment, in reality, the attainment of many goals. Some of these are the official goals of a school: the broad, formal, publicly stated objectives that a school seeks to achieve (e.g., educating the citizens of the state, providing services for the hand-icapped, providing taxpayers with the highest possible quality of education on their investment). In addition, schools facilitate the attainment of many of the personal goals of teachers. We all join organizations and continue to participate in them for a variety of reasons which go well beyond the formal goals of schools. Teachers may decide to join a particular school because it may satisfy some social needs such as providing interaction with other people, or because it offers opportunities to exercise skills that they couldn't practise elsewhere, or simply because the school has certain financial incentives that fulfill such goals as receiving a regular salary or health benefits. These personal goals are likely to prove as important as the formal goals of the school. If a school were unable to satisfy the personal goals of teachers, it would lose those members, resulting in serious problems rising from the shortage of personnel. Thus staff de-velopment must consider both personal and organizational needs.

In addition to motivating teachers to join and remain in a school, goals – both formal and personal – also serve at least two other functions. First, they serve to guide behavior and stimulate effort at work; and second, formal goals in particular serve as a basis for evaluation. Schools are judged in terms of the extent to which these goals have been attained. If they are not achieved, the overall effectiveness of the organization is questioned. Similarly, the overall performance of individuals or teachers can be evaluated against chosen goals. Meeting or exceeding a goal is considered good performance, while failing to meet one is considered poor performance. In sum, goals motivate people to join schools and continue participating in them; they provide a source of work motivation, and they are useful for assessing performance.

Administration

It was suggested previously that schools are systems of coordinated be-haviors and that in order to achieve school goals, such behaviors need to be directed by others. Administrators perform such a task. Administration or management involves the coordination of human and material resources toward the accomplishment of formal goals. In every school teachers perform a variety of activities, and they need physical and informational resources at different times to do so. The responsibility for coordinating, regulating, and integrating all these activities falls largely upon school administrators. Therefore, school administrators must know the technical aspects of work, and must understand human behavior in order to be successful. In addition to having technical and behavioral knowledge school managers must be aware of some other aspects of schools that affect the way they manage, such as complexity, size and organizational struc-ture.

Complexity and Size

Not so long ago most schools were small. They involved simple divisions of labor, relatively few specializations, and lines of authority that were very clear. But times have changed. Schools come in all shapes and sizes and in general many have become increasingly large and complex (McCarty, 1989). These changes have brought benefits as well as problems to school administrators with regard to the management of teachers' behavior. For example, with the development of different programs (e.g. special education, counseling, and the like), we find increasing division of labor and specialization. We have more complicated school units and problems; we have many different teachers doing many different kinds of jobs.

This complexity creates problems with or tensions between two important elements involved in school operation: goals and management. With increased complexity, organizational members – teachers included – develop differing orientations. Consequently, the goals of schools become more difficult to define. For example, the assistant superintendent for financial services in a large school district may see the primary goal of their schools to be the minimizing of costs. Social studies teachers, on the other hand, may be relatively unconcerned about minimizing costs and may instead view the goal of providing the child with 'holistic education' as primary. In contrast to social studies teachers, science and math teachers may view schools as a means of providing only academic education to students rather than holistic education.

These differing views frequently produce internal conflict and can cause problems in determining school procedures, for without agreement about goals, it is hard to make decisions about the proper means of attaining them. In their task of coordinating and integrating the various values and goals, administrators as managers find their leadership roles much more difficult to fulfill as they work to achieve joint, agreed-upon action.

Directly related to complexity is the size of school districts. McCarty (1989) indicated that districts vary greatly by size, citing large districts such as the state of Hawaii, the cities of Chicago and New York, in contrast to small districts like Colman, South Dakota. With increases in size, problems have developed. School administrators can no longer know first hand what is being done in different school buildings. Teaching staff may have less identification with the goals of the district; they do not know most of their colleagues within the district. Thus it is much more difficult for the school district to motivate employees and to coordinate their ongoing activities. In summary, modern schools are faced with a number of problems, many of which have to do with their size and complexity. If schools are to be run efficiently, administrators must learn how to deal with these challenges.

Structure

Another characteristic of schools is the organizational structure – that is, the sum total of the ways in which a school divides its labor into different tasks and then achieves coordination among those tasks. The facts that the high school of a large school district usually has its own budget apart from the elementary school, and that each building may have its own principal and vice-principal are formal features of that organization as are the systems of pay, promotion, tenure and performance evaluation. All of these make up the formal structure of a school. Though no two school districts are likely to have exactly the same structure, all will have some sort of structure.

A few characteristics of the school structure that affect the way administrators manage include vertical differentiation, centralization and formalization. Vertical differentiation has to do with the number of vertical levels of authority in the organization, essentially the degree to which administrative activities are divided. Generally, as schools get larger they also develop more hierarchical layers. This makes sense, since the more teachers employed in a school district the more effort it takes to coordinate their behavior. For instance, large school districts such as the city of Chicago may have a great number of associate superintendents in charge of different areas of the city. These associate superintendents may also have a number of assistant superintendents to coordinate areas such as curriculum, staff development, budgets or personnel evaluation.

The degree of differentiation can significantly affect the job satisfaction of administrators and teachers. For example, Berger and Cummings (1979) suggested that administrators working in highly differentiated organizations experienced higher levels of job satisfaction than administrators working in less differentiated organizations.

A concept closely related to differentiation is centralization which refers to the locus of decision-making authority in schools. If all or most important decisions about school operations are made at the top by a few individuals, the school is said to be highly centralized. However, if decision-making authority is delegated to lower levels of the school so that those who actually have to implement the decisions become more involved in the decision process, the school is said to be highly decentralized. Like differentiation, the degree of centralization is on a continuum, with school districts varying in the extent of centralization they exhibit.

As stated previously, the literature has argued for both greater school decentralization and centralization. There are pros and cons for both arguments. For example, it could be argued that in a decentralized school district the teachers who are actually implementing curriculum policy are likely to have greater technical expertise, in the sense that they are more familiar with the problems they face. On the other hand, they may lack the experience and the overall district perspective possessed by those administrators in higher level positions. Moreover, decisions can be made more quickly in decentralized school districts than otherwise, thus making decentralized school districts somewhat more responsive to changing conditions.

The final structural feature of schools to be mentioned is formalization. Formalization is the degree to which a school district has clearly specified rules and regulations that govern the work-related behavior of teachers and administrators. Highly formalized school districts typically have thick manuals of procedures, rules and regulations, and detailed job descriptions that specify the expectations for employees. In addition, highly formalized school districts generally require an extensive amount of paperwork in the form of frequent memos and reports. In contrast, a school district that is not highly formalized operates with many fewer rules and regulations, has general job descriptions and usually requires less paperwork. Furthermore, less formalized school districts encourage direct communication among individuals from different organizational levels. Communication through the formal chain of command is less characteristic.

The literature on formalization indicates that a primary benefit from it is that formalization coordinates behaviors; there is little ambiguity about who is doing what and when. Formalization also serves as an objective standard against which performance may be judged. However, there is a negative side to this. Formalization tends to focus attention on the rules and procedures to the exclusion of the overall goals that they are intended to serve. For example, an employee or teacher may decide to follow the rules rigidly, even when doing so is not in the best interest of the school district. Such problems are less likely to occur in less formalized school districts.

In summary, a review of some of the basic organizational features of schools has focused in particular upon the nature of goals and goal-setting, upon the coordinating role of administrators, upon the factors of complexity and size, and finally upon a few characteristics of the structure of schools. All of these aspects have significant impact upon the way managers and teachers behave at work. Yet the intricacies of their interaction may not be as obvious as one might think, particularly to the new or inexperienced employee. It may take years of working at the same school or district to understand the complexities. Staff development is a facilitating design that may be used to clarify the complexities for both experienced and inexperienced employees.

Restructuring Schools

Over the past several years, there has been a major push for reforming schools. This movement has focused at the level of improving educational excellence. Parents and legislators have called for increased rigor in schools in response to findings which indicate that our young people are not performing as well on standardized tests as they did in earlier years. Moreover, the National Commission on Excellence in Education (1983) also identified poor staff morale and poor-quality teaching as factors needing serious attention by school officials. Most reports of this kind call for restructuring schools.

A body of knowledge that attempts to deal with restructuring schools is the research on school effectiveness. This research has identified numerous variables that seem associated with school effectiveness such as high student achievement, positive school climate, high teacher morale, and the like. This research has stimulated possible solutions for school improvement such as innovative instructional strategies and reorganized curriculum (e.g., cooperative learning, increasing course requirements and graduation standards), changes in personnel practices (e.g., merit pay, teacher competency testing) and institutional changes (e.g., school-based management, voucher systems, etc.) (Brophy, 1983; Odden and Dougherty, 1982; Purkey and Smith, 1983; Rosenshine, 1983; and Stedman, 1987).

Because the research on effective schools has concentrated only on 'excellent schools', it must be considered as having limited application to most schools around the country, particularly those undergoing significant change. (See Stedman, 1987 for more detail.) Moreover, the vast majority of research on school improvement ignores the internal structures and the group dynamics within the schools. Thus, it seems imperative that staff development be used to incorporate both research and practice. This would provide innovative ideas that get at the root of the matter: meeting the goals of both the teacher and the organization, while working to meet the encompassing needs of the students.

One issue that needs careful attention is the context in which schools operate, i.e., the culture. Schools do not exist solely as closed environments. The school's culture reflects and is intertwined with that of the larger society (Sarason, 1982). This means that values and norms of staff and students will impinge upon any innovating or restructuring that is undertaken. In other words, we need to build cultures that emphasize both the individual and the organization rather than only one or the other. The school culture should be one in which the teacher and the student become active learners and partners in the learning process (Lightfoot, 1983). We need to build teacher commitment to effectiveness and school commitment to the teacher.

Another issue that needs rethinking is the idea of participative decision-making in schools. The literature has advocated the concept of school-based management (Guthrie, 1986), an idea which proposes to alter the governance structure of school districts by decentralizing decision-making in the areas of budget, personnel and programming, thus increasing local autonomy and accountability (Malen, Ogawa and Kranz, 1989).

We need to move away from the traditional top-down approach existent in most schools, to full participatory systems which reflect the democratic principle that governance should be shared among those directly concerned with the functioning of a particular building or activity. This means that we should give thoughtful consideration to the roles and responsibilities of teachers. They must be given greater discretion concerning goal-setting, curriculum development and personnel policy.

Finally, we need to address issues related to the knowledge base of teachers, content and pedagogical issues. School districts must provide teachers with many opportunities to engage in critical thinking concerning their knowledge of the subject matter while involving them in creative thinking about innovative and effective instructional strategies. Moreover, schools should encourage the concomitant development of curriculum which emphasizes thinking rather than memorization (Lewis, 1989). Teachers must be involved in these kinds of inquiries and activities to be successful in providing a failure-free and academically rich environment for all children, a significant implication being that school organizations must provide teachers with the tools to rethink their professional roles and responsibilities – preparation time, reflective time.

To summarize, restructuring must incorporate a many-faceted approach. There must be continuing attention paid to the needs and goals of practitioners as human beings and professionals. There must be continuing awareness of the nature and structure of the school organization. There must be commitment to new and improved instructional strategies, to improved curriculum. But above all there must be total commitment of both teachers and administrators to staff development programming to build a culture of school effectiveness in which authority and power are shared among all.

References

ANDERSON, M.B.G. and IWANICKI, E.F. (1984) 'Teacher motivation and its relationship to burnout', *Educational Administration Quarterly*, 20, pp. 109–132.

ASHTON, P.T. and WEBB, R.B. (1986) *Making a Difference: Teacher's Sense of Efficacy and Student Achievement*, White Plains, NY, Longman, Inc.

BARTH, R.S. (1988) 'Principals, teachers, and school leadership', *Phi Delta Kappan*, 69, pp. 639–642.

BERGER, C.J. and CUMMINGS, L.L. (1979) 'Organizational structure, attitudes, and behaviors', in STOW, B.M. (Ed.) *Research in Organizational Behavior*, Greenwich, CT, JAI Press.

BREDESON, P., KASTEN, K.L. and FRUTH, M.J. (1983) 'Organizational incentives and secondary school teaching', *Journal of Research and Development in Education*, 6, pp. 52–58.

BROPHY, J.E. (1983) 'Classroom organization and management', *Elementary School Journal*, 83, pp. 265–285.

CHISOLM, G.B., WASHINGTON, R. and THIBODEAUX, M. (1980) 'Job motivation and the need fulfillment deficiencies of educators', paper presented at the Annual Meeting of the American Educational Research Association, Boston.

GUTHRIE, J. (1986) 'School-based management: The next needed education reform', *Phi Delta Kappan*, 68, pp. 305–309.

LEWIS, A. (1989) *Restructuring America's Schools*, American Association of School Administrators, Arlington, VA.

LIEBERMAN, A. (1988) 'Turf, tension, and new tasks', *Phi Delta Kappan*, 69, pp. 648–653.

LIGHTFOOT, S.L. (1983) *The Good High School*, New York, Basic Books Inc.

LORTIE, D.C. (1975) *Schoolteacher: A Sociological Study*, Chicago, University of Chicago Press.

MAEROFF, G.I. (1988) 'A blueprint for empowering teachers', *Phi Delta Kappan*, 69, pp. 472–77.

MALEN, B., OGAWA, R.T. and KRANZ, J. (1989) 'What do we know about school based management? A case study of the literature — a call for research', paper presented at the Conference on Choice and Control in American Education, University of Wisconsin-Madison.

MASLOW, A.H. (1954) *Motivation and Personality*, New York, Harper.

McCARTY, D.J. (1989) 'The school district: A unique setting', in REYNOLDS, MAYNARD, C. (Ed.) *Knowledge Base for the Beginning Teacher*, New York, Pergamon Press.

McCLELLAND, D.C. (1961) *The Achieving Society*, New York, Harper.

McCLELLAND, D.C. (1978) 'Managing motivation to expand human freedom', *American Psychologist*, 33, pp. 201–210.

McCLELLAND, D.C. (1985) *Human Motivation*, Glenview, IL, Scott Forsman.

McCLELLAND, D.C. and BURNHAM, D.H. (1976) 'Power is the great motivator', *Harvard Business Review*, 54, pp. 100–110.

MIZRUCHI, M.S. (1983) 'Who controls whom? An examination of the relation between management and boards of directors in large American corporations', *Academy of Management Review*, 8, pp. 426–435.

NATIONAL COMMISSION ON EXCELLENCE IN EDUCATION (1983), US Office of Education, Washington, D.C.

ODDEN, A. and DOUGHERTY, V. (1982) *State Programs of School Improvement: A 50 State Survey*, Denver, CO, Educational Commission of the States.

PURKEY, S.C. and SMITH, M.S. (1983) 'Effective schools: A review', *Elementary School Journal*, 83, pp. 427–452.

ROSENSHINE, B. (1983) 'Teaching functions in instructional programs', *Elementary School Journal*, 83, pp. 335–351.

SARASON, S.B. (1982) *The Culture of the School and the Problem of Change*, Second Edition, Boston, Allyn and Bacon Inc.

SIMON, H.A. (1958) *Organizations*, New York, The Free Press.

STEDMAN, L.C. (1987) 'It's time we change the effective schools formula', *Phi Delta Kappan*, 68, pp. 215–224.

STIMSON, T.D. and APPLEBAUM, R.P. (1988) 'Empowering teachers: Do principals have the power?', *Phi Delta Kappan*, 70, pp. 313–316.

TRUSTY, F.M. and SERGIOVANNI, T.J. (1966) 'Perceived need deficiencies of teachers and administrators: A proposal for restructuring teacher roles', *Educational Administrative Quarterly*, 2, pp. 168–180.

WEICK, K.E. (1979) 'The social psychology of organizing' (2nd ed.), Reading, MA, Addison-Wesley.

Part 2
Focusing the Perspective

4   The Teacher as Leader

Ralph Fessler

Teachers represent a reservoir of untapped leadership potential which, if released and channeled, could greatly improve teaching and learning in schools. The challenge is to develop strategies to direct teacher leadership into activities related to staff development and instructional improvement. This must be done in a manner that does not force our best and most creative teachers to leave the classroom in order to pursue leadership positions in administration or supervision. Numerous opportunities for leadership reside within the role of teaching, and these must be reinforced and nourished. Examples of potential school improvement leadership roles for teachers include designing and conducting inservice sessions, routinely engaging in peer coaching activities, serving as mentors for new teachers, actively participating in pre-service training of prospective teachers, writing and refining curriculum, engaging in action research, and, in all of these activities, taking responsibility for aligning school goals with classroom instructional activities.

In this chapter the rationale for a teacher leadership model will be explored, and a model for such a program will be presented.

Rationale for Teacher Leadership Model

In recent years a variety of emerging issues and developments have converged, creating a climate conducive to empowering teachers with increased responsibility and leadership. The following are key illustrations of this trend:

Expanded Role of the Principal

The expanding responsibilities and roles of the principal make it imperative that power be shared with teachers. It is impossible for one person to perform all of the roles being currently assigned to principals. In Maryland, for example, a recent state task force (The Maryland Commission on School-based Administration, 1987) called for the following as responsibilities and roles for a school principal:

- Instructional maintenance and improvement
- Professional development and service
- Pupil development and service
- School and community relations
- Administration of facilities and finance
- Organizational relationships and responsibilities

In order to perform these role functions, the Maryland report states that principals must demonstrate conceptual understanding in *nineteen* separate areas (including such diverse topics as human growth and development, theories of instruction, adult learning theory, curriculum theory, supervision theory, change theory, leadership theory, community and public relations, technology, business management, personnel and labor relations, pupil services, and research related to effective educational practices). Moreover, the report calls for principals to demonstrate competencies in ten separate skill areas (instructional supervision, planning and goal setting, problem analysis, decision-making, communication, coordination, interpersonal relations, staff development, conflict resolution, and stress management). Similar descriptions of the principal's expanded role have been cited in national studies (The University Council for Educational Administration, 1987; Danforth Foundation, 1989).

Although the various duties expected of principals (and the competencies and skills necessary to fulfill them) are important, it is unrealistic to expect one person to perform all of those functions well. Charged with reconciling unrealistic role expectations with the everyday realities of school life, principals are forced to make choices. Priorities are set on the basis of personal strengths, interests, and day-to-day pressures. Activities related to teacher development and instructional improvement may be high on the list of some principals but viewed as less important by others. Rather than diluting principals' energies and efforts with important but unrealistic expectations, it makes much more sense to share power, leadership and decision-making with teachers. Given the expanded responsibilities and expectations being placed on principals, this may be the only practical approach.

Principal Role Conflict

A dilemma often faced by principals is the conflict between their accountability and staff development roles. As principals, they are expected to represent the interests of the school system in evaluating teachers for purposes of contract renewal, tenure and related personnel matters. Activities in this sphere often include classroom supervisory visits to assess teacher performance, evaluative conferences, and written comments which become permanent parts of personnel records. These are reasonable role expectations from a management point of view. In order to fulfill the staff development function, however, it is necessary to build open trust relationships with faculty. Teachers must have confidence that the supervisor is there to help, not to 'snoopervise'. This necessitates open communication, sharing of strengths and weaknesses, and confidentiality.

Some principals possess the management and interpersonal skills to play effectively both the accountability and helping relationship roles. This is a rare combination of skills, however, and many well-intending administrators have difficulty wearing both hats. An alternative approach is to separate the functions, with the principal maintaining the management accountability function and the teachers empowered to work with their peers to support teacher development.

School Restructuring Movement

In recent years there have been numerous attempts to 'restructure' schools to make them more responsive to changing needs. Several models have called for various forms of 'school-based management', a term used to describe efforts to transfer resources and decision-making from the central office to schools (Guthrie, 1986). Examples include restructuring efforts in Chicago, Miami, Buffalo and Rochester. Approaches to school-based management are compatible with the notion of teacher empowerment. In order to implement school-based management programs, it is essential to share with teachers the decision-making and leadership related to teacher devolopment and curriculum that traditionally have been the responsibility of central office personnel and principals.

Teacher Plateauing

A problem inherent to the teaching profession is the tendency for teachers to 'top out' or 'plateau' in job mobility almost as soon as they enter the classroom. Except for a few school districts that have experimented with career ladders and lattices, teachers have limited career options. A teacher

who desires the challenges of leadership, mobility, and expanded responsibility is often forced to leave teaching, either by making an exit from
education completely or by opting for non-classroom education roles such
as administration, supervision or counseling. Many teachers who remain
in the classroom are forced to repress their leadership needs. The teacher
leadership options presented in this chapter offer the opportunity for
creative and energetic teachers to experience new challenges without
having to leave the classroom to find them. Expert teachers are kept
where they do the most good – in the classroom with students.

Support from Research and Literature

The concept of teacher leadership is supported by the literature and
research on participatory management. Thomas Sergiovanni (1979) has
drawn extensively on the work of Maslow (1966) and Herzberg (1959) in
analyzing motivation and incentive factors important in a school climate.
Sergiovanni's modified version of Maslow's hierarchy of needs emphasizes
the importance of establishing security for teachers in the form of money,
benefits, tenure and role consolidation before concerns switch to social
need satisfaction, self-esteem, autonomy and self-actualization. The addition of autonomy as a basic need is an adaptation of special note. Sergiovanni argues that the need for professional independence in decision-
making is a very high order need for teachers, surpassed only by the need
for self-actualization.

The work of Herzberg is also applicable to teacher motivation and
teacher incentives. Herzberg's two-factor theory differentiates between
'hygiene factors' and 'motivational factors'. The former refers to lower
level needs such as salary, growth possibilities, status, working conditions,
policy and administration and job security. These hygiene factors are
considered 'dissatisfiers', in that their absence will lead to a decreased
level of performance that does not meet minimally acceptable standards.
The adequate fulfillment of lower level needs will lead to 'a fair day's work
for a fair day's pay', but not much more. According to Herzberg and
Sergiovanni, merely increasing the fulfillment level of these needs will not
result in professionals moving above a basic level of performance because
needs that are already met to an adequate degree no longer serve as
motivators. In order to create a climate that encourages higher levels of
performance, motivational factors must be present. These include higher
level needs such as the need for achievement, recognition, excitement
inherent in the work itself, responsibility, and advancement. Satisfaction
derived from fulfillment of these needs will lead to performance that
exceeds 'a fair day's work for a fair day's pay', but removing them will not
reduce performance below that basic level. It seems clear that these

motivational needs would be well-served in an environment of teacher empowerment.

Other work in education and management offers additional support for empowering workers and teachers for leadership and decision-making. Examples include the work of McGregor (1960) and the various approaches to participatory management that are found in Japanese management strategies (Ouchi, 1981).

Expanded Teacher Union Agenda

Finally, in recent years the agenda of teacher unions has been expanded to include advocacy of teacher empowerment for purposes of leadership (Shanker, 1987; Futrell, 1987; Vaughn, 1987). During the formative period of the teacher union movement, the focus was on salary, fringe benefits, job security and related issues that tended to fall into Herzberg's list of 'hygiene factors'. In recent years, however, the agenda has expanded to include topics related to teacher autonomy and participation in decision-making. Issues of teacher leadership are now a priority for teacher unions.

In summary, numerous converging factors seem to be supporting a climate receptive to the notion of teacher leadership. The time is right for expanding role options for teachers.

Teacher Leadership Options

Teacher leadership can take many forms. Some leadership options are summarized in Figure 4.1. This is not meant to be an all-inclusive list, nor are all of the options mutually exclusive. Indeed, there is much overlap among categories. The key here is that teachers should be given the opportunity to experience leadership roles without being forced to leave the classroom permanently. Support for this approach may require some scheduling and role modifications, and more will be said about this later in the chapter. The following are descriptions of the expanded role options summarized in Figure 4.1.

Teacher as Pre-service Teacher Educator

The potential for teacher leadership in pre-service teacher education expands beyond the traditional role of supervision of student teachers. Classroom teachers should be involved in methods classes as well as hosting practicum experiences in their classrooms. They are in a unique position to apply theory to practice as teachers, mentors and role models.

Ralph Fessler

Figure 4.1   Strategies for Teacher Empowerment and Leadership

Source: Ralph Fessler, The Johns Hopkins University

Partnerships with universities can lead to the designing of structures that will provide leadership outlets for teachers as well as improvement of teacher education. The concept of the 'clinical professorship' is not new but has taken on a fresh perspective in light of recent calls for reform of education and teacher education (Holmes Group, 1986; Carnegie Forum on Education and the Economy, 1986). Teachers working in partnership with universities also become leaders in areas such as mentoring, teacher-led inservice and staff development, and teacher research.

Teacher as Mentor of New Teachers

Experienced teachers have a key role to play in supporting the efforts of beginning teachers (Thies-Sprinthall, 1986). Mentor teachers can provide novices with guidance and structure in the context of a trusting relationship. Specific activities can include assisting new teachers in 'learning the ropes' regarding school and system policies, practices and politics, as well as assisting them with specific classroom management and instructional techniques.

62

Teacher as Researcher

Teachers live and work in a living laboratory. They are constantly faced with decisions among alternative courses of action. The teacher researcher would accept the challenge of constantly applying the questions of an applied social scientist to everyday problems and decisions. Activities would include observing problems that emerge in everyday classroom situations, gathering data about the problems and alternative solutions, formulating hypotheses about potential solutions to the problems, gathering data to test and retest the hypotheses, and drawing tentative conclusions. A research orientation to teaching and learning raises the potential for continuous teacher renewal and school improvement. In addition, a teacher-as-researcher model could provide the basis for collaborative field-based research between schools and universities.

Teacher as Organizational Leader

Opportunities for leadership in professional associations provide an excellent source for teachers' higher level need satisfaction by providing recognition for their expertise and leadership. Opportunities such as these should be encouraged by school systems, and support should be provided in the form of released time and financial assistance for travel.

Teacher as Staff Developer

Teacher-led staff development is often the most effective format for school-based inservice activities (Howey, *et al.*, 1981). Here teacher leadership can include working with peers to identify school and individual teacher growth needs, identifying available resources to assist in meeting those needs, and, when appropriate, delivering the inservice or professional growth activity.

There is a great deal of talent in the ranks of teachers, which too often goes unrecognized and unrewarded. Teacher leadership in staff development activities provides opportunities for talented teachers to share their expertise with others and to gain well-deserved recognition.

Teacher as Peer Coach

The role of the teacher as peer coach is to provide assistance to other teachers in the context of a supportive, helping relationship (Joyce and Showers, 1982). The ambiguity of roles that confronts the administrator-supervisor would not be present here. Specific strategies and skills that would assist teachers in this role include suggesting appropriate alternative strategies, and providing constructive and continuing feedback on modifications attempted.

Teacher as Curriculum Developer

Teachers have an important role to play as curriculum developers. Participation in curriculum-writing workshops can be a means of tapping their expertise and directing their experience into the process of developing new curriculum materials. Not only is the product likely to be better if teachers are directly involved in this process, but the probability of implementation is greatly enhanced as well. Teachers who have an investment in curriculum-writing projects are more likely to use the products of their efforts and to encourage their peers to do so as well.

Organizational Support

The key to implementing a teacher leadership model is an organizational commitment to empowering teachers to seek leadership opportunities. While some implementation problems exist, an organization with a commitment to this approach can develop reasonable solutions. The following are some suggested strategies:

Empowering Teachers Through Training and Development

School systems should encourage teachers to develop the expertise necessary to assume the leadership roles described above. This should include identifying teachers with interest in and potential for leadership and providing them with the necessary support and training. Opportunities should include university coursework, self-study, conferences, workshops, and, perhaps most important, opportunities to try new ideas.

A new master's degree program to support teacher leadership has been established at The Johns Hopkins University. The curriculum of this program centers on preparing teachers for school-based leadership by developing skills in areas such as peer coaching, curriculum development, staff development, field-based research and advanced instructional strategies.

Team Teaching

Team teaching options provide opportunities for teachers to work and plan together in ways that maximize individual strengths. Open communication, planning and cooperation are essential to effective teaching teams. The climate created by such activities may facilitate natural expressions of teacher leadership in areas such as curriculum development, peer coaching and mentoring.

Career Ladders/Lattices

A key feature of career ladders is the differentiation of teacher roles to provide opportunities for teacher leadership. Numerous examples appeared in the 1950s and 1960s (Christensen, 1987) and have surfaced again in recent years (Jundura and Burke, 1989). Such models provide for differentiated roles for teachers as they move up a ladder of responsibility and leadership. A fresh approach offered by Christensen, McDonnell, and Price (1988) advocates a 'Career Lattice' approach, which differentiates among roles for specific activities and projects without presuming a one-directional, 'up the ladder' concept. (See Chapter 7.) Such approaches provide specific strategies for empowering teachers for leadership.

Modest adaptations of role structures that provide opportunities for teacher leadership include the creation of positions such as team leaders, grade-level leaders and chairs of school staff development committees.

Flexible Employment Patterns

The notion of flexibility in employment patterns offers additional support for teacher leadership opportunities. One example of this would be summer curriculum-writing teams, where teachers engage in planning and writing curriculum they will be using. Other examples include teacher internships in leadership positions as well as sabbaticals to enable teachers to gain new leadership skills.

One rather innovative option deserving special mention is the temporary assignment of teachers to work as resource specialists in teacher centers. Both the Howard County Teacher Center in Maryland and the Regional Staff Development Center in Kenosha, Wisconsin, have utilized this approach, (see Chapter 9). Teachers are 'loaned' to the center to work with other teachers in curriculum and instructional improvement projects. After a specified period of time (one or two years) these individuals return to their schools, where their roles as teacher leaders continue.

Ralph Fessler

Summary

Providing teachers with leadership opportunities supports current reform activities such as school-based management, school restructuring and teacher empowerment. In addition, the notion of teacher leadership addresses issues such as expanded, unrealistic job expectations for principals and the conflict between the accountability and staff development roles experienced by supervisors.

Teachers are in a position to provide leadership in areas such as preservice teacher education, mentoring, research, professional organizations, staff development and inservice, peer coaching, and curriculum development. Empowering teachers for such leadership roles provides opportunities for teachers' higher level need satisfaction, and brings valuable expertise to the problems of school improvement.

The ideas presented in this chapter are offered as a challenge to school supervisors and administrators. Effective leaders should utilize all of the resources at their disposal to enhance teaching and learning in their schools. Empowering teachers for school leadership can only increase the potential for school improvement.

References

CARNEGIE FORUM ON EDUCATION AND THE ECONOMY (1986) 'A nation prepared: Teachers for the 21st century', Washington, DC, The Carnegie Forum.

CHRISTENSEN, J.C. (1987) 'Roles of teachers and administrators', in BURDEN, P. (Ed.) *Establishing Career Ladders in Teaching*, Springfield, IL, Charles C. Thomas.

CHRISTENSEN, J.C., MCDONNELL, J.H. and PRICE, J.J. (1988) *Personalizing Staff Development: The Career Lattice Model*, Fastback 281, Bloomington, IN, Phi Delta Kappa Educational Foundation.

DANFORTH FOUNDATION (1989) 'Searching for the right reforms', *A Report on the Danforth Program for Professors of School Administration*, April.

FUTRELL, M. (1987) 'Career ladders: An NEA perspective', in BURDEN, P. (Ed.) *Establishing Career Ladders in Teaching*, Springfield, IL, Charles C. Thomas.

GUTHRIE, J.W. (1986) 'School-based management: The next needed educational reform', *Phi Delta Kappan*, 68, pp. 305–309.

HERZBERG, F., MAUSNER, B. and SNYDERMAN, B. (1959) *The Motivation to Work*, New York, John Wiley and Sons.

HOLMES GROUP (1986) 'Tomorrow's teachers: A report of the Holmes Group', East Lansing, MI, Michigan State University.

HOWEY, K.R., BENTS, R. and CORRIGAN, D. (Eds) (1981) *School-Focused Inservice: Descriptions and Discussions*, Reston, VA, Association of Teacher Educators.

JOYCE, B. and SHOWERS, B. (1982) 'The coaching of teaching', *Educational Leadership*, October, 40, 4–8, p. 10.

JUNDURA, R. and BURKE, P. (1989) *Differentiated Career Opportunities for Teachers*, Bloomington, IN, Phi Delta Kappa Educational Foundation.

THE MARYLAND COMMISSION ON SCHOOL-BASED ADMINISTRATION (1987) *Improving the Effectiveness of School-Based Administration in Maryland*, Baltimore, MD.

MASLOW, A.H. (1960) *Motivation and Personality*, New York, McGraw Hill.

McGREGOR, D. (1960) *The Human Side of Enterprise*, New York, McGraw Hill.

OUCHI, W. (1981) *Theory Z: How American Business can Meet the Japanese Challenge*, Boston, Addison-Wesley.

SERGIOVANNI, T. and STARRATT, R. (1979) *Supervision: Human Perspectives*, New York, McGraw Hill.

SHANKER, A. (1987) 'Support for career ladders from teacher associations: New School teachers', in BURDEN, P. (Ed.) *Establishing Career Ladders in Teaching*, Springfield, IL, Charles C. Thomas.

THIES-SPRINTHALL, L. (1986) 'A collaborative approach for mentor training: A working model', *Journal of Teacher Education, Vol. XXXVII*, December, 6, pp. 13–20.

THE UNIVERSITY COUNCIL FOR EDUCATIONAL ADMINISTRATION (1987) 'Leaders for America's schools', *The Report of the National Commission on Excellence in Educational Administration*.

VAUGHN, J. (1987) 'The role of teacher unions in the development and implementation of incentive programs: Attracting excellence', *Proceedings of a Seminar on Incentives That Enhance the Teaching Profession*, Elmhurst, IL, North Central Regional Educational Laboratory.

5   The Practitioner's Perspective

Barbara Herzog and Patricia Koll

The perspective of the practitioner – that is, teachers, principals and staff developers – has long been one focused on the nuts and bolts of everyday activities. In contrast, the theorist has been conceived of as one in the ivory tower who is out of touch with the realities of everyday circumstances. Thus, the long standing theory-practice gap.

It has been our experience that the gap is more myth than reality. We firmly believe that theory lays a solid foundation for effective practice and our experiences with applied research, including the study reported here, have confirmed John Dewey's contention that 'theory is, in the end, the most practical of all things' (Griffiths, 1959, p. 10). Griffiths goes on to explain that theory describes the 'what is' of practice (1959, pp. 14–15).

Of particular concern to practitioners in recent years have been instructional leadership and the professional development of those who are instructional leaders. Since the effective schools research pointed up the importance of strong instructional leadership, it seemed appropriate to target that area for applied research to determine the extent to which theory and practice are in harmony.

More specifically, the study reported in this chapter is part of a more comprehensive research project undertaken in Wisconsin to determine the frequency of participation, the motivation to participate, the value of participation, and the role of the principal in promoting professional development activities. Although this report focuses primarily on the role of the principal in encouraging the professional development of teachers, it also highlights the implications of the study for teacher education and for staff development. The perspective taken is that instructional leadership, to be most effective, must be a team enterprise (Glickman, 1989). Staff developers and teachers themselves must be equipped to assume responsibility for decision-making about professional growth and school improvement.

68

This larger study is a follow-up to an earlier research project by one of the authors (Herzog, 1984) on the motivation of Wisconsin 'Teachers of the Year' to participate in professional development activities. The earlier study also examined frequency of participation, motivation to participate, value of participation, and the role of the principal in promoting professional development activities. The sample and population in the earlier study were smaller than in this study. The theoretical framework for determining motivation in both the Herzog study and this study followed the work of Maslow (1954).

Purpose of the Study

A general problem exists for practitioners and theorists alike in that there are both contradictory and inconclusive studies regarding motivation and staff development. Important questions need exploration: what motivates teachers to develop professionally, and how can a principal nurture the motivation to enhance teacher participation in professional development?

The first purpose of the study was to identify factors which motivate both teachers and principals to engage in continuing professional development. The second and equally important purpose was to examine the role played by the school principal in encouraging continuing professional development on the part of teachers. It was important to attempt to determine more precisely the role of the principal in encouraging the continuing professional development of teachers due to the rhetoric in the literature related to the role of the principal as instructional leader, the effective schools research, and the theory-practice connection for practitioners.

Given the lack of mobility of many of today's teaching staffs and the rising average age of teachers in numerous districts, it is increasingly imperative to keep present teaching staffs and principals professionally up-to-date and vital. Means must be found to encourage their continual professional development. According to Evans, schools must support staff members' ongoing development in order to sustain staff competence (1989, p. 10).

> To remain current, to assist in the dynamics of societal and world change, schools must reflect the ability to adapt and to improve. Fundamental in this process is the notion that individuals currently in the field must be improved. The hallmark of a true profession is one where the most recent and vital information is disseminated and used by its members. We have arrived at a juncture where to remain static while the world demands change is exceptionally precarious. (Hansen, 1980, p. 67)

One of the purposes of inservice education, staff development, or continuing professional development is to adapt and improve educator performance, concomitant with societal and professional changes. It is important to identify factors which motivate educators to engage in such improvement activities as well as to promote the critical role of the principal as a leader of instructional leaders if positive changes are to be effected in schools. According to Glickman, 'the principal is not seen as the sole instructional leader but rather as the leader of instructional leaders' (1989, p. 6).

The research questions that guided the segment of the study reported in this chapter were:

1 to what extent do teachers and principals regularly engage in different continuing professional development activities?
2 what motivates teachers and principals to engage in continuing professional development?
3 to what extent do professional development activities contribute to their growth?
4 what is the role of the principal in encouraging the continuing professional development of teachers?
5 what are the implications of the study for teacher educators, principals and staff developers?

Answers to these questions could not only illuminate the realities of instructional leadership and professional development, but could also bridge the theory-practice gap for practitioners in varied settings.

Design of the Study

The population of the study included all of the teachers nominated by their respective school districts in 1986 for the annual Teacher of the Year (TOY) Award (n = 125) conferred by the Wisconsin Department of Public Instruction (DPI), and all of the principals nominated by their respective school districts in 1986 for the annual Wisconsin DPI's Principal of the Year (POY) Award (n = 30). Teachers were nominated for the award in one of the four categories: elementary, middle/junior high, senior high, and special services. Principals were nominated in one of three categories: elementary, middle/junior high, and senior high.

Random samples of Wisconsin teachers (RT) and principals (RP) in numbers equivalent to the numbers of teachers and principals nominated for the above mentioned DPI awards were also surveyed. These random groups were included in the study in order to make the results more generalizable to all Wisconsin teachers and principals and to gain additional insights that would be instructive to teacher educators, school principals and staff developers.

A written survey questionnaire was mailed to each teacher and each principal involved in the study. The survey contained a list of thirty professional development activities for which respondents were asked to assess the frequency and extent of involvement as well as their motivation for participation. The principal and teacher versions were identical except for an additional page of nineteen items on which teachers were asked to give their perceptions of their own principal's actions in encouraging professional development of teachers, and principals were asked to describe their own actions relative to the same nineteen items. The survey was based on the one used in Herzog (1984) with appropriate modifications and additions.

A follow-up mailing sought additional responses to the survey and ultimately resulted in an overall response rate of approximately 86 per cent. Frequency data and t-tests were used to analyze the responses of the four subgroups to each of the questions addressed in the study. A t-test is a statistical test which allows for comparison of two means to determine whether the difference between the means is a real difference or a chance difference (Tuckman, 1978, p. 257). Implications for teacher educators, principals and staff developers were extrapolated from the data.

Data Analysis

Respondents were asked to identify the frequency of their participation in the thirty professional development activities over the past two years from none to five-or-more occurrences. Mean responses of the four subgroups (principals of the year, random principals, teachers of the year and random teachers) were used to identify top priorities from the responses to frequency of participation. Four items out of the thirty total were selected by all four groups as top priorities. The mean values for the highest responses to frequency of participation are given with rank orders in Table 5.1.

In order to analyze the data in the section dealing with motivation, the thirty professional development activities were grouped into seven categories. These categories included (1) attending conventions, conferences and workshops; (2) making presentations at conventions, conferences and workshops; (3) reading professional journals; (4) observing other teachers teaching; (5) taking educational television (ETV), educational telephone (ETN), university, or vocational school (VTAE) credit or non-credit courses; (6) attending curriculum, staff development, task force, or professional organization meetings; and (7) writing or reviewing student textbooks or writing journal articles.

The reasons for participation follow the work of Maslow as modified by Porter (cited in Hoy and Miskel, 1982). The levels provided for

Table 5.1 Highest priorities for frequency of participation

ITEM	POY		RP		TOY		RT	
	Mean	Rank	Mean	Rank	Mean	Rank	Mean	Rank
Observing other teachers teaching	4.8	(1)	4.7	(1)	1.9	(4)	2.0	(4)
Attending meetings as a member of a curriculum committee	4.3	(2)	4.3	(2)	3.9	(1)	2.9	(2)
Reading professional journals	4.1	(3)	4.2	(3)	3.6	(2)	3.2	(1)
Attending an in-district workshop	3.9	(4)	3.7	(5)	3.3	(3)	2.8	(3)
Attending meetings as a member of an inservice council	3.8	(5)	3.8	(4)	*		*	

* Not in top five
POY = Principal of the Year (n = 29)
RP = Random Principal (n = 30)
TOY = Teacher of the Year (n = 104)
RT = Random Teacher (n = 107)

selection by respondents were (A) security, (B) belonging, (C) self-esteem, (D) autonomy, and (E) self-actualization. It was interesting to note that the most popular responses for participation in staff development programs were (E) self-actualization and (C) self-esteem, followed by (A) security. These results were similar to those reported in the Herzog study (1984).

A summary of the reasons for participation for each of the seven categories follows:

1 Attending conventions, conferences and workshops: although both teacher groups were more likely to attend conventions, conferences, and workshops for security reasons, all four groups identified self-actualization followed by self-esteem needs as their primary motivators.
2 Making presentations at conventions, conferences, and workshops: the principals of the year were more likely to make conference or workshop presentations than were members of the other three groups. Self-esteem and self-actualization needs were the primary reasons cited by all four groups.
3 Reading professional journals: all four groups reported self-actualization and then self-esteem needs as their two main reasons for reading professional journals.
4 Observing other teachers teaching: more principals identified security and autonomy as reasons for observing teachers teaching than did the teachers. Observation of teachers is traditionally part of a principal's job description. For teachers, self-actualization and

self-esteem were most often identified, whereas self-actualization and autonomy were more often identified by principals.

5   Taking ETV, ETN, university or technical school credit or non-credit courses: although overall few of the subjects in the study reported having taken ETV (educational television), ETN (educational telephone network), university, or vocational school courses, those who did in the principal of the year, random principal and teacher of the year groups cited self-actualization and self-esteem as their primary motivators. For random teachers, security ranked just behind self-actualization as a motivator.

6   Attending curriculum, staff development, task force, or professional organization meetings: teachers of the year, principals of the year, and random principals were motivated to attend curriculum, staff development or professional meetings to meet self-actualization and self-esteem needs. Random teachers were motivated first by self-actualization and second by security.

7   Writing or reviewing student textbooks or writing journal articles: few of the subjects reported having written articles or having reviewed textbooks. For those who did in all four groups, self-actualization and self-esteem were identified as the primary motivating factors.

In response to the section of the questionnaire asking the extent to which various activities have contributed to their professional development, respondents could select from a five-point scale which varied from 1 for none to 6 for a great extent. Teachers and principals identified taking university non-credit courses and reading of professional journals as contributing the most to their professional development. These same activities were also rated high by the subgroups in terms of frequency of participation. Professional development activities cited by teachers as contributing the most to their professional development included taking a university non-credit course and reading of professional journals. Professional development activities cited by principals as contributing the most to their professional development included observing teachers teaching, taking a university non-credit course, attending meetings as a member of a building or district curriculum committee, attending an in-district workshop, and reading of professional journals. Thus, those professional development activities cited as contributing the most to the growth of the subjects were also the ones for which they reported the highest frequency of participation.

In the last section of the survey nineteen items dealt with perceptions of the role of the principal in promoting continuing professional development among teachers from the respective viewpoints of principals and teachers. The five-point scale for responses varied from 1 for no involvement to 5 for great involvement. The perceptions of both groups of principals as to how they promoted staff development were significantly higher than the perceptions of both groups of teachers as indicated by the t-test values reported in Table 5.2. All differences between teachers and principals were statistically significant at the .01 level. In other words, principals perceive themselves as doing more to enhance staff development than teachers acknowledged.

For each of the nineteen principal behaviors, the mean values for the principals of the year were higher than those for the teachers of the year; sixteen of these differences were statistically significant. The three principal behaviors for which the differences between the principals of the year and the teachers of the year were not statistically significant at the .05 level were: providing access to school funds for professional travel, keeping written records of teacher participation in continuing professional development and encouraging/requiring each teacher to have an annual plan for continuing professional development.

Table 5.3 compares the mean values for the perceptions of the four groups relative to the top-ranked principal behaviors for encouraging professional development. As shown in Table 5.3, the four respondent groups included the same four principal behaviors among the top five ranked items.

Positive school climate, an important characteristic of an effective school (Edmonds, 1982), was ranked by teachers and principals at the top of all lists. Teacher leadership, a concept in the forefront of current literature in teacher education (Howey, 1988, Zimpher, 1988), was ranked second or third by all four groups. Out of nineteen possible activities, all groups ranked the same five or six items at the top of their lists as strategies that principals use to encourage teacher professional development.

Implications of the Study for Principals

The research reported here supports the findings of others (Fielding and Schalock, 1985; Mazzarella, 1983; McEvoy, 1987) that principals can enhance professional growth within their schools. As a result of this research and the findings of others related to the role of the principal, we stress the importance of the following:

1　Acting as staff developers: Administrator preparation programs should prepare school principals for the roles they must play in motivating the professional growth of their staff. At present, the topic of staff development does not receive a great deal of attention in administrator preparation programs despite the fact that staff development is a key to school improvement.

2　Acting as instructional leaders: Administrator preparation pro-

Table 5.2   Perceptions of principals' behaviors to encourage professional development

ITEM (Ranked by Principals' Means)	MEAN ALL PRINCIPALS n = 59	MEAN ALL TEACHERS n = 211	t* VALUE
1. Actively works at establishing a positive school climate	4.8	3.6	−6.26
2. Encourages development/implementation of new curricular/instructional ideas	4.4	3.3	−6.13
3. Provides opportunities for teachers to assume leadership	4.3	3.3	−5.12
4. Cooperates with a building inservice/staff development council	4.1	3.4	−3.86
5. Sets an example by participation in continuing professional development himself/herself	3.8	2.9	−5.15
6. Serves as a mentor for key teachers who have potential for professional development	3.7	2.6	−5.99

7. Acknowledges teacher participation in
    continuing professional development in oral
    or written form to the teacher
	3.7	2.5	−5.83

8. Provides access to school funds for
    professional travel to conferences,
    conventions, workshops, etc.
	3.6	3.0	−3.38

9. Includes continuing professional development in the yearly teacher evaluation	3.6	2.6	−4.93
10. Discusses staff development expectations during interviews with teacher candidates	3.6	2.3	−6.90
11. Allocates funds for a school professional library	3.3	2.5	−4.64
12. Encourages teachers to engage in self- assessment	3.4	2.5	−5.36
13. Plans for continuing professional development within faculty meetings	3.4	2.6	−4.17
14. Provides information about or suggests graduate courses for faculty to take	3.4	2.3	−5.80
15. Encourages inter-class or inter-school visitations	3.4	2.2	−6.45

16. Acknowledges teacher participation in
    continuing professional development in the
    school bulletin or newsletter
	3.3	2.2	−5.54

17. Keeps written records of teacher participation in continuing professional development	3.2	2.6	−3.08

18. Encourages and/or requires each teacher to
    have an annual plan for his/her continuing
    professional development
	2.8	2.0	−3.57

19. Offers to teach classes for staff members in
    order to demonstrate specific instructional
    strategies
	2.8	1.5	−8.30

*   All t values significant at the .01 level

Barbara Herzog and Patricia Koll

Table 5.3 Perceptions of principals' strategies to encourage professional development.

ITEM	POY		RP		TOY		RT	
	Mean	Rank	Mean	Rank	Mean	Rank	Mean	Rank
1. Actively works at establishing a positive school climate	4.9	(1)	4.7	(1)	3.7	(1)	3.6	(1)
2. Provides opportunities for teachers to assume leadership	4.6	(2)	4.1	(3)	3.5	(3)	3.2	(2)
3. Encourages development/ implementation of new curricular/ instructional ideas	4.4	(3)	4.3	(2)	3.4	(4)	3.1	(4)
4. Cooperates with a building inservice/ staff development council	4.3	(4)	4.0	(4)	3.6	(2)	3.2	(3)
5. Provides access to school funds for professional travel	*		3.8	(5)	3.1	(5)	2.8	(5)

* Not in top five
POY = Principal of the Year (n = 29)
RP   = Random Principal (n = 30)
TOY = Teacher of the Year (n = 104)
RT   = Random Teacher (n = 107)

grams must emphasize the instructional leadership role of the principal and deemphasize the school-manager role. Such programs must provide concrete examples as to what instructional leaders do that distinguish them from school managers. Reasons for emphasizing the need for instructional leadership must be provided to aspiring administrators.

3   Motivating professional growth: Principals need to be ready to discuss motivational forces with their staffs as an integral part of the supervision and evaluation program. Principals should encourage staff to engage in self-analysis of their motivation as it relates to professional growth. Staff need to know that their principals have high expectations when it comes to supervision for the improvement of instruction and the professional growth of staff. Continued growth needs to be seen as the norm in our schools.

4   Working closely with committees: Principals need to work more closely with district or building staff development committees to design alternative approaches to staff development that will be motivational and will facilitate the meeting of self-esteem and

self-actualization needs. Too often principals view themselves as separated from the staff development programs designed for their staffs.

5 Effective communication: Improved communication should occur between principal and staff so that the principal's verbal and non-verbal behaviors communicate a clear message relative to the importance of professional growth and the ways in which they are nurturing it. Discussion of staff development expectations should begin with the initial job interview and should continue throughout a staff member's tenure. Principals need to communicate more effectively to their staffs the ways in which they do promote staff professional growth.

6 Involving teachers: Principals need to share their instructional leadership role with other staff members to effect the greatest impact. Principals need to nurture instructional leadership among members of their teaching staffs. They also need to provide opportunities to involve teachers in decision-making about professional and school improvement. Teacher empowerment can become a reality only if principals have the skills and the predispositions to make it happen.

Implications of the study for Staff Developers

Staff developers and principals who both share the primary responsibility for professional growth need to be better prepared to deal with the issue of motivation. With that in mind, we offer practitioners the following seven recommendations. These recommendations are most germane to a school system large enough to employ a practitioner to serve at least half time as a staff development specialist.

1. Staff developers' relationship to principals: Staff developers should serve as coaches to principals in their role as instructional leaders, and, as a result of their training and experience, are generally more sensitive to motivational concerns and instructional improvement than are principals. As they work with principals, they will need to encourage principals to assume more of an instructional leadership role and less of a school-manager role. Staff developers may need to put themselves in a coaching role in working with principals for whom the instructional leader role may be an unfamiliar and, perhaps, a threatening one. This role should be as important to staff developers as their role in training teachers.

2. Encouraging motivation: Staff developers should encourage self-assessment of motivation. Both staff developers and principals must encourage teachers to engage in self-analysis of their motivation as it relates to professional growth. Self-assessment and needs assessment strategies that incorporate motivational concerns should be provided by staff developers on at least an annual basis. Some helpful resources in this area include the Job Preference Questionnaire which enables teachers to diagnose their own level of motivation in the Maslow hierarchy. Results could be discussed in conferences with staff developers or with principals. Curwin and Fuhrman in *Discovering Your Teaching Self* (1975) provide a variety of self-assessment instruments that include motivation and value-oriented emphases along with performance proficiencies. The Harris-Hill (1982) DeTEK system incorporates teacher self-assessment as one component of the assessment.

3. Meeting staff needs: Staff developers should design alternative approaches to staff development to meet both self-esteem and self-actualization needs. They can enlist the aid of principals and staff development committees in designing alternative approaches to staff development that will meet self-esteem and self-actualization needs, needs identified in both this study and the Herzog study (1984) as being the main motivators. Staff developers should also be familiar with and promote the kinds of activities that participants in this study reported as being frequent and effective vehicles for their professional growth. Observing other teachers teaching, reading professional journals, taking university non-credit courses, and the like can be integrated into the menu of alternatives for staff development. Observing other teachers can generate perspectives on teaching style, teaching strategies and classroom management practices that could be adapted/adopted and utilized in the observer's classroom.

Professional journals often provide specific suggestions for new materials, instructional strategies, student activities and current curricular directions. University non-credit courses can be designed to respond to local professional needs and are often delivered by classroom teachers. Staff developers can facilitate the scheduling of interschool or interclass observations, the securing of budget support for professional libraries in every building, as well as working with university outreach offices to plan appropriate non-credit courses.

4. Meeting district expectations: Staff developers should collaborate with principals in meeting district expectations. Both staff developers and principals must communicate clear messages about the importance of professional growth. In order that a consistent message is communicated, staff developers may need to work with principals who send mixed messages through their verbal and nonverbal behaviors. Clearly, the principal's supervisor must articulate these expectations and hold principals accountable for professional growth. However, staff developers can be a key resource for and collaborator with principals in meeting these expectations.

5. *Enhancing motivation:* Staff developers should broaden the range of incentives to enhance motivation, and may also need to encourage districts and schools to provide more varied incentives. Motivation is too often assumed; administrators may 'take it for granted' that teachers will be motivated to grow professionally. Because of the number and complexity of variables that affect teacher motivation, such is not always the case. Staff developers must stand ready to provide suggestions for appropriate incentives that can move from extrinsic to intrinsic in nature.

6. *Encouraging university participation in staff development:* Staff developers and teacher educators should crusade for non-credit university involvement in career-long professional development (Larson, Koll, and Cozad, 1988). To this end staff developers need to acknowledge the accepted findings relative to credit courses as a part of continuing professional growth. Teachers and principals in this study reported a comparatively low interest in taking credit courses to enhance their professional skills. Rather, the course activities that engage them more are of a non-credit nature (such as make-it and take-it workshops and local inservice education programs) a fact that is incongruent with the way in which most universities are funded. Staff developers and teacher educators must join the crusade to change that circumstance. They must tell boards of regents, legislators, and others who control budgets, both public and private, that professors must be available to work with staff development in a variety of non-credit modes on a part-of-load basis. These types of non-credit activities are critical to the professional development of teachers and principals. If teacher education institutions are to play a vital and collegial role in staff development, a mechanism to fund university involvement on a part-of-load basis must be designed and implemented (Larson, Koll, and Cozad, 1988). Anything less is an empty promise of the collaboration of higher education in staff development programs.

7. *Selection of principals as instructional leaders:* Staff developers should encourage the selection of principals who are instructional leaders. Staff developers should support the hiring of principals who are committed to continuing professional development for both themselves and for their staffs, and they need to use opportunities to serve on screening committees to crusade for the hiring of principals who see themselves first and foremost as instructional leaders. Principal candidates should be asked the right questions:

> What incentives have you used to encourage professional growth?
> What is your role in facilitating professional growth and working collaboratively with staff developers?
> What have you done in the past three years to provide professional growth to your staff?

It is only with such instructional leaders on board that staff development will be seen as a team enterprise between staff developers and principals.

Clearly, further work is needed to determine the staff developer's role in motivating professional growth. Just as clearly, dramatic results will occur only when staff developers and principals collaborate in achieving this goal.

Implications of the Study for Teacher Educators

The research reported in this chapter supports the findings of other earlier studies (Mazzarella, 1983; Fielding and Schalock, 1985; McEvoy, 1987) that show that principals can actually stimulate and enhance professional growth within their schools. It also sends a message to teacher educators relative to the important role they can play. Six recommendations for teacher educators are listed below.

1. Screening for motivation for professional growth: Preservice programs may need to screen candidates for teacher training relative to their motivation for entering the profession. Those who are admitted should be those who clearly express a commitment to the concept of career-long development. Motivation for professional growth should be a topic that is included in one or more professional studies courses, and students should be encouraged to compare themselves to inservice teachers with regard to the research findings on motivation. Do they find satisfaction in knowing that they are performing well and in having others acknowlege their achievements?

2. Preservice teachers' motivation: Preservice teachers should be expected to analyze both the needs and motivational forces which promote their performance and improvement efforts. Such self-analysis should be nurtured as an on-going process throughout the preservice preparation program. The emphasis throughout should be on the development of those intrinsic forces that have the potential for making a significant difference in the classroom behavior of teachers.

3. Expectations theory: Preservice programs must also prepare our future teachers to communicate their expectations relative to continuing professional growth to the principals with whom they will interview and work. We contend that expectations theory is relevant in this dimension just as it is in others; principals will play out those behaviors that staff members have clearly expressed as expectations of their role. Principals who have seen themselves as building managers instead of as instructional leaders and catalysts for professional development undoubtedly will not modify their behavior until or unless there are enough voices demanding a change or at least setting the wheels of the 'self-fulfilling prophecy' in motion.

4. Local staff development programs: The implications are also clear for the teacher educators who are involved with local staff development programs. As staff development programs are planned, district staff developers and their colleagues in higher education need to pay heed to motivational considerations. More precisely, they need to plan programs that appeal to teacher motivation in the areas of esteem, autonomy, and self-actualization. Approaches that enable teachers to feel good about themselves, enhance feelings of competence and empowerment, and push them to peak performance are those that are most likely to make a difference in subsequent classroom performance.

5. Options for participation: Staff development programs provided by teacher educators must include options for participation so that choices will facilitate a fit or match between motivation and activity. Teacher educators can do much in working with local districts to channel staff development monies away from the one-day 'dog and pony shows' or 'one-shot, hot-shot' approaches that still characterize far too many inservice education programs.

6. Continuing professional development: Teacher educators along with principals and staff developers need to acknowledge the findings relative to credit courses as a part of continuing professional development. They should, along with staff developers, launch a crusade to change the financing of universities and colleges so that non-credit activities are also incorporated into the funding structure of the institutions.

In conclusion, the study reported herein describes the 'what is' as well as the 'what should be' of practice based on Maslow's motivation theory as applied to professional growth and the role of the principal (Hoy and Miskel, 1982). Thus, we believe that the theory lays a solid foundation for effective practice and for carrying out the suggested recommendations.

It is evident that motivation, professional growth, and the role of the principal are critical components in the effectiveness of our schools. As educators and practitioners, we must keep them in the forefront of our efforts. When all staff see themselves as vital members of a school's instructional leadership team, school improvement outcomes will lead to the self-actualization of the school.

References

BOYER, E.L. (1984) 'Reflections in the great debate of '83', *Phi Delta Kappan*, 65, 8, pp. 525–530.

CURWIN, R.L. and FUHRMAN, B.S. (1975) *Discovering Your Teaching Self*, Englewood Cliffs, NJ, Prentice-Hall.

EDMONDS, R.R. (1982) 'Program of school improvement: An overview', *Educational Leadership*, 40, 3, pp. 4–11.

EVANS, R. (1989) 'The faculty in midcareer: implications for school improvement', *Educational Leadership*, 46, 8, pp. 10–15.

FIELDING, G.O. and SCHALOCK, H.O. (1985) *Promoting the Professional Development of Teachers and Administrators*, Eugene, OR, Center for Educational Policy and Management, University of Oregon.

GALL, M.E. *et al.* (1984) *Involving the Principal in Teacher's Staff Development: The effects on the quality of mathematics instruction in elementary schools*, Eugene, OR, Center for Educational Policy and Management, University of Oregon.

GLICKMAN, C. (1989) 'Has Sam and Samantha's time come at last?', *Educational Leadership*, 46, 8, pp. 4–9.

GRACE, V., BUSER, B. and STUCK, O. (1987) 'What works and what doesn't, characteristics of outstanding administrators', *NASSP Bulletin*, 71, 502, pp. 72–76.

GRIFFITHS, D.E. (1959) *Administrative Theory*, New York, Appleton-Century-Crofts.

HANSEN, J.M. (1980) 'Why inservice? An obligation of schools to provide the best', *NASSP Bulletin*, 64, pp. 67–73.

HARRIS, B.M. and HILL, J. (1982) *Developmental Teacher Evaluation Kit*, Austin, TX, Southwest Educational Development Laboratory.

HERZOG, B.J. (1984) *Factors that Motivate Effective Wisconsin Teachers to Engage in Continuing Professional Development*, unpublished doctoral dissertation, University of Wisconsin, Madison, WI.

HOWEY, K.R. (1976) 'Putting inservice teacher education into perspective', *Journal of Teacher Education*, 27, pp. 101–105.

HOWEY, K.R. (1988) 'Why teacher leadership?', *Journal of Teacher Education*, 39, 1, pp. 28–31.

HOY, W.K. and MISKEL, C.G. (1982) *Educational Administration: Theory, Research and Practice*, New York, Random House.

KOLL, P., HERZOG, B. and BURKE, P. (1989) 'Collaboration between staff developers and school principals to promote professional growth', *Journal of Staff Development*, 10, 3, pp. 54–61.

KOLL, P., HERZOG, B. and BURKE, P. (1988–9) 'Continuing professional development: Implications for teacher educators', *Action in Teacher Education*, x, 4, pp. 24–31.

LARSON, C., KOLL, P. and COZAD, L. (1988) 'Funding university involvement in staff development', *Journal of Staff Development*, Winter, 9, 1, pp. 44–49.

LEZOTTE, L.W. (1982) 'Effective schools research and implications', *Citizen Action in Education*, 9, 1.

LIPHAM, J.M., RANKIN, R. and HOEH, J.A., Jr. (1985), *The Principalship, Concepts, Competencies, and Cases*, New York, Longman.

MASLOW, A.A. (1954) *Motivation and Personality*, New York, Harper and Row.

MAZZARELLA, J. (1983) 'Instructional leadership: Profile of a high school principal', *OSSC Bulletin*, January, 26, 5, pp. 1–37.

McEVOY, B. (1987) 'Everyday acts: How principals influence development of their staffs', *Educational Leadership*, 44, 5, pp. 73–77.

PORTER, L.W. (1961) 'A study of perceived needs satisfactions in bottom and middle management jobs', *Journal of Applied Psychology*, vol. 45, pp. 1–10.

PURKEY, S.C. and SMITH, M.S. (1983) 'Effective schools — a review', *Elementary School Journal*, 85, 3, pp. 353–389.

TUCKMAN, B.W. (1978) *Conducting Educational Research*, 2nd edition, New York, Harcourt Brace Jovanovich, Inc.

ZIMPHER, N.L. (1988) 'A design for the professional development of teacher leaders', *Journal of Teacher Education*, 39, 1, pp. 53–60.

Part 3
Staff Development in Action

6   A Prototypic Human Resource Model

Linda S. Parker

Why Staff Development?

I think the only way we're going to get from where we are to where we want to be is through staff development. When you talk about school improvement, you're talking about people improvement. (Ernest Boyer)

Few educators would disagree with Ernest Boyer's viewpoint that, if educational institutions are to improve, the individuals within them must change. However, as noted by Lortie (1975), change in individual teachers is seriously impeded by isolation. This chapter will discuss the effect of teacher isolation on efforts to improve schools, the part that staff development has to play in educational renewal, and the current status of staff development as it relates to such efforts. A human resource model for planning for staff development programs will then be described — a model that breaks down the barrier of teacher isolation and empowers teachers to participate fully in their own professional development as well as school renewal efforts.

Isolation — A Constraint to Change

The effect of isolation, according to Lortie (1975), is that it contributes to a 'more-of-the-same syndrome' among classroom teachers. Lortie goes on to describe the effects of isolation: '... the vast majority of classroom teachers continue to work apart from other adults. Opportunities for mutual consultation are limited during the working day, and contacts between teachers are peripheral to their major obligations' (p. 232). Lortie points to the 'cellular' organization of schools as one of the causes of teacher isolation.

In *A Place Called School*, Goodlad (1984) also likens classrooms to 'cells'. He, too, cites this cellular nature of schools as one of the reasons for teachers' isolation from one another, thus restricting their access to 'ideas beyond their own background of experience'. Not only does this isolation make it difficult for teachers to provide mutual assistance to one another, but it limits collaborative school improvement efforts as well.

Lieberman and Miller (1984), in discussing the social realities of teaching, also provide a very descriptive picture of the 'lonely enterprise' of teaching:

> Once graduated from a preparation program, teachers find themselves alone in the classroom with a group of students without a peer or supervisor in sight. The neophyte teacher is left with degree in hand, high expectations internalized, a fistful of untried methodologies, and few adults with whom to share, grow, and learn. (p. 4)

It is indeed true that most educators engage in their profession separated from one another in the workplace. Teachers in the K-12 system enter their buildings in the morning, perhaps exchanging a few words with their colleagues before and after school or in the lounge over lunch, and exit the building in the evening after having spent most of the day alone in their classrooms with a group of students. Discussions about teaching strategies seldom take place during these limited interactions between teachers, and few have time during their busy workday to reflect upon their success — or lack thereof — with their students.

Because teachers are separated from one another in the workplace, there is a serious need for the development of collaborative relationships. As noted by Joyce and Showers (1988), collaborative activities and relationships are growth-producing. Furthermore, a staff development program that has as its goal the development of cohesion as well as the professional growth of each individual will be one that helps to promote change within the organization.

Staff Development and School Improvement

A strong human resource development program is, as previously noted, a necessary ingredient for school improvement. Dillon-Peterson (1981) points out, however, that staff development and organizational development are *both* necessary for maximum growth of individuals *and* change in the institution. Dillon-Peterson defines staff development as 'a process designed to foster personal and professional growth for individuals within a respectful, supportive, positive organizational climate having as its ultimate aim better learning for students and continuous, responsible self-renewal for educators and schools'. She defines organizational development as 'the process undertaken by an organization, or part of an organization, to define and meet changing self-improvement objectives, while making it possible for the individuals in the organization to meet their personal and professional objectives' (p. 3).

One can readily discern the interrelationship between the definitions of staff development and organizational development and see that they are representative of 'two sides of the same coin'. To ignore this interrelatedness is to invite what Goodlad (1984) describes as fragmentation of staff development. Fragmentation may result in the adoption of whatever teaching strategy is currently 'in fashion' as well as an inability to resolve chronic problems at the school or district level.

Parkay and Damico (1989) would argue that one of the greatest barriers to school improvement is the lack of staff input and control, resulting in improvement efforts that are not congruent with their aims and beliefs. Goodlad (1984) also contends that, for renewal or school improvement to occur, 'authority and responsibility must be distributed across the system'. In addition, McGreal (1989) identifies what he calls 'leadership density' (i.e., leadership that is dispersed throughout the organization) as a necessary ingredient for instructional improvement.

The message is clear: when there is little effort to develop staff cohesiveness and broad-based involvement in the planning and implementation of staff development/organization development programs, change is unlikely to occur.

Present Status of Inservice Education

The present status of most efforts at human resource development fall far short of the model for change that is required for staff renewal and school improvement. Few staff development programs are embedded in overall efforts at organizational development, and efforts to break down the barriers of isolation by programs that promote collegiality and cohesiveness are only now beginning to emerge.

In 1975, Lortie described the 'state-of-the art' of staff development in a way that still describes most current programs when he said that inservice training 'rarely rises above a superficial level'. He went on to say: '. . . it seems to consist primarily of occasional short "workshops", faculty meetings, and infrequent visits to the classroom by central office supervisors. School systems generally have not assumed responsibility for systematically improving staff performance through serious training programs' (p. 234).

Edelfelt and Lawrence (1975) describe inservice education in terms such as piecemeal, patchwork, and haphazard. They also contend that inservice education 'is seldom based on teacher need and is often conducted in a manner that negates good teaching and learning' and argue that neither the institutions of higher education nor the local school districts have embraced inservice as a basic commitment.

Almost ten years later, Joyce and Showers (1983) described staff development efforts in this way: '... in any given year the average teacher in the United States participates in only about three days of inservice work, rarely more than a day at a time, and usually in brief workshops that feature "inspiring" speeches and demonstration of discrete skills' (p. 1).

More recently, Joyce and Showers (1988) made the following observation concerning the status of staff development efforts:

> As this is written, the field of staff development is evolving gradually from a patchwork of courses and workshops into a system ensuring that education professionals regularly enhance their academic knowledge and professional performance. States, school districts, intermediate agencies, and teachers' organizations are searching for ways to enlarge the investment in staff development and generate better forms of it. They are trying to develop a system that will embed professional growth opportunities into the work life of teachers and administrative and supervisory personnel. (p. 1)

The human resource model described in this chapter is, indeed, such a system. The elements of the model include (1) assessment, (2) planning, (3) implementation, (4) evaluation, and (5) participant empowerment. Comprehensive programming to meet the needs of individual teachers is at the heart of the model. Consequently, the elements of assessment and planning are closely intertwined, but for the purpose of clarity, will be presented as two separate elements.

Assessment

Staff development programs obviously exist within the broader milieu of district-wide goals and priorities as well as state and federal guidelines and requirements. Thus, priorities must be set, making an analysis of current conditions an essential element of any effective staff development program. A picture of 'what is' must be developed by means of a combination of methods to provide the input needed to design an effective program that will, as Boyer (1983) put it, take a district to where it wants to be. In order to accomplish this task, two questions must first be answered: (1) what data sources are most important to us? and (2) what data collection methods will be used?

School versus Individuals as Priority

In conducting needs assessment, those persons responsible for planning and implementing staff developmnent programs should keep in mind three general purposes to be served by the program (Joyce and Showers, 1988, pp. 6–7):

1   enhancement of individual clinical skills and academic knowledge
2   the study of school improvement
3   district-wide initiatives to improve the educational program

Staff development personnel must also keep in mind, however, that even though professional development efforts need to provide a balance between those activities desired by educators and those needed to have significant impact on school and/or district-wide programs, the highest priority should go to improving the competencies 'to do one's job' (Wood, Thompson and Russell, 1981). Consequently, even though multiple data sources should be used in setting priorities, assessment techniques described below will focus primarily on identifying the needs of individual staff members.

Methods of Assessing Need

Needs assessments usually take three forms (Dillon-Peterson, 1981, p. 4):

1   Supervisors determine needs based on their assessment of the quality of work being performed by persons reporting to them.
2   Staff members are asked to report their perceived needs on a survey questionnaire or to respond to a checklist.
3   Groups of individuals (i.e., departments, schools, district-wide councils) collaboratively identify needs and develop plans to bring about change.

Dillon-Peterson cites the third method as being supported by research on change as the more effective method because the individuals who are going to be 'developed' will be more committed to 'carrying out plans which they feel reflect a genuine need and which they helped to develop'. However, each of the methods described below has its place in developing the data base needed to design an effective human resource development program.

Personnel evaluation. In discussing teacher assessment and staff development as 'links in the same chain', Fessler and Burke (1988) made the following observations:

> The purpose of teacher assessment ought to be the identification of growth needs that will serve as the basis for planning appropriate strategies for development. Conversely, the purpose of staff development ought to be to provide the necessary structure and support for teachers to fulfill their identified growth needs. (p. 14)

Unfortunately, personnel evaluations are frequently ignored as a data source for an assessment-based staff development model. However, the results of teacher assessment can reveal both needs that should be addressed by individual professional development plans as well as consistently occurring needs (e.g., weaknesses related to classroom management skills or instructional strategies) that could be effectively addressed by an inservice training program.

In order to incorporate teacher evaluation as part of the needs assessment effort, Fessler and Burke suggest three guidelines for implementation (pp. 17–18):

1 Teachers should be encouraged to engage in self-assessment.
2 Teachers and supervisors should engage in frequent sharing and conferring sessions.
3 Staff development activities should be based on growth needs agreed upon by teachers and supervisors.

Interviews. An informal technique that may yield data that would not surface in a more formal technique is the free exchange of ideas through a one-to-one interview. Although such interviews may be limited in usage because they are time-consuming and sometimes difficult to analyze, structured interviews utilizing written protocols can provide valuable information. Such inteviews can be especially useful as a follow-up to a survey questionnaire for clarifying expressed needs of respondents.

Interviews may also take the form of extended discussions held with groups of district and building administrators, teachers, school board members and other parents, as well as students. Parkay and Damico (1989) report using such a technique in order to gain a broader perspective on the curricular and instructional needs confronting their schools. The use of the 'on-site diagnosis' was part of a seven-step school improvement model which was developed to 'empower teachers to design staff development programs based on their own needs'.

Questionnaires. Data from questionnaires are very helpful in determining the magnitude of a problem because they are a quickly obtained and simple source of information from a broad range of respondents. Because of the breadth of input, such surveys are useful in prioritizing district-wide needs.

Survey questionnaires may be of two types: an open-ended survey or a list of items to be checked and/or ranked (Glickman, 1985). Open-ended surveys may be used to 'document and add to the information already received through eyes and ears', but it is important to keep such surveys brief. Questionnaires that ask staff to check or rank priorities should also be kept brief, preferably within two back-to-back pages. Such questionnaires are most useful after preliminary data have been collected by other methods to generate ideas relative to perceived needs and/or weaknesses in current programs.

Nominal Group Process. The Nominal Group Process, which is primarily for problem-solving and decision-making in groups, is a highly structured sequence of group activities designed to regulate interactions so that all group members have an opportunity to give input. It is another very helpful method of identifying inservice needs (Wood, Thompson and Russell, 1981). The process follows five steps (pp. 69–70):

1 Listing — participants list their responses to a clear statement of a problem to be addressed; no interaction is permitted at this time.
2 Round-robin — participants present items from their lists, one at a time in round-robin fashion, which are recorded for later use; no other interaction is permitted.
3 Voting — using cards or ballots, each participant ranks/prioritizes the items on the master list; again, no interaction is allowed.
4 Discussion — ranking results are tabulated and discussed.
5 Final voting — each participant votes a final time, listing his/her priorities (four-six) from the master list.

After the five-step process has been completed, results are tabulated and analyzed to determine the group's ideas and priorities for solving a problem.

Delphi Technique. The Delphi Technique might be described as a paper and pencil version of the Nominal Group Process. It is a written method of prioritizing needs which was originally developed to forecast future trends but may also be used for needs assessment (Glickman, 1985). The overall process involves the dissemination of an open-ended survey questionnaire, after which participants' comments are reproduced and returned to them for developing an individually written synthesis of the various ideas. A new list of all synthesized ideas is returned once again to participants for ranking, and this process continues until clear priorities emerge.

Official records. Documentary evidence for supporting needs identified by other approaches may be found in a variety of materials (Glickman, 1985). For instance, the results of students' achievement test scores and diagnostic tests may point to weaknesses in the curriculum or the instructional program itself. Records regarding the number of discipline referrals being made by teachers may point to weaknesses in classroom management techniques. Such findings may suggest staff development needs related to these issues.

Each of the data collection procedures just described has advantages and disadvantages, and each is more useful for some purposes than for others. As noted earlier, needs assessment data should be gathered from multiple sources using a variety of techniques. Those planning staff development programs will want to use those methods that are best suited for a particular purpose, keeping in mind, however, that the primary sources of information should be the potential participants for whom the activities are being planned.

Planning

As already indicated, this human resource development model is based on the premise that educators' needs can best be addressed if they are involved in identifying their own priorities and planning collaboratively to meet those needs. This is a departure from past practice, as one of the problems with traditional inservice education has, in fact, been failure to address individual needs and concerns adequately (Leggett and Hoyle, 1987). This section will detail how teachers can become actively involved, both at the building and district level, in designing staff development programs that will transform their priorities into activity formats and delivery systems. The outcome of such involvement will be a greater sense of ownership on the part of teachers, who will then participate more enthusiastically in staff development programs. This planning process is divided into two stages — a readiness stage and a plan development stage.

Getting Ready

Readiness is a crucial but frequently forgotten stage in the planning of staff development programs (Wood, Thompson and Russell, 1981). It is the stage where resistance to change must be overcome and where commitment to high quality programming is established. It is, therefore, a stage that planners dare not omit, because broad-based support is essential for successful implementation of a comprehensive human resource development program.

Involvement of building and district-level administrators, teachers and support staff — as well as school board members — is necessary at this stage to help establish a climate that supports school improvement efforts. Emphasis during this stage of planning is on developing new role expectations and responsibilities for both teachers and administrators, providing opportunities for collaborative planning, and developing new channels of communication (Wood, Thompson and Russell, 1981). Specific activities are: (1) establishment of a governance structure, (2) development of a rationale or mission statement, and (3) establishing program goals.

Governance structure. Establishment of a district-wide staff development council or committee will enhance the relationship between individual schools and district office personnel (Joyce and Showers, 1988). The district council is responsible for activities such as conducting the needs assessment, selecting the areas that will receive system-wide support during any given period, and coordinating staff development activities. The council also provides support to individual school committees that are formed to engage in problem-solving and to establish building-level staff development priorities.

Representation on the district staff development council should be broad-based and include teachers, administrators and support staff who can provide a variety of grade level and subject area perspectives. In addition, both regular and special education teachers should be represented on the committee. It is also advisable that at least one school board member be a part of this group so that he or she can keep the board informed and generate support when it is needed from the board (McGreal, 1989).

In order to function effectively, a spirit of cooperation is essential as members of the advisory council approach decision-making tasks (Joyce and Showers, 1988). Individual members need to understand that the entire district organization must be of concern to them, not just their own individual needs or that of their school. Consequently, the committee chairperson will need to be concerned with building cooperative relationships within the group.

Communication will also be a high priority. Within the council, open discussion and the free exchange of ideas and opinions will need to be encouraged. In addition, regular channels for effective inter-building communication will need to be established.

Philosophy/mission statement. One of the first activities of a newly formed district staff development committee must be the writing of a philosophy or mission statement. The mission statement should express a philosophy that encourages growth and life-long learning (Loucks-Horsley, *et al.*, 1987) and should establish mechanisms for responding to local school improvement needs. The philosophy should be written in such a way that it clearly defines the scope of the program in terms of responding to curricular and instructional needs. It should also define which groups in the community will be served. It is desirable that the mission of the staff development program be inclusive of all those with a vested interest in education: teachers, administrators, support staff, non-certified staff, school board members and the community at large.

This mission statement may become part of a policy statement that is approved by the school board. Board approval of such a policy is crucial for establishing development of the district's human resources as a high-priority enterprise. This policy may include elements such as the board's responsibility for professional development of the district's staff, purpose of the program, assignment of responsibility for overall leadership, incentives for participation (i.e., reimbursement of a percentage of tuition), and who will be served.

Goal-setting. Program goals should flow naturally from the philosophy/mission statement. Goals are general statements of desired outcome, broad in nature and few in number, which may guide programming for as long as three to five years. Since good staff development recognizes the value of the individual as well as the school community to which he or she belongs (Loucks-Horsley, *et al.*, 1987), the goals established by the staff development council will include goals related to system needs as well as individual needs. A comprehensive set of goal statements could include all of the following areas (WASCD, 1988):

1. Performance improvement — individual needs related to performance evaluations or to school or district goals and priorities
2. Job orientation — benefits and labor contract orientation, specific job/position requirements, other information related to 'how we do things here'
3. Career development — related to career or responsibility change, including retirement planning
4. Personal health — may include intervention as well as prevention and maintenance.

Once the staff development council has prepared a philosophy statement and written a set of clear, well-understood goals that are congruent with individual as well as institutional goals, it is ready to move on to the next phase of the planning stage. It should not begin the process of planning delivery systems, however, unless activities up to this point have established a climate that is conducive to growth and until a commitment to professional development has been made by the district (Wood, Thompson and Russell, 1981). The reason for this caveat is clear: an educational innovation will not be sustained unless 'there is a shared understanding of its purpose, rationale, and processes' (Joyce and Showers, 1988).

Developing the Plan

Planning at this stage focuses upon translating goals and identified priorities into activity formats and delivery systems. Staff development planners will also need to consider the nature of adult learners, the change process, and teacher career stages when determining specific objectives and planning activity formats. Thus, to be relevant and effective, staff development activities need to be planned not only according to prioritized topics, but must also consider factors that promote optimal adult development (Glickman, 1985).

Translating needs into objectives. Needs assessment techniques for establishing priorities have already been discussed in detail. This function is coordinated and carried out by the district-wide staff development council, although building-level faculty committees should also be engaged in problem-solving and decision-making activities to establish priorities for school-based staff development activities. These identified needs are, of course, a major consideration in designing the staff development plan as they form the basis for program objectives.

Objectives are different from goals in that they are short-term and highly specific in nature. The objectives should spell out what will happen, when it is to be accomplished, and who will be involved. Activities (to be discussed later) for meeting these objectives will tell how it will happen. The objectives, which should also set standards of achievement and tell how results will be measured, are of three types: knowledge objectives, strategies or skill objectives, and attitude objectives (Wood, Thompson and Russell, 1981).

Considering the nature of the adult learner. Those responsible for planning staff development programs require an understanding of principles of adult learning as they make decisions about the design and delivery of staff development programs (Moore, 1988). Adults learn differently from children and will become disillusioned with staff development programs which do not recognize those differences. Principles and practices, which were developed and tested by Moore, should be applied to staff development programs. According to Moore, adult education programs should (pp. 3–4):

- have a climate of respect
- help learners achieve self-direction and empowerment
- have a collaborative mode
- capitalize on learner's experiences
- foster participation
- foster critical, reflective thinking

- foster learning for actions
- foster problem posing and problem-solving.

Understanding the change process. An understanding of the Concerns-Based Adoption Model, CBAM, (Hall, Wallace and Dossett, 1973) which provides a framework for understanding the stages of teachers' concerns about a specific innovation or change, can be useful in planning inservice (Bents and Howey, 1981). Assumptions arising from the model are relevant to planning staff development programs (p. 31):

1 The change (innovation) is appropriate.
2 Change is a process, not an event.
3 Change is a personal experience.
4 The individual has to be the focal point.

Understanding the change process is important because of the fact that some people more readily accept change than others. Thus, understanding how people develop in their feelings and skills as they implement something new has relevance to staff development planners.

Giving attention to teacher career stages. Professional development needs of new teachers are very different from those of experienced teachers. For instance, the more experienced teacher is less likely to change his or her practices as a result of participation in training activities and requires a more individualized, personal approach (McLaughlin and Marsh, 1978). Consequently, teacher career stages are an important variable in planning staff development programs.

Teacher career stages have been classified in different ways. For instance, Fuller and Bown (1975) identify three stages of learning to teach: the survival stage comes first, followed by a mastery stage when teachers strive to improve their performance, with the third stage occurring when teachers either settle into stable routines and become resistant to change or become more concerned about their students. Burke, Christensen, and Fessler (1984) describe eight components of the career cycle: pre-service, induction, competency building, enthusiastic and growing, career frustration, stable but stagnant, career wind-down, and career exit.

Regardless of the labels used to define career stages, there is no doubt that teachers have different concerns at different times during their teaching careers that have implications for staff development programming. For instance, beginning teachers will be very concerned about effective classroom strategies whereas experienced teachers may be more interested in educational activities that promote health and wellness. Thus, an awareness of the fact that needs change throughout the teaching career cycle should be reflected in program offerings.

Designing activity formats. In addition to the fact that teachers' individual needs and concerns were rarely addressed, other problems with traditional inservice education have included the preponderance of one-shot workshops and the failure to provide follow-up support and feedback at the school level (Leggett and Hoyle, 1987). It is important that such pracitices be eliminated when designing activity formats. Instead, the human resource development program should consist of activities that become an integrated aspect of school change.

Joyce and Showers' (1988) extensive research on training has identified five training components for staff development planners to choose from: (1) exploration of theory and concepts, (2) demonstration or modeling of the skill(s), (3) opportunities to practice the skill(s), (4) feedback about performance, and (5) coaching in the workplace (pp. 67–68). Implications for designing activity formats drawn from their research on training follow (p. 72):

1 Participants must have sufficient opportunity to develop skills that they can eventually practice in classroom settings.
2 Training will have to be more extensive if the content is new to trainees than if it is relatively familiar.
3 If transfer into the workplace is the training objective, follow-up coaching in the workplace will probably be necessary.

Obviously, it is unnecessary for all staff development activities to include all five components. Some activities will have only knowledge or awareness objectives. For instance, an informational session may be held to explain the district's new insurance program or other benefits to employees. In other words, the purpose of the activity will determine the most suitable format for accomplishing the desired outcome.

Selecting delivery systems. Staff development delivery systems are not all planned and implemented in the local school district. A wide array of options may be provided by universities, state education agencies, vocational/technical centers and intermediate education agencies. Offerings for staff to choose from fall into three broad categories (WASCD, 1988):

1 *District activities* such as building-planned training programs, on-site university courses, induction programs for beginning teachers, curriculum development, conducting action research, and serving as a cooperating teacher
2 *Continuing education activities* such as advanced degree studies, seminars, conferences, and workshops
3 *Professional involvement activities* such as participation in professional organizations, research, and reading.

Figure 6.1   *Staff Development Delivery Systems**

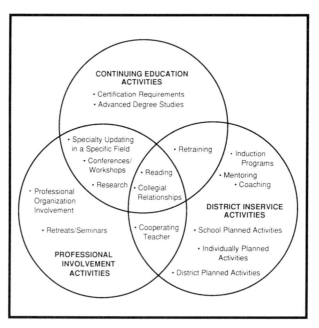

* Original concept from WASCD, *Planning Effective Staff Development*. Madison, WI:
Wisconsin Association for Supervision & Curriculum, 1988.

Activities from these three broad categories are interrelated and, in some instances, overlapping in nature (Figure 6.1). For instance, serving as a cooperating teacher is a professional involvement activity carried out at the local level.

The important thing for staff development planners to remember is that professional involvement activities frequently are initiated by the individual teacher and often take place outside the local school district. Contribution of all of these sources to the continued professional development of staff should be recognized in planning the overall human resource development program.

Implementation

When does planning end and implementation begin? Does planning end when the 'welcome' is given at a seminar and end once the participants have completed evaluation forms and returned to their classrooms? That might be the case when the seminar is an isolated 'one shot' event that has little or no relevance to the daily lives of the participants and is not related

to the instructional needs in their buildings. However, in a human resource development model which is based on the participants' needs and
is embedded in the overall instructional program, the point where planning and implementation become separate elements of the staff development process is not so easily discernible.

So far, the first two elements of the human resource development
model, assessment and planning, have been discussed. Teacher involvement with collaboration was emphasized in the planning of a needs-based
staff development program. Such collaboration will continue to be emphasized as the implementation phase is explained in terms of (1) roles and
competency modeling and (2) monitoring tasks and activities. It will become obvious that, just as in the case of assessment and planning, the
elements of planning and implementation are interwoven with one
another.

Roles and Competency Modeling

Just as few educators would disagree with Boyer's (1983) observation that
'when you talk about school improvement, you're talking about people
improvement', few would disagree with Goodlad's (1984) argument that
the individual school is the unit for improvement. However, if school-
based improvement is to live up to its promise of producing substantial
change in our schools, there must be a new way of thinking about the way
we should operate in our schools as well as at the district level because it
will involve new expectations and roles (Caldwell and Wood, 1988).

As educators assume new roles and develop new competencies,
modeling will become an important ingredient of the human resource development program. In fact, Killion and Harrison (1988) have identified
modeling as one of three critical elements of any training program, the
other two critical elements being reflection and application. Bents and
Howey (1981) also speak of the importance of 'role-taking experiences' as
well as the need for 'careful and continuous guided reflection'. Modeling
will, in fact, be important to all the key players.

The role of the teaching staff. Teachers are an untapped gold mine and
must be used extensively as staff developers (Wu, 1987). Not only will
they assume leadership roles and serve on both school-based and district-
level staff development committees, but they should assume roles as
trainers of teachers. These roles include but are not limited to serving as
workshop presenters and instructors for courses/training programs, peer
coaches who observe and provide feedback to colleagues as they practice
new skills in their classrooms, and mentors who provide assistance and
support to beginning teachers.

Teaching adults is not the same as teaching children (Kowalski, 1984).

Consequently, time and effort will need to be spent in training teachers to assume roles as staff developers. It will be time and effort well spent, however, because 'the importance and effectiveness of teachers as staff developers have been thoroughly documented throughout the literature' (Wu, 1987). According to Sousa (1987), advantages to using teachers as staff developers include benefits such as (p. 39 adapted):

- The comfort most teachers feel with a teacher/staff developer during classroom visits to observe/give feedback because the threat of evaluation is removed
- Teachers recognizing staff developers as classroom colleagues and more readily accepting their suggestions as realistic and practical
- Watching a colleague teach a lesson which provides a model for effective use of skills thus encouraging apprehensive teachers to try them
- Providing an opportunity for professional growth for the staff developer.

One caveat in particular should be kept in mind when teachers are involved in training other teachers. The selection of the workshop leaders/ trainers must be judiciously handled. In a state-wide school improvement effort in Delaware reported by Barkley, McCormick, and Taylor (1987), it was found that training was well received by teachers where the trainers were selected by their peers. However, in a few cases where trainers were chosen by unpopular principals, the impact of the training itself was clouded by resentment over the selection process.

Peer coaching and mentoring are two roles that are increasingly being assumed by teachers (Berlin, *et al.*, 1987; Chase and Wolfe, 1989; Chrisco, 1989; Gomery and Crouse, 1987; Joyce and Showers, 1988; Krupp, 1987; Leggett and Hoyle, 1987; Parker, 1988a; Westhoff, Carter and Bailey, 1987; and Wright, 1987). Both are powerful human resource development techniques if implemented in supportive environments where a trusting relationship is continually nurtured.

The major purpose of peer coaching programs, according to Joyce and Showers (1983), is 'implementation of innovations to the extent that determination of effects on students is possible'. More specifically, the process of coaching serves three functions (pp. 83–84):

1 to build communities of teachers who continually engage in the study of their craft
2 to develop the shared language and common understandings necessary for the collegial study of new knowledge and skills
3 to provide a structure for the follow-up to training that is essential for facilitating the transfer of new instructional skills.

Mentoring, which is 'the process by which a trusted and experienced person takes a personal and direct interest in the development and education of a younger or less experienced individual' (Krupp, 1987), may or may not involve peer coaching that incorporates classroom observation and giving feedback. Mentorships are a very effective means of providing assistance and support to new teachers. In fact, mentoring or a 'buddy system' is the teacher induction practice that has received the widest support in the research literature (Elias, Fisher and Simon, 1980; Houston and Felder, 1982; McDonald, 1980; Parker, 1986; Ryan, 1979). In addition, mentoring provides a staff development opportunity for both beginning and experienced teachers, especially mid-career teachers, with mentors citing benefits such as revitalization of their own teaching and re-evaluation of their own teaching techniques and beliefs (Parker, 1988b).

Several guidelines should be observed when implementing either type of program. First, providing training to teachers prior to assuming either a peer coaching or mentorship role is absolutely essential. Second, teachers' participation should be voluntary. Third, teachers should never breach confidentiality by sharing information with other teachers, their principal, or other administrators. Finally, neither relationship should be tied to evaluation. If implemented with these guidelines in mind, both mentoring and peer coaching can open doors between teachers, reduce loneliness and isolation, and enhance communication and respect.

The role of the district administrator. Successful implementation of the human resource model requires administrative leadership and support (Berlin, *et al.*, 1987; Duttweiler, 1989; Loucks-Horsley, *et al.*, 1987; Wood, Thompson and Russell, 1981). Both active participation as well as verbal commitment to the staff development effort are absolutely essential.

Demonstrations of support by the district adminstrator play a major role in ensuring success of a staff development program. Monetary support for released time is a major part of the financial support. However, funding for items such as clerical support, travel costs and training materials should also be budgeted to the extent needed for a sustained effort at human resource development. Superintendents can also provide non-monetary support in the form of philosophical support, sharing of ideas and reinforcement for trainers (Daniel, 1987).

The role of the principal. The building principal plays a key role both in promoting and maintaining an effective professional development program as well as in providing leadership for school improvement (Killion, Huddleston and Claspell, 1989; Lieberman and Miller, 1984; Lyons, Jr., 1989; Wood, Thompson and Russell, 1981). The attitude of the principal is, in fact, critical. One especially important way in which principals can demonstrate their active support is to participate in training sessions. By doing so, principals not only indicate that they are committed to new initiatives, but their participation will enable them to provide supervisory support as the new instructional techniques are introduced into the program.

The role of 'people developer' is a new one for principals. Consequently, success in this role entails both commitment and flexibility (Killion, Huddleston and Claspell, 1989):

> A principal needs to choose when to be a cheerleader, who encourages, motivates, and builds enthusiasm; a coach, who facilitates growth through questioning, advising, or suggesting; an expert, who directs and sets standards; or a resource who provides access to information, people, budget, time, or space. (p. 3)

A key role indeed! And just as teachers require training and preparation in order to assume new roles, the principal's role may require a new set of skills, knowledge, and beliefs. A willingness on the part of principals to become actively involved in their own professional development will, in effect, demonstrate their commitment to renewal, thus serving as powerful role modeling for teachers.

The role of central office staff. The support and interest of central office administrators, in addition to that of the superintendent and principals, are also very important to the outcome of local change efforts (Bertani, *et al.*, 1987; Dillon-Peterson, 1981; McLaughlin and Marsh, 1978). Providing leadership for the district staff development advisory council may be one role assumed by personnel such as a director of personnel and/or staff development. Assisting principals and school faculties in developing and implementing building-level plans is another role for staff development personnel. Serving as instructor for courses and workshops and designing and delivering staff development programs for principals and the school board are also likely responsibilities. Care should be taken, however, to ensure that both responsibilities and leadership for new initiatives are shared. Otherwise, school improvement efforts will not be sustained (Caldwell and Wood, 1988).

The role of school board. Adequate economic support must be provided by the school board for the sustained effort needed to bring about change (Dillon-Peterson, 1981). As already mentioned in the section on planning, a school board will be much more inclined to provide sufficient resources if one of its members serves in a planning role on the district staff development advisory council. It must also be remembered that providing inservice education opportunities for the entire board is a human resource development activity that may pay large dividends and should not be ignored by staff development planners.

Media presentations. Video/audio feedback as an instructional technique has an important role to play in implementation of new instructional techniques (Duttweiler, 1989; Gomery and Crouse, 1987; Leggett and Hoyle, 1987; Wade, 1984/5). Videotapes may be used as an effective subsitute for participant or presenter modeling of instructional strategies. For instance, videotaped teaching episodes may be used for training peer coaches in observational techniques. During workshop sessions, teachers may also view videotapes of each others' teaching and provide feedback to one another regarding skill acquistition.

Video- and audiotapes may also be used after training for self-monitoring during implementation of new instructional strategies (Wood, Thompson and Russell, 1987). The video- and audiotape recordings of classroom activities can be played back by the teacher to help examine his or her own behavior. Additionally, their use as part of the supervision process enables the teacher and principal to analyze together the effectiveness of an instructional skill.

Networks/linkages. The expanding of resources is a primary benefit of cross-organizational collaboration and is, therefore, a means of providing cost-effective staff development. The sharing of ideas and human resources results in other benefits to districts that establish such linkages, including instructional improvement and the enhancement of curriculum development efforts (Taylor, Thompson, and Schmuck, 1989).

Linkages may take many forms (Cameron, 1988). Several school districts may form networks or consortia to plan joint training activities and/or to share the expertise of specific staff members in a consultant or program support role. Linkages with intermediate education agencies, colleges or universities, and state education agencies may enable a district to provide on-site courses or workshops. Since school-based staff development programs are the most effective, the advantage to the district becomes apparent.

States which have intermediate education agencies provide a unique opportunity for the development of networks between and among school districts. Wisconsin, with its twelve Cooperative Educational Service Agencies (CESAs), is such a state. A wide range of staff development activities is coordinated with and for the CESA's member districts, one example being the CESA 5 Beginning Teacher Assistance Program. Two training components, a mentor training program and a series of seminars for beginning teachers, are provided on a regional basis whereas other aspects of the program are school-based (Parker, 1988a).

In Chapter 9, Letvin and Klobuchar describe the Regional Staff Development Center, another collaborative effort in Wisconsin. The alliances, networks and study committees which are part of the Center's program bring together educators from all grade levels and disciplines to learn from one another. The University of Wisconsin-Parkside is also involved in the Center's program and, in fact, took the initiative to establish the relationship between the university and the school districts.

Both of these examples are just two among many types of linkages that need to be considered by educational organizations. This is especially true in the case of small rural districts where central office staff developers are not available. Since dollars for staff development are not plentiful, no district can afford to ignore the value of cooperation with outside agencies.

Monitoring Tasks and Activities

During this stage of implementation, which might be called the maintenance stage, continuous review and monitoring should take place to determine whether new behaviors are still being practiced and goals being met (Wood, Thompson and Russell, 1981). Monitoring may take many forms, including the regular supervisory process. Incentives for teachers, including those which might be provided as part of state certification programs, are important during this phase of program implementation.

Support by administrators. Supervisors, particularly the building principals, have a crucial role in the monitoring of staff development programs. Informal classoom visits show support for the teachers, especially when they are made for the purpose of giving encouragement or expressing an interest in how implementation is progressing. Such support is often cited as being crucial to the implementation of peer coaching programs (Chrisco, 1989; Garmston, 1987; Krupp, 1987; Leggett and Hoyle, 1987).

On a more formal basis, a systematic process for classroom supervision must be implemented. Sergiovanni (1988) notes that supervision, if well done, is a form of staff development. He continues: 'A thin line exists between supervision and staff development and, in the ideal, the two are brought together as a single process in the school's daily routine' (p. 402).

Incentives. Recognition and rewards provide encouragement for participation in staff development programs. Incentives also help to stimulate the enthusiasm and commitment that is needed to sustain an innovation. Wade (1984/5) found that being selected to participate in a training program, whether by being designated to represent a particular group or by a competitive process, is a powerful incentive. Released time and college credit have also been found to provide a significant incentive for continued professional development. Districts that reimburse teachers and administrators for all or a portion of their tuition for graduate courses may reap large dividends.

Certification programs. Many states no longer issue life licenses for professional school employees. For instance, in Wisconsin regular licenses are now issued for a term of five years, and renewal of the regular license requires the completion of six semesters of credits at an accredited college or university. Thus, renewal of one's license becomes not only a requirement for remaining in the field of education but an incentive for continued professional development.

Providing alternatives to obtaining college credit is a service found in some states. The State of Wisconsin provides educators with the opportunity to meet its continuing education requirement through its Equivalency Clock Hour Program. Teachers who attend or participate in non-credit programs may earn equivalency credits (thirty clock hours equal one semester credit) at preapproved workshops, seminars or conferences. Credit is based on the principle of preapproval of programs offered by appropriate providers, which include agencies such as the Wisconsin Department of Public Instruction, accredited colleges and universities, and Wisconsin's cooperative educational service agencies (CESAs).

Evaluation

Any educator who has attended a workshop, seminar or conference has undoubtedly completed at least one evaluation form in his or her professional career. Such evaluations usually consist of a one-page questionnaire, frequently incorporating a rating scale, that asks the participant to identify the strengths and weaknesses of the program. Evaluation forms of this nature, sometimes referred to as 'user satisfaction' questionnaires, may also ask respondents to indicate how they benefitted from participation in the program. In fact, evaluation of staff development efforts is based almost entirely on the opinions of participants and 'success rests on whether they enjoyed the activity and whether it was perceived as helpful' (Dillon-Peterson, 1981).

Evaluation of training programs is, of course, an important aspect of the overall evaluation function of an effective human resource development model. However, data collected to determine the perceived effects of a workshop on participants are only one assessment measure to be considered. In addition to evaluation of training, assessment information should include evaluation of the extent of implementation of the staff development plan as well as effects on performance in the workplace.

Outcomes to be Evaluated

The purpose of evaluation is to aid decision-making about the future of the program. That being the case, a major question to be answered by evaluation efforts is whether the program is making any difference. Planners also need to know what, if any, relationship exists between those differences and program activity (Loucks-Horsley, 1987). To answer these questions, information is needed about both program processes and program effects, including but not limited to how program activities are being implemented and received by participants.

Evaluation efforts must, if they are to have any meaning, be directly related to the overall long-term goals established by the advisory council as well as to the objectives selected for specific training activities. Data collection and measurement strategies will depend upon the nature of the intended outcomes which should include changes in participants, changes in the organization and changes in students (Castle, 1988; Joyce and Showers, 1988; Loucks-Horsley, et al., 1987).

Changes in participants. Objectives for staff development activities should, as previously mentioned, include attitude, knowledge and skill objectives. Consequently, changes in all of these areas will become the focus of evaluation efforts. Pre- and post-testing is an effective method of collecting data to gauge changes in participants' knowledge base as well as, to some extent, changes in attitudes and feelings. Collecting information on the participants' immediate satisfaction with a specific training event will continue to be of interest to planners, and traditional workshop evaluation forms may be used to collect such information while at the same time giving participants an opportunity to report unanticipated learnings.

Changes in participants' skill level and use are not as easily measured, which is probably one reason this area of program evaluation is usually neglected. Documentation of initial skill acquisition can be accomplished during the actual training if participants are provided with opportunities to practice skills in micro-teaching situations. Clinical supervision or peer coaching are useful in observing and helping teachers practicing the new skills between training sessions as well as after the training is completed. Such observations would also yield information on how well teachers have learned and are using the target skills (Loucks-Horsley, et al., 1987).

Changes in the organization. One of the overall goals of the human resource development model is increasing collaboration/collegiality as well as expanding the roles and responsibilities of participants. As with skill acquisition, such outcomes are not easily measured. However, qualitative perceptions and opinions regarding such changes can be drawn from both survey questionnaires and interviews. In addition, supervisors' observations of increased ability and willingness of staff to work collaboratively in resolving problems or initiating a new problem can provide impressions of changes within the organization.

Changes in students. Standardized test scores are frequently cited as a method for measuring student outcomes following a new innovation or efforts at school improvement. For example, the ACT and SAT results are cited as evidence that schools are either improving or being engulfed by a 'rising tide of mediocrity'. However, it is very difficult to relate student progress directly to new practices or teaching techniques being implemented in the classroom (Loucks-Horsley, *et al.*, 1987).

Despite the fact that it is difficult to find connections between staff development activities and student performance, because it takes time for significant student change to be readily observable, a variety of measures may be used to look at student performance. Outcome measures that may be used include standardized test scores, competency-based test results, attendance and discipline referral records, student products, various survey techniques, as well as classroom observations.

Loucks-Horsley, *et al.*, provide a schematic drawing that organizes and summarizes various methods of documentation and measurement of changes in outcomes (Figure 6.2). Staff development planners will find this model useful as they develop their own evaluation plan.

Extent of Implementation

In addition to the effects upon participants/teachers, students and the organization, the extent of implementation of the staff development process itself is a fourth variable that must be considered in the overall evaluation process (Castle, 1988; Joyce and Showers, 1988). Four components for evaluating the staff development process include: (1) the staff development council, (2) the needs assessment process, (3) staff development activities, and (4) the evaluation process itself (Castle, 1988).

Another evaluation model that may be useful when planning for evaluation of all four components of the staff development process has been developed by Castle (1988). The model consists of the following steps (pp. 24–25):

1   Determine the evaluation criteria and standards
2   Determine questions to be answered based on the evaluation criteria
3   Select and/or design and administer the instruments
4   Analyze and interpret the data and develop conclusions
5   Disseminate results and conclusions to all concerned parties
6   Make decisions based on results and conclusions.

Additional guidelines for planning an effective evaluation process follow: First, both formative and summative information should be collected

Figure 6.2   Methods of Documentation and Measurement for Different Outcomes**

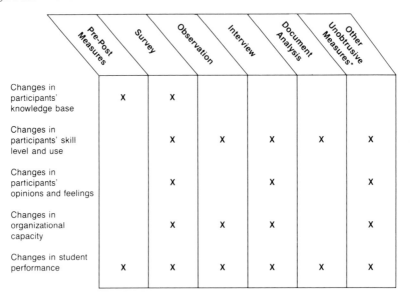

	Pre-Post Measures	Survey	Observation	Interview	Document Analysis	Other Unobtrusive Measures*
Changes in participants' knowledge base	X	X				
Changes in participants' skill level and use		X	X	X	X	X
Changes in participants' opinions and feelings		X		X		X
Changes in organizational capacity		X	X	X		X
Changes in student performance	X	X	X	X	X	X

*   Unobtrusive measures refer to observations of people, their environment, and their processes, carried out in an informal manner, in such a way that informants are not asked to respond in any special way for the purposes of the evaluation.

**   Original concept from Loucks-Horsley, et. al., Continuing to Learn — A Guidebook for Teacher Development. Andover, MA: The Regional Laboratory for Educational Improvement of the Northeast & Islands, 1987.

(Loucks-Horsley, *et al.*, 1988; Moore, 1988; Wood, Thompson and Russell, 1981). Formative data should be collected as the program unfolds aimed at describing activities and events in order to improve the program and to decide what to do next. Summative evaluation data aims to 'sum up' program results and to help make global decisions about the continuation of a program.

Second, it is important to look at both process and outcome variables so that planners can be sure the program is being implemented correctly as well as determine if the program is making a difference. It is crucial to look at both variables, since outcomes will be directly affected if the program is not being implemented as planned (Loucks-Horsley, *et al.*, 1988).

Finally, both the content and the delivery process used in the training program need to be examined (Joyce and Showers, 1988; Killion and Harrison, 1988). Planners must check to be certain that the skill, knowledge and attitude objectives have been adequately reflected in the activity format selected for the training program or workshop. In addition, factors such as principles of adult education and teacher career stages should also be reflected in activity formats as well as in the overall staff development plan.

Participant Empowerment

Maeroff (1988) acknowledged that a linkage exists between staff development and empowerment when he said, 'A vehicle for pursuing empowerment is already in place. It is an old and familiar part of every teacher's life: inservice education' (p. 474). He went on to observe, however, that a thorough overhaul of staff development programs is needed if such efforts are to fulfill their potential for 'prying open the door to empowerment'. The human resource development model does not pry open the door to empowerment – participant empowerment is what it's all about. When teachers and other professionals share both authority and responsibilities while engaging in collaborative assessment, planning, implementation and evaluation, that *is* participant empowerment.

Maeroff (1988) argues that, if we are going to empower teachers, we need to 'lift' them in three key areas: status, knowledge and access to decision-making. All of these facets of teacher empowerment are included in the human resource development model. First, it provides status for teachers by putting them in leadership positions. Second, it increases participants' knowledge and skills and, in addition, provides opportunites for them to share their talents with others. Third, the model not only provides participants with access to decision-making but directly involves them in the decision-making process. Let us examine each of these facets of participant empowerment.

Assuming Leadership Positions

It goes without saying that a leadership position usually provides status for the person filling such a position. A true position of leadership also provides the kind of power and authority that enables or permits the leader to get things accomplished. In discussing empowerment, Maeroff (1988) noted that, for teachers, empowerment 'has more to do with deportment than the ability to boss others'. He goes on to observe: 'It is the power to exercise one's craft with quiet confidence and to help shape the way the job is done' (p. 475).

The human resource development model provides numerous opportunities for teachers to assume leadership roles in the overall staff development program. They serve on both building-level and district-wide staff development committees, and thus are able to see their needs and opinions reflected in the policies and activities which become the overall design of the program. Teachers also assume direct responsibility for the training of their colleagues, not only by serving as workshop leaders/presenters but also by serving as peer coaches or mentors.

One of the primary reasons that staff involvement in a committee process is so important is that 'the process helps develop leadership in the members of these groups that can then influence the rest of the staff' (McGreal, 1989). Therefore, suggests McGreal, teachers who serve as members of such groups should be selected on the basis of their credibility and influence with their colleagues, because such status can be important when a new initiative represents a dramatic or threatening change. Persons who serve in such leadership positions also develop management skills that can be an asset to overall school or district-wide initiatives.

Increasing Participants' Knowledge

Francis Bacon has been quoted as saying 'Knowledge itself is power'. Obviously, one must be sufficiently educated and informed to exert authority, so providing opportunities for teachers to become more knowledgeable is a necessary step in enhancing their power. They need opportunities to leave the isolation of their classrooms and to 'gain an overview that teachers do not ordinarily obtain' (Maeroff, 1988).

As both teachers and administrators assume new roles, then, adequate training becomes a must. Opportunities must be provided for them to increase their knowledge base in order to make informed judgments. Collaborative skills will also need to be practiced so that collegiality can flourish both at the building and district level. Thus, staff development planners must be committed to the belief that appropriate training and support will be provided for those who assume new roles. Failure to do so may mean that teachers and administrators will be unable to achieve the desired results in carrying out their new responsibilities.

Simply making staff development opportunities available, however, will not be sufficient for empowering participants in a staff development program. The human resource development model requires both teachers and adminstrators to assume responsibility for their own growth and development as well as that of their colleagues.

Involving Participants in Decision-Making

In an interview with Ron Brandt (1989), Ann Lieberman defined teacher empowerment as 'involving people authentically in dealing with their own professional lives'. She went on to explain that teacher empowerment means:

Real participation by teachers reflecting their vision of participation.... It means empowering teachers to participate in group decisions: to have real decision-making roles in the school community, which in most places they don't have now. (p. 24)

Decision-making is, as noted by Lieberman, a very significant aspect of empowerment. The human resource development model provides many opportunities for involvement in decision-making, one of the first decisions being, as previously mentioned, the decision to become involved. Adult learners will, however, be more motivated to risk becoming involved and learning new behaviors if 'they have control over the learning situation and are free from threat of failure' (Wood, Thompson and Russell, 1981). Modeling during training sessions, as well as in the classroom, reduces the risk of failure and encourages teachers to become active participants in their own learning.

In the human resource model, teachers are provided with many choices beyond whether or not to become involved in their own learning. A menu of staff development opportunities is provided so that teachers are able to make choices based on their particular career stage. Participants are also involved in making choices about objectives, activities and materials for training programs. This involvement responds directly to the adult learner's need for control over his or her own learning (Wood, Thompson and Russell, 1981).

Attention to all three key areas — status and leadership, increasing participants' knowledge, and involvement in decision-making — encourages teachers' continued participation in the staff development program and, in the process, empowers them to recognize that they can make a difference.

Summary

If staff development programs are to be successful in enhancing the professional lives of educators and in fuelling and guiding school improvement efforts, they must be customized to meet the needs of the school district as well as the individual needs of educators within the system. Thus, school districts can no longer be content to design and implement the typical kinds of staff development programs that have been provided in the past as 'instant solutions' to long-term problems. As described by Dillon-Peterson (1987), these programs have been:

... crash training courses in new techniques, cursory introduction of new 'teacher proof' curriculum materials, sensitivity training sessions prior to court-ordered desegregation, brief workshops on new state or federal regulations. These may involve an occasional inservice day with little or no follow-up, college-type courses, or large group presentations by an outside consultant. (p. 5)

The human resource model presented in this chapter is not a 'typical' staff development program. It is one that would be described by Dillon-Peterson as an example of 'what works in staff development' because it is one that has the potential for bringing about substantial change in the individual through a group process that provides for support, the exchange of ideas, the maintenance of enthusiasm and problem-solving capabilities.

References

BARKLEY, W.W., McCORMICK, W.J. and TAYLOR, R.R. (1987) 'Teachers as workshop leaders: A model for teachers training teachers', *Journal of Staff Development*, 8, 2, pp. 45–48.

BENTS, R.H. and HOWEY, K.R. (1981) 'Staff Development — change in the individual', in DILLON-PETERSON, B. (Ed.) *Staff Development/Organization Development*, Alexandria, VA, Association for Supervision and Curriculum Development, pp. 11–36.

BERLIN, B.M., CONYERS, J.G., FRICKER, W., JENSEN, K.B. and ROONEY, J. (1987) 'Teacher-2-teacher: The Palatine peer coaching program', *Journal of Staff Development*, 8, 2, pp. 21–23.

BERTANI, A., TAFEL, L., PROCTOR, J. and VYDRA, J. (1987) 'Teachers as leaders: A district plans for new roles, new directions', *Journal of Staff Development*, 8, 1, pp. 36–38.

BOYER, E. (1983) *High School: A Report on Secondary Education in America*, New York, NY, Harper and Row.

BRANDT, R. (1989) 'On Teacher empowerment: A conversation with Ann Lieberman', *Educational Leadership*, 46, 8, pp. 23–26.

BURKE, P.J., CHRISTENSEN, J.C. and FESSLER, R. (1984) *Teacher Career Stages: Implications for Staff Development*, Bloomington, IN, Phi Delta Kappa Educational Foundation.

CALDWELL, S.D. and WOOD, F.H. (1988) 'School-based improvement — Are we ready?', *Educational Leadership*, 46, 2, pp. 50–56.

CAMERON, J. (1988) 'Using networks to promote staff development', *Journal of Staff Development*, 9, 1, pp. 40–43.

CASTLE, D.K. (1988) 'Evaluating the effects and the process of staff development', *Journal of Staff Development*, 9, 11, pp. 20–26.

CHASE, A. and WOLFE, P. (1989) 'Off to a good start in peer coaching', *Educational Leadership*, 46, 8, p. 37.

CHRISCO, I.M. (1989) 'Peer assistance works', *Educational Leadership*, 46, 8, pp. 31–32.

DANIEL, L.D. (1987) 'District administrative support: A must for the teacher/trainer', *Journal of Staff Development*, 8, 1, pp. 46–48.

DILLON-PETERSON, B. (1981) 'Staff development/organization development — perspective 1981', in DILLON-PETERSON, B. (Ed.) *Staff Development/Organization Development*, Alexandria, VA, Association for Supervision and Curriculum Development, pp. 1–10.

DUTTWEILER, P.C. (1989) 'Components of an effective professional development program', *Journal of Staff Development*, 10, 2, pp. 2–6.

EDELFELT, R.A. and LAWRENCE, G. (1975) 'In-service education: The state of the art', in EDELFELT, R.A. and JOHNSON, M. (Eds) *Rethinking in-service education*, Washington, D.C., National Education Association, pp. 1–23.

ELIAS, P., FISHER, M.L. and SIMON, R. (1980) *Helping Beginning Teachers Through the First Year: A Review of the Literature*, Princeton, NJ, Educational Testing Service.

FESSLER, R. and BURKE, P.J. (1988) 'Teacher assessment and staff development: Links in the same chain', *Journal of Staff Development*, 9, 1, pp. 14–18.

FULLER, F.F. and BOWN, O.H. (1975) 'Becoming a teacher', in RYAN, K. (Ed.) *Teacher Education: The Seventy-Fourth Yearbook of the National Society for the Study of Education*, Chicago, IL, University of Chicago Press, pp. 25–52.

GARMSTON, R.J. (1987) 'How administrators support peer coaching', *Educational Leadership*, 44, 5, pp. 18–26.

GLICKMAN, C.D. (1985) *Supervision of Instruction: A Developmental Approach*, Boston, MA, Allyn and Bacon, Inc.

GOMERY, J. and CROUSE, R. (1987) 'The Oregon consortium for instructional coaching', *Journal of Staff Development*, 87, 8, pp. 18–20.

GOODLAD, JOHN I. (1984) *A Place Called School — Prospects for the Future*, New York, NY, McGraw-Hill Book Company.

HALL, G., WALLACE, R. and DOSSETT, W. (1973) *A Developmental Conceptualization of the Adoption Process Within Educational Institutions*, Austin, Texas, Research and Development Center for Teacher Education, The University of Texas.

HOUSTON, W.R. and FELDER, B.D. (1982) 'Break horses, not teachers', *Phi Delta Kappan*, 63, 7, pp. 457–460.

JOYCE, B.R. and SHOWERS, B. (1983) *Power in Staff Development Through Research in Training*, Alexandria, VA, Association for Supervision and Curriculum Development.

JOYCE, B. and SHOWERS, B. (1988) *Student Achievement Through Staff Development*, New York, NY, Longman, Inc.

KILLION, J.P. and HARRISON, C.R. (1988) 'Evaluating training programs: Three critical elements for success', *Journal of Staff Development*, 9, 1, pp. 34–38.

KILLION, J.P., HUDDLESTON, J.P. and CLASPELL, M.A. (1988) 'People developer: A new role for principals', *Journal of Staff Development*, 10, 1, pp. 2–7.

KOWALSKI, T.J. (1984) 'Research and assumptions in adult education: Implications for teacher preparation', *Journal of Teacher Education*, 35, 3, pp. 8–10.

KRUPP, J.A. (1987) 'Mentoring: A means by which teachers become staff developers', *Journal of Staff Development*, 8, 1, pp. 12–15.

LEGGETT, D. and HOYLE, S. (1987) 'Peer coaching: One district's experience in using teachers as staff developers', *Journal of Staff Development*, 8, 1, pp. 16–20.

LIEBERMAN, ANN and MILLER, LYNNE (1984) *Teachers, Their World, and Their Work — Implications for School Improvement*, Alexandria, VA, Association for Supervision and Curriculum Development.

LORTIE, DAN C. (1975) *School Teacher — A Sociological Study*, Chicago, IL, The University of Chicago Press.

LOUCKS-HORSLEY, S., HARDING, C.K., ARBUCKLE, M.A., MURRAY, L.B., DUBEA, C. and WILLIAMS, M.K. (1987) *Continuing to Learn — A Guidebook for Teacher Development*, Andover, MA, The Regional Laboratory for Educational Improvement of the Northeast and Islands.

LYONS, JR., V.E. (1989) 'A practical approach to building-level staff development', *Journal of Staff Development*, 10, 1, pp. 32–34.

MAEROFF, G.I. (1988) 'A blueprint for empowering teachers', *Phi Delta Kappan*, 67, 7, pp. 473–477.

McDONALD, F.J. (1980) *The Problems of Beginning Teachers: A Crisis in Training*, Princeton, NJ, Educational Testing Service.

McGREAL, T.L. (1989) 'Necessary ingredients for successful instructional improvement initiatives', *Journal of Staff Development*, 10, 1, pp. 35–41.

McLAUGHLIN, M.W. and MARSH, D.D. (1978) 'Staff development and school change', *Teachers College Record*, 80, 1, pp. 69–94.

MOORE, J.R. (1988) 'Guidelines concerning adult learning', *Journal of Staff Development*, 9, 3, pp. 2–5.

PARKAY, F.W. and DAMICO, S.B. (1989) 'Empowering teachers for change through faculty-driven school improvement', *Journal of Staff Development*, 10, 2, pp. 8–14.

PARKER, L.S. (1986) *The Efficacy of a Teacher Induction Program in Providing Assistance and Support to First-Year Teachers*, unpublished doctoral dissertation, University of Wisconsin-Madison.

PARKER, L.S. (1988a) 'A regional teacher induction program that works for rural schools', *Journal of Staff Development*, 9, 4, pp. 16–20.

PARKER, L.S. (1988b) 'Mentoring the beginning teacher: A professional development opportunity for both beginning and experienced teachers', *Forward: Wisconsin Journal for Supervision and Curriculum Development*, 13, 2, pp. 29–38.

RYAN, K. (1979) 'Toward understanding the problem: At the threshold of the profession', in HOWEY, K.R. and BENTS, R.H. (Eds) *Toward Meeting the Needs of the Beginning Teacher*, Minneapolis, MN, Midwest Teacher Corps Network, pp. 35–52.

SERGIOVANNI, T.J. and STARRATT, R.J. (1988) *Supervision: Human Perspectives*, New York, NY, McGraw-Hill Book Company.

SOUSA, D.A. (1987) 'Training teachers to be staff developers', *Journal of Staff Development*, 8, 2, pp. 38–40.

TAYLOR, V.S., THOMPSON, K. and SCHMUCK, R.A. (1989) 'Cross-organizational collaboration: A study of staff development and school improvement efforts in Oregon', *Journal of Staff Development*, 10, 2, pp. 16–20.

WADE, R.K. (1984–5) 'What makes a difference in inservice teacher education? A meta-analysis of research', *Educational Leadership*, 42, 4, pp. 48–54.

WASCD (1988) *Planning Effective Staff Development*, Madison, WI, Wisconsin Association for Supervision and Curriculum Development.

WESTHOFF, M., CARTER, Y. and BAILEY, L. (1987) 'Collaborative roles to improve instructional skills', *Journal of Staff Development*, 8, 2, pp. 25–29.

WOOD, F.H., THOMPSON, S.R. and RUSSELL, SR. F. (1981) in DILLON-PETERSON, B. (Ed.) *Staff Development/Organization Development*, Alexandria, VA, Association for Supervision and Curriculum Development, pp. 59–91.

WRIGHT, L.V. (1987) 'A program for improving teacher decision making through peer coaching and reflection', *Journal of Staff Development*, 8, 3, pp. 54–57.

WU, P.C. (1987) 'Teachers as staff developers: Research, opinions, and cautions', *Journal of Staff Development*, 8, 1, pp. 4–6.

7 The Career Lattice — A Model for Structuring Personalized Staff Development

John H. McDonnell and Judith C. Christensen

Moving Toward Professional Involvement

The reform efforts of the 1980s coupled with the educational research of the past twenty years has set the stage for potentially dynamic changes in the 1990s. The timing is right for teachers to assume greater leadership roles in their profession. More emphasis on local control and a ready pool of veteran teachers along with a recognition of the teacher as decision-maker are all elements which create a climate for positive changes in the profession. There is also recognition of teachers' potential to assume leadership positions within the school structure without having to leave classroom teaching completely. Role changes which are backed by professional organizations and teachers' unions open the doors for change wider still. As teachers work through new role definitions, the shifts in leadership and authority will become a reality. However, change will take time as principals and central office personnel as well as teachers redefine and prepare for new roles.

Many attempts to upgrade the teaching profession were included in reform packages during the 1980s although many programs were considered experimental and funding was not being provided for future implementation (Cornett, 1988). Career ladders, merit pay and incentives of many types were implemented in districts and states. In December 1988, for example, thirty-four states had planned or were planning career ladder or incentive programs with state funding.

Teachers are ready for involvement in decisions that directly influence their lives. A study of incentives considered appropriate by teachers (McDonnell, Christensen, and Price, 1988) revealed that control over instructional decisions, influence in school decision-making, and control over issues in the work environment ranked higher than money issues with teachers. Worthy of note is that the greatest discrepancy appeared when appropriateness of being designated master or lead teacher was compared to availability of the position. It was seen by teachers to be very appropriate but seldom available to them.

The Metropolitan Life Survey of the American Teacher (1986) found that 97 per cent of teachers queried think that school districts should have a team approach to school management and that the teacher's biggest role should be in academic, pedagogical and student-related areas. Boyer (1988) in a state-by-state analysis of teacher involvement found that teachers most frequently took part in decisions about textbooks and materials and curriculum but were very uninvolved in activities such as selecting new teachers or administrators or even designing staff development.

The need for involvement and role change has been stated throughout the past decade. Teachers' unions, professional organizations and individuals within the school structure recognize the effects of such a movement and generally support the intent. The agenda for the 90s is implementation.

Change, however positive, is not easy. Fullan (1985) identified seven points concerning change: '(1) change takes place over time; (2) the initial stages of any significant change always involve anxiety and uncertainty; (3) on-going technical assistance and psychological support assistance are crucial if the anxiety is to be coped with; (4) change involves learning new skills through practice and feedback — it is incremental and developmental; (5) the most fundamental breakthrough occurs when people can·cognitively understand the underlying conception and rationale with respect to "why this new way works better"; (6) organizational conditions within the school (peer norms, administrative leadership) and in relation to the school (external administrative support and technical help) make it more or less likely that the process will succeed; and (7) successful change involves pressure, but it is pressure through interaction with peers and other technical and administrative leaders' (p. 396). Although Fullan was summarizing research conducted on curricular innovations, the points are salient ones to consider as roles change and schools restructure.

Involving Teachers in Change

As the 1990s begin, a shift toward decentralization and site-based management is evident. This movement reflects many of the research findings of the past decade. Wood (1989) summarizes some of the assumptions about staff development which come from the research:

1   The school, not the district, is the primary unit of change.
2   Significant change in educational practice takes considerable time and is a result of long-range staff development programs conducted for three to five years.
3   Those who are changing their behavior must make personal and group commitments to the new programs and practices.
4   All school personnel should be involved in staff development throughout their professional lives.
5   As adult learners, educators are motivated to learn when individual differences are recognized and when educators have some control over what and how they learn.
6   Leadership in designing and implementing staff development should be shared by administrators and learners (pp. 27–28).

These assumptions reflect a change in attitudes about teachers and their roles in professional development. They point to the need for active involvement in needs assessment, planning and implementation as well as the need to provide alternatives and leadership roles for teachers. Overall, they indicate a shift away from a deficit model for staff development to a professional growth model based on individual and organizational needs.

Individual needs of teachers have become more important as the teaching force has matured. The turn-over in teaching has diminished leaving a veteran staff in most schools. Keeping teachers up-to-date and vital while recognizing their expertise is a challenge. Professional development has been forced to change.

Adult development theorists such as Levinson, Gould, Erikson, Kegan, Loevinger and others have shed some light on the developmental needs of adults. Using their insights, professional development specialists have stressed the need to tailor activities to meet personal levels of development. Judy Arin-Krupp (1989) suggests that staff developers recognize differences by (1) using both personal and professional knowledge about participants; (2) involving the learners in planning; (3) using evaluation information to reassess needs; (4) helping participants tie their individual needs to school and district goals; (5) encouraging participants to write a proposal for their own staff development (pp. 45–46).

Levine (1989) sums up the need for meeting individual needs while maintaining collegiality:

> Adults in schools need to work with each other in mutually supporting, collegial relationships focused on important facets of teaching and learning. School people must have expanded roles in decision-making about issues that affect their work lives. To professionalize education, control must revert to those in the business of teaching and administering. Giving teachers and administrators

discretion over their work is an essential form of empowerment. (p. 30)

Teacher empowerment is a complex process which can appear simple and therefore have 'token' efforts which will create surface and nominal changes rather than true changes within the organizational structure. Maeroff (1988) provides an in-depth discussion of four areas he sees as essential to empowerment: status, increased knowledge, increased collegiality and decision-making power. Incentives as simple as having access to telephones or comfortable meeting rooms to more complex incentives such as involvement in scheduling, and time to develop curriculum are essential for empowerment.

Little (1988) emphasizes needed changes in the professionalization of teachers. Two areas she outlines are the structure of the career including opportunities for advancement/promotion and expanded or job enlargement opportunities. She argues that a proposal to develop teacher leaders will satisfy two needs: 'It will present attractive opportunities and rewards for teachers, and it will direct greater institutional attention to the quality of teaching' (p. 81).

The importance of teacher empowerment seems clear. Empowerment allows the development of teaching from a quasi or emerging professional status to that of a full profession — to the degree that this can be accomplished within a bureaucratic organizational structure. Among characteristics that make teaching a profession are the sense of a career, a knowledge base, a professional culture and a degree of autonomy and accountability within the sphere of professional responsibility — the teaching of the nation's children and youth. The implications of the above characteristics highlight the need for continual, individualized professional development within the confines of the organizational environment's goals and objectives.

Professional development has historically been limited in terms of amount, quality and organization. In many districts, perhaps most, inservice education has been a laughing stock among teachers — a subject for derision and jokes. At best it has been benign; at worst it has been seen as an impediment to the teachers' fundamental task of being alone in classrooms preparing for their students. Yet the logic inherent in the professionalization of teaching is that teachers must be in charge of providing professional staff development to maintain and improve levels of expertise in the knowledge base and professional culture of their field. The programs must be based on short- and long-term planning and goals and must be continuous in nature. Incentives should be part of the organizational scheme. Finally, some model for planning and organizing staff development is needed. Teachers as educational leaders might well be the end result.

Professional Development and Bureaucratic Structures

The traditional salary schedule purports to reward professional growth in two ways. First, it is assumed the more experience one has the better the person is as a teacher and the more salary one should receive. The authors, however, are unaware of research which supports this assumption. Rather, research undertaken by the authors in collaboration with the members of the Collegial Research Consortium (McDonnell, Christensen and Price, 1988) demonstrate that neither age nor time in teaching correlate with a teacher's career stage. A young teacher can readily be in career frustration; a veteran teacher can as readily be enthusiastic and growing. Personal and organizational factors are the key determinants of career stage and effectiveness. (It should be pointed out that many salary schedules do not go beyond eight to fourteen years except perhaps in footnoted, periodic increments.)

The second assumption behind the traditional salary schedule is that additional college units and/or higher degrees improve teaching effectiveness and thus should result in additional salary, at least up to a point. The corollary to this seems to be that when one reaches some arbitrary point, say MA + 30, one knows all there is to know. Typically, salary incentives are dropped as a reward for additional professional development.

The type of professional staff development that occurs under this structure is mixed. Often advanced degrees are required at some point with little thought as to their usefulness to teacher development. Some degrees, especially in the sciences, are so research oriented that they have little positive effect on the teacher's classroom performance. These degrees may even create dysfunction in the classroom. Other degrees, in administration or counseling for example, while of worth in their own right, may have little effect in the classroom. If utilized for career development, they tend to lure teachers out of the classroom into other fields, at the taxpayer's expense. Traditionally, steps to salary advancement have been limited to college/university units. Increasing recognition is being given to providing salary credit for other types of staff development activities. Yet if these do not transfer to the common currency of transcript credits, they place teachers at a disadvantage if and when they change districts because such activity credits are not transferable. No wonder teachers are cautious about taking non-credit workshops unless they are already at the top of the salary schedule. Some districts with traditional schedules do have adequate, even excellent career development programs, and the trend to develop and implement quality programs seems to be on the increase as part of the empowerment movement. While the traditional schedule does not prevent high quality staff development, it certainly does not ensure it and may in fact serve to inhibit the necessary change in outlook and organization which supports and provides incentives for engaging in district or school-based staff development programs.

Merit pay, traditionally defined, does not focus on professional development either. The intent in these schemes is to reward teachers by some type of accountability system so that those rated as more effective teachers benefit from a higher salary in some fashion. This system has trouble taking into account various aspects of student characteristics. In addition, the intuitively effective teacher is more highly rewarded regardless of the degree of participation in professional development activities. To the degree that salary is an incentive, and research indicates that it is a positive incentive but not significantly greater than several others (McDonnell, *et al.*, 1988), merit pay would seem to encourage on-going education at least on the part of less effective teachers.

Yet merit pay, regardless of its value, is probably not worth the effort of implementation for at least three reasons: teachers seem to be egalitarian in their outlook on teaching. They feel that all have strengths and weaknesses; all deserve the same financial reward based on some easily determined, non-judgmental, objective criteria. Second, teachers have great suspicion of the rater and the instrument in any accountability system. Here, the individualistic nature of the teaching enterprise comes to the fore. Each teacher is an individual and has his or her own repertoire of effective techniques. How can one instrument rank an almost infinite variety and combination of teaching styles and relationships? And further, can one trust the rater? The third impediment to merit pay is the collective bargaining movement. Teacher unionism has placed the administration and teachers in an adversarial relationship. While the collective bargaining movement has resulted in an empowerment of teachers within a bureaucratic structure and has historically been important, one residue is a 'them or us' mentality lacking in mutual trust. No wonder that less than 5 per cent of the teachers in the US work under a merit pay system.

Even if the preponderance of evidence indicated that such systems provide incentives for professional growth and effective teaching, the nature of teacher sentiments seems not to provide a fertile environment for the acceptance of such a system. Further, as long as the ultimate evaluation is in the hands of the administration, the professional characteristic of peer autonomy is violated.

Since the *Nation at Risk* report was published in 1983, the idea of upward career movement has become the fad purported to professionalize teaching — and this may be the case. Based on old models of differentiated staffing from the 1960s, career ladder models took off. Tennessee, North Carolina, Texas, and Florida (with several different models) developed career ladders early; then interest seemed to peak. More recently, Rochester, New York, has received considerable attention with its negotiated career ladder. Whether ladders last through the 1990s is an open question, but some of the same obstacles which impede the growth of merit pay may also limit career ladders. Further, the massive and costly programs that have been put into place may not prove cost effective. While claiming to provide a career line within teaching, thus providing more effective instruction, career ladders do not provide in and of themselves any scheme for professional staff development. This fact is recognized by the California Roundtable on Educational Opportunity (1985). While it called for the development of a career ladder model for the state, it realized that some mechanism which ensures professional growth and development must also be provided. It recommended the development of a career lattice to meet this important goal.

The Career Lattice Model (Christensen, McDonnell and Price, 1988) is a planning device for career-long teacher growth and development which can operate in conjunction with any type of salary scheme. In the conservative district wishing to maintain a traditional schedule, the career lattice can be used to focus on staff development for the person moving upward on the schedule, as well as providing for those teachers who have 'topped out'. For those districts interested in experimenting with merit pay or career ladders, the career lattice just as effectively provides for a planning model and a focus on staff development. And for the more adventuresome, the career lattice could stand alone as the major organizer for salary determination.

In this way, professional staff development and effective teaching would become the central focus for determining a wide variety of incentives, both material and non-material. In this way, both the socially oriented and the individualistic sentiments of teachers could be harnessed for professional growth. And in this way the variety of career stages of teachers could be accommodated across the career span of the teaching professional.

The Career Lattice: A Model for Structuring Personalized Staff Development

The Model

The Career Lattice Model (Figure 7.1) is made up of four aspects of a teacher's professional development activity. The first two are contained in a lattice or matrix with intersecting spaces. On the horizontal axis are those roles usually taken by teachers as they go about their work. Some roles are more common than others with a teacher often serving in several roles at the same time. The attempt here is to sort them out and identify them so that a teacher may better analyze needs and organize a multi-step plan of professional development. These categories include some of the roles teachers can assume to meet personal and professional needs.

- *Learner.* In this role the teacher is learning new skills or content to use in the classroom to be shared with others in some way. For

Figure 7.1   The Career Lattice Model

Teaching Responsibilities	Career Lattice Role Options					
	Learner	Knowledge Producer	Peer Coach	Teacher Educator	Mentor	Leader
Student Evaluation						
Planning						
Curriculum						
Instructional Strategies						
Materials						
Classroom Management						
Discipline						
Climate (School/Classroom)						
Communication						
Professionalism						
Co-Curricular						

Examples of Empowerment Experiences:
1. Education or training
2. Experience
3. Development activities such as: travel, conferences, workshops
4. Organizational work
5. Research or reading
6. School/Classroom visitation
7. Released time

Initiated by:
1. Self
2. Peers
3. Administrators
4. Students
5. Parents

example, a school might need someone with expertise in computer education so a teacher is selected to become the 'resident expert'. Coursework and classroom visits might be the professional development plan for this teacher as new skills are learned. Later the teacher could serve in a leadership role within the school to achieve a future professional development goal.

- *Knowledge Producer.* This role involves the teacher in collaborative or action research in the classroom or in the development of new materials and techniques. It might involve writing new curricula or teaching units.
- *Peer Coach.* In this role the teacher serves as collegial adviser, offering support and constructive feedback, suggesting alternative useful strategies to a fellow teacher.
- *Teacher Educator.* This might be a collaborative role with a college or university either as a teacher of preservice teachers, or as a colleague sharing knowledge with other experienced teachers.
- *Mentor.* In mentoring the teacher assumes a long-term role supportive of a colleague in some or all areas of teaching responsibili-

ties. A teacher could be a mentor for a beginning teacher or for any other teacher in need of support.

- *Leader*. The category of leader in the matrix can take many forms. It can involve leadership at a grade level or in a content area, in curriculum development at a local school district level, or even within a professional organization.

The role functions described here are examples of some options for professional development and change for teachers. With a career lattice, there will of necessity be a change of role definition from those traditionally held for teachers, principals and central office personnel, role changes which might require some budget modifications with different ways of spending money allocated for staff development.

The vertical axis identifies those responsibilities that teachers have as they carry out their various roles. These responsibilities focus on the usual classroom activities of teachers, but they also have broader implications for other education professionals such as staff developers since they represent the activities and conditions under which effective teaching and learning occur. These responsibilities will have different meanings dependent upon the role option chosen for development.

The teaching responsibilities listed in the model characterize those typically assigned to teachers of any grade or subject. Evaluating students, planning for instructional strategies, and selecting curriculum or materials are all part of the teaching cycle of diagnosing, planning, teaching and evaluating. Related areas could include managing the classroom, dealing with discipline, and developing a positive classroom climate. Communicating with students, other teachers, parents, administrators and community members are other responsibilities, Exhibiting professionalism is a multifaceted responsibility which includes gaining knowledge of the field as well as participating in the profession through formal and informal organizations and networks. Co-curricular responsibilities are the related, extra duties teachers are asked to perform such as acting as advisers of yearbooks, newspapers, or drama clubs, acting as coaches and in other similar capacities.

The third aspect of the career lattice involves identification of the initiators of the activity. These appear at the lower right of the model. To be significant, the activity must flow out of both the personal environment of the teacher but also must be supported by the organizational environment. This support comes when the activity is based on goals and objectives of both the district and the local school. The person initiating the activity will vary. It may be the teacher who takes a personal interest and works to expand it into a school activity. Peers may decide on an important school need and enlist a group of teachers to develop appropriate programs to solve some specific problems. Administrators may also identify school needs and request interested teachers to attack the problem through professional development activities. An administrator may identify a specific problem in a classroom and suggest that a plan be developed by the teacher to remedy the deficiency. Students and parents are, or should be, significant participants in planning for school improvement and identifying specific needs from their unique perspectives.

Once the roles and responsibilities of the professional development plan are decided upon and the plan is initiated, it is necessary to attend to the fourth component of the model, the actual experiences which empower the teacher proceeding with an individualized development program. These activities, listed on the lower left side of the model, must be varied both to meet the particular career stage of the teacher and to focus on the development goals. Diversity is also necessary in order to meet the many goals of the schools within a district as well as to implement the overall district decisions for school improvement. Finally, these empowerment activities will serve as incentives to enhance the profession for teachers. In some cases they may be as important as the salary base itself if not more so.

Means to Empowerment — The Experiences

Education or training is the most common type of professional activity that teachers undertake. This may assume the form of classroom courses and/or advanced degrees either in a content area or in education techniques and methodology. It can also include training in specific areas as new information comes to light. Accommodating different learning styles and cooperative learning are examples.

Any experience which focuses on a specifically identified role and responsibility can help advance one's understanding and insights, thus enhancing growth and development of the individual teacher. This might include other work activity, volunteer work in the community and past learning experiences. Avocational activities, such as hobbies, as well as one's vocational history form an important empowerment base for growth and development in new realms of endeavors.

A variety of activities should be included in any development program. Specific workshops can support advanced learning and acquisition of knowledge. Conferences can serve several functions; the participant usually has various options to attend meetings particularly attuned to new areas of developing expertise. Perhaps more important is the chance to network, to develop a collaborative group of professionals interested in the same issues and types of development. To learn from your colleagues, to interact and exchange ideas is a type of peer activity characteristic of professional work. It can be an important, eye-opening activity for many teachers. Finally, travel can be used profitably in developing areas of knowledge and skills. Such activities need to be focused through the professional development plan. Objectives and goals for the particular experience need to be firmly in place.

Organizational work is an often overlooked arena for enhancing professional development. A teacher can develop and hone leadership skills as well as broaden the network of expertise in a particular area; and a mentoring relationship with other teachers just beginning to gain knowledge in a new area can be developed, too. Such work can do much to provide a sense of autonomy, self-esteem and efficacy — a key characteristic of professionals.

Reading information about current research should be a continuing activity for teachers. It becomes an empowering experience when it is focused on an emerging area of knowledge and should be considered as an appropriate activity for many professional development plans. Furthermore a growing knowledge base can support active field research thus producing more information and expanding the horizon of understanding. Schools and classrooms are natural habitats for this type of activity and teachers have more ready access to this kind of action research than most other actors in education. As teachers pursue increasing professionalization of their field, this type of empowerment activity should come increasingly to the fore.

Teachers can learn a great deal from visiting other schools and classrooms if the nature of the development plan lends itself to such activities. Development of new techniques and methodologies in particular fall into this category. What better way of cementing knowledge of new techniques than by observing an expert in the technique using it with a class? Peer coaching and mentoring roles particularly call for this type of empowerment activity.

Released time is seen by most teachers engaging in professional development activities as not only essential but as the key incentive in research (McDonnell, *et al.*, 1987). This was true regardless of the teacher career stage, with available time a more powerful incentive than increased salary or some other stipend. Districts wishing to provide high quality professional development must take this into account. Time often equates with money, but other organizational arrangements should be considered as the search continues for this illusive element. Released time will very likely become an empowerment component essential to professional development activities.

The Career Lattice Model is a support structure for professional growth and development and for teacher empowerment. It is an attempt to put into rational form the teaching act and to identify teachers' various roles as they go about their professional lives. By identifying and separating these elements it is hoped that a teacher and supporting staff can think more knowledgeably about professional career development and plan for both short- and long-term results. Since these goals come from several sources, the articulation between the needs of personal environment and

Figure 7.2   *Personalized Professional Development Plan*

Teacher Plan and Record Form

Name: _____

School: _____

Address: _____

_____

Telephone: _____

Topic: _____

How does this plan meet the goals of the following constituents:

1. Your personal goals?_____

_____

2. Your school's goals? _____

3. Your school district's goals? _____

_____

		Empowerment				
Role Option	Area of Teaching Responsibility	Activity:	How will you achieve your objectives?	Resources Needed/ Incentives	Evaluation: Evidence of Completion	Evaluator's Comments/ Approval

those of the organizational environment are critical. Without synchroniza-tion here, professional development activities will neither empower the teacher nor move education toward meeting the needs of the children in a particular school or building. The Career Lattice Model is designed to enable thoughtful discussion and adequate planning of effective profes-sional growth activities.

The Career-Lattice Model Personal Professional Development Plan — Its Use

The authors have developed a format to implement the Career Lattice Model (Figure 7.2). An effort has been made to provide a written docu-ment for teachers and staff developers to use when planning professional growth activities.

The document consists of the Lattice Model itself with an appropriate discussion of its four facets as previously discussed in this chapter. The teacher, often with consultation of a staff development leader, is then directed to consider areas of professional growth and development which are pertinent goals to work on. Short-term and long-term aspects must be considered as well as a time line for final attainment of the goals specified.

The mesh with organizational goals and needs must also be specified. The teacher then identifies the specific role(s) to be played and the area(s) of teaching responsibility which are most representative. The intersecting boxes thus become a guide to action. These questions — ones of empowerment — then need to be asked:

1 What activities would allow you to meet your goal(s)?
2 How much time will it take to accomplish your goal(s)?
3 What resources are needed to complete the activities you have planned?
4 What evidence will you provide for document completion?

On the record form of the plan, sections are provided for listing of the role option and of the teaching responsibility. Empowerment choices are then listed, with activity(s), time and the resources needed. These resources themselves can be seen as incentives of various types which can provide a spur to action for teachers — a motivation for self-improvement toward more effective teaching. Some of these may be material incentives such as increased salary or stipend and some may be non-material such as various allocations of time. Finally, a column for evidence of completion and for the evaluator's comments and approval are incorporated. The criteria for evidence of completion should be clearly delineated during the planning stages and be part of the agreed-upon plan. Of course, modification to any aspect of this plan is possible over time as new knowledge is gained and new challenges appear. The teacher is now ready to pursue the planned professional development activities. The following section details a hypothetical case of how a teacher might assume a new role as a staff development leader.

A Prospective Staff Developer Uses the Planning Model

Evelyn is interested in becoming an educational leader in the area of staff development. She has been an elementary teacher for ten years, having spent the prior eight years at home raising her children. She taught five years before parenthood. She is now in her mid-forties and the children are away at college. Evelyn has decided that it is time for professional development activities which will expand her career opportunities and extend her options as a leader. Evelyn, it is generally agreed, is in the Enthusiastic and Growing Stage of her teaching career (see Burke, Christensen and Fessler, 1984).

The district in which Evelyn teaches is convinced of the need for life-long learning for teachers and has established staff development as a district-wide goal. It is believed that the best level for effective change and growth to occur is at the building level through the designation of a teacher in every building to function as a staff development leader on a part-time basis. Appropriate adjustments are made in Evelyn's teaching schedule. She is provided with a full-time intern who team teaches with her but can also be in charge of instruction independently, thus providing released time for Evelyn to participate in staff development functions.

Evelyn uses the Personalized Professional Development Plan (PPDP) to organize the short and long-range goals for her professional development activities. Her first role option is clearly that of being a learner. Responsibilities of importance that she will need to pursue include the following:

1 Instructional Strategies — Individualizing staff development while incorporating the goals of the district in her building through needs assessment, and alternate delivery methods, thus effecting change.
2 Communication — Understanding and gaining experience in human relations and interpersonal relations. Using presentation strategies in small and large group settings. Understanding needs of adult learners.
3 Professionalism — Gaining knowledge and understanding of the history of professions and the teaching profession in particular. Developing awareness of the stages that teachers go through during their careers. Using appropriate staff development methods and incentives for teachers in each stage.

Evelyn has clearly identified her goals as she makes plans to become a staff development leader. She must now decide on how she will best become empowered to carry out these increased responsibilities. Because this is a new area for her and a major undertaking in knowledge acquisition, Evelyn decides to enroll in a master's degree program in educational leadership with a focus on staff development. Several new programs have been developed at higher education institutions in her area which are designed to provide alternate roles for teachers within a teaching setting as opposed to educational administration which tends to pull teachers out of the profession. She also chooses a program which is a good balance between theory and practice. While providing for the knowledge base she needs in this new field, it also incorporates several practica and an internship which allows her practical experiences.

Evelyn has developed her time line — two years part-time and one year full-time to complete the work. She has requested financial assistance from the district to start the degree with specific courses which would allow her to obtain her knowledge goal. For the third year she will request a sabbatical leave to finish her degree. In addition, she has identified two new professional organizations she will join which focus on staff development, supervision and curriculum. Continual contact with the literature provided by these organizations as well as district support to attend their annual meetings will provide vehicles for keeping current in her field and ideas for use in her own school. As she develops and hones her skills in staff development, these organizations may well provide options for presentation of knowledge she has acquired in her new role as well as a potential leadership role. Because this first part of Evelyn's professional activity is in higher education, evidence of completion includes transcripts.

A second important role Evelyn has identified is that of knowledge producer. She will gradually enlarge this role as her role of learner is successfully completed. During her degree programs, and especially during the practica and internships, she will develop plans and strategies for establishing a staff development program in her own school. Activities will gradually be moved from the higher education classroom to the school setting with experiences obtained through the practica and internship, attendance at conferences and workshops, and organizational work increasingly becoming the activities which support her role as knowledge producer. Visits to other sites which have model staff development programs and her own research and reading will become more significant as she moves away from the directed learning of academe and becomes empowered to develop her own staff development plan for her school. The sabbatical leave experience provides her the much-needed time. This phase as knowledge producer will be completed at the end of her first year back from sabbatical leave when she plans to have a staff development plan ready to submit to her colleagues in her school.

Evelyn is now ready to assume the role of educational leader as she works with her peers to implement an effective staff development program in her school. The responsibilities defined early on as necessary to become a good staff developer are still in place. However, her role relationship with them has now changed. She must use the knowledge learned and strategies developed to facilitate a staff program for professional development. She is now responsible for putting into effect that which she has worked toward. She now has the responsibilities and role functions which are characteristic in professions: she is now responsible for her own development and the facilitation of the individual professional development of her colleagues.

In this leadership role Evelyn finds that she must develop other roles over time. In a real sense she has become a teacher educator. Her intern is a local college student and Evelyn is responsible for many of her pre-service career activities. She is also responsible for keeping her staff current with research and finds herself learning and developing workshops as new information arises. Another new role for Evelyn has been in the area of peer coaching. The staff identified a building need for more collegial relations in working with each other and decided, upon Evelyn's suggestion, to use peer coaching. Her coaching role is an ever-expanding one as her peers become more comfortable in working with her as a colleague and fellow teacher as opposed to administrative leader and evaluator of the staff. Finally, Evelyn is developing as a mentor. For the teachers in their induction year a First Year Assistance Program has been developed. As mentor, Evelyn will be responsible for working with new teachers in various areas identified as needing further development. In much the same way Evelyn will be working with experienced teachers in the career stages of Frustration or Stagnation to provide coaching and staff development which, it is hoped, will bring renewal and enthusiasm.

Evelyn is an example of an 'Enthusiastic and Growing' teacher who has stayed in the classroom part-time and enlarged her professional role options. She has used the Career Lattice Model as a way of conceptualizing and planning for her career goals and development as an educational leader. Other teachers would have different plans and different time lines dependent on their own grade level, academic area and past education and experiences. Nevertheless, the Personalized Professional Development Plan and the Career Lattice can be utilized as they plan their future options.

The authors worked with a group of elementary grade teachers, personalizing their professional development needs. The Career Lattice Model Personalized Professional Development Plan was used to help them identify and plan a specific short-term area of professional growth in which they had a specific interest and which also met defined goals of the district and/or school. These teachers were all veteran teachers. Several of them had 'topped out' on the salary schedule but they were still motivated by other incentives to pursue professional development. What follows is a sampling of several of their PPDPs.

Precautions in Developing Career Lattice Plans

Career Lattice Models should be developed over time, with adequate planning and care. This is true whether they will be utilized as an incentive system on their own or in conjunction with some other salary structure such as the traditional salary schedule, merit pay, or a career ladder. To be successful, certain criteria should be maintained. Career Lattices should be teacher initiated; since the goal is teacher empowerment, it makes little sense to impose bureaucratically the use of a lattice on teachers. As in so many other aspects of the teaching profession, if even lattices are arbitrarily imposed, teachers will find a way to subvert them. Again in light of the goal of empowerment, time and work demands on teachers must be carefully considered. If a career lattice is seen as simply another task which takes away from teacher time, as another of the myriad of administrative demands, then such a plan has little chance of improving professional staff development in a district. The Career Lattice Model need not be limited to teachers; it can be opened to all professional staff provided it is used flexibly to meet the needs of all participants and changed when necessary as 'glitches' are discovered and improvements are suggested.

There are several professional considerations which should be taken into account when developing a career lattice for use in staff development. Procedures must be clear and objective. Criteria for placement, rewards, and utilization must be universal and clearly communicated. Within the procedure must be incorporated a method for teacher decision-making. This process should be on-going and fully utilized. It cannot be seen as simply a means for co-opting teachers. In addition to any incentives inherent in the lattice, other extrinsic incentives must be available to teachers. Research has documented how important a rich selection of available incentives is to the motivation of teachers dependent on specific career stages. Rewards and recognition for classroom teaching should be part of a district's incentive structure over and above a career lattice. Nor will a career lattice replace overall salary improvement. A professional salary, regardless of how it is structured, is critical in any school district.

Finally, a career lattice should not be confused with career ladders. Career ladders are attempts to reward capable teachers by placing them on a different and higher salary schedule. Some ladders do little more than this, while others endeavor to differentiate responsibilities as one moves up. Often they are seen as competitive devices. They certainly have not yet been fully accepted by teachers. Career lattices are not competitive. They accommodate the importance of professional development and establish a way of planning for it. They accommodate the fact that teachers may have different career paths they wish to pursue, none inherently better than another. Career Lattices have the potential for being considered by teachers as a useful method for thinking about their future goals and developmental activities.

Case Study #1

Name: Sandra K.
Grade level: 2nd
Topic: Creative Writing — to develop a writing program that is comfortable and workable
Personal goals: Smooth sailing through the year with a manageable program
School/district goals: Effective writing
Role option: Learner
Area of teaching responsibility: curriculum; materials; classroom management; instructional strategies

Empowerment Plans:

Activity	Time	Resource/incentive
1. Read relevant professional literature	ongoing	Library time
2. Attend Ralph Fletcher Writing Workshop	June 20– 24	2 hours credit
3. Look at children's literature throughout the year to use with students' writing	ongoing	Literature Conference Children's/adult bookstores
4. Visit other writing programs outside the district, with focus on logistics and organization	whenever possible	Released time

Evaluation: grade report; students' writing

Case Study #2

Name: Karen
Grade level: 4th
Topic: Problem Solving — Logical Thinking
Personal goals: Not waste the students' time reviewing concepts in math already known
School/district goal: Improve math scores; promote teacher collegiality

Phase I

Role option: Learner
Area of teaching responsibility: Instructional strategies; materials
Empowerment plans:

Activity	Time	Resource/incentives
1. Spend time working with colleague, examine her materials	1 week	Released time
2. Take class on problem-solving Re-examine materials from Iowa. Look for appropriate inservice activities	1 week open	Tuition/travel support Support for inservice
	May 5–8	Support for attendance at State Math Conference

Phase II

Role option: Knowledge producer
Area of teaching responsibility: Student evaluation; planning; curriculum; instruction strategies; materials
Empowerment Plans:

	Activity	Time	Resource/incentives
1.	Develop program for 4th grade	1 year	Released time; support to attend math conference
2.	Work with gifted and top math group in 4th grade	1 year	Released time; support to attend State Conference for the Gifted and Talented

Evaluation: Written report on conference activities; curriculum in place by end of project

Case Study #3

Name: Virginia
Grade level: 5th
Topic: Reading Comprehension — Instruction
Personal goals: This is an area that has come up in research as needing our attention; I therefore want to know what needs to be improved.
School/district goals: To provide the best education possible

Phase I

Role option: Learner
Area of teaching responsibility: Instruction strategies
Empowerment Plans:

	Activity	Time	Resource/incentives
1.	Locate research by D. Durkin	3 months	ERIC search
2.	Read articles that address comprehension instruction	4 months	*Reading Teacher* articles and other periodicals

3. Attend reading conference — focus on comprehension seminars	1 week/ weekend	Funds to attend conference

Phase II

Role option: Knowledge producer
Area of teaching responsibility: Materials
Empowerment Plans:

Activity	*Time*	*Resource/incentives*
1. Design and implement new strategies in the classroom	1 year	Freedom to be flexible with the basal series in order to incorporate these strategies

Phase III

Role option: Communication
Area of teaching responsibility: Instructional strategies; materials
Empowerment Plans:

Activity	*Time*	*Resource/incentives*
1. Meet with other teachers at same grade level to share ideas	Concurrently	Released time

Evaluation: Report progress to principal or supervisor over a 2-year period. Observation by supervisor in the classroom

References

ARIN-KRUPP, J. (1989) 'Staff Development and the Individual', in CALDWELL, S.D. (Ed.) *Staff Development: A Handbook of Effective Practices*, Oxford, OH, National Staff Development Council, pp. 45, 46, 49, 50, 54.

BOYER, E.L. (1988) *Teacher Involvement in Decision Making: A State-by-State Profile*, The Carnegie Foundation for the Advancement of Teaching.

BURKE, P., FESSLER, R. and CHRISTENSEN, J. (1984) *Teacher Career Stages: Implications for Staff Development*, Fastback 214, Bloomington, IN, Phi Delta Kappa Educational Foundation.

CALIFORNIA ROUND TABLE ON EDUCATIONAL OPPORTUNITY (1985) *Teaching: Making It an Effective and Attractive Profession*, Sacramento, CA, Author.

CHRISTENSEN, J.C., McDONNELL, J.L. and PRICE, J.J. (1988) *Personalizing Staff Development: The Career Lattice Model*, Fastback 281, Bloomington, IN, Phi Delta Kappa Educational Foundation.

CORNETT, L. (1988) *Is 'Paying for Performance' Changing Schools?*, Atlanta, GA, Southern Regional Education Board.

FULLAN, M. (1985) 'Change processes and strategies at the local level', *The Elementary School Journal*, 85, 8, pp. 391–421.

LEVINE, S.L. (1989) *Promoting Adult Growth in Schools*, Boston, Allyn and Bacon.

LITTLE, J.W. (1988) 'Assessing the prospects for teacher leadership', in LIEBERMAN, A. (Ed.) *Building a Professional Culture in Schools*, New York, Teachers College Press, pp. 78–106.

MAEROFF, G.I. (1988) *The Empowerment of Teachers*, New York, Teachers College Press.

McDONNELL, J.H., CHRISTENSEN, J.C. and PRICE, J.R. (1988) 'Incentives and teaching career stages: Influences and policy implications', in BARTELL, C.A. (Ed.) *Incentives that Enhance the Teaching Profession: A Discussion of the Policy Issues*, Elmhurst, IL, North Central Regional Educational Laboratory.

METROPOLITAN LIFE INSURANCE COMPANY (1986) *American Teacher*, New York, Author.

NATIONAL COMMISSION ON EXCELLENCE IN EDUCATION (1983) *A Nation at Risk: The Imperative for Education Reform*, Washington, DC, US Government Printing Office.

WOOD, F.H. (1989) 'Organizing and managing school-based staff development', in CALDWELL, S.D. (Ed.) *Staff Development: A Handbook of Effective Practices*, Oxford, OH, National Staff Development Council, pp. 27, 28, 35, 36.

8   A Model for District Staff Development

Nancy Blair and Ronald Lange

This chapter provides a practicable design that school districts can use to formulate staff development programs. The key phases of this design involve creating awareness and readiness for staff development, conducting a needs assessment, and planning, implementing and evaluating the program. Additional important characteristics and components of effective staff development are incorporated throughout the presentation.

Staff development is a process that can exist at all levels of school operation: district, building, department/grade-level and individual. At the district level, several key perspectives must be kept in mind when preparing effective staff development programs. The practitioners' perspectives on inservice typically have been less than positive, mostly due to ineffective programs over the years; it is critical to keep a clear focus on the practitioners' viewpoints when generating any staff development program. As key decision-makers regarding staff development, the school board and administration also have opinions about what constitutes a worthwhile program. Finally, staff development planners need to be well aware of the effective staff development practices that research has highlighted within the past decade. These varied perspectives will be examined in this chapter as the phases of developing a district program are presented.

Overview

Too frequently local staff development programs are 'activity'-based in response to the attractiveness of popular presenters or programs in vogue at a given time. Currently, one might find district workshops being offered on thinking skills, cooperative learning, teaching the gifted and talented, computer applications, reading comprehension strategies and so on. The question to be asked is, 'Do these activities fit into an overall plan or framework that exists in the district to meet the diagnosed needs of the district, the teachers or the students?'

The design suggested in this chapter offers an organizational umbrella under which a district can provide a systematic approach to staff development. It includes a sequence of phases that a district should consider as the program is developed. These phases are not necessarily mutually exclusive nor are they prescriptive. Any two districts following the phases could end up with very different programs. What they will be assured of is a carefully considered, systematic plan that fits the specifics of their district and has the commitment of the central players — staff, administration, school board and community.

Phase One — Creating Readiness

In this phase, which is often ignored, the current level of expectations for staff development is analyzed and a baseline for the future is established. In this phase questions such as these are explored: 'Are current expectations adequate for staff development in this district? How do we change or raise our expectations over time? Are the key people in this district committed to the staff development process? Do we have a solid rationale for staff development that is easily communicated to the public?' Once these questions are addressed, governance structure, policy and goal formulation will be considered to complete the phase.

Phase Two — Conducting a Needs Assessment

Every program needs a solid foundation for short- and long-term success. The discrepancy between what currently exists in the district and the general goals agreed to in the readiness phase form this foundation and become the basis for the staff development program.

Phase Three — Planning a Comprehensive Staff Development Program

In this phase, a district will consider various staff development components such as district inservice and continuing education activities. Multiple delivery systems will be described as well as evaluation questions formed early in the planning process.

Phase Four — Implementing the Staff Development Program

Historically, this is where districts have expended most of their efforts, often without the strong foundations of readiness, assessment and planning. Once phases one through three have been carried out, the main concerns for implementation are to follow the district plan to utilize current research on effective staff development practices, and to monitor the program during its progress. Monitoring and adjusting the program during the implementation phase will ensure a healthier program along the way as well as lay the groundwork for the last phase, evaluation.

Phase Five — Evaluating the Staff Development Program

Evaluation deals with staff development outcomes that are measurable and reportable. This phase also takes into consideration the audience for and design of evaluation procedures. And finally, evaluation cycles back to the next planning phase for revision and program improvement. (WASCD, 1988).

Perspectives

Before launching into the phases for building a district staff development program, it is important to reflect a bit on the different perspectives that groups within a district bring to the process. These varying perspectives need to be kept in mind throughout all five phases to ensure that readiness and commitment can truly be incorporated.

We can start with classroom teachers. Typically, teachers are interested in staff development programs that are directly related to their day-to-day responsibilities of delivering instruction to their students. Beyond this, teachers have varying needs dependent upon the stage of development in their careers (Fuller and Bown, 1975). A beginning teacher wants a program that will meet his/her survival needs first, while a veteran teacher may be refining and honing skills at a mastery level, teaching a completely new curriculum at a higher instructional plane. In the readiness, needs assessment, planning and implementation phases, these varying yet valid perspectives of the teaching staff must be taken into account.

The perspectives of building level administrators are often complementary to those held by the teaching staff but have the added breadth of a building-wide view. A principal or assistant principal may be interested not only in the individual skill development in the teaching staff (and may indeed perceive those needs somewhat differently from the teachers themselves), but also may have interests that lie in the arena of school improvement. The school-wide perspective should not be lost in either the needs assessment phase or the planning phase. Utilizing the principal as the instructional leader can have direct benefits for any staff development model.

District level administrators and the board of education bring yet another perspective to the formulation of a staff development plan. System-wide goals, responsiveness to the taxpayers, cost effectiveness, measurable outcomes and accountability are realistic concerns that must be addressed in all phases of development. The school board shoulders the ultimate responsibility for the success or failure of the staff development program to deliver its promised outcomes.

Finally, recent research in staff development has established key characteristics that should be considered by planners as programs are developed. These characteristics include participant involvement, support for the staff development structure, continuity, clarity of expectations, opportunity for participation and feedback, choice of content and format, expertise of trainers and ongoing assessment (NSDC, 1987).

In summary, as a district works its way through the phases of defining a staff development program, varying and sometimes discrepant viewpoints must be considered and actively addressed. From the readiness phase through evaluation, teacher, administrator and school board opinions and needs, as well as research priorities, will have to be addressed specifically and frequently. Without this understanding, neither the necessary commitment to nor clarity of goals for the staff development program will exist, nor will the program garner the support needed for sustenance and success.

Phase One: Creating Awareness/ Readiness for Staff Development

What is Readiness?

Readiness for staff development is that phase which promotes effective engagement in and commitment to professional growth by school boards, administrators, district planners and participants. Because growth and change hinge on the recognition by school personnel of the need to make a strong commitment to the identification of instructional and program needs as well as possible solutions to meet those needs, a critical step in the readiness phase is to generate support for the necessary changes.

During the readiness phase, the focus is on creating new expectations for teachers and administrators, new behaviors and new commitment to changes in carrying out their professional roles (Wood, Thompson, and Russell, 1981). A climate for change needs to be established through the leadership both of the central office and of the building principal. This climate supports collegiality, experimentation, joint decision-making, and trust and confidence in professional judgment. The readiness phase also incorporates the development of a rationale, formation of a foundation of commitment, the establishment of governance, and the construction of written policies, program philosophy and broad goals.

Rationale

Early in the process of establishing a district staff development program, all affected parties — board of education, administration, program planners, program participants — must reach consensus on a rationale for their staff development program. The rationale should answer the question, 'Why should our district provide staff development opportunities for its employees?'

Statements of rationale typically incorporate ideas such as the following:

- School districts are labor-intensive organizations which employ a substantial work force to act on their purposes. The degree to which they accomplish their purposes is largely dependent on the competence of their employees. Employee competence can be positively influenced by improvement opportunities provided through a district staff development program.
- Staff development can help a school district assure local control by providing mechanisms for responding to local improvement needs.
- Staff development can contribute to both the accomplishments of organizational goals and the job satisfaction of individual employees.
- Staff development can be a primary means for creating and maintaining ownership and commitment by district employees to their job roles and responsibilities.
- Those responsible for the growth and development of students should be model learners themselves, continuing to learn as they help students learn. Staff development programs can facilitate this life-long learning by district employees.
- Changing societal conditions continually alter the expectations held for schools. In addition, the methods and technology available for school personnel to use to act on these expectations continually improve. A staff development program can provide the means for school personnel both to adapt to change and to remain current in their fields (WASCD, 1988).

Commitment

Obviously, no district can establish an effective staff development program without gaining commitment to do so from all affected parties — board of education, administration, program planners, program participants. Commitment means agreeing to a level of intensity of involvement that can bring about whatever is to be accomplished.

What commitments are necessary from those involved?

- From the board of education: resources (time and money) for continuing long-term improvement efforts
- From the administration: leadership which empowers program planners and participants to use the available resources toward meaningful improvements
- From the program planners: wise decisions (based on research and experience) regarding what can be reasonably done in their local situation to effect desired improvements
- From the program participants: willingness to invest in individual and collective efforts to improve their professional practices
- From all of the above: a vision of what can make school life better for the students served accompanied by a set of collective and individual plans for ways to realize that vision.

Developing a Governance Structure

An effective staff development program develops a governance structure and process for decision-making to determine staff development needs, the plans to meet them, and finally the methods of implementation. Governance embodies formal authority to develop a mission statement and is based upon collaboration to determine membership and operational guidelines.

This structure should be formed in a way that ensures the inclusion of various perspectives along with a broad base of support. This can best be accomplished through the establishment of a multi-constituent district council. Councils will vary from district to district, but each council should include administrators and teachers, with consideration given to parents, students and community members. Regardless of the actual make-up it should include people who are open-minded, sensitive to the needs of the district and capable of working well together. However, the council should also be characterized by diversity of ideas, people and support. If master contract or policy provisions apply, the governance structure should be developed to meet such requirements.

There are five major principles of shared governance (Koll and Cozad, 1981):

- Representation in decision-making for meeting school or district needs is crucial. All levels need to be involved to develop a feeling of ownership and commitment.
- A collaborative relationship among council members is a common sense approach. Teachers, administrators and boards of education may have objectives others cannot totally support.
- Governance relationships cannot exist in isolation from other district planning.
- The larger the district and the size of the staff development council, the more the planning can be done by subcommittees.
- It is important for council members to check with district personnel in whatever ways possible before decisions are made. If individuals have a 'voice', they participate in programs more positively.

The planning council. The initial task in planning a staff development program is to decide who should be involved in the planning council. Some districts have ongoing inservice committees or other groups that are already in place. The council's expertise should be used to strike a balance between the content being addressed and the process skills being developed.

Three primary criteria should be considered in the council formation: relevance, expertise and jurisdiction (Owens, 1981). Relevance refers to those most affected by the staff development program. Expertise refers to those having expert knowledge in the considered area. Jurisdiction refers to those who have the authority to carry out decisions. Council members must have authority to carry out whatever is planned or the time will be wasted and frustration will result.

Responsibilities will vary depending on the goals for the council, whether mandated by local, state or federal government or based upon district needs and interests. The responsibilities may be very specific or quite general, commonly including assessment and goal-setting, identification of resources available, program design and evaluation, and dissemination of information to others.

Time should be allowed for reading, sharing and reflecting on what constitutes a successful staff development program, along with creative consideration of what the staff development program should be. The focus should be on educating, re-educating and building collegiality in an ongoing process.

Developing a Philosophy Statement and Program Goals

Once commitment and support have been engendered, a rationale clearly stated and the governing board constructed, policy and philosophy statements and broad goals must be developed — the last step in creating readiness.

Policy statement. The school board needs to approve a policy statement concerning the purpose of the staff development program in order to provide the members of the council with a legitimized and official position recognized by all district staff members. Pertinent master contract provisions need to be taken into consideration in the development of the policy statement.

Philosophy statement. The philosophy statement provides a common basis in the school district for communication, program development, and commitent to staff development. The statement describes decisions made about curriculum and concomitant instructional needs for growth and development in the district; it addresses the question of 'Why staff development?'

Goals. Goals should be broad-based statements of intent about staff development efforts in the district and should complement or be directly linked to the district policy statements.

An effective staff development program should provide opportunities for district staff members to acquire knowledge, skills and attitudes related to performance improvement, job orientation, career development, personal health and school climate. A thorough assessment of the needs of the district staff will focus attention on the goals to be stressed for an annual plan.

The following is a possible set of goal statements:

- Performance Improvement: all employees of the district should receive appropriate opportunities to improve their job performances.
- Job Orientation: new employees of the district and those transferred to different positions should receive orientation to the district as an organization, to their specific work locations, to their specific job/position requirements, and to the benefits associated with their employment.
- Career Development: employees of the district should receive appropriate opportunities to develop their careers within the district.
- Personal Health: employees of the district should receive

appropriate assistance in achieving and maintaining a high level of personal health — physical, mental and emotional.

- School Climate: school employees should have an opportunity to contribute to the well-being of the organization. Issues such as collegiality, experimentation, shared decision-making and trust and confidence building may be included.

The five goals described are proposed as boundaries within which an effective staff development program should operate. However, the five goals are not proposed as necessarily having equal importance, nor is it proposed that an equal amount of staff development activity should necessarily occur within each goal at any given time. In fact, 'Performance Improvement' may receive considerably more attention over time than any of the other four goals.

Summary

Creating readiness for staff development involves establishing a commitment of all interested parties to promote changes to meet curricular, instructional and related needs in the district. A supporting rationale statement facilitates gaining a commitment from all involved. The development of a governance structure, policy statement, philosophy statement and program goals completes the readiness phase. More specific staff development programs can then be established based upon a thorough needs assessment.

Phase Two: Conducting a Needs Assessment as a Basis for Planning

In the field of education, the term 'needs assessment' is used many times as a desired or necessary component of a planning process but is usually not clearly defined. Often, educators regard a needs assessment as an opportunity to list their wants or wishes relative to any or all aspects of their work environment. The results of such needs assessments are often of little value; few specific desired changes can be identified and targeted. For the purposes of this chapter, a need is defined as the discrepancy or gap between what is (current practice) and what should be (desired practice). Furthermore, the needs to be considered should be targeted to the specified goals such as performance improvement, career development, job orientation, personal health/wellness, or school climate. Too often, educators fail to assess needs in relation to specified goals within the school district and an unmanageable list of needs results. As an example, a needs assessment related to the goal of performance improvement could focus on specific skills, on knowledges or on attitude changes desired by the participants. Needs also can relate to broader issues within the district such as involvement in decision-making, communication opportunities, use of resources, school atmosphere and related concepts.

Key Components of a Needs Assessment Process

The desired *outcomes* of effective needs assessment will set the framework. Throughout the process the following underlying assumptions should be kept in mind:

- Needs can be assessed through the collection of information from participants.
- Needs and conditions within the district are often changing.
- All people affected by goals of the staff development program should participate in the needs assessment process.
- Staff development objectives and outcomes should be stated in specific, measurable terms to facilitate evaluation processes and future needs assessments.
- Needs can be assessed at various levels: district, building, department, grade or individual.

A variety of assessment sources may be used in this process:

- Staff: teachers and administrators can supply information regarding the desired versus current situations concerning instructional methodology, curriculum implementation, student assessment and adequacy of resources.
- Students: current students as well as graduates can provide input relative to curriculum sufficiency, instructional effectiveness, and attitudes.
- Research and Current Trends: present curriculum programs and instructional practices can be compared to state-of-the-art programs and new concepts to determine needs.
- Program Evaluations: the process of thoroughly evaluating a program can identify curriculum areas as well as instructional deliveries that are in need of improvement. Organizational issues such as communication and articulation often are identified as the result of program evaluation.
- Personnel Evaluations: needs often become apparent through the established process of staff evaluation, Typically, needs are often identified in the areas of performance improvement such as classroom management, instructional delivery or student assessment.

- Assessment/Testing Programs: student achievement testing, whether norm or criterion-referenced, can provide valuable data for program improvement in specific content areas as well as in broad areas such as thinking skills or cognitive instructional strategies.
- Strategic Planning: districts that employ a long-range strategic planning model often will identify staff development needs as a result of the planning or implementation aspects of that process.

The needs identified from the above sources _must_ bear a direct relationship to the goals of the staff development program. Without that focus, needs can become so diverse that the staff development relationship is lost.

Steps in Conducting a Needs Assessment

A sequence of steps exists in preparing for and conducting an effective needs assessment. The major steps are highlighted as follows:

Step One — Planning for the needs assessment. During the planning process, careful attention should be given to the following questions:

- What overall staff development goals will be addressed in the needs assessment?
- What kind of information will be sought concerning these goals?
- What needs sources will be used and how will the data be collected? Will instruments be selected from outside sources or be locally developed?
- What kinds of problems may be encountered in conducting the needs assessment, including acceptance of, and commitment to, the process?
- What is a reasonable time schedule to conduct the assessment?
- How will the data be processed and analyzed? Will sampling be used to keep the amount of data manageable?
- How can the best information be obtained for the lowest cost?

Step Two — Collecting information. Multiple sources should be used in collecting needs assessment data. A variety of procedures is available and often the use of several procedures is more effective than reliance on one since each has unique strengths and weaknesses. The common methods of collecting data include:

- Individual Interview: structured interviews seek out specific input via a questionnaire, but are limited in nature. Unstructured interviews involve one or two key questions and ask for additional information. Semi-structured interviews may be most useful in many needs assessments since they ask for specific input, but allow for additional information. Individuals selected for interviews should be able to provide a complete picture of the areas being addressed.

- Focus Group Interviews: specific groups of a generally homogeneous nature can be interviewed about their opinions of a specific area. This procedure often is used to validate perceptions or hunches that seem to be prevalent or have arisen from other data collection techniques.

- Nominal Group Process: this process is used generally with six to nine individuals to generate needs statements that represent the consensus of the group. The statements are then prioritized by the group after an initial brainstorming process that moves from the individual to the group level. Larger groups may be subdivided and the results from each subgroup consolidated and prioritized by the total group (Delbecq, Van de Ven, and Gustafson, 1975).

- Questionnaires: these devices are generally quick and easy to administer. Quantitative responses are easy to tabulate if a multiple response format is used. The response scale should be four-point in nature and the length of the questionnaire relatively short. (The four-point scale forces a choice and doesn't allow the non-answer of '3' available on a five-point scale.) The questions should be readable. Selective sampling is often highly effective, but the use of questionnaires limits spontaneous participant input.

- Documentary Evidence: many kinds of data are archival in nature; they already exist in the district. Test scores, curriculum guides, schedules, minutes, budget records, policy statements, student enrollment records, etc. are usually available. These kinds of data can support needs statements generated in other ways.

- Other Procedures: observational data, strategic planning processes, and other group processes are also available to generate data for needs assessments.

Through the use of these methods, both descriptive and judgmental data will emerge. Descriptive data are more factual and involves written descriptions of numerical records. Judgmental data evolve from opinions, beliefs, and ratings.

Step Three — Determining program objectives and outcomes. The data collected in step two should reveal the greatest discrepancies between current and desired practices or conditions. Again, the use of multiple assessments and multiple data sources will help ensure the validity of the identified needs. The analysis of the needs assessment data should help the local district to:

- Validate the staff development program goals and enable specific program objectives to be identified.
- Rank program objectives in order of priority, particularly if resources are limited.
- State the program objectives in specific and measurable terms so that subsequent staff development activities can be evaluated in terms of attainment of the program objectives.

Summary

An effectively conducted needs assessment will provide a list of prioritized, measurable program objectives linked to the overall goals of the staff development program. In addition, the needs assessment provides an overview of the current status with respect to the staff development program goals. Since the identified needs are directly related to the ultimate goals of the staff development program, the needs assessment process lays the foundation for the next phase, planning the staff development delivery system.

Phase Three: Planning the Program

Once a district has established a climate that supports staff development, has provided for governance and policies, and has conducted appropriate needs assessments, it is time to plan the program. *A comprehensive program consists of district staff development activities, continuing education activities and professional involvement activities.* District staff development programs consist of those activities formulated by the district planning council intended for various groups in the district or the entire district staff. These activities are scheduled for regular sessions usually built into the school calendar. Continuing education programs can be planned by the district staff development council or can be offered by other institutions or agencies. Continuing education activities normally occur outside the regular school calendar and are voluntary in terms of staff participation; the credits or hours often can be applied to salary schedule advancement and/or recertification. Professional involvement activities represent the choice of the individual staff member to participate in various professional organizations, to participate in college or university activities and to participate in district or building level committees such as those concerning curriculum or evaluation.

Activities from the three broad categories of staff development, of continuing education and of professional involvement are interrelated as they make their impact upon the individual professional. However, the specific focus of this chapter is upon two of the categories — district staff development activities and continuing education activities planned by the staff development planning council.

Identifying Objectives

Based on the results of the needs assessment and the overall district goals, specific objectives for each program will be developed by the planning committee. These objectives will define opportunities for staff to acquire knowledge, skill and attitudes.

Knowledge objectives deal with learning and using specific content. The knowledge objectives in staff development provide opportunities to acquire new information and understandings. For example, current efforts to incorporate cooperative learning into classrooms require specific knowledge objectives. Teachers will need to become aware of the definition of cooperative learning, to understand the differences among cooperative, competitive and individual goal structures and to learn the role of the teacher in preparing cooperative learning activities. Initially, staff development programs will be designed to make sure that basic knowledge objectives are achieved.

Skill objectives pertain to changing teaching behavior. Staff development strategy or skill objectives provide opportunities to develop new teaching behaviors. Knowledge alone is not enough to implement cooperative learning in the classroom, as an example. Teachers would need to learn and be able to use new procedures for planning, managing and evaluating students during instruction using a cooperative learning format.

Attitude objectives identify the commitments, values and other affective variables necessary to implement changes in professional behavior. Staff development attitude objectives provide opportunities to develop new outlooks and feelings. In order for teachers to make the effort to change some of their teaching behaviors to incorporate cooperative learning in their classroom — to use the same example — and to stick with it through the initial learning phases, teachers must feel a commitment to the methodology to retain their motivation. Attitudes are typically changed after initial knowledge and basic behaviors have been successfully developed. Research has shown that commitment flows from competence, rather than preceding it (Miles and Huberman, 1984). Essentially, without extensive training, people do not have sufficient knowledge or experience to 'buy in' (Showers, Joyce, Bennett, 1987).

It is critical that the objective, whether in terms of knowledge, skill or attitude, be specific and measurable. Evaluation of the program objectives will depend directly upon the specificity and measurability of those objectives. If the objectives are vaguely worded or cannot be measured, program evaluation will suffer. It is *imperative* that the objectives be constructed with attention paid to evaluation (see Phase Five) before the staff development activities have been implemented. Evaluation planned 'after the fact' is too often a characteristic of less-than-effective staff development programs.

Translating Objective into Activity Formats

As plans for the staff development program in a district are initiated, the first step, after setting goals and developing specific objectives, is to plan an activity format that matches the objective. Some are far more efficient than others and can be every bit as effective as those formats that may be more elaborate.

Informational formats match knowledge objectives. If the objectives deal with the acquisition of knowledge, a variety of informational formats will be best suited to accomplish the objectives.

- *Basic Information* — There are many times during a school year when staff need to be made aware of federal regulations, state statutes, board policies, etc. The objectives are strictly informational in nature and can be met quickly and efficiently. Often a written newsletter or memo will suffice. But if it appears that the information will generate questions, then the topic might best be presented in a faculty, department or grade level meeting.
- *Exploration of Ideas* — When the objectives deal with theoretical or abstract ideas, an exploratory format might be selected. This format allows for small groups of people to exchange ideas and to 'explore' concepts. Meetings should be informal, in relaxed settings where participants can easily discuss ideas. Time for reading and reflecting can be included, extending the activity over a period of time.
- *Formal Instruction* — Many staff development activities require formal instruction at some point to develop the theoretical and knowledge base of the content identified. A year-long study of the elements of effective teaching might require a series of lecture-discussion and simulation activities provided by an expert in the field. Since knowledge alone will not be sufficient to effect any

change in teaching behaviors, this type of activity often will need to be linked to the next type of format dealing with skill and attitude objectives.

Experiential formats match skill and attitude objectives. If the objectives fall within the realm of changing staff behavior (use of a different teaching strategy), or developing new skills (use of computers), or changing attitudes (willingness to use computers for instruction), the staff development activity format should provide for opportunities to grow in performance or to master new skills.

- *Field Experiences* — Often teachers visit other locations for study. This type of format allows for real-world models or demonstrations by other teachers in other classrooms or schools. Teachers may either observe others in an educational environment demonstrating the skill to be learned or may 'shadow' a noneducator professional in the 'world of work'.

- *Demonstration, Practice and Feedback* — This type of format provides participants with a clear linkage of action to objectives, through active viewing of demonstrations or models, and the opportunity to practice and receive feedback in a safe, supportive environment. Demonstration-feedback formats need to be organized around small group instruction, to provide time for practice and feedback to refine behaviors, and to provide time for evaluation. Because of these components, this format is demanding in terms of commitment of time and personnel.

- *Coaching* — This format allows teachers to practice learnings in the real world of the classroom and to receive specific feedback and support while doing so. Coaching is usually linked to preceding staff development activities that have provided the knowledge base, demonstration, practice and feedback, in a protected environment. Coaching can be conducted by the course instructor, a supervisor or a fellow teacher. The strength of the latter, called peer coaching, comes from the firm bond of collegiality and support that can result. As teachers try new methods of teaching, many are unsure of themselves and feel uncomfortable with only administrative feedback. Peer coaching removes any stigma associated with evaluative feedback. While peer coaching is the most demanding on district resources, research conducted by Joyce and Showers (1983) suggests that it is the most effective format to promote transfer of new practices into consistent and effective classroom use.

- *Embedded Activities* — Embedded staff development allows for professional growth through the daily work of the teacher. Self-observation and analysis, observation and surveys of students, team teaching, participation on child-study teams, and taking on leadership roles within the school and the district provide avenues for ongoing professional growth. The key to embedded activities is the inclusion of systematic observation/feedback, experimentation with curriculum and/or instructional behavior and gaining more understanding of one's self as a professional.

Variables Which Affect Learning Through Staff Development

As programs are being planned, certain variables which can increase the effectiveness of the activity should be considered.

The change process: The Concerns-Based Adoption Model (CBAM) provides a useful reference for understanding the change process (Hall, Wallace and Dossett, 1973). It emphasizes how people develop in their feelings and skills as they are introduced to and implement something new. These naturally-occurring concerns should be considered as plans are made:

- First concerns are self-oriented; 'What is it, and how will it affect me?'
- Later concerns change to wanting to master the new practice and getting organized to use it comfortably.
- Lastly, when the practice has been mastered, concerns are focused on how it affects the students, and what changes can be made so that it will have a greater impact (NSDC, 1987).

Incentives. If participants feel a strong need to meet the objective guiding the staff development program, motivation for participation and achievement of the objective are very likely to be present. However, if the perceived need level is low (i.e., if this is something administrators think is very important but teachers aren't buying into), incentives may be necessary. Since money is not the most effective incentive for staff development programs, the staff development planner needs to be aware of the incentives available to the program implementation process as well as those most valued by the personnel who will be involved. Extrinsic rewards dealing with continuing education units for college credit for recertification can supplement intrinsic rewards of satisfaction, increased productivity/effectiveness, and increased recognition and reinforcement of new behaviors or activities.

Group size: Any staff development planner must be concerned with group size. A common mistake is to group all teachers together for staff development activities, or perhaps separate the teachers according to secondary or elementary teaching responsibilities. Neither method may be appropriate for determining group size and composition. A staff development planner needs to ask several questions:

- What would be an effective group size to meet the objective?
- Do all teachers need to participate? Is there a way to assess specific need before prescribing the learning?
- If the size of the group needs to be smaller than the number of participants who need to participate, how could small groups be formed?

Remember, the size of the group will greatly determine the amount of involvement and the amount of importance the participant will feel in the group.

Room/location: Some staff development activities are formal, yet still effective; others need an informal setting for effectiveness. Some activities require participant communication — at tables or in chairs from which people can move easily to talk to each other. Some activities simply require that people listen. The room and/or location will enhance or detract from a staff development activity and must be chosen after the objectives for the activity are set.

Leadership: Certain objectives might require leadership for the activity to come from outside the district. If this is the case, flexibility in scheduling as well as in feedback and follow-up becomes limited. Planners can develop local leadership through long-range planning by setting objectives more than a year in advance so district personnel can have the time to receive the training necessary to provide local leadership. This is particularly important when a district objective is translated into a professional growth activity format.

Involvement of the staff: The organizational format chosen should reflect the level of involvement needed. Some types of activities promote passive participation. Many objectives require very intense involvement of the participants in order for the objective to be achieved.

Summary

The program planning committee builds upon the staff development philosophy and goals to develop specific and measurable knowledge, skill and attitudinal objectives for staff, based on needs that surfaced in the assessment phase. The formats for staff development activities should match the objective so that experiences provided have the greatest likelihood of helping participants to reach the objective(s). In addition, variables such as group size, incentives, length and breadth of activities, and leadership need to be considered in the planning process. *It is critical that evaluation of the staff development program be planned prior to the implementation of activities.* (Phase Five details the evaluation process.)

Phase Four: Implementing Effective Staff Programs

Conditions of an Effective Delivery System

Staff development is a process of achieving individual and organizational growth through planned change. The implementation phase of the staff development program is a critical part of the process during which the efforts of the planners are carried out. Certain conditions should be established that provide an environment in which staff development efforts can be successfully and effectively delivered:

Administrative involvement: A level of support from the top administration must be evident from the outset of the program. The interest of the district leadership must be genuine and visible. Involvement in the program is necessary to model the behavior expected of participants.

Structured activities: As mentioned in the description of Phase Three effective staff development activities directed at skill improvement should employ the training components of presentation, demonstration, practice, feedback and coaching — as appropriate. The activities should be conducted on a long-term continuing basis as opposed to the 'one-shot' sessions found in many programs. Scheduling activities on this basis allows for intervening practice and feedback to occur, preferably in a coaching setting. In addition, the amount of program content should be kept manageable for each session or activity particularly if practice and feedback are to be built in.

Learning options: Inservice opportunities work best when individuals can freely choose a particular kind of activity from options which accommodate professional needs and learning styles. A series of alternative activities should be offered during the course of a particular professional development effort. Programs that have different educational experiences accommodating different states of development are more likely to accomplish their objectives. Opportunities for teachers to become involved in demonstrations, trials and feedback are more effective than those in which teachers merely absorb ideas.

Well-chosen experts: Programs should make use of district resource people whenever possible. Effective leadership can be developed when personnel within the district utilize their strengths in roles as instructors, consultants or trainers. Leaders of staff development activities should be selected according to their expertise rather than their positions. This expertise relates to the skills and knowledge involved as well as to the ability to deliver the skill or knowledge effectively. Most programs could be greatly enhanced by the recognition and use of local talent. Because of the need for ongoing assistance and staff support, in-house experts may be generally more effective than outside consultants. When outside consultants direct staff development activities every attempt should be made to have them available for follow-up classroom consultation and inservice activities. The critical element is not who conducts the program, but the design and delivery of the program.

Congenial setting and climate: Staff development activities are generally not very successful in an 'after hours' format. Provisions need to be made for released time, regularly scheduled inservice sessions, summer or weekend workshops or combinations thereof. A comfortable, low-key setting, preferably with small group size is desirable. Participants need to recognize that the district values the staff development activities enough to provide sufficient time in a desirable setting, preferably away from the school when in session.

The climate for staff development should be positive in nature. Participants should recognize that experimentation and risk-taking can take place; the emphasis is upon learning new skills or knowledge. Teachers should be prepared to make a commitment to change in terms of new learning and behavior. An atmosphere of collegiality is highly desirable for all participants.

Responsibilities for Implementation

For a staff development program to be successful, it must be seen district-wide as something that is valued, expected and supported. If staff development is district-wide, then school board members, superintendents, assistant superintendents, staff developers, curriculum coordinators and teachers can all assume leadership functions. At the building level, principals, assistant principals, department heads, team leaders and teachers can each play leadership roles. The following responsibilities are outlined for each group:

Board of education: the role of the board of education in staff development is to provide support through board goals, policy and financial
support. Involvement of one or more board members in program activities
is highly recommended.

Superintendents/principals/assistant principals: staff need to know from
superintendents and principals that professional growth is something they
value, expect and support. In one school district, for example, the superintendent visited with several staff members individually and informally
discussed the importance of professional growth. This was followed by
discussions at faculty meetings led by the building principals/assistant
principals and faculty members of the staff development teams. Again,
involvement of key leaders in the actual program is important to the staff.

Assistant superintendents/staff developers/curriculum coordinators: it is
generally the responsibility of these people to coordinate the district
efforts in staff development. They may or may not serve as chairs of
district staff development teams. They provide leadership for implementing the staff development activities. In addition, staff developers are also
involved as trainers or presenters.

Team leaders/department heads: these key leaders in many school districts have already been singled out as having responsibility for curriculum
and professional growth. They often are the key people serving on staff
development committees.

Teachers: because staff development programs are generally focused on
instructional improvements, teachers need to be totally involved in planning, developing, and evaluating each program. They should serve as key
elements on the district/building staff development teams. For any staff
development program to be successful, it needs to be infused with faculty
who are valued and respected by their peers.

Monitoring

The process of monitoring newly acquired skills is a shared responsibility
between the staff and administration. The implementation and the eventual maintenance of those skills should be considered as final steps in the
fulfillment of the staff development program objectives. A number of tasks
and activities are identified below to guide understanding of the process.
It should be noted that monitoring is considered not as evaluation but as
facilitation of the successful practice of the desired outcomes. Testing the
efficacy of the staff development program objectives should be part of the
evaluation plan. Monitoring tasks and activities include:

- Providing support services to those staff practicing desired skills
- Providing recognition/reward for staff efforts
- Visiting classrooms to assist teachers in refining their skills
- Encouraging peer coaching and collegial team modes of monitoring and providing feedback
- Using a systematic process for coaching to monitor new skills
- Involving students to provide feedback where applicable
- Establishing a working philosophy which maintains that desired outcomes are dependent on both teachers and administrators.

Summary

Implementation of the staff development program involves ensuring that the delivery system is effectively carried out. Key characteristics of effective staff development programs need to be built into the delivery system. The responsibilities for implementation should be carried out by the staff development planners, administrators, and participants. A system needs to be established for monitoring the program delivery and the transfer of activities, skills or attitudes into the classroom setting.

Phase Five: Evaluating the Staff Development Program

Rationale

Evaluation of the staff development program addresses the issues of program and process effectiveness. The accountability of staff development programs is necessary so that decision-makers in the district may continue provision of resources (time, personnel and funding). Future program planning is contingent upon assessing the results of current programs. Programs which are effective should be continued while ineffective programs should be terminated or modified.

Staff development participants also need to be informed of the results of programs in which they have participated. It is more likely that staff members will participate and make a commitment to programs for which definite positive outcomes can be documented. It is also desirable that staff members recognize that their input and suggestions for changes are being used to improve program delivery. During the planning phase (Phase Three), program objectives were developed and written in specific and measurable terms to facilitate ultimate evaluation. It is these objectives that form the basis for evaluation.

What is Evaluated?

The evaluation of a staff development program needs to be linked directly to the overall goals and specific objectives of the program. From the outset, program objectives need to be stated in measurable terms which reflect the following possible outcomes:

- Changes in participants in terms of skill or performance levels, knowledge acquisition, or expressed attitudes/beliefs/feelings
- Changes in student learning (cognitive, affective or psychomotor)
- Changes within the organization such as increased collaboration or collegiality or expanded roles of the participants.

These outcomes can be assessed at the district, school, department/grade or individual level.

Processes — or elements thereof — evolved during the planning and implementation of a staff development program also need to be evaluated to improve the planning and delivery of programs. Examples include the kinds of activities used in the program, the opportunities provided for staff input during program planning, the effectiveness of trainers or presenters and the schedule/time structure provided for programs.

Types of Evaluation

In planning for the evaluation of the staff development programs, consideration should be given to the following two types of evaluation:

- *Process evaluation:* in order to improve the program in terms of the next steps or activities, attention should be focused upon monitoring the program delivery and making adjustments where necessary. To do this, periodic assessments of the implementation activities are necessary. Questions to ask are: What has worked well? What activities are effective or ineffective? What have participants' reactions been? Is the program being implemented as planned? If not, what has been changed? Each of these questions should be linked to a corresponding program objective.
- *Outcome evaluation:* eventually, a final decision is needed regarding the continuation of a program. Did the program work? What changes occurred as a result of the program? What specific outcomes (anticipated or unanticipated) have been attained? (NSDC, 1987) Outcome evaluation provides answers to these questions and is of particular significance in a long-term program.

Consideration of Resources

When formulating an evaluation design, attention needs to be paid to resources available to carry out the evaluation. Complex evaluation designs can require sophisticated analysis techniques, evaluation skills and potential costs beyond the resources of the district. The staff development planners need to consider how much can be done realistically in relation to how much needs to be done. The basic maxim is to keep the evaluation simple and directly related to the outcomes of the program. The data collection inherent in the evaluation plan must be viewed in terms of the data analysis required later.

Designing the Evaluation

Once the staff development committee has reviewed program objectives and considered evaluation types, the following key questions need to be addressed:

- What are the program goals, objectives or outcomes that need to be evaluated?
- What measures can be used to assess the attainment of the goals and objectives? What are the critical evaluative questions to be asked and answered?
- How will information be collected for each of the measures/ questions? Is there provision to measure unanticipated outcomes? Who will collect the data? When?
- How will the collected information be analyzed or summarized to answer the evaluation questions?
- How will the evaluation data be reported and to whom?
- Will the assessment-measures and resulting information satisfy the questions of the various audiences for the program, whether participants or observers?

A systematic approach to addressing each of the above will lead to a sound plan for evaluating the staff development program.

Evaluation Models

Careful planning should have been done prior to the implementation of the staff development program so that a comprehensive evaluation component is included. The plan will specify the kinds of measures to be used to assess the attainment of the program goals, objectives and outcomes. A variety of formats may be used in the evaluation process, each with its

Figure 8.1   *(National Staff Development Council, 1987)*

Evaluation Question	Information Sources	Collection Method	Responsibility	Timeline
How do the training and follow-up affect participant's classroom behavior?	Teachers Supervisors Students	Observations using checklist Interviews	Teachers Staff Development Committee Classroom Observers	Oct–Nov (before training) April–May (after training)
Have this year's staff development offerings been relevant to teacher's needs?	Teachers	Written Survey	Staff Development Coordinator	May
What changes are desired for next year?	Teachers	Written Survey	Staff Development Coordinator	May

Permission for reprinting this table has been granted by the National Staff Development Council and the Regional Laboratory for Educational Improvement of the Northeast and Islands.

Figure 8.2   *(Ryan & Crowell, 1982)*

Assessment Level	Example
LEVEL I Teacher Perceptions	The teacher's self-report of what s/he gained from a staff development experience, the effectiveness of the presenter, materials, etc.
LEVEL II Teacher Knowledge	The teacher's acquisition of knowledge required to apply a new skill, etc. The assessment should be more than a measure of the information acquired. It should determine whether a teacher can make decisions that are appropriate for using the new skills, etc.
LEVEL III Teacher Behavior	The teacher's ability to apply a strategy or technique. Measurement at this level necessitates observation of classroom behavior.
LEVEL IV Student Classroom Behavior	The teacher's ability to cause students to change their behavior or to engage in activities in line with the teacher's instructional strategy or technique. Again, classroom observation is the appropriate method of assessment.
LEVEL V Student Outcomes	The student's acquisition of knowledge, skills, or values that a new instructional strategy or technique would be expected to generate or facilitate.

Permission for reprinting this table has been granted by the National Staff Development Council.

strengths and weaknesses. Figure 8.1 gives a model that is brief and easy to use. Another approach to evaluation is to use criteria at different levels of assessment. The key is to link the assessment level to the purpose of the staff development activity and the use(s) of the data as demonstrated in Figure 8.2. Making assessments at the first level is the most frequent practice and also the most often criticized because it cannot objectively demonstrate teacher or student change. However, when linked to personal and/or professional development activities, these data may be found to be useful and meaningful and may lead to important decisions about future staff development programs.

The anticipated outcome of an activity often can be assessed in more than one way. For personal and professional development, the collection of more than one type of data where possible will increase the meaningfulness of the evaluation. Figure 8.3 illustrates detailed evaluation possibilities for staff development programs.

Please note that surveys or questionnaires often can be conducted using machine-scorable forms to facilitate tabulating data. Computer software is available to compute statistics (percentages, averages, etc.) for tabulated data.

Using the Evaluation Data

Analysis and interpretation of the evaluation data involve looking at information in terms of the original evaluation questions. Judgments will need to be made regarding the answers to the evaluation questions. 'Do the data indicate positive staff perceptions? Do they show significant participant skill or attitude changes? Do the data show changes in student learning? Do they support the overall staff development program? Are the data valid?' Tests (e.g., pre/post scores) can be employed to demonstrate statistical significance where appropriate, adding to the validity of the final conclusions.

In preparing to report the evaluation results, the key elements are simplicity and conclusiveness. The prospective audience will determine the kind of report to be delivered and the information to be included. Program participants, staff development planners and decision-makers have different needs for evaluation results, including recommendations for the future based upon conclusions from the current as well as past programs. Such recommendations should be utilized in preparing the next annual staff development plan.

Evaluating the Evaluation Plan

Following the conclusion of the evaluation of the staff development program, the evaluation component itself should be analyzed in terms of effectiveness. Questions such as the following should be asked (from Duke and Corno, 1981):

Figure 8.3 (Little, 1982)

Can Be Evaluated By:	Staff Development That is Designed to				
	Be Satisfying to Participants	Build Knowledge and Skill	Foster Actual Use of New Ideas and Practices	Contribute to Greater Collegiality	Improve/Alter Students' Performance, Behavior, Attitudes
Direct observation (performance-based evidence)	Participants' specific observations of the clarity of objectives, adequacy of instruction, opportunity for practice, usefulness of feedback Observers' records of frequency and nature of selected program design components (e.g., instructor's modeling of intended behavior)	Staff developers supervisor's or peer observation of practice: • peer teaching • microteaching • other (e.g., team-building) Observation of actual implementation Criterion-referenced knowledge or skill tests	Recorded classroom observation Teacher self-reports of nature and frequency of use (seminar 'debriefing,' question-naires, logs) Student reports of specific teacher practices	Direct observation of collaborative work (e.g., observation of team-building exercises; record of actual opportunities such as committee meetings) Participant's logs of actual work sessions	Classroom (or other) observation of specific performance, behaviors Student self-reports of behavior; peer reports, criterion-reference tests of knowledge, skill (pre-post) Norm-referenced tests of knowledge, skill Teacher logs, charts
Asking for perceptions, experiences	Participants; summary judgments of relevance and perceived utility of topic; participants' overall rating of program effectiveness Reviewers' judgments of program prospects for achieving intended effects, based on review of design materials and activities Interviews	Participants' reports of main knowledge or skill gained Participants' anticipated gain on specific objectives or program Others' reports of participants' gains	Teachers' and others' reported attitude toward (approval/disapproval) new practice Reported confidence; commitment to future use; support by peers and others; willingness to advocate to others, train others Interviews	Perceived sanctions for collaborative work Reported willingness to work with others Reported usefulness of working with others Perceived symmetry/equity in members' involvement, influence Interviews	Teachers' perceptions of student performance Students' perceptions, views, attitudes
Official records and other documentary evidence	Records of requests for new or follow-up participation			Collaboratively designed curriculum, lesson plans, other materials, classroom experiment, inservice sessions	Historical records of achievement, disciplinary referrals, etc., across time, groups, teachers, individual students, buildings

Permission to reprint this table has been granted by the National Staff Development Council.

- Was the evaluation *comprehensive* enough? Were there sufficient data, preferably from multiple sources, to answer the questions? Can decisions be made based upon the evaluation?
- Did the evaluation design possess *technical quality*? Were the data presented clearly and understandably? Were the results valid?
- Was the evaluation *useful*? Did the participants, planners and decision-makers make use of the data? Were the conclusions warranted by the data?
- Was the evaluation conducted *appropriately*? Were the participants involved, informed and cooperative? Were expenditures justifiable?

A well-designed evaluation component is absolutely necessary in the original staff development plan. Too often, staff development planners think about evaluation of the program after the program has occurred. Prior planning enables the planners to make sure that the desired data are collected before the time of collection is past. In today's era of accountability, staff development planners need to be concerned with program evaluation from the onset of program planning.

Conclusion

A district level program for staff development should be developed while keeping in mind the perspectives of the practitioners and administrator/ board members, as well as current research. This program can be developed by working through the following phases:

- Creating awareness and readiness for staff development that establish a definite commitment at all levels, creating a shared decision-making governance structure, a well-defined philosophy statement and a set of program goals
- Conducting a needs assessment within the district that is linked to the goals of the overall program, that prioritizes the important needs
- Planning the staff development program to include key components of effective staff development programs
- Implementing the staff development program while building in critical elements of effective staff development delivery systems
- Evaluating the staff development program throughout the process in terms of specific program objectives linked to the overall goals, and reporting the results to various district groups.

The resulting program will be unique in that it is customized to meet the existing conditions in the local district. By working through the phases outlined above, the essential components and key characteristics of effective staff development practices will be incorporated within the program. With careful planning, implementing and evaluation, a long-term staff development program can provide for meaningful and positive change which will eventually transfer into an improved learning environment for students in the district. In addition, participants in the staff development program will develop a stronger sense of collegiality and purpose through the professional interactions and expectations built into the program.

References

DELBECQ, A., VAN DE VEN, D. and GUSTAFSON, D. (1975) *Group Techniques for Program Planning: A Guide to Nominal Group and Delphi Process*, Glenview, IL, Scott Foresman and Co.

DUKE, D.L. and CORNO, L. (1981) 'Evaluating Staff Development', in DILLON-PETERSON, B. (Ed.) *Staff Development*, Association for Supervision and Curriculum Development (ASCD Yearbook).

FULLER, F. and BOWN, O. (1975) 'Becoming a Teacher', Chapter 11 in *Teacher Education: The Seventy-fourth Yearbook of the National Society for the Study of Education*, Chicago, IL, University of Chicago Press.

HALL, G., WALLACE, R. and DOSSETT, W. (1973) *A Developmental Conceptualization of the Adoption Process Within Educational Institutions*, Austin, Texas, Research and Development Center for Teacher Education, The University of Texas.

JOYCE, B.R. and SHOWERS, B. (1983) *Power in Staff Development Through Research on Training*, Association for Supervision and Curriculum Development.

KOLL, P.J. and COZAD, L. (1982) *Staff Development: A Process Approach*, University of Wisconsin System.

LITTLE, J.W. (1982) 'Making Sure: Contributions and Requirements of Good Evaluation', *Journal of Staff Development*, April, 3, 1, pp. 25–47.

MILES, M. and HUBERMAN, M. (1984) *Innovation in Education*, Englewood Cliffs, NJ, Prentice-Hall.

NATIONAL STAFF DEVELOPMENT COUNCIL (1987) *Continuing to Learn — A Guidebook for Teacher Development*, The Regional Laboratory for Educational Improvement of the Northeast and Islands and the National Staff Development Council.

OWENS, R.G. (1981) *Organizational Behavior in Education*, Englewood Cliffs, NJ, Prentice-Hall.

RYAN, T.F. and CROWELL, R.A. (1982) 'Evaluation for Non-Evaluators: Assessing Staff Development Outcomes', *Journal of Staff Development*, April, 3, 1, pp. 156–169.

SHOWERS, B., JOYCE, B. and BENNETT, B. (1987) 'Syntheses of Research on Staff Development: A Framework for Future Study and a State-of-the-Art Analysis', *Educational Leadership*, November, 45, 3.

WISCONSIN ASSOCIATION FOR SUPERVISION AND CURRICULUM DEVELOPMENT (WASCD) (1988) *Planning for Effective Staff Development Programs.*
WOOD, F.H., THOMPSON, S.R. and RUSSELL, SR. F. (1981) 'Designing Effective Staff Development Programs', in DILLON-PETERSON, B. (Ed.) *Staff Development/Organization Development*, Alexandria, VA, Association for Supervision and Curriculum Development (ASCD Yearbook).

9 A Regional Staff Development Center Model

Esther Letven and Judith Klobuchar

Introduction

History

The Regional Staff Development Center serves the professional development needs of educators in twenty-six school districts and three postsecondary institutions in a two-county region of southeastern Wisconsin. Within the two-county service area are both urban and rural populations. School districts vary in size from eleven (11) professional staff to 1700. The Center, which not only is a place but also embodies a philosophy, grew out of the commitment of this educational community to high-quality education.

In the summer of 1983 all members of the local education community were rocked by the national wave of criticism of American education. By invitation of the chancellor of the University of Wisconsin-Parkside, a group of educational leaders from large and small school districts, unions, boards of education and post-secondary institutions met to discuss their reactions to the reports and the resulting negative publicity.

The eventual formation of the Southeastern Wisconsin Educators' Consortium — composed of administrative, board and teacher association leaders — was a major step in uniting educators in the area. This diverse group eventually decided to examine the one issue they all agreed on: the need for more, and more effective, professional staff development. The Consortium's first major project was the creation of the Regional Staff Development Center in 1985.

Purpose

In defining staff development, the Regional Staff Development Center works on the premise that training is not enough. Educators need collegial support and recognition if they are to remain challenged and enthusiastic about the important work they do. Recognizing that training, support and recognition must occur at the district and building levels, the Center seeks to supplement, not supplant, local efforts. Its role in helping meet district and building level needs is determined by the district's size and access to resources, both fiscal and personnel.

While serving as a clearing house for regional resources, the Center also acts as a consortial agent for districts seeking grants, making it possible for them to secure resources and to implement special projects they would have difficulty undertaking on their own. Using this strategy, the Center now administers a variety of grants from federal agencies, the state of Wisconsin, and private foundations.

The Center's consortial structure permits a far more comprehensive staff development program than any district could provide individually, particularly those in small rural areas. Bringing together educators from multiple districts and from a variety of grade levels breaks down the physical and political isolation characteristic of many school districts.

As the demands of teaching become more complex, it is imperative that the doors of isolation be opened. Through the Regional Staff Development Center, educators in the southeastern corner of Wisconsin are finding ways to work together as colleagues. By working together on issues of common concern, individuals are experiencing a renewed professional enthusiasm.

The Mission and the Method

The heart of the Center's mission is promoting professional growth for educators throughout their careers. Programs and services incorporate principles of adult learning and thrive on the energy released when educators connect with and learn from one another. College and university faculty offer research and content expertise while public school teachers provide a wealth of practical knowledge. The Center's activities reflect the belief that collegial interaction facilitates professional growth and that true staff development is far more than courses and speakers.

The specific mission of the Center is three-fold: the Regional Staff Development Center promotes *support, recognition,* and *training* for the educational community of Kenosha and Racine Counties. A number of programs and services have been developed to achieve these goals of support, recognition and training. Examples of Center programs which illustrate each goal are provided below. Keep in mind, however, that while each example supports primarily one goal, the other two, to a lesser extent, are also being addressed.

Support

By working together on issues of common concern, individuals are finding support for their professional needs and expertise. Collaborative efforts which cross geographic and grade-level barriers continue to expand through the Center's alliances, networks and study committees. Pilot programs emerging from these support groups capitalize on the entrepreneurial skills and research interests of the educators involved.

Academic Alliances: The Academic Alliances developed by the Center are modeled on the national project begun by Claire Gaudiani, Director of the Academic Alliance Project and they function as educator support groups. An alliance is a group of school and university/college faculty who meet together regularly as a 'community of scholars' to share experiences, knowledge and interest in their common disciplines. The collegiality which results transcends the levels at which they teach. School and college faculty meet as colleagues to identify their needs and concerns and to design ways to improve the quality of their intellectual and professional lives.

New alliances form with each year of the Center's existence. Currently, groups are established in the subject areas of chemistry/physics, English composition, elementary science, family and consumer education, foreign language, general science, international education, mathematics, physical education, teaching Shakespeare and technology education.

Through these alliances, members help each other maintain the spirit of inquiry crucial to the healthy intellectual life of all faculty members, regardless of the levels at which they teach. At a recent Physics/Chemistry Alliance meeting a college professor showed the participants how he demonstrates the mirage phenomenon in his classroom. During the follow-up discussion, an elementary teacher described the approach he uses with young children; the professor enthusiastically responded by deciding to use this simpler strategy with his college students. Collegial respect is an important by-product of such an exchange of ideas, as is the sense of renewal. Commenting on her participation, one teacher remarked, 'The science alliance has given me new skills and fresh enthusiasm for my entire job — not just in teaching science. It's been a cool glass of water on a hot, dusty road. Really hits the spot!'

Networks: Similar in design to alliances, but different in focus, networks operate as professional idea exchanges among educators with mutual interests or common challenges. Some networks are position-specific involving personnel such as counselors, exceptional-education teachers, library/media specialists, social workers, and speech and language therapists. Others are grade level-specific involving teachers of early childhood/kindergarten, first grade, second grade, or third grade, while still others attract those who share a common interest in such areas as cooperative learning, the gifted and talented, the middle level child, middle/secondary reading, multicultural education, and women in administration.

Networks generally share a similar initial experience. A steering committee, convened by the Center, plans a 'kick-off' event which reaches out to all educators in a specific discipline or interest area. For example, the Cooperative Learning Network began with a dinner meeting open to all interested educators. The speaker, a local middle-school principal, led a discussion that appealed to the full range of teaching levels represented, elementary through postsecondary. From the discussion at this initial gathering, the planning committee set the direction and developed themes for successive meetings. Each meeting had a special focus. At one, practitioners of cooperative learning shared techniques they had found particularly successful; at another, a newsletter was prepared for regional distribution. Subsequent meetings were devoted to making non-practitioners aware of the various techniques and models of cooperative learning.

Because networks are organized by their own members, no two are alike; however, some common features exist. All have program coordinators and planing committees, all assess their members' needs, set goals for themselves, and draw members from across different levels throughout the geographic area.

Study committees: Classroom teachers rarely have the opportunity to analyze and then act on the conditions affecting their professional lives. Study committees are one vehicle the Center uses to help teachers escape the intellectual stagnation and isolation that often plague their daily workplaces. Each study committee, working toward a tangible product, helps build teacher self-esteem. As an elementary teacher said after an all-day meeting of a study committee, 'I came away with a feeling of pride. I was treated as an intelligent adult. It was wonderful to spend a day sharing ideas with "adults". I went home refreshed and eager to go to school the next day'. This teacher helped design a beginning teacher assistance program which now serves all twenty-six school districts in the Center's membership area.

Project Assist, a beginning teacher/mentor program, emerged from a six-month study by an interdistrict committee of teachers, school board members and administrators. From this Beginning Teacher Study Committee, a comprehensive program emerged with support seminars for new teachers, mentor training for experienced teachers, and an orientation checklist for administrative use with teachers new to buildings. These tangible outcomes were important to committee members, but the collegial relationships that developed during the study committee's deliberations exceeded everyone's expectations. Working together on a common concern blurred the lines of authority among administrators, teachers and board members. Teachers found it stimulating, board members learned more about the needs of teachers, and administrators were reminded of the everyday demands on classroom teachers.

A second study committee emerged when a humanities professor came to the Center concerned about her students' lack of knowledge of different cultures, even within their own communities. Her college students were unable to understand, much less discuss, the issues of cross-cultural communication. Center staff responded by inviting educators with teaching experience in multicultural settings to meet and react to these concerns. Subsequent meetings of this group resulted in a human relations handbook and an external grant which initiated, and now maintains, the three-year-old *Multicultural Education Program.*

Study committees are created as needs emerge. Strong concerns and frustration often provide the commitment and energy for a group to explore and examine an issue in depth. As long as challenges are present in the work lives of educators, new approaches to problem-solving, such as study committees, will play an important role in their professional development.

Recognition

An often neglected, but vital component of any staff development program is recognition of creativity and excellence. A school culture survey conducted by representatives of area schools indicated that recognition efforts received little attention in most districts. Through the Center, several programs have been initiated to encourage the recognition of good work.

Educators' Hall of Fame: Each year five exemplary educators from the area are honored and recognized for their contributions to the educational community by being inducted into the *Southeastern Wisconsin Educators' Hall of Fame.* Nominees must have had a significant impact on education in southeastern Wisconsin. The involvement of teachers and administrators in the nomination of colleagues and the support of local newspapers in conducting the annual ceremony contribute to the meaningful recognition of educational excellence. Recipients of the honor have included teachers from kindergarten to college level and administrators from the building level to the superintendency. Position is unimportant; quality and impact are the determining factors.

A formal dinner and recognition ceremony are held to celebrate their induction. At the same time recent education graduates from the two local teacher education programs are recognized for their choice of career and welcomed into the profession by the Wisconsin State Superintendent of Public Instruction.

Educators' Showcase: Public education and awareness are the goals of the *Educators' Showcase*, held each year at an area shopping mall. Individual schools, as well as the Center's networks and alliances, exhibit state-of-the-art educational techniques, materials and student work during the two-day event. Performances and demonstrations on the mall stage show the general public the best of what schools are offering in the sciences and arts.

Mini-grants: Each year, competitive grants ranging from $50 to $250 are awarded to area teachers to pursue innovative and exploratory projects of direct benefit to students. Grants for the 1989–90 school year ranged from an interdisciplinary/intergrade project where eighth-grade students designed and sewed costumes for a fifth-grade physical education square dancing unit, to one in which qualified laboratory personnel assisted a rural fifth-grade science teacher by providing cholesterol screening during a science unit on the circulatory system.

Training

The Regional Staff Development Center provides workshops and seminars which emerge from the needs and interests of local educators. The types of training experiences range from single-session information-passing to weekend conferences to multi-session all-day programs spaced throughout the academic year.

Developing drug-free schools: Twenty-two school districts in the two-county rural areas form the *Southeastern Wisconsin AODA Consortium* through the Regional Staff Development Center. The purpose of this consortium is to develop and expand effective drug-free school programs which increase drug and alcohol awareness in school personnel, students and parents. By training and empowering school-based advocates and community members, more sharing of effective programs and materials is occurring among districts, and new school/community partnerships are emerging.

Science Fellows: Initiated with state funds, and continued with federal support, the Partnership of Industry and Education's *Science Fellows Program* was implemented by the University of Wisconsin-Parkside and the Regional Staff Development Center to improve elementary science education in Kenosha and Racine counties. Forty-two 'science-anxious' teachers, selected annually from public and private elementary schools in the area, attend a series of eight mini-courses in physical science using hands-on teaching strategies. Upon completion of the program, these fellows become resource teachers within their school buildings. The goal of the program is to have a core of teachers in each elementary school trained in process science instruction. This cadre of teachers also support one another with information and ideas through the Elementary Science Alliance.

From its inception, the program has continued to expand. Three former science fellows have become full-time elementary science specialists, bringing updated knowledge and techniques into classrooms through demonstrations. The partnership with business and industry has resulted in a roving science mobile, linkages between classroom teachers and working scientists, and class field-trips to area laboratories, trade shows and expositions.

Regional Inservice Day: A major event of each year is that Friday in February, when 4,500 educators in the two-county area convene to attend a series of speeches, workshops and seminars coordinated by the Regional Staff Development Center. Regional Inservice exemplifies the collegial nature of the Center and synthesizes the three goals of the mission statement: support, training and recognition. Under the guidance of a Regional Core Planning Committee, a number of groups representing member districts, alliances, networks, and special interest groups develop the program and monitor its success. Teachers not only plan the program (support), but also serve as presenters (recognition). Regional Inservice Day provides teachers with convenient access to a major conference complete with a wide variety of workshop choices and recognized speakers (inservice training).

Specialized Roles Lead to Learning

Beyond the collegial learning inherent in support groups and study committees, special interactive leadership roles assumed by educators through the Regional Staff Development Center are rich in professional growth experiences.

Staffing the Center

The innovative staffing structure of the Regional Staff Development Center encourages teacher participation and leadership. Teachers fulfilling several different roles augment the permanent administrative team comprised of the director, assistant director and clerical staff. While center associates, program coordinators and contact teachers do much of the Center's work, functioning as leaders, they are at the same time expected to learn.

Center associates: Experienced classroom teachers on leave from their districts, spend a year working full-time at the Center. Selected through administrative recommendation, application and an interview process, they represent a cross-section of the Center's membership. This work experience involves far more than merely staffing an existing organization and monitoring on-going programs. Working together to facilitate staff development for all teachers in the two counties, center associates gain an understanding of the 'big picture' in education by discovering the joys and challenges of teachers, administrators and board members.

Doing the work of the Center is only part of the associate experience. Learning and growing as an educator are important products of this year at the Center. To help focus the experiences, each associate develops a professional development plan, with funds and support available to facilitate the successful accomplishment of his/her goals. Each plan identifies areas of desired growth and specific strategies for achieving that growth. Activities might include participating in national and/or regional conferences, taking credit courses, team teaching with a college faculty member, supervising student teachers, conducting research, and/or becoming members in professional organizations. In doing the Center's work, associates also build a number of skills such as facilitating support groups, leading group discussions, making presentations, writing grants and producing a monthly newsletter.

Program coordinator: As the Center's membership and numbers of programs grew, its organizational structure creatively expanded. Every support group (alliance, network, or study committee) has at least one program coordinator who organizes and facilitates the activities of the group, with the help of the center associates. These coordinators are full-time classroom teachers who receive a modest stipend for their after-school efforts. Occasionally they meet as a group to discuss their particular programs and encourage each other. Adult learning styles and leadership skills are examples of the topics discussed.

Contact teachers: Contact teachers are the communication link between schools and the Center. Each of the more than 100 school buildings served by the Center has one or two contact teachers. These teachers are responsible for all communications to and from the Center, including distribution of the monthly newsletter. They also serve as in-house advocates of Center activities, sharing their knowledge of programs and encouraging participation.

Additional Leadership Roles

Through the Center's pilot induction program, experienced teachers serve as *mentors* for beginning teachers. Mentors introduce new teachers to the building and the faculty, help them learn the curriculum, provide appropriate feedback on instructional skills, and impart 'tricks of the trade'. Mentors benefit from these relationships as well, learning new approaches, even reevaluating their own practices.

Teachers serve as *staff development advocates* on the County Staff Development Council which was formed to provide the region's non-urban school districts with the equivalent of the inservice committees of larger districts. Each school building from the twenty-four non-urban districts has a teacher representative on this committee who attends monthly meetings designed to accomplish three goals: 1) collect and dispense information, 2) develop leadership opportunities, and 3) discuss current educational trends.

Teams of *grant writers* often emerge from study committees. The resulting collegial writing experiences give classroom teachers the opportunity to put their own practitioner experiences to meaningful use. By contributing their expertise in the development of proposals, teachers remind college/university faculty of the realities of the classroom. Working with higher education faculty or other K-12 educators, these teachers learn how to develop need statements and how to formulate plans to address those needs. Since the writing and rewriting process demands hard work, a true sense of accomplishment accompanies the completion of a grant proposal.

Assessment of Needs

The range of programs offered through the Regional Staff Development Center requires a variety of assessment procedures. Some have involved the membership-at-large while others target specific programs.

An early regional assessment included a sixteen-part survey completed by educators during the Center's first year (1985–6). Its purpose was to determine general professional development needs and interests while at the same time making the teachers aware of the Center's existence. This survey helped shape the general program direction of the Center and clarified the need for the three approaches to staff development (support, recognition and training). In 1986–7, teachers participated in a Career Stages Assessment Inventory which linked interests with such criteria as years in education and career attitudes. Through this inventory, professional development avenues and incentives for participation were identified for teachers at different career stages. These data helped shape the scope and delivery of the Center's services and programs.

The Regional Staff Development Center, as an organization, was carefully analyzed in its 1987 Strategic Plan using three assessments: an environmental (community) scan, an internal (staff) assessment and a market (client) assessment. The resulting seven strategic goals and their action objectives continue to guide Center activities.

Special surveys which are position, grade-level, or discipline-specific are also used. Examples include the Program Coordinator Year-end Survey, the Elementary Science Needs Survey, and Regional Inservice Surveys. Alliance and network program coordinators also conduct need assessments as part of their group planning processes to establish yearly themes and special workshops.

Special programs such as Project Assist, Elementary Science Fellows, and the Multicultural Education Fellows Program undergo formal evaluation. Strategic goals, developed by a broad-based committee of administrators and teachers, serve as the foundation for program evaluation. Formal evaluation of special programs is done through pro- and post-inventories with research assistance from the university faculty.

Finally, informal assessment is ongoing. Due to its flexible nature, the Center is in a unique position to respond quickly to the expressed needs of administrators and teachers. Through the *Center Exchange*, the monthly newsletter, or during various presentations, individuals are encouraged to contact the Center directly with ideas for new projects or suggestions for initiating professional support groups.

Organizational Structure

Policy Making

The Center's management system is influenced by the same collegial culture that permeates the entire operation. The Southeastern Wisconsin Educators' Consortium, which founded the Center, now serves as its governing body. Members of the Consortium include the director of the Center, the CEO, a board member and a faculty member from each large institution/district, representatives from the clusters of rural districts, and representatives from the three local teachers' associations. These superintendents, college presidents, teacher union officials, and school board members meet monthly as a consortium to make policy decisions about the use of resources, access to programs, and relationships to outside community agencies. Urban and rural, large and small, K-12 and post-secondary — all meet as equals and make decisions by consensus.

While policy decisions are made by the Educators' Consortium, the Program Advisory Board is responsible for needs assessment, program development and evaluation. This advisory board includes members of all the constituent groups (teachers, administrators, union officials, board members and post-secondary representatives). Program Advisory Board meetings often include lively discussions about how best to deliver staff development. Many issues are explored such as how to use the professional day for training, how to involve career stagnant teachers, and how to develop collegial relationships between college faculty and K-12 teachers.

Program Implementation

Implementation of programs is the responsibility of the director. Assignments are given by the director to staff members and are monitored by the assistant director. Associates are expected to keep the assistant director informed of their projects; weekly staff meetings are dedicated to information sharing and problem-solving. Decisions are made by consensus. When differences surface, they are resolved by staff discussion; if necessary, final resolution is the responsibility of the director. In this collegial model, differences are often the healthy result of intense program ownership on the part of planners and participants. Respecting divergent perspectives and opinions is an important element of the Center's culture.

Resources

Resources needed to operate the Center are generated in three ways: 1) each district/institution contributes a fee based on its number of staff members, 2) grants from public and private sources fund special programs and often include monies for Center support services, and 3) the University of Wisconsin-Parkside furnishes support for the director's and lead secretary's positions and also provides the physical facility and its maintenance.

On an annual basis the director develops the budget and monitors the spending. The Consortium, upon approving the budget, contracts with UW-Parkside to serve as the Center's fiscal agent. Fiscal resources are spent in direct relation to program priorities. It is a priority-driven system based upon a clear vision of program direction.

Collegiality, then Ownership

The philosophy and structure of the Regional Staff Development Center capitalize on local expertise and energy. This structure of cooperation affords 4,500 Wisconsin educators the opportunity to learn from each other through alliances, networks, study committees and specialized roles. Recognizing and showcasing the positive contributions of area educators enhances self-esteem and creates a climate for continuing professional growth.

The Center offers professional development within a culture that recognizes human development as a function of engagement with others in a professional culture that offers choice, authority and responsibility. It is the Center's belief that staff development is more than courses and speakers. Through the Center, educators are learning by choosing *new roles* (center associates, program coordinators, mentors), *new relationships* (alliances and networks), *new instructional strategies* (science fellows, multicultural education), and *new learning opportunities* (study committees, video conferences).

The Regional Staff Development Center attributes its success to the spirit of collegiality and feelings of ownership experienced by its members. Decision-making resides with those closest to the programs since the Center's philosophy is to invite educators to their 'own' programs, not to those of the 'Center'. Together, regardless of level or position, both the challenges and joys of being an educator are celebrated through the Regional Staff Development Center.

Reference

GAUDIANI, C. *Academic Alliances*, Philadelphia: University of Pennsylvania.

10   A Statewide Staff Development Model

Anne Conzemius

Introduction

It has become a fundamental responsibility of the state to provide and oversee public education. Implicit within that very basic role is the responsibility to ensure that all children in the state's elementary and secondary schools are provided equal access to educational opportunities regardless of where they reside. It follows then that the state must assume some level of stewardship for ensuring that the individuals who provide those opportunities have some uniformity of qualification. Additionally, individual local units of education should have equal access to those equally qualified teachers.

This theory, if followed to its reasoned end, might readily lead one to conclude that both preservice and inservice training for teachers must be a responsibility of the state. Yet, as logical as this may seem, there is not a clear consensus about what the nature and extent of a state's involvement in teacher training and renewal should be. Nor is there a clear consensus about the desired nature and extent of the state's involvement in continuing inservice opportunities for teachers. Instead there exists a continuum of beliefs about the role and function of state government relative to staff development.

If one is to build a case for the role of a state educational agency in staff development, then a variety of influences must be considered. Such influences include the political, philosophical, economic, psycho-social and logistical conditions which contribute to the larger picture. This chapter will provide a framework for the development of a state model for inservice training. Each of the influences mentioned above will be examined and then reconsidered as the framework is developed into a model for educational improvement on a statewide level.

The State Educational Agency (SEA) is a government unit which exists within a larger political realm. Its function and responsibilities are constitutionally defined. At a minimum, SEAs are charged with the responsibility to provide and supervise public education and to license its practitioners. In providing education, the state ensures that financial and human resources will be available. In fulfilling its stewardship to provide those resources, each state takes on some degree of responsibility to recruit, train and retain competent professionals to staff its public schools.

The task of licensing is relatively straightforward. Criteria for preparation and renewal are established and then licenses are issued to individuals who meet those criteria. Such a statement is not meant to minimize the complexities involved in establishing the criteria and procedures for licensing, but to provide a contrast to the relatively ambiguous nature of the state's duty to supervise public education — which can mean anything from simply overseeing to inspecting and directing. Decisions about where a state agency will operate along the supervisory continuum are guided by its history and by the philosophical viewpoints of its political leaders.

Whether written or unwritten, SEA leaders have a philosophy about the state's relationship to local education agencies (LEAs), teacher preparation institutions, and the educational community in general. This underlying philosophy guides state policy-making and in so doing establishes the boundaries of its authority and its activities. For example in states with a philosophy of strong local control there are no state-adopted textbooks or curricula. State mandates do not define schools' organizational structures; local boards of education have tremendous flexibility in decision-making relative to school organization, policies and procedures. As long as certain minimum standards are met, LEAs in states such as these have the right and responsibility to decide what each will do to educate the youth of their communities. On the other hand, states which exercise maximum authority over local units of education come to very different conclusions about state involvement in the governance of schools.

Once a state agency defines the conditions of its involvement in local affairs, the manner in which it goes about fulfilling its constitutional obligations begins to unfold. A balance must be found between what the state is obligated to provide and how far it is willing to go to oversee or direct its implementation. It is a question of balances between political authority and philosophy, between duty and stewardship.

The issue of a state's involvement in staff development offers a perfect forum for this type of discussion. In particular, in states with local control it is difficult to define the point at which the state agency's responsibility to provide competent professionals overlaps with the local district's right and responsibility to support professional growth. The question of supervision also arises relative to this issue. Since the improvement of teaching contributes to the overall effectiveness of schools, the SEA would certainly have a legitimate right to be concerned about teacher training and renewal. The state is the level at which both initial and continuing licenses are issued, so it stands to reason that the state agency would have added cause to extend its jurisdiction from preservice to inservice education. Finally, the state does have a contribution to make in the overall economy of effort. As the institution responsible for overseeing public education, the SEA has a perspective that can be helpful to the individual districts and/or intermediate units. By identifying common needs and trends, the state can assist in facilitating linkages among and between districts to match available resources with a given set of needs. The state is able to provide consultation, build networks of skilled trainers and operate as a motivating force for the recruitment and retention of highly qualified teachers and administrators.

Having established at least some justification for state involvement in staff development, it is important to examine the economic influences that play a part in determining the nature and extent of that involvement. Obviously it is neither efficient nor wise for a state to assume the full expense of providing continuing professional development for all of its educators. Sheer numbers, the geographical distances between districts and the diversity of professional needs make state-controlled staff development prohibitive. From the identification of state trends and needs to the implementation and evaluation of programs and services, the costs of staff development can become astronomical. One must continually assess the potential contribution and expense of each program element in relation to attainment of the final goals, e.g., large numbers of participants cause any single expenditure to become a major budget item. Thus, unless a particular cost can be considered vital to the process or the quality of the eventual product, it probably will not be included.

There are other factors which militate against coordinating all staff development at a state level. The relevance and ownership of any learning experience is heightened with local focus and support. When training is localized, there is a much higher probability that the focus of that training will better meet the needs of the student population it was meant to affect. Additionally, efforts to institute subsequent changes in behavior, procedures, curricula and the like are much more apt to occur when training has been locally developed, implemented, and fiscally supported. Thus, local time and dollars spent on training have a greater chance of producing the desired outcomes at an earlier stage.

The nature of the logistical problems facing a state agency will depend upon the kind of intervention or assistance it wishes to offer. Certain constraints, other than those already mentioned, have a profound effect upon how a state ultimately delivers its services. For example, the differences of the conditions of one district's employment contract compared to those of another can be vast. Such issues as released time, board-approved salary credits, professional development time, and district level support for tuition, travel, substitute teachers, etc. all play their part in making the process yet more complex.

Another kind of constraint has to do with timing. Though the summer months seem to be the logical time to offer direct services to teachers, it is not that simple. Many teachers use the summer months for personal renewal. Others, for financial reasons, are forced to become employed during those months. Many teachers find it more profitable to spend their summers earning new graduate degrees or credits which will ultimately move them ahead on their district's salary scale. The influences of family and vacations present further challenges to program planners.

Last, but not least, state agencies can rarely function with great speed. The size of the agency would certainly make a difference to the ultimate efficiency with which it is able to operate. In very large bureaucracies it is conceivable that, to ensure quality programming with adequate public exposure, planning would have to be well underway before a budget was ever approved. This is particularly problematic for states which do not operate under biennial budgets, but must have annual approval for reallocation of funds for ongoing programs.

The Model

Background

This model represents one way a state agency can provide leadership and service to staff development programs on a statewide basis, while at the same time recognizing the importance of local contributions. It was designed to address needs related to the recruitment, retraining and retention of qualified science teachers in Wisconsin. The model incorporates the following considerations:

- Wisconsin has a long history of local control of school governance;
- Teacher availability in Wisconsin will soon become a significant problem, particularly in chemistry, physics and mathematics;
- Recruitment, retraining and retention efforts are integrally related to teacher motivation, recognition, prestige and opportunity for financial and professional advancement;
- Retraining efforts should be multi-dimensional, i.e., development opportunities must include new learning in the areas of pedagogy, content and curriculum development;
- Improving science education in Wisconsin requires a K-12 focus.

These five considerations provided the backdrop for the creation of a model which addresses both the priorities of the state as well as the needs of individual teachers and districts. Under the consultation and direction of an advisory panel of business representatives, political leaders and educators (elementary, secondary, university, vocational/technical, state agency consultants, school board members, etc.) the plan's framework was developed. The panel developed four broad goals: (1) to encourage the state's top science educators to remain in the profession; (2) to provide an effective and efficient means for teachers to learn from and motivate one another; (3) to improve teachers through increased knowledge, skills and confidence in developing and delivering a science curriculum which would enhance students' abilities to think critically and to solve problems; (4) to increase the public's awareness of the need for greater scientific and technological literacy among the population in general.

Acknowledging that an individual teacher's needs will vary depending upon the grade level he or she teaches, the advisory panel recommended that the substance of the program be developed by groups of teachers representing the different grade levels. Each group was to have the flexibility to build in objectives and activities unique to the needs of their participants. The final product was to be the result of the cumulative effort of practicing science teachers (elementary, middle and high school) working cooperatively with state agency consultants and representatives from the state's institutions of higher education.

The Planning Process

The first step of the planning process was to decide what kind of format would (a) accomplish the goals identified by the advisory council; and (b) reach the greatest number of teachers most efficiently. Ultimately, a 'trainer-of-trainers' format was chosen. A small group of 'master' science teachers would be selected to design and present a program to the best science teachers in the state. These teachers would then be designated and trained as inservice leaders and curriculum consultants. Eventually, this group would present inservice programs, provide consultation and coaching to other teachers in their districts or regional areas and would assist district curiculum specialists in curriculum planning and in the implementation of direct community-based science education projects.

By adopting this format, the state could identify its key teacher resources at all levels, provide an opportunity for them to expand upon their professional competencies, and through them, reach a greater number of teachers and communities across a wide geographic area. Additionally, the teachers who comprised this group would be recognized for their leadership, thus earning further professional and financial rewards as a result of their new roles within their districts. It was anticipated that recognition would serve as a motivating factor to keep these top-notch professionals from fleeing the educational arena. By recognizing the accomplishments of outstanding teachers and providing a vehicle by which those teachers could share their common as well as their unique talents, teaching as a profession would be highlighted. Financial and professional growth rewards enhance the prestige of educators both in the eyes of their colleagues and in the eyes of the public.

To summarize, in and of itself the program format has the potential to make an important contribution toward meeting the identified needs of retention and retraining. Further, the problem of teacher availability and recruitment is addressed indirectly as more and more people are touched by the enthusiasm of these top teachers. There is a contagious excitement which has the potential to spark new energy among educators statewide, and in the public as well.

This powerful idea of multiplying efforts by 'training the best to train the rest' left a question: who would train the best? Step two of the planning process was to find the right combination of people uniquely skilled both intellectually and pedagogically, with personalities socially and psychologically balanced. These were to be the state's 'master' science educators, three groups of three to four teachers each, representing the very best in elementary, middle and high school science education in Wisconsin. This cadre of experts was selected by state agency personnel who were familiar with the research and continuing education pursuits of the state's most active science teachers through joint experiences in professional state and national science organizations and joint participation on state and national teacher award selection committees. Though it proved to be difficult to coordinate schedules and travel, the commitment of the state to having the very best practicing teachers designing and delivering the training program ultimately enhanced the credibility of the total project.

The third major step in the planning process was to select the criteria for choosing the teachers who would comprise the cadre of ninety trainees. The core of master-teachers worked with state agency staff to develop the criteria. There was relatively little argument about the characteristics that would be sought: classroom effectiveness, innovation, professional involvement, leadership potential and academic strength. Of course, in the final selection an equitable geographic distribution, equitable balance of sex, race, and school affiliations and a good mixture of grade level representation were also considered crucial.

Selecting the criteria was not nearly as difficult as deciding how they would be qualitatively defined or measured. Use of a nomination procedure provided the initial screening. District administrators, principals, science chairs, university professors, and known leaders in the scientific and educational community were told of the program and asked to submit names of individuals they felt met the stated criteria. Each nominee was then sent an application package including a letter of congratulations, an application form and a brochure describing the program. The items on the application were designed to evoke responses that involved innovative and critical thinking and demonstrated a broad professional perspective. Later it was discovered that the extensive nature of the application form, both in length and content, itself served as an effective screening device. The application forms, along with letters of reference and nomination papers were ultimately reviewed by a selection committee comprised of three state agency consultants and the master-teachers. Thirty teachers and three alternates were chosen for each grade level team (K-6, 6–9, 9–12).

Program Development

All nine master-teachers worked together with state agency consultants to establish a set of common program strands which would run through each training experience. The strands included training and activities in curriculum development, exposure to new teaching techniques and strategies, instruction in the principles of adult learning, and in the development, presentation and evaluation of effective inservice programs. After the common threads had been selected, the master-teachers broke into their grade-level teams to plan the curriculum and schedules that would best suit the needs of the teachers they would be training. The end results were three very different programs yet with similar objectives and major points of emphasis.

Program Delivery

It was felt that, to accomplish the amount of work that had been outlined, the best setting for this kind of training was one that would present a minimal number of distractions. Since each group of trainees would have just one week together, it was imperative that camaraderie be established as quickly as possible, as much of the learning that was to occur required a confident, cohesive group of learners. Thus a remote research facility situated on a small lake and bog in the midst of one of the state's national pine forests was selected as the training site.

One distinct advantage of the site was its natural environment, highly conducive to the study of science. The beautiful surroundings were both quietly calming and stimulating but, more importantly, participants felt their attention could be more clearly focused in this kind of atmosphere. Total immersion, concentration and closeness of living conditions helped develop and maintain a feeling of family among participants.

The program was offered in six, one-week increments for fifteen teachers at a time. Grade-level teams were kept together and a weekly rotation was established — first fifteen middle-school teachers, then fifteen elementary, fifteen high-school teachers, etc. Room, food, recreation and all materials were provided. Each trainee also received a stipend to help defray the cost of transportation or to assist in the paying for graduate credit. The master-teachers divided responsibilities with two of the team of three working as trainers during each weekly session, thus bringing the ratio of participant to master-teacher to about seven to one. In addition, guest speakers from business, higher education, professional organizations and the state were brought in on a regular basis to assist in providing instruction.

However, by all indications, the greatest amount of valuable new learning occurred when the participants taught one another. Each was asked to bring a lesson or activity that he/she used in the classroom which was particularly innovative, effective and/or motivating. Blocks of time within each week were devoted to professional sharing among the participants. Evaluation results revealed that this type of activity empowered the individuals, giving them both the confidence and the inspiration to expand professionally.

In keeping with Wisconsin's tradition for local control since there is no mandated state curriculum, it was important to design a program which deliberately allowed participants to choose from among a variety of theories, practices and resources. Clearly, the opportunity for professional sharing is a method designed for choice and adaptation to local issues and practices. This opportunity for choice was also the manner in which training for adult learning and staff development were approached. Participants learned about an array of theories and programs including Bernice McCarthy's 4-Mat (1982), the Concerns-Based Adoption Model, CBAM (Hall, Wallace and Dossett, 1973), Teacher Career Stages (Burke, *et al.*, 1984) and peer coaching, etc. This multi-theoretical approach was anxiety-producing for some of the trainees, especially those who had little background or experience in working with older or adult learners. Though these teachers were some of the most innovative, confident, and effective teachers of children, they often expressed concern about their ability to facilitate adult learning. In many ways, it would have been simpler to advocate one particular theory or method, but that would have been contradictory to the general premise of choice and local adaptation upon which the overall program was built.

Throughout the week participants were reminded that their selection had not been random. They had been nominated and selected on the basis of their leadership abilities. A special opening reception and final ceremony recognizing their status as top-notch educators helped add to the feelings of prestige — prestige they so rightly deserved. This element of recognition was one way of emphasizing the importance of the commitment of these participants to education as a profession.

Finally, no matter how successful a one-week experience is, without follow-up and renewal, it is unlikely that long-term improvement can be sustained. Thus in the fall of the year, all participants and staff were reassembled. Since each trainee was required to develop and deliver some sort of leadership project, this follow-up activity provided an excellent means for monitoring progress and providing additional needed support. Participants presented their projects in small group settings. Discussions about their successes and frustrations helped to clarify the next step each needed to take to implement his/her final goal.

Participants also had the opportunity to meet their counterparts from the other five weeks. Part of the follow-up weekend was devoted to discussion in geographic groupings so that networking could begin. This was especially helpful to those who resided in the more remote regions of the state. These follow-up activities were organized to facilitate discussions across grade-level teams. Thus, new groups of individuals with a variety of common concerns were established. Participants soon discovered that feelings of isolation and apprehension were shared by all regardless of the age of the students they taught or the area of the state in which they lived.

Elements of Success

In order for a program of this nature to be transportable to other states or regions, it is important to analyze the basic elements which contributed most to its success. First, recognition was a key element. The evaluations overwhelmingly revealed that having been nominated by an administrator or colleague was an essential part of the process. It made the participants aware that they truly stood out among their peers. In addition to the honors and certificates each received during the week of training, other forms of recognition were employed. Each teacher's nominating administrator was sent a letter of congratulations along with a press release to give to the local media. After the week's experience, another letter went from the state agency to the district administrator describing the work that his/her staff member had done. This letter also encouraged the administrator to utilize the participant's new skills as a consultant, as an inservice presenter or as a curriculum leader within the district. Finally, all the participants submitted project summaries and identifying data. These were compiled as a resource book and were distributed across the state.

A second key element was the opportunity for ongoing assessment. Daily logs were kept by the participants and reviewed nightly by the master-teachers. This was an excellent way to provide on-going feedback about the clarity of goals, individual needs and progress of the group. The logs also provided a means for individuals to reflect upon the day's activities and learning thus synthesizing personal daily goals and objectives.

Group bonding proved to be a third key element of success; so much of what occurred during the week depended upon group cohesiveness and an overall atmosphere of trust. Since the instructional format so heavily involved active cooperative learning, it would have been virtually impossible to accomplish the extensive agendum without this important element.

This leads to perhaps the most basic and absolutely essential element of success: master-teacher leadership. Because group cohesiveness was so important, it was imperative that the master-teachers be able to create that bonding quickly while remaining sensitive to individual apprehensions and resistance. They needed to be able to perceive subtle indications of withdrawal and then provide just the right balance of support and encouragement without lowering expectations for achievement. Keeping in mind that only one week was available for each group, the leaders needed to be effective managers of people, time and programs.

Finally, the importance of the follow-up sessions cannot be underestimated. In addition to the opportunities these sessions afforded for discussion, feedback and support, they also sent a clear message that educators at the state level were committed to the program and its participants. The follow-up activities were a way to say, 'We're serious about wanting you to succeed'. Ultimately, for this model to work, the newly-trained cadre of leaders must know that they are partners in a statewide effort which cannot come to fruition without their commitment and follow-through. Thus, the follow-up sessions served to reaffirm interest among professionals at the state level in maintaining and nurturing that sense of partnership.

Summary

This model for staff development puts the state educational agency in the role of agent or 'broker' of human resources. As such, its responsibility is one of creating opportunities, marketing resources and assistance in the match-up between district or regional need and trainer qualities, skills and knowledge. Through ongoing commitment to this type of program, the state agency is helping to assure that high-quality resources continue to be available and up-to-date. This can be done by expanding opportunities for the already identified cadre of master-teachers, identifying new groups of teacher-leaders and assisting in the establishment of strong networks among program participants.

This model also allows for considerable local district choice. It keeps the responsibility for the professional development of teachers at the local level, while assuring that qualified leaders are available to provide training. As previously mentioned, district–sponsored staff development increases the probability that subsequent training efforts will be more effective and meaningful. Having been trained in the assessment of needs, program design and implementation, and in the consultative skills of instituting change, the trainers from the model program are able to 'customize' their work within districts. This is one way in which the model contributes to the increased effectiveness of local level programming. Though this model was developed in a state with local school governance, it lends itself to modification and could certainly be adapted by any state or region regardless of its philosophy about local versus state control. The transportability of the program rests in the key elements of recognition, ongoing assessment and program flexibility, group cohesiveness, leadership and follow-up.

References

BRANDT, R.S. (1987) 'On teachers coaching teachers: A conversation with Bruce Joyce'. *Educational Leadership*, February, 44, 5.

BURKE, P., FESSLER, R., CHRISTENSEN, J. (1984) *Teachers Career Stages: Implications for Staff Development*, Fastback 214, Bloomington, IN, Phi Delta Kappa Educational Foundation.

HALL, G., WALLACE, R. and DOSSETT, W. (1973) *A Developmental Conceptualization of the Adoption Process Within Educational Institutions*, Austin, Texas, Research and Development Center for Teacher Education, The University of Texas.

McCARTHY, B. (1982) 'Improving staff development through CBAM and 4-Mat', *Educational Leadership*, October.

11 A Staff Development Model for Post-Secondary Education

Howard L. Stone

As renewed attention is being given to upgrading the quality of education at all levels, staff development is seen as an important component of high-quality education. Staff development is not a new activity, although its focus and primary goal have become more clearly defined, that is, increasing the competence of teachers to facilitate learning in order to increase the competence of students.

Since learning is a process within the control of the learner, teaching must be a facilitating process. The teacher may be viewed as a member of one of the helping professions. Staff development, therefore, can be defined as an activity designed to facilitate the learning of how to facilitate learning. The question that is crucial to the success of all those activities we label staff development is, 'What kind of learning are we trying to facilitate?'

Staff development at the post-secondary level provides both unique challenges and opportunities. Teachers at the post-secondary level come prepared as content specialists, with advanced degrees in specific disciplines. The challenge is to turn these content specialists into people who understand the art of teaching so thoroughly that they can teach their subjects to others. However, very few have experienced any formal training in teaching as a discipline. The knowledge of education they bring with them is what they themselves experienced as students. Thus these non-expert 'experts' present a unique challenge.

In discussing his thoughts on learning how to teach, Lee Shulman points out reasons why it is that of all the professions, teaching is so difficult:

One of the reasons learning to teach is so difficult is because unlike other professions where you can use the discipline as a basis for your practice, in teaching the disciplines play a dual role. They are both the basis for practice, and they are what you practice. For instance, if I'm a physician and understand anatomy, I've learned well enough not to confuse the aorta with the superior vena cava — I'm okay. But, if I'm a teacher of anatomy that's not enough. I've got to understand it enough to explain it to somebody else.

A second reason it is so difficult to learn to teach is that unlike many other professions, people who learn to teach learn it after having completed a seventeen-year apprenticeship of observation. They have spent seventeen years, more or less, and nearly 20,000 hours as observers of teaching and they've learned an enormous amount about it.

One of the things that comes out very clearly is the enormous influence content course teachers have on students' conceptions of teaching. Whether they like it or not, university and college teachers in the discipline are teacher educators. They are educating future teachers every time they represent their subject in a particular way, every time they either do or don't make the evaluations they conduct compatible with the goals of the instruction in which the engage, every time they present their pedagogy in a particular way.

A third reason learning to teach is difficult is that much of learning to teach depends on learning from experience. The whole idea of learning from experience is: I do something, it doesn't work, so I try something else until I finally find something that does work. It's a kind of thoughtful trial and error, but it's predicted on two assumptions: one, we have reasonably accurate access to what we do, and two, we are reasonably accurate in identifying the consequences of what we do. But it is very difficult to establish those two assumptions (Shulman, 1987: Assessment Conference).

Perhaps some of the greatest obstacles facing staff development in postsecondary education are the rewards of teaching per se — perceived or actual. A faculty position in an institution of higher education carries with it the responsibilities for providing research, teaching, and service, all areas presumably of equal importance. In reality, however, excellence in teaching alone will rarely be considered sufficient cause for promotion. Yet teaching is the central focus of everything we do in universities and colleges and it ought to be the primary concern for all involved. Currently, however, only one part of the university — the school of education — takes the responsibility for preparing people to engage in teaching.

However, all who teach should be obliged to think about how they teach, as well as about the content of what they teach.

Another obstacle may be the attitudes faculty members have developed about their competence as teachers. Faculty are meticulous about their research methodology and the results obtained, and they take pride in their service functions. Most of them would like to take equal pride in their teaching, but most of them do not have an array of techniques available to them. They rely on past experiences and role models which may or may not be appropriate for what they are attempting to achieve. They know that they are not as proficient as teachers as they are practitioners of their disciplines, and some are defensive and resistant to efforts to modify their teaching behavior. Staff development at the post-secondary level must not be perceived as punishment for doing something wrong, but instead, should be perceived as a positive happening. Faculty in colleges and universities are well-trained academically and have demonstrated excellence as researchers and practitioners in their fields, but most have received no formal training as teachers. They have little problem dealing with feedback on how to improve their skills as researchers or practitioners; peer review and client feedback are an accepted way of life. However, in their role as teachers, some may be defensive and hostile regarding such feedback. The issue of academic freedom is often raised as a means to avoid such feedback.

An axiom to be followed in changing human behavior is that people are unwilling to change unless they themselves see a discrepancy between what they are achieving and what they hope to achieve. Staff development at the post-secondary level should be approached as an activity designed to provide staff with a wider range of alternatives in performing an essential activity — teaching. It is not an effort designed to train them to accept additional responsibilities. As researchers, few staff would reject the opportunity to explore the use of alternatives with which they might not be currently familiar; as teachers they need to be equally receptive.

The field of medicine at the post-secondary level has proved to be uniquely capable of benefiting from staff development opportunities in the area of teaching. Medical educators have long recognized the need to accept the responsibility for the development of teaching skills among the staff. Furthermore, physicians accept the fact that teaching is a responsibility they accept when they take a position in an academic medical center. Yet few physicians consider themselves expert in the field of teaching. They have readily sought out and accepted the advice of educators — many times more readily than have educators themselves.

Of the 125 medical schools in the United States, almost all have established offices of Medical Education Research and Development. There is a national Group on Educational Affairs that is part of the Association of American Medical Education and a national publication, *Academic Medicine*, that is devoted to reporting results of research projects in medical education. There is also a national society of the Directors of Research in Medical Education.

Many insightful doctors have promoted a thoughtful approach to the problems of teaching in medical education. William S. Middleton, MD, the late Dean Emeritus of the University of Wisconsin Medical School, reflected in 1951 that,

> ... medical education has suffered immeasurably from the old adage that teachers are born, not made. Until recent years there has been no studied effort to establish the validity of this position. Yet the techniques of education have grown apace. It is high time that we invite specialists in the field of pedagogy to advise us in this matter.

He went on further to present his views on teaching as follows: 'The best teachers are profound and sustained students of their respective subjects (who) direct rather than dictate thought'. (Middleton, 1972)

Phil Manning, MD, Professor of Medicine, University of Southern California, indicated that,

> The very nature of medicine requires that physicians be teachers. Teaching is an impetus for study; it requires the teacher to acquire, review, and organize the knowledge to be taught. In good teaching, teachers are also learners and exchanges of ideas, challenges, and feedback make learning a lively affair. (Manning, 1987)

J. Willis Hurst, MD, Candler Professor of Medicine, Emory University School of Medicine, also commented that,

> Teaching and learning go hand in hand. Physicians should live up to their title, doctor, which means teacher. One can always find someone to teach. Practicing physicians should teach patients, just as they should interact instructively with colleagues ... Instead of giving details, the teacher should discuss concepts. The purpose of lectures should be to create interest, stimulate students' curiosity, and motivate them to seek further information. The teacher must also have a good sense of timing and know when to bring up each subject. Part of a teacher's success depends on personality, and the common denominator in the personality of good teachers is their ability to stimulate students to work on problems when the teacher is not there. The successful teacher checks the ability of the student to think rather than regurgitate facts. (Hurst, 1987)

Charles H. Mayo, MD, stated, 'The safest thing for a patient is to be in the hands of a man engaged in teaching medicine. In order to be a teacher of medicine the doctor must always be a student' (Mayo, 1927). And finally, Leigh Thompson indicated three ways teaching helps him to learn. 'First, it stimulates me to search published materials, learn new facts, and update my knowledge. Second, it forces me to organize my knowledge for my presentation. Third, it provides the opportunity for feedback from the audience'. (Thompson, 1987)

Given this often-expressed desire for improvement in medical education by medical educators themselves, what then is an appropriate approach to staff development at the post-secondary level, especially in an established professional school? One common denominator among staff in a medical school is knowledge of the *practice* of medicine, whatever the particular medical specialty or subspecialty. The model that the author developed was rooted in the idea that, 'Good medical practice is good educational practice'. Indeed there is great similarity between the decision-making models used in medicine and education, though each uses a different vocabulary.

The initial step in the staff development process was to determine the means of providing appropriate and significant feedback to the faculty on their practices as educators. A feedback system was carefully constructed and incorporated into a model of self-management developed by the author. This Self-Management Model proposes the development of skills and techniques that enable the professional to obtain evidence of his/her own accountability as a teacher. As John W. Gardner pointed out, 'One of the greatest dangers in modern society is that men and women will forfeit their opportunities to participate in meaningful decisions concerning their own lives and work'. (Gardner, 1981) The Self-Management Model is designed so the professional may be involved in those decisions.

One of the common concerns regarding feedback is that the recipient may view that activity as a means of placing blame for something not being accomplished. In the Self-Management Model placing blame does not become an issue; the professional's needing to know the consequences of his/her actions is the issue. If the basic tenets of professionalism — autonomy and self-regulation — are to be retained, professionals must be involved in monitoring the consequences of their actions. In the Self-Management Model discovering that areas of practice are in need of improvement is not important in itself. What the professional is held accountable for is what actions he/she takes in response to such information. After all, Somerset Maugham once stated that only a mediocre person is always at his best.

The Self-Management Model

The basic principles of the Self-Management Model used as the means for providing feedback on teaching to the faculty are as follows:

- Criteria for evaluation of performance are developed in terms of specific roles to be performed within the context of specific programs to be implemented. The teaching faculty are actively involved in determining the appropriate criteria for evaluation.
- Teaching personnel are evaluated on the basis of their ability to respond to data over a period of time, rather than on isolated observations, and in a variety of contexts.
- Specific objectives for the organization of information and the methods of instruction must be made known — whether the objectives involve departments, instructional years, or individual classrooms.
- Individual faculty assume responsibility for making known the activities they expect will accomplish the goals and objectives which they helped establish. Thus the main burden for the analysis of teaching rests with the teachers themselves.

The process for providing feedback to faculty consists of several steps:

A Database is Created

Students: Students experience what goes on in a classroom on a daily basis and thus, if asked appropriate questions, can provide unique insights into teaching. The important point is that students are not asked to make direct value judgments of the teaching, but rather they should be asked focused questions about what they observed and/or experienced. Such information creates a database that peers use to make value judgments. Faculty should be required to secure student reactions to their teaching and examinations every time a course is taught.

Peers: One of the most important functions for peers is to monitor faculty input, e.g., 'Is what is presented appropriate for that level?'; is the information accurate?' etc. If the proposed input is flawed, delivery becomes relatively unimportant. Occasionally, peers do actually observe classroom teaching. Peers also monitor the quality of examinations and, most importantly, make judgments regarding the database after it has been created. These are not impossible or unreasonable tasks for peers to perform.

Achievement Data: Data from valid and reliable faculty-prepared exams and/or standardized exams are used to measure the extent of student learning if appropriate data are available. Invalid and unreliable examinations are not apt to provide usable information anymore than invalid and unreliable medical tests produce useful data.

- Peers evaluate the data and identify both strengths and areas needing improvement.
- Peers discuss their observations with the faculty member being reviewed.
- The faculty member outlines a plan of action for improving performance.

An important factor to consider in providing feedback to faculty is the need for criteria which can be used to compare observations to anticipated outcomes. If there is no reference point, valid judgments cannot be made. It is also important to monitor the effort faculty put into their teaching activities, especially the efforts made to respond to those areas needing improvement, those areas identified by peers.

Once the feedback system was in place and faculty had become accustomed to receiving and using such information, the author identified those essential elements of effective teaching in which the faculty would need to develop competence. These elements were then incorporated into a teaching model infused with the concept that good educational practice is analogous to good medical practice.

The elements of effective teaching are:

- deciding what should be taught
- prioritizing learning objectives
- providing a framework of expectations
- designing appropriate learning experiences which incorporate problem-solving and systematic decision-making
- providing frequent feedback to students in relation to their achievement of the objectives
- providing alternate learning experiences, either remedial or enrichment, based on the achievement of stated objectives
- providing positive reinforcement
- establishing helping relationships with students and colleagues that embody human warmth, spontaneous concern, assisting, receiving, rewarding

When asked to teach medical students, physicians are sometimes at a loss; they frequently ask how they should begin or what they should be doing. Since good educational practice is analogous to good medical practice, the answers to these questions are embedded in the way a medical practitioner would interact with a patient: good education does not happen by chance any more than good medical care happens by chance.

Table 11.1   The medical and educational problem-solving models

Medicine	Education	Function
Database	Assessment of Needs	To obtain accurate information on which to base decisions. To define target behavior or condition.
Problem List	Statement of Objectives	To establish objectives designed to change or attain the target behavior or condition.
Treatment Plan	Teaching Plan	To develop and implement activities designed to achieve established objectives.
Evaluation of Patient Progress	Evaluation of Student Progress	To assess accomplishments. To determine degree to which objectives were attained.

Dr Daniel Tosteson, former Dean of the Harvard University Medical School, restated the thesis that, practicing medicine is a kind of problem-solving. 'Each medical encounter is unique in a personal, social, and biological sense ... these aspects of uniqueness impose on both physician and patient the need to learn about the always new situation to find the plan of action most likely to improve the health of that particular patient at that particular time'. (Tosteson, 1983) With this perspective the physician functions as a teacher, helping patients to learn about the possibilities for living a healthier life. And the same conscientiousness exhibited by physicians in delivering health care should be applicable when they assume the role of teacher in providing education.

A commonly used problem-solving model in medicine is the problem-oriented patient record that contains four basic elements: a database, a problem list, a plan of medical intervention and patient management, and an evaluation of patient progress. John Dewey, noted educational philosopher, also stated the premise that the practice of education requires a problem-solving approach. Learning happens on an individual basis, and it occurs when an experience has personal meaning for the student — that is, when it is incorporated into an individual's frame of reference so that he/she is changed in the use of knowledge, skills, or developing new values and attitudes. Therefore, the problem-solving task for the teacher is to find the most effective learning alternatives for the students.

The problem-solving model used in education is based on the 'learning cycle' and contains four basic elements: a needs assessment, a statement of objectives, a plan of instructional intervention, and a plan for the evaluation of student achievement. Table 11.1 shows the comparisons between the medical and education problem-solving models. The point in summarizing these comparisons is that if the same care exhibited by physicians in the delivery of health care were practiced when they assume

Table 11.2   Course development matrix

1. Assessment of Needs	Indicate information necessary to formulate course objectives.
2. Goals and Objectives	Indicate unit of instruction and specify learning objectives.
3. Performance Criteria	Indicate how to determine whether students have achieved each objective.
4. Teaching Plan	Design teaching/learning activities to help students achieve objectives.
5. Evaluation and Feedback	Stipulate how program and teaching effectiveness will be evaluated and how feedback will be used to improve the course.

the role of teacher, we would see great improvement in programs of medical education.

In addition to pointing out the similarities of the medical and educational problem-solving models to which the medical practitioners could relate, the staff development program for medical educators presented them with a course development framework that could be used as a guide for developing and implementing a specific course of instruction. (Table 11.2) Having these guides for designing an educational program or teaching plan based on sound problem-solving models is essential, although it is only the first step in the educational process. The method of implementing the plan or program is equally important.

Medicine and education are both 'helping' professions. In addition to having special knowledge and skills, members of both professions are required to be thoughtful, disciplined, and creative. They must also exercise skill in judgment and uphold the high standards of their respective disciplines. Success in either profession requires establishing helping relationships with patients or students. The basic elements that make such a relationship possible are a thorough knowledge of subject material and technical skills, plus warmth and concern, and the ability to give immediate feedback and positive reinforcement. Teaching without creating a helping relationship makes no more sense than providing health care without caring. A comparison of educational and medical practice indicates that the two professions involve many similarities, and it is these similarities that formed the basis for staff development activities in a post-secondary education program, medicine. It was an idea to which the staff could readily relate.

Although these similarities do exist, it can also be pointed out that physicians change many times as they take on the role of teacher. What actually happens when the medical practitioner changes from the role of doctor to teacher? Is a good problem-solving model adhered to? Are the

Table 11.3   *Comparison matrix*

Medical Practice	Frequent Medical Education Practice
Medical intervention is not begun until medical problem is diagnosed.	Often instructional methods are identified before the learning objectives are specified.
Once medical treatment has begun, the doctor is continually reassessing the patient's progress to determine the effectiveness of the treatment.	Formative evaluation is seldom done and feedback to the student is often lacking. The student is 'terminal' before problem areas are identified and corrected.
If a patient does not respond to treatment, the patient is not condemned and the treatment is not repeated without determining why it was not effective.	In education, the student is frequently blamed for failure to learn and then subjected to the same instruction for the same amount of time as a punishment.
In medicine, the constant is the effectiveness of treatment and improved health. Time is the variable.	In education, too often time is the constant.
A doctor assumes all patients are treatable.	Medical teachers often assume that a given percentage of students will fail even before instruction begins.
If a doctor used a malfunctioning sphygmomanometer he/she would not trust the blood pressure reading from such an instrument.	In education, the results of invalid and unreliable examinations are frequently utilized as measures of the extent of student achievement.
A doctor's effectiveness is judged in terms of his/her ability to diagnose medical problems, prescribe appropriate treatment, and manage the patient's medical progress.	In education, the teacher's effectiveness is not usually judged in terms of his/her ability to diagnose learning problems, select appropriate instructional intervention, and manage the student's learning progress.

components of an effective helping relationship found in the student-teacher interaction? Table 11.3 compares desirable medical practices with some of the illogical behaviors that were found in medical education, practices that the staff development process was designed to change.

The staff development model described in the foregoing discussion has filled an important need in post-secondary education. The fact is that many current post-secondary educational practices are not based on what is known about learning theory or research on teaching. Too often we perpetuate myths about education or we teach as we are taught, and too often alternatives are not readily available to the post-secondary educator. This model has enabled the faculty in one medical school to relate educational practice to a field in which they are already knowledgeable, namely medical practice. However, the strength and power of such an analogy-based program lies in its potential for transferability to other academic disciplines and to other professional schools. Indeed it has been used successfully in the field of nursing, the comparisons between nursing and education being very similar to the comparisons between medicine and education. It has also been used as the basis for a course entitled, 'Basic Principles of Educational Practice in Higher Education' taught to faculty and graduate students across the Madison, Wisconsin campus. No matter what the discipline, staff development can and should become a significant and vital part of higher education.

References

GARDNER, JOHN W. (1981) *Self-Renewal*, New York, W. W. Norton and Co., Revised Edition.

HURST, J. WILLIS, MD. (1987) 'Personal essay', *Medicine: Preserving the Passion*, New York, Springer-Verlag, Inc.

LUDMERER, KENNETH M., MD. (1985) *Learning to Heal*, New York, Basic Books, Inc.

MANNING, PHIL R., MD and DEBAKEY, LOIS (1987) *Medicine: Preserving the Passion*, New York, Springer-Verlag, Inc.

MAYO, CHARLES H. (1927), quoted in 'Proceedings of the staff meetings of the Mayo Clinic', 28 September, 39, 2, p. 233.

MIDDLETON, WILLIAMS S., MD (1972) *Values in Modern Medicine*, Madison, Wisconsin, The University of Wisconsin Press.

SHULMAN, LEE S. (1987) 'Assessing content and process: Challenges for the new assessments', an address presented at the AAHE Assessment Forum, Second National Conference on Assessment in Higher Education.

SHULMAN, LEE S. (1987) 'Learning to teach', paper published in the AAHE Bulletin, 40, 3.

THOMPSON, LEIGH, M.D. (1987) 'Learning from teaching', *Medicine: Preserving the Passion*, New York, Springer-Verlag, Inc.

TOSTESON, DANIEL, M.D. (1983) *New England Journal of Medicine*, November, Boston, MA, 314, 22, pp. 1530–1536.

Additional Source Material

All the printed and audiovisual material listed is available from: The Office of Medical Education Research and Development, University of Wisconsin-Madison Medical School, 1300 University Avenue, Madison, Wisconsin 53706.

Printed Material

- *Handbook for Writing Educational Objectives*
- A collection of position papers and research reports on the evaluation of teaching effectiveness.
- Simulated exercises for considering the evaluation of teaching effectiveness.

- Data-gathering instruments for evaluating educational programs and teaching effectiveness.
- Booklets on specific teaching activities:
  - *Guiding Students to Discover*
  - *Preparing and Presenting an Effective Lecture*
  - *Using Questions to Teach*
  - *Guidelines for Facilitating Learning: A Medical School Faculty Handbook, 105 pages.*

Audiovisual Materials

- *Teaching: Activities Designed to Facilitate Learning.* A 45-minute videotape demonstrating the teaching techniques of lecturing, of using questions to teach, and of guiding students to discover. The videotape is available in 3/4", Beta, and VHS videocassette format.
- A series of four tape/slide programs entitled *Self-Management: A Model for Professional Accountability in Education.*
  - Part I: The Theory of Self-Management
  - Part II: The Role of the Individual Instructor
  - Part III: The Administrative and Organizational Role
  - Part IV: Format for Implementation
- *Good Medical Practice is Good Educational Practice: A Framework for Faculty Development.* The University of Wisconsin-Madison Medical School. A tape/slide program with discussion guide.

Part 4
Looking Ahead

12 Future Directions for Staff Development — The Staff Development Specialist

Peter Burke

The basic construct for staff development that permeates all chapters of this book is one which incorporates needs assessment, planning, implementation, evaluation and participant empowerment. An emphasis on global concerns, as well as local, regional and national concerns, is implicit in all of the stages of this construct. Each stage also serves as an organizing element in the chapters that describe staff development models for elementary, secondary and post-secondary staff members.

Staff development is not a static practice but a constantly evolving process that is based on the ever-changing needs of the individual participants. This emphasis on change has resulted in a dynamic evolution of the basic construct into the several staff development models presented. This chapter builds upon the previous chapters to design a future agenda for staff development. This agenda specifically describes a preparation program for staff development specialists, those professionals who must provide the leadership and expertise in determining our future directions.

Implications for the Future

In this chapter seven implications for staff development have been synthesized from the previous chapters, implications which can serve the practice of staff development as a checklist of constructs to be considered. They can also serve research in staff development as concepts to be challenged or confirmed, or as a foundation for the design of future hypotheses. Finally, they can suggest directions for the training of staff development specialists.

Peter Burke

Adult Learners

Professional staff members in educational institutions are adults. As such, these people have special learning needs and special learning styles. Knowles (1970) referred to the education of adults as 'andragogy' and differentiated it from the 'pedagogy' of teaching children and youth. His stages for the practice of adult education are quite close to the stages of the construct given at the beginning of this chapter. The chapters in Knowles' book include 'Assessing Needs and Interests ...', 'Defining Purposes and Objectives', 'Designing a Comprehensive Program', 'Operating a Comprehensive Program' and 'Evaluating a Comprehensive Program'. Participant empowerment is the one additional concept this book has added for the purpose of defining staff development as the education of adults.

It has been indicated throughout that adults have different learning needs, learning styles, strategies and preferences. The literature from research on adult learning was summarized by Bryant (1981) in the statement 'They require learning that is self-paced, self-directed, relevant to personal or career interests and participatory in nature ... A process design is favored over a content design' (p. 60).

The first implication for staff development is:

<u>Adult learners have special needs that must be considered in program planning.</u>

Learning to Learn

Once individual needs are assessed the plan developed should not be a content-driven, lecture-oriented approach. There should be a problem-solving, interactive approach to learning; adults learn by doing and by sharing. In discussing problems in continuing education Apps (1979) stated that one purpose of continuing education is 'to help people learn how to learn'. His rationale for this statement is that the traditional methods of teaching do not give individuals the '... responsibility for organizing what they plan to learn' (p. 98). The staff development process must have built-in strategies that are aimed at helping the participants learn how to plan and continue the educative process on their own.

Adults have to see a personal or professional need for change if they are expected to participate fully in staff development activities. In addition, their individual styles must be respected and the learning activities must be structured in a systematic fashion that is appropriate for each learning style. Encompassing all of the planning should be a goal of preparing each person for individualized life-long learning (Burke, 1987).

A second implication for staff development is:

Programs must be structured to help participants learn how to learn.

Teacher-Leaders

Another characteristic of adult learners is that they need control over the learning situation (Wood, Thompson and Russell, 1981). Elements like peer support, the environment or climate, trust, open communication, and freedom from failure are all important aspects of successful staff development. One of the most effective ways to provide the necessary control and to help structure the positive environment is to have teachers themselves act as staff development leaders.

Two types of expertise are needed for teacher-leaders to assume staff development responsibilities. These are content and process expertise (Luke, 1981). Teacher staff development leaders already have or can gain the content expertise and may then share that knowledge with colleagues. Several examples of teachers training teachers are given in the earlier chapters. Teachers also may have expertise in the process of learning that would be a valuable asset to the planning of staff development. In each case, the teacher-leaders are participants who take a leadership role, they are teachers who have been empowered, to provide a positive environment for their peers as they go through the learning activities together. The Career Lattice of McDonnell and Christensen in Chapter 7 is an example of one way this leadership might be structured.

A third implication for staff development is:

Teacher-leaders are essential to program success.

Career-long Education

Teacher education is a career-long process (Burke and Heideman, 1985). So, too, is staff development a career-long process that must focus on professional responsibilities and be based on a systematic (strategic) long-range plan (Wood, Thompson and Russell, 1981). We have seen in this book that access to staff development opportunities can stem from local, regional, state or national programs and perspectives. As the needs of the individuals change and the sophistication of their learning becomes more complex, the structure of the programs must change to meet the needs.

Ward (1977) saw staff development as lifetime education and he said 'Lifetime education, therefore, is a comprehensive theory for the practice of general education designed for the strategic reformation of educational practices that ... have grown ineffectual and obsolescent' (p. 21). Topics, structure, focus and sophistication of programs must all change with the changing needs of the participants as they move through their career stages and as they mature in their careers.

A fourth implication for staff development is:

Learning must be a career-long activity.

Program Direction

Teacher leaders in the delivery of staff development are crucial. Another type of leadership, however, is equally important to the success of a staff development program. This is the administrative leadership that provides structure, continuity, evaluation and feedback to the process. Lassey (1971) said that the basic task for this kind of leadership is 'to arrange organizational conditions and methods of operation so that people can achieve their own goals best by directing their own efforts toward organizational objectives' (p. 43). It is essential that there should be someone in the organization who is able to keep the long-range goals in perspective during short-range program planning, and someone who keeps a balance between organizational and personal goals in program delivery.

This type of leadership comes from a staff development specialist – from a person whose main goal is to create and move forward a comprehensive long-range plan for staff development which includes '... academic, fiscal, physical, personnel, research, organizational, and evaluation concerns' (White and Belt, 1980, p. 222). The authors of the chapters describing models in this book are exemplars of this type of leadership. They depend on effective communication and coordination to accomplish their tasks both with and through people. The examples given in the previous chapters demonstrate the coordinative skill necessary to accomplish the defined tasks.

Successful staff development depends on a clear distinction between the needs for teacher empowerment and the need for program direction. In essence, the program director must be a sensitive and democratic leader who allows the participants to share in the design and implementation of the program. This leadership cannot be *laissez-faire*, it cannot be rigid delegation, nor can it be cooptation. Program direction for effective staff development must be responsible and informed decision-making with accountability accepted by the program director.

A fifth implication for staff development is:

Administrative leadership is crucial for program direction and success.

Collaboration

Educators at all levels of the profession must collaborate to ensure successful programs. Smith (1975) called for '. . . an open collaborative effort among those representing the public, the university of scholars, school administrations, and teacher organizations at different levels of decision-making' (p. 33). The reason for this collaboration was to improve staff development programs.

The responsibilities of each of the groups mentioned by Smith have been outlined in several of the chapters of this book. One crucial collaborative effort to be emphasized here is that between the university and the school. Following up on his call for lifelong education, Ward (1977) identified the responsibility of higher education in this type of collaboration:

> Training and facilitation preparation for education . . . is the proper function of the scholastic institution . . . supportive facilitation, required services for the essentially independent pursuit by individual and peer group of any and all knowledge of interest, should be the institutional function during adulthood. (p. 22)

The topic of school-university collaboration has received continual attention in the literature of education. It has been just recently that formal collaboration for the development of experienced teachers and staff has received careful scrutiny (Arends, 1990). Collaboration, to be successful, must include all of the partners as professional equals. As in cooperative learning, the supportive facilitation necessary for lifelong education includes all of the participants acting as equals in their collaborative efforts.

Schools and universities must work together to identify, research, reflect upon and solve the problems that stand in the way of good educational practice. This process of working together, probably as much as the product of the work itself, is staff development. One essential avenue of collaboration must become the preparation and professional growth of staff development specialists.

A sixth implication for staff development is:

Schools and universities must collaborate to ensure continued professional growth.

Preparation

In a recent look at the goals of staff development, Sparks and Loucks-Horsley (1989) described five models for staff development. These models were synthesized from a review of the varied program offerings described in the literature — program offerings not unlike those described in this book. The models Sparks and Loucks-Horsley identified included individually guided, observation/assessment, a development/improvement process, training and inquiry (pp. 40–57).

These five models for staff development could be represented as five plates spinning at the end of five sticks, with the staff development specialist as the artist who keeps the plates from falling. One aspect of the collaborative efforts mentioned above was the preparation of staff development specialists. It should be the responsibility of the universities to help specialists learn how to get the plates spinning in the first place, and then continue to help them keep the plates from falling.

Two institutions have published outlines of preparation for staff development specialists. Syracuse University has a graduate program with courses in leadership, supervision, organizational change, curriculum, administration, finance, program evaluation and current research on teaching. Reviewers of this program recommend an internship with a mentor, seminars and reflection on theory and practice as continuing parts of the program (Tallerico, 1989).

A program for the preparation of staff developers at the University of Maryland covers three aspects: first, the roles of trainers, consultants and administrators are studied. Second, the cognitive and affective domains are reviewed. Third, competencies in knowledge, skill and individual characteristics are built into the program. Recommendations for program improvement at this institution include reflection, organizational development, and a holistic, experiential approach to continuing development (Henkelman and Bahn, 1989). These two examples suggest new directions for what must become integral components of future staff development.

A seventh implication for staff development is:

Universities must design preparation programs for staff development specialists.

Preparation of Staff Development Specialists

The two examples given above describe institutions on the cutting edge of designing leadership programs for staff developers. In the first example, an institution combined existing graduate courses into a comprehensive program that would serve as a foundation for prospective staff development specialists. In the second example, a cognitive structure was designed that gave prospective staff development specialists an understanding of the underlying principles that would lead to effective staff development programs.

Both included recommendations for specific components that would make these good programs even better. These components included reflection, guided experience with seminars, and an expanded look at organizational development as a consequence of staff development.

Reflection

Perhaps the most basic element of problem-solving, or of a staff development program structured to allow participants to learn how to learn, is reflection. Staff developers need to step back from the process to take a close and critical look at what is happening. In some instances, this type of procedural review is referred to as formative evaluation, that is, the critical reflection on the success or failure of a staff development process. Formative evaluation offers ongoing corrective measures when areas are identified for improvement. It also allows the program director an opportunity to select positive features of programs for use in future programs.

A group of staff developers and researchers, in an attempt to prepare a future agenda for staff development, coined the phrase 'thoughtful education' (Strong, *et al.*, 1990). Thoughtful education is reflection. It is a paradigm of the collaboration of program developers and researchers designed to study and solve the problems of professional growth. The authors contend '. . . the time has come for those of us who create the models, programs, and strategies to work together' (p. 29). Collaboration is crucial to successful reflection.

Reflection should result both in explanations of the reasons or rationale for program occurrences and in questions that need to be answered either before or during future programs. Reflective thinking can give a logic to what has happened and can provide an agenda for future site-based action research. These two responsibilities of reflective action substantiate the need for collaboration between schools and universities on this process. The right questions must be asked, and past experiences of others must be used to begin answering the questions. Practitioners and professors must work together.

Guided Practice

The theory of adult developmental stages identifies the search for a mentor as important early in the lives of all adults. Each of the two university-based programs described above made recommendations for an experiential component to be part of a preparation program for staff development specialists. A key element of this guided practice would be the selection and assignment of a mentor who would be responsible to guide and give advice to the neophyte staff developer.

Mentor programs have been implemented and are seen as successful in teacher preparation, in business, and in the preparation of school administrators. Two national programs are focused on the mentoring of school principals and superintendents. The National Association of Secondary School Principals has a leadership program established in several states that includes a mentor component. The federal government established a fund for Leadership in Educational Administration Development (LEAD) where many of the state programs use the mentor concept in their developmental efforts.

Schools and universities can work together to structure a mentor program for prospective staff developers to offer guided practice in program development. This collaboration is especially critical since the specialist is often one-of-a-kind in a school or district. As a consequence, the pairing of mentors and protégés, in many cases, must cross district lines. Seminars for the discussion and reflection on practice also could be structured by a regional agency or institution of higher education, another example of collaboration.

Organization Development

If staff members change and improve through conscious developmental efforts, then the organization should change and develop as well. Dillon-Peterson (1981) defined organization development to be '. . . the process undertaken by an organization . . . to define and meet changing self-improvement objectives, while making it possible for the individuals in the organization to meet their personal and professional objectives' (p. 3). Staff development, for her, is embedded in organization development.

A recent synthesis of the research on staff development and organization development affirmed this view. Shroyer (1990) said 'Staff development must be viewed as a comprehensive and continuous process of personal growth and self-actualization within the context of organizational growth and improvement' (p. 4). She goes on to list nineteen separate guidelines for staff development program directors. All of these recent guidelines, in total or in part, are represented in the chapters in this book describing models.

Collaborative efforts to design staff development training programs for specialists could have the effect of improving both the schools and the universities as organizations. The university self-improvement objectives should be to design programs that include responses to the implications listed in this chapter, and prepare specialists to deal with the program models described in the previous chapters of this book.

Graduate Programs —
the Burke-Heideman Eighteen-Point Guide

The foundation for the preparation of specialists to deal with models such as those described in this book should be embodied in higher education graduate programs. It is imperative that higher education institutions be introspective and find ways to design programs for future staff development leaders. Arends (1990) warns that 'institutional insularity and lack of connectedness to the larger profession, along with slowness and inability to respond to criticism . . .' (p. 141) have disadvantaged colleges of education. Change in college programs can and must occur.

Two examples of such programs have been given, and other examples exist at other institutions. An effective graduate program designed to prepare staff development specialists should include, or at least consider, the following components:

- knowledge of school organization and administration
- knowledge of cultural and ethnic diversity
- knowledge of teacher career stages and career development
- preparation for dealing with conflict resolution among adults
- awareness of teacher empowerment
- awareness of adult development theory and adult learning styles
- a coherent vision of what schools should be
- integration of global demographics and their implications for education
- knowledge of characteristics of school effectiveness
- ability to assess professional needs accurately
- a research base, especially action research or field-based research
- strategies of participatory or shared decision-making
- preparation in critical thinking or problem-solving skills
- preparation in techniques of collaborative programming
- preparation in strategic planning including long and short-range goal setting
- individualization to meet participants' needs
- an experiential component, including a mentorship
- a development of a continuing commitment through career-long activities

Continuing Development

The long-term future of staff development is dependent upon the attention given to the career-long involvement of staff developers. The program components outlined above form a framework for the initial preparation of staff development specialists. Still needed is a strategy to continue this preparation and continue the professional growth of these specialists.

There is no doubt that the need exists. Not content with the attention paid to staff development as a cognitive field by existing professional organizations, these specialists formed an organization of their own. The National Staff Development Council (NSDC) became an answer to the inability of groups such as the Association of Teacher Educators or the Association for Supervision and Curriculum Development and others to respond to the needs. The growth in membership in NSDC has been phenomenal, testimony to the increase in the number of people in school districts assigned to staff development responsibilites, and to their needs for continued growth.

Annual conventions and publications of professional groups have long been the method of development for experienced educators. The NSDC followed this model and now has extensive conventions and an excellent publication in *The Journal for Staff Development*. Both the conventions and the journal, along with other occasional publications, serve as positive examples of development opportunities for specialists. State and regional affiliates of this national organization are beginning to emerge, signaling the continuing need for on-going developmental efforts for specialists.

The regional staff development center model described by Letven and Klobuchar in Chapter 9 is an excellent example of career-long education for staff development specialists. This model blends several important characteristics. There is a strong school-university partnership that includes several schools and three post-secondary institutions. There is ample opportunity for teacher leadership as well as interactive opportunity for program planners from different districts. Finally, both content and process are considered in designing programs to meet identified needs. More collaborative efforts of this type, given time and resources, should be the model for staff development in the future.

Conclusion

The theoretical framework, practical models and summary implications of this book are intended to inform intelligent practice in staff development. There has been an explosion of activity in this area for several and varied reasons. Change is, essentially, a neutral term. To make the changes in the process of staff development and in the programs themselves become positive change will take careful study and practice. It is the hope of the editors and chapter authors that the information in this book will help schools, universities, agencies and organizations continue to keep staff development as a priority in education.

References

APPS, J.W. (1979) *Problems in Continuing Education*, New York, McGraw-Hill Book Company.

ARENDS, R.I. (1990) 'Connecting the university to the school', in JOYCE, B. (Ed.) *Changing School Culture Through Staff Development*, Alexandria, VA, Association for Supervision and Curriculum Development, pp. 117–143.

BRYANT, B.L. (1981) 'A review of the literature in selected areas of educational research', in ANDREWS, T.E., HOUSTON, W.R. and BRYANT, B.L. (Eds) *Adult Learners (A Research Study)*, Washington, DC, Association of Teacher Educators.

BURKE, P.J. and HEIDEMAN, R.G. (1985) *Career-long Teacher Education*, Springfield, IL, Charles C. Thomas.

BURKE, P.J. (1987) *Teacher Development: Induction, Renewal and Redirection*, Philadelphia and London, The Falmer Press.

DILLON-PETERSON, B. (Ed.) (1981) *Staff Development/Organization Development*, Washington, DC, Association for Supervision and Curriculum Development.

HENKELMAN, J. and BAHN, J. (1989) 'A holistic approach to the graduate training of staff developers', *The Journal of Staff Development*, Summer, 10, 3, pp. 2–10.

JOYCE, B. (Ed.) (1990) *Changing School Culture Through Staff Development*, Alexandria, VA, Association for Supervision and Curriculum Development.

KNOWLES, M.S. (1970) *The Modern Practice of Adult Education: Andragogy Versus Pedagogy*, New York, Association Press.

LASSEY, W.R. (1971) *Leadership and Social Change*, Iowa City, Iowa, University Associates.

LUKE, R.A. (1981) *Teacher-Centered In-Service Education: Planning and Products*, Washington, DC, National Education Association.

SHROYER, M.G. (1990) 'Effective staff development for effective organization development', *The Journal for Staff Development*, Winter, 11, 1, pp. 2–6.

SMITH, E.B. (1975) 'Improvements of in-service education: A collaborative effort', in EDELFELT, R.A. and JOHNSON, M. (Eds) *Rethinking In-Service Education*, Washington, DC, National Education Association.

SPARKS, D. and LOUCKS-HORSLEY, S. (1989) 'Five models of staff development for teachers', *The Journal of Staff Development*, Fall, 10, 4, pp. 40–57.

STRONG, R.W., SILVER, H.F., HANSON, J.R., MARZANO, R.J., WOLFE, P., DEWING, T. and BROCK, W. (1990) 'Thoughtful education: Staff development for the 1990s', *Educational Leadership*, February, 47, 5, pp. 25–29.

TALLERICO, M. (1989) 'New directions in university-based preparation of staff developers', *The Journal of Staff Development*, Summer, 10, 3, pp. 12–15.

WARD, V.S. (1977) 'Staff development through lifetime education', in BEEGLE, C.W. and EDELFELDT, R.A. (Eds) *Staff Development: Staff Liberation*, Washington, DC, Association for Supervision and Curriculum Development.

WHITE, T.J. and BELT, J.R. (1980) 'Leadership', in KNOX, A.B. and Associates, *Developing, Administering and Evaluating Adult Education*, San Francisco, Jossey-Bass Publishers.

WOOD, F.H., THOMPSON, S.R. and RUSSELL, S.F. (1981) 'Designing effective staff development programs', in DILLON-PETERSON, B. (Ed.) *Staff Development/Organizational Development*, Alexandria, VA, Association for Supervision and Curriculum Development.

Notes on Contributors

Blair, Nancy, PhD Head of Graduate Education and Director of the Educational Leadership Program, Cardinal Stritch College, Milwaukee, Wisconsin.

Burke, Peter, PhD Chief, Standards Implementation and Technical Assistance Section, Bureau for School Improvement, Wisconsin Department of Public Instruction, Madison, Wisconsin.

Christensen, Judy, PhD Director, Master of Arts in Teaching Program, National College of Education, Evanston, Illinois.

Conzemius, Ann, MS Director, Office of Employee Development and Training of Department of Employment Relations, State of Wisconsin. Formerly Director, Education for Economic Security Act Program, Department of Public Instruction, State of Wisconsin.

Fessler, Ralph, PhD Director, Division of Education and Professor of Education, The Johns Hopkins University, Baltimore, Maryland.

Heideman, Carroll, BM., MS. Retired. Elementary Teacher, Madison Metropolitan School District, Madison, Wisconsin.

Heideman, Robert, PhD Retired. Distinguished Service, Director Educational Placement and Career Services, School of Education, University of Wisconsin-Madison, Madison, Wisconsin.

Herzog, Barbara, PhD Director of Curriculum, Oshkosh Area School District, Oshkosh, Wisconsin.

Klobuchar, Judith K., BS Social Studies Teacher, Burlington Junior High School, Burlington Area School District, Burlington, Wisconsin. Center

Associate (1988–89) Regional Staff Development Center, University of Wisconsin-Parkside, Kenosha, Wisconsin.

Koll, Patricia, PhD Associate Dean, College of Education and Human Services, University of Wisconsin-Oshkosh, Oshkosh, Wisconsin.

Lange, Ronald, PhD Assistant Superintendent of Instruction, School District of Elmbrook, Brookfield, Wisconsin.

Letven, Esther M., MS Director Regional Staff Development Center, University of Wisconsin-Parkside, Kenosha, Wisconsin.

McDonnell, John H., PhD Professor of Education, Beloit College, Beloit, Wisconsin.

Parker, Linda S., PhD Assistant Administrator/Director of Instructional Services, Cooperative Educational Service Agency 5, Portage, Wisconsin.

Reyes, Pedro, PhD Assistant Professor of Educational Administration, School of Education, University of Wisconsin-Madison, Madison, Wisconsin.

St. Maurice, Henry, PhD Director of Field Experiences and Assistant Professor, School of Education, University of Wisconsin-Stevens Point, Stevens Point, Wisconsin.

Stone, Howard, PhD Professor, Department of Continuing Medical Education. Director, Office of Medical Education Research and Development, University of Wisconsin-Madison Medical School, Madison, Wisconsin.

Index

I.A.A.E. Occasional Paper No. 2

The Rural Challenge

Contributed Papers Read at the
17th International Conference
of Agricultural Economists

Edited by
Margot A. Bellamy,
Commonwealth Bureau of Agricultural Economics
and
Bruce L. Greenshields,
Economics, Statistics and Co-operatives Service,
U.S. Department of Agriculture

INTERNATIONAL ASSOCIATION
OF AGRICULTURAL ECONOMISTS

Gower

© The International Association of Agricultural Economists 1981

All rights reserved. No part of this publication may be reproduced, stored in a retrieval system, or transmitted in any form or by any means, electronic, mechanical, photocopying, recording, or otherwise without the prior permission of Gower Publishing Company Limited.

Published by Gower Publishing Company Limited, Gower House, Croft Road, Aldershot, Hampshire GU11 3HR, England.

British Library Cataloguing in Publication Data

International Conference of Agricultural Economists
   (17th: 1979: Banff, Canada)
   The rural challenge. (-Occasional paper/
   International Association of Agricultural
   Economists; No.2)
   1. Agriculture - Economic aspects - Congresses
   I. Title   II. Bellamy, Margot A.
   III. Greenshields, Bruce L.
   338.1   HD1405

ISBN 0 566 00472 0

Printed in Great Britain by
Biddles Ltd, Guildford, Surrey

Contents

iii

iv

Foreword

This book is the second in the IAAE Occasional Papers series. It contains 40 full papers and 40 abstracts of contributed papers presented at the 17th International Conference of Agricultural Economists, held in Banff, Alberta, Canada, September 3-12, 1979. In addition, it contains the openers' remarks and rapporteurs' reports of the discussions that ensued, and four papers presented at a special session on Canadian agriculture. The titles of sessions in which the papers were presented are in the contents along with the names of those persons who chaired the sessions.

The conference theme was "Rural Change: The Challenge for Agricultural Economists." The program was structured to correspond to the levels at which agricultural economists work--micro, subnational, national, supranational, multinational, and disciplinary. The inclusion in this book of the reactions of the conference participants provides an unusual opportunity for the reader to experience the flavour of the discussions and to judge the quality and relevance of the papers. The reader will discover that, in addition to the contributed papers, the openers' remarks and the comments from other participants are substantial contributions to the professional dialogue.

The 80 contributed papers were selected for presentation at the conference from over 300 proposals. The Contributed Papers Selection Committee members were Kenneth R. Farrell (Chairman), John H. Cleave, Yair Mundlak, Allen B. Paul, G. Edward Schuh, Shamsher Singh, Juan Zapata, and Bruce L. Greenshields (Executive Secretary). I served on the committee in an ex officio capacity.

The support of the Economics and Statistics Service of the U.S. Department of Agriculture, and the Institute of Agricultural Economics of Oxford University in the preparation of this book is gratefully acknowledged. In particular, the Association and I are deeply indebted to Margot Bellamy and Bruce Greenshields for many hours of careful work in editing the manuscript (received in varying condition) for publication, and much credit is due to Patricia L. Beavers who typed the camera copy, often from handwritten notes. The views expressed in this book are not necessarily those of the IAAE or the institutions with which the authors are affiliated.

Glenn L. Johnson
Vice President--Program
1977-79

The Rural Challenge
at the Micro Level

MICRO LEVEL RESEARCH ON RURAL MARKETING SYSTEMS

Roger W. Fox and Michael T. Weber

This paper focuses on micro level marketing research to support the design and implementation of rural development programmes. Contemporary rural development efforts are directed primarily at promoting change so as to simultaneously affect the distribution and growth of income, employment, nutrition, health, and other dimensions of the quality of life in rural areas. Although there is a continuing debate over the appropriate rural development strategy, adequate analyses of the essential growth and equity issues will not be forthcoming until we better understand the micro behaviour of both production and marketing systems in rural areas.

Although our focus is on rural marketing systems, we recognize that food and agricultural markets are ultimately national and in many cases international in scope. Consequently, our plea for more micro research on rural marketing systems does not imply that micro analysis of urban marketing systems, macro analysis of national marketing systems, or international trade analysis be reduced. We believe all of these are necessary, but none alone is sufficient for the design and implementation of rural development programmes. And while none of these research areas has enjoyed high priority in national economic planning and development programmes, we contend that there is a critical shortage of micro understanding and analysis of the rural portions of national marketing systems (Abbott).

Shortcomings of Previous Marketing Research

Much of the marketing economics research in low income countries has been guided by the traditional efficiency concepts tied closely to the relatively static, perfectly competitive economic models. Important dynamic questions involving growth and equity have been largely ignored. Likewise, much of the research has been concerned with macro issues involved in testing for conditions of structure, conduct, and performance predicted by the perfectly competitive model. These studies frequently include assumptions of homogeneous behaviour on the part of farmers and marketing agents, and use data that are averages of many observations (for example, monthly price data), thus obscuring important variations in market behaviour. Furthermore, there is a "top down" orientation to the research that emphasizes urban and export markets with only minor attention to input and rural consumer goods markets. The results of existing marketing research are often inappropriate for making specific recommendations for improvements in rural markets, especially if the objective is to extend improved services to specific target groups such as small farmers and other low income rural residents. Consequently, the design of rural development schemes continues to be based upon popular beliefs about excessive margins, exploitative middlemen, and uninformed farmers. These views, in turn, lead to strong pressures for direct government intervention in marketing. But as Lele found in studying some 17 rural development programmes in sub-Saharan Africa, "The foremost shortcoming of the approach adopted in many of the programmes is that it has paid little attention to making the traditional forms of marketing organization work."

Micro level marketing research carried out by other disciplines also has its shortcomings. Little of what has been done contains analyses that yield policy recommendations. For example, geographers interested in the location of economic activities have undertaken a large number of descriptive studies of market places, periodic markets, and itinerant traders in rural areas of developing countries. This research is important because it provides knowledge of how these traditional trading institutions function. Unfortunately, by geogra-

3

phers' own assessments, much of their research suffers from the inability to offer answers to questions concerning policy and planning of rural marketing systems (Ghosh and McNulty, and R. H. T. Smith).

Anthropologists and sociologists have observed and described rural household behaviour relative to production, consumption, storage, and sales decisions. Anthropologists also have a tradition of conducting individual village studies. Although their research provides valuable descriptive information about rural populations and economic processes, it rarely contains a policy focus. Currently, a group of economic anthropologists is seeking to use concepts from regional science to put their village studies into a more useful framework for understanding and promoting rural development (C. A. Smith).

The field of business administration also has potential for contributing to better rural development policy and programmes. Improved private and public business management practices are fundamental to rural marketing system reform. Yet there is very little micro level research indicating what the potentials are and how change can be introduced.

Knowledge about technical alternatives in marketing is another necessary component of rural marketing systems research. Engineers and marketing technicians often conduct feasibility studies of new methods of storage, food processing and preservation, packaging, and transportation. Unfortunately, their analyses and recommendations can easily escape sufficient socioeconomic content and rigour. This has often resulted in an overendorsement of capital intensive technologies, underutilization of new facilities, and insufficient emphasis on local capacity for continued development of skilled labour and management personnel (Riley and Weber).

A Suggested Rural Marketing Systems Approach

The conceptual framework of a rural marketing system which we envisage involves the integration of many components. It includes a geographical dimension that may correspond to the area of a typical rural development project. Within this area there are farms, villages, and one or more rural towns (county seats). The marketing activities occurring within the area are viewed in terms of their interrelationships involving economic, social, geographic, and technical variables. The parameters and variables defining these interrelationships form an endogenous system. At the same time, external or exogenous factors are viewed as having important impacts on the operation of the rural marketing system. These external factors include (1) market linkages with other rural market systems, (2) market linkages with large urban and industrial areas, (3) international market linkages, and (4) government policies and programmes.

The endogenous relationships involve the interaction of rural households and rural markets. The rural household is seen as the basic production and consumption unit. Its output consists of labour, crop and livestock products, nonagricultural products, and service activities (marketing is an example of the latter). Some of these outputs are initially sold in local markets while others are retained for household consumption (food and home produced consumer goods) and for production (labour and home produced inputs). Sales of labour, agricultural output, home produced goods, or services result in cash income which rural households can use to make purchases of consumer goods and services, labour inputs, agricultural inputs, inputs for nonagricultural products, and to save and invest. The rural markets which facilitate these exchanges are normally identified as product (output) markets, input markets, consumer goods markets, and financial markets. The rural financial markets provide important services to the other three markets and directly to rural households. In practice the demarcations between the various rural markets are not nearly so clear. Individual marketing agents may provide services in all four of the markets. It

4

is through these and other rural marketing institutions that important internal and external linkages are developed and maintained. The internal linkages involve the transactions within a particular rural marketing system and the external linkages are with other rural market areas, urban and industrial areas, and export markets.

The internal and external relationships of the rural marketing system, as conceived above, have been independently studied by several disciplines. The integration of these approaches is needed to achieve more policy relevart work supporting rural development. We suggest the following set of objectives for developing an integrated rural marketing system framework:

1. To develop an understanding of how the system functions, thereby providing a better basis for identifying the economic, social, and technical factors which constrain improvements in the system.

2. To estimate the growth and equity impacts on the rural population of pontaneous and planned changes in rural marketing institutions.

3. To predict and evaluate the impacts on rural marketing institutions of changes in the volume and composition of rural household output.

4. To evaluate the growth and equity impacts on the rural population of changes in external markets, policies, and programmes.

5. To prescribe policy and programme changes that will result in major improvements to the rural marketing system and that are consistent with the rural development goals concerning growth and equity.

The above objectives begin to acquire meaning and focus only when specific problems and issues are discussed. Work on the first objective provides a good basis for developing understanding among the relevant disciplines. Because of the emphasis on equity as well as growth, it is important to focus on the operation of the system in terms of the distribution of wealth and income, access to government services and political power, social status and organization, geographic considerations, and technical performance. Qualitative as well as quantitative information is required. The integrated study of a rural marketing system should lead to a better understanding of the factors which constrain its improvement. This involves the determination from the viewpoint of the participants of the rigidities in the private and public components of the system. Technical, social, and institutional constraints are involved. The traditional constraints involve various aspects of exchange, transportation, storage, planning, information, and policy.

The emphasis of the second objective is on what happens if specific internal changes are made in rural marketing institutions and services. For example, what would be the growth and equity effects of alternative feeder road systems in a rural development area? An analysis of the feasibility and impacts of group marketing activities by small scale producers is another example. Clearly, there are interactive effects among possible changes; for example, access to transportation services of a cooperative could assist small farmers in reaping greater benefits from improved feeder roads.

Since a significant portion of the rural development effort is directed towards expansion of agricultural output, it is imperative that the impact of actual or proposed changes in the volume and composition of output be examined (objective 3). Bottlenecks and rigidities associated with traditional marketing systems can restrict the spread of Green Revolution technologies by lowering their profitability. Lele observed that proportionally large increases in supply often result in severe price decreases at the farm level. The impact of

5

production specialization on the nutrition of rural households is another issue. Also, the ability of the rural marketing system to provide efficiently and effectively the required production inputs and the increases in consumer goods demand (resulting from higher rural incomes and specialization) needs to be investigated. The complementarity of production and marketing research and improvements is clearly articulated in this objective.

Pricing, market intervention, international trade, and credit policies are good examples of external government policies that would be investigated under objective 4. These are often evaluated in the aggregate or macro sense, but their equity, growth, and efficiency impacts on rural households need to be studied. For example, how does national price policy affect small farmers' production, consumption, storage, and marketing decisions? Also, how do general employment and income expansion programmes affect demand and income distribution at the rural level? Likewise, what are the local impacts on growth and equity of export expansion programmes?

The final objective involves the recommendation of policy and programme changes to improve the rural marketing system. We conceive of this as a marketing package composed of an externally and internally consistent set of prescribed actions which will lead to significant improvements in the well-being of the rural population, particularly the rural poor. Since external linkages to individual rural marketing systems can be strategic, it is important to realize that the minimum marketing package may well include needed improvements in other rural, large urban, or export markets.

Methods and Strategies for Conducting the Research

The principal requirements for conducting the research are that (1) the major part of the research will have to be multidisciplinary, (2) substantial portions of the research will have to occur in rural areas, and (3) a long run byproduct of the research should be the development of local marketing research teams and extension workers who receive continuing institutional support.

Successful multidisciplinary research requires that a general conceptual framework exist on which all relevant disciplines agree. We are therefore calling for the building of a more comprehensive and systematic conceptual framework which permits a clearer understanding of the interdependencies in the economic, social, political, nutritional, managerial, and technical dimensions of rural marketing processes. We are not sure that the present state of the arts, either in systems science or in our understanding of the full complexities of the rural marketing system, would produce a useful quantitative systems model to assist in analysis and policy formulation. However, rural development project designers and administrators need a conceptual rural marketing systems model to assist them in arranging for appropriate design and evaluation research. This research should have a cumulative impact on project managers and help them recognise and evaluate the dynamics of endogenous and exogenous changes associated with the system.

Our attempt to define the major elements of the rural marketing system is a first step in building a comprehensive model. But this conceptual framework needs to be reviewed by the other disciplines and extended to reflect more fully the social, political, economic, and technical variables, and institutions that comprise the system. All relevant disciplines would be expected to broaden their performance accounts to include (1) growth in outputs and associated changes in price levels, (2) income distribution patterns, (3) employment impacts, and (4) nutritional impacts. The units of analysis include, as previously identified, rural households and rural marketing institutions. An important task of the research would be quantifying and describing (1) the production, marketing, and consumption relationships among the various subgroups of households and marketing agents, and (2) the linkages of households and

6

marketing agents to the exogenous components.

Finally, the importance of creating local applied agricultural marketing research and extension capabilities must be recognized. Even an equity with growth rural development strategy involves constant structural transformation of the rural economy. Research and extension services are continually needed to assist farmers and rural marketing firms in discovering and adopting new technologies, management methods, and institutional forms. Furthermore, the knowledge generated by these services is needed at all levels in the continuing process of agricultural policy formation. Self-sustaining rural development depends heavily upon the availability and leadership that such permanent research and extension capabilities provide. Donor agencies and foreign researchers need to place high priorities on helping to design and implement specific rural development projects which contribute to the establishment of these longer run local capabilities. Micro level research on rural marketing systems can contribute substantially to this goal.

References

Abbot, J. C. (1981) Technical assistance in marketing: A view over time, in Rural Change: The Challenge for Agricultural Economists (edited by G. L. Johnson and A. H. Maunder). Farnborough, England; Gower Publishing Co.

Ghosh, A.; McNulty, M. L. (1978) Locational analysis and spatial planning of marketing systems in developing countries. Paper presented at the International Geographical Union Working Group in Marketplace Exchange Systems Symposium, Zaria, Nigeria, July 23-30, 1978.

Lele, U. (1975) Marketing of agricultural output, in The Design of Rural Development--Lessons From Africa. Baltimore, Maryland, USA; Johns Hopkins University Press, chap. VI.

Riley, H. M.; Weber, M. T. (forthcoming) Marketing in developing countries, in Frontiers in Agricultural Marketing Research (edited by P. L. Farris). Lafayette, Indiana, USA; Purdue University, chap. 16.

Smith, C. A. (1976) Regional economic systems, linking geographical models and socioeconomic problems, in Economic Systems (edited by C. A. Smith). New York; Academic Press, vol. I, chap. 1.

Smith, R. H. T. (1978) Market Place Trade--Periodic Markets, Hawkers and Traders in Africa, Asia, and Latin America. Vancouver, Canada; University of British Columbia.

OPENER'S REMARKS--Louis F. Herrman

How does one conceptually organize a field as amorphous and heterogeneous as agricultural marketing so that it becomes possible to study it coherently and comprehensively, with the aim of formulating specific recommendations for improvement? The earliest approaches to this problem proceeded commodity by commodity, function by function, and firm by firm, guided by efficiency concepts tied to perfectly competitive models. Experience has brought growing dissatisfaction with the results of this kind of research, mainly because we do not get answers to certain kinds of questions that are becoming increasingly urgent.

The concepts of efficiency and competition are not at fault. Failure to abolish certain popular beliefs about middlemen and to generate certain needed recommendations requires a new framework within which to organize micro level research on rural marketing, but the classic ideas of efficiency and competition will remain essential elements of that framework.

The concept of systems is being applied increasingly in many fields of study. We must thank Fox and Weber for their effort in formulating an application to the field of micro level research in rural marketing. As to carrying out research along these lines, I am somewhat daunted by the implication that micro level projects must henceforth encompass full systems models with a complete set of data collected in the project locale. Constraints of time and money will continue to make this impractical in most cases. Constant awareness of the systems concept, however, will improve the design of smaller studies. Also the concept will beneficially affect the interpretation of results. Some work approching a full systems model will be useful in most countries, nationalistic proclivities being what they are.

It is difficult to acquire a real down to earth, grass roots understanding of the marketing process at the rural level: the marketing behaviour of farmers, the conditions affecting success of marketing innovations, and so on. There are deeply ingrained public prejudices against the middleman, analogous to formerly held notions about peasant attitudes toward new technology. If a few good systems oriented studies at the micro level can lead to deeper understanding and eradicate some of the prejudices, there will be a more favourable environment for economic development in the marketing sector.

RAPPORTEUR'S REPORT--Aloysius C. Nwosu

How should micro level marketing research be designed to produce more meaningful results? Efforts should be made to understand how the existing marketing system has evolved rather than simply impose preconceived ideas about market structure, conduct, and performance on the system under investigation. Similarly, agricultural economists should lay more emphasis on operational efficiency; that is, how to get the job done in terms of delivering food and other agricultural products to consumers, rather than their present preoccupation with economic efficiency.

There is a need to investigate to what extent rural markets are competitive with a view to assessing the bargaining power of primary producers, the status of rural marketing infrastructure, and rural processing.

A distinction ought to be made between multidisciplinary research as advocated in the paper and interdisciplinary research which is preferred for micro level work. What is probably required is a methodology for making researchers from the various disciplines cooperate and work together harmoniously.

Contributing to the discussion were Osama A. Al-Zand, Ijoyi Fendru, Michael Haines, C. Govind Ranade, and Ammar Siamwalla.

8

THE ANTI-MIDDLEMEN ATTITUDE OF FARMERS IN GREECE: CAUSES, REPERCUSSIONS, AND SOLUTIONS

Christos Kamenidis

In the early stages of economic development, the production of raw agricultural products is generally considered the major productive economic activity, while marketing is considered a "surplus cure" activity. This has led various public policy makers to emphasize production and almost totally neglect marketing in preparing national development plans. Furthermore, the anti-middlemen attitude which generally prevails among farmers and consumers, and sometimes among government authorities, has also played some role in the underdevelopment and inefficiency of the agricultural marketing system. This attitude seems to have contributed considerably to the retardation of agricultural and overall economic development.

The main aim of this research is to determine the extent and causes of the prevailing anti-middlemen attitude among Greek farmers, to evaluate its major repercussions, to propose certain policy measures to remedy this problem, to specify whom farmers mean by middlemen, and to outline some possible directions of future research.

This study refers to almost the entire area of Greece, since the farmers from whom the data have been obtained are scattered all over the country. However, not all provinces are equally covered, mainly for financial reasons. The primary data used in this analysis were collected from 524 farmers during 1976-78. Questionnaires were used for this purpose, completed either by personal interviews or by mail. According to the method of data collection, these can be divided into the following categories:

1. Data collected by mail from 186 farmers of central Macedonia. The original sample size was 510 farmers, determined by stratified sampling. Taking into account the conditions prevailing in Greece (farmers' education, the value which Greeks still put on research, and so forth), this response rate of 36 percent is considered satisfactory.

2. Data collected by the author's personal interview of 218 farmer members of agricultural cooperatives all over the country.

3. Data collected from 120 farmers of various areas of Greece through personal interview by four University students.

To determine the extent of the anti-middlemen attitude, farmers were asked to state their opinion about the middlemen; that is, whether or not middlemen are useful. Not unexpectedly, all the interviewed farmers answered that middlemen are harmful to them. They even went on to characterize middlemen as "parasites of society" and "exploiters of farmers and consumers." Of course, this is farmers' opinion, not always based on their own experience or justified by the facts. It is a matter of further research to find out if or the extent to which farmers are right.

Next, farmers were asked to clarify whom they mean by middlemen, because the type of middlemen farmers have in mind makes a lot of difference for public policy makers. The vast majority (42 percent) of the interviewed farmers mean brokers; that is, those marketing agents who are placed between farmers and any buyer and who conducts negotiations on product prices and other terms of trade. Few (10 percent) of the interviewed farmers mean both brokers and dealers; 13 percent mean brokers, dealers, and local traders; 15 percent mean brokers, dealers, local traders, and wholesalers; 18 percent mean all but retailers; and very few (3 percent) include retailers.

The anti-middlemen attitude of farmers is not directed equally against all types of middlemen. The direction and magnitude of farmers' anti-middlemen attitude depends mainly on the marketing system of the product under consideration. Thus, in certain product sectors (tobacco, for example) farmers usually mean brokers. Producers of fruits and vegetables most frequently mean wholesalers, processors, and exporters.

Causes

Dissemination of false information. The reason most frequently cited by farmers for their anti-middlemen feelings is middlemen's dissemination of false information about the current and future prices of farm products, conditions of supply and demand, imports and exports, and so forth. Farmers state that such information psychologically forces them to sell their products at prices which are generally below what they could achieve under conditions of perfect information. This reason was cited by 20 percent of the sample of 524 farmers. Those citing this reason are mostly livestock producers, and tobacco and cotton growers.

Purchase of farm products at prices lower than government guaranteed prices. Despite the fact that the government determines floor prices for agricultural products, there are cases in which middlemen buy such products below these prices. This reason was claimed by 16 percent of the sample, mostly producers of fruits, vegetables, poultry, and livestock.

Price offerings unrelated to product quality. Another reason which farmers cited to explain why they are against middlemen is the latter's tactic of buying farm products at prices which do not reflect product quality but rather the bargaining power of farmers. This factor was claimed by 15 percent of the sample, mainly producers of fruits, vegetables, tobacco, and cotton.

Delayed payment to farmers. In some instances, certain middlemen delay their payment to farmers for a long time, even a whole year, as a means of making profits. To achieve this delay, middlemen sometimes issue cheques for which no credit exists in the banks. Such a tactic has frequently been utilized by tomato processors. This reason was cited by 13 percent of the sample.

Issue of false invoices. Certain middlemen, to avoid any punishment by the state authorities for purchasing products at prices lower than the government guaranteed prices, sometimes issue false invoices to farmers. In such invoices, while prices are recorded correctly, purchased quantities are knowlingly underestimated. Such cases were cited by 9 percent of the farmers interviewed, mainly broiler, livestock, and cotton producers.

Cheating farmers in weighing their products. Sometimes farmers complain that middlemen underrecord the quantity of the product. This reason was cited by 8 percent of the sample, mostly meat producers.

Introduction of higher percentage of foreign material into the farm products. This is one of the methods which middlemen utilize for making profits, if the other methods cannot be proved efficient. This reason was claimed by 7 percent of the sample, mostly tomato, cotton, rice, and wheat producers.

Violation of the terms of production contracts. Some farmers blame certain middlemen, especially processors and exporters, for violating the terms of production contracts which they have made with them. More specifically, farmers say that while these middlemen have asked them to produce a certain quantity of a product with an agreement to buy it all at a specified price, they did not buy any of it. Thus the product is left on the farms, partially or totally deteriorated, yielding the farmers little or no income. This case was cited by 5 percent of the sample, mainly producers of watermelons, cucumbers, carrots, peas, and okra.

Purchase of only some part of the total quantity of a product available. Another reason for which farmers accuse middlemen is that sometimes they do

10

not buy all the quantity of a product available for sale. They buy only some amount of it, and usually the best quality, leaving the rest to the farmers who have difficulty in selling it. This is the case with fruit, vegetable, cotton, and tobacco growers. This reason was cited by 3 percent of the sample.

Payment of a small proportion of the product's total value. Sometimes certain middlemen (wholesalers and exporters, for example) do not pay farmers (fruit producers, for example) the total value of their products. This happens especially when products are sold on a commission basis. In such cases, middlemen complain to farmers that a significant proportion of their products has deteriorated. This reason was cited by 2 percent of the sample.

No payment at all to farmers. There are cases in which farmers do not get any money from middlemen, simply because after they purchased the products from the farmers on a credit or on a commission basis they disappeared. Some of these cases came into court. This reason was cited by 1 percent of the sample, all of whom refer to their own experience. This usually happens with livestock producers and fruit growers.

Miscellaneous. Payment to farmers at prices lower than those agreed upon with middlemen can be mentioned here. Such an instance was noticed with certain cherry producers in northern Greece. Miscellaneous reasons were cited by 1 percent of the farmers.

The above cases do not apply to all middlemen in the country. No doubt their performance varies from good to bad. However, farmers, having in mind those middlemen who do not operate well, generalize their feelings against all and thus create a nationwide anti-middlemen attitude. In this light, the task of an agromarketing researcher is to identify those middlemen who do not perform well and to take all the necessary measures to force them to improve their marketing performance.

If all these accusations of farmers against middlemen are true, the next question which arises is, Why do middlemen in Greece behave in such a way that they create an attitude against them not only from farmers but also from consumers and government authorities? It seems that the answer to this question lies mainly in the theory that middlemen in Greece generally behave on a short-run basis. This means that middlemen see themselves temporarily in the marketing business. For this reason, they try to make the highest possible profits in the shortest possible time.

The main reasons why middlemen behave on a short-run basis in Greece seem to be the following:

1. The relatively high risk which prevails because of the: frequent changes in the government trade and price policies; high rate of inflation; lack of adequate infrastructure; lack of adequate number and properly equipped transportation modes and warehouses; limited food processing industries; tariffs and other restrictions of the European Community; and lack of government marketing services (such as grading).

2. The fact that state laws and regulations regarding the marketing of agricultural products are not strict and powerful, so they can be easily ignored by middlemen without any severe punishment.

3. The lack of well organized cooperatives and other organizations of farmers to compete successfully with existing private marketing firms and thus force them to improve their marketing efficiency.

4. The lack of substantial requirements for any firm going into the marketing business, especially the wholesaling and exporting of farm products.

Repercussions

Distrust. The general outcome of the anti-middlemen attitude is distrust among the various participants in the food production and distribution system which necessitates personal participation of middlemen in the transactions, and long and hard bargaining negotiations among the participants to come to agreement about the product prices.

Wide product output and price fluctuations. Farmers dissatisfied with middlemen may stop producing the product the next year, resulting in output and price fluctuations. This implies an irregular flow of food products to consumers, which is one of the important dimensions of market performance.

Misallocation of farm resources. If farmers, reacting in such situations, go into the production of those products which bear low risk but do not yield high farm incomes, farm resources will be misallocated.

Deterioration of product quality. While an agreement is negotiated between farmers and middlemen about product prices, product quality might deteriorate. For example, in 1977, while producers and processors of peas negotiated their final price, the peas lost their tenderness and thus became unsuitable for processing. For this reason, the peas in question were not purchased by processors. As a consequence, both producers and processors lost a considerable amount of income.

Solutions

Since the anti-middlemen attitude of farmers (and government authorities as well) has negative repercussions upon the market performance of the various agricultural industries, the question which arises next is, What should be done to eliminate this attitude and improve the marketing system?

Certainly you cannot expect that farmers will stop having such an anti-middlemen attitude just by advising or educating them to do so. It seems that the most effective way to convince farmers to change their attitude towards middlemen is to improve the marketing system and benefit them accordingly.

To achieve this, certain measures must be taken, among which are: (1) educate middlemen how to do good business; (2) establish strict laws and regulations for the food distribution system, so that certain unethical tactics cannot be used; (3) organize an efficient agricultural information system which will contribute to improvement of the overall food marketing system; (4) take steps to reduce the marketing risk, so that middlemen can operate on a narrower margin; (5) help organize efficient marketing cooperatives, which will benefit farmers by performing the marketing functions more efficiently and by forcing middlemen to operate their business activities more efficiently; and (6) set certain minimum requirements for entering into the food marketing business, especially in exporting and wholesaling agricultural products.

Obviously, this research does not cover all the problems of middlemen. For this reason, it is worthwhile to continue to seek answers to the following important questions:

1. What marketing services do middlemen offer to the various participants in the marketing system as agricultural products flow from producers to consumers?

2. What is the cost of the marketing services offered at different seasons for each product?

3. How can the marketing cost be minimized through achieving economies of size in various marketing functions, such as processing and advertising; reduction of product deterioration by utilizing properly equipped transpor-

tation modes and other facilities (warehouses, for example); elimination of unnecessary marketing institutions or functions; better organization of the marketing system; greater labour productivity by employing well trained people and placing them in the right job; and use of advanced technology in the marketing process.

4. What are the behavioural characteristics of the middlemen and what are their repercussions upon producers, consumers, and society?

5. What are the options open to farmers in selling their products? Why do they have to deal with brokers?

OPENER'S REMARKS--Henry E. Larzelere

Since an anti-middlemen attitude is almost universal among farmers of both developing and developed countries, we can admit it readily. Whether there is some differentiation in the attitude toward various types of middlemen is more significant. The attitude may be a general concern for what happens between producer and consumer both in price and quality, or it may specifically refer to the individual agencies with which the farmer deals.

Kamenidis' study indicates a predominance of "brokers" under the classification of "middlemen" to whom farmers in Greece referred. Brokers in U.S. parlance function by arranging sales without taking title to or physically handling produce. Unless there is something lost in translation or in individual country custom, brokers are not the middlemen with whom farmers in the United States and numerous other countries have direct contact.

It is important that in universalizing the results of this study we know the functions of different middlemen. Furthermore, in any attempts to improve the performance of the middlemen in the eyes of farmers or others, whether by government agency or others, the target group needs to be specifically identified. Farmers in Greece or elsewhere would likely have varying opinions regarding different types of middlemen. Certainly the opinions of farmers regarding local traders with whom there is frequent contact would be different than opinions regarding an exporter who is seldom if ever known or contacted.

Twelve causes of the anti-middlemen attitude of farmers are listed in Kamenidis' survey. Each is pertinent in individual cases. The causes of farmers' attitudes toward individual middlemen can probably be summarized as resulting from perceived relative bargaining power between the farmer and the middleman. The farmer infrequently takes part in a bargaining exercise, whereas the middleman develops considerable bargaining skill by almost constant practice. Bargaining includes such aspects as opinions of quality and shrewdness in calculating premiums and discounts.

In addition I believe that farmers' attitudes toward middlemen in general are often fueled by politicians seeking scapegoats for low prices to farmers or high prices to consumers.

These attitudes may even go back to the physiocrat philosophy of several centuries ago when only product creators, such as farmers, were productive, and service creators, such as middlemen, were nonproductive. Service is in reality what middlemen create.

Many of the reasons listed by Kamenidis for middlemen behaviour are related to the political and physical situations in the area involved. The middlemen tend to make wider margins as the physical and political situations become more complicated or uncertain.

Middlemen in general tend to have a smaller proportion of their capital investment in fixed assets than is the case of farm production where land is a major asset. Such a situation provides middlemen with more flexibility in

13

changing operations to match the conditions which prevail, and such a situation frequently accentuates the dominance that middlemen may appear to have over the farmers.

Kamenidis listed four types of measures which might make the overall production and marketing system work efficiently. One, establishment of strict laws and regulations regarding the food system warrants some attention, but such a procedure can be overdone. Excessive measures can create the need for more service or paperwork to be performed by nonfarmers with larger margins needed by the middlemen. Two, an efficient and unbiased agricultural information system is highly desirable. Three, steps to reduce marketing risk should mean improvement of general conditions of transportation, storage, and processing. Four, creation of cooperatives is a worthy type of improvement. Adequate education of potential farmer members is essential, especially with the realization that a cooperative must be programmed to perform some or all of the middlemen's functions better and more efficiently than is currently being done, and with the realization that some of the services, costs, and margins of present middlemen cannot be eliminated by a cooperative. Education in management skills to direct the cooperative is a necessity where cooperative formation is contemplated.

RAPPORTEUR'S REPORT--Aloysius C. Nwosu

A major criticism of the paper, which echoed throughout the discussion, was that the paper is biased in favour of farmers; participants argued that the impression is created that the author shares the attitude of the farmers toward the middlemen. Greater objectivity could have been achieved if the author had gained a more balanced picture of the farmer-middleman interaction in the marketing process. This lack of balance not only limits the policy implications of the findings but raises questions about why farmers have continued to sell to middlemen and why other arrangements have not arisen to displace the middlemen.

Many participants stressed the fact that marketing has costs. A study of marketing costs, marketing margins, and profits of middlemen would therefore be required to present a more balanced picture. It was even suggested that the more relevant question should be, How would marketing be affected if middlemen withdrew their services, or if they were replaced entirely by institutions like cooperatives?

Finally, the general thinking seemed to be that there was the need to conduct similar research in other developing countries to augment the author's experience in Greece.

Contributing to the discussion were Glenn T. Magagula, S. Mbogoh Mubyarto, John M. Staatz, and Ken W. Stickland.

SMALL SCALE FARMING AND THE WORLD FOOD PROBLEM: AN APPRAISAL WITH LESSONS FROM NORTHERN NIGERIA

George O. I. Abalu and Brian D'Silva

Shortfalls in food production and increased incidence of malnutrition are both familiar characteristics of many developing countries. While grain supplies have increased on the world level (mostly due to favourable growing conditions and bumper harvests in North America and the Indian subcontinent), large food deficits are still projected for many developing countries (World Bank). It is apparent that food production in developing countries is not keeping pace with demand.

It is now generally accepted that developing countries, if they are permanently to meet their food demands, will have to rely on their soil, their other resources, and their farm economies. Many developing countries, with the assistance of international bodies, are now embarking on various strategies to attain food independence. However, considerable confusion continues as to the most effective way of meeting national food needs. There is still confusion and uncertainty as to whether increased agricultural production should be achieved through a complete overhaul or replacement of existing farming systems or through their modification with the aim of making existing systems function more efficiently.

Efforts to replace existing farming systems have to a large extent laid emphasis on rapid agricultural growth through large scale capital intensive production schemes. The frequent inability of many of these types of schemes to meet growth targets, and the increasing amounts of inequality associated with them, are causing considerable concern (Nkom). At the heart of this concern has been a growing awareness that in the majority of low income countries, even in those displaying the most successful records of growth, strategies of change have failed to meet the most basic objective of economic development—the reduction of poverty (Matlon).

The failure of this rapid growth, or "top down" approach to increasing agricultural development in developing countries (Hardin), has resulted in a rethinking of the appropriate strategy to pursue. Increasing emphasis is now being placed on modifying rather than replacing existing farming systems to meet national food and equity goals. This approach is often referred to as being "bottom up."

In this paper we seek to examine the potential of the "bottom up" approach to increasing agricultural production and to identify obstacles inherent in it. Although the focus of the paper is on technologies currently existing or being introduced in northern Nigeria (a semiarid zone), we hope that the lessons from our analysis will prove useful in other parts of the world.

Farming Systems in Northern Nigeria

The bulk of agricultural production in northern Nigeria is undertaken by small scale farmers. Most of the labour force, management, and capital originate from the household. Output is usually consumed on the farm or traded in local markets. Although the decisionmaking process is hampered by imperfections in marketing and political institutions, there are indications that there are considerable logic and rationale behind the way the small scale farmers live and grow their crops (Abalu and D'Silva).

The existing farming system is, however, incapable of meeting the food requirements of the country. This fact is highlighted by a huge food import bill. Food imports have increased dramatically from nearly 44 million naira in 1963 to over 468 million naira for the first six months of 1977 (Abalu and D'Silva). The need for a workable strategy to increase agricultural production and diminish poverty is therefore very obvious.

Small Scale Improved Technology

A vast amount of improved technologies is already available and being used in many parts of the world. It is now generally accepted that adoption, however technically feasible, often proves to be inappropriate in terms of equity in the distribution of the benefits between households and families.

National planners and international donors are becoming increasingly committed to the idea of "growth with equity." Matlon reports, however, that in spite of this new commitment, efforts to incorporate equity as an operational planning objective have often floundered due to insufficient knowledge of how to design, implement, and measure the attainment of equity oriented policies. In the rest of this paper, we examine the potential of some equity oriented technologies in northern Nigeria and identify the obstacles to implementing them.

Two levels of technology are examined--a traditional level and an improved level involving small scale farmers. Data used in the analysis are based on surveys involving two groups of farmers from villages in the area. Technologies aimed at improving the income and poverty situation of small scale farmers were made available to one group of farmers and not to the other. The difference between the improved and traditional technologies lies in the improved seed variety used, the application of recommended amounts of fertilizer, the adherence to planting specifications, and the timeliness of farm operations.

Without minimizing the well-known limitations of production function analysis, the impact and potential of the improved level of technology is analysed by treating total factor productivity as an index number, and computing it as a shift in the production function. The traditional level of technology is chosen as a base for comparison. Production functions for maize, sorghum, cotton, and groundnuts were estimated using the Cobb-Douglas form. Rates of change from the traditional level of technology were then calculated. (See Abalu for details on the procedures used in the calculation.)

Empirical Results

The average levels of output and inputs under the two levels of technology under consideration are presented in table 1. Ordinary least squares were employed to estimate the production functions. The coefficients appearing in each of the regression equations are given along with their standard errors of estimate in table 2. The corrected square of the coefficient of multiple correlation and the sample size are as given in the table. The rates of change from the traditional level of technology to the improved small scale technology are presented in table 3, together with estimates of output per man-hour that were obtained as a result of the change in technology and the value added net of the change in technology.

The results from table 3 suggest that a "bottom up" approach to increasing agricultural production has good potential in the Nigerian context. Adoption by small scale farmers of these equity oriented technologies implies a rate of technological change of 33 percent for maize and groundnuts, 36 percent for sorghum, and 61 percent for cotton. These figures represent impressive improvements and suggest that there may not necessarily be a conflict between growth and equity in increasing agricultural production in the area.

However, experiences from northern Nigeria suggest that efforts to incorporate

16

Table 1. Average levels of output and inputs under traditional
and improved technology levels

Variable	CROPS							
	Maize		Sorghum		Cotton		Groundnuts	
	Tradi-tional	Impro-ved	Tradi-tional	Impro-ved	Tradi-tional	Impro-ved	Tradi-tional	Impro-ved
Output (kg)	924.87	1201.69	1272.52	1088.21	633.56	1178.11	426.77	1178.11
Capital (ha)	0.40	0.43	2.02	0.81	1.94	1.57	0.49	0.52
Labour (man-hours)	162.63	149.5	316.00	252.32	459.37	648.50	342.50	285.32

a) Land in hectares was used as a proxy for capital due to high
correlation between capital and land.

Table 2. Estimated coefficients of production functions for
improved technology levels

Independent Variable	Crops and Coefficients[a]			
	Maize	Sorghum	Cotton	Groundnuts
Intercept	154.20*** (.36)	16.21** (.51)	7.33** (.19)	10.28** (.48)
Capital	0.04 (.27)	0.57*** (.19)	0.34** (.19)	0.58*** (.11)
Labour	0.41*** (.15)	0.76*** (.21)	0.75** (.15)	0.76*** (.19)
R^2	.12	.44	.64	.67
n	39	43	60	27

Note: Standard errors in parentheses
***Significant at the 1% level; **Significant at the 5% level
*Significant at the 10% level

Table 3. Technological change and labour contribution to output
growth for maize, sorghum, cotton and groundnuts

Crops	Technological Change (%)	Labour Contribu-tion to increased output[a] (kg/man-hour)	Value added net of Technological change[b] (kg/man-hour)
Maize	33	8.03	6.04
Sorghum	36	4.31	3.16
Cotton	61	1.82	1.12
Groundnuts	33	1.84	1.38

a) Average output per man-hour obtained as a result of the shift in the
production function.
b) Corrected value added net of technological change. Estimate represents
increase in output per man-hour attributable to increase in other factors
of production.

the small scale farm sector into this type of strategy have met several obstacles, prominent among which are obstacles with regard to implementation. In the next section, we examine some of these obstacles.

Obstacles to Implementing Improved Small Scale Technologies

The rationality of farmers, at least of those in northern Nigeria, is not in doubt (Abalu and D'Silva). If a suitable technology is developed, if it adds greatly to the yield, and the added yield can return a relatively secure profit beyond the enhanced costs of the new technology, farmers would adopt the technology provided that the following other requirements are met (Hays and Norman):

1. Technical feasibility—the technology must be capable of increasing productivity given the technical elements.

2. Economic feasibility, dependability, and compatibility with the farming system—the technology must be profitable and exhibit a level of risk the farmer can accept as well as have attributes which enable it to fit into the farming system.

3. Social acceptability—the technology must be compatible with community structures, norms, and beliefs.

4. Infrastructure compatibility—the technology must have attributes which can be accommodated by the present level of infrastructure.

The technologies we have described above would appear to meet the first two requirements. However, efforts to implement them have floundered in the past because national planners and donor agencies have had insufficient knowledge about the operation of community structures, norms, and beliefs, and have been unable to provide adequate infrastructural support systems.

These community structures play a crucial role in the succcess of equity related technological change. Northern Nigeria has a strong hierachical and stratified community structure dominated by a few local officials responsible to traditional rulers. Consequently, the success or failure of equity related development will depend to a large extent on how successfully the effort performs within existing social strucutres. The difficulties in working within existing structures are often so great that many agricultural planners and donor agencies have, by default, gradually but conspicuously moved their emphasis away from equity and toward growth. For example, initial attempts to achieve both equity and growth in an agricultural development project in northern Nigeria have ended up concentrating most effort on "progressive farmers," since it is not the project's responsibility "to start social revolutions" (Huizinga).

The second obstacle to successful implementation of equity oriented technologies has to do with the provision of adequate infrastructural support systems. Even if the technologies were technically and economically feasible, difficulties of implementation would arise unless a set of infrastructures compatible with the technologies evolved. The infrastructures in the area have failed to provide adequate support for the technologies being developed. The quality of market channels is still hampered by lack of timely information, lack of grading and standardization of agricultural products, lack of storage facilities, and poor communication. Extension efforts have largely been imported versions of successful efforts created elesewhere to provide answers to problems and aspirations of farmers who already had access to land, social status, and political and economic power. In northern Nigeria, where the average farmer does not live much above a culturally determined subsistence level and has little economic and political power, the end result has not been very promising (Abalu and D'Silva).

Farmers will also be encouraged to adopt a new technology if they are reassured that they will receive the necessary new inputs at the right places and the right times, and if the financial resources they need to pay for the improved technology are available when they need them. Recent studies in northern Nigeria indicate that there are major problems inherent in the input distribution systems, prominent among which are problems of procurement and equitable distribution (Huizinga). Inadequacies in all these infrastructural elements have contributed to the failure of even well-meaning equity related agricultural projects.

Conclusion

In this paper we have attempted to examine the feasibility of rapidly increasing agricultural production in northern Nigeria through the small scale farm sector. Our analysis suggests that equity related technologies have good potential for increasing food production in the area even if they are "bottom up" in their structure. There are, however, many constraints to this "bottom up" strategy, the most serious of which appear to be those related to social and infrastructural compatibility. These constraints would need to be removed if equity related development projects in the area are to be able to achieve their welfare objectives.

References

Abalu, G. O. I. (1977) Relevant technology and agricultural development: Some experiences from northern Nigeria. Zaria, Nigeria; Department of Agricultural Economics, Ahmadu Bello University, unpublished paper.

Abalu, G. O. I.; D'Silva, B. (1979) Socio-economic aspects of semi-arid tropical regions of Nigeria. Paper presented at the Workshop on Socio-Economic Constraints to Development of Semi-Arid Tropical Agriculture, ICRISAT, India, February 19-23, 1979.

Hardin, L. S. (1977) Discussion: Social science and related implications. American Journal of Agricultural Economics, 59, 853-854.

Hays, H. M.; Norman, D. W. (1978) Developing suitable technology for small farmers. Lindsborg, Kansas, U.S.A.; Department of Economics, Bethany College, mimeograph paper.

Huizinga, B. (1979) The guided change project: An experiment in small farmer development administration amongst the Hausa of Nigeria. Zaria, Nigeria; Department of Agricultural Economics, Ahmadu Bello University, unpublished paper.

Matlon, P. J. (1977) The size distribution, structure, and determinants of personal income among farmers in the north of Nigeria. Ithaca, New York, U.S.A.; Cornell University, unpublished Ph.D. dissertation.

Nkom, S. A. (1978) Bureaucracy, class formation, and rural development: A critique of rural development programmes in Nigeria. Paper presented at the Social Science Seminar, Ahmadu Bello University, Zaria, Nigeria.

World Bank (1977) Developing country foodgrain projections for 1985. Washington, D.C., U.S.A.; World Bank Staff Working Paper No. 247.

Abalu and D'Silva present evidence to illustrate the gains in productivity and equity to be expected from introducing simple technological changes within the reach of the small scale farmer. They show that by using timely planting, improved seeds, and fertilizer, a small scale farmer can substantially raise the output of various crops. It is then suggested that if thousands of small scale farmers employ these simple technical changes, they can produce substantial food surpluses which will not only help alleviate the world food problem, but will also help reduce inequities in income distribution. This proposition sounds very appealing and plausible, but the authors themselves immediately start complaining about the problems involved in the implementation of the programme.

While I agree with their submission, it does not go far enough. We are all witnesses to the dramatic performance of the small scale cocoa farmers in Nigeria and Ghana and the groundnut producers in Senegal and Nigeria. Why have the successes of the midfifties eluded our food producing farmers in the seventies? I suggest as reasons: the neglect of the farmers by policy makers who preferred to hold down domestic food prices; the lack of incentive for farmers to stay and work hard on farms when apparently less effort in urban areas yielded what appeared to be better standards of living; the progressive decline in the number of farm labourers; and the lack of capacity on the part of the farmers to plan and manage large scale farms. In their anxiety to satisfy the wishes of the politically articulate urban pressure groups, policy makers opted for large scale state owned farms that were badly managed with woeful results. They compounded the problems by allowing imports of food crops like rice and maize to compete with local production. Thus rather than improve the rural infrastructure, Nigeria spent huge sums on food imports to alleviate the suffering of the city consumers. It has been very difficult to assure farmers a reasonable share of the economic boom in the country and the younger ones have deserted the countryside.

There is no doubt that marginal improvements by thousands of small farmers will greatly increase the country's total output. But attention must be focused on the difficulties in assembling, processing, and distributing the increased output, and on ensuring that the producer receive a fair share of the consumer's dollar. Persistent inefficiency in this area will continue to result in failure to meet the food needs of large concentrations of urban populations and in recourse to imports to bridge the gap, assuming that other countries, notably developed countries, will continue to have the exportable surpluses, that developing countries can pay for them, and that food is not used as a political weapon. In addition, technological change which requires more labour appears doomed to fail in the Nigerian context as the hard core of devoted farmers declines rapidly. The rural to urban drift and the dislike of drudgery are much in evidence. Even if yields and total production increase, can the increases be handled advantageously?

My suggestion is that more farmer cooperatives be established so that farmers can (1) develop the countervailing power needed against the exploitative middlemen, and (2) form powerful lobby groups to influence government decisions. In this way farmers can obtain higher income and greater equity in income distribution. The farming population must no longer leave its fate in the hands of urban based politicans, but must participate to get what it needs. Do the small farmers merely want to subsist? Or are they more interested in the good things available to urban dwellers? If the latter is the case, would it be fair to continue holding down farm prices? It is of great importance that agricultural economists work to ensure that farmers participate in shaping their own future.

RAPPORTEUR'S REPORT--Karl T. Wright

Increased management complexities follow the introduction of tractors to small scale farmers. New sets of decisions have to be made on inputs, harvesting, marketing of surplus, and maintenance of tractors. The small farmer may not have adequate management capacity for new tractor efficiency. Tractors must be introduced selectively only by those who can use them profitably. In developing countries, cars have been serviced adequately, but tractors have not, because terms of trade do not favour farmers; that is, they can not adequately pay for service. The motor industry has shown the way, but without improving the terms of trade, mechanization will not appeal to small farmers. The implementation of mechanization brings problems of improved seeds, improved planting methods, and management. Importation of rice and maize, farmers leaving the land, and the needs of cooperatives are additional problems. To subsist or improve must be the farmer's decision.

We need to think of food problems of urban as well as rural people and whether the excess of food over consumption is affected by new technology changes. Rice self-sufficiency changed the technological problem of maize and millet. Work is currently being done on the increased output of food provided by new technology.

Livestock should be brought into the studies because of the complexities and advantages of integrating crop and livestock production and the effect that livestock production has on the distribution of income. In Nigeria, livestock is produced by nomads, crops by farmers. Bringing these two groups together appears to be a good idea, but the difficulties are many. In Libya, it is difficult to improve the small farmer in desert areas if the big problem is machinery use and lack of knowledge. It may not be possible to generalize the lessons from Nigeria to other countries.

Contributing to the discussion were Puran C. Bausil, Judith Heyer, and John R. Raeburn.

THE PROBLEMS AND STRATEGIES OF RURAL DEVELOPMENT IN HILLS WITH SPECIAL REFERENCE TO NEPAL

Ramesh Chandra Agrawal

Abstract

Hills are important to the economy of Nepal, but have been at a disadvantage with regard to infrastructure, supply of fertilizer, credit, and seed. This has already increased the disparity between the hills and the plains. Smaller size of highly fragmented holdings, lower productivity, lower level of education and extension, cultivation of marginal lands, soil erosion, lack of alternative sources of employment in villages and consequent migration, and limited quantities of marketable surplus are all responsible for the vicious circle of lower levels of farm incomes, limiting the capability of the small hill farmer to reinvest or buy new inputs.

Agriculture alone can not sustain the rural economy in hills where development has to be a continuous and long term process, and the basic approach to which has to be an integrated one. This integration must be sectoral, spatial, and temporal. Rural change in hills has to encompass agriculture, horticulture, livestock, forestry, agro-based industries, necessary infrastructure, social services, and even tourism. These efforts must be supplemented with special programmes designed to help small farmers, rural poor, and women so that the benefits of development are shared by the whole rural populace. The paper points out some areas where agricultural economists can make a very useful contribution.

OPENER'S REMARKS—Geoffrey G. Antrobus

Agrawal gives a very clear view of physiographic and socioeconomic characteristics of rural Nepal. The problems faced by small farmers in the hill areas are similarly clearly spelt out. The consequences and reasons for the proposed strategies of rural development are, however, less clear. To what extent can the inhabitants of the hills expect to receive a larger share of government revenue, credit facilities, and education and extension services, given the very limited total resources of Nepal? If the hill area is treated "more equally," as is suggested, by how much would the present situation improve in the light of the reported overpopulation and low and declining crop yields, and how receptive is the hill farmer to extension advice?

Considering the proposed development strategy for the hills--the improvement of existing enterprises and practices, the introduction of new crops, varieties and inputs after field evaluation, and the preparation of "model farm plans" in isolated pockets--on what basis should hill farmers, as opposed to other farmers in Nepal, be given credit "on a priority basis on special terms"? In the light of the plea made in the paper that hill farmers of Nepal need special treatment, is the message relevant only to the situation in Nepal or is it applicable to other developing countries as well? And can a generalized theory be hypothesized for hill areas in developing countries in terms of a strategy for development?

RAPPORTEUR'S REPORT--Karl T. Wright

The hill farmer is rational within the constraints of his resources, information, social conditions, transportation, and communication. He is receptive to extension advice given in due regard to these constraints. Deforestation has been reckless in the hills. We cannot exclude forestry and forest based industries from a long term strategy of rural development in the hills. Land productivity is higher and labour productivity is lower in the hills than on the plains. Intensified land use exists on some lands with minor changes in cropping practices, but caution is needed for ecology and conservation. Intensified land use is also dependent on the availability of irrigation, inputs, and extension services. The farming is chiefly done by women. Men migrate to off-farm work, coming back to the villages for ploughing and sale of produce. Off-farm cash income is higher than farm cash income for all classes of hill farmers. The strategy of better treatment in receiving credit, when funds are limited, should be secondary to maximizing the net returns of the available funds. Development of agriculture alone is not enough to make small farms viable. It is therefore vital that cottage industries also be developed.

Contributing to the discussion were Donald S. Ferguson, Tirath R. Gupta, Ryohei Kada, Rajan Kasturi Sampath, and Garland P. Wood.

POTENTIAL PRODUCTIVITY OF MODERN RICE TECHNOLOGY AND REASONS FOR LOW PRODUCTIVITY ON ASIAN RICE FARMS

Robert W. Herdt

Abstract

Results of a collaborative project involving over 28 agronomists and economists are reported. Over 800 agronomic experiments conducted in ten locations in six Asian countries comparing farmers' production with maximum yield levels of modern rice technology are analysed. Under wet season conditions, yields were raised by an average of 0.9 tonnes per hectare, but the cost of obtaining the increased yields exceeded their value in six out of ten locations. Under dry season conditions, yields were increased by an average of 1.3 tonnes per hectare, and were profitable in nine out of ten locations. High levels of fertilizer and insect control contributed roughly equally to raising the yields, but the increased cost of high insect control exceeded the value of its yield contribution in most cases. The opposite was generally true for fertilizer. One result has been that rice entomologists have reoriented their research to try and achieve more cost effective protection. There was a distinct negative correlation between the increased yield obtained by adding fertilizer above the farmers' levels and the price of fertilizer in terms of rice, dramatizing how price policies affect incentives.

OPENER'S REMARKS--Morag C. Simpson

Discussion of this paper could logically centre around the validity of the findings and their policy implications. Neither time nor the available information allows a discussion of the validity of the findings. Results drawn from a very wide sample raise the question whether all other things were equal. The samples cover two seasons in each of three years and came from six different countries, each presumably with different taxation, government support services, and market situations.

To simplify the situation, let us assume that the results are valid and that the broad picture is that there is a gap of around one tonne of rice per hectare between what farmers actually got and what they could have got if they had used available additional inputs (mainly fertilizers, insecticides and herbicides).

Why did they not use these inputs? Because at existing ratios of input to output prices, it did not pay them to do so. In that these inputs have a large petrochemical component, then if it does not pay farmers to use them now, they will be highly unlikely to do so in the future. Hence the gap will remain unless new farming practices are adopted which rely on renewable natural resources.

Farmers are notorious for being weak sellers and buyers and thus are adversely hit by imperfection in the marketing systems for inputs and outputs, and also tend to bear a higher than intended incidence of taxation. Hence, if it is thought desirable to narrow the yield gap, some attention could profitably be given to marketing and taxation policies.

No generalizations have been made from this study, which is defined only as yield research to find what farmers did and what they could have done. It does not now pay to use high levels of inputs, whether fertilizer or labour, and will not pay later. Inputs and outputs depend to a large extent on government policies.

This study in technical and economic efficiency and social strategy is a good example of the systems approach. The methodological problem of Herdt's partial approach is that it has not reflected true relationships. Why not use a simulation model where yield gaps, levels of input utilization, product prices, input prices, and other relevant factors are all brought in? It would be interesting to observe the nature of relationships that would then emerge between yield and relative prices from a complete model as against the positive zero order relationships which Herdt has implied in his paper.

The meaning of potential productivity is not clear. Productivity is more concerned with attitude and quality of farming population than with policy measures and extension activities.

Contributing to the discussion were Takeo Misawa, David Norman, Mario Jose Ponce, and R. Thamarajakshi.

THE EGYPTIAN FARM MANAGEMENT SURVEY:
AN APPROACH TO UNDERSTANDING A
COMPLEX AGRICULTURAL SYSTEM

Ahmed A. Goueli and Mohammed Kamel Hindi

Abstract

This paper reports on the Egyptian farm management survey which covers some 822 farmers selected from 56 villages scattered throughout the main old lands farming area of the country. The Egyptian experience is of interest to other countries which, like Egypt, seek to expand or update their data base on farmer practices and cost structure. The survey took a year to conduct and involved a large group of agricultural economists. Results were used to analyse a variety of relevant issues including those pertaining to prices, incomes, and mechanization policies. A number of lessons of interest to other countries were learned, including valuable experience with the FAO farm management data collection and analysis system.

SUBJECTIVE PRODUCTION FUNCTION PARAMETERS AND RISK: WHEAT PRODUCTION IN TUNISIA

Terry L. Roe and David Nygaard

Abstract

At the time of seed bed preparation for the production of durum wheat, Tunisian farmers form subjective estimates of the parameters of the underlying production function. If their estimates are not accurate, resources are not optimally allocated. If farmers behave as though their estimates are not known with certainty, they face risk. Based on a survey of 125 Tunisian farmers, the parameters of the underlying production function and farmers' subjective estimates of these parameters are estimated. The level of farmers' risk aversion is also estimated. The results suggest that at the time of seed bed preparation, Tunisian farmers overestimated the yield they would obtain at harvest, but that the cause of this overestimation was unusually low rainfall. Otherwise, farmers apppeared correctly to perceive the true parameters. Years of experience are found to affect farmers' subjective estimates. The results also suggest that about 80 percent of the farmers in the sample are risk averse and discount the market price for durum wheat of 7.1 dinars by a sample average of 2.7 dinars per quintal. The method used in the study is unique and appears to be a reasonable approach to measure and identify the cause of allocative errors, risk, and the value of information to farmers which results in more accurate subjective estimates of the parameters of the true underlying technology.

OPENER'S REMARKS—R. J. McConnen

The price assumption of Roe and Nygaard may be realistic for Tunisian wheat, but their methodology is poor. Some heroic assumptions are employed to estimate a risk discount factor. Some of these assumptions cannot be tested and I understand this. However, alternative checks—even if they are not rigorous—should be run on the estimated risk discount factor. If Roe and Nygaard can measure allocative errors, then it is possible to consider the costs and benefits of policies which could decrease them.

I am not surprised that 80 percent of the farmers are risk averse. I am surprised that 20 percent are not. I am surprised that education turns out to be a significant variable in estimating the subjective production function. But has the technology—high yielding varieties of durum wheat—become, in fact, a traditional technology variety in Tunisia? What would happen if the technology were really new? What if the production function were more complex, involving multicrop irrigated areas? What would happen if we look at farming systems and not merely a single commodity? What do the results have to say with regard to policy variables?

PROBLEMS AND PROSPECTS OF SMALL FARMERS
AND LANDLESS IN INDIA

I. J. Singh and U. K. Pandey

Abstract

Small farmers and the landless are faced with the vicious cycle of low or negative incomes, low investment, and uneconomic size of farm holdings. Discriminant analysis indicates that the area in high yielding crop varieties, and per acre fertilizer use are the major factors affecting the viability of small farmers. India's Small Farmer's Development Agency has significantly increased the viability of small farmers. Through resource reallocation and by providing credit facilities, small farmers and landless may be made viable in the developing countries. International financing agencies such as the World Bank have, therefore, a major role to play in improving the lot of small farmers and the landless in the developing countries, particularly in Southeast Asia.

OPENER'S REMARKS—A. S. Kahlon

[As summarized by the rapporteur.]

The paper is not applicable to all of India. The small farmer definition is one of the major contributions of the paper. As for the creation of special small farmer institutions as a solution to the small farmer problem, this is not consistent with experience. Rather, there is a need for more general economic development.

In relation to the importance of credit, there is a need for technological inputs to be considered. Synthetic farm plans are not applicable as a generalization for small farmers, even within a region, due to the varying degrees of resource imbalances. On a worldwide basis, production is not the most difficult task; marketing is essential and more difficult. The need for marketing infrastructure is a serious omission in the paper.

I propose an integrated strategy with at least the following elements: (1) credit to the person who works the land, not to the land owner; and (2) improvement of the extension programmes by means of with a system of rewards to those who work with small farms.

RAPPORTEUR'S REPORT—Carlos A. Zelaya

Concern was expressed about scepticism over the future of small farmers. One of the problems is to whom the credit goes. There is a need for change in the power structure.

The authors need to define more clearly who the small farmer is. The owner operator? The share cropper? Policy depends on that definition.

The authors need to look into differentiated planning for small farms. The socialist option is always open.

Farmers' service societies present a solution to the supply of credit, inputs, and marketing services.

Contributing to the discussion were Mahmood Hasan Khan, J. S. Sarma, Wolfgang M. Schultz, and Rudolf Sinaga.

AGRARIAN POLICY TOWARDS PRIVATE AGRICULTURAL HOLDINGS AND THE ASSOCIATION OF PRIVATE PRODUCERS WITH THE SOCIAL SECTOR IN AGRICULTURE

Dusan Tomic

Socialist Yugoslavia has chosen industrialization as the basic pattern of economic development. This orientation has been given a vigorous impetus by the development of socialist self-management socioeconomic relations based on social ownership of the means of production.

Development and Structure of the Private Sector in Agriculture

Accelerated industrialization and increasing demand for food have contributed to a continuous growth of agricultural production as well as enormous structural changes. The private sector has undergone complex socioeconomic change within the general development of Yugoslavia's agriculture. In the 1962-1976 period, the private sector's agricultural production increased 2.0 percent per year while agricultural production in the social sector increased 6.5 percent per year. In 1977, the private sector accounted for 75 percent of the agricultural production and 53 percent of purchases of agricultural products, used 80 percent of total arable land, and owned 89 percent of the cattle weighing over 500 kilograms. That sector's share of income and commodity production, which was considerably lower than its production potential, indicates the extensive and low productive character of private agricultural production in Yugoslavia.

The proportion of agricultural population to the total population decreased from 67 percent in 1948 to about 31 percent in 1977. The process of the social division of labour is still not completed, and I envisage a further decrease in the total agricultural population.

The structure of private, small sized agricultural holdings constitutes one of the main obstacles to the development of agricultural production. The total number of private holdings in Yugoslavia is declining. Private holdings having 5 hectares or more account for 75 percent of all private holdings, but own only 41 percent of the land. The average size of a private holding is 3.8 hectares of arable land, but each holding has an average of eight parcels.

Along with the economic development and qualitative changes in the economic and social structure of the population, the process of diversification among holdings has rapidly developed so that one notices an increased number of holdings acquiring a mixed character. Mixed private holdings already make up about 59 percent of all private holdings. In 1976, income earned through work outside the holding already made up 70 percent of total income.

Goals of a Socialist Transformation

The basic goal of the socialist transformation of agriculture and the village consists of turning private, small sized agriculture into intensive and productive, socially organized agricultural production by means of the pooling of labour and other inputs on the basis of self-management and income relations.

The essence of the process of turning private labour into social labour in Yugoslav agriculture consists of: (1) the formation of large scale production as the basis of modern technological progress and modern organization of work; (2) overcoming the structure of small sized private holdings without violating private ownership of land; (3) asociated private producers enjoying status which makes it possible for them to manage agricultural production and carry out the distribution of joint income, depending on the labour and resources they invested in production; (4) a vertical integration of associated private producers with the processing, distribution, and consumption of agricultural and food products; and (5) associated private producers earning more income, increasing their standard of living, and improving their economic and social status.

The process of socialist transformation of agriculture must be neither coercive nor achieved by means of administrative measures, but should develop gradually under the principle of respecting private producers' free will and independence when making decisions on the pooling of labour and other inputs.

Agrarian Policy with Regard to Private Holdings

A more efficacious use of private holdings' production potential constitutes an essential component of increased agricultural production. Such a policy's point of departure is that a fuller and higher engagement of private producers' production potential saves social investment, makes possible fuller employment of the rural work force, increases income, and incorporates the agricultural population in the self-management and social mechanism.

Agrarian policy has a complex effect on the strategy of agricultural production's improvement and rise. Its measures and instruments are based on a uniform socioeconomic system and development of self-management production relations with the aim of creating conditions for increased labour productivity and ensuring an equal footing for workers in the social sector and associated farmers in the creation and earning of income.

National agrarian policy defines the common bases and directions of investment policy and the sources of resources to be used for financing enlarged production, as well as the mode of foreign credit distribution. Terms and measures with regard to the use of resources of private producers for investment are separately defined. Favourable terms of credit provisions exist for certain forms of investment.

The policy of agricultural and food product prices is based on the principle of ensuring their being formed freely on the basis of the operation of market laws and social contracts, and self-management agreements on prices. With the aim of assuring stability of production and consumption of food, social control of prices is exercised for wheat, maize, sunflowers, sugarbeets, tobacco, cotton, wool, fresh meat, and livestock for slaughter. Producer and retail prices are defined for those products.

Policy for the functioning of the agricultural product and food markets starts from social plans, food supply to demand ratios, and the fixed national annual commodity balances. It is oriented in four directions: (1) long term contracts of production and placement; (2) strengthening of the function of commodity reserves; (3) building up of technical equipment of the market; and (4) improvement of the organization of purchase and placement of agricultural products, from private producers in particular.

With the aim of assuring an undisturbed development of production and distribution of food, credit policy is applied to overall socially organized agricultural production and stocks of all agricultural products, the prices of which are socially controlled.

The development and working out of the general principles and measures of national agrarian policy is done in the republics and autonomous provinces because it is there where the actual production, eocnomic, and social problems of the development of the private sector in agriculture are being resolved. This means that agrarian policy with regard to private holdings bears the traits of a regional character.

Agrarian policy towards private holdings is characterized by numerous measures, conditions, and forms, the purpose of which is to stimulate the development and association of the private sector's agricultural production. An analysis of the degree of development as well as of the characteristics of the measures and instruments points out the significance of the directions of the agrarian policy's operation at the regional level.

The process of the transformation of private ownership into social ownership is characterized by numerous transient forms of the formation of large productive units suitable for the development of modern agricultural production. Private ownership of land does not create special obstacles to the process of transformation for two reasons: (1) in the plains area, private tenure is limited to 10 hectares of arable land, while in the hilly, mountainous regions, the limit is 20 hectares of land; and (2) the process of removing private holdings from agricultural production results in insufficient use of land. That is why numerous measures have been undertaken, such as land reclamation, redistribution of fields, irrigation, grouping of land in large complexes for the sake of modern cultivation, lowering input costs, and higher taxation of nonagricultural owners of land.

In all the regions, a policy of socially controlled retail prices of agricultural products is pursued. If these retail prices are lower than the producer prices to protect the population's standard of living, then compensation is given to producers. Corresponding measures are undertaken and premiums given to give impetus, on private holdings, to the production of milk, use of quality seeds and plants, and improvement of purebred livestock. The policy of giving credit to private holdings through social organizations is directed to a better use of production capacities, development of joint production, specialization of production, and joint investment.

To improve and increase production, tax policy offers a number of facilities to private producers, such as a changed use of land, specialization of production, exemption from the payment of taxes for new seedlings, improved treatment where labour and other inputs are pooled, and differentiated taxation in the turnover of land. Special attention is paid to the improvement of the system of training of private producers, in particular young agriculturists. Social security for private producers is an important element of agrarian policy. The inclusion of private producers in the health, disability, and pension insurance system is solved through the gaining of increased income and association in agriculture. Aging households attain the right to a pension by giving their land to the social sector.

Agrarian policy's intention is that every agricultural region and village should form social agricultural organizations which will try not only to assist the improvement of agricultural production and the pooling of labour and inputs of private holdings, but also to associate private producers with the processing, distribution, marketing, and consumption of food. On the basis of the concept of the long term development of agriculture, development programmes are prepared, by regions, for associating private holdings with socially organized agricultural production, taking account of the various types of private holdings, as well as for the sake of improving living conditions in the village.

The long term policy of economic development has increasingly been oriented towards the industrialization of rural areas. The dispersion of industry, the building up of infrastructure, the development of services, the spread of the network of projects for accepting, stocking, and distribution of agricultural products will vigorously stimulate private producers to pool their labour and inputs on the basis of joint production and joint gaining of income.

The association of private agricultural producers with the social sector on a self-management basis is a strategic question of the future development of the agroindustrial complex. The setting up of integrational links within an agroindustrial complex is a historical process, characteristic of all the developed countries. This historical process has developed through various organizational forms which are characterized by a particular economic content depending on the socioeconomic system.

In Yugoslavia, the farmers' association has a long tradition. It has particularly developed in the post-war period through various forms of association between agricultural cooperatives and private agricultural producers. Cooperation in production has constituted the essence of all these various forms of integration and improvment of agricultural production on private holdings. Along with the development of productive forces and the food market, cooperation in production has gradually lagged behind because it has developed on a short term basis, and upon sales relations, so that it has not assured stability in production.

An accelerated development of productive forces and of the demand for food create conditions for a more rapid activation of production potential and private producers' incorporation into the social division of labour through pooling labour and inputs. Such a pooling creates conditions for a gradual integration of individual labour and inputs into associated labour with socially owned means of production.

Theoretically viewed, the economic essence of associated labour and inputs is the creation of more income for all the associated subjects, and participation, on an equal footing, in management of production and the formation and distribution of income, depending on invested labour and inputs.

The model of pooling labour and inputs on a self-management basis and income relations makes possible a concentration of social resources and a social organization of agricultural production and income gained in agriculture, incorporation of private agricultural producers in the uniform self-management sociopolitical system, and a vertical integration of primary agricultural production with the other sectors of an agroindustrial complex.

RAPPORTEUR'S REPORT--Carlos A. Zelaya

There is far more government involvement in agriculture in Yugoslavia than in North America. Within the so-called agroindustrial complex, there is a need for a better definition of the role of self-management and the implications and meaning of proper regulation of socioeconomic relations within the social sector.

There is a potential conflict in resource use, especially in relation to urban and industrial use of agricultural land. Since World War II, yearly per capita income has increased from U.S.$129 to U.S.$2,000, with structural changes in all fields of life. While in the first phase of this development, rural to urban migration was encouraged by industrialization policies, now the policy is to intensify the industrialization of rural areas in order to balance conditions betwen the rural and the urban areas and thus keep the population in rural areas. As a policy objective, pricing of agricultural commodities should be accomplished through a free market (without distortions). However, there are guaranteed prices for certain commodities in order to insure an income to the producer and to protect the consumers' standard of living.

The objective of Yugoslav policy is to create a socialist society with democratic participation. Therefore, both private sector farmers and social sector farmers are free to manage their operations, and that includes associations between the two sectors through their own arrangements. Fifty percent of the individual farmers cooperate with the social sector in input supply and product marketing, while 10 percent have gone as far as pooling resources and cooperating in joint production.

Contributing to the discussion were A. S. Kahlon, Hiroyuki Nishimura, Kenneth H. Parsons, and William E. Phillips.

THE EVER PRESENT PROBLEM OF DETERMINING
OPTIMUM FARM SIZE

Jacques Brossier

Abstract

Do economies of size actually exist? What has been learnt by the experience of socialist countries? Following a recap of the basic problem of determining economies of size (facts and theories), new light is shed from analysis of concentration in some socialist countries. Did concentration in Bulgaria and in Cuba allow a rapid growth of agricultural production? Did concentration disregard the existence of economies of size? What conclusions can be drawn for the future of the family farms in western countries? The analysis is based on the construction of a linear program model for a large dairy farm in Cuba. For cereal, milk, and cattle production, the author does not observe technical economies of size. But socialist concentration which is neither a complete failure nor a complete success can be coherent with respect to the historical situations (external economies) and to the social objectives (equalization of the conditions). It is possible that private ownership of land constitutes an obstacle to the appearance of slight economies of size in western countries. Furthermore, family farms produce at less cost than the capitalist farms because the political, social, and economical situations oblige the farmers to accept underremuneration for the factors furnished by the family (capital and labour). Following the increasing role of family farms in nonsocialist agricultural production, the author concludes with a plea for a real economic analysis of family production. What does the family mean to the economy? Perhaps we must develop new methods of analysing these family but diversified farms.

OPENER'S REMARKS--Ivan Oros

Concentration in the family farms and the large scale holdings of the socialist countries is an irreversible process, but increasing size of the holding is neither self-contained nor a dogmatic process pressed by the government. Thus in Hungary, for instance, concentration is hampered by agricultural policy. The main goal of the industrylike concentration consists in the realization of an industrylike production pattern in agriculture and the abolition of differences between village and town, and between industrial and peasant work.

I think it is more correct to speak about the optimal size of a production line than about the optimal size of a holding in general. Modern technology and equipment define the optimal size of a production line (for example, sown area of a crop) rather than the size of the entire holding. In concentrated holdings, overhead costs are smaller. By means of machinery of higher performance, if the holding has a satisfactorily large area at its disposal, agricultural work can be carried on with higher productivity and profit than on a smaller plot. In the large scale holdings of the socialist countries, the aforementioned possibilities are generally available and there is a chance to carry on specialized productive activity as well as to adjust farm size to technical endowments.

The scale or structure of the holding was of greater importance in agricultural economics in the past when production lines were superimposed on each other within the holding. Today, in the era of increasing specialization, the question of the scale has lesser importance, and can by no means be considered any more as a decisive factor in determining the size of several production lines.

AN ANALYSIS OF THE DYNAMICS OF
TECHNOLOGICAL CHANGE IN AGRICULTURE

Yoav Kislev

Technological improvements are generally conceived in economics as identical increases in productivity for all producers. Reality is more complicated--the diffusion of new technologies is generally associated with differential changes in the scale of production, with entry into promising new lines of activity, and in the exit of producers who cannot keep up with the technological pace and are forced out by deteriorating terms of trade. These are the economic processes that revolutionize the technological and social structure of the rural communities in the process of development. This paper outlines a few assumptions and findings of a theory of structural change associated with technological improvement and illustrates it with developments in the dairy and the poultry industries in Israel.

Theoretical Outline

The theory is presented in terms of the dairy industry. Equation (1) defines the density of cow distribution:

(1) $n(m,t) = N(m,t)/N^*(t)$,

where:

m $(0 \leq m \leq 1)$ is the index of the level of management of the dairy operation;

$N(m,t)$ is the number of cows in year t in herds of management level m;

$N^*(t)$ is the total number of cows in the country; and

$n(m,t)$ $(0 \leq n \leq 1)$ is the density of cow distribution by management level.

Let milk yield y be a function of the genetic level of the herd $G(t)$ (both measured in kilograms of milk per cow per year) and management level m:

(2) $y(m,t) = mG(t)$.

In Israel, all cows are bred by artificial insemination. It is therefore reasonable to assume that the genetic potential of all herds is the same. Cows differ in their genotypes, but these differences wash out at the herd averages. Actual, realized yield differences stem from differences in operator management abilities. The industry's milk supply will, therefore, be:

$$(3) \quad Q(t) = \int_0^1 y(m,t)N(m,t)dm$$
$$= G(t)N^*(t)\int_0^1 n(m,t)mdm$$
$$= G(t)N^*(t)E(m,t).$$

$E(m,t)$ is the country average management level (the average weighted by the distribution of cows by management levels.)

Income of the better farmers—those with higher management abilities—will be higher and they will tend to expand their operations; the worst farmers are will lose and have to exit. These developments will be reflected in the factor determining supply expansion, which can be seen by differentiating the second line in equation (3):

$$(4) \quad \dot{Q} = \dot{N} * \int_0^1 G(t)n(m,t)mdm \qquad \text{[expansion effect]}$$

$$+ \ G(t)N * \int_0^1 n(m,t)mdm \qquad \text{[genetic effect]}$$

$$+ \ G(t)N * \int_0^1 \dot{n}(m,t)mdm \qquad \text{[concentration effect]}.$$

The expansion effect is the increase in supply resulting from a change in the size of the national herd, leaving constant the genetic level and the distribution of cows by management level. The genetic effect is the increase in production due to genetic improvement, holding constant the size and the distribution of the herd. The concentration effect is the increase in milk production due to the shift of the production between operators of different management levels. Empirical estimates of equation (4) are presented in the next section.

Empirical Illustration

Concentration of producers is affected by the terms of trade, defined here as the ratio of the price of the product to the price of feed concentrate. Another factor which is important in determining the dynamics of the industry is the proportion of purchased inputs in total cost; this last proportion is termed the selection stress. The tighter the selection stress, the stronger the financial effect of a change in the terms of trade and the faster the adjustment process to this change. (Government intervention in the credit market--prevalent in Israel--mitigates these effects and modifies the dynamics of the industry.)

Table 1 reports the terms of trade and the selection stress in eggs, broilers, and milk production and their changes between two years—1967 and 1972. Terms of trade stayed constant in egg production, deteriorated substantially in the production of broilers, and changed slightly in the milk industry. The selection stress is the tightest in broilers; eggs are second, and milk is last.

Figures 1, 2 and 3 depict the cumulative distributions of production by efficiency levels for the years 1967 and 1972 (1971 for milk production). Efficiency, a measure of the level of management, has been defined in the dairy industry as annual yield per cow, and for the poultry industry as the number of eggs per tonne of feed (with meat from the egg production flocks converted into eggs at the rate of 1 kilogram of meat equal to 20 eggs), or the numbers of tonnes of meat per tonne of feed in broiler production. These definitions are justified by the assumption of constant marginal product to feed ratios and constant fixed costs.

Figure 1 indicates exit of the lower tail of the distribution between 1967 and 1971 (compare the broken line to the solid line) and improvement in yields in the upper tail. Average yield rose over that period from 5,039 to 5,312 kilograms per cow per annum. Though potential genetic improvement is the same in all herds, it is only the better producers that realize yield increases. The relatively low selection stress and the just slight deterioration in the term of trade (due in part at least to government intervention) permitted many of the weaker dairy operators to stay in the industry—the graphs for 1967 and 1971 coincide in the moderate efficiency zone.

35

Table 1: The Terms of Trade and the Selection Stress.

Product	Unit	Terms of Trade (Ratio of the price of 1 unit of the product to 1 kilogram of concentrates)		Terms of Trade in 1972[a]	Selection Stress (Ratio of outlays on purchased inputs to value of product)[b]	
		1967	1972		1967	1972
Eggs	egg	.368	.368	1.00	.68	.77
Broilers	kg	6.69	5.75	.86	.77	.80
Milk	kg	1.478	1.433	.97	.67	.68

a 1967 - 1.00
b at the sample mean

Source: Institute of Farm Income Research, Tel Aviv.

Table 2: Components of Supply Increments.

	Milk	Broilers	Eggs
Period	1960-74	1967-75	1967-75
Production increment [a](%)	110	170	36
Partition of increment [b](%)			
Total	100	100	100
Expansion	73.5	88.0	93.3
Concentration	7.4	11.9	4.4
Genetic	9.9		
Residual	9.2	0.1	2.3

Source: Kislev and Rabiner, 1979, and Michal Reiss, Master Thesis, in preparation.

a End of period minus first year over first year's level.
b See equation (4).

Figure 1:   Distribution of Milk Production.

Figure 2:   Distribution of Egg Production.

Figure 3:   Distribution of Broiler
Production.

The picture for the poultry industry (figures 2 and 3) is more complex and more interesting. Average productivity in the country increased in broiler production and deteriorated in egg production--the last from 4,608 to 4,488 eggs per tonne between 1967 and 1972. Examination of the graphs leads to the impression that both high and low efficiency producers left egg production and only the mediocre stayed. There was a general increase in productivity in this product. Here it also seems as if the weaker producers either exited or improved the efficency of their operation. Faster technological changes may have attracted the more efficient operators into broiler production--those who can hope to reap an appropriate rent for their abilities to be technological pioneers. These producers may have left egg production. On the other hand, the technological stagnation in egg production made this line of activity comparatively simple. Everyone can produce eggs, including producers with relatively low alternative costs. This permits the sector to operate even at low income levels, but the efficient operators--those with better alternatives--leave.

Concentration of production in the hands of the more efficient operators contributes to increased productivity. Table 2 attempts to partition supply increments in the three lines of production to the effects of equation (4). Efficiency is defined in terms of yield per cow or production per tonne of feed as in figures 1-3. The calculation will be illustrated with milk production. The national milk producing herd is divided (and this division was employed in table 2) into registered and nonregistered herds. The registered dairies are generally larger (mostly in Kibbutzim), have higher yields, and their yields—as a group—increased through time. The nonregistered herds are mostly in relatively small family operated dairies with low and stagnant yields. The share of the registered dairies grew over the last two decades, from 30 to 50 percent of the national herd (Kislev, Meisels, and Amir). This growth is the measure of concentration used in table 2.

Total milk supply in 1974 was 210 perent higher than in 1960, at the beginning of the period considered. Of this supply increment (taken as 100), 73.5 percent was due to the mere increase in the number of cows. The concentration effect was calculated as the differential growth of the registered herd times the yield differences between the registered and the nonregistered herds. The estimate is that this effect is responsible for 7.4 percent of the supply increment. The genetic effect was calculated under the assumption that the genetic process was taken from breeders' estimates prepared in progeny tests. The residual, the complement to 100 percent, can be attributed to general technological changes: improvements in husbandry, veterinary practices, and the like. The calculation can be summarized in rough terms as indicating that 30 percent of milk supply increment over the 15-year period 1960-74 was due to productivity improvements. Of these, a third was due to each of the productivity components: concentration effect, genetic effect, and more general technical change.

In the poultry industry, the expansion effect was taken as the increase in feed input times the base year product to feed ratio. Unlike the situation in milk production, estimates of genetic progress in the poultry industry have not yet been prepared. The residuals in the broiler and egg columns include, therefore, the genetic effects. These estimates of the residual technical change indicate, if we accept the method used, that there could not have been substantial genetic progress in broiler production. This finding is somewhat puzzling and will probably not be accepted by breeders who claim to have introduced several superior types during the period covered by the analysis. On the other hand, many changes in structure and equipment were introduced--mostly by the better producers—while expanding the scale of operation (part of the concentration process), and it could be that the efficiency gains resulting from these changes can be attributed to the genetics of the new lines. A better answer to this puzzle can be expected to come out of a detailed study of poultry breeding in Israel, now underway.

The empirical findings illustrate, I trust, the significance of the dynamic perspective suggested by the theoretical assumptions of the paper. The work in this area is far from completion and several extensions are worth mentioning: (a) the explict analysis of a multiproduct farming firm; (b) explicit recognition of government's role in shaping the dynamic processes in agriculture; and (c) incorporation of the effects of omitted variables, such as alternative income opportunities outside agriculture.

Reference

Kislev , Y.; Meisels, M.; Amir, S. (forthcoming) The dairy industry of Israel, in Animal Production Systems (edited by B. L. Nestel).   Amsterdam, The Netherlands; Elsevier Scientific Publishing Co.

DEVELOPMENT PROBLEMS OF THE AGRICULTURAL SECTOR IN LABOUR MANAGED MARKET ECONOMIES

Gunther Weinschenck

Organizational Characteristics

General characteristics.   A labour managed market economy with a mixed structure is defined by the following characteristics:

1.   There are three sectors: a social sector which consists of labour managed enterprises; an individual sector which consists of family enterprises with nonfamily or limited nonfamily labour, and a capitalistic sector which consists of capitalistic enterprises with workers who are employed at an agreed wage, which is not directly dependent on the economic success of the enterprise.

2.   The decisionmaking process is decentralized and relies on the market mechanism in principle.

3.   In the labour managed sector, the firms observe the following basic rules: the process of management is based on democratic majority rule; the income of the firm is shared by all members; and the members of the firm collectively enjoy the usufruct of the enterprise (including the accumulated capital), but they are not owners in the sense that neither the members collectively nor each member individually may sell the assets of the firm.

Particularities of the Yugoslavian agricultural sector.   Yugoslavia has only a social and an individual sector.   The individual sector produces less than 15 percent of the GNP, and is of major importance only in agriculture. In 1977 in the individual sector, 75 percent of the GNP of the agricultural sector was produced by 96 percent of the total active agricultural population, who cultivated 84 percent of the agricultural land on 2.6 million holdings with an average size of 3.9 hectares. The social sector employed 4 percent of the active agricultural population in about 2,000 enterprises, which occupied 16 percent of the cultivated land and produced 25 percent of the social product of agriculture. There is a considerable bias of the distribution of natural conditions between the two sectors in favour of the social sector.

Economic Factors Supporting the Development of a Dual Structure

The idea of the labour managed system requires that newly employed workers share fully in all rights of those already employed.   Consequently, from the viewpoint of the workers' council, it is only advantageous to increase (decrease) the existing labour force if the increase of the net income earned by an additional (the "last") worker is above (below) or at least equal to the average income of the workers already employed. The appropriate objective function is to maximize the average labour income. The labour capacity of the individual farm household is determined predominantly by noneconomic reasons.   Its distribution between farm work and off-farm work is strongly influenced by economic principles--it would be sensible to remove parts of the family's labour capacity from farm work as long as the opportunity earnings of off-farm work are above the marginal productivity of farm work.

Obviously only two stable situations can exist in the labour market under these conditions:

1. **The full employment situation.** The labour managed system offers so many employment opportunities that everybody from the individual sector for whom it is advantageous to work there may do so.

2. **The underemployment situation.** The employment opportunities in the labour managed sector are so rare that the possibility of work there does not appear as a realistic opportunity in general for the active population in the individual sector.

In labour managed enterprises the optimal labour input is achieved in both situations if the marginal productivity of labour equals its average productivity. Hence, it is independent from the price of labour (from the minimum income at which additional employees would be willing to work in the enterprise).

Family farms try to maximize the family income taking into account the existing possibilities for off-farm work. If sufficient employment opportunities are available in the labour managed sector, the marginal productivity of family labour on the farms tends to become equal to the average labour income in the labour managed sector. However, in a structural underemployment situation, labour income in the social sector and marginal productivity in the individual sector are not directly related. The marginal productivity of family labour can amount to any value above zero, depending on the profitability of farming, particularly of labour intensive farming, and on the given land to worker ratio.

No difference exists in both sectors concerning the optimum combination of yield increasing inputs (fertilizer and irrigation) at a given structure of production and given natural and economic conditions. The optimal combination of labour and predominantly labour saving inputs is also determined by the same economic principle in both sectors. However, the price of labour to be used for the determination of the minimum cost combination differs. In family farms with a given labour force and a given land input, the marginal productivity of labour is the relevant price. The optimal use of labour saving capital inputs at given input prices is determined by the profitability of labour intensive crop production or of animal production on the basis of purchased feed. In labour managed farms, the average labour income is the relevant price. It is advantageous for the remaining labour force to substitute labour for capital as long as the average earnings per worker are higher than the costs of capital to substitute the "last" worker. As in the full employment situation, the equilibrium capital to labour ratio tends to approach its technical maximum, since average labour productivity increases with continuous substitution, thus at least partly compensating for the effect of the normally decreasing substitution rate.

Countervailing Factors

The different "labour price" applies also to the calculation of relative profitability of farm enterprises within farms and results in different comparative costs favouring the division of labour with respect to the satisfaction of demand. Labour managed farms are the marginal producers of labour intensive products (products like most vegetables and soft fruit, of which the production function indicates a relatively wide technical range of substitution between land and yield increasing inputs, but a relatively small technical range of substitution between labour and labour saving inputs). Family farms with relatively small land to worker ratios are the marginal producers of labour extensive products (products like cereals with a relatively small technical range of substitution between land and yield increasing inputs and a relatively large range of substitution between labour and labour saving inputs). The production of these products in family farms is usually due to one of the following reasons: (1) self-sufficiency; (2) submarginal conditions for farming for which no alternative exists under given natural and economic conditions, and the possibility to remain in business mainly rests on the possibility of reducing the remuneration of labour in the individual sector to basic subsistence; or (3) to use the land capacity which cannot otherwise be used due to crop rotation reasons or because the labour capacity in critical seasons is exhausted by producing labour intensive products. Both sectors have comparative advantages for basically different production systems for products like pigs and eggs which require little or no direct land input and which can be produced within a wide range of substitution between labour and labour saving inputs. Displacing competition—if it occurs—is likely to begin at these markets.

Preliminary Conclusions

Labour managed enterprises are likely to follow the most capital intensive development path in any stage of growth. This does not necessarily affect the differentiation of yield increasing inputs in agriculture between the social and the individual sector. However, the stage of structural underemployment is likely to last longer and provide less off-farm work opportunities than in capitalistic economies. The capital to labour ratio will develop differently in the two sectors of agriculture during structural underemployment. No general statement is possible with respect to the resulting income differences, since the individual sector is forced to maintain capital extensive (usually small scale) production under marginal conditions, but also has the chance to compete successfully in labour intensive crop production and—the more capital is scarce in the social sector—in small scale animal production on the basis of purchased feed. Three main factors influence the development of income differences between the sectors besides capital formation in the social sector: (1) the land to worker ratio in the individual sector; (2) the distribution of natural conditions between the sectors; and (3) the relative importance of the individual sector.

Economic factors suggest the need for employment of labour in both sectors after the employment in the labour managed sector reaches a level at which everybody from the individual sector who wants to work there can in principle expect to find an opportunity. The resulting exodus of workers from the individual sector causes either a change in the farm size structure in the individual sector, accompanied by an increase in predominantly labour saving capital inputs, or a decrease in production in the individual sector.

Institutional Factors

Institutional arrangements, especially those concerned with access to the capital market and diversification of technical progress, could be set up, in principle, in ways which avoid any discrimination of sectors. However, they will very likely favour the social sectors for which the implementation normally has strong ideological and political motivations. In Yugoslavia, economic policy did little to moderate the dual structure which the labour managed system finally established in 1965 had inherited, and did much to encourage it. The distribution of capital has been and still is determined by the government and the distribution of power in the banking system, both of which favour the social sector. Individual farms only have access to credit via labour managed firms by organized cooperation with them. Organized cooperation was (and in many parts of the country still is) practically the only organized way for the distribution of technical progress in the individual sector. The growth of single firms by increasing the land input is restricted by the agrarian law limiting the maximum size of private holdings to 10 hectares of farm land and 25 hectares of woodland except in the very mountainous regions.

A few institutional arrangements that have the tendentious effect of at least moderating the rigidity of the duality of the development are: (1) the institutionalized cooperation between the two sectors; (2) the opening of the labour markets of the industrialized economies of Western Europe to Yugoslav workers; and (3) the possibility of temporarily employing part-time workers in the social sector at an agreed wage rate without giving them the status of members of the enterprise.

Table 1--Share of the production of the individual sector
as a percentage of total production (a) and relative
yields (b) in 1977

	(a) Percent	(b) Social=100
Social product	75	1/56
Wheat	60	60
Maize	84	66
Sunflower	49	93
Sugarbeets	30	94
Tobacco	100	--
Paprika	94	na
Potatoes	98	60
Tomatoes	92	na
Milk	91	33
Wool	95	na
Lamb	2/95	na
Pig meat	2/80	na
Cattle	2/75	na

1/ Social product per hectare of cultivated land.
2/ Estimates.
na = Not available.

Development in Yugoslavia

In 1975--ten years after the final establishment of the labour managed system—labour productivity in the social sector was 4.5 and land productivity almost twice as high as in the individual sector. The biased influence of institutional factors appears most distinctly in the distribution of investments since 1965 which were about 2-2.5 times higher in the social sector, and in the development of yields (table 1) which, however, also reflects the biased distribution of natural conditions. The production share of different goods has developed largely according to the comparative cost advantages of the two sectors, which in turn also reflect the distribution of investment and technical knowhow that is predetermined by policy, as well as the biased distribution of natural conditions. The farm size structure in the individual sector remained almost unchanged between 1965 and 1975 under the influence of lack of employment opportunitites and the institutional limitations to farm growth. However, income from off-farm work increased relative to income from farm work, especially in smaller farms. The reduction of underemployment in the individual sector, which has been achieved in recent years by the growth of employment opportunities in the social sector and the opening of the West European labour markets, signals that development may approach the end of the structural underemployment period in the near future. The resulting reduction of the labour force in the individual sector means the end of the dual development period. The unavoidable change in farm structure can be acieved either by gradual absorption of the individual sector by the social sector or by structural changes similar to those which happened in highly industrialized capitalistic countries. For political reasons, the government is likely to favour the first possibility.

OPENER'S REMARKS—Augustyn Wos

What Weinschenck calls the social sector does not develop according to the rules of market economies, therefore I do not accept the term labour managed. In Poland as well as Yugoslavia, labour transfer occurs between the social and private sectors in agriculture as specific states of dynamic balance are being established. Polish economists, however, do not term this situation a labour managed economy. The concept seems rather artificial to me, and does not render the essential characteristics of a mixed economy in agriculture. However, since I do not consider the definition to be the most important issue, we may accept the one suggested by Weinschenck.

It is risky or even dangerous for a social enterprise to increase employment in a situation where increase of the net income earned by an additional worker is below or at least equal to the average income of the already employed workers. A similar situation occurs in collective farms, many of which guard against admitting new members if they do not contribute an adequate land area or if their productivity is lower than average. This gives rise to harmful closing of some collective farms. It should be emphasized, however, that such a situation holds only for a very early development stage of those farms. Later on, when the farms face problems brought about by too small a production scale, these limitations give way to the second phase—economic expansion. Then the collective farms strive for new members. These problems are well known from experiences of all socialist countries. Thus, the situation analysed by Weinschenck on the model of Yugoslavia refers only to the initial development phase of the social sector in agriculture. The advanced development phase brings quite new problems which are, however, not covered by Weinschenck's analysis. The change of rules of running social farms in single phases of their development is a vital problem for discussion. Agricultural economic literature of socialist countries has considerable achievements in this field.

The next problem dealt with in the paper concerns the choice of more or less labour intensive products according to land to worker ratios on different types of farms. The statement that labour managed farms are the marginal producers of labour intensive products is generally right. At the time when the family farms and the labour managed farms are operating on a mass scale, the problem of choice of production lines is determined explicitly. But what does the problem look like when the number of small scale family farms is decreasing rapidly? Then the production of labour intensive products is started by big state or cooperative enterprises, which essentially changes the economics of the latter and requires a determination of new price relations between work and technique. With the developing and changing social sectors, the economic rules or choice of production structure are also changing.

The matter of choice of optimum production structure is of significance not only for the relations between the social and private sectors, but as it appears from experience, it is one of the most vital development problems of private farms, particularly if there are possibilities to hire farm labour. In Poland, where one-third of the total number of individual farms are part-time farms, and where nonagricultural sectors constantly offer a considerable number of jobs, tendencies for extensification of production structure of part-time farms appeared. However, a thorough analysis indicates that it need not necessarily be so. The main problem consists in the choice of a production structure which suits the economics of those farms. Products which ensure income per labour unit comparable to that attainable outside agriculture get high priority. A typical peasant farm is maximizing the overall profit or the profit per land unit, which is the constraint. On the other hand, part-time farms maximize profit per labour unit, and this rule shapes the choice of production structure. In this respect, the situation in Poland differs from that described by Weinschenck. His analysis and conclusions are right for structural underemployment, which presumably exists in Yugoslavia, but they cannot be generalized for conditions of the dual economy. I would be inclined to admit that Weinschenck's paper refers to a specific case of dual economy at an early phase of its development under circumstances of structural underemployment. Weinschenck's theses can, however, hardly be accepted as a general theory.

LENDING TO RURAL POOR THROUGH INFORMAL GROUPS: A PROMISING FINANCIAL MARKET INNOVATION?

Dale W. Adams and Jerry R. Ladman

Abstract

A number of low income countries have recently experimented with group lending as a way of providing more rural poor with financial services. Five advantages are claimed for this financial market innovation: (1) repayment rates are improved, (2) lender loan costs are reduced, (3) technical assistance costs are reduced, (4) more rural poor can be serviced, and (5) borrowers expend less resources to get loans. The paper summarizes results of research on these issues.

The authors report that group lending often does not improve repayment performance and that it may increase the lender costs due to expenses of loan supervision and group formation. In most cases the borrower's costs of getting group loans are reduced in comparison with individual loans. Innovations in financial markets, such as group lending, have a better chance of success if more realistic and flexible interest rate policies are in force.

RAPPORTEUR'S REPORT--James O. Wise

The best basis for the formation of a viable, cohesive and informal group of borrowers is that it have some reason for existence prior to the extension of credit, and that it be economically and socially homogeneous. Interest rates must cover the costs of lending and provide a profit to the private lender if he is to lend to the rural poor without inflation. Credit may be extended to the rural poor in order to increase productivity, but also to meet other development goals such as reducing rural to urban migration and promoting rural solidarity.

Afghanistan has a successful group lending programme, particularly in terms of its repayment record, which is running at about 90 percent or higher after three years or more of experience. However, repayments could be good and the programme still not be achieving the desired goals. Repayment records can also vary depending on how borrowers view the credit program and the credit institution. For example, farmers may view the credit programme as a handout.

ONE AGENT OF RURAL CHANGE:
PROVISION OF CREDIT IN TANZANIA, ZAMBIA, AND SUDAN

Jean M. Due

Abstract

This is a study of one agent of rural change--credit--as used to implement government agricultural policy in Tanzania, Zambia, and Sudan. In all three countries, agricultural development banks have been established to channel credit to the agricultural sector. In Tanzania, the major thrust of this credit has been to ujamaa villages for communal production. In Zambia, it has been to small private farmers. And in Sudan in recent years, the emphasis has shifted from small size cotton farms on irrigated land to large scale dryland farms.

In Tanzania, the villages whose major source of income was tobacco (an export crop) had good repayment rates of 89 percent in 1973 and 1974 and 76 percent in 1976. The food crop growing villages producing maize had high negative net returns and low repayment rates. In Zambia, repayment rates were 64 and 88 percent in 1975 and 1976. These loans were only for seasonal inputs which were given in kind except for a small cash component for hired labour. In Sudan, although the Agricultural Bank was established to furnish capital primarily to small farmers and cooperatives, its focus in the seventies has been shifted to large scale farmers, many of whom are business and professional people or civil servants. Thus the current focus is a further distortion of income distribution in favor of high income families. This is in marked contrast to the focus in Tanzania and Zambia.

OPENERS REMARKS--Sing Ming Yeh

Credit alone is by no means a panacea for the problem of raising the productivity or income of the rural poor. To effectuate rural change, a credit programme should be closely linked to the provision of farm inputs, extension, marketing services, and price stabilisation measures.

Good repayment rates of farmers in Tanzania and Zambia might be attributable to the compulsory delivery of farm products such as maize, groundnuts, cotton, and tobacco to marketing boards. While it might be the intention of the Sudanese government to boost the agricultural output and increase the marketable surplus of major crops from commercial farms, the Agricultural Bank should furnish capital primarily to small farmers and their cooperatives and leave the needs of large and medium farmers to the commercial banks.

We do not have an idea from Due's paper to what extent the small farmers are covered by the public credit programmes. We are not informed of the prevailing interest rates of the public farm credit programme, or whether there is any mobilization of savings.

RAPPORTEUR'S REPORT—James O. Wise

The period of time covered by the study was one of radical change for Tanzania and may explain some of the results. More background information would have been helpful as well as more information on how production was changed by the extension of credit. The farmers included in the sample were the "best and brightest," thus the results may be different for other groups of farmers.

AGRICULTURAL BANKS OR MULTIPURPOSE BANKS?
THE GROWTH AND DEVELOPMENT OF
THREE COOPERATIVE BANKS IN EUROPE

Andre Neveu

The Credit Agricole Mutuel in France, the Deutsche Genossenschaftsbank in the Federal Republic of Germany, and the Raiffeisen-Boerenleenbank in the Netherlands have many points in common, or at least many similarities: their history, nature, development in an agricultural and rural environment neglected by the traditional banking system, and primary mission, which is financing agriculture and the cooperative sector. However, after becoming sufficiently large, they began to more closely resemble their competitors, the multipurpose commercial banks. Do the limitations imposed by the need to develop and to use modern management systems create a danger for these banks? Will they lose their originality in a world where uniformity is common fare?

Impact of Agricultural Development

At the end of the 19th century, specific needs led to the creation of specialized credit for financing farming and its complementary activities in the form of storage and marketing cooperatives. Conventional banks had long neglected the credit needs of small and medium sized farms. These farmers had limited needs, lived far from the cities, make small profits, and did not keep records.

Banks had even greater reservations about farm cooperatives. Weak financial structures (particularly the nearly total absence of any net worth), numerous management problems, and the ticklish problem of controlling creditors in case of liquidation, caused bankers to regard cooperatives with great caution.

In France, Germany, and the Netherlands, the vacuum left by the conventional banking system was gradually filled by small mutual credit associations, formed by farmers or other rural people. These banks prospered, gradually bringing credit to the vast majority of farmers and many other rural people. At the beginning of this century, these banks merged or were federated at the regional level. Later, a central bank formed an umbrella over the whole system.

Cooperative banks have developed along with agricultural modernization. This modernization has been especially marked since World War II. Modernization was largely a result of cooperative banks. In return, the banks also profited. In fact, by neglecting agriculture, conventional banks have overlooked a number of factors which have become valuable assets in the hands of the cooperative banks: (1) the virtual absence of any risk in financing farms which at the outset are relatively debt free and whose production is protected by effective barriers in the form of tariffs; (2) the size of the farm and rural populations whose earnings, and therefore savings potential and loan needs, rose sharply since the end of War War II; and (3) the development of business relations between farmers and agribusinesses has made it a common occurrence for farmers to use bank services.

Maintaining a very decentralized structure has, in effect, been an effective management tool. Constraints in agricultural financing and history (multiple cooperative credit banks) offer an explanation as to why the structure has remained more decentralized than in other banking systems (except for peoples' banks).

At present, cooperative managements still exist at the local and regional levels. It is, however, less noticeable at the national level, in spite of the fact that representatives of the lower level banks control the activities of the central bank. This control is very limited in Germany and especially so in France, because the central banks are public institutions.

Credit for Small and Medium Sized Farms

From the beginning, cooperative banks have striven to offer, within the limits of their possibilities, three large credit categories related to the farmers' three big needs: short term credit for financing floating assets; medium term credit for financing normal equipment; and long term credit for financing purchases, land development, and, occasionally, buildings.

Loans are usually made on a longer term basis than those made by commercial banks. This provides better conditions for slow turnover activities requiring large amounts of capital. These terms may extend to 20 or 30 years.

Although loans to farmers are made on a particularly long term basis, cooperative banks usually offer farmers preferred interest rates. In addition, these rates are often lowered by the government, which may subsidize interest rates. This is justified on the basis of the small profits made on capital invested in agriculture. Of course this practice is relatively limited in the Netherlands. It is more widespread in Germany (one-third of agricultural financing). Both of these countries have a system in which this subsidy can be used by the beneficiary in the bank of his choice, not necessarily a cooperative bank. The government of Germany also provides public funding, with very favourable conditions, for certain particularly expensive investments. In this case, the bank serves only as an intermediary between the government and the farmer. In France, subsidized loans represent a large proportion of all agricultural financing (about 40 percent). Credit Agricole Mutuel has a monopoly on the allocation of government subsidized farm loans in France.

Among the various guarantees usually demanded of borrowers, joint security is a specific characteristic of cooperative banks. There are many different types of farm guarantees used, all in relation to the large variety of assets. In all totally or partially owned farms, farmers can offer prime quality guarantees—mortgages. This is an advantage for their banker who consequently runs nearly no risk. Cooperative banks have not neglected to make extensive use of this type of security.

Tenant farmers, on the other hand, cannot be offered the possibility of a mortgage becaue they are not property owners. There are, however, other forms of security whch are commonly used, including one that is completely original: one or more farmers agree to pay the debt if the borrower defaults. This system is not used as often now and because of the risks involved for the surety and because credit is more readily available to tenant farmers.

Recently the approach of financing for specific objectives has been giving way to a global approach, in which all of the farmer's needs are considered. This development has come into sharper focus with the application of the 1972 Common Market directive on agricultural modernization. This directive anticipates drawing up actual farm development plans. In this way, cooperative banks finance several thousand development plans each year in France, Germany, and the Netherlands.

Expansion into Nonagricultural Sectors

There were technical, economic, banking, and financial reasons that led to this change. The technical reasons result from the fact that farmers have been tending to get involved in pre- and post-production activities: pre-production through the financing needed for supplies, but also for various necessary services in running a farm (veterinary, insemination, farm machine repair, builders, farm machine manufacturers); and post-production, through financing storage, packaging, processing, and marketing agricultural produce. This expansion was further encouraged by the fact that these businesses were frequently run on a cooperative basis.

The economic reasons are based on the relatively slow development (even lately) of farm activity. This has led the cooperative banks to look for other clients and other sources of capital outside of agriculture. The banking reasons are based on the fact that a modern bank's services largely exceed what is necessary for managing a farm. These services include investments as well as loans and auxiliary services (keeping accounting records, travel agency, currency distributors, and money exchange).

Finally, purely financial reasons have led cooperative banks to look for resources outside of agriculture, with special emphasis on family households. In fact, the agricultural sector used to save more than it borrowed, but now the situation is reversed. Like other productive sectors, agriculture borrows more than it saves. A purely agricultural bank would therefore lack sufficient resources to cover its financing.

Organization and Management of Cooperative Banks

Cooperative banks have successfully avoided transforming their local banks into simply powerless branch offices. Local banks in Germany and the Netherlands, as well as regional banks in France, are true banks with at least a high level of independence in terms of implementing business policy and allocating normal loans. Nevertheless, financial resources are frequently pooled for large loans. At this point the central bank steps in, either participating in the financing (in the Netherlands and Germany), or as the coordinator of activities between regional banks (in France).

With the diversification and enormous complication of banking functions, it is difficult to find members who really participate in running their bank. Many members only participate in management by attending general meetings. It is difficult to find competent persons who are available to perform normal management tasks (in principle, administrators are not paid).

Increasing the field of activity creates the problem of extending membership to other professions. The problem seems relatively minor in Germany and the Netherlands, where the membership was never limited to farmers. It is, however, a more delicate problem in France where farmers still have a very large majority of the responsibilities.

The development of large banking groups really poses the problem of a bank's relationship with the government. This relationship is based on certain points: (1) legal control of everyday management, especially in France where the Caisse Nationale is a public institution; (2) utilization of the banking group to distribute certain state aids; and (3) orienting allocation of resources.

Conclusion

Cooperative banks are gradually becoming more like other banks, even if they maintain certain individual characteristics, a very decentralized management, and decisionmaking power that remains at least partially in the hands of its members.

COMPARISON BETWEEN THE THREE INSTITUTIONS

- Crédit Agricole Mutuel
- D.G. BanK
- Rabobank

1977

	FRANCE	GERMANY	NETHERLANDS
Gross domestic product (U.S. $ billions)	380,66	516,20	106,39
Final agricultural production (U.S. $ billions)	27,0	24,0	9,0
Total population (Millions)	53,0	61,4	13,9
Number of agricultural farms	1.148,0	858,7	137,0

31.12.1976

	Crédit Agricole Mutuel	D.G. Bank	Rabobank
I - Organization			
Local and Regional Banks	3.094	5.014	1.028
Offices	9.800	19.500	3.130
Members	2.945.500	8.000.000	890.000
Current accounts	8.989.700		2.345.000
II - Assets			
Total Assets of the Group (U.S. $ billions)	51,7	89,4	20,7
III - Deposits			
Total deposits (U.S. $ billions)	41,9	83,1	19,8
Part of the Institution in the source of funds (in %)	15,8	20,0	40,0
IV - Loans and Credit			
Total loans (U.S. $ billions)	34,0	59,1	17,9
i.e. - loans to farmers (in %)	44,0	7,0	18,5
- loans to cooperatives (in %)	12,0	7,?	11,5
Part of the Institution in total domestic credit (in %)	12,5	15,0	17,5

AN ANALYSIS OF PLANNED VERSUS ACTUAL
ALLOCATION OF AGRICULTURAL CREDIT IN COLOMBIA

Robert C. Vogel and Donald W. Larson

Abstract

Like many developing countries, Colombia follows a policy of concessionary interest rates for agricultural credit in an attempt to promote agricultural production and to subsidize farmers, especially small farmers. These concessionary interest rates lead to excess demand for credit which in turn necessitates rationing devices and procedures. The primary purpose of this paper is to examine these rationing mechanisms and to evaluate the planned and actual allocation of credit for major seasonal crops.

The principal finding of this study is that the planned allocation of credit has virtually no impact on the actual allocation of credit among the seasonal crops, and, more importantly, little or no effect on crop production. Furthermore, the credit planning process is costly and time consuming in terms of scarce human resources. Due to fungibility, credit is diverted from the planned allocation to uses where rates of return based on profit expectations are highest. There seems to be little justification for concessionary rates of interest if the main purpose is to influence the allocation of credit and thereby promote the production of certain crops. In addition, the credit planning process tends to concentrate agricultural credit in large loans to large farmers and thereby to make the distribution of income more unequal.

OPENER'S REMARKS--Herman Jacobs

How far is a credit programme influenced by the economic and social setting that the authors indicate exists in Colombia? What conclusions can be drawn from the statistical work done? Is this case study an example of the pros and cons of a credit programme, or is Colombia just a special case? Credit programmes are implemented on the basis of theoretical arguments and it is very necessary to see what comes about in practice. This is what the authors did.

The International Monetary Fund and the Economic Commission for Latin America statistics differ from the authors' figures on prices and discount rates. The authors also used data for years with economic problems after which the government changed the economic policy. I question if one can judge the credit policy in these extreme years. One should take average normal years on the one hand and extreme years as special cases. The UN data do not support the conclusion that nonagricultural investment is more profitable.

The outcome of the correlation analyses is striking, as there is no significant relationship. Is it possible that in normal years a correlation could be found, but not in extreme years and situations because in those periods the credit allocation process cannot function well? Use of multivariate techniques to see what factors do influence real credit allocation would have been a better approach.

One objective of the credit policy was to increase production, which happened. Without the programme, would production have increased? And certain crops were to be promoted, so that the production would be diversified. The composition of production could have been the dependent variable. Then one could perhaps better see how far the credit programme influenced the composition of agricultural production. The problem that large amounts of crops are grown and only changed at the margin is then reduced and the question that matters (Did the programme change the use of land for different crops?) could be investigated.

If the study gave a more balanced impression of Colombia, one would attach more importance to the report and possibly be convinced about the failure of credit programmes in general, and especially in Colombia. Did the credit programme fail because Colombians in particular could not effectively implement it, or would a credit programme fail in any country? The paper is too much of a verbal attack on Colombia and did not investigate the subjects enough to support the conclusions drawn. I would suggest that the study be deepened before we can say that this case is sufficient to judge the possibilities of credit as an aid to agricultural development. I would not generalize these results for other countries or use Colombia as an example before the study is in a more definitive state.

References

International Monetary Fund (1979) International Financial Statistics (May).
Economic Commission for Latin America (1975) Economic Survey of Latin America.

RAPPORTEUR'S REPORT--James O. Wise

The point was made that governments are using credit as only one method of influencing the production of certain commodities. Furthermore, producer groups exert influence on credit distribution and thus the allocation may differ from the production goals of governments.

The Rural Challenge
at the Subnational Level

CHANGES AT THE URBAN-RURAL INTERFACE:
THE CONTRIBUTION OF OFF-FARM WORK BY FARMERS

Ray D. Bollman

A common characteristic of rural change in most countries has been the net flow of human resources from the farm to the nonfarm sector. Off-farm work by farm family members has been identified as an important factor influencing this flow (Baumgartner; Hathaway, 1960 and 1967; Hathaway and Perkins, 1968a and 1968b; Kaldor and Edwards; Perkins, 1973; Perkins and Hathaway; and Szabo.) The purpose of this paper is to investigate the interrelationships between off-farm work and entry to and exit from farming. Data are drawn from a longitudinal micro data file on Canadian farmers from the 1966, 1971, and 1976 Censuses of Agriculture (table 1). The data are ideally suited to the study at the micro level of the impact of off-farm work on the movement of farmers to the nonfarm sector.

The first important point to note is that the relatively small change in the number of farmers between census periods is comprised of a surprisingly large rate of gross entry and gross exit. From 1966 to 1971, the number of census farm operators in Canada declined by 64,397 (14.9 percent), which was due to a gross exit of 152,354 (35.4 percent of the 1966 number of operators) and a gross entry of 87,957 (which was 24.0 percent of the number of 1971 operators) (table 2). Similarly, the net change in the 1971 to 1976 period was a decline of 27,527 (7.5 percent) which was due to a gross exit of 129,922 (35.5 percent of the 1971 operators) and a gross entry of 102,395 (30.3 percent of the 1966 operators). Thus, the number of gross entrants and gross exiters is so large that the determinants of both gross entry and gross exit must be understood in order to comprehend the changes at the urban-rural interface. The analysis of this paper is constrained to the impact of off-farm work.

Does Off-farm Work Influence Entry and Exit of Farmers?

Off-farm work appears to facilitate the entry of individuals into farming. The greater the number of days of off-farm work reported in 1976, the greater the proportion of operators who had entered in the 1971 to 1976 period (see the last row of table 2). However, in the 1966 to 1971 period, more than 25 days of off-farm work were required before the rate of entry became greater than the rate of entry of operators with no off-farm work (Bollman, 1979). Overall, 54.3 percent of the operators with full-time off-farm work in 1976 (greater than 228 days) started farming in the 1971 to 1976 period.

When we control for the demand for the operator's labour in farm work (measured by the size of farm in terms of total capital value), we find that the proportion of entrants tends to increase as the days of off-farm work increases, for each size of total capital value (table 2).

Off-farm work also facilitates the exit of individuals from farming. The greater the number of days of off-farm work reported in 1971, the greater is the proportion of operators who have exited in the 1971 to 1976 period (see the last row of table 3). However, nearly full-time off-farm work is required before the rate of exit is greater than for operators with no off-farm work. Similarly, in the 1966 to 1971 period, more than four months of off-farm work were required (Bollman, 1979). Thus, it appears that small amounts of off-farm work retard off-farm movement by farmers.

In this case, when we control for the demand for the operator's labour in farm work (again measured by the size of farm in terms of total capital value), we find that the proportion of exiters increases as the number of days of off-farm work increases, for each size class of total capital value (table 3). However, in each total capital value class under $25,000, the exit rate is greater if no off-

Table 1. Number and Percent of Census-farm Operators(1) who Entered(2) and Exited(3) between 1966 and 1971 and between 1971 and 1976, Canada(4) and Provinces

	Year	Number of Census-farm Operators(1)	Net Change	Percent Change	Gross Entry(2)	Percent Entering	Gross Exit(3)	Percent Exiting
Canada	1966	429,731			-	-	152,354	35.5
			-64,397	-15.0				
	1971	365,334			87,957	24.1	129,922	35.6
			-27,527	-7.5				
	1976	337,807			102,395	30.3	-	-
Newfoundland	1966	1,704			-	-	1,166	68.4
			-687	-40.3				
	1971	1,017			479	47.1	611	60.1
			-153	-15.1				
	1976	864			458	53.0	-	-
Prince Edward Island	1966	6,348			-	-	2,598	40.9
			-1,813	-28.6				
	1971	4,535			785	17.3	1,666	36.7
			-856	-18.9				
	1976	3,679			810	22.0	-	-
Nova Scotia	1966	9,593			-	-	5,154	53.7
			-3,605	-37.6				
	1971	5,988			1,549	25.9	2,698	45.1
			-569	-9.5				
	1976	5,419			2,129	39.3	-	-
New Brunswick	1966	8,689			-	-	4,457	51.3
			-3,222	-37.1				
	1971	5,467			1,235	22.6	2,433	44.5
			-933	-17.1				
	1976	4,534			1,500	33.0	-	-
Quebec	1966	80,146			-	-	31,129	38.8
			-18,992	-23.7				
	1971	61,154			12,137	19.9	23,846	39.0
			-9,642	-15.8				
	1976	51,512			14,204	27.6	-	-
Ontario	1966	109,805			-	-	43,128	39.3
			-15,167	-13.8				
	1971	94,638			27,961	29.6	34,551	36.5
			-5,918	-6.3				
	1976	88,720			28,633	32.3	-	-
Manitoba	1966	39,708			-	-	11,115	28.0
			-4,764	-12.0				
	1971	34,944			6,351	18.2	11,456	32.8
			-2,892	-8.3				
	1976	32,052			8,564	26.7	-	-
Saskatchewan	1966	85,431			-	-	24,083	28.2
			-8,728	-10.2				
	1971	76,703			15,355	20.0	23,336	30.4
			-6,029	-7.9				
	1976	70,675			17,307	24.5	-	-
Alberta	1966	69,250			-	-	20,789	30.0
			-6,726	-9.7				
	1971	62,524			14,063	22.5	20,574	32.9
			-1,565	-2.6				
	1976	60,959			19,009	31.2	-	-
British Columbia	1966	19,057			-	-	8,735	45.8
			-693	-3.6				
	1971	18,364			8,042	43.8	8,751	47.7
			1,030	5.6				
	1976	19,394			9,781	50.4	-	-

Source: Canada, Statistics Canada, 1966-1971-1976 Census of Agriculture Match.

(1) Operators of institutional farms are excluded.
(2) An entrant is an individual who was a census-farm operator in the latter period, but not in the former period.
(3) An exiter is an individual who was a census-farm operator in the former period, but not in the latter period.
(4) Canada excludes operators of farms in the Yukon and Northwest Territories.

farm work is reported than if full-time off-farm work is reported. For total capital value classes over $25,000, operators with full-time (or nearly full-time) off-farm work have a greater probability of exiting than if no off-farm work is reported (compare columns 1 and 11 in table 3). However, the mere incidence of off-farm work tends to retard off-farm movement for all total capital value classes less than $74,950 (compare columns 1 and 12 in table 3).

Summary and Implications

The movement of human resources from the farm to the nonfarm sector has been a predominant feature of developing economies. Such a movement has often been identified as a method of improving the welfare of the farm population. Off-farm work has been suggested as a means to facilitate this transfer (see the references cited in the first paragraph; Perkins, 1972; and Herndier).

The magnitude of gross exit and entry (table 1) suggests that the best way to increase net outward migration may be to employ policy measures to restrict entry. The size of gross exit appears sufficiently large without attempting to increase it still further.

An analysis of the impact of off-farm work on the gross entry and exit of farmers indicates that off-farm work promotes entry (table 2) but retards exit, except for the larger capital value classes (table 3). Thus, an increase in off-farm work will tend to reduce the net outward migration of farmers.

However, the major income source for census farm operators is off-farm work (Bollman, 1973). Thus, if the policy objective is to increase the welfare (specifically, the money incomes) of farmers, off-farm work should be promoted. The incomes of farmers will rise. The movement of labour out of agriculture will be retarded, but the increased substitution of off-farm work for farm work is, in itself, an adjustment of human resources from the farm to the nonfarm sector.

References

Baumgartner, H. W. (1965) Potential mobility in agriculture: Some reasons for the existence of a labour transfer problem. Journal of Farm Economics, 47 (February) 74-82.

Bollman, D. (1973) Off-farm work by operators of Canadian census-farms— 1971. Canadian Farm Economics, 8 (6) 1-5.

Bollman, D. (1979) The contribution of off-farm work to entry and exit by farmers. Unpublished paper, Agriculture Division, Statistics Canada.

Hathaway, D. E. (1960) Migration from agriculture: The historical record and its meaning. American Economic Review, 50 (May) 379-391.

Hathaway, D. E. (1967) Occupational mobility from the farm labour force, Farm Labor in the United States (edited by C. E. Bishop). New York; Columbia University Press, 71-96.

Hathaway, D. E.; Perkins, B. (1968a) Farm labour mobility, migration, and income distribution. American Journal of Agricultual Economics, 50 (May), 342-353.

Hathaway, D. E.; Perkins, B. (1968b) Occupational Mobility and migration from Agriculture, in Rural Poverty in the United States, A report by the President's National Advisory Commission on Rural Poverty. Washington; Government Printing Office, 185-237.

Herndier, G. W. (1973) An evaluation of the effectiveness of part-time farming as an adjustment vehicle. Unpublished thesis, University of Saskatchewan.

Kaldor, D. R.; Edwards, W. M. (1975) Occupational adjustment of Iowa farm operators who quit farming in 1959-61. Agricultural and Home Economics Experiment Station Special Report, Iowa State University, No. 75.

Table 2

Number and Percent of Entering Farmers[a] in the 1971 to 1976 Period, by Size of 1976 Total Farm Capital Value, by Number of 1976 of Off-farm Work, CANADA[b]

Size of Total Farm Capital Value (1976)	Number of Days of Off-farm Work (1976)											Subtotal, some days	Total
	0	1-6	7-12	13-24	25-48	49-72	73-96	97-126	127-156	157-228	229 & over		
< 2,950													
Number (1976)	245	—	—	5	10	10	10	5	5	30	70	145	385
Entrants, 71-76	169	—	—	3	7	8	7	4	3	18	58	110	271
Percent Entrants	69	—	—	67	70	78	67	71	50	61	83	76	71
2,950-4,949													
Number (1976)	375	—	—	5	10	15	10	15	15	35	100	210	590
Entrants, 71-76	201	—	—	3	5	8	7	9	11	28	76	149	353
Percent Entrants	54	—	—	50	55	50	69	60	71	79	76	71	60
4,950-7,449													
Number (1976)	825	10	10	10	20	35	15	50	35	95	205	485	1,310
Entrants, 71-76	415	6	6	3	13	17	9	37	24	62	154	332	747
Percent Entrants	50	60	60	33	65	48	62	74	68	66	75	69	57
7,450-9,949													
Number (1976)	880	5	5	15	25	45	25	50	35	115	245	565	1,445
Entrants, 71-76	403	3	1	5	9	20	12	22	22	70	182	346	749
Percent Entrants	46	50	20	36	35	45	48	44	64	61	74	61	52
9,950-14,949													
Number (1976)	2,820	20	20	55	90	115	110	175	115	365	835	1,910	4,730
Entrants, 71-76	1,117	8	7	23	39	48	57	98	69	232	542	1,128	2,245
Percent Entrants	40	42	33	41	43	42	52	56	60	64	65	59	47
14,950-19,949													
Number (1976)	3,280	25	30	45	110	140	135	245	175	565	1,110	2,580	5,855
Entrants, 71-76	1,144	11	15	20	48	67	62	113	81	311	714	1,446	2,588
Percent Entrants	35	44	48	44	43	48	46	46	46	55	65	56	44

19,950-24,949													
Number (1976)	4,030	40	40	90	145	195	150	250	230	715	1,300	3,165	7,190
Entrants, 71-76	1,433	13	20	42	56	86	57	113	111	385	810	1,698	3,129
Percent Entrants	36	32	50	47	39	44	38	45	48	54	62	54	44
24,950-49,949													
Number (1976)	23,975	255	265	485	1,050	1,140	1,065	1,620	1,315	4,285	8,200	19,695	43,670
Entrants, 71-76	6,786	79	78	175	379	437	436	665	572	2,207	4,855	9,890	16,676
Percent Entrants	28	31	30	36	36	38	41	41	44	52	59	50	38
49,950-74,949													
Number (1976)	27,220	260	335	545	1,095	1,110	975	1,675	1,195	4,520	8,635	20,340	47,565
Entrants, 71-76	6,895	69	105	166	385	398	395	708	521	2,354	4,868	9,968	16,865
Percent Entrants	25	27	31	30	35	36	41	42	44	52	56	49	35
74,950-99,949													
Number (1976)	24,270	270	320	490	880	920	780	1,255	885	3,335	6,830	15,960	40,230
Entrants, 71-76	5,712	64	89	154	281	355	298	544	376	1,642	3,721	7,522	13,233
Percent Entrants	24	24	28	31	32	39	38	43	43	49	54	47	33
99,950-149,949													
Number (1976)	38,595	475	480	770	1,260	1,310	1,065	1,790	1,160	4,435	7,950	20,700	59,290
Entrants, 71-76	8,379	101	119	216	370	454	380	681	495	2,007	4,017	8,841	17,219
Percent Entrants	22	21	25	28	29	35	36	38	43	45	51	43	29
149,950-199,949													
Number (1976)	26,630	370	375	525	910	775	645	975	595	2,200	3,755	11,120	37,750
Entrants, 71-76	5,260	94	105	136	245	248	240	340	231	955	1,838	4,429	9,689
Percent Entrants	20	26	28	26	27	32	37	35	39	43	49	40	26
199,950 and over													
Number (1976)	70,090	1,025	1,065	1,385	1,910	1,480	1,095	1,580	920	2,815	4,395	17,670	87,760
Entrants, 71-76	12,879	233	210	290	471	415	353	524	318	1,034	1,872	5,719	18,598
Percent Entrants	18	23	20	21	25	28	32	33	35	37	43	32	21
Total													
Number (1976)	223,235	2,770	2,950	4,420	7,530	7,285	6,090	9,680	6,680	23,505	43,635	114,545	337,785
Entrants, 71-76	50,792	689	757	1,233	2,315	2,559	2,318	3,855	2,835	11,303	23,715	51,578	102,371
Percent Entrants	23	25	26	28	31	35	38	40	42	48	54	45	30

a. An entrant is an individual who was a census-farm operator in 1976 but not in 1971.
b Operators of institutional farms and farms in the Yukon and Northwest Territories are excluded.
Source: CANADA. Statistics Canada. 1966-1971-1976 Census of Agriculture Match

Table 3

Number and Percent of Exiting Farmers[a] in the 1971 to 1976 Period by Size of 1971 Total Farm Capital Value,
by Number of 1971 Days of Off-farm Work, CANADA[b]

Size of Total Farm Capital Value (1971)	Number of Days of Off-farm Work (1971)											Subtotal, some days	Total
	0	1-6	7-12	13-24	25-48	49-72	73-96	97-126	127-156	157-228	229 & over		
<2,950													
Number (1971)	1,105	10	10	30	45	35	40	60	60	105	250	645	1,750
Exiters, 71-76	904	6	7	24	38	26	25	48	42	80	179	474	1,379
Percent Exiters	82	56	73	79	84	75	62	80	70	77	71	74	79
2,950-4,949													
Number (1971)	1,845	15	20	40	75	90	75	130	90	210	515	1,250	3,100
Exiters, 71-76	1,406	8	14	37	48	55	50	93	68	146	362	874	2,283
Percent Exiters	76	50	71	92	64	61	67	72	75	70	70	70	74
4,950-7,449													
Number (1971)	3,870	45	50	90	180	180	175	230	230	525	1,105	2,800	6,675
Exiters, 71-76	2,763	32	33	47	107	105	111	148	148	323	705	1,753	4,519
Percent Exiters	71	71	67	52	59	58	64	65	64	62	64	63	68
7,450-9,949													
Number (1971)	4,670	65	65	145	225	230	190	315	270	685	1,395	3,595	8,265
Exiters, 71-76	3,041	31	33	80	124	118	95	176	141	394	791	1,988	5,029
Percent Exiters	65	48	51	55	55	51	50	56	52	58	57	55	61
9,950-14,949													
Number (1971)	11,685	160	185	375	655	560	570	835	730	1,855	3,845	9,765	21,445
Exiters, 71-76	6,809	77	87	164	303	245	291	406	357	922	2,028	4,879	11,684
Percent Exiters	58	48	47	44	46	44	51	49	49	50	53	50	54
14,950-19,949													
Number (1971)	12,815	205	220	425	720	680	640	915	760	2,030	4,110	10,705	23,520
Exiters, 71-76	6,646	95	102	161	303	263	252	390	320	885	1,896	4,666	11,312
Percent Exiters	52	46	47	38	42	39	39	43	42	44	46	44	48

19,950–24,949													
Number (1971)	13,840	240	255	430	765	685	660	925	745	2,100	4,380	11,190	25,030
Exiters, 71–76	6,474	80	89	158	271	247	265	340	288	830	1,933	4,502	10,976
Percent Exiters	47	33	35	37	35	36	40	37	39	40	44	40	44
24,950–49,949													
Number (1971)	65,495	1,300	1,285	2,030	3,325	3,075	2,550	3,545	2,530	8,095	15,510	43,240	108,740
Exiters, 71–76	24,502	427	376	605	997	905	793	1,071	862	2,744	6,063	14,842	39,345
Percent Exiters	37	33	29	30	30	29	31	30	34	34	39	34	36
49,950–74,949													
Number (1971)	45,405	1,160	990	1,395	2,085	1,760	1,395	1,840	1,205	3,865	6,080	21,775	67,180
Exiters, 71–76	13,306	278	205	302	503	430	382	468	342	1,107	2,066	6,081	19,387
Percent Exiters	29	24	21	22	24	24	27	25	28	29	34	28	29
74,950–99,949													
Number (1971)	27,680	805	665	950	1,175	895	700	855	580	1,635	2,305	10,565	38,245
Exiters, 71–76	6,858	154	131	188	243	201	152	188	129	440	807	2,631	9,489
Percent Exiters	25	19	20	20	21	22	22	22	22	27	35	25	25
99,950–149,949													
Number (1971)	26,575	765	650	785	1,050	780	540	715	390	1,190	1,555	8,415	34,995
Exiters, 71–76	6,064	128	123	145	216	167	121	163	98	280	516	1,956	8,022
Percent Exiters	23	17	19	18	21	21	22	23	25	24	33	23	23
149,950–199,949													
Number (1971)	10,175	300	225	285	385	230	165	210	145	335	555	2,840	13,015
Exiters, 71–76	2,289	54	43	58	74	56	32	42	37	109	232	737	3,026
Percent Exiters	23	18	19	20	19	24	20	20	25	32	42	26	23
199,950 and over													
Number (1971)	10,925	260	200	265	285	220	135	185	125	275	495	2,445	13,370
Exiters, 71–76	2,820	59	38	56	59	40	33	49	30	86	192	651	3,471
Percent Exiters	26	23	19	21	21	22	24	26	24	31	39	27	26
Total													
Number (1971)	236,095	5,335	4,830	7,240	10,970	9,410	7,840	10,760	7,855	22,900	42,095	129,240	365,333
Exiters, 71–76	83,885	1,429	1,285	2,022	3,283	2,862	2,605	3,583	2,855	8,345	17,767	46,037	129,922
Percent Exiters	36	27	27	28	30	30	33	33	36	36	42	36	36

^a An Exiter is an individual who was a census-farm operator in 1971, but not in 1976.

^b Operators of institutional farms and farms in the Yukon and Northwest Territories are excluded.

Source: CANADA. Statistics Canada. 1966-1971-1976 Census of Agriculture Match.

63

Perkins, B. B. (1972) Multiple Jobholding among farm operators: A study of agricultural adjustment in Ontario. Guelph; School of Agricultural Economics and Extension Education, University of Guelph, May.

Perkins, B. B. (1973) Farm income and labour mobility. American Journal of Agricultural Economics, 55 (December) 913-920.

Perkins, B. B.; Hathaway, D. E. (1966) The movement of labor between farm and nonfarm jobs. Agricultural Experiment Station Research Bulletin, Michigan State University, No. 13.

Szabo, M. L. (1965) Depopulation of farms in relation to the economic conditions of agriculture on the Canadian prairies. Geographic Bulletin, 7 (3 and 4) 187-202.

OPENER'S REMARKS--John R. Raeburn

My greatest surprise on reading the paper was at the high rates of gross entry and exit. These obviously make the policy issues all the more important. What would such a high gross entry rate really imply for the policymakers, including those concerned with education?

I have quickly and rather roughly determined from Bollman's tables--including some from his fuller paper--that rough annual exit rates were greater than the 3.3 percent that one would expect on the assumption of a 30 year age gap between father and son.

Bollman included more about ages at entry and exit in his longer paper, and we should understand that the age class intervals in which lie the median ages of leavers are generally as low as 45-54, with a slight tendency for the percentage of leavers who are over 59 to decrease in Nova Scotia and increase in Saskatchewan. And the age class in which the median age of entrants lies is 35-44, but 45-54 in Nova Scotia and 25-34 in Saskatchewan, in the 1971-76 period. The percentage of entrants who were older than 54 dropped substantially between 1966-71 and 1971-76.

I think all this and more is desirable as a background before we consider the regressions of exit and entry rates on age of operator, on farm capital value, or on other "size" measures. We do not have the provincial figures to help with these regression curves--but the all-Canada figures do require explanation against the background indicated, particularly if there are any policymakers thinking of promoting off-farm work or restricting it so as to reduce entry rates and thereby increase net outward migration. Policymakers should have more information on what and where off-farm work is; where it is available and where not; who wishes to do it and who does not; and who (in relation to their own farm business planning) could economically do it and who could not.

RAPPORTEUR'S REPORT--Linda Chase

What is a census farm and what constitutes off-farm work? Bollman used a constant farm definition of at least one acre and $50 gross sales. He distinguished between off-farm work and nonfarm work; full definitions appear in previous publications. It was noted that since new entrants may include the small shift from farm worker to farm operator, information on the origin of entrants would be useful. What is the impact of off-farm work on productivity? Bollman replied that in looking at resource use, part-time farmers may be less productive but still efficient. It was suggested that off-farm work seems to raise commercial farm numbers, indicating income stability at this level. Finally, there was interest expressed in the reasons for the upward trend in off-farm work. Bollman suggested that an incentive is the nonfarm demand for labour--as unemployment increases, participation in off-farm work declines.

OFF-FARM EMPLOYMENT AND FARM ADJUSTMENTS:
IMPLICATIONS OF PART-TIME FARMING FOR RURAL DEVELOPMENT

Ryohei Kada

Statistical evidence shows that farm families in most of the developed countries are increasingly dependent on income from off-farm sources. In the United States, for example, over 50 percent of all farm operators worked off the farm in 1969, which is almost twice the percentage of forty years ago. The percentage of income from off-farm sources, as a result, increased from 29 percent in 1935 to 54 percent in 1976 (U.S. Department of Agriculture).

The taking up of off-farm employment by one or more members of a farm family is probably one way to counteract the cost-price squeeze and to adjust to the rapidly changing economy and technology of a modern society. Little attention has been paid, however, to the nature and mechanism of adjustments through off-farm employment, especially at the micro level. Furthermore, very few economists have attempted to make intercountry comparisons of part-time farming from this viewpoint, due mainly to the lack of comparable data in most developed countries (Gasson).

Taking the farm family as the unit of account, the main objective of this paper is to present and discuss the direction of on-farm and off-farm adjustments, labour allocation decisions, and the life cycle pattern of employment and income of the part-time farm family.

Research Method and Data Characteristics

Case studies from the United States and Japan, each essentially different in the nature of labour and land market situations and institutional settings, are compared. It is hoped that the intercountry comparison will make it possible to analyse how a different structure of opportunities in these two countries affects and determines the adjustments made by farm families with respect to factor use (land, labour, and capital), types of farm technology, and other farm and family organizations.

Primary data, collected by me in 1976-77 in Wisconsin, USA, and Shiga Prefecture, Japan, serve as the main source of the analysis of part-time farming. A total sample of 193 part-time farm families from Wisconsin and 239 from Shiga were interviewed and analysed. A part-time farm family is defined here as one in which one or more members is engaged in off-farm work, including self-employed enterprises, for 30 days or more per year, and thus earns off-farm income.

The average size of farm operation is 59 hectares in the Wisconsin sample, compared with only 0.9 hectare in Shiga. Various types of farm operation exist in Wisconsin: 42 percent of the sample are in dairying, 38 percent in beef and hog enterprises, and 11 percent in cash cropping. In Shiga, in contrast, over 95 percent of the sample specialized in rice cropping, with only a few engaged in other speciality crops.

Although income components are quite different, off-farm income makes up a significant part of the total family income in both countries. The average income derived from off-farm employment in Wisconsin amounts to U.S.$13,018, about 71 percent of the total family income. The dependence on income from off-farm sources is much heavier in Shiga, where nearly 80 percent of the total family income comes from off-farm sources.

Wisconsin data also show that part-time farm families are not homogeneous. Two major types are classified by the criterion of the existence of urban-rural relocation of residence: the first is the group of farm families who are on a long-standing farm but who for some reason shifted the farm operation from a full-time to a part-time basis (type A); the other group comprises those previously established in urban areas, but who thereafter acquired farmland, relocated residence to a rural area within commuting distance to off-farm employment, and started the farm enterprise as a supplementary source of income (type B). Nearly 30 percent of the total Wisconsin sample of part-time farm families belong to type B, which reflects the high mobility of labour and land market situations in the USA. Part-time farm families in Shiga are not so diversified as in Wisconsin, the majority are heavily dependent on off-farm income for their livelihood and also specialize only in rice farming. In fact, no farm families in the Shiga sample have ever relocated their residence from urban to rural areas.

Major Findings

On-Farm and Off-Farm Adjustments

Various on-farm and off-farm adjustments are made by dual job holders in order to relieve the burden of dual job holding. In Wisconsin, among the major adjustments made on the farm are: to get other family members' help; to ask outside help; to change the size or type of farm operation; and to work harder or longer on the farm. The nature of these on-farm adjustments is significantly related to the type of farm operation, the pattern of labour allocation, and the size of farm. For example, dual job holding operators of relatively larger size farms mentioned other family members' help to be the most important on-farm adjustment; those of smaller size farms have more frequently changed their type of farm operation into less labour intensive ones and relied more heavily on outside help such as custom work.

The nature of on-farm adjustments made by Shiga farmers is similar to those in Wisconsin except for the following two points. First, a great majority of dual job holding farmers mentioned using labour saving machines as a most important adjustment, which reflects the recent rapid development and diffusion of rice farming mechanization. Second, there are almost no farm families that have changed the type of farm operation; almost all part-time farms have basically remained in rice cropping with unchanged farm size, though intensity of land use has been reduced by eliminating the winter crops on paddy fields.

A remarkable impact of off-farm employment on agricultural production is the change in the nature of farm operation in the two countries: in Wisconsin, the type of farm enterprise has often been shifted to a less labour intensive one, such as from dairy to beef or cash grains, and such changes occurred more frequently in areas relatively proximate to large cities; in Shiga, the heavy dependence on off-farm employment has brought about the elimination of winter crops, resulting in the monocropping pattern of rice everywhere.

Though the extent and possibility of off-farm adjustment are somewhat limited due mainly to the institutionalized nature of the nonagricultural employment pattern, more than half of the dual job holding farm operators in both countries made off-farm adjustments in one way or another. Among the major off-farm adjustments made by Wisconsin farmers are: to use paid vacation weeks to work on the farm; to select flexible off-farm employment including self-employed businesses; and to make nonregular work shift arrangements. In Japan, the widespread self-employed businesses, including putting out arrangements, are commonly found in rural areas where modern urban employment opportunities are limited. Hence, the selection of flexible off-farm employment was suggested as the most important off-farm adjustment made by Shiga farmers.

Labour Allocation Patterns

The decision as to how the farm family allocates its available labour between farm and off-farm is taken into consideration, because it determines not only the level of incomes obtained but also the nature of the adjustments and resource use pattern. As shown in figure 1, the direction of labour allocation is quite different among various members of the family. The farm operator (or family head) and spouse tend to take major responsibilities on both farm and off-farm almost equally. Members of the older generation tend to contribute more on the farm in both countries. The younger generation members devote more time to on-farm employment in Wisconsin, whereas they allocate more time to off-farm employment in Shiga.

Interdependency of labour allocation decisions among various members of the part-time farm family is another important finding of the present study. The nature of interdependency is, however, essentially different in the two countries. In Wisconsin, farm labour input is composed of as many family members in the working population as possible, with some school children helping on the farm. And the nature of family interdependency is complementary; the greater the farm labour inputs of the operator and the spouse, the heavier the farm contribution made by those of the younger generation. With respect to the off-farm labour inputs in Wisconsin, however, the extent of such interdependency seems relatively weaker than the case of farm labour input (figure 1).

In Shiga, on the other hand, such interdependency appears to exist in off-farm rather than on-farm labour inputs. Due to the limited farm size and its expansion potential, farm tasks are carried out sufficiently well by the elderly and the female members, with seasonal help from young male members in machinery operation. In contrast, off-farm labour input is composed of as many members of working age as possible in the family.

It is also found that the labour allocation pattern is influenced by various farm and family factors. Among those factors of importance, farm size and the type of farm operation are far more significant in Wisconsin than in Shiga. The varied types of farm operation and the greater opportunities to expand farm size in Wisconsin account for this difference. Among family related factors, the family structure and the stages of the family life cycle are shown to have significant influence on the pattern of the family's labour allocation in both countries. In Wisconsin, such influence appears more clearly with respect to the on-farm labour input, whereas in Shiga the influence is much stronger in the off-farm labour input.

The Impact of the Family Life Cycle

The aging structure of the farm family over life cycle stages has a substantial impact on the nature of labour allocation, the amount of income received and

FIGURE 1

the type of farm operation. Two idea types of family structure are compared: one is the nuclear family system as a typical situation of the Wisconsin farm family, the other being the extended family system representing the Shiga farm family.

The pattern of family labour allocation and the composition of income received from the two sources show a marked difference between the two systems. As is depicted in figure 2, in Wisconsin the aggregated farm labour input increases at early stages but decreases at later stages, reflecting the aging structure of the farm family. The movement of the aggregated off-farm labour input somewhat complements that of on-farm labour input. As a result, the realized total family income is almost equalized at different life cycle stages. From this it is inferred that off-farm employment makes a significant contribution in smoothing out the family income stream at a high, stabilized level over time.

In Shiga, however, no such complementary relationship can be observed; both farm and off-farm labour input patterns take a U-shaped curve over the development stages of the farm family. Under the extended family system, there is no end or contraction of the family or the family farm operation (figure 3). This sharp contrast regarding employment and income characteristics is due mainly to the different family systems, but it is also attributable to the different inheritance and property tax systems of the two countries.

Another significant finding in the life cycle approach is that farming changes are also related to the life cycle stages in Wisconsin. The Wisconsin data show that the change of the type of farm operation into a less labor intensive one mostly took place either at the time of the generational transfer of the family farm or when the physical capacity of family labour was sharply declining. Here again, such farming changes according to life cycle elements were minimal, if they occurred at all, among Shiga farm families.

Conclusions and Implications

The most significant role played by off-farm employment is in additional income to the farm family, which, combined with net farm income, brings about a more stabilized and improved level of family well-being. If farm adjustments can be appropriately made, then disadvantages attached to dual employment, such as reduced time for leisure, limited access to services, and lower returns to investment in the farm operation are more likely to be offset by the utility derived from off-farm employment and off-farm income.

Policy implications of part-time farming are twofold. On the one hand, the dual employment pattern is likely to bring about more efficient use of family labour resources. That is, when stable off-farm employment opportunities are provided within commuting distance, excess family labour may be absorbed, resulting in higher productivity per unit of labour as a whole. On the other hand, nonlabour farm resources are more likely to be used less efficiently by the part-time farm family, farmland may be used at a lower level of capacity, and farm machinery and equipment may be used fewer hours per year, implying lower output per unit of capital investment. Therefore, policy planners need to take into consideration these twofold productivity characteristics of part-time farming. For the purpose of reducing rural poverty problems, the dual job holding appears to be an effective vehicle to enhance the well-being of the rural population.

The findings of the present study are largely inconclusive on the future of part-time farming, although the majority of the sample farm families expressed their intention to maintain the dual employment pattern, at least for the foreseeable future. But part-time farming, as broadly defined in this study, seems likely to remain, if not increase substantially, as an important part of rural settings considering that: (1) the labour-saving technological change within the farm sector will likely continue; (2) farmers with relatively small, insufficient farm units will find it increasingly difficult to realize an adequate income from farming; and (3) the relative advantage of and preference for living in a rural area and taking up farming will likely be enhanced.

References

Gasson, R. (ed.) (1977) The Place of Part-Time Farming in Rural and Regional Development. Proceedings of a seminar held at Wye College, July 11-14, 1977. Wye College, England; Centre for European Agricultural Studies.

U.S. Department of Agriculture (1976) Agricultural Statistics.

RAPPORTEUR'S REPORT--Linda Chase

Discussion of Kada's paper focused on the direction of the flow of income between sectors, and on his use of the farm family unit. In Japan, does the farm support an off-farm worker or does off-farm work help finance higher levels of farm investment? Kada felt that the latter was more common, but that the issue is complex. The author's use of the farm family unit was supported, although where a farm family has a full-time, off-farm worker, the definition of a part-time, off-farm unit becomes less clear. It was noted that the unit labels in figure 1 are ambiguous; they appear to indicate an even scale where the author intended proximate figures. For example, "3" indicates 100-200 days of farm labour.

FIGURE 2

FIGURE 3

DILEMMAS WITH MULTIJOB HOLDERS
(PART-TIME FARMERS) IN AGRICULTURE

Stane Krasovec

In 1964, I presented a study on the future of part-time farming to the 12th International Conference of Agricultural Economists at Lyon. That study drew attention to the relatively high proportion of part-time farmers (paysans-ouvriers) in both developed and developing countries and went on to argue that part-time farming is a transitional phenomenon in the process of rapid economic growth, and that it gradually declines in significance in highly developed regions. The validity of that prognosis was subsequently the subject of prolonged discussion in numerous economic publications. Statistical evidence used in those discussions is often oversimplified and open to question. First, the trend is not identical by size classes. Second, while individual type II and part-time farmers leave agriculture en masse, a large number of type I and full-time farmers may change between censuses into type II. The census does not indicate the movement or degree of mobility of individuals through decades and generations, which can be established only through demographic studies. In addition, the class status of many farmers may be changed as a result of movements in farm prices and incomes. Thus, the actual position in many countries seems to confirm Professor Niehaus' dictum, "stehende Welle" (standing wave).

The share of part-time farms in the total number of holdings has increased in many countries, but some of my critics overlooked a statement in my study to the effect that, in brief, as the marginal size for a viable holding increases, so, for a time, will the number of part-time holdings. Farmers with a lower acreage will have to seek means to maintain their incomes, such as greater mechanization and larger capital investment. Farmers on the smaller holdings could not afford to make these changes without additional income. Moreover, farmers are no longer willing to accept a lower standard of living than their urban counterparts. Even farmers with medium sized or larger holdings who could not increase their acreage found that with increased mechanization they were able to take on supplementary work off the farm. They were encouraged to do so in order to satisfy their desire for a wider range of consumer goods. Shorter working hours in industry and dramatic changes in transport facilities helped them to achieve this end. In short, part-time farmers are no longer the poor paysans-ouvriers whom I had primarily in mind in 1964. Rohm has stressed that part-time farming has always and everywhere "changed in quantitative and qualitative respects and will change further."

The economic motivation and conditions of part-time farmers have already been examined in considerable detail by distinguished economists of various countries as well as by national and international institutes and agencies, but up to now no one has attempted an exposition of a general and overall policy toward part-time farming as such. This may in part be explained by the lack of clear and credible appraisals in research, and therefore an absence of agreement whether to encourage or discourage part-time farming (Bergmann and Laurent).

The attitude of goverments has been essentially one of laissez faire. It is only very recently that part-time farmers have been taken into account in the formulation of economic policies, and, even so, only to a very limited extent. First, it has been frankly admitted in the EC that there is much to be said in the restructuring of agriculture for those giving up farming to go through a transitional period of part-time farming in order to make the change to another occupation less painful. Second, and more important, the EC has provided, under the less favoured areas directive, that financial aid may be given from EC funds to farmers who derive or may derive a substantial proportion of their income from nonfarm activities such as tourism, thereby helping to prevent the depopulation of remote mountainous areas and a possible subsequent soil erosion.

The extent to which part-time farmers qualify for state aid to agriculture differs from country to country. In France, Italy, the United Kingdom, Canada, and, to some extent, Sweden, pressure from farm organizations--who regard part time farmers as non-bona fide or undersellers--has resulted in their being largely excluded from credit facilities, investment aids, tax concessions, and the like, on the grounds that their nonfarm income should enable them to do without help. By contrast, in Austria, Finland, Norway, and Switzerland, part-time farmers are classified with "low income" farmers and qualify for various income support payments. In socialist countries such as Poland and Yugoslavia, no distinction is made between full-time and part-time farmers in general government policies or in the operation of farmer cooperatives.

The above examples, however, reflect specific ad hoc policies rather than any defined attitude toward part-time farmers as such. This indifference to the technological and economic destinies of these people may be of little consequence for the economies of countries like the United States, Canada, the United Kingdom, and the Federal Republic of Germany, where the production on part-time farms has little effect on the total available food supply. The position is, however, entirely different in some other countries where up to two-thirds of the available agricultural area may be occupied by part-time farmers and land is very scarce and industry poor. In these countries, a wide variety of approaches to the subject could be made (leading in some cases to conflicting results), bearing on land use, general economic policies, employment and income policies, population distribution, ecology, tourism, and even housing and architecture. In addition, political and ideological considerations come into play.

Part-time farming is criticized for low economic and technological efficiency, low yields per acre and per worker, low capital to output ratios and low land mobility. In those socialist countries where part-time farms exist, they are regarded as an obstacle to the expansion of large agricultural units. Similarly, in most capitalist countries, part-time farmers are nowadays looked upon as an impediment to agricultural structural reform since they impede the creation of larger, viable holdings. They may, however, be tolerated in areas where, because of topography or soil, land cannot be cultivated in larger units. It is also recognized that a high degree of efficiency may be achieved on part-time farms in the production of specialty products such as wine, fruit, vegetables, and honey, but this applies to only a minority of part-time farms.

The aggregate income earned per person and per household in part-time farming is a relevant factor in the context of economic growth. On average, the aggregate income derived from farming plus nonfarm work is higher, in similar size classes, than that of full-time farmers, irrespective of the possibly lower yield per acre and the lower level of industrial wages in rural areas. Further, in households where the housewife and one or two adult children earn wages for off-farm work, or replace the "occupier," the family labour potential is fully realized in gainful work, instead of being restricted to work of little or no economic value. While it may be true that the low productivity per acre on part-time farms--whether commercial holdings or not--means that the food supply on the home market is lower than it would be otherwise, it is also true that the subsistence production of part-time farms results in a commensurate reduction of demand. It is surely advantageous to the agricultural industry generally if the extra income earned on part-time farms is used for investment in agriculture, but even if, instead, it is used for consumer goods, provided these goods are home produced, the internal market is expanded. Experience in Japan could be cited in support of this view. Others supported this analysis, contending that part-time farmers act economically as multipliers and may contribute to faster economic growth.

The two conflicting standpoints outlined above on the value of part-time farming to national economies could be reconciled if part-time farmers were considered by category, as they are far from being a monolithic population. Economists have, in fact, identified a wide variety of types with differing origin, motivation, and structure. For the purposes of this paper, two main types with opposing economic behaviour and propensities are basically relevant.

Type I is defined as households where the agricultural holding is the main source of income or represents the farmer's main occupation. In some countries, farmers on such holdings are referred to as paysans-ouvriers. In the Federal Republic of Germany, such farms are called agricultural main income holdings. Farmers on these holdings are entirely dedicated to their farms; they use their savings from off-farm work for farm investments, and, particularly on the smaller holdings, their results are superior to those on full-time holdings of a similar size.

Type II is defined as households where the main source of income or main occupation is off the holding, in some countries called ouvriers-paysans. In the Federal Republic of Germany, such farms are called agricultural supplementary income holdings. Operators of these farms, as a rule, have only one foot in agriculture. They care little about yields, they are willing to reduce their already small acreage, and, in some cases, the holdings are left uncultivated and kept as "social fallow" as a hedge against bad times.

This latter classification has been used in agricultural statistics for some time, originally in Japan and subsequently in many other countries, including the Federal Republic of Germany and Austria, and in the OECD. It reflects the historical pattern of transference from farming into other work via part-time farming. If this distinction is not made, the facts are liable to be distorted and the conclusions reached inaccurate. If type I part-time farms were designated instead as full-time farms--as is done in some countries, including Yugoslavia--the yields of full-time farms would be artificially inflated. The merging of type I part-time farms and type II into a single group of part-time farms can have the general effect of eliminating the differences in yields between part-time and full-time farms.

The situation of type II part-time farmers (and in certain circumstances also of type I), as described above, is, however, subject to some qualification. It is true of classical part-time farmers or ouvriers-paysans in developing regions. In other words, it is true of subsistence farmers practicing old-fashioned polycultural (or "mixed") production. In those parts of Europe where subsistence or semisubsistence farming still prevails, it would be useful if a decision were reached as to whether part-time farmers (particularly type II) are subsistence or commercial producers.

The subsistence part-time farmer is on the whole a weak, conservative producer, usually associated with traditional peasantlike mixed agriculture. Sooner or later the farmer gives up cattle, abandons meadows and pastures, and cultivates what remains without manure or fertilizers. Thanks to (often increasing) off-farm income, low yields do not worry the farmer, and, indeed, unless the holding is mechanized or mechanical help is available and the family is large, the farmer could hardly work the holding at all.

The commercial part-time farmer, in the first instance, usually cultivates a proportion of land for the market and then gradually increases that proportion, in some cases ending up with only a single crop. This enables the farmer not only to spend substantially less time on the farm, but, in addition, to achieve often much higher yields than the full-time farmers of the same size farms. The possible loss through crop failure is compensated either by off-farm income or by savings from earlier good years. In this way, the producer may become comparatively wealthy and have a working day no longer than that of a full-time farmer. The succeeding generation may well be ready to retain its footing on the land.

In different environments (different education, tradition, length of the working day or week, transport conditions, and marketing and credit institutions) the behaviour of the above types and subtypes can be modified to a greater or lesser extent.

The implications of various economic types of part-time farming, both for the agricultural industry generally and for the national economies, should be taken into account in the formulation of agricultural policy. National statistical services should be geared to provide information on the frequency distribution of each of the types referred to above. This information should form an integral part of the criteria used in assessing individual regional situations—availability or scarcity of land, lack or excess of national food production, developed or developing economy, and significance of agriculture for the balance of payments. Thus equipped, policymakers would be better able to make optimal decisions on part-time farming; that is, whether, for instance, to adopt a laissez faire policy, or to encourage greater commercial production, or to concentrate on efficient land use, or to encourage specialization and monoculture. These decisions would be given effect in the usual ways—through price supports, credit facilities, tax concessions, legislation, and so on. In some countries, many policies on these lines are already in operation; in others, no action whatsoever has yet been taken.

References

Bergmann, D.; Laurent, C. (1977) Research needs and priorities, in The Place of Part-Time Farming in Rural and Regional Development (edited by R. Gasson). Ashford, Kent; Centre for European Agricultural Studies, Wye College.

Rohm, H. (1973) Entwicklungsprobleme der Nebenerwebslandwirtschaff. Grune Reihe, No. 5.

OPENER'S REMARKS—Hiroyuki Nishimura

This paper has brought us some meaningful insights into part-time farming. I agree that part-time farming has played a significant role in increasing farmers' income and thus their well-being. Basically, part-time farming or off-farm employment is an important phenomenon in the industrial society.

In the last part of the paper, Krasovec distinguishes between subsistence and commercial part-time farmers. That may be possible on theoretical grounds. At the practical level, however, the separation of these is somewhat doubtful for various reasons. Use of the statistical methods, as he suggests, may be possible only after the clarification of subsistence and commercial part-time entities. For regional types of agriculture or forms of nonfarm employment, some qualification is also essential. For example, if we extend our observations to a stable type II part-time farmer near and within the urban areas and to a depressed type II part-time farmer in the rural areas, it would be necessary to have more details and adjusted distinctions. I would like to know more about the feasibility of his concepts and their application to actual cases.

As regards the definition of part-time farming, Japanese statistics have added more detailed groupings for part-time farmers of type I and II since the 1970 census. There are now four categories, by status of labour force, of those engaging in off-farm jobs. They are: (1) both head of household and his or her successor; (2) head of household only; (3) successor only; and (4) other family members.

In addition to those cases mentioned by Krasovec, mainly for Western European countries, it may be useful to refer to part-time farming in Japan. First, part-time farming has increased to 87 percent of all farms. The share of type II is about 68 percent. Off-farm jobs of this type are fairly stable, because of the limited amount of acreage in farmland and the unavailability of large size farming. The main source of income in part-time farming, therefore, depends on a stable salary. Actually, the influence of part-time farming on the agricultural production is large enough that it cannot be entirely ignored.

Second, in most cases in Japan, farming is characterized by rice monoculture, which, in addition to the influence of the monsoon, is predominant partly because of its simple cultural practices and its decreasing use of labour. Moreover, monoculture has resulted in farmers having more time to seek off-farm jobs.

Third, type II part-time farmers usually keep their land as an asset for prospective capital gain or old age insurance. Thus, it brings about unused land and a shortage of supply for residential usage.

Fourth, there is no particular policy to support specific part-time farmers. However, evaluating their role is now a focus of attention because we need to keep a sufficient level of self-supply of foods and to seek a sound society to ensure comfortable living in a safe environment.

RAPPORTEUR'S REPORT--John Hardie

Studies in individual countries to obtain a more precise knowledge of the principal economic behaviour of each of the two types were recommended. All the type I farmers are not completely concentrated in agriculture and do not always obtain better yields than full-time farmers, nor are all the type II waiting for an opportunity to reduce their acreage. In the alpine valleys of France and Italy, there is a trend toward renewal of part-time farming by people who previously were nonfarm workers in the French mountain region of Vosges.

Given the different methods of statisticians working in different countries under different sociological constraints, we will have great difficulty in obtaining comparable data at an international level. Some are already using the share of income between farm and nonfarm sources, and others the percentage of labour time devoted to one of the activities. In France, one can still only use labour time, and the results are estimates based on conventional measures. So the borderline between the two types is imprecise in some countries, whereas it is more accurate elsewhere, for example in the USA.

Should the national contributions of part-time farmers be enhanced through more explicit public policies? Should such policies encourage farm consolidation and enlargement for part-time commercial or type I farmers? And should they help accelerate the transition of type II farmers to urban or nonfarm living? How would such policies best interface with policies to enhance the production of larger commercial farms and policies to promote tourism, dispersed settlement, and other activities?

The adoption or rejection of certain public policies for part-time farmers has implications for larger commercial farms, for international trade, and for the very way of life in some countries. Part-time farmers are far from a monolithic class. They vary greatly in their economic and social characteristics, even within the types presented by Krasovec. Accordingly, Krasovec offers a plea for more data on their circumstances so that appropriate public policies, including the laissez faire option may be identified and implemented. But here is a dilemma. We need more adequate data to formulate policies. But without relevant questions based on feasible policy alternatives, we cannot specify what data will be adequate.

Contributing to the discussion were Alan R. Bird (in absentia), Sven Holmstrom, Claude Laurent, and Takeo Misawa.

RURAL LABOUR FORCE IN THE FUTURE: THE JAPANESE CASE

Takashi Matsugi

Abstract

This paper deals with the decreasing trend of agricultural labour inputs and its future consequences. A simple extrapolation of the trend shows that labour shortage will occur in late 1980s when domestic income parity is a main concern and in the mid-1990s when Japanese agriculture should be more efficient. Less use of labour is desirable to raise productivity, but the outflow of labour from the agricultural sector can be promoted only through the creation of abundant job opportunities outside agriculture. To meet the new situation of labour shortage, policy measures which are to contribute to rural development should aim (1) to help enlarge farm size through improved land mobility, (2) to afford the younger generation educational facilities required for effective large scale farm management, and (3) to introduce factories into rural areas to create more jobs for those willing to leave farming.

OPENER'S REMARKS--Garland P. Wood

What assumptions are made regarding energy costs in the growth rate projection of 4 percent? Energy costs have more than quadrupled since 1973. Various experts project the real costs of energy to triple and perhaps go to a factor of five by 1995. What would happen if not only the costs went up at these alarming rates, but if Japan were faced with a situation of fixed or decreasing available energy units per capita?

In the United States, and perhaps Japan as well, the growth rate of the economy is expected to slow. Cheap energy is no longer the driving force for industrial growth. Labour will be relatively cheaper compared to energy costs in industry and agriculture. We would expect a more labour intensive agriculture. There are many unknowns and much speculation as to the future of industrial nations under energy restrictions including quantity, quality, and costs of energy. These factors will have a dominant effect on any agricultural projections, including labour needs.

Why should Japan compete in the world market with its agricultural production? Is it not perfectly logical for Japan to continue to subsidize its agricultural production if it assures a safe food supply and allows a flexible labour supply?

What policies or lack of policies led to the projected labour shortage in 10 to 15 years? Why is it recommended to introduce factories into rural areas to absorb the present labour surplus if in 10 to 15 years shortages are expected? Are there other more feasible alternatives?

My major concern with the paper is that it is tied to a 4 percent growth rate. What would a 2 percent or zero percent growth rate do to the projections? Two or three such projection rates would give policymakers a better idea of their choices.

OFF-FARM LABOUR SUPPLY:
THE CASE OF LAGUNA, THE PHILIPPINES

Dwight A. Smith

Abstract

Recent studies show that off-farm earnings are important for low income rural households. Little is known about the supply of labour by these households to off-farm work. This paper reports on research concerning off-farm labour supply response of small rice producing farms in Laguna, the Philippines. The Philippines government is attempting to alleviate rural poverty through increased off-farm employment.

The research is based on a theoretical labour supply model for a two person household. Off-farm labour supply is specified as a function of farm and off-farm wage rates, nonearned income, and a series of farm and household characteristics. Tobit analysis is used to estimate the relationships. The results show that men in the household are very responsive to off-farm wage rates. The labour supply elasticity with respect to off-farm wage rates approached four. Farm size had a negative effect on off-farm work, while the number of children had a positive effect.

Rural households are likely to be responsive to off-farm employment opportunities. Decisionmakers in the Philippines and elsewhere must attempt to reverse the large scale bias found in current policies if small scale rural enterprises and off-farm employment are to realize their potential in reducing rural poverty and improving income distribution.

RAPPORTEUR'S REPORT--John Hardie

The assumption of a highly elastic availability of off-farm work was queried, as was the general applicability of the results to Southeast Asia. Such studies should account for the variation in behaviour and seasonal labour requirements by type of enterprise; for example, rice and coconuts. In fact, the case study sample was mostly rice intensive farms, and the inclusion of work on the other farms nearby as off-farm work tended to increase its variability. Migration to urban areas for part of the year was accounted for by including the resulting wage as income from remittances. The residency status of off-farm workers was recognized as having important policy implications. The cost of transport between farm and off-farm work was accounted for in the study.

THE IMPACT OF INTERSECTORAL MIGRATION
ON DEMOGRAPHIC DYNAMICS IN RURAL AREAS

Joachim von Braun

Abstract

Sectoral changes of structure also lead to demographic structural changes. This becomes particularly clear in rural areas. This process is investigated using the Federal Republic of Germany as an example of an industrialized country with a decreasing population.

In rural areas, shrinking economic sectors are proportionally overrepresented. Through mobility out of these sectors and through interregional migration, the younger age groups in particular are numerically reduced during their period of greatest fertility, as mobility is prevalent in this age group. This has far reaching effects on regional population development. It is demonstrated by means of a demographic model that the agricultural population will decrease more rapidly than the nonagricultural population. In this way, the changing demographic structure itself becomes a dynamic component in rural change.

This phenomenon of the influence of population and economic development on each other is more closely investigated with the aid of an interdependent demographic econometric model of the agricultural labour force. The model yields better results in explaining labour developments than econometric models, which neglect demographic components as intruding factors. With the help of a projection of the development of agricultural labour in 42 regions, the possibilities for applying this new model as an aid to political decisionmaking are demonstrated.

OPENER'S REMARKS--Sadako Nakayasu

Japanese agriculture has been subjected to structural change through the influence of both demographic and economic development. In many countries, the percentage of the older age groups in the current agricultural labour force is much higher than that in the nonagricultural labour force. The labour mobility and altered demographic structure caused many problems in the agricultural sector and rural areas.

Braun mentioned that intersectoral mobility, combined with interregional migration of the younger employees may result in a vicious circle. I agree, but are there any different problems in the regions where intersectoral mobility does not necessarily entail interregional mobility? For instance, is there a problem of less efficiently used land?

We must seek a way to bring about more favourable results of mobility, if we cannot avoid it. The investigation of regional differences is useful for this purpose.

RAPPORTEUR'S REPORT—Anthony E. Ikpi

Why are young people moving from farming to other occupations in the Federal Republic of Germany? Is this due to unfavourable terms of trade in agriculture? If this is the case, governments need to provide agricultural programmes for the rural poor, and developing countries in particular must be ready to provide all that is needed for implementing such rural projects.

Contributing to the discussion was James A. Akinwumi.

RURAL DEVELOPMENT:
LATIN AMERICA IN THE NEXT DECADE

Stephen E. McGaughey

Rural Development Issues

Rural development projects are aimed at reducing: (1) the large differences in income between urban and rural areas; and (2) the income inequality that persists within rural areas because of the large differences in access to agricultural assets (particularly land), to social services (such as health, education, and housing), and to productive services (such as credit, marketing, and processing facilities). The lack of these facilities and services and the disparities in income and wealth have led some Latin American governments to promote projects which supply the deficient facilities and services to poor rural areas. This emphasis on integrated rural development has also been promoted by the international lending agencies--the World Bank and the Inter-American Development Bank in particular. While rural and agricultural development projects have been initiated in a number of countries, this paper emphasizes examples in Latin America in which the Inter-American Development Bank has been involved. Specific references to these projects do not represent an official viewpoint, however, and opinions expressed herein are exclusively mine.

In executing agricultural and rural development projects in Latin America, most problems have arisen because of inattention to: (1) beneficiary partic-ipation in designing and implementing the projects; (2) dealing with changes in the existing institutional structure and public organization; (3) finding criteria for the selection of beneficiary persons, groups, and regions; and (4) resolving the debate among those espousing a product oriented development strategy and those supporting a social development oriented strategy. Two major project categories may be differentiated--the agricultural development project and the rural development project. Mosher has suggested a practical classification scheme for these projects. The former emphasizes supplying missing production services (marketing, credit, extension, and research) while the latter emphasizes public social services (education, health, and sanitation).

Rural development projects should increase the participation of the rural poor in the planning stage of the projects. This is emphasized in the rural development programmes of Mexico and Colombia, but is absent from many other agricultural investment programmes in Latin American countries. For example, it has been common for governments to design and execute agricultural projects (such as irrigation) without a careful consideration of the receptiveness and the social characteristics of the beneficiary groups. This has given rise to serious problems such as frequent dissatisfaction of beneficiaries, underutilized investment works, high project unit costs, production failures, low rates of return, and heavy government subsidization of the beneficiaries. See, for example, the survey of Colombian agrarian reform projects by Howard.

The candidate beneficiaries of rural development projects are the inhabitants who historically have been excluded—the small subsistence farmer, the landless worker, and the population in the small urban centre in predominantly rural regions. To the extent that the rural poor are concentrated in well defined regions, rural development projects may benefit this group, but if the rural poor are spread out through all rural and small urban areas, there is a reduced prospect that specific regional rural development projects will have the desired effects. It is clear that middle income rural inhabitants may benefit from traditional public programs because of the access they have to the programs. For example, school nutrition programs often do not reach the lowest income groups because the children of the poor attend school with much less frequency than other income classes (Offedal and Levinson).

The separate components of rural and agricultural development projects have been integrated in only a haphazard way. See especially McInerney for an excellent statement on the need for looking at the direct and indirect linkages among all project components. Thus, in the past, marketing facilities have been created for agricultural projects without considering, for example, the need for local credit facilities or a new farm to market road. Penetration roads have been built which have not been accompanied by an effective organization for land settlement, titling, agricultural credit, or extension. Thus, the promotion of rural development projects is a response to past failures to include key project elements which have limited the success of past projects. On the other hand, designers now seem to be trying to include every possible missing project element, even ones which a project may not absolutely require to be feasible and cost effective. Thus, there is a tradeoff between the degree of "completeness" of the individual rural development project and its cost effectiveness and manageability, which has not always been recognized in Latin America.

Rural development projects contain new institutional arrangements. Social services are usually separately provided by government entities--for example, health services by the Ministry of Health, and rural education by the Ministry of Education--with little coordination among the ministry budgets. Thus, traditional budgetary procedures have to be substantially altered to fit the demands of rural regional project allocations. These budgetary changes are being made by some Latin American governments because the functional ministry budgetary procedures have done little to reach the most needy groups. Hence, traditional budgetary systems are most likely to reinforce, or at least may be neutral toward, the traditional inequity in the allocation of public resources to groups or regions.

Rural Development Experience in Latin America

Major national rural development programmes are underway in Mexico and Colombia, and while these national programmes are called "projects" by external lending agencies, in practice they are sectorial and regional development programmes.

Mexico. The Investment Program for Rural Development (PIDER) evolved since the late 1960s under two government administrations and began operating in the 1972-74 period. The programme, as originally designed, projects an eventual expenditure well in excess of US$1 billion in about 50 microregions. Eventually, the programme should benefit several million rural inhabitants and extend to roughly 100 microregions.

A unique feature of the PIDER programme is a new institutional structure to consolidate central government budgetary control over the programme. A mix of productive support and social service investments is chosen for each microregion after formal consultations with local and state government leaders. State authorities participate by refining political and economic decisions leading to regional expenditure programming. There are more than a dozen public agencies that participate in PIDER, and each of the separate ministries is assigned funds which must be employed directly in it. Hence, the traditional separate planning of these entities is now coordinated through a unified budgeting and planning process.

PIDER appears to have achieved initial success, especially by altering the budgetary process in favour of the rural poor, by achieving production gains in certain microregions, and by obtaining greater participation of local political leaders and farmers. It is too early to judge whether the programme will give rise to a significant increase in rural incomes and employment, but the political commitment is high and this should ensure that federal and state officials continue to promote the programme.

Colombia. In the early 1970s, Colombia initiated a rural development strategy. It is intimately related to a national food programme (PAN), the purpose of which has been to increase the supply of food especially by increasing the output on small farms where the bulk of the national food supply is produced. In order to further the objectives of the food programme, a national, integrated rural development programme (DRI) was designed to increase the productivity of small farmers in priority regions. DRI is based on the central notion of improving the technological package of the small farmer in order to expand agricultural productivity, and, therefore, 60 percent of the expenditures will be to expand agricultural production through agricultural research, extension, credit, and marketing services.

An effort has been made in the DRI programme to operate a new institutional system, coordinating the separate programmes of the individual public sector agencies. But the lines of institutional authority are confusing. The DRI institutional structure is headed by a national coordinating committee which brings together the directors and chiefs of all the 13 participating public agencies. While the National Planning Department plays an essential role in programming the budget activities, the Agricultural Bank is responsible for executing and administering the funds and a quasi-independent coordinating body composed of national, district, and municipal coordinating committees is responsible for reviewing the programmes, policies, and activities. DRI gives the impression of separate planning and budgetary activities, with the national government having limited authority to enforce compliance with the goals set out by the national coordinating committee.

Other countries. Rural development projects have also been undertaken in several other Latin American countries, but not on the scale and complexity as those in Colombia and Mexico. The Inter-American Development Bank has supported several rural and agricultural development projects and colonization projects in the Dominican Republic, Venezuela, Peru, Bolivia, Brazil, and Paraguay designed to supply rural infrastructure, such as irrigation or production credit to medium and small holders. Major irrigation investments have been financed in Mexico.

Conclusions. While there has been considerable political rhetoric in support of rural development in Latin America, the practical consequences have fallen well short of these high expectations. Each country is slowly developing its own practical rural development programme--some countries emphasizing production infrastructure and social services (PIDER) and others production technology and extension services (DRI). A few countries have rejected, at least implicitly, a strategy of increasing direct aid to the rural poor, emphasizing instead commercial agricultural production and an urban industrial development policy. Many Latin American countries are still only supporting local rural development projects which have relatively high per beneficiary investment costs. They have not taken steps toward comprehensive national programmes with all of the public expenditure and institutional reallocations which follow.

Prospects for Latin American Rural Development

The "triage" approach (see the searching commentary by Myrdal) to allocating external assistance by the advanced countries emphasizes that middle income countries in Latin America should receive a declining share of total foreign assistance--with a greater share going to lower per capita income countries in Asia and Africa. Likewise, there is rising political pressure to increase the proportion of the remaining assistance received by Latin America that is channeled to low income countries and beneficiaries. While this approach appears consistent with the desire that funds be received by the neediest groups, Latin America still has a large segment of rural poor, and it has reached a stage in which it can now absorb more funding than in the past. The World Bank, the United States, and the Inter-American Development Bank together loaned Latin America the equivalent of about US$1 billion for narrowly defined rural development, integrated agricultural development, colonization, and agrarian reform projects during the period 1970-78. However, a current manifestation of the weakness of public support for agriculture is the scarcity of agricultural investment projects suitable for external financing. The region's overall investment coefficient is rising, but the domestic revenue structures are still strained to generate sufficient resources to meet expenditure goals. Thus, the total net financial requirements to undertake massive rural development programmes are still beyond available domestic and external savings.

New rural development efforts, over the short term, would compete with investments for industrial and basic energy programmes, and this would require unacceptable political sacrifices as the urban population rapidly increases. Hence, large amounts of external resources are needed for both a concerted urban industrial and rural agricultural development effort in Latin America over the coming decade. Even if national savings grow, external assistance will still be required. Lacking "soft" funds, governments will have to utilize private commercial sources. If international public financial resources are limited, the region will increase its external debt burden over the period, which should not surprise financial observers.

Latin America cannot avoid supporting agricultural and rural development. The shape of this development may not accord with preconceived views of all outsiders, but an effort will have to be made, for several reasons. Latin America has experienced one of the largest population growth rates of any region of the world and this has direct implications for rural development investment strategies in years to come. The labour force has expanded at unprecedented rates, placing a strain on the ability of the industrial and urban centres to supply productive employment. A declining share of employment is in agriculture—falling from 53 percent of the active labour force in 1950 to 41 percent in 1970—while the industrial sector has barely increased its share of employment—from 19 to 22 percent of the labour force.

There is a serious need to increase rural development activities because they are highly beneficial to both agricultural and industrial development. Industrial development, which will become increasingly export oriented, would be stimulated because of an increased demand for agricultural inputs and services. This in itself will contribute to an increase in urban industrial employment. Simultaneously, the introduction of modern agricultural technology will increase productivity and income in rural areas. It will be easier to transfer labour out of agriculture and to absorb it into higher paying employment in urban centres.

Before Latin America can initiate this strategy, a number of fundamental policy changes will have to be made, breaking with traditional economic policies toward agriculture. The most important changes concern: (1) agricultural pricing policies; (2) government budgetary allocations for agricultural research and extension; and (3) administrative institutional biases against agriculture. These needed changes go against fundamental historical trends which have accompanied the rise in the political dominance of the urban centres and the continuing weakness of the public agricultural bureaucracy.

Unless Latin American governments make major improvements in the policy elements just noted, then one can expect continuing social, economic, and political problems in rural areas, which further increase the costs of rectifying the gap between the rural poor and the urban beneficiaries of government economic policies. Unforeseeable political instability should be anticipated if rural and urban poverty continue to grow. Such fundamental problems will not be resolved by occasional investment in a rural or agricultural development project, but rather by the transformation of public priorities to give rural development an equal political status with urban and industrial development. This has yet to occur in most Latin American countries. Lessons have been learned by some countries which have undertaken agrarian reform programs (the Andean region), but they have failed to produce the income and production benefits in rural areas or to avoid large food imports for the growing urban population.

References

Howard, E. H. (1976) The approach to agrarian reform in Colombia and the role of the external lending agencies. Ph.D. dissertation. Cambridge, Massachusetts, USA; Harvard University.

McInerney, J. P., The technology of rural development. Staff working paper no. 295. Washington, D.C.; The World Bank.

Mosher, A. T. (1972) Projects of Integrated Development. New York; Agricultural Development Council, December.

Myrdal, G. (1975) The equality issue in world development. Swedish Journal of Economics, 77 (4) 413-432.

Offedal, O. T.; Levinson, J. F. (1977) Equity and income effects of nutrition and health care, in Income Distribution and Growth in the Less Developed Countries (edited by C. R. Rank, Jr. and R. C. Webb). Washington, D.C.; The Brookings Institution, 381-433.

RAPPORTEUR'S REPORT--Anthony E. Ikpi

The rule of thumb that was used in deciding whether the investment projects in Latin America were profitable and beneficial to the rural poor was the value of the output resulting from these projects plus the degree of local involvement and participation in the project. Local involvement and participation may sometimes turn out to be expensive in terms of both time and money. Political implications of nonlocal involvement and participation often dictated the need for involving local participation. Empirical evidence of this is obtainable only in the form of consequences that follow in event of nonlocal participation.

Contributing to the discussion was Earl D. Kellogg.

ACCOUNTS, PROSPECTS, AND METHODOLOGY
FOR RURAL DEVELOPMENT IN TANZANIA

Rameshchandra M. Shah

Abstract

This paper looks at rural development from a broad national point of view, beginning with an historical sketch of Tanzania. It then outlines and justifies the country's present ideological stand and related meaning of rural development. It describes and critically evaluates the technological, sectorial, social, financial, foreign aid, and regional aspects of rural development.

Special emphasis is put on the question of advanced technology being used in underdeveloped rural areas, the role of financial institutions, and the limited role of traditional cash crops grown for foreign markets. The findings show that food crops have better future prospects than cash crops. Finally, the paper touches on the criteria for determining agricultural price policies and regional development strategies.

OPENER' REMARKS--Gary C. Taylor

Shah's point that programmes such as tractorization and introduction of high yielding varieties are doomed to limited success without significant improvement in the physical and service infrastructure is an important one. That the primary emphasis in development should be put on transportation and primary education is perhaps an oversimplification, but these were vital components in the initial development of rural areas in North America.

The most significant omission from Shah's paper is a discussion of policy and strategy to cope with the rapidly rising costs of energy and the resulting impacts on rural development. Energy costs escalated some 18 percent in Tanzania in 1978. Price increases in 1979 and the prospect of continuing escalation will have a severe impact on the structure and prosperity of the rural economies of countries which lack oil. Rural development policies must be reshaped to recognize this important factor.

Programmes aimed specifically at rural development--that is, at problems of low income and equity in rural areas--have enjoyed only qualified success. There are numerous failures of rural development projects sponsored by governments in African countries. There are relatively few specific rural development programmes anywhere that have clearly achieved their objectives except at enormous costs. Why is this so? I would have liked to learn more from this paper about how and why successes and failures have occurred in Tanzania.

RAPPORTEUR'S REPORT--Anthony E. Ikpi

Rural development programmes should not be confused with agricultural development programmes, especially in India where rural development programmes differ from the usual large agricultural projects, because most rural development projects are social and not just economic in content and character. Rural development projects are usually planned to affect both institutional and administrative structures.

Contributing to the discussion was Prafulla K. Mukherjee.

AREA PLANNING APPROACH TO RURAL DEVELOPMENT
AND THE PROBLEM OF CONSISTENCY BETWEEN
LOCAL AND NATIONAL PLANNING

Kamta Prasad

The centralized approach to planning pursued so far in poor countries of Asia and Africa has not succeeded in bringing about widespread change in rural life. The trickle down effect has failed, and with it has come a growing realization of the need to make a direct attack on the problem of rural poverty by initiating action at the local level through an area planning approach whereby plans for the integrated development of small areas would be formulated and implemented by local people (Nyerere; and Government of India, 1978a). This planning from below, or grass roots planning, is expected to result in plans for better utilization of rural resources, through local people having better awareness of their needs and preferences and fuller information on the conditions and possibilities of their areas. The area level planners, having a more intimate knowledge of the interdependence of activities at the micro level, would be in a better position to develop integrated programmes which avoid duplication and produce maximum impact with minimum cost. Moreover, a better implementation of development programmes would be ensured through more realistic planning and greater involvement of local people in plan formulation and implementation (Government of India, 1978b).

However, it is not always realized that, in view of the economies of scale which may be present, an overriding concern with decentralized planning, in particular with the objectives of local self-reliance and full utilization of local resources to the neglect of comparative advantage and regional specialization, may tend to offset the beneficial aspects of area planning mentioned above, and, therefore, need not result in an optimal situation. Whether or not it will result in a consistency between local and national plans in an interdependent, multiregional economy is another and a far more important question; for the failure of aggregate supply to match with aggregate demand, or of the structure of production to be in harmony with the composition of national demand is bound to have an unfavourable effect on the pace of development, especially in a public sector dominated economy like India's where supply and demand imbalances tend to provide grounds for slow working of enterprises resulting in delayed execution of projects. However, in the absence of much work on decentralized planning, very little is known on this aspect (Arrow and Hurwicz, Goreux and Manne; Malinvaud; Uzawa; and Westphal). Hence, it is proposed to examine this question in some detail, spell out its implications for rural development, and deal with the manner in which the problem posed here can be resolved. The discussion will be conducted primarily in the light of the institutional characteristics of the Indian economy and against the background of its considerable experience of development. However, the treatment of the subject matter will be made as general as possible.

The Consistency Problem

The establishment of autonomous area planning units in a country of the size and dimension of India would result in a multiplicity of public agencies entrusted with the task of making decisions on economic activities affecting production and consumption. Whether or not consistency between micro level and economywide plans would be brought about under such conditions would depend upon the type of assumptions made about the institutional framework of an economy. For example, the problem does not arise in a traditional society with village or local self-sufficiency as the basic motto, where production is for self-consumption, the local market, or both. Nor does it arise in an exchange but centrally planned economy where decisions at different levels are subservient to those taken at higher or national levels. The problem could arise in a pure capitalist society having millions of independent producers, but, as is well known, is automatically solved due to the working of the competitive market mechanism which brings about equilibrium in the economy at the level of full employment of resources.

Actual reality is far more complex and cannot be fitted into the simplistic theoretical frameworks outlined above. For example, prices in modern capitalistic societies do not conform to the assumption of continuous variation in either direction; they tend to become rigid. Downward and even upward revisions are made by finite steps at discrete time intervals so that equilibrium between demand and supply of goods is often established at the cost of excess capacity and unemployment of resources. The situation in India is still more complex in view of the mixture of several systems. India has an exchange economy with a regional or national market for domestically produced goods, and its scope is increasing. But the market mechanism is not perfect on account of several distortions, including restrictions imposed by the government. Prices of several basic inputs (for example, coal, electricity, steel, cement, and fertilizer) are subject to government control and regulation. And the free adjustment of prices of a number of agricultural commodities such as rice, wheat, raw cotton, and sugarcane is interfered with by the policy of support prices. In addition, there are price rigidities and restrictions on trading and production in several other sectors. Parts of the labour market are subjected to wage rigidity imposed by the trade unions, and parts by the operation of a government regulation prescribing minimum wages. In a strict sense, the labour market does not function and therefore cannot be relied upon to bring equilibrium in the economic system.

Under these conditions, if production decisions come to be taken at the area level in an autonomous manner, equilibrium at the macro level can be brought about only if there is an area (residual) which can absorb all shocks coming from other areas. No such area exists and in its absence there is no mechanism to ensure consistency between local and national planning. Inconsistency may arise on account of the differences in the goals and objective functions of the different decisionmaking units. For example, maximum growth of national output, national integration, and regional specialization may be objectives of national policy, whereas local self-sufficiency and full employment of local resources may be the goals of area units. Like independent producers in a capitalist system, the area authorities draw up their plans for optimization in the context of their objectives, resources, technology, potential, and problems. But, unlike the capitalist system, there is no automatic mechanism to ensure demand and supply balances at the national level in view of the imperfections of the market mechanism. Due to the intrusion of administered prices into the system, price paid to producers of certain commodities might be prevented from falling even if supply is rising ahead of demand. Disequilibrium may show up in the form of stockpiling with government marketing agencies, which, in due course, may necessitate sale at subsidized rates. Subsidies may be justified only to the extent they are based on differences between shadow prices and market prices. But it is doubtful whether there would be much scope for using shadow prices as policy variables under these conditions. Thus, equilibrium can be brought about only at the cost of massive subsidies by using funds which could have been better spent on rural development programmes. This sort of a situation has arisen quite often in India. Khadi and village industries, foodgrains, and sugarcane are some of the more prominent recent examples. The probability that this situation will occur is high in most of the developing economies because the productive capabilities at the local levels are mostly of traditional goods such as handspun and handloom clothes and village handicrafts, while the structure of demand at the national level has been changing in favour of newer goods such as nylons, plastics, stainless steel, and aluminum, which require the use of sophisticated equipment and skilled labour not found everywhere.

However, the above line of reasoning is not valid for the nontradable activities like land contouring and leveling, drinking water supply, construction of dug wells, distribution of water from an outlet, social forestry, or primary education, which are no less important for rural development. This list can be extended to cover commodities having only a local market. The problem really arises in the case of commodities entering regional and national markets, and may become more acute for areas producing specialized products for widespread markets, such as copper in the Singhbhum district of Bihar in India, whose development plans cannot be finalized until the micro plans of other areas are known, and vice versa. We may generalize this and state that consistency between local and national planning is easy if decisions made in one area do not cause economic scarcities in the rest of the economy. The smaller the area, the more difficult it becomes to fulfil this condition. Therefore, in such cases, complete autonomy of planning at the area level is ruled out. The need to take the overall demand and supply balances into account requires that the area level plans are prepared within a macro framework.

The problem is not confined to products alone, but extends to factors of production like labour and capital, which are mobile and have a market which goes beyond the area boundary. Here, also, there is no mechanism to ensure consistency between the total demand by all areas and aggregate supply. Various types of problems may arise in practice. For example, if jobs for all labour in an area are provided in the area itself under some sort of an employment guarantee scheme (of the type attempted in some states of India) and at some minimum wage rate high enough to meet their reasonable needs, then there will be little incentive for labour to move from surplus to deficit areas, in which case optimum development would not be assured. In the case of capital, which is usually very mobile, a disproportionately greater part may find its way from the less developed rural to more developed urban areas on account of several factors, including the operation of the economic forces of prices, wages, credit, and interest rates. Such problems can be resolved only within a macro framework with a suitable mix of general and differential policies formulated at the national rather than area level.

The problem of inconsistency may also arise with respect to use of resources like river water held in common with other areas. The possibility of the aggregate requirements of different areas turning out to be more than the total supply of the resource cannot be ruled out. Moreover, if every area started preparing plans for its own optimization without looking into the adverse effects of its policy on neighbouring areas (that is, external diseconomies), the result would be utter confusion and a gross misutilization of resources, which would not be in the best interests of rural development. For example, in the case of flood control, an embankment on one side of the river or in one area tends to produce adverse effects on the other side or in upstream or downstream areas. Similarly, a drainage scheme for an area may result in drainage congestion for the contiguous area below. Similar problems of reconciling inconsistent area plans may arise in the case of the creation of such infrastructural facilities as major roads and bridges, railway lines, power plants, storage, or marketing, which are necessary for rural development but go beyond area boundaries. Such activities should be taken out of the purview of area planning and decided at the appropriate regional or national level.

Multilevel Planning

It follows from the above that the problem of consistency as posed here can be resolved by formulating area plans for marketable commodities within a macro framework and by an appropriate devolution of functions at different levels:

local, regional, and national. The planning exercise would be carried out, not at any one level (area or national), but at several levels with appropriate links established between them so as to arrive at a mutually consistent set of quantitative allocations and prices. This would imply disaggregation of economic activities and plan targets by regions and areas. On the other hand, the need to ensure demand and supply balances would require the planning exercise to be disaggregated with respect to specific kinds of activities or sectors of the economy as usually takes place in economywide planning models. Thus both the regional and sectorial ramifications of multilevel planning are relevant here. This would require formulation of multisectorial and multiregional planning models. It will take a long time before such models are developed and come to be generally accepted. Meanwhile, an attempt may be made to identify and demarcate the fields of activities where planning bodies at different levels should have exclusive, dominant, or marginal responsibilities. It can be inferred from what has been said earlier that the scope for the devolution of functions at the area level is not insignificant in the context of rural development. Activities like soil conservation, social forestry, land reclamation, village roads, minor irrigation, animal husbandry, education and social services, water supply, health, housing, and local transportation are liable to planning at the area level. Given the low capital base and low level of productivity in rural areas, the thrust of rural development in the initial years would be on development of activities of the type mentioned above. It is therefore feasible to make use of the area planning approach for bringing about rural development.

Iterative Procedure

An important question that arises here is whether plans at the higher level would be prepared first and those at the lower levels be worked out within the framework already decided at the higher level or vice versa. In other words, should planning be from above or below? India, which has explicitly recognized the role of multilevel planning, seems to have opted for the first alternative. "It has been decided that a block will be taken as the primary area for local planning. At the same time, it is realized that the block level planning will have to be built in a framework of district level planning which has to be adjusted to the overall state plan. The state plan already forms a part of the national plan" (Government of India, 1978a). This is in keeping with the centralized approach to planning pursued so far, which, though justifiable on grounds of efficiency and administrative ease, has been found inadequate to bring about widespread rural development. However, the other alternative of planning from below is also not the ideal solution because it may result in inconsistency at different levels; that is, the totality of plans prepared by the units on a level of hierarchy may not be compatible with the plan of the higher level of units of which they form constituent parts.

Hence, what is needed for rapid rural development is neither planning from above nor planning from below but something in between, which can be brought about by an iterative procedure in which the planning agencies at the area, regional, and national levels would participate, each giving information related to the productive activity to be undertaken by it and revising its programme in the light of information received from lower and higher agencies. As compared to purely centralized planning, the process will take more time and pose greater administrative problems. Conflicts between different regions may arise, and, if not properly handled, may vitiate the development atmosphere. There is also a risk that iterative planning may degenerate into mere horse trading. But, ultimately a consistent plan should emerge if the planning agencies at various levels of the hierarchy adopt a flexible approach having more than one variant of their plans to start with, and respect the right to make certain decisions which necessarily have to be made at a higher or lower level. In this way, it is possible to reconcile the apparently conflicting objectives of decentralized planning to foster maximum utilization of local resources and local talent on the one hand and central monitoring and control to ensure the overall balance between demand and supply on the other.

References

Arrow, K. J.; Hurwicz, L. (1960) Decentralization and computation in resource allocation, in Essays in Economics and Econometrics (edited by R. W. Pfouts). Chapel Hill, USA; University of North Carolina Press.

Goreux, L. M.; Manne, A. S. (editors) (1973) Multi-Level Planning: Case Studies in Mexico. Amsterdam; North Holland Publishing Co.

Government of India (1978a) Five Year Plan, 1978-83, A Draft Outline.

Government of India (1978b) Report of the Committee on Panchayati Raj Institutions.

Malinvaud, E. (1967) Decentralized procedures for planning, in Activity Analysis in Theory of Growth and Planning (edited by E. Malinvaud and M. O. L. Bacharach). MacMillan.

Nyerere, J. K. (1975) Socialism and rural development, as quoted in The Design of Rural Development: Lessons from Africa (by U. Lele). Baltimore, Maryland, USA; The Johns Hopkins University Press, p. 151.

Uzawa, H. (1958) Iterative methods for concave programming, in Studies in Linear and Non-Linear Programming (edited by K. J. Arrow, L. Hurwicz, and H. Uzawa). Stanford, California, USA; Stanford University Press.

Westphal, L. E. (1975) Planning with economies of scale, in Economy-Wide Models and Development Planning (edited by C. R. Blitzer, P. B. Clark, and L. Taylor). Oxford; Oxford University Press.

RAPPORTEUR'S REPORT--Theodora S. Hyuha

Inconsistency is among many problems in planning programmes. Other problems include balanced versus unbalanced growth, imperfect knowledge, lack of knowledge, and lack of feedback processes. We are dealing with constrained optimization with many constraints. It is hard to define a micro unit because macro and micro regions differ from place to place. Using decomposition models may be too complex and too theoretical to be of any use.

USING ECONOMIC OPTIMIZATION MODELS TO FIT INVESTMENT MEASURES FOR AGRICULTURE TO A REGION (ILLUSTRATED BY MEANS OF EXPERIENCE GAINED IN THE GERMAN DEMOCRATIC REPUBLIC)

Helmut Schieck

The adoption of scientific and technological advances in order to increase agricultural production implies rising demands on the scientific management of these advances. It has become necessary to use economic optimization models to help managers make decisions in an increasingly scientific way. Decisions regarding the modernization and renewal of the material and technological bases of crop and animal production in cooperative and state farms have a long term and lasting effect on production efficiency and, as a rule, are of a highly complex nature. For example, a model was developed to provide information relating to the agricultural use and development of a given region as comprehensively as possible. This was intended for large scale investment; for example, in the animal production sector, for rationalization and reconstruction of existing facilities or for new buildings, as appropriate. The mathematical background of the model consists of the algorithm for static linear optimization. It was possible to formulate the problem in 140 lines and 170 columns, and about 2,000 coefficients were used to quantify the relationships, conditions, and limitations.

The model links with major prerequisites which are being worked out for development according to the plan for socialist agriculture in the German Democratic Republic. These include long range draft plans for regional development which can be set up for administrative regions, such as counties or districts, or for regions that are distinguished by their special natural or economic conditions.

Once it is known, in principle, which are the preferred large regions for integrating investment measures for crop and animal production, the location has to be defined more precisely, and a decision made based on economic analysis. This is done by choosing macro locations, defined as regions in which the major production relations between the investment and its environment are being realized; for example, in animal production units, these are production and supply of feed, utilization of slurry, supply of labour, slaughtering and processing, and repair and services. Integration of investment measures result from the necessity of meeting the farm's need to extend its production capacity, and, in doing so, of making use of the possibilities of concentrating and specializing production, and, in this context, of optimally utilizing the production conditions of the macro location, and thus stimulating social development in the region concerned. Altogether, this approach is meant to contribute to (1) raising the output and effectiveness of production and (2) gradually improving the working and living conditions of the people working in agriculture.

The model described above was worked out to facilitate recording the most essential relationships--the input-output relationships--for making scientific decisions for such a complex task. It is meant to help in making statements on whether or not a proposed macro location would have sufficient resources for the regional integration of an intended investment and whether or not its use would be effective when compared with other locations, and measured by the initial investment cost and operating costs. At the same time, it is necessary to decide what the profile of agricultural production should be, and what the pre- and post-agricultural sectors in the given region should look like, given the long range objective of the overall national economy. This, in turn, provides conditions for a more precise detailing of long range and complex development plans for the whole region.

The investigations and model computations must allow for the major factors influencing the choice of location and the regional integration. According to the experience gained so far when integrating investment measures aimed at the expansion of animal production by rationalization and reconstruction of existing facilities or the construction of new units, the following factors proved to be most essential:

1. Securing adequate feed supplies for the livestock in the facilities, which are to be either newly erected or expanded by rationalization and reconstruction, and for livestock in the other units already producing in the given region.

2. Choosing the location of such investments, and making decisions on the concentration of animals to be kept, with due consideration to the existing or intended possibilities of effective utilization of slurry. Taking account of the requirements of socialist working and living conditions as well as of environment protection, the projected expenditure on slurry management should be low. An independent model for several variants of slurry management is first used for this purpose. The investment and technological costs, and the labour, energy, and material requirements are determined with due consideration given to the special local conditions. Slurry utilization has to be harmoniously integrated in the overall system of improving soil fertility for crop production by the appropriate organic and mineral fertilization.

3. Having the technical infrastructure, especially allocation of land, the local adaptation of the construction site, the development of the transport system, and water and energy supplies. Land use for construction purposes is subject to legal regulations. From the standpoint of the overall national economy, it should be confined to poor soils. The local adaptation for the most part comprises the preparation of the site when using standard projects. The inputs required depend on features of the terrain, the type of soil, and the groundwater table. Its site is, at the same time, an essential factor in overall building costs. The development of the transport system, even with extensive use of existing roads, often requires the tracing out of new routes and the fixing of their technological parameters. New animal production units or those extended by way of reconstruction make great demands on the regional water resources. Investment expenditures vary with the production profile of the unit and the related standard water requirement, as well as with the kind of water supply involved (public network or domestic wells). Parameters for energy supply and transformer plants are based on general practices for planning and project preparation of energy supply systems.

4. Meeting sanitary, safety, and veterinary requirements as stipulated in acts and regulations. Essential sanitary and veterinary aspects include, among others; avoiding excessive odours which might disturb dwellings and recreational areas; routing of roads, paths, and pipelines for the transport of animals, feed, and waste products to bypass built-up areas; providing sufficient land for the disposal of waste products with due consideration to ground and surface water conditions; excluding all possibility of emission hazards to the unit by existing or planned industrial plants; and maintaining safe distances between facilities to curb the spread of contagious diseases.

5. Increasing transport operations needed for both production proper and distributing the produce obtained. Transport distances should, as a rule, be kept as small as possible to minimize costs and losses, road load, and the

time cooperative farmers and workers need to reach their places of work.

6. Supplying replacement animals for the new or extended production units. It must be borne in mind that often there will not be sufficient animals available within the given macro location to secure replacments in line with the new requirements.

7. Having the necessary amount of labour available with the right qualifications. The investigations must therefore include the labour fund of the given region, its structure (age, occupation, and qualifications), and the possibilities of using it efficiently. It is also necessary to allow for the labour required for existing animal production as well as for the additional labour required for crop production in the macro location.

Most of the above factors for justifying the choice of a certain macro location and for regional and sector fitting of such investment measures can be quantified, and thus can be considered in model computations. When such investment measures are implemented in a given region, attention must also be paid to providing adequate living conditions for the people. The social infrastructure should be improved in an efficient way with as low an investment as possible. The following social infrastructure complexes are of prime importance: housing construction; institutions for care of children; education and public health services; trade and service sectors; and institutions and facilities for satisfying intellectual and cultural needs, and for sports activities.

Decisions on fixing the location and regional adjustments of investment projects can be prepared with due consideration of these aspects and of model computations. The model described above was worked out to provide the relevant information as comprehensively as possible. By using this model, it becomes possible to record and assess the essential factors involved in fixing locations and regional and sector fitting with all their multifarious inter-relationships.

Starting from the planned growth of production, the following target functions are determined: minimizing production cost and investment, and maximizing net product and profit. With relatively low additional input, the model can be used to test several variants for the location under review so as to make full use of its available natural and economic resources. The model, therefore, is flexible and permits the testing of possibilities and consequences of fitting investment projects related to cattle and pig production. With certain modifications, it can also be used for investment projects in crop production, such as drying plants and processing and storage facilities.

The model can easily be used by enterprises other than the one where it originated. When it is applied to the same problem in another region, a large number of coefficients can be reused. The model computation provides information on the possibility, in principle, of fitting one or several investment objects into the macro location under review. This is essentially dependent on the results affecting the utilization of regional production resources. Thus, if the model shows demands on limited resources beyond those available in the location, it is necessary to clarify whether potential for expanding capacity would be available. If it is not, the intended scope of the investment project cannot be fitted into the regional scheme. In this case, it may be necessary to use another macro location with more substantial resources or to reduce the scope of the investment project.

If the regional production conditions are not sufficiently utilized, analogous adjustments have to be made in the opposite direction. When harmony is achieved between the expected use of the resources in the chosen location (or that considered to be correct) and the location requirements of the chosen investment project, the efforts can be concentrated on detailed information

91

regarding further consequences for the regional production structure.

The model results can be used to derive to what extent the major production sectors (including their land, labour, feed, and input requirements) would have to be developed so as to reach optimal targets in the macro location by combining new investments and existing production capacity. From this, it becomes obvious that results are worked out not only for new investments but rather for all the production within the territory of the macro location, and that this approach prevents one-sided decisions. Detailed results are computed for the scope and structure of land use, gross crop product (subdivided as market product, seed and planting material, and feed), feed conservation and use for the various species of animals, livestock by type and uses, gross animal product, labour input in animal production and crop production, level of investment, import and export of breeding animals and productive livestock in the territory of the macro location, and value coefficients of the production process.

Experience gained so far in using this methodology suggests that the approach described is suitable for scientific investigation of location and regional fitting of investment projects for animal production units, crop production, feed production, and other agricultural investments. This is not, however, sufficient in itself for scientific decisionmaking. Such decisions can only be made taking full account of the overall framework set by agricultural policy and of the socioeconomic conditions in the macro location concerned, in combination with the utilization of the results of the linear optimization model. In future work, the methodological instruments will see further improvement and definition and be supplemented by other methods. In principle, it is a first step towards the ever more fully planned and long term solution of the difficult and complex decision problems faced by cooperative farmers and workers in cooperative and state farms, as well as by government management agencies, so as to benefit every individual farm and enterprise as well as the socialist society of the German Democratic Republic as a whole.

RAPPORTEUR'S REPORT--Theodora S. Hyuha

Criticisms were made of underlying assumptions in the model about predetermined prices, social systems, and demand. There are agencies in the socialist system to determine prices and demand. These are external to this model. How relevant is the model to reality since it is linear and nondynamic, and since data may not be available in developing countries? There are limitations to the application of the model to developing countries. The model assumes that there is no trade, although its existence would hardly affect the predictions of the model. In the German Democratic Republic, the social system is determined by the socialist ideology. There is no difference between cooperatives and the state as they both serve the same purpose.

THE IMPLICATIONS FOR RURAL CHANGE OF PHASING OUT RICE PRODUCTION IN MAIN MARGINAL AREAS AS MEASURED BY SECTOR INCOME, ON-FARM EMPLOYMENT, AND FOOD PRICES: THE PHILIPPINE EXPERIENCE

Leonardo A. Gonzales

Abstract

Phasing out marginal rice lands would not adversely affect rice production in the Philippines, if the current cropping intensity index of 134 percent of palay irrigated land were increased to at least 230 percent, at an average yield level of 45 cavans per hectare. At higher technology levels assumed for palay, sector income, credit, and exports would tend to increase. On-farm employment would, however, tend to drop as marginal lands planted to palay are phased out. These results were estimated by the MAAGAP programming model that provides guidelines for the optimum allocation of available resources in the Philippine agricultural sector under competitive market conditions. Relative to the reliability of the results generated by the model, users should be constantly aware of its static equilibrium nature. Results may not accurately reflect reality because the sector is dynamic in actuality. In this regard, therefore, estimates as shown in this report should not be interpreted in their absolute quantitative magnitude but rather in terms of the directional changes that they intend to convey.

OPENER'S REMARKS--Ngo Huy Liem

That self-sufficiency was not adversely affected by phasing out rice production in marginal areas is logical. But the gap between technological progress available for rice production on the one hand, and actual rice yields in the Philippines on the other hand, is tremendous. There are also nontechnological factors which act as important constraints to the targeted production, and which are not included in the model (high prices of fertilizers and pesticides, overpricing of certain production inputs, delays in providing credit, and so forth). In phasing out rice production in marginal areas in favour of other crops, one must also take into account the tenure system. In addition, motivation and participation of the farmers should be seen as a precondition for successful rural change.

RAPPORTEUR'S REPORT--Max T. Colwell

Although there are substantial data available in the Philippines, some data limitations were encountered in model development. Policy decisionmakers have taken note of the model results, including the fact that the simulation model was not designed to solve income distribution problems. Because the Philippine growers traditionally undertook a rice monoculture production programme, some problems occurred in the adoption of a diversification programme. The problems were reduced when successful new crop demonstrations were achieved. Substantial rice surpluses do occur, and support price setting involves a compromise between production costs and consumer purchasing power.

Contributing to the discussion were A. S. Kahlon, A. Rodrigo Mujica, and Ammar Siamwalla.

LESSONS OF 50 YEARS OF PARASTATAL AGENCIES IN DEVELOPMENT OF IRELAND'S AGRICULTURE AND RURAL ECONOMY

A. Desmond O'Rourke

Abstract

The Republic of Ireland has made extensive use of parastatal agencies in developing its agriculture and rural economy. They have played an important, though changing, role in transforming Ireland from an impoverished ex-colony in the 1920s to full membership of the European Community in the 1970s. Initially developed to meet specific needs, their aggregate importance in national economic planning has become recognized. This paper outlines both the expected and unexpected, direct and indirect, effects of the Irish use of parastatal agencies. It spells out the possible benefits and pitfalls which must be faced by developing countries which are short of natural resources, capital, management, and trained workers when using parastatal agencies to promote development. The problems of interaction between parastatal agencies and the private sector in the mixed Irish economy are also explored.

OPENER'S REMARKS--John Duncan Watt

O'Rourke, in a very diverse paper (in terms of the variety of subjects covered which are of interest to agricultural economists) and in the limited space available to him, was able to outline the environment in which the agencies operate, their diversity (reflecting their objectives), and their diverse impacts on the agricultural sector. In essence, he described their possible use as instruments of change in developing countries. He also attempted to produce criteria for evaluation of their usefulness.

Perhaps the major lesson from the Irish experience has been the problem of tenure; once these agencies and associated government support are established, it is very difficult to shift them. It is, for example, apparent from the paper that the Coras Iompair Eireann may have outlived its usefulness. Other lessons are the tradeoffs between entrepreneurship, monopoly, planning, accountability, and monetary costs to the exchequer. It was not proven that the benefits of parastatal agencies exceeded those which may have ensued from the operation of "encouraged" private enterprise. There is, of course, the inevitable difficulties of the tradeoff between economic and social objectives, and of changes in the objectives over time.

RAPPORTEUR'S REPORT--Max T. Colwell

The legal status of Irish parastatal agencies has been altered with minimal effect on their functions as a consequence of Ireland's entry into the European Community. Some Irish parastatal agencies were unsuccessful in diversifying into different markets, and some other agencies (for example, transportation and electricity) were successful due to more appropriate mechanisms.

Contributing to the discussion were A. Rodrigo Mujica, Robert O'Conner, and Roland E. Williams.

THE PLACE OF ACCELERATED PRODUCTION CAMPAIGNS IN EFFORTS TO EXPAND AGRICULTURAL OUTPUT

Delane E. Welsch

Abstract

The accelerated production campaign has become popular in recent years as a vehicle for increasing the aggregate output of a particular crop by substantially raising the per hectare yields on enough farms to make an impact on output at the national level. One could almost say that production campaigns have become a "style of development." Masagana 99 is selected as an example of a successful campaign, and those factors which appear to be necessary preconditions are available technology, a credit system, incentive prices, and political support and leadership. Activities that must be set in motion once a decision has been made to initiate a campaign include: organizing for planning, implementation, and control with a structure that goes from the local village to the highest level of government; selecting target areas and concentrating effort in them; training farmers and field technicians, and making the technicians mobile; supplying and coordinating inputs and credit; and publicity. If the preconditions are not in place, resources should be used to establish them rather than on a campaign that is likely to fail. While they require to be backed up by research and extension, accelerated production campaigns are basically promotional activities, and can be incompatible with research and extension organizations. Overshadowing all of these factors is weather, which can make or break a campaign.

OPENER'S REMARKS--M. Rafiqul Islam Molla

In its essence and outlook, Welsch's paper reflects the philosophy that if growth occurs, rural welfare will improve automatically. But for the families in the rural areas characterized by a segmented special order and an unequal land distribution, the outlook depends as much on distribution as on production. This latter view is so widely and strongly held that this has become commonplace sociopolitical judgment of the day in these countries, and, according to this view, the crux of the problem is not growth per se but how to attain growth with equity.

I, however, support the view that the main hope for supporting the expanding (and poor) population in these countries lies with rapid agricultural growth through high yielding technology. In a basically poor country, equity cannot be substituted in any manner for growth. Moreover, the effect of growth through high yielding technology in these countries, in reality, does not seem to pose any serious problem of the rich getting richer. Most of the farmers there have either subsistence or marginal land holdings. In addition, the existing high rate of population growth largely neutralizes the wealth accumulating effect of such growth towards the rich gaining more and more economic and social power, as indicated by the fact that the large holdings are continually being subdivided into small units. With the effects of growth, most of the farmers with large holdings are at best merely able to maintain their holdings, income, or both.

If the underlying objective of equity and welfare goals is not one of sharing the poverty, I believe that in these countries the emphasis on equity related growth is a self-defeating and futile approach.

The crop campaign as a strategy for accelerating agricultural growth is found to be consistent with the classic example of the programmatic approach to development policy in the developing countries. It is a highly effective and promising tool for rapid expansion of aggregate production. It has the inherent ability to promote rapid and wide application of modern high yielding technology.

Modern high yielding seed and fertilizer technology has the feature of flexibility in use. It can be usefully applied even in part. Therefore, weather variation, with which Welsch is overly concerned, is not an overriding factor seriously limiting the scope of crop campaigns. Weather changes can cause fluctuations in production only up to 20 percent. Moreover, early maturing and drought resistant crop varieties and small scale irrigation can be included in the technology package as adjustment elements to overcome the problems of uncertain weather situations.

Welsch has not talked about the duration of the campaign. In my opinion the campaign efforts should last for two years to be followed by supportive programs on a regular basis.

Accelerated agricultural production growth in the face of an ever increasing population is a critical, sensitive, and perplexing problem confronting these countries. The problem, however, is made unduly complex by the untimely introduction of distributional equity as a goal in the development process.

RAPPORTEUR'S REPORT--Max T. Colwell

Production campaign programmes are most appropriate where a country has a production crisis, and they are a frequently used mechanism for mobilization of people.

Contributing to the discussion was Anthony E. Ikpi.

THE ENERGETICS OF AGRICULTURAL PRODUCTION
IN EASTERN EUROPE AND THE USSR

Mieczyslaw Adamowicz

The Issue

Although agriculture uses only a small share of the world's total energy consumption, it is generally recognized that its needs are crucial, since the existing technologies for increasing production rely so heavily on energy intensive inputs. It therefore becomes imperative to find ways of economizing in the use of the expensive and rapidly depleting supplies of fossil fuel, to develop alternative sources of energy, and to better utilize existing agricultural energy sources as substitutes for expensive energy produced outside agriculture.

Most studies of energy use in agriculture have described the developed western countries. Less information is available about agricultural energy use in developing and in the centrally planned countries. In the latter two groups of countries, large increases in food and agricultural production are required. Since these countries now possess relatively abundant supplies of agricultural labour, and modest supplies of capital and industrial energy, it is possible that they may have alternatives to the energy intensive path of agricultural development followed in the most technically advanced western agriculture.

Now is a good time to study the energetics of agricultural production in Eastern Europe and the USSR because the agriculture of these countries has been undergoing dynamic change characterized by more intensive use of capital, increased specialization of agricultural enterprises, strengthening of vertical and horizontal integration, and a growing scale of production. Concentration of land, labour, and capital in the big state and cooperative farms under state and social control creates a system of agricultural production which could be quite easily adjusted to changed economic and energy situations.

With current technology, agriculture in these countries would require extremely high direct and indirect energy inputs to bring crop yields and animal productivity to the full potential. Perhaps alternatives exist. In times of energy scarcity, energy analysis of agriculture in different countries can give insights into the viability or competitiveness of different agricultural systems.

This study covers seven socialist countries which are members of the Council for Mutual Economic Aid (Bulgaria, Czechoslovakia, the German Democratic Republic, Hungary, Poland, Romania, and the USSR). To gain a perspective on the energy situation, it is necessary to know the actual amounts and productivity of the energy used in the agriculture of the countries under consideration. Therefore, the purpose of this study is: to describe the energy inputs into agriculture in the seven countries and outline changes in these inputs during the period 1960-1977; to measure agricultural output in energy units; and to compare energy inputs with the energy content of agricultural output in order to estimate the efficiency of energy use.

The method used in this study has been adapted from FAO. Energy used in agricultural production was divided into two categories: (1) energy incorporated in agricultural production inputs produced outside agriculture; and (2) energy used directly as fuel and power within agriculture. In the first category are such items as agricultural machinery, tractors, combines, trucks, horse drawn equipment, as well as fertilizer and pesticides. Energy in food was measured on the basis of crops in final form including grains, field beans, potatoes, oilseeds, sugar, vegetables, fruits, and animal products (meat, eggs, and milk). Animal feed was not counted as part of energy output. The energy value of the animal product was multiplied a factor of 7.0 to account for the energy value of the feed. Thus all figures for energy output are converted to crop production equivalents.

Energy Inputs

The years 1960 to 1977 were characterized by a rapid increase in the use of energy in the seven countries, from 849,716 to 2,793,162 million gigajoules (TJ), an increase of 229 percent. The USSR showed a 236 percent increase, with a 1960 use of 597,881, and a 1977 use of 2,006,856 TJ. The six countries of Eastern Europe, taken as a group, exhibited a rise from 251,835 to 786,306 TJ, a 212 percent increase. Material energy (machinery, fertilizers, and pesticides) as a component of farm inputs increased 350 percent. The use of operational energy (energy used directly as fuel, electricity, horse power, and human labour) rose by an average of 143 percent--a 243 percent increase in fuel and electricity and a 42 percent decline in horse power and human labour.

Table 1--Sources of energy inputs into agriculture

	1960	1977	1960	1977	1977/1960
	------TJ--------		-----Percent----		Index
Farm machinery	170,448	406,562	20.0	14.6	239
Fertilizers	169,776	1,120,415	19.9	40.1	660
Pesticides	9,067	44,824	1.0	1.6	492
Subtotal	349,281	1,571,801	40.9	56.3	450
Fuel	271,584	716,851	31.9	25.6	264
Electricity	45,838	373,312	5.4	13.4	814
Subtotal	317,442	1,090,163	37.3	39.0	343
Horses	91,178	52,804	10.8	1.9	57
Labour	93,836	78,394	11.0	2.8	84
Subtotal	186,014	131,198	21.8	4.7	71
Total	849,716	2,793,162	100.0	100.0	329
(of which) USSR	597,881	2,006,856	70.4	71.8	336
Eastern Europe	251,835	786,306	29.6	28.2	312

Changes in energy use occurred from 1960 to 1977. The proportion of material energy obtained from outside agriculture increased. The share of operational energy decreased. In 1960, only in Czechoslovakia and the GDR was more than 55 percent of energy use in the form of machines, fertilizers, and pesticides. In the USSR, the rate was 37 percent; in Romania it was barely 26 percent. The increase in the share of material energy for the seven countries was in the range from 41 to 56 percent. Hungary increased its share by 75 percent. Bulgaria, Czechoslovakia, and the GDR increased their proportion by 66-69 percent. For Romania and Poland, the figure was 58-60 percent and for the USSR about 53 percent.

In 1960, energy used in the form of farm machinery and fertilizer each accounted for about 20 percent of total energy use. The intensification process caused the share of energy use for fertilizer to rise to 40 percent by 1977 for the seven countries taken together. The fertilizer share rose from 14 to 36 percent in the USSR and from 34 to 51 percent in Eastern Europe.

A rapid increase also occurred in the use of energy in the form of pesticides and herbicides. However, it only amounted to 2 percent of 1977 energy inputs. The use of energy embodied in farm machinery increased gradually, so the proportion of energy inputs thus expended decreased. In the USSR, it fell from 23 percent in 1960 to 16 percent in 1977. In Eastern Europe, the share went from 14 percent in 1960 to 11 percent in 1977. The greatest relative increase in the use of energy embodied in machines was in Poland and Romania. There the 1960-77 period was one of accelerated progress in mechanization.

The use of energy in the form of liquid fuel increased in pace with mechanization. For the seven country group, liquid fuel use increased by a factor of 2.6, while in Eastern Europe there was a fourfold increase. Energy from liquid fuels in the seven countries fell from 32 to 26 percent over the 17 year period. However, for Eastern Europe the share of energy use from liquid fuels increased. For Eastern Europe it was a small increase, from 19 percent in 1960 to 23 percent in 1977. For the USSR, energy use from liquid fuels fell from 38 to 27 percent.

While the portion of energy used directly in agriculture as electricity is modest, rates of increase in use are very high. It increased by a factor of 8 over the 17 year period. Electrical energy, as a share of total energy inputs, increased from 4 percent in 1960 to 7 percent in 1977 in Eastern Europe. In the USSR, it increased from 6 to 16 percent. Although rates of increase in energy use in the form of electricity have been high, agricultural use as a percentage of all electrical energy produced remains low.

For the seven countries taken together, the share of energy from outside agriculture which was used directly rose only slightly and amounted to 39 percent in 1977. Total energy inputs from outside of agriculture rose from 78 percent in 1960 to over 95 percent in 1977.

Energy in the form of work by people and horses declined in relative and absolute terms. Energy from horses went down from 13 percent in 1960 to 2.3 percent in 1977 in Eastern Europe. In the USSR, it went from 10 to just under 1.7 percent in the same period. In Eastern Europe, energy from human labour in 1977 was 64 percent of the 1960 figure. In the USSR, the 1977 human labour input was 75 percent of the 1960 level. In 1960, human work amounted to 15.5 percent of the energy input in agriculture in Eastern Europe and 9.2 percent in the USSR. The comparable figures for 1977 are 3.5 percent for Eastern Europe and 2.5 percent for the USSR.

While the area under cultivation and the number of persons employed in agriculture both declined and the use of energy from outside of agriculture increased, energy inputs per unit of land increased. For the entire region, the use of energy per hectare of agricultural land increased threefold—from 1,478 to 4,558 megajoules (MJ). The increase for Eastern Europe was from 4,143 to 13,046 MJ, and in the USSR from 1,166 to 3,632 MJ. The GDR and Czechoslovakia achieved striking increases in energy intensity.

Energy use per person employed in agriculture increased faster than did energy per unit of land. Energy used per person increased by a factor of four for the entire region, from 17,972 to 70,250 MJ. In Eastern Europe, it increased from 13,844 to 60,921 MJ, and in the USSR from 20,588 to 74,743 MJ.

Energy Outputs

From 1960 to 1977, the energy content of crop production destined for human consumption and for fodder increased in the whole region by 47 percent. In Eastern Europe, it increased by 44 percent and in the USSR by 48 percent. Particularly large increases were registered in Bulgaria, Romania, and Hungary.

Crop production destined for direct consumption grew more slowly than animal production expressed in a crop product form. In Eastern Europe, crop production grew by 25 percent; in the USSR by 35 percent. Comparable figures for animal production are 55 percent for Eastern Europe and 57 percent for the USSR. The crop product share of total energy output for the whole region was, as a result, reduced from 37 percent in 1960 to 32 percent in 1977. The ratio of food crop products energy to total food energy output decreased from 80 to 77 percent in Eastern Europe and from 83 to 81 percent in the USSR.

The energy output of agriculture per unit of land and labour rose. From 1960 to 1977, energy output rose from 23.5 to 34.5 gigajoules (GJ) per hectare. Energy produced per person employed increased from 78.6 to 161.1 GJ. The largest energy output per hectare (55 GJ) and per person (484 GJ) in 1977 was in the GDR. Czechoslovakia followed with 40 GJ per hectare and 312 GJ per person.

Energy Efficiency of Agricultural Production

The energy efficiency ratio is computed by dividing the energy output by total energy input. This calculation allows a comparison of seven quite diverse agricultural systems. A sizable drop in the energy efficiency occurred between 1960 and 1977. For the whole region, the following indices prevail (1960=100): energy inputs, 329; energy produced in agriculture, 147; and energy produced as food products, 136.

The energy efficiency ratio decreased from 5.01 to 2.27 in the entire region. It fell from 5.68 to 2.64 in Eastern Europe and from 4.83 to 2.13 in the USSR. In the entire region, energy produced in the form of food products divided by energy inputs declined from 2.47 to 1.03. In Eastern Europe, the ratio fell from 2.61 to 1.10, and in the USSR from 2.41 to 1.00. A ratio of less than 1.00 indicates that for each unit of energy contained in foodstuffs more than one unit of energy input is needed. In the years 1975-77, such a situation prevailed in the GDR, Czechoslovakia, and the USSR. In the remaining countries, the ratio of energy output to energy input is approaching 1.00. It is noteworthy that two of the countries with the lowest value of energy efficiency are those with the highest energy inputs per unit of land and labour.

Table 2--Ratio of energy output to energy input

Countries	Ratio of energy produced in agriculture to energy inputs			Ratio of energy produced in the form of food products to energy inputs		
	1960	1970	1977	1960	1970	1977
Bulgaria	3.68	2.13	2.31	2.12	1.19	1.17
Czechoslovakia	5.14	2.80	2.51	2.15	1.09	0.98
GDR	4.77	2.93	2.66	1.84	1.04	0.93
Hungary	6.11	2.59	2.72	2.97	1.17	1.27
Poland	7.39	3.53	2.65	3.31	1.30	1.03
Romania	5.01	2.37	2.85	2.77	1.16	1.42
USSR	4.83	2.85	2.13	2.41	1.41	1.00

Conclusions

As a result of an increase in the input intensity of agriculture during the years 1960-77 in all of the countries of the region, there was a great increase in energy use. More energy of industrial origin was employed, especially energy in the form of fertilizer and electricity. At the same time, the amount of energy delivered by people and horses declined.

The energy content of agricultural output increased but more slowly than did the energy content of agricultural inputs. As a result, the ratio of energy output to energy input declined. The decline was accelerated by the increase in animal production.

One of the main goals of agricultural policy in Eastern Europe and the USSR will be to continue to increase agricultural production. At the same time,

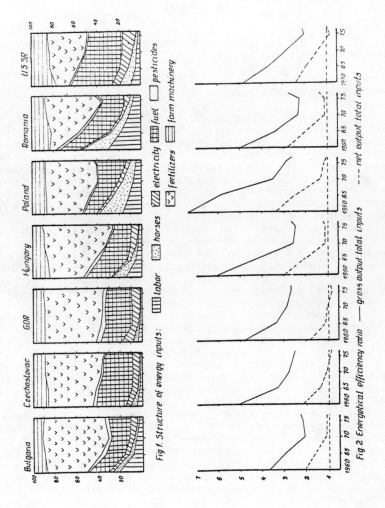

Fig 1. Structure of energy inputs:

⊟ labor   ⊡ horses   ▨ electricity   ⊞ fuel   ☐ pesticides

⌄⌄ fertilizers   ▦ farm machinery

Fig 2 Energetical efficiency ratio —— gross output total inputs --- net output total inputs increases in the cost of energy and possible further declines in the energy efficiency ratios will spur the search for more economical energy management systems and for more effective methods of energy use. Problems of energy efficiency in agriculture will be a matter of concern both at the level of the production unit and the national level of policymaking. Solutions to energy problems will involve those who produce energy and agricultural inputs. As new information becomes available, what is taught by agricultural information and extension services will need to be changed.

References

COMECON, Yearly Statistics.
FAO (1977) Energy and agriculture, in The State of Food and Agriculture. Rome; Food and Agriculture Organization of the United Nations.

OPENER'S REMARKS--John S. Nix

The derived energy efficiency ratios are very different from those calculated by Renborg, but no doubt an explanation could be found if one had time to study both papers in detail. Both are invaluable in instructing farm management economists to stop thinking entirely of resource use and optimal resource allocation simply in terms of land, labour, and capital (measured in both physical and financial terms), and to consider factors other than the profitability of the individual farm. We have been quite properly forced to think much more broadly--in terms of the whole world and of the future--about the increasing use of energy and its finite supply. We now need to concentrate on the problems posed in the second paragraph of the paper--economizing in the use of energy, developing alternative sources, and making better use of existing resources.

In the 1920s, when UK farms were first mechanized, 10 to 20 MJ of energy were required to substitute for one hour of labour. Today the figure is estimated to be 230. Furthermore, energy in the 1920s (and even the 1950s) was very cheap and in apparently inexhaustible supply. Thus the marginal revenue is now very much lower and the marginal cost very much higher.

We know the main possibilities for increasing the energy efficiency ratio: using more legumes in place of nitrogenous fertilizer; reducing machinery inputs (for example, by nonploughing, minimal cultivation, and direct tilling); reducing waste; making greater use of animal faeces and straw for manuring, fuel, and feed; and, most destestable and difficult of all to contemplate when improved nutrition standards are needed by so many of the world's population (but especially vital), reducing the dependence on animal products and increasing the emphasis on crop products for direct human consumption.

Above all, there is the problem of the developing countries whose needs for agricultural development mean that they are bound to increase their demands for energy substantially. Developed countries are clearly in no position to preach about energy conservation, especially that just to feed each person in the UK and USA takes about three times the average per capita energy used for all purposes in the developing countries. But perhaps we can at least help develop techniques that use additional energy more economically than we have done in our own agricultural development. Obviously, the rapidly increasing price of energy will to a large extent dictate that this is done, through sheer economic necessity; that is, the price mechanism will operate as it should.

Of course, we can argue that agriculture is responsible for a comparatively small part of total energy use--estimated to be one or two percent in the UK and about three percent in the USA--although in the developed countries the total percentage is considerable if the amount used to make farm products available for final consumption is included (transport, processing, packaging, and so forth).

The proportion is then estimated to be 12 to 16 percent in the UK and USA--or even 25 percent by the time the food is prepared and ready to eat. Thus a small redirection in the proportion of energy used beyond the farm gate would save far more than even a large reduction in its use in agricultural production itself.

Still, this does not save those of us working in agriculture from having to face up to this large problem and doing our best to tackle it--even if we agree with Renborg that the situation is far from desperate. Certainly I very much support Renborg when he argues that the blunderbuss "make cuts" approach is too gross and simplistic, and that here surely is an area which cries out for economic analysis.

Reference

Renborg, U. (1981) Energy analysis of agriculture: Biology or economics--A survey of approaches, problems, and traps, in Rural Change: The Challenge for Agricultural Economists (edited by G. L. Johnson and A. H. Maunder). Farnborough; Gower Publishing Co.

RAPPORTEUR'S REPORT--John P. McInerney

The main points raised in the discussion were concerned with the focus on energy efficiency ratios as a single factor approach to efficiency measurement. In the context of a complex production system such as agriculture, with its dependence on both natural and processed energy sources, and a role in the economy that could not be adequately reflected simply in terms of energy processes, the nonenergy aspects of inputs and food output cannot be ignored.

It was insisted that the approach presented in the paper was of little diagnostic use and would not provide a basis for improving efficiency, as it was necessary to look at all possible combinations of factors at each stage in the production system. The need for any specific emphasis on energy aspects was questioned anyway, since there is little evidence of a consistent rise in the real price of energy in the long term.

The issue of energy input associated with labour was raised and related to the earlier paper by Renborg. It was suggested that if the total energy required for the life support of labour is employed in calculating energy inputs, then the computed efficiency of energy use in agriculture remained unchanged between 1956 and 1972, even allowing for the highest energy requirement needed to support the increased living standards employed by labour over the same period.

Contributing to the discussion were John S. Nix, Geoff W. Edwards, George T. Jones, Martin Popescu, and Ulf Renborg.

103

REGIONAL AND FARM LEVEL ADJUSTMENTS TO
THE PRODUCTION OF ENERGY FROM AGRICULTURE:
BRAZIL'S ALCOHOL PLAN

Reinaldo I. Adams and Norman Rask

Introduction

An impending world shortage of oil has prompted many to call the energy crisis a liquid fuel problem. This is especially true for Brazil where a commitment to major use of liquid fuels is responsible for a serious emerging energy problem. About 80 percent of Brazil's petroleum needs are imported, and petroleum price increases since 1974 have severely strained the balance of payments. Domestic supplies of oil and coal are inadequate and show little promise of ever meeting more than a small percentage of domestic energy needs. In response to this situation, Brazil has adopted some short run policies to slow the growth in demand for petroleum products. More importantly, Brazil is implementing a pioneer plan to produce a significant amount of its liquid fuel needs in the form of alcohol derived from sugarcane, cassava, and other energy crops. This effort presents the world with the first major experiment in the commercial competition between food and energy production.

The outcome of this experiment is generally important for a world short of both energy and food. It is of special interest to many developing countries located in tropical areas with limited fossil fuel reserves. For many of these countries, energy from biomass, and specifically liquid fuel production, may be an attractive alternative to costly oil imports. Brazil represents many developing country characteristics, having biomass production potential, limited fossil fuel reserves, and foreign exchange problems exacerbated by a heavy oil import bill. Brazil does, however, have abundant land resources. Alcohol production is being initiated on prime developed agricultural land (Sao Paulo), and the research results reported below do not consider an expansion of agricultural land area.

The purpose of this paper is to report initial results of a farm level regional analysis of the Brazilian alcohol plan. Alcohol production from energy crops is presently not competitive with world oil prices. However, within Brazil, a price regulated energy market insures a competitive price for alcohol. The analysis examines both the regulated market and a free market for energy. The free market analysis is conducted to measure the anticipated response to rising energy prices.

Energy price increases are reflected in regional farm level models in several ways, including derived farm level prices for energy crops, differential energy inputs to farm production technologies (mechanized and nonmechanized), uses of specific technologies by farm size, energy inputs to alcohol processing, and transportation costs of raw products and alcohol to processing plants and distribution centres. Energy prices are set at various levels in specific regions, with both regional and central demand centres competing for the final product. Regional land and labour use, crop competition (between sugarcane and cassava, and between food and feed crops), and technological change (energy intensity) are all studied in relation to energy price changes and volume of energy production.

The Alcohol Plan

The alcohol plan is a product of the energy realities faced by Brazil and the agricultural potential for producing alcohol. Over the past 20 years, Brazil has embarked on an ambitious industrialization programme that has relied substantially on an automobile industry, truck transport, and areas of highly mechanized agriculture. This path of development has necessitated a strong reliance on petroleum as a source of energy to supply the liquid fuel needs of the automobile and truck transport sectors. Imports have accounted for 80 percent of petroleum needs, and lack of major fossil energy sources has forced the country to initiate a search for other sources of energy while controlling internal consumption of petroleum products. Brazil has been using a limited amount of alcohol mixed with gasoline (gasohol) for many years. This alcohol has been produced as a byproduct of a substantial sugar refining industry.

In 1975, Brazil initiated a plan to increase the alcohol production from sugarcane and to investigate the possibility of using other crops, especially cassava, sweet sorghum, and babacu (palm) for alcohol production. The long run goal is to replace most petroleum needs with domestically produced alcohol. A public control system was also established to develop and control the production and distribution of alcohol, to fix prices and conversion quotas, and to propose new policy measures for the future development of the alcohol plan.

The initial goal was to produce about 2.6 billion litres of alcohol a year by 1980, equal to about 20 percent of all gasoline consumed in the country in 1975. This alcohol is to be utilized in a mixture with gasoline. Initial alcohol production and use has occurred in the established sugarcane areas near major consumption centres such as Sao Paulo. However, it is felt that regional production of alcohol will be both desirable and necessary in order to meet the production goals in the alcohol plan, to spread alcohol use throughout the country, and to provide a broader distribution of the expected income and employment increases associated with expanded alcohol production. Thus, new areas, with substantially different agricultural production resources and crop alternatives, are to be integrated in the plan.

The plan has significant implications for a broad spectrum of domestic and international activities for Brazil. The dimensions of these issues are only beginning to be recognized and addressed. The private sector is reluctant to undertake substantial capital investment in distillery plant capacity, knowing that the cost of petroleum is still below alcohol production cost. Therefore, rapid expansion of distillery capacity must be based on government support and incentives.

In addition, there is competition for the use of basic resources for the production of sugar, alcohol, and other exportable crops, and a tradeoff between them and imported petroleum. Price relationships will naturally be an important determinant of the allocation of these resources. Thus, emphasis in the analysis was placed on resource competition within the agricultural sector as determined by international and domestic price relationships between petroleum, alcohol, sugar, cassava, and other competitive domestic crops.

Regional Farm Level Models

Four regions were selected for study. The first is Campinas, in the State of Sao Paulo, representing the most concentrated sugarcane production area in Brazil. This area is characterized by large mechanized farms in a labour deficit area. It is located near the largest consumption centre of Brazil--the city of Sao Paulo. Contrasting with this area are three other regions selected from the southern states of Brazil--two in Santa Catarina and one in Rio Grande do Sul. These areas represent regional production and consumption centres in which small farms predominate in a labour surplus area.

Rio Grande do Sul has a major regional consumption centre, the city of Porto Alegre, and a regional production area with both sugarcane and cassava. Agricultural technology is intermediate, with both modern mechanized and small traditional farms. Santa Catarina is a minor regional consumption area, but a major regional production area, with mostly small farms, surplus labour, and traditional technology. It has subregions with both sugarcane and cassava and with cassava only. The regions selected thus represent a cross section of alcohol production and consumption conditions for testing the impacts of the alcohol programme.

The model for analysis was defined at three levels: agricultural production, alcohol processing, and alcohol and gasoline blending and marketing, with connecting transport linkages. Special emphasis in the analysis, however, is given to agricultural production where the alcohol producing crops--sugarcane, cassava, and eucalyptus (firewood)--compete with other agricultural products for land and labour resources. Five different processing activities are established using sugarcane, cassava, or both as raw materials for alcohol production. Finally, four mixing plant locations (consumption centres) are defined in Campinas (Sao Paulo), the city of Sao Paulo, Itajai (Santa Catarina) and Porto Alegre (Rio Grande do Sul).

Analysis and Conclusions

The analysis was conducted in two parts: first, the 1976 (base year) price and policy relationships were used to estimate alcohol production and use relationships under conditions existing then. In 1976, diesel oil--used mostly for agricultural production and merchandise transportation--was priced at Cr$2.07 per litre at the retail level. The retail gasoline price was Cr$4.07 per litre and the alcohol wholesale price was Cr$3.26 per litre. The minimum wage rate of Cr$4.36 per hour was adopted for the region of Campinas, which is a labour deficit area. For the other regions, a value of Cr$3.00 was used. Under these conditions, alcohol was competitively produced in the model at all four production regions, mostly for local consumption.

In the second part of the analysis, a free market price system for energy was simulated to test the competitiveness of alcohol production and its effect on resource allocation. Energy and alcohol prices were set at various levels to characterize alternative energy price levels. Under these conditions, alcohol produced competitively in all regions for local consumption at wholesale prices ranging from Cr$2.43 to Cr$2.55 per litre, or roughly double free market wholesale gasoline prices. Distant markets could be supplied at higher energy prices only.

TABLE 1: Breakeven Alcohol Wholesale Price Levels
by Production and Consumption Regions [a]

Production Regions	Consumption Centres			
	Campinas	Sao Paulo	Itajai	Porto Alegre
	(Cr$ per litre)			
Campinas (Region 1)	2.43	2.65	3.73	4.55
Santa Catarina North (Region 2)	3.49	3.32	2.45	3.08
Santa Catarina South (Region 3)	3.75	3.46	2.55	2.65
Rio Grande do Sul (Region 4)	4.18	3.88	2.91	2.44

[a] Shaded area represents prices for consumption centres within or adjacent to production regions.

The imported wholesale cost of gasoline was Cr$1.20 per litre which was equivalent to approximately U.S. $0.43 per gallon.

Family farm labour is an abundant resource in many small farm regions of Brazil. Energy crops are labour intensive, and their relative profitability is strongly dependent on the value assigned to the family labour input. Part of the analysis focused on the impact of variable costs on competitive alcohol prices. Family labour costs were set at various levels to evaluate this impact. No changes occurred for alcohol prices and resource allocation within the Campinas model. However, within the Santa Catarina and Rio Grande do Sul labour surplus area models, alcohol prices were sensitive to labour costs. A reduction of one cruzeiro per hour in family labour cost resulted in a reduction of about Cr$.18 per litre for breakeven prices for alcohol in Santa Catarina and Cr$.08 in Rio Grande do Sul.

In the model, energy crop activities competed directly with other activities for the use of land and labour. An increase in alcohol production, therefore, could occur only with activity substitution at the farm level. The activities most affected were cattle and maize production. Labour use also increased because the energy producing crops are more labour intensive than most of the activities replaced. Energy price increases reduced mechanization in favour of non-mechanized activities.

The general economic interpretations of these results are as follows. First, with present world petroleum prices, alcohol cannot be produced competitively. However, alcohol production is competitive at the energy prices now existing in Brazil and within present price estimates for other alternatives to petroleum (coal liquefaction and shale oil). Within the agricultural sector, regional production centres, labour surplus areas, and alternative source crops are all competitive with centrally located major sugarcane production areas. While increased energy prices reduce agricultural income through increased input costs, energy crop production more than offsets this loss, resulting in a net aggregate gain for agricultural income especially in nonmechanized areas. Employment in agriculture also shows net gains with energy crop production.

Implications for Brazil

Brazil's current energy situation--a lack of fossil energy resources, a liquid fuel based transportation system, and foreign exchange problems caused by high petroleum imports--has forced it to make early decisions about liquid fuel use and source of supply. The decision has been made to continue high use of liquid fuels and to produce a significant portion of these in the form of alcohol from biomass. The results of this analysis in some measure support this decision and point to some development steps that will facilitate this change.

The competitive price analysis demonstrates that, while subsidies are necessary to stimulate alcohol production at the present time, a projected two to threefold increase in real petroleum prices within a few years will place alcohol in a competitive range using present technology. Any improvements in production or processing technology will enhance this comparison.

The competitive nature of regional production areas opens up the possibility of spreading the employment and income generating impacts of the alcohol plan more broadly throughout the country. In fact, from the income and employment perspective, needs are greater and gains more apparent when alcohol is produced in regional rather than central areas.

Finally, since this is a pioneering effort, policy planners, technical personnel, and industries have little experience on which to base decisions. Technical developments are also at early levels in some areas such as miniplant design, processing techniques, and energy crop production development. Each of these areas must receive adequate research support if the plan is to move ahead at an efficient level.

Many developing countries have resource situations similar to Brazil. As noted earlier, most developing countries are located in tropical areas with the physical environment to produce significant biomass yields. A surplus labour situation on small farms is also a common characteristic of developing areas. Finally, most tropical countries are fossil fuel poor since the principal coal and oil deposits are located in temperate areas. There are significant differences among developing countries in the relative availability of land for nonfood uses. However, since the model used in this study forced energy crops to compete with food crops for a fixed land resource, the results should be meaningful for land short countries as well.

The implications of the results for developing countries take several forms, including competitive alcohol price levels and labour employment and income generation possibilities. For example, tropical, low income, labour surplus countries may have a comparative advantage in biomass energy production using sugarcane and cassava as raw products. Both are labour intensive, and, combined with a lower opportunity cost for farm family labour, this will allow developing countries to produce alcohol at lower prices. This alcohol may be used for domestic energy needs, or in exceptional cases, exported. In either case, it will substitute for petroleum imports. In addition, a domestic alcohol programme can provide expanded job opportunities in both agriculture and industry, leading to increased incomes.

There is, however, a very important food energy tradeoff to be considered by developing countries. This is especially true in situations where land resources are limited. This tradeoff will be determined in part by the relative productivity and price of energy and food crops. Sugar production may be one of the first crops affected as energy prices rise and alcohol production becomes a plausible option for sugar producing countries. Sugar prices will possibly follow the path of energy price increases as alcohol becomes competitive with other energy sources. In the longer run, other sources (like cassava) may become preferred options even in the sugar producing countries, and thereby reduce the competition between alcohol and sugar.

RAPPORTEUR'S REPORT—John P. McInerney

A dominant theme in the discussion was the basic economic viability of energy from biomass, it being suggested that the more conventional fuel sources would in general be consistently cheaper over the long term. For example, the breakeven price necessary to make oil shale extraction competitive has consistently risen so that it still remains just uneconomic, and the same is likely to happen with alcohol production.

The potential economics of producing alcohol as demonstrated in the paper were questioned as being specific to Brazil which, as an energy deficit country, has established an artifically high domestic price for alcohol; thus, if opportunity costs (as reflected on the world market) for inputs and outputs had been used, the conclusions would have been both different and more correct. The view was expressed, however, that for certain isolated and small country situations (Papua-New Guinea and Samoa were cited as examples) which could not justify high capital costs of petroleum refining, the smaller scale possibilities of producing energy from biomass represented a valuable economic alternative, and this was where its future probably lay.

Contributing to the discussion were Graham F. Donaldsen, James B. Fitch, Robert C. Kramer, and Alfred Thieme.

COMPARISON OF THE POTENTIAL FOR PRODUCING ENERGY FROM AGRICULTURE IN BRAZIL, INDIA, AND THE UNITED STATES

Wallace E. Tyner

Abstract

This paper examines energy from agricultural programmes in Brazil, India, and the United States. It begins with a review of energy supply and demand conditions and factor endowments of the three countries. With this background, it goes on to examine in more detail one biomass energy source and policy for each country.

What clearly emerges from these three different countries and perspectives is that each country is concentrating on an area of energy from biomass that is particularly suited to its energy supply and demand and factor endowments. India is particularly in need of fuel and fertilizer in rural areas to increase the productivity of the agricultural sector and the living standard of rural people. Hence, India has adopted a programme to increase the efficiency of resource use in rural areas by producing both fuel and fertilizer from animal manure via a biogas process. However, social and institutional problems were shown to be important barriers to successful adoption of the biogas technology in rural India. Brazil is particularly dependent on foreign sources of oil, has an abundance of land, and has adopted a programme to use that land to produce liquid energy. The U.S. has advanced the least in the field of producing energy from biomass partially because the U.S. energy markets are somewhat insulated from world energy prices by controlled domestic prices. However, it appears that the United States could economically convert its surplus agricultural production capacity to energy crops and produce a small fraction of its current gasoline consumption. Overall, it appears that economic rationality, when viewed from a social perspective, has prevailed in the policy decisions of these countries regarding energy from biomass.

The Rural Challenge
at the National Level

THE CHALLENGE FOR AGRICULTURAL ECONOMISTS IN EFFECTING LAND REFORM IN THAILAND

S. Chirapanda and W. Tamrongthanyalak

This paper is intended to provide a brief outline of the land reform programme in Thailand and discuss the problem areas which offer the challenge for agricultural economists in land reform implementation. It also attempts to make general observations on the role played by agricultural economists which could have some relevance to other countries with land reform experience.

Historical Background

The agrarian problems facing Thai agriculture have much in common with other economies. Agricultural productivity is low and there is little or no indication of any tendency for it to increase within the foreseeable future. For example, the 1972-77 average yield of paddy rice was virtually the same as for the preceding 5-year period—about 1.7 tonnes per hectare. The same pattern is also found in the case of maize and cassava, which are Thailand's major crops. This stagnation on yields combined with low and fluctuating farm prices has often led to low farm income. In 1976, the average farm income was only US$1,304 per household. The average size of the farm household was about seven persons.

The overall tenurial situation distorts the regional picture. For the entire country, 2.2 million hectares (out of 18.1 million hectares of cultivated land) are operated by tenant farmers. The rate of tenancy is about 20 percent of the total farm households. This is equivalent to about 1 million households. However, with a breakdown into four regions, the central region, which accounts for less than one-fourth of the country's total cultivated acreage, is the hardest hit. About 1.3 million hectares are operated by tenant farmers, whereas 41 percent of the total number of farm households in the region rent land from others. Thus, the tenurial conditions are serious and are likely to deteriorate without effective land reform measures.

The impact of population growth is alarming. Although the rate of population growth has declined in recent years to about 2.5 percent per annum, the sheer size of the existing population and the entry of additional labour mean that the population will be constantly exerting pressures with differing degrees on various sectors of the economy. One of the devastating effects of population growth is the denudation by farmers of 4-5 million hectares of public land, which is mainly national forest reserves. These agrarian problems led to farmers' unrest throughout the country during 1973-74. The farmers were organized into mass rallies in major towns. Some even marched to Bangkok and submitted an ultimatum to the government to meet their demands. Consequently, the agricultural Land Reform Act was passed as a major concession to the farmers, to solve the economic ills of the rural masses. The law became effective in 1975.

The Land Reform Programme

The main characteristics of the land reform programme consist of the transfer of land ownership to tenant farmers, and the provision of basic supporting services to the land reform beneficiaries. The implementation procedure is, however, divided into two parts—private and public land. The private land reform implementation procedure concentrates mostly on the transfer of landownership, in which case land is acquired through voluntary sales or expropriation with compensation, and resold to tenant and landless farmers. In contrast, the public land reform programme is focused on the reallocation of land to the landless farmers, which inevitably includes the legalizing of the squatters, and on the provision of specific supporting services needed to render farming viable. The latter is under the direct responsibility of the Agricultural Land Reform Office (ALRO) which is the main executing government agency. The supporting services consist of three items--domestic water supplies, village roads, and small water resource development for farm use. Other supporting services, which are perhaps more important, are provided by other government departments through coordination with ALRO.

The Thai land reform programme, now in its fifth year, is facing a wide range of problems. At present, ALRO is operating in nearly 1,000,000 hectares, most of which are public land (formerly forest reserves). The amount of land purchased up to the end of June 1979 was only 13,570 hectares. If the past record is any indication, land reform in Thailand still has a lot of ground to cover. Furthermore, despite the land acquired by the government, land redistribution has not been carried out on any major scale.

Problems Identified

Problems confronting land reform are multidimensional and multidisciplinary. It is, however, our purpose to restrict ourselves mostly to those problems in the land reform proper. Although ALRO is the main executing agency, it does not carry out all land reform activities. Other government departments are also taking part, and interagency conflicts often lead to an ill defined line of responsibility, resulting in duplication of work, and waste of financial resources. The government is trying to draw the line among various departments, but it is not known yet whether this will be successful. Even with successful coordination of efforts, some conservative agricultural policies can undermine the strength of land reform. For example, the policy on rice premiums, which is equivalent to an imposition of export taxes, constitutes evidence of an urban bias against the rural poor.

Land reallocation among land reform beneficiaries represents another source of problems. The land plots are to be equal and redistributed among farmers. But resistance from the farmers--tenants and squatters alike--with large holdings is rather strong. At the moment, there is a tendency for the government to offer compensation. The next questions are probably how much the compensation payment will be and whether this is practical on a nationwide basis. In the public land domain, the main emphasis is laid on the squatters. This inevitably tends to encourage further encroachment of forest reserves, thereby creating more problems for land reform. It also results in a dilemma because the government consistently aims to stop illegal squatting.

Land valuation constitutes another problem area. On the one hand, it is preferable to establish guidelines for local government authorities to follow in land value appraisal, owing to the fact that conditions which influence land value vary from place to place. On the other hand, mere guidelines are likely to lead to irregularities, ambiguities, and corruption. This offers a strong case for a strict, centralized valuation procedure. The government chose the latter, and found it necessary to revise the adopted valuation procedure because of its impracticality in many areas. The newly revised version will soon be in operation, but some problems still remain unsolved.

Certain complementary measures which could provide effective preconditions for successful land reform have not been adopted. Land policy and land taxation (and tax structure in general) are obsolete in themselves, but with careful and deliberate manipulation, they could facilitate land reform. Another set of problems seems to stem from the actual implementation. ALRO personnel are relatively inexperienced and lack capable and effective leadership at almost all levels. Like other departments, ALRO faces the usual bureaucratic hurdles. Decisions are often made without sufficient assessment of the kinds of effects and repercussions which may be included.

It is generally recognized that land reform problems can, to a great extent, be solved by agricultural economists. It would not be an overstatement that agrarian problems are basically economic, and, as a consequence, agricultural economic solutions are clearly needed. Agricultural economists are directly involved in the planning aspects of land reform, which would cover the establishment of long term and annual targets, land reform project sites (in cases where land reform does not extend over the entire economy), basic needs among the poor, suitable farm size and land ceiling, land value appraisal, financing, and even land reform training. But land reform planning in this context is directed toward the policymaking level as well as the operational level. The final decisions must, for the most part, take other factors into consideration. Probably the greatest challenge to agricultural economists is the extent to which final decisions are influenced by them.

The multidisciplinary and multidimensional nature of land reform supports the need for agricultural economists to seek mutually acceptable solutions. They must pay sufficient attention to the social problems in the poverty stricken areas; for example, education, organization, and welfare. Free and easy access to supporting services would guarantee the land reform beneficiaries some form of security and, in a sense, an element of basic needs. There are times when straightforward recommendations offered by agricultural economists are subject to scrutiny by political scientists. For example, if farm size is fixed smaller than the average holding operated by tenant farmers, this may tend to alienate the tenants whom the government is supposed to help in the first place. The concept of optimality in traditional economic theory is usually overridden in favour of the simple rule of thumb in determining viable farm size. There are numerous factors influencing optimal farm size, such as soil quality, farm capital, land use, cropping pattern, location, and family size. But, in the land reform programme, simplicity tends to prevail. In the Thai case, farm size depends, at present, mainly on the average land holding and the expected level of income. With respect to land value appraisal, agricultural economists often find themselves caught between two extremes; that is, a detailed and scientific valuation method and an oversimplified method. They must formulate a set of rules which takes into account some major determinants of land value and which, at the same time, is simple enough for all parties concerned to understand. It thus appears that in effecting land reform, agricultural economists must operate in an environment which demands second best solutions. Agricultural economists are, nevertheless, undoubtedly the best qualified people to effect land reform.

In addition, successful land reform cannot be realized without prior assessments of its full impact on the economy as a whole or without creating the necessary and sufficient preconditions for success. Land reform implies basic changes in land tenure and structure relating to production and supporting services. Thus, it cannot be treated in isolation. To the extent that landowners are forced to sell their land under the land reform programme, the government must ensure that adequate measures are designed to prevent unnecessary polarization of power groups. The urban elite could be brought in to either directly or indirectly participate in the land reform process. The costs which may be incurred in land reform should somehow be met by the benefits to the society of which everyone is a part. It is this delicate balance among various interest groups on which the success of land reform so vitally depends.

In making policy recommendations, agricultural economists must recognize the importance of the prevailing political environment. Land reform is political, and political will is needed continuously in the execution of land reform implementation. The challenge lies in the involvement of agricultural economists at the policymaking level and in the implementation of policy decisions. Lack of proper understanding of the ramifications of land reform at the policy level often contributes to lack of successful implementation and consequent erosion of political support. Top level decisonmaking depends, to a considerable extent, on the degree of persuasiveness the agricultural economists can command in offering solutions to agrarian problems. The situation is complex and difficult to handle when decisionmakers comprise landlords and rural elite who indulge in preserving the status quo and protecting their own vested interests. In this way, it is an art and not a science in which the agricultural economists are involved and must in due course practice.

But the degree of persuasiveness should be seen in the light of the structural organization which is responsible for implementing land reform, and also the practical aspects in which land reform is carried out. In many countries, a full ministry is created especially for land reform, in which case the need for coordination and cooperation among government agencies is probably minimized. In contrast, ALRO, which is the main executing agency, is only one of many departments within Thailand's Ministry of Agriculture. There is a built-in tendency for overlapping and duplication of work, especially in the provision of production and supporting services. This could lead to interagency conflicts, waste, and unnecessary diffusion of scarce budgetary and skilled human resources. Within the Thai context, there is a need for multidepartmental coordination and cooperation in land reform activities. The basic needs of the land reform beneficiaries must be identified and systematically grouped. The delegation of responsibilities of implementation is then made to various government departments concerned, with ALRO as the major coordinating agency. This, in fact, was achieved in 1978 (with some modifications), but it remains to be seen how far this will go. It is rather unfortunate that given the potential and wide ranging effects that land reform might have in the economy, the structure of the organization is not conducive to swift implementation or subsequently to a successful land reform programme. This presents another challenge to the role of agricultural economists in effecting land reform.

Summary

Agricultural economists have been actively involved in advancing the cause of land reform. Since 1975, when the land reform programme was initiated, they found themselves confronted with the multidimensional and multidisciplinary set of problems which increasingly demanded both traditional agricultural economic solutions and politically oriented, mutually acceptable solutions. In concert with the current international acceptance of land reform as a much broader concept, the role of the agricultural economists becomes more comprehensive, especially in recognition of the utmost importance of relationships and interlinkages between basic tenurial reform and reform of supporting services in agriculture. The challenge to agricultural economists lies in decisionmaking at the policy-making and operational levels. Perhaps the most important challenge involves the extent to which value judgments made by agricultural economists affect top level decisionmaking. In so doing, the agricultural economists are no longer restricted to their own professional area, but extend over and beyond to the art of decisionmaking.

OPENER'S REMARKS—David Freshwater

Land reform is a major source of problems from both an efficiency and equity perspective. The authors note that yields and incomes are low in Thai agriculture, and attribute this, in part, to the rice premium policy which keeps farm receipts low. Clearly, land reform will not affect this cause of low income. The claim for land reform on efficiency grounds rests on the difference in incentives between owner and renter. An owner is hypothesized to be more

116

willing to adopt cultivation practices that increase the long term productive power of the land than a tenant who lacks security of tenure. However, past experience with land reform indicates that ownership is not enough to ensure increased yield.

The new owners need access to credit for equipment and advice on farm management if they are to take advantage of the opportunity. Where credit and education programmes are absent, land reform can result in yield and output declines. Although the Thai Land Reform Act has provisions for improving the infrastructure through support services, no mention is made of credit or extension programmes to complement the Act. Given the authors' statements regarding the lack of coordination and cooperation between government departments, there is cause for concern as to the likelihood of the current reform measures being successful in increasing output.

On an aggregate basis, land reform may lead to resource misallocation between sectors as well as within agriculture. Conversion of forest land to agriculture implies a shift of resources from forestry to agriculture largely as a result of squatters' actions. The effect of this conversion on aggregate income may be one of the costs of the land reform process.

From an equity standpoint, land reform involves the taking of resources from some individuals and distributing them to others. Although a more equal distribution of resources is likely to increase social welfare where resource ownership is highly concentrated, there is a point at which equality of the distribution conflicts with equity, and social welfare declines. Legitimizing squatters raises another equity problem. Although such an action may be inevitable for political reasons, it results in rewards to a group that has acted outside of the existing set of rules governing the society. Thus, those who violate the social contract are being rewarded. The authors note that the opposition to compensating those giving up the land comes from owners, tenants, and squatters. Thus, the Land Reform Act appears to be geared to reducing farm size irrespective of the type of tenure system. Such a policy--without evidence that low productivity can be directly attributed to farms that are too big--suggests that political considerations dominate economic considerations.

The authors correctly point out that land reform is essentially a political matter and that the role of the economist is to ensure that the policymaker is informed of the costs and benefits of decisions. Where land reform must take place to maintain order in the system, economists should recognize that land reform may in fact not be a cost minimizing solution. Land may have to be reallocated at the expense of reduced output and efficiency in order to prevent greater polarization of society. This should not suggest that agricultural economists neglect their area of expertise and fail to point out the costs of this reallocation. It suggests that they should determine why land reform is taking place so that they can offer relevant advice. As the number of effective constraints increase, the set of feasible solutions declines, and the economist must recognize this and convey this recognition to the policymaker.

I would disagree with the author's claim that the role of the agricultural economist in land reform is clear, positive, and definite. The pressures leading to land reform and the effects of reform are complex and numerous. Value judgments are necessary at every step in the process, and economists, by their nature and training, have only one particular perspective on the problem. They should make their views known, but the extent to which they should advocate them is unclear.

HOW A POLITICAL CHANGE ROUSES A STRONG SOCIAL IMPACT IN THE AGRICULTURAL SECTOR: AN ATTEMPT AT AGRARIAN REFORM IN PORTUGAL

A. Sebastiao Goncalves

Portugal Before the Political Change

People working in the agricultural sector had a very low standard of living, below the minimum level of culture and sanitation. In one northern area, families lived alongside their cattle, without water and sewage systems. In 1972, about 16 percent of the farms had no access roads for trucks, and in 1960 only 14 percent of the houses had water. In 1968, 97 percent of farms were less than 20 hectares and 39 percent less than 1 hectare. Owners directly managed 64 percent of the farms and 14 percent were managed by someone appointed by the owner. About 56 percent of the farming units did not use any mechanical equipment. Emigration was the only solution for the men, leaving their wives behind to manage the farms, with the result that one-third of the farming units were managed by women, or men over 65 years old.

For economists, the situation was very complicated. Henrique de Baros wrote that "the people working in the agricultural sector are always dominated by economic forces which have done all that they could to keep them in very poor economic and social conditions." However, such a situation does not seem difficult for most politicians. In 1964, one politician said that he tried to find "the way to give a more equitable compensation to the farmers, so they can meet their basic needs and their justifiable wants." But the main political leader for almost fifty years, before 1974, said that "in the country there are not any privileged or underprivileged social classes." Others have said more or less the same; very odd words for an economist. About 20 years ago, a politician clearly said that "agricultural technicians must stay in the fields as long as necessary to take account of producers' needs, and to prepare the rural people." Those are demagogic words. More than 30 years ago, the most important political leader said: "I am always trying to develop government services to increase production." However, relations between the producers and the government departments were rather poor, and beyond the technicians' responsibility.

Agricultural credit was based on a tangible guarantee, mainly a mortgage, so it was practically impossible for nonowners to get a loan. In 1957, a law set up a bank "to promote an accelerated development" of the national economy, with many of its rules borrowed from an official institution nearly 100 years old. The loans were also mainly based on mortgages, and very often the new bank used the money of the old. The new bank's first undertaking was to get a showy building as its head office, near the very people who had no money to improve their production. We must see the reality of credit and its use; quite often landowners got a loan and used the money to make loans to nonowners at a higher interest rate. Loans for equipment were also granted according to the "tangible guarantees" underestimated by the creditor, and the credit repayment not tied to the needs.

Data provided by producers were not comprehensive enough to allow a plan. In 1970, in one district, 43 of the farm managers were illiterate. Nevertheless, in 1949, a national agricultural plan was established, and three years later a politician said that technicians and the government had no relevant data. Nearly 30 years later, a technical meeting was told of the necessity of minimum accounting practices to help manage farming units. How can plans be implemented if the population does not have the basic knowledge to take advantage of them? Can we expect the help of government agencies?

Some of those who attended the 1970 World Conference on Agricultural Education and Training did not understand the need to solve the problem of

118

technicians who do not like going to rural areas, preferring to stay behind closed doors in their offices in the main cities, or to emigrate. Those who know the situation in Portugal could easily understand the technicians' behaviour in spite of political statements on this matter.

A national plan placing emphasis on the development of technology in the face of emigration was needed, accompanied by modification of the means of production. A long time before, another plan had said that management centres had been expanded to improve productivity. In 1969, the only political party said that "the government was trying to provide technical assistance for a more dynamic agriculture." In 1974, a few days before the overthrow of the government, a politician talked about the possibility of quickly developing the agricultural sector to solve the needs of the country.

We can get an idea of the gap between those wishes and what could be achieved by the available resources. The only political party said: "The Government gave the farmers, owners, and workers the means to promote agricultural development on the basis of cooperatives, and training centres have been set up all over the country." Such a statement is a way to put the responsibility on the technicians, landowners, and workers.

If the landowner has basic knowledge and the necessary means of production, he tries to use his land according to its specific qualities. But, in Portugal, 54 percent of the area is occupied by agriculture and only 24 percent should be used by this sector; in the most extensive agricultural district, only 14 percent of the land has conditions for agriculture and cattle, in spite of being 82 percent used. Because of this situation, even specific products are more expensive in this country than in others with higher wages, and it is not possible to avoid rigid and responsible state intervention. To increase agricultural productivity, technicians working in the public sector have a very important part to play.

Two other factors are very important to increase production: (1) credit managed by a public institution; and (2) price fixing schemes to pay the producer for the more important products. Credit should not be granted free. Many people favour a specialized credit institution, but it is not realistic. It is not possible to have one department able to study all the different aspects usually incorporated in the word agriculture. Each specialized department should carry out the analysis: the amount involved, repayment conditions, and the interest rate. The credit institution is responsible for the monitoring of the credit policy included in the master plan and for the flow of funds. This all depends on cooperation between the producer and the technicians.

Portugal After the Political Change

Political change came in 1974 from a bloodless military coup, and the agricultural sector was very much affected. Before 1974, there were no organized small or medium sized farms managed in accordance with the law (PMA), or workers' associations. The PMAs were a reaction against the situation of an underprivileged class, especially following Joao XXIII's speech on the need for such associations. In regions with large scale farms, occupation of land--often called wild occupation--started soon after 1974 by workers and small owners. "The land for those who work it" was the slogan included in the text of the new constitution. These takeovers scared away some large scale owners and others stopped cultivating.

Early after 1974, production collective units (UCPs) were established. Workers got together and I have seen them working very hard, even without proper inputs or basic knowledge. In 1975, the government decided to help the UCPs through a special credit scheme and creation of Centres for Agrarian Restructuring. But those decisions were not enough to solve the basic problem of instability. One politician said that the agrarian reform should be carried out in the legal order, and also said that agricultural problems could not be solved by laws. People really did not know what agrarian reform meant.

Instability was very widespread. Technicians gave advice about the need to develop conditions for improved production, but the rural population heard about theft of livestock and equipment and house burnings. This all increased instability, mainly from the government and state departments.

After the land takeovers occurred, a law established the conditions for expropriation according to the quality of land and the size and volume of production, giving to the owner the right to keep part of the expropriated land. Another law established the right to a payment, and that afterwards, according to the new constitution, there would be no possibility of further compensation. Practically, this all involved difficult problems, causing friction and difficulties for land reform.

Another regional agency was created: the Regional Centres for Agrarian Reform (CRRAs) with extensive legislative power to implement new policies to solve regional problems such as acts of sabotage and complaints about agrarian reform. Furthermore, the CRRAs can requisition equipment from large scale farms and put them on UCPs. This short presentation of the goals of CRRA is enough to make clear the conflicts between the owners of large scale farms, the local population, and even members of the government. Such a task would be very difficult if the CRRAs want to operate within the law. But how is it possible without suitable means? Uncertainty is the worst danger in an organization covered by theoretical laws and government instability. In 1976, some CRRAs were closed, and many of their technicians laid off.

Another government agency--SADA--was set up to inform the PMAs about agrarian reform legislation, and to put forward the problems of people working in agriculture. This is another difficult task; to give information about complicated legislation to a people lacking basic education.

One more government agency was set up: the Commission for the Analysis and Study of the Problems of Agrarian Reform (CAEP), directly under the Minister of Agriculture. According to the new constitution, the agrarian reform implied the setting up of collective forms of ownership under the sponsorship of the state. But the social atmosphere did not permit the forecast results to be attained, and there is even an association which stands against all collective forms. It is easy to understand the difficulty of achieving cooperation between farmers and governmental agencies owing to the political environment which puts emphasis on individual cases. Although the constitution stipulates that technical assistance is a producer right, this general condition is not adhered to, in spite of the musical words of one of these new agencies that "the leaders of the agricultural sector can quickly and efficiently make relevant decisions for each region." The same situation exists now as previously: a lot of words, conforming neither to economists' or technicians' recommendations, nor to the real need to improve the social welfare of the people.

Right after 1974, a law was presented making a provision for "changing the credit policy very shortly so to give an impetus to agricultural development." One year later, the financial situation of farms was more precarious, and another law made pronouncements about credit policy; a month later, the Minister of Agriculture made public his decision about "reformulation of credit policy," fifteen days before the law about special credit for PMAs was made. Four months later, another law made provisions for giving aid to all the collective farms so they could pay salaries. It is interesting to note what this law says: "The Minister has the power to manage the credit and to take care of its correct application." Farmers know the real meaning of such power.

The distribution of loans was easy, but repayment was not easy, owing to the financial situation of the farm units. In 1976, the government decided to collect back payments through the judicial system. But who is responsible for such a situation, the government agencies or the farmers?

Commercial banks do not really have the right conditions to provide credit for agriculture and cannot promote the adaptation of the sector to production needs. One of the so-called "revolutionary decisions" has been the nationalization of the banking sector; before that, an old public institution existed for agricultural credit, more or less like private banks.

After the great number of revolutionary decisions--very often opposed to each other--by nine governments, the main cause of the risky economic and social situation was the general and demagogic statements about the "rosy days ahead." In 1975, the press wrote that the two main political leaders thought that social discipline was the basis of development. But to have efficient and responsible management of governmental services is an essential condition. And how can we have such management if decisions are inconsistent? It is easy for a politician to initiate reform, beginning with the government and state departments, following a decree that "the government has the means to implement the agrarian reform in an orderly way," because a politician has enough power. But is it possible to have authority without responsibility? For agricultural economists, the responsibility is a necessary prerequisite, beginning with political leaders.

In September 1977, a basic agrarian reform law was issued, with bylaws eight months later. After the nationalization of banking, the system is operating without any policy integrating it with the growth in production. Two years after the approval of the first law relating to agrarian reform, legislative standards started to be more inflexible. In 1977, two basic laws relative to lease contracts, expropriation, and economic and technical aid to the UCPs were repealed. Some UCPs no longer operated, owing to a feeling of frustration, mainly due to police intervention in giving back the land to its owners. It is a duty of the government to set the example of order and responsibility.

Economists--not politicians--are the people working to obtain the means of promoting economic growth. But it is not possible to do so as long as rural people live with a sense of frustration, seeing the economic and political problems topple all their hopes for a change in the situation.

We are thus facing a real challenge for agricultural economists.

OPENER'S REMARKS--Phillip M. Raup

A fundamental task of a government is to establish the rules governing the conduct of business. This obligation is especially critical for agriculture, since long run commitments of labour and capital must be made. The most critical of these rules concerns the tenure under which land is held.

Goncalves documents the disastrous consequences for agriculture that can result from instability in governmental policies, and from uncertainty with regard to rights in land. The point of departure is the political events of 1974 in Portugal, and the subsequent and often spontaneous efforts to carry out agrarian reform. Agrarian reform efforts in Portugal after 1974 did not constitute a formal programme. They were instead a happening--an occurrence--and this complicates any attempt to assess their results by measured performance or stated goals.

An essential prerequisite for successful agrarian reform is the existence of a local network of supporting institutional arrangements. The most important is a tradition of effective local government. Where this is absent or weak, an agrarian reform effort may be defeated before it begins. An equally critical institutional structure is the system of agricultural credit. When rights to land are highly concentrated, are then broken up and redistributed, and are not carefully documented and registered, there is no adequate foundation for land based or mortgage credit. Any credit extended by government resembles welfare payments. A weak base is thus created for the use of credit as a device to guide land use and promote more intensive agricultural production.

The Portuguese experience adds another chapter to the long history of government attempts to promote agrarian reform by creating new forms of organization from the top down. Inadequate attention was given to local units in the organizational structure, although they were the critical ones in the implementation of the programmes that were ultimately attempted.

There was apparently a related neglect of informal and nongovernmental organizations that might have been helpful in mobilizing support for the agrarian reform. This applies especially to paraprofessional organizations of crop producers, livestock producers, marketing agencies, and local merchants.

A basic conflict between objectives is introduced when pricing policies for agricultural products are dominated by a desire to provide cheap food in order to reduce urban unrest. A cheap food policy cannot succeed if the rural sector is itself undergoing a major transformation. A policy for the cities, in this setting, must look first to the countryside. This has been, in all countries, one of the most difficult lessons to learn.

The consolidation and ultimate success of agrarian reform efforts depend upon the quality of the new farm managers. This, in turn, is a function of the availability of local schools which stress vocational training for agriculture. A neglect of this educational component has doomed agrarian reforms in a number of countries. It is extraordinarily difficult to provide this essential link when an entire countryside is torn by political unrest, but this is the time when a widespread network of agricultural vocational schools is most needed.

Underlying the many issues touched upon in this perceptive paper is the problem of congested rural population. Together with Spain and Ireland, Portugal has had the highest rate of population increase among the countries of Western Europe in recent years. Although low by developing country standards, much of this increase has been rural. This has enormously complicated the tasks of agrarian reform.

ISSUES IN THE AGRARIAN REFORM OF THE PLANTATIONS: A CHALLENGE FOR AGRICULTURAL ECONOMISTS

Nimal Sanderatne

Abstract

Plantations--an outgrowth of colonial economic exploitation--are an excellent example of an economic organization which promoted growth without development. A three tiered authoritarian structure ensured high profits to owners and high remuneration to managers, but the skill specific and often indentured labour obtained only bare subsistence wages and poor housing, educational, and health facilities. Agricultural economists must face the challenge of demonstrating alternative organizational forms for cultivating plantation crops which would combine the objectives of increased production with improved distribution. They must make comparative studies of plantation and small holder cultivation of crops, and determine how a slave driven plantation system could be converted to an incentive oriented structure, and how economies of scale on plantations could be reaped by smaller units, perhaps by a system of group farming. They must not only evaluate alternate land use patterns and plans for mixed farming, but suggest and devise realistic and practical measures for developing institutional structures which could effectively deliver an intensive, diversified, and multicultural agriculture which integrates plantations with rural agriculture.

OPENER'S REMARKS--John F. Timmons

Sanderatne characterizes the plantation as essentially a colonial and transitional type of organization built around the monoculture of sugarcane, tea, bananas, rubber, or other export crop, through "exploitation of people and natural resources." But plantations are indigenous as well as exogenous, regarding a particular country. This distinction may well be important. Probably the paper should be entitled "Issues in agrarian reform of foreign owned and operated plantations," since strengths and weaknesses are presented within the "foreign owned and operated" and "colonial" contexts.

There is need for investigations on similarities and differences of externally and internally financed plantations in terms of productivity, employment, income distribution, resource use, and participation of workers and their families in the social, political, and economic affairs of the community and nation. Investigations are needed on plantation organization and management which identify advantages and disadvantages of plantations and suggest alternatives for maintaining their production advantages and for overcoming their labour use disadvantages in keeping with the agricultural objectives of the country.

As the basis for agrarian reform, studies made within the country as well as reviews of experiences gained from other countries might well encourage alternatives to the plantation, including individual owner operators, cooperatives, collectives, and other tenure forms. Also, adjustments within the plantation ownership and management structure, wherein labourers would become organized in a manner similar to various industrial firms, or wherein the plantations would become reorganized into a firm with direct participation of labourers in its management and operation may also be possible remedial alternatives.

The paper's implied challenge for agricultural economists consists of research needs in analyzing plantations in the early process of agrarian reform as an inherent part of a country's economic and social change. There exists an extensive reservoir of experience in the transformation of plantations to other forms. These experiences largely remain to be analyzed. Such analyses might well be subjects of thesis and dissertation research or other professional undertakings.

A DYNAMIC, MULTISECTOR MODEL OF THE
WORLD AGRICULTURE-INDUSTRY-ENERGY COMPLEX

Yiu-Kwan Fan and Louis J. Cherene

Abstract

Agricultural development brings with it an increasing interdependence between the agricultural and industrial sectors and a new competition between them for energy and nutrient resources. This involves rapid social and economic adjustments which are not always anticipated and are in general imperfectly coordinated. The imbalances thus created should affect the dynamic performance of the world economy. To study these aspects, an adaptive, dynamic, multisector, temporary equilibrium model is presented. Applying the framework developed by Cigno, the model consists of the agricultural, industrial, energy, and household sectors, describing a von Neumann economic system with 27 commodities and 39 economic activities. Joint production is allowed. The world economy collectively maximizes the accounting value of its capital stocks at the beginning of each period, using accounting prices updated by the previous shadow prices, and subject to constraints partly set by the myopically optimal activity levels of the previous period. As it evolves, period by period, the economy traces a sequence of temporary equilibria. The model is simulated and some qualitative results are reported. The simulation runs demonstrate, inter alia, the significant role of exhaustible natural resources in affecting future economic growth, and the intersectorial imbalances resulting from the competition between the agricultural and industrial sectors for labour, energy, and other nutrient resources. Some extensions of the model are also suggested.

OPENER'S REMARKS--Michael H. Abkin
[Remarks read by Chester B. Baker.]

The model presented in this paper can be faulted for an almost total reliance on economic behaviour, with little or no regard for technological change (that is, constant technology coefficients in the LP matrix) or social and political adjustments. Maximizing the value of carryout capital stock can hardly be an adequate explanation of global behaviour in response to energy constraints. The use of the imputed value of capital in t+1 as equivalent to the total future profit stream generated by that capital is questionable.

It would be all right if the multiperiod problem were already solved and the imputed value were indeed the discounted profit stream. However, lagged shadow prices from a single period LP can hardly be expected to have this meaning. Can an LP model, particularly a single period, globally aggregated LP, explain even economic adjustments adequately enough (and purely economic adjustments themselves are not enough) to provide meaningful information for policy analysis or even for just understanding the problems involved?

RAPPORTEUR'S REPORT--Anders Wallenbeck

A multiperiod LP model can be reduced to a two period model if the economy under consideration is assumed to be in equilibrium. The first step model outlined here has to incorporate all the important constraints. But it is still worthwhile to study the behaviour of a simplified model based on sound theoretical grounds--in this case equilibrium theory. It is a little bit better to say that people optimize when looking forward then to say nothing about the future because we do not know how people behave.

124

NATIONAL PLANNING FOR AGRICULTURE
IN A DEVELOPED AGRICULTURAL EXPORTER:
THE CASE OF NEW ZEALAND

Robin W. Johnson

Abstract

This paper is concerned with planning in agricultural ministries at the national level. Planning in New Zealand is based on the British system of government and its relevant institutions. After briefly outlining the agricultural background, the paper discusses the relationship between the elected representatives and the paid administrators, the functioning of government and the recognition of felt needs, the coordination of national government aims and objectives, the role of the export sector in national planning, and the planning mechanism for government intervention. The aim of the paper is to describe the national administration of agricultural policy in a developed economy so that general discussion can develop with participants from other comparable systems of government.

RAPPORTEUR'S REPORT--Anders Wallenbeck

The compatability of economists, politicians, and pressure groups is much more important to incorporate in the analysis of the decision process in Canada than it is in New Zealand. In Canada, for instance, the pressure groups have almost no impact. How to keep farmers operating in the domestic market when the government policy is supporting the development of new export markets is an important problem for exporting countries. As it seems to be easier to introduce instruments for marketing control in New Zealand, they can better handle this problem in New Zealand compared to the situation in Canada. There seems to be a greater demand for better decision tools than economists and the state of the art in economic sciences can supply.

Contributing to the discussion was Richard Day.

U.S. AGRICULTURE IN AN INTERDEPENDENT WORLD: CLOSING THE GAP BETWEEN ANALYTICAL SYSTEMS AND CHANGING REALITY

Leroy Quance and Mihajlo Mesarovic

Abstract

Modeling developments in long range analysis of food and agriculture in the U.S. Department of Agriculture are offered as evidence that models are becoming more global, integrated, interdisciplinary, long run planning oriented, balanced in terms of labour and capital components, explicit with respect to policy and management decision options, and thus more useful. The development and use of the grains, oilseeds, and livestock (GOL) world trade model, national-interregional agricultural projections (NIRAP) system, Case Western Reserve University's world integrated model (WIM), and their linkage in the agriculture in the world integrated model (AGWIM) are offered as positive progress toward a more realistic analytical ability to analyze emerging issues with respect to food and agriculture in an interdependent world.

OPENER'S REMARKS--I. J. Singh

That economists need to go back to the drawing board to develop a new model of agriculture in an interdependent world is a sweeping generalization that the authors have not substantiated through their own work or by proving the futility of past work. To close the gap between analytical systems and changing reality, methodological research issues related to food and agriculture should have been discussed. For example, how do these models improve existing techniques for collecting and processing the large amount of data required to predict the outcome of the various policy decisions? The discussion of the models is mechancial and lacks the touch of economics. For example, how could AGWIM be used to determine the costs of meeting commodity needs from various domestic and foreign sources of supply and what pattern of supply would minimize those costs? Discussion of these issues would have provided a useful framework for organizing and maintaining information on food and agriculture through AGWIM.

RAPPORTEUR'S REPORT--Allan N. Rae

Both the WIM and NIRAP have been validated reasonably successfully. A validation problem that remains, however, arose in projection work when data values used in the model fell outside the range of data values used in the estimation phase. Confidence intervals surrounding projected estimates increased the further into the future such projections were made. This raises the question of just how complicated these models need be. Confidence intervals were generally of the order of 6-8 percent in these models. However, in relation to the degree of model complexity, researchers need to have managerial control over the model, and all its component parts. The pyramid model structure of aggregate, regional, and individual commodity components is useful in this connection.

Contributing to the discussion were Stefan Tangermann and Gunther Weinschenck.

BUILDING ANALYTICAL CAPACITY FOR AGRICULTURAL DECISIONMAKING: AN ISSUE OF TECHNOLOGY TRANSFER AND INSTITUTION BUILDING

George E. Rossmiller and Michael H. Abkin

The Issue

Many national governments, research institutions, and international organizations have been investing heavily in development of large scale computerized models as analytical aids to agricultural sector planning and policy decisionmaking. A complete list of all the modeling efforts currently on line or under development is not available, but as of December 1977 there were at least 21 active national level models of the U.S. agricultural sector alone, out of a total of 75 world, national, single commodity, food reserve, and other models with agricultural implications or components, not including modeling work done by other countries or international organizations, other than the World Bank and FAO (Boss and others).

Few, if any, of these efforts can be judged as unqualified successes, and most have failed to perform up to original expectations. This dismal record is not the result of technical modeling problems per se, since many examples of technically operational models can be found. Why then do we find modelers and model based analysts complaining that they are ignored or even berated by decisionmakers? Why are decisionmakers frustrated with what they find to be unusable and irrelevant information being thrust upon them by the modelers and the policy analysts? Even more curious, why do decisionmakers continue optimistically to support modeling efforts when the track record of so many models has been so poor? The immediate answers to these questions are really quite simple, while the understanding necessary to remedy this apparent paradox is much more complex.

The difficulties lie in the problems associated with technological innovation and transfer and with institution building and adaptation to accommodate the decisionmaking system and the new technology to each other. Only when these problems are properly identified and understood by all participants will it be possible to redesign the system to incorporate and use such models to their full potential. In this paper, we develop a framework for approaching a solution to fuller use of such a model based capacity to provide analytical input to the information required in the decision process.

We can begin to understand the origin of this multifaceted problem and clear the confusion surrounding its nature if we look at it from three perspectives. Indeed, these three perspectives will provide a framework for finding a solution. They are:

1. The necessary existence of motivation and means to improve the analytical capacity for decisionmaking, possibly through the adoption of innovative technologies;

2. The nature and proper role of analysis and models in the decisionmaking process; and

3. The need to plan for the institutional changes required for continued evolution, maintenance, and use of the expanded capacity and associated analytical technologies.

Motivation and Means

Forrester, in writing of the rapid evolution in the military application of the computer, states that by 1961 "the speed of military operations increased until it became clear that, regardless of the assumed advantages of human judgment decisions, the internal communication speed of the human organization simply was not able to cope with the pace of modern warfare. This inability to act provided the incentive." The inability to act has since become evident in many other quarters of the socioeconomy in most countries, with agricultural sector decisionmaking as no exception. The inability to act has been brought about by the increased complexity of the interdependent relationships between the rural and urban economies, the increased number of voices with the political power to influence the agricultural policy agenda, the increasing interdependence among nations, and the increased complexity of the technical and institutional aspects of the agricultural system and its environment. The need has been created for: more information; better, broader, and more detailed analysis; and more rapid and timely communication between the decisionmaker and analytical staff.

Almost in desperation, decisionmakers and analysts alike have turned to the computer and computer modeling as a potential means to relieve the pressures of their increasing burdens. While the results have been disappointing in not living up to expectations, no better alternative has magically appeared. Thus, decisionmakers are caught on the horns of a dilemma. If, on the one hand, they refuse the challenge of attempting to incorporate the technology of the computer into their decision processes, they are certain to find the increasing complexity and speed of events overwhelming their ability to manage them. If, on the other hand, they embrace the computer technology as a means of delivering them from their management problems without fully understanding that technology and how to use it wisely and efficiently, they will more than likely not achieve their objectives or expectations, possibly doing harm in the process. In order for improvements to be made in either situation, however, the motivation must occur at a level of decisionmaking where there is power; that is, the means to take appropriate action with respect to budgeting, staffing, and organizational adjustments.

Analysis and Models

The confusion and disappointment can be traced back to both frustrated expectations and unwarranted fears and distrust of quantitative models, especially computerized, mathematical simulation models. Many decisionmakers and their analytical staffs, unfortunately frequently encouraged by modelers themselves (Greenberger), have built up inflated expectations of what "the computer model" would do for them--give them answers or tell them what they should do--only to be disappointed by the results. Conversely, many others have rejected the notion of computer models, sometimes even quantitative models of any sort, repulsed by the seeming dehumanization involved in reducing the affairs of people to numbers, and of machines dictating what course people should take. Both of these views display a basic misunderstanding--frequently on the part of the modeler as well as that of model users--of the nature and proper role of models in analysis and of analysis in decisionmaking.

Analysis is the third stage of the iterative, six stage process of decisionmaking. It is preceded by, first, definition of the problem requiring a decision, and, then, based on that definition, observation of relevant aspects of the real world situation. In Bonnen's sense, observation corresponds to data collection, and the following analysis stage corresponds to the processing and interpretation of those data into information bearing on the decision to be made. Analysis generally includes projecting, over a relevant time horizon, the likely consequences of alternative courses of action. There is, therefore, a great deal of interaction with decisionmakers during analysis in order to formulate and reformulate the alternatives to be tested. Following analysis, the remaining three stages of the process are the decision itself, implementation of that decision (actually another level of decisionmaking in its own right), and, finally, evaluation of and bearing responsibility for the actual results.

Anybody making a decision invariably uses some model to perform analysis prior to the final decision. Here we are defining model in its broadest sense to mean an abstraction or representation of relevant aspects of the real world, where the relevance is determined by the problem definition. Thus, models used in analysis can range from vague intuitive or mental images, to scaled down physical replicas, to physical analogs, to formal mathematical symbols. Mathematical models, particularly with the advent of the digital computer, afford the opportunity to incorporate into the analysis many more complex relationships in a logically consistent way that can be done with informal, mental, or "seat of the pants" models.

It is a mistake, however, either to expect or fear that a given mathematical model can provide all the information needed for a decision. No such model can ever prescribe what action is "best." That can only be done by the decisionmaker using information from a variety of sources, together called a "problem solving model." This can typically include one or more formal mathematical models, or relevant portions of them, and, also, very importantly, the decisionmaker's own mental model of the situation.

A final point we can make here concerns the usefulness of distinguishing between structure and data as basic ingredients of a model, mathematical or otherwise. Data are taken here to include both initial conditions and parameter values, while structure means the relevant set of endogenous and exogenous variables (including policies) and their causal relationships, including dynamic feedback links. Experience has shown that the structure of a mathematical model can be generalized for application in a variety of contexts and problem areas. It is, therefore, important to consider the costs of developing such a model, which can be substantial, as an investment, and the resulting model as capital stock from which a flow of services can be derived for various purposes. In evaluating the benefits and costs of a model from this standpoint, then, one can consider returns on the investment, maintenance costs, and perhaps even the payback period.

Planning for Institutionalization and Use

In the past, the provision of analytical information for decisionmaking was a much simpler matter. Not only were the problems less complex and interrelated but the traditional techniques for analysis were simpler and thus more transparent to the analysts and decisionmakers who used with confidence the information derived from their application. But to make full use of the analytical technology available to deal with the problems and complexities of the present real world requires a high degree of task and skill specialization.

In a large scale model based effort to improve the organizational capacity for planning and policy analysis, an effective team must include a stable, critical mass of modelers, computer programmers, subject matter specialists, analysts, and, of course, decisionmakers. Such a team must be organized under a common set of objectives to permit a free flow of information and feedback to assure a relevant focus and a quick response capability from the standpoint of the decisionmaker who is the end user of the effort. Team members must be well qualified in their own area of speciality and be of a persuasion to work well in a multidisciplinary team setting.

The whole institutional approach and infrastructure needed must be planned with care at the time the project is launched, and it must be able to sustain its relevance and usefulness in the long term. This includes the capacity to do continuous model development and adaptation as the problems and the reality being modeled change. It includes the ability to routinely maintain and update the data and information base in a timely and consistent manner. And, it includes the capability to transfer the necessary knowledge and technology over time as the team members change. None of these are trivial functions when dealing with large scale model based analytical capacities. The histories of modeling projects indicate that few, if any, of these projects have paid adequate attention to these aspects, and thus they have not developed the necessary institutional infrastructure.

In the final analysis, no single blueprint for success in building, institutionalizing, and using an analytical capacity can be found. Each situation will have its own unique environment, institutional setting, technical requirements, economic and political constraints, uses, and personalities that will necessitate adaptation and flexibility for any prescribed approach. We can, however, summarize the major requirements which will make the task more tractable and more likely to achieve a useful and relevant model based analytical capacity as an integral part of a dynamic decisionmaking structure.

1. Recognition on the part of decisionmakers that analytical input for decisionmaking can be improved, and a political will on their part to make the necessary improvements.

2. An understanding by decisionmakers, analysts, and modelers alike that the development of a comprehensive, model based capacity requires a substantial commitment of resources, trained personnel, and effort over a sustained period of time before the additional quantity and quality of decision information (that is, the benefits) will justify the cost, which can be substantial, of the initial investment to accumulate the capital stock to build the capacity.

3. Initial planning for development and use of a large scale, computerized, model based technology which includes the necessary conditions for making the new technology part of the ongoing decision process. This will frequently require adaptation of the existing organizational structure to accommodate the new technology and to assure that the institutional infrastructure provides the functions required for sustaining and using the new capacity provided by the new technology.

4. Recognition by all participants that the provision of timely information for decisionmaking is a dynamic process that must adapt to changing needs, changing problems, and a changing real world. Flexibility by all participants (modelers, analysts, decisionmakers) in the process, in the model technology itself, and in the institutional infrastructure is necessary to maintain a useful and relevant decisionmaking analytical capacity over time. Models must, in particular, contain the richness and flexibility to be easily adapted, manipulated, and put together in various configurations at appropriate levels of aggregation in order to meet particular analytical needs of decisionmakers at the time they are needed.

References

Bonnen, J. (1975) Improving information on agriculture and rural life. American Journal of Agricultural Economics, 57 (5) 753-763.

Boss, G.; and others (1978) Food and agriculture models for policy analysis, in System Theory Applications to Agricultural Modeling (edited by A. H. Lewis and C. L. Quance). Washington, D.C.; U.S. Dept. of Agriculture and the National Science Foundation.

Forrester, J. W.; Greenberger, M. (editors) (1972) Managerial Decision Making in Management and the Computer of the Future. Cambridge, Massachusetts, USA; MIT Press, pp. 52-53.

Greenberger, M.; and others (1976) Models in the Policy Process. New York; Russell Sage Foundation.

RAPPORTEUR'S REPORT--Allan N. Rae

When individual institutions carry out research in isolation, conflicting policy solutions can be given for the same problems. Therefore, is there need for a suprainstitution to coordinate research? No, coordination is best left to the researchers in the various institutions--that is, a removal of horizontal barriers. In the United States, coordination is a matter of individual communications among researchers. There are many models of U.S. agriculture; for example, at USDA and at the universities. Coordination is up to the researchers and appears to work successfully as the various models are each aimed at different problem areas. Too much coordination in research is harmful because it limits useful competition among researchers.

Interaction between the policymaker and the research team is vital. Models gain credibility through time as they are used, and as the users become trained in the features of the model.

Continual adjustment of the model to changing circumstances is required, giving little time to fine tune the model which after a period of time becomes a hybrid with an outdated structure and data base. Such a model would not then perform as well as it could, and credibility problems could arise. A model is basically an accounting system, and should therefore correspond to the accounting systems with which policymakers are familiar if the model is to be acceptable.

Contributing to the discussion were Choong-Yong Ahn, Hans-Ake Jansson, Lyle P. Schertz, and Gunther Weinschenck.

ADJUSTMENT PRESSURES ON THE AGRICULTURAL SECTOR
OF AN OPEN ECONOMY: THE AUSTRALIAN SITUATION

D. P. Vincent and G. J. Ryland

Introduction

The Australian economy has undergone substantial compositional changes since the early 1960s. The relative position of agriculture has declined following the more rapid growth rates of other sectors, especially mining. The uneven growth rate between sectors has led inexorably to adjustment pressures emerging on the slower growing sectors and on the slower growing industries within sectors. The agricultural output mix has changed markedly. Value shares of output and exports represented by wool, fruits, and dairy products have declined, while those represented by beef and wheat have increased. Numerous factors have contributed in recent years to the adjustment pressures facing the agricultural sector and its constituent industries. These include changes in international trading conditions, the mining boom of the late 1960s, real wage increases in excess of productivity gains in the domestic economy, and increased protection from imports afforded key manufacturing industries.

From the late 1960s to the mid-1970s, world prices for textiles, footwear, and other manufactured products fell relative to the prices of agricultural and mineral products and processed and unprocessed energy products. The Australian economy as a whole benefited from these changes, though adjustment pressures emerged in certain sectors (Freebairn). In particular, export and export related industries expanded at the expense of industries competing with imports which experienced the largest relative price declines. On the debit side, restrictions on the access of Australian products to overseas markets, particularly the EC, have severely curtailed a number of rural industries.

Unprocessed mineral export earnings jumped from A\$64 million in 1962/63 to A\$1,753 million in 1974/75. The effects on the balance of payments and subsequently the exchange rate, standard of living, and industrial structure have been the subject of several recent studies (Dixon, Parmenter, and Sutton; and Gregory). The basic mechanism involves a lowering of the domestic price of traded relative to nontraded goods either by revaluation of the Australian dollar or by a higher local inflation rate.

Real wage costs net of productivity gains increased at an annual rate of over 3 percent for the period 1968 to 1975. In addition, despite a 25 percent across the board tariff cut in 1973, substantial increases in protection, primarily by way of import quotas, have since been granted to key domestic industries. The competitive position of the export oriented agricultural sector is especially vulnerable to increases in domestic production costs.

Our paper investigates the medium term impact on the Australian agricultural sector of two of the previously mentioned adjustment pressures: (1) changes in international demands for and supplies of agricultural and other commodities of importance to Australian trade; and (2) a further expansion of Australian mining activity. It then explores the effectiveness of reducing tariffs on import competing industries as a means of dissipating adjustment pressures on agriculture arising from the combined effect of (1) and (2).

Analytical Framework

Our projections are derived from Australia's multisectoral model of industrial and workforce composition (ORANI) (Dixon, Parmenter, Ryland, and Sutton). ORANI is a predominantly neoclassical model based on a 115 x 113 commodity by industry input-output matrix, and a labour force disaggregated into nine occupations. Computing difficulties associated with size and nonlinearities are avoided by using the linearization technique of Johansen. The model's main behavioural postulates are that producers minimize the costs of producing their outputs (subject to appropriately specified production functions), and that consumers maximize their utility subject to an aggregate consumption constraint. Competitive pricing behaviour is imposed via zero pure profit constraints. The model contains a number of advances over previous models of its type which make it particularly well suited to analyzing policy issues related to international trade. These advances include: (1) the treatment of domestically produced and imported commodities as imperfect substitutes; (2) downward sloping foreign demand curves for export commodities; and (3) an agricultural sector specification which recognizes both the joint production features of agricultural enterprises and regional differences in their production functions. The agricultural sector consists of a 10 x 8 commodity by industry submatrix. Agricultural industry production functions are of the multiinput-multioutput form, such that:

$$(1) \quad g(Y^r) = f(X^r) = Z^r,$$

where Y^r and X^r are vectors of outputs and inputs respectively in region r, and Z^r is a scalar index defining region r's production capacity. Function f is of the Leontief form among intermediate inputs and between them and primary factors, and of the CRESH form (Hanoch) among the primary factors (labour, land, and capital). Function g takes the CRETH form (Vincent, Dixon, and Powell). The representative farmer is viewed as buying a bundle of nonspecific inputs (labour, fertilizer, and so forth) to combine with the fixed factor, land. The level of nonspecific inputs determines the location of the product transformation curve. The farmer then has a choice of feasible output combinations (wheat, sheep, and so forth) with production possibilities described by transformation frontiers exhibiting less than infinite elasticities.

A feature of the model is that the division between endogenous and exogenous variables is user determined. In a study of the effect of, say, the motor vehicle tariff on the output of wheat, the motor vehicle tariff would be set exogenously and the output of wheat would be endogenous. If, however, we wanted to know the level of protection needed by the tobacco industry to boost its output by 10 percent, then tobacco output is exogenous and its tariff endogenous. Of particular relevance to this study is the switch between industry rates of return and industry capital stocks. With fixed capital stocks and endogenous rates of return, the model is cast in the short run mode. The alternative long run specification employed here involves fixing industry rates of return and allowing capital stocks to adjust. The model then provides a snapshot of a single year, the assumption being that the snapshot year is far enough into the future such that changes in relative rates of return induced by the initial disturbance are eliminated by capital mobility between industries.

Projection Scenarios

Our focus is on prospective developments in the Australian economy to the mid-1980s. We first provide the model with projections of annual changes in world relative prices for imported commodities (the small country assumption is imposed for imports), and annual percentage shifts in the foreign demand schedules for Australian export commodities together with estimates of their foreign price elasticities of demand. These projections are based on an IMPACT study (Freebairn) of likely developments affecting demands, supplies, and prices of internally traded commodities. They refer to average trade opportunities in a nominal year and abstract from seasonality, business cycle, and other transient phenomena. World prices of machinery, equipment, appliances, and motor vehicles are assumed to rise most slowly. These assumptions reflect an anticipated continuation of technological innovation and more capital intensive production techniques in the production of such commodities. The next slowest to rise group (price increases of 2.6 percent per year faster than the first group) are those products produced by (or anticipated to be soon produced by) developing countries (for example, steel and most metal products not highly fabricated). The fastest rising prices are for wool, meat, and dairy products, and developed country exports (other than machinery). These prices are assumed to inflate from 4-5 percent higher than those of the most slowly increasing group. Prices of wheat and sugar are projected to increase by 2.8 and 2.6 percent, respectively, relative to the most slowly increasing group. Oil prices are projected to increase only at the same rate as prices in general. Annual percentage increases in prices are cumulated for the 5 year period.

Australia's apparent comparative advantage in mineral exports may lead to a further comparatively rapid growth of the mining sector with the restoration of global macroeconomic health. In simulating this, we assert that the direct effects of new mining activity on domestic demands and employment are likely to be small by comparison with the indirect effects arising from the additional foreign exchange earned. We assume that additional mineral exports yield an addition to foreign exchange of A$500 million by the fifth year.

Our third simulation involves a further across the board reduction in ad valorem tariffs of 25 percent.

Since we wish to consider the adjustment forces independently of short run business cycle phenomena, the macro environment is assumed to be one of full employment. Occupational wage relativities are fixed, but the overall level of real wages adjusts to maintain full employment. The endogenous exchange in real absorption from the exogenous shocks is allocated among its components (aggregate consumption, investment, and government expenditure) according to their initial shares.

Results

TABLE 1 : IMPACT OF CHANGES IN WORLD PRICES, TARIFFS AND A MINING BOOM

Variable Projected	Simulations of Effects of:			
	World Prices	Mining 'Boom'	Tariff Reductions	Total Impact
	(percentage change)			
Real Absolute Wage	1.09	0.81	1.04	2.94
Aggregate real Absorption	1.43	1.93	0.28	3.64
Aggregate real Exports	2.00	-10.91	3.68	-5.23
Aggregate real Imports	1.69	2.18	3.11	6.98
Rural Employment	6.04	-2.86	0.58	3.71
Agricultural Commodity Outputs				
Wool	6.61	-1.78	0.38	5.21
Sheep	9.75	-2.13	0.46	8.08
Wheat	-1.32	-2.19	0.51	-3.00
Barley	0.81	-1.89	0.45	-0.63
Other cereal grains	1.33	-0.99	0.29	0.63
Meat cattle	10.27	-2.23	0.51	8.55
Milk cattle and pigs	3.75	-0.75	0.18	3.18
Other farming exports	-4.38	-2.55	0.73	-6.20
Other farming import competing	1.24	-0.05	0.13	1.32
Poultry	3.33	-0.70	0.16	2.79
Industry Sector Outputs				
Agriculture	3.67	-1.72	0.41	2.36
Mining (Existing Industries)	-2.01	-17.81	6.72	-13.10
Processed foods	1.19	-1.07	0.27	0.39
Other Manufacturing	-3.28	-0.93	-0.61	-4.82
Services	1.18	1.26	0.32	2.76

A summary of results is contained in table 1. We concentrate on some key macroeconomic aggregates and agricultural commodity outputs. Industry outputs have been aggregated to sectors. The figures in the table refer to percentage changes in the variables in a typical year, 5 years hence from the levels they would have reached in the absence of the shocks. Thus, column 1 indicates that, in the fifth year, exports would be 2 percent higher under the world price scenario than they would have been had world prices not changed.

Column 1 shows that the projected world price scenario implies a terms of trade gain to Australia. Exports exceed imports and real wages and real domestic absorption increase. However, the tendency for world price increases for export commodities to exceed those for import competing commodities in itself leads to adjustment pressures. Output contractions occur for export commodities such as minerals whose prices are projected to decline relative to most agricultural commodity prices. Most agricultural commodities and industries (and hence rural employment) gain. Exceptions include wheat and the other farming export groups (mainly sugar) whose price prospects are unfavourable. The processed foods and services sectors, which have substantial linkages to domestic consumption, benefit from the increased aggregate absorption. The growth in domestic absorption is also an important factor in offsetting the output contractions of import competing industries resulting from the decline in the relative prices of most imported commodities.

Column 2 demonstrates the adverse effect on export industries from the additional foreign exchange generated by the mining boom. Note that the simulation captures only the indirect (foreign exchange) effects; the existing mining industries therefore suffer in the same manner as other export industries. Agricultural outputs are considerably less volatile than mining outputs because of the presence of fixed (industry specific) land. While the mining boom also leads to adjustment pressures on the manufacturing sector through stronger import competition, the increased absorption helps cushion these effects. The clear beneficiaries are the nontraded (services sector) industries.

Column 3 indicates that the tariff cut is beneficial to the economy as a whole and to the export oriented sectors in particular. The essentially import competing manufacturing sector contracts. The services sector expands because of its consumption linkages and the increase in domestic absorption, while the processed foods sector expands because of its linkages to exports and domestic consumption.

Concluding Remarks

We have attempted to quantify the medium term effect on the Australian agricultural sector of two pressures for adjustment—changes in world prices of traded goods and an accumulation of foreign exchange (which we attribute to a projected expansion in mining exports). Our analysis overlooks a number of other potential adjustment pressures. These include technological developments and demographic factors, both of which are likely to contribute to changing patterns of industrial demand and occupational employment. Both of these issues are amenable for analysis within the ORANI framework. While we believe that the pressures we have dealt with will operate in the medium term, our projection scenarios remain speculative. Our price scenario implies an extremely favourable outlook for the agricultural sector as a whole but with differential effects within the sector. Our simulations demonstrate the adverse effects on traded (especially export) industries of foreign exchange from an expansion in mineral exports. Unlike the import competing industries, the export oriented agricultural industries gain little from the overall expansion in domestic absorption afforded by the mining boom. The tariff reductions go some of the way to reducing the cost-price squeeze on the agricultural sector arising from the foreign exchange effects of the mining boom. Given, however, the tentative nature of our scenarios, we would not want to place too much emphasis on the numerical projections. A more fundamental aim has been to illustrate the importance of a multisectoral framework in analyzing policy issues of this type. While our results remain specific to the Australian economy, our quantitative approach is applicable to any market oriented economy.

References

Dixon, P. B.; Parmenter, B. R.; Ryland, G. J.; Sutton, J., M. (1977) ORANI: A general equilibrium model of the Australian economy. First progress report of the IMPACT project (an economic research project sponsored by a number of Australian government departments), Canberra, Vol. 2.

Dixon, P. B.; Parmenter, B. R.; Sutton, J. M. (1978) Some causes of structural maladjustment in the Australian economy. Australian Economic Papers, No. 57, January.

Freebairn, J. W. (1978) Projections of Australia's world trade opportunities: Mid and late 1980s. IMPACT working paper, Melbourne, No. I-07, December.

Gregory, R. G. (1976) Some implications of the growth of the mineral sector. Australian Journal of Agricultural Economics, 20 (2) 71-91.

Hanoch, G. (1971) CRESH production functions. Econometrica, 39 (5) 695-712.

Johansen, L. (1974) A Multi-Sectoral Study of Economic Growth. Amsterdam; North Holland Publishing Co., 2nd edition.

Vincent, D. P.; Dixon, P. B.; Powell, A. A. (forthcoming) The estimation of supply response in Australian agriculture: The CRESH/CRETH production system. International Economic Review.

OPENER'S REMARKS--George T. Jones

Many would be interested in derived elasticities for agricultural products in general and in detail but doubtless this is too much to ask. How strong are the forces obliging visible trade to balance? Is the projected expansion in mining to be financed by external sources of investment, and are other net inflows of investment into Australia predetermined? Who gets the profits and where do they go? There is a strong analogy with the projections of the impact of North Sea oil on the UK economy.

While not having very severe qualitative disagreements, I did wonder from exactly what date the price assumptions are measured and whether the beef prices start very low. I recognize that any price trend for beef looks sharper in percentage terms from the other side of the world. But I was trying to fit higher real beef prices into the UK framework and was coming up with less than zero growth in demand. At much higher prices, the impact of novel protein food seemed serious, especially for the kind of beef Australia sends us. I know less about the other UK markets for beef, but wonder if the authors are not overguessing the prospects.

Perhaps the most important point of the model itself is that the supply elasticity for production of agricultural products in general is separated from the problem of determining the composition of supply. This makes it rather easier to handle, but does it avoid some kinds of questions that one would like to ask; for example, is it intrinsically more difficult to expand production of less intensive products like wool because of links with land?

Am I right in writing the model like this?

(1) $\quad 1 = \Sigma\, d_i(Y_i/Z)^{b_i} \qquad$ [for g]

(2) $\quad 1 = \Sigma\, c_i(X_i/Z)^{a_i} \qquad$ [for f]

136

In this formulation, are the short run inputs such as feed, fertilizer, and services tied to the factors X or to the products Y in a Leontief manner, and are they the net outputs or the gross outputs that are described in Y? Are they the gross costs including renovation of capital that are included in X? Was consideration given to any other generalization of the CES function (using no more parameters) such as the two stage CES in which some capital may substitute more closely for land while most of it may be substituted more closely for labour? How does technical progress enter into the projections--through factor saving technologies in f or through specifying more product in g? It would appear that the model allows no supply elasticity for land while allowing unlimited supply elasticity for capital (in spite of difficulties farmers may have in raising it). Is this entirely the right balance in such a big place? How is the labour specified that relates to agriculture, and has it been made too easy to exchange it for other factors, even within the same region?

LEONTIEF INPUT-OUTPUT TECHNIQUE AND THE DEVELOPMENT OF AGRICULTURAL DATA SYSTEMS

K. S. Howe

Introduction

This paper suggests that a Leontief type input-output technique has an unrealized potential as the basis for efficient data systems. A model in the process of development for the UK livestock, meat, and meat products industry is used as an example. An expansive discussion of agricultural data systems is beyond the scope of this paper, but a thorough examination of the principal issues and an extensive bibliography are given by Barnard.

The Contribution of Leontief Input-Output Technique: A Case Study

Origins

The Meat and Livestock Commission in the United Kingdom requested a "network analysis" of the entire UK livestock and meat industry, the origins of which are described by Duckworth. Briefly, since the Commission is charged with increasing industrial efficiency, it was felt essential to obtain a detailed description of the industry's economic structure. In this context, "increasing efficiency" is broadly defined as providing the environment wherein economic objectives can be more easily achieved. From an awareness of areas where information is limited, research effort can be directed to increase the level of knowledge. In turn, this knowledge should assist in guiding policy decisions.

Requirements

A "network analysis" implies the need to account for the salient features of the industry and particularly the interrelationships between economic activities. The industry which the Commission serves demands that expression of interrelated features must include information significant to a wide range of personnel. For example, within the Commission there are specialist divisions and services concerned with a mix of both economic and technical data. Clearly, these two aspects are not independent, but they do set the extremes.

The need for a data system for the livestock and meat industry is evident. Since the data are explicitly problem oriented for the reasons described, it may be preferable to speak of an information system as distinct from a data system. Eisgruber appears to favour the distinction, regarding data as messages which are unevaluated for a particular use at a particular time. Once associated with a problem, the data become information. The distinction is more attractive in principle than practice, however. The term "data system" is retained here, although the distinction between data and information is sometimes useful.

The data system should be easily understood because of the variety of users. Physical and value data for the demand and supply of all inputs and outputs, and the interrelationships between enterprises, products, supply, and demand must be shown in an uncomplicated manner. The importance of minimizing technicalities when economists are providing data to nonspecialist policymakers is emphasized by Capstick.

Conceptual Framework

It is implicit that the data system requires a simple yet comprehensive model of the industry. The extent of the sector suggested that a systems approach would be helpful. The ideas developed subsequently have much in common with the frameworks developed by French and Nieto-Ostolaza. The livestock and meat industry is essentially a system bounded on the one hand by industries generating inputs used by farmers, animal product processors, and distributors, and on the other hand by exogenous final demand determinants. The system comprises four subsystems representing pig, poultry, beef, and sheep products at all stages of production, processing, and distribution. These subsystems can be disaggregated into first stage production (farm production) and second stage production (processing and distribution). Furthermore, these two stages contain conceptually distinct activities such as rearing systems for livestock, and distributive networks for products as between, say, household and catering consumption, small goods manufacturing, and exports. These characteristics will be reflected in the structure of the data system.

The stringency of the requirements precludes any complex mathematical systems model. However, the link between the systems model and the data system can be established by assuming that the flows of outputs and resources throughout the total system are described by linear functions. A review of the possible methods for formalizing the industry model pointed directly to a Leontief input-output framework.

Advantages of the Input-Output Approach

The Leontief input-output technique is a type of programming model. Petit aptly summarizes the attraction of such models in that they "are very efficient instruments to organize coherently a huge mass of information; the very specificity and explicit character of the assumptions on which they are based lead to their thorough discussion--a definite advantage."

The application of instructions to elementary data (that is, physical co-efficients and unit values) for each product sector generates the corresponding transactions submatrices. Within each product sector matrix is described the nucleus of the subsystem in the form of intermediate transactions, with primary inputs as inflows and final demand as outflows. Interaction between the subsystems is described by aggregation into the industry matrix. It is through this initial manipulation of data that fundamental gaps in knowledge become apparent. For example, it was quickly found in constructing the beef sector matrix that store cattle movements and the relative importance of rearing and fattening systems are poorly documented. Data gaps become apparent from simple description and the importance of filling them may be assessed via sensitivity tests at this stage, but other facets of the input-output technique also contribute.

In the input-output technique, a distinction is often drawn between its uses for description and analysis. The explanation above shows that even simple description has an analytical function. The more usual analytical applications are for economic planning, impact analysis, optimization of some objective function, study of price effects and the comparision of policies. These applications are clearly explained in O'Connor and Henry, and their relevance in the present context is discussed with extensions by me (Howe). The vital point is that the structure of the basic matrix showing total resource flow and the technical coefficients from it are easy to understand. Even the principles of obtaining the interdependence coefficients do not require a profound knowledge of matrix algebra (see O'Conner and Henry). Most important is that the whole exercise focuses attention on the basic data inputs and how these are used.

If it is thought that there may be errors in assumptions about the existence and magnitude of intraindustry flows, then the structure of transactions can be changed to simulate different possibilities. Armed with any new transactions matrix, the subsequent computations are carried out as usual and results similarly appraised.

Organization and Administration of the Data System

A number of facilities are envisaged, each intended to contribute to the desirable qualities of modern data systems outlined above. At the present developmental phase, the model is being explained on index cards, with two sets for each of the total system and its four subsystems. One set explains the calculations and the other sources of data. Cross referencing enables sequential calculations to be traced and matched with data inputs. It is anticipated that adoption of the data system will be accompanied by transfer of these records to computer files. A possible generalized structure is shown in figures 1 and 2. The flow diagrams are largely self-explanatory, but some supplementary explanation is needed.

The "read year" command in figure 1 shows that the data system is geared to recording and manipulating time series information. If desired, users may call lists of instructions, data, and sources. These are essential facilities because improvements can materialize only from scrutiny by authorized and informed parties. Alternatively, data or sources listings may be extracted by researchers who wish speedy access to information for their own purposes.

Figure 2 continues figure 1 and shows the options for producing matrices and manipulating these for both the industry and its subsectors. Both data and instructions may be altered, and the consequences investigated on recomputing. The changes may well require new matrix dimensions. The broken box for sensitivity tests and comparative options is so presented because it includes a range of possible subroutines. For example, it may be useful to compute measures of variance for matrix coefficients calculated from different data sets under different assumptions.

Conclusions

It is contended that the application of a Leontief input-output technique to the problem of establishing data systems meets many of the objectives identified in appraisal of the existing situation. The UK meat industry model provides examples.

First, the model is avowedly oriented towards the enduring problems of understanding the fundamental structure of the industry and monitoring developments over time. Second, the model is holistic in that it encompasses the entire industry. Traditional preoccupation with obtaining farm production data has hindered documentation of the processing sectors, but the data gaps are defined and improvements can be initiated. Third, a particular strength of the model is that it is explicitly constructed from elementary data on unit prices, costs, and physical coefficients. This maximizes flexibility in the data system as circumstances and data requirements change. Moreover, matrix entries can be altered to simulate changes in economic structure and technical coefficients. Contrast this property with the accounting framework of Carlin and Handy, an improved though nevertheless rigid structure which may itself be rapidly outdated. An input-output model could be used to set up data in a corresponding form. It is interesting that, in common with other accounts of data systems, Carlin and Handy employ a variation of the input-output approach.

More generally, the input-output technique has potential as the basis of a much wider data network. In the United Kingdom, a network can be envisaged in which the Department of Agriculture and other organizations including, say, the Meat and Livestock Commission, the Milk Marketing Boards, and the Home Grown Cereals Authority establish and integrate compatible data systems. In principle, the apex of the integrated network would be a transactions matrix for the national agricultural industry. Decentralization meets the objective of exploiting particular areas of expertise.

The inherent assumptions of linearity may be considered a limitation, but extravagant claims are not being made for the technique. If construction of more flexible models is appropriate for certain aggregate or subsector problems, there is nothing to prevent it. On the contrary, the data system provides the optimal route to relevant information.

The mere development of a single industry model must necessarily have a long gestation period. In the longer term, the demands on resources will be high, but results of the kind produced by Hayami and Peterson indicate the considerable benefits which can accrue. The potential contribution of the Leontief technique appears to have been overlooked. It is considered that the method warrants serious discussion and investigation in other sectors of agriculture and in other countries.

Figure 1 Basic facilities provided by the data system

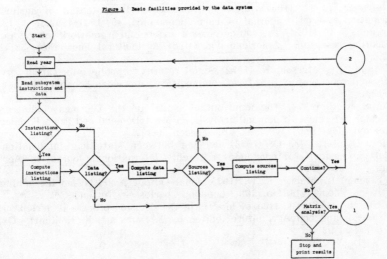

Figure 2 Computation and manipulation of matrices.

TC = technical coefficient
IC = interdependence coefficient

141

References

Barnard, C. S. (1975) Data in agriculture: A review with special reference to farm management research, policy, and advice in Britain. Journal of Agricultural Economics, 26, 289-331.

Capstick, C. W. (1977) Agricultural policy and the contribution of agricultural economics research and analysis, in Decision-Making and Agriculture (edited by T. Dams and K. E. Hunt). Oxford; Alden Press, 47-61.

Carlin, T. A.; Handy, C. R. (1974) Concepts of the agricultural economy and economic accounting. American Journal of Agricultural Economics, 56, 964-975.

Duckworth, J. E. (1973) The role of the economist in research for the meat and livestock industry. Journal of Agricultural Economics, 24, 479-492.

Eisgruber, L. M. (1967) Micro and macroanalytic potential of agricultural information systems. Journal of Farm Economics, 49, 1541-1552.

French, B. C. (1974) The subsector as a conceptual framework for guiding and conducting research. American Journal of Agricultural Economics, 56, 1014-1022.

Hayami, T.; Peterson, W. (1972) Social returns to public information services: Statistical reporting of U.S. farm commodities. American Economic Review, 62, 119-130.

Howe, K. S. (1977) The input-output model of the UK meat industry with particular reference to demand analysis, in Meat Demand and Price Forecasting. Bletchley; Meat and Livestock Commission, 1-13.

Nieto-Ostolaza, M. C. (1973) Balance between statistical information and models in agricultural economic research. International Journal of Agrarian Affairs, 5, 458-470.

O'Conner, R.; Henry, E. W. (1975) Input-Output Analysis and Its Application (Statistical Monograph No. 36). London; Charles Griffin and Co.

Petit, M. (1977) The role of models in the decision process is agriculture, in Decision-Making and Agriculture (edited by T. Dams and K. E. Hunt). Oxford; Alden Press, 62-76.

RAPPORTEUR'S REPORT--Andre Brun

Howe's model can effectively be taken as a data system. Its input-output nature, in aggregate terms, makes it possible to describe activities, but not to explain production decisions. As Howe argued, it can be progressively disaggregated with the help of more accurate data, when its utility is recognized. For instance, the lowland steppe activity could be subdivided to account for different products such as wool and meat; but, it is clear that to attempt to achieve a once and for all universal and detailed collection of data is impossible and would be a waste of time. The author emphasizes the possible use of this kind of model, through the interdependence coefficients, to investigate the perturbations caused by a change in any input or output. The fact that he has been driving the model by the output (demand) does not imply that he cannot proceed by the input side.

The need for exploring the meaning of the input-output coefficient by clarifying the structure of any subbranch and the technologic spectrum is recognized; but this kind of test has not been implemented. The validation of the input-output coefficient remains a must whatever the kind of test.

Contributing to the discussion were Denis K. Britton, Wilhelm Henrichsmeyer, John O. S. Kennedy, and Alfred Thieme.

A DYNAMIC SECTOR ANALYSIS AND PROGNOSIS SYSTEM (DAPS) WITH SPECIAL REFERENCES TO THE AGRICULTURAL SECTOR IN THE FEDERAL REPUBLIC OF GERMANY

S. Bauer

Abstract

In order to combine the advantages of activity analysis models and econometric models, an agricultural sector analysis approach has been developed which is mainly based on a dynamic coupling of these two model types. The change in the production and factor input level is explained by the shadow prices and other economic factors (market prices, income, general economic variables, and so forth). The shadow prices are computed in a specially formulated LP model at given (modeled) agricultural technology and fixed production and factor input levels. The whole system contains other submodels in order to consider the circulation and dynamic interdependencies within the agricultural sector. The model has been empirically specified and tested for the agricultural sector of the Federal Republic of Germany in the period 1955-75. The policy oriented applications show that the model gives a detailed picture of the consequences of policy and general economic changes.

RAPPORTEUR'S REPORT--Andre Brun

Bauer's model cannot be referred to as a data system. It is a sector model in which the prices are exogenous. The prices concern only the inputs and serve to feed the behavioural submodel.

This very complex model, carefully based on time series data (20 years), has been built for explaining or predicting the effects of policy decisions. The different hypotheses made, consisting of price cuts or increases (general or selective), changes in the rate of taxation or inflation, or in the opportunity cost of labour, or some mix, are experimental in order to test the reasonableness and sensitivity of the model. The behaviour of investment following a general commodity price cut of 10 percent reflects only the variation in investment flows (not the variation in stocks) and shows a new rise after 9 years, which represents an adjustment lag during which equipment is only partially renewed.

It is necessary to convince policymakers of the capacity of such a model to appraise the whole sector and of the consistency of such a framework. This should be done through a simplified version so policymakers can understand the different stages necessary to complete the working of the model.

Contributing to the discussion were Denis K. Britton, Wilhelm Henrichsmeyer, John O. S. Kennedy, and Alfred Theime.

PUBLIC PRICE FORECASTING AND PRICE VARIABILITY

Donald MacLaren

Abstract

This paper is concerned with exploring the influence which public price forecasting might have on the variability of market price. From the autocovariance function of the stochastic model employed, measures of asymptotic variance and periodicity are obtained as indicators of market price variability. The conclusions from a simulation of the model suggest that holders of inventories who act on the public price forecast have a greater impact on price variance than do producers, while producers influence the periodicity to a greater extent. However, given alternative assumptions about the speed of adjustment to price changes, public price forecasting may increase variabilty rather than diminish it. This is more true of producers than of inventory holders. Hence, in a real commodity market, public price forecasting might require careful analysis of the structural parameters before implementation.

OPENER'S REMARKS--Rex F. Daly

Stability is not the issue in North American markets. Usually the government's public information package provides objective basic commodity statistics and interpretations, primarily to assure greater equity among farmers and traders and to avoid private manipulations in the market. Point forecasts of prices are not all that helpful to farmers and other business people. They are much better informed if they understand the basis for developing price forecasts and the most likely ranges of uncertainty about them.

Although MacLaren's model is quite standard, such oversimplified models, even though necessary, always raise questions about possible impacts of a more complete specification. The results seem to be more of an exercise in arithmetic than economic analysis. Would it be possible to provide an economic rationale for some of the major results? Is it logical to expect price variance to increase "without bound"? Surely something happens to producer and stockholder actions before this happens. Are the variations a quirk in the simple model or perhaps due to a misspecified model?

RAPPORTEUR'S REPORT--Michael S. Igben

If the producer's reaction to point forecasting is less than the reaction of traders, then point forecasting has little application. Even if a limited usefulness of point forecasting is accepted, there is the need to incorporate an economic interpretation to the results to further enhance its usefulness. If policymakers are to accept the recommendations of this paper, then there is the need to amend the constant elasticities and present a well defined concept of "socially desired gains."

Socially desirable forecasting is aimed at quantifying economic surplus, which in itself is a measure of social welfare. Even though a knowledge of the magnitude of the economic surplus is important, farmers really do not appreciate point forecasting.

Contributing to the discussion were Ramesh C. Agrawal, David I. Bateman, and Abhijit Sen.

THE VALUE AND COST OF INFORMATION

W. L. Nieuwoudt

Introduction

Mathematical models are derived measuring the social benefit and cost of information in comparison to the social benefit or cost of an input (fertilizer) subsidy under different factor market assumptions. In 1975, 54 countries subsidized fertilizers (FAO). In the following countries, the subsidy was as high as 50 percent of the average price of all fertilizers: Ghana, Libya, Niger, Tanzania, Uganda (certain farmers), Iran, and Sri Lanka. In Togo, the subsidy on urea in 1974 was 82 percent (FAO).

Economic Model

The economic model is an industry demand and supply relationship for an input (fertilizer) where the area under the demand function is assumed to measure income generated through the application of the resource while the area under the resource supply represents opportunity costs of resources.

Statistical Model

Demand functions for fertilizer have been estimated for various countries; for example, the United States (Griliches; and Tweeten), Japan (Hayami), the United Kingdom (Metcalf and Cowling), and South Africa (Nieuwoudt and Behrmann). Input demand elasticities estimated in these studies showed a remarkable conformity. The phenomenal increase in the application of fertilizers during the post-war period was largely attributed, in all these studies, to a fall in the fertilizer product price ratio. These findings indicate that fertilizer purchases are sensitive to fertilizer price changes as through a subsidy.

Social Cost of a Subsidy Under Equilibrium Conditions

In the following analysis, it was assumed that farmers, on the average, apply fertilizers at optimum levels (figure 1). In figure 1, AB represents the industry demand curve for an input and S_1 the supply, assuming that the supply is not entirely elastic. A percentage subsidy shifts the supply from S_1 to S_2. Supply shifts more at higher prices because the input subsidy represents a constant proportion of cost.

The social cost of an input subsidy--triangle GHD in figure 1--can be approximated by:

$$(1) \quad S_c = (1/2)S^2 \epsilon\phi \, X_1/(\epsilon + \phi)P_1,$$

where S is the subsidy as a fraction of input expenditure, ϵ the elasticity of input supply, ϕ the absolute value of elasticity of input demand, X_1 the initial consumption, and P_1 the initial price of fertilizer. Wallace and Johnson adopt a similar mathematical procedure in determining the welfare cost of product price supports. Use of integration to obtain the social cost would require complete specification of demand and supply functions.

Equation (1) is in agreement with economic theory in the sense that if either ϵ or ϕ is zero, implying that if either demand or supply is inelastic, then social costs become zero. Social costs increase with an increase in either S, ϵ, or ϕ. The squared subsidy term means that social costs increase at an increasing rate if the subsidy is raised. Elasticities of demand and supply in equation (1) carry equal weights in determining social costs. In the long run, both demand and supply would be more elastic, implying that social costs would be greater in the long run.

Because of the distinction between long and short run elasticities and the uncertainty concerning the input supply elasticity in particular, social costs were calculated with different parameters.

Certain qualifications need to be made in the above analysis. If the average cost of the industry supplying the input falls over the entire range of output, then a subsidy would promote welfare and not reduce it (Hyman). The above analysis is also of a partial nature in the sense that no other input subsidies were assumed to exist. In reality, other inputs in agriculture are subsidized in many countries, and Friedman shows where other market distortions (subsidies) exist; it is not clear whether a further distortion (subsidy) reduces or promotes welfare.

Welfare Benefit of a Subsidy Under Non-Pareto Conditions

In the following analyses, it was assumed that farmers underrate the true value of fertilizer applications as portrayed in figure 2, and respond according to demand ab and not to AB. Slopes of ab and AB are drawn to be parallel but in the subsequent analyses this assumption is relaxed. Figure 2 depicts the situation where a subsidy increases welfare. The subsidy stimulates consumption from Q_1 to Q_2 which is still to the left of the optimum consumption (point H, figure 2). The social welfare area NMGD is approximated as follows:

$$(2) \quad [\text{Welfare gain}] = [(1/2)SQ_2\eta\epsilon/(P_1\epsilon + P_2\eta)][2P_3 - 2P_2$$

$$+ S\eta(P_2\phi + P_3\epsilon)/\phi(P_1\epsilon + P_2\eta)],$$

where ϵ is the elasticity of supply, η the elasticity of demand ab, ϕ the elasticity of demand AB, and Q_2 the current fertilizer expenditure with a subsidy. Social benefit is positively related to absolute values of demand and supply. Equation (2) is in agreement with economic theory in the sense that if either η, ϵ, or S is zero, then social benefit becomes zero.

price of factor

Figure 1 Social cost of an input subsidy under equilibrium conditions

Figure 2 Welfare effects of information and of an input subsidy under Non-Pareto conditions

146

Value of Information

The annual benefit of information is measured by triangle NMH in figure 2. The procedure adopted to measure NMH was to determine GHD separately before adding it to previous estimates of NMGD. Area GHD is approximated by the following equation:

$$(3) \quad [\text{Area GHD}] = (1/2)(P_3 - P_2)^2 Q_2 \, \phi\varepsilon/(P_3\varepsilon + P_2\phi).$$

Estimates of the benefit stream of information increase with an increase in assumed values of P_3, ε, ϕ, and η.

Yields of crops in most countries have increased substantially in post-war years (FAO), and over time curve AB (figure 2) shifts outward, while curve ab may shift toward AB. In order to introduce some dynamic elements into the previous static analysis, an attempt was made to estimate the capital value of information as the present value of a stream of annual benefits. The following proportionate adjustment pattern was assumed:

$$(4) \quad [\text{Capital value}] = A_0 + A_0 M(1 + g)(1 + i)^{-1}$$
$$+ \, A_0 M^2(1 + g)^2 (1 + i)^{-2}$$
$$+ \, \ldots \, + \, A_0 M^n(1 + g)^n(1 + i)^{-n} = A_0/(1 - K),$$

where $K = M(1 + g)(1 + i)^{-1}$, which is a converging series if $K < 1$.

A_0 represents annual benefits of information (triangle NMH, figure 2) measured in monetary values at constant prices. The inflation premium cancels out from the discount rate and the benefit stream (Howe). M measures the proportionate shift of the ab curve towards AB (figure 2) in the absence of an additional expenditure on information. It is thus assumed that farmers are in the process of adjusting to an optimum level of fertilizer, and that an expenditure on information expedites this process. The introduction of new technologies increases the benefit of information annually by a proportion g through a shift in the AB curve to the right.

Empirical Results

According to expert opinion such as the South African Fertilizer Society, the South African Sugar Association, and numerous research reports too extensive to mention (Mohr; and Nieuwoudt and Behrmann), sugarcane producers in South Africa apply fertilizers at approximate optimum levels, while maize farmers underrate their value. Mohr summarized the findings of 143 different fertilizer trials, the majority carried out over long periods. The Sugar Association alone analyzed 33,000 soil samples during 1977. Cane farmers have reached the point where excessive fertilization depresses the quantity of sucrose. This conflicting phenomenon could partly be attributed to the fact that the Sugar Association supplies free soil testing to its members while maize farmers have to pay for such an analysis. The marginal product of fertilizer application on maize was estimated between 1.2 - 1.5 UK pounds for 1 pound spent on fertilizer.

In the case of sugarcane, social cost estimates (figure 1 and equation 1) as a percentage of fertilizer expenditure varied from a low of 0.059 percent with an input supply elasticity of 0.25 and a short run input demand elasticity of -0.75, to a high of 0.78 percent if input supply is perfectly elastic and the long run input demand elasticity is -2.50. The current subsidy is 7.9 percent of the average price. For estimates of short and long run fertilizer demand elasticities refer to Nieuwoudt and Behrmann.

Welfare benefits of a fertilizer subsidy as a percentage of fertilizer expenditure in the case of maize producers were estimated for two extreme sets of parameter values (refer to equation 2). Social benefit was estimated between a low of 0.05 percent if the value marginal product $(P_3) = 1.2$, $\eta = -0.75$, $\phi = -2$, and $\varepsilon = 1$, and a high of 5.7 percent if VMP $(P_3) = 1.5$, $\eta = -2.50$, $\phi = -1$, and $\varepsilon = 4$. Elasticity of demand AB (ϕ) is of lesser importance in determining social benefit because prices and quantities depend on the intersection of the supply and demand ab, and thus the elasticities of the latter relationships. The smaller social benefit with a higher ϕ value is because P_3 in figure 2 is a fixed point leading to a smaller gain, the more elastic the curve AB.

The fact that about 65 percent of South Africa's fertilizer consumption is applied to maize suggests that the social gain created by the present subsidy outweighs the social cost. A possible solution may be different subsidies on different crops as prevailing in Spain, Cameroon, and Fiji (FAO). Different farmers in the same industry may, however, have different perceptions of the value of the input. Further, according to expert opinion, many farmers tend to overfertilize low potential soils and underfertilize high potential soils in the maize areas. Subsidizing the information service would thus be more efficient than subsidizing fertilizers.

Estimates of the annual benefit of information (area NMH in figure 2) as a percentage of fertilizer expenditure were derived from equations (2) and (3). Using the two previous sets of extreme parameter values, estimates ranged from a low of 1 percent to a high of 14 percent. The annual monetary benefits of fertilizer information to maize producers were estimated to be within the narrower range of 4 million to 11 million pounds.

The cost of providing this information needs to be considered. According to experts at the Sugar Association, a soil sample should ideally be taken for every 10 hectares of land once every 3 to 4 years. Using the current area under maize of 4,453,000 hectares, the number of soil samples taken every 3.5 years comes to 127,000. Experts at the Fertilizer Society independently estimate the optimum number of soil samples at 30,000. Fertilizer firms offer a soil testing service at 3.3 pounds per solid sample, which is probably below cost because it is furnished in anticipation of future sales. Other private firms undertake soil testing on a profit basis at 6.7 pounds per sample. Estimates of the cost of information thus derived range from a low of 105,000 to a high of 851,000 pounds. The annual benefit of information thus exceeds the cost of supplying it by more than tenfold. The current annual fertilizer subsidy is 14 million pounds while a free soil testing service may cost a fraction of that.

Estimates of the capital value of information were estimated from equation (4) for two extreme sets of parameter values. Estimates ranged from a low of 13 million pounds if $i = 0.07$, $g = 0$, $M = 0.75$, and $A_0 = 4$ million pounds, to a high 268 million pounds if $i = 0.04$, $g = 0.05$, $M = 0.95$, and $A_0 = 11$ million pounds. An M value of 0.95 implies that after each year the benefit of information is reduced by 5 percent as farmers adjust towards an optimum input level. It is clear from these estimates that the payoff from an investment in information could be significant.

As a last thought, furnishing of soil testing information on an individual farm basis should be seen in a wider context such as in systems analysis whereby fertilizer information is supported by other information; for example, recommended suitable varieties.

Conclusion

Using mathematical models, the welfare effects of fertilizer subsidies were compared with a subsidy on information. Empirical estimates indicate that in the case of South African agriculture, social benefits of a fertilizer subsidy outweigh social costs. A subsidy on information is clearly superior to that of an input subsidy as the benefits of information exceed the cost of supplying the information, through a free soil analysis service, by more than tenfold.

References

FAO (1975) Production Yearbook. Rome; Food and Agriculture Organization of the United Nations.

Freidman, M. (1962) Price Theory. Aldine.

Griliches, Z. (1958) The demand for fertilizer: An economic interpretation of a technical change. Journal of Farm Economics, 40, 591-606.

Hayami, Y. (1964) Demand for fertilizer in the course of Japanese agricultural development. Journal of Farm Economics, 46, 766-779.

Howe, C. W. (1971) Benefit-Cost Analysis for Water System Planning. Publication Press.

Hyman, D. N. (1973) The Economics of Government Activity. Holt, Rinehardt, and Winston.

Johnson, P. R. (1965) The social cost of the tobacco programme. Journal of Farm Economics, 47, 242-255.

Metcalf, D.; Cowling, K. (1967) Demand functions for fertilizers in the United Kingdom, 1948-65. Journal of Agricultural Economics, 18, 375-385.

Mohr, P. (1973) Guidelines for fertilization of maize on soil series of the Avalon and Hutton forms. Journal of the South African Fertilizer Society, 2, 75-82.

Nieuwoudt, W. L.; Behrmann, H. I. (1972) Demand functions for fertilizer in South Africa. Agrekon, 11 (4) 18-23.

Tweeten, L. G. (1962) An economic analysis of the resource structure of U.S. agriculture. Ph.D. thesis. Ames, Iowa, USA; Iowa State University.

Wallace, T. D. (1962) Measures of social costs of agricultural programmes. Journal of Farm Economics, 44, 580-597.

RAPPORTEUR'S REPORT—Michael S. Igben

This paper does not violate any important neoclassical assumptions relating to the economic analysis of the value of information, and in this respect the empirical evidence presented here, although circumspect, provides a good study of the economic use of information.

Since information has differential distribution, with several factors playing important roles in the capacity of the individual to absorb information (such as different abilities and education), the methodology needs to be modified to take this into account. This is especially so because there is other empirical evidence of differential absorption of information, even when the cost of providing information about a given innovation is the same. Since the high cost of information is not the only reason preventing farmers from adopting a given innovation, the quality of this paper could have been improved if other possible factors were identified. The nonuse as well as the differential use of fertilizer by farmers was due principally to the existence of an information gap.

Contributing to the discussion were James T. Bonnen, Rex F. Daly, James H. Johnston, A. S. Kahlon, Hassan Aly Khedr, Morag C. Simpson, and M. L. de Sward.

NATIONAL INTEREST IN INTERNATIONAL BUFFER STOCKS

Ulrich Koester

Introduction

There seems to be wide agreement that international buffer stocks for certain commodities such as wheat may help to increase world welfare. However, it is not possible to establish buffer stock schemes for all of those commodities where buffer stocks might have a favourable effect. This may be partly due to conflicts between broad national interests and economic benefits. It therefore seems worthwhile to examine the determinants of national interest, which is done in this paper. The analysis is restricted to some special aspects. Since for the world as a whole total export earnings must be equal to total import expenditures, the analysis can be restricted to analyzing the effects on total export earnings. In the following formulation, we assume that an international buffer stock can achieve stabilization of an equilibrium price. Without the buffer stock, prices are assumed to fluctuate only due to supply fluctuations. Given this set of assumptions, it follows that export earnings can only fluctuate due to changes in supply if the buffer is in operation. We get:

$$(1) \quad dR/R = dq^S/q^S,$$

where:

R = world export earnings for the commodity exported; and

q^S = total world market supply.

According to (1), the percentage change in revenue is equal to the percentage change in world market supply. This fluctuation of export earnings under the buffer stock has to be compared with a situation without a buffer stock. To work out this effect, we start with the following set of equations:

$$(2) \quad R = pq^S,$$

$$(3) \quad q^S = q^S (p, a),$$

$$(4) \quad q^D = q^D (p),$$

$$(5) \quad q^S = q^D,$$

where:

p = world market price,

a = shift parameter due to weather conditions, and

q^D = total world market demand.

From (2) to (5) it follows that:

$$(6) \quad dR/R = [(\varepsilon^D + 1)/(\varepsilon^S - \varepsilon^D)1(- \, da/a),$$

where:

ε^D = price elasticity of world market demand, and

ε^S = price elasticity of world market supply.

A comparison of equations (1) and (6) shows that price stabilization can only stabilize export earnings if $|(\varepsilon^D + 1)/(\varepsilon^S - \varepsilon^D)| > 1$. Hence, two necessary conditions for a stabilization effect can be given: the absolute value of the demand elasticity must be less than 0.5 and the value of the supply elasticity must be less than 1. The elasticity of demand has to be smaller (in absolute terms) the higher the supply elasticity. If, for example, the supply elasticity were 0.8, the price elasticity of demand has to be smaller than 0.1 to get a positive stabilization effect on export earnings via price stabilization. Taking into account that the supply elasticity on the world market may be much higher than short term domestic production elasticities due to domestic storage policies, and the fact that domestic export elasticities are determined by domestic supply and demand elasticities as well as by the degree of self-sufficiency, it could be questioned if the necessary conditions are met for many commodity markets. However, even if total world export earnings cannot be stabilized via price stabilization, it may, nevertheless, be possible to stabilize an individual country's export earnings.

In working out the effects on an individual country, the general set of assumptions stated above is applied again. The only modification of the above model is given by the following equations:

(7) $\quad q^S = q^S (p, a_i)$,

(8) $\quad R_i = pq^S$,

where:

q_i^S = world market supply country i,

R_i = export earnings of country i, and

a_i = shift parameter of country i's world market supply curve.

Solving the set of equations (2) to (5) and (7) to (8) with respect to R_i results in:

(9) $\quad dR_i/R_i = (- da/a)[(1 + \varepsilon_i^S)/(\varepsilon^S - \varepsilon^D)] + da_i/a$,

where:

ε_i^S = price elasticity of world market supply of country i.

Equation (9) gives the magnitude of revenue fluctuations under free market conditions for country i. Hence, these fluctuations have to be compared with those under a buffer stock which are:

(10) $\quad dR_i/R_i = da_i/a_i$.

A comparision of (9) and (10) highlights the following results:

1. If domestic fluctuations in supply are negatively correlated with world market supply fluctuations, domestic export earnings will always be stabilized via a buffer stock.

2. If domestic and world market fluctuations are positively correlated, the likelihood of a stabilization effect with given elasticities is higher the

151

smaller the magnitude of domestic supply fluctuations are relative to world market supply fluctuations. According to this result, exporting countries with far above average fluctuations in domestic supply may not be at all interested in an international buffer stock. Their export revenue may be more stable under free market conditions.

3.   Given domestic and world market supply fluctuations, a stabilization effect will more likely arise if all elasticities under consideration are small (in absolute terms). However, it does not hold any longer that the above are necessary conditions for a stabilization effect. This means that an individual country's export earnings may be stabilized even if total world market export earnings are destabilized.

To work out the effects of an international buffer stock on fluctuations of an individual country's import expenditure, the same model is applied. The following equations are postulated:

(11) $Ex = pq^I$,

(12) $q_i^I = q_i^D - q_i^S$,

(13) $q_i^S = q_i^D (p)$,

(14) $q_i^S = q_i^S (p, a_i)$,

(15) $q_o^D = q_o^D (p)$,

(16) $q_o^S = q_o^S (p, a_o)$, and

(17) $q_i^I = q_o^S - q_o^D$,

where:

Ex =   expenditure on imports of the product under consideration,

q_i^I =   import quantity of country i,

q_i^D =   domestic demand for the product under consideration in country i,

a_o =   shift parameter of world market supply curve,

q_o^S =   international supply of all other countries, and

q_o^D =   international demand of all other countries.

Solving this set of equations with respect to Ex results in:

(18) $dEx/Ex = (- da/a)[(1 + \varepsilon_i^{ID})/(\varepsilon^{ES} - \varepsilon_i^{ID})] - [S/(1 - S)](da_i/a_i)$,

where:

S = q_i/q_i^D = degree of self-sufficiency of country i,

ε_i^{ID} =   import elasticity of country i, and

ε^{ES} =   export elasticity of all other countries.

152

Equation (18) stands for fluctuations in import expenditures under free market conditions. Hence, this equation has to be compared with an equation which indicates fluctuations on expenditures in the case of a buffer stock in operation. This is:

(19) $dEx/Ex = - [S/(1 - S)](da_i/a_i)$.

A comparison of (18) and (19) highlights the following results:

1. When there is positive correlation between domestic and world market supply, and the value of the import elasticity is less than 1, price stabilization will lead to reduced fluctuations in import expenditures. Such a situation will very likely prevail for countries with a small degree of self-sufficiency.

2. If the absolute value of the import elasticity is greater than 1, and if fluctuations are negatively correlated, price stabilization will lead to reduced fluctuations in import expenditures. Such a situation may prevail for importing nations with a high degree of self-sufficiency.

3. If fluctuations are positively correlated and the absolute value of the import elasticity is greater than 1, detailed information is needed to check the stabilization effect. It depends on the magnitude of domestic and world market fluctuations and on all parameters given in the above formula.

4. If fluctuations are negatively correlated and the absolute value of the import elasticity is less than 1, the same statement as above (3) is valid.

National Versus International Stabilization Schemes

An individual country's decision concerning whether to join an international stabilization scheme does not depend only on expected net benefits, but also on a comparison with the possible costs and benefits of a national stabilization scheme. This may be a further source of national interest in international programmes. This consideration is explored here in some detail.

If exporting as well as importing nations were to aim at stabilizing export earnings or import expenditures by national stabilization schemes, a crucial difference of interests would appear: it would be very costly for exporting nations to stabilize export earnings via a national stabilization scheme because the individual countries would have to accommodate all potential world market fluctuations with a national storage programme. The costs of such a programme would very likely be higher than the possible benefits, and the national costs would be the same as total costs for an international buffer stock with the same benefit.

For an importing nation, however, the result of such calculations may turn out to be quite different. Storage capacity has to be larger in the case of positively correlated national and world market supply fluctuations. Domestic storage capacity should be great enough to accommodate domestic supply fluctuations and the effects of world market price changes on import expenditures. With increasing world market prices, some of the stocks should be released to stabilize the level of import expenditures. The necessary condition for stabilizing import expenditures via a national stabilization scheme is, therefore, a negative import demand elasticity. Such a situation may be assumed as realistic in most cases.

The necessary storage capacity is expressed in the following equation:

(20) $C = dq^S + (dP/P)(q^D_i - q^S_i),$

where:

C = storage capacity,

dq^S_i = change in domestic supply,

q^S_i = domestic supply,

q^D_i = domestic demand, and

dP/P = percentage change in the world market price.

The second term on the right side of equation (20) indicates that a 1 percent change in world market prices has to be compensated for by a 1 percent change in the quantity imported. It is very simple to calculate from (20) the necessary storage capacity as a percentage of total domestic production. We get:

(21) $C/q^S_i = dq^S_i/q^S_i + [(q^D_i - q^S_i)/q^S](dP/P),$ and

(22) $C/q^S_i = dq^S_i/q^S_i + [(1 - S_i)/S_i](dP/P).$

Even with an international stabilization scheme, some national storage capacity up to the percentage change in domestic supply is needed. The storage capacity saved by an individual country through an international stabilization scheme comes to:

(23) $C_S/q^S_i = [(1 - S_i)/S_i](dP/P),$

where:

C_S = storage capacity saved.

Equation (23) shows that the national storage capacity which is needed to compensate for world market price fluctuations is determined entirely by the degree of self-sufficiency and the expected fluctuations in world market prices. For a S_i of 0.9 and a 10 percent change in world market prices, the storage capacity has to be 1.1 percent of national production, and for a S_i of 0.4 it should be 15 percent. This shows that the storage capacity necessary to compensate for world market price fluctuations increases progressively with decreasing self-sufficiency.

This finding has important political relevance. Because the comparative disadvantage of national stabilization schemes versus international schemes is much smaller for importing countries with a degree of self-sufficiency of nearly 100 percent than for highly deficient regions or exporting countries, the bargaining power may be quite unequal. The unequal benefits derived by individual countries from an international stabilization scheme should be taken into account when setting the level of national contributions, so that those who benefit most are required to pay most. If countries which only benefit marginally from a stabilization scheme are asked to make large contributions, they may refuse to cooperate, thus endangering the stability of the entire scheme.

The proposed models are elegant and of considerable conceptual value in dealing with a relevant set of problems. Some suggestions for improvement included expanding the models to deal with the cumulative aspects of storage and abnormal behaviour of demand and supply schedules caused by cross price elasticity and joint product effects.

The approach might be adapted for the purposes of decisionmakers in individual countries to include the effects of incomplete cooperation in an international buffer stock. There could also be complementary relationships between national and international objectives in controlling commodity markets which might be explored.

The conclusions in the paper would be more convincing if support could be found in the extensive literature on this subject, and if the assumptions made and the results of the models could be tested empirically.

DYNAMIC MODELS FOR STABILIZING FOOD PRICES

Harold G. Halcrow and Takashi Takayama

Multiyear dynamic spatial models of the U.S. grain, oilseed, and livestock (GOL) economy show how to stabilize prices in this part of the world food economy. The standard GOL model can be operated at modest cost, well within the limits of previous price support and storage programmes operated by the U.S. government. Appropriate application of the model and its derivatives will stabilize the U.S. GOL economy within a relatively narrow price band, and this will help to stabilize prices in other trading countries as well.

Identifying the Problem

The task to be performed by the model was established in this study by identifying the causes and extent of instability inherent in the U.S. GOL economy. The test assumed that from 1976 to 1980 the market would clear at the end of each year with no reserve stocks. The export demand was fixed and perfectly inelastic. Then, eight alternative yield scenarios were selected, each with a unique yield sequence for wheat, maize, and soybeans. These produced yearly model solutions that proved to be infeasible in 1979 and 1980 in the sense that the next year's planted acreage corresponding to the scenario price was negative, or production was not enough to cover the total demand of the United States and the rest of the world.

The instability was attributed to the basic supply-demand structure of the U.S. GOL economy operating under the assumption that the markets must clear at the end of each year. The fact that this assumption does not hold in the real world permits the GOL economy to function. But, since all scenarios became infeasible under this assumption, the findings emphasized that the GOL economy has a tendency to be highly unstable if there is no government reserve stock programme.

Multiyear Stabilizing Programmes

Use of specific forward looking price bands and stocking operations, treated as a primal and dual relationship, transform the structurally unstable U.S. GOL economy into one that is structurally stable, providing that the government of the United States employs a sequence price and reserve stock plan of operations over time consistent with the known dynamics of the GOL economy. An optimum price band width can be established; and there is a least cost, price stabilization, reserve operations policy that can be designed. This proves to be a multiyear spatially coordinated program with specified beginning and ending inventories and designated price band limits.

Simultaneous stocking operations and market prices were developed for 1976 to 1980 for each of the eight alternative yield scenarios. One of the eight is presented as an example, comparing price fluctuations within each of three arbitrarily selected price bands. Price band A is the widest, allowing maximum price fluctuations above and below a price trend line, of $65 per metric tonne (mt) for wheat, $55/mt for maize, and $110/mt for soybeans. Price band B is narrower, allowing maximum price fluctuations above and below the trend line of $35/mt for wheat, $15/mt for maize, and $25/mt for soybeans. This is equivalent to about $.94/bu for wheat, $.375/bu for maize, and $1.34/bu for soybeans. Price band B also includes a trend increase in each price, as consistent with an assumed increase in demand relative to supply. Price band C has no width, allowing no deviation in price above or below the established trend line.

Following the establishment of these price bands, stocking or reserve operations consistent with each price band were generated for each year by solving a single period, one commodity model within the floor and ceiling price constraints. If the floor price is hit in the solution, its dual withdrawal quantities will be generated in the solution algorithm and will appear in the solution simultaneously. If the ceiling price is hit, then the dual injection quantities will appear in the solution.

Price Band A

Most stock operations under price band A tended to become undesirably large (and some were not feasible). As the required withdrawals and injections escalated, stock operations became incapable of containing prices within the band. In the first four of the eight scenarios, a good maize crop in 1977 suppressed its supply price to the minimum level of $69/mt, and 5.2 million metric tonnes (mmt) of maize were withdrawn from the market to maintain the minimum market price. This low maize price sharply decreased the acreage for maize, and, at the same time, sharply increased the acreage for soybeans. As a result, the price of maize rose to the maximum level, and an injection was required. This was followed by a withdrawal in 1979 and another injection in 1980.

Soybean operations were correlated with maize. The increased soybean production in 1978 decreased its price to the minimum level and required a withdrawal of 8.5 mmt. Because of this low price, soybean acreage decreased by about 10.7 million acres in 1979 and maize increased almost the same amount. The stock withdrawal in 1978 was followed by an injection of 11.5 mmt in 1979, and a withdrawal of 9.2 mmt in 1980. Wheat was also subject to the withdrawal-injection operation.

In the fifth and sixth scenarios, the withdrawal of maize started in 1978, followed by an injection in 1979, and a withdrawal in 1980. The quantity of withdrawal in 1980 was 45.7 mmt. The seventh and eighth scenarios resulted in a withdrawal of 32.3 mmt in 1979, and an injection of 28.6 mmt in 1980.

Several difficulties were encountered in operating the programmes: (1) in 1979, if scenarios 7 and 8 are realized, the United States cannot meet the quantity of maize to be injected into the market, even though all the carryover stock of maize existing at that time is depleted; (2) the sum of withdrawals and injections is the largest of the three alternative price bands; (3) quantities of withdrawals and injections are larger in the later years than in the earlier years of the projection period, which suggests that there is a tendency for the models to explode; and (4) the soybean sector is exposed to violent year to year fluctuations of prices, production, and consumption.

Price Band B

Stock operations under price band B were more manageable in magnitude, and generally feasible. When price band B is implemented, a withdrawal or an injection is required almost every year for each scenario. Important differences in the operational characteristics of price bands A and B are the following: (1) price band B requires withdrawal-injection operations more often than price band A--in the 5 years, price band B required such operations 79 times, while price band A used them 66 times; (2) the sum of withdrawals and injections in the eight scenario is the smallest among the three price bands, however; (3) quantities of withdrawals and injections required by price band B are more evenly distributed among years than those of price band A; (4) unlike price band A, there are no shortages of stocks of any commodity in any year to meet required injections, and price band B mitigates fluctuations of price and production in the soybean sector rather substantially.

Price Band C

In price band C, a withdrawal or an injection is required every year for each commodity. Prices are completely stabilized, though moving upward along a trend. In terms of quantities of withdrawals and injections, however, this narrowest price band does not produce the highest degree of stability. The sum of withdrawals and injections is not as small as in price band B. In fact, for wheat and maize alone, the sum is close to that of price band A. The price of soybeans is almost completely stabilized, however, which indicates that price stability for a given commodity is possible, providing certain conditions are met.

Alternative Model Costs and Optimality

The price stabilization reserve stock programme has shown that the GOL economy can be stabilized, even though it is structurally unstable without such a policy. The policy alternatives are very large in number and variety, however, and it is important to know whether there is a least cost programme that will provide the desired degree of stability. The exercises with the three alternative price bands show that price band B, which has the intermediate width, resulted in the smallest quantity of withdrawals and injections. This result implies that an optimal price band stocking operation can be found, with optimality defined as the operation that entails the minimum quantities handled by the withdrawal and injection operations of the government. This can be pursued much further, of course, to search for still more optimal results.

The carryover stock operations in the United States must be large enough and timely enough to achieve the desired results. In the case of price band B, the maximum carryover quantities are about 34 mmt for wheat, 51 mmt for maize, and 20 mmt for soybeans. In comparison with historical data, these quantities are well within the capacity of the U.S. GOL economy, but the results generated by the model scenarios indicate clearly that a policy oriented deliberate government program is required. Although private storage firms may be motivated to increase their stocks when there is a drop in price, it is doubtful that they will voluntarily inject their stocks into the market before prices rise above program levels. Owing to this asymmetric tendency, some form of government participation in this operation is necessary to achieve the degree of price stability that is consistent with export goals of the United States, and the desires for price stability as generally expressed by producers and consumers in the United States and the rest of the world.

Costs and Benefits of Stabilization Policy

An additional set of models, which allows for some elasticity in export demand, reduces the magnitude but not necessarily the frequency of stock operations required to stabilize prices within a given price band. This would tend to reduce the total costs of the reserve stock programme. Yearly increases and decreases in export demand are an important destabilizing factor in domestic markets, however. If the reserve stock programme is designed to offset these to a significant degree, the required magnitude of the programme would be at least as large as suggested above.

The benefits of an effective stabilization policy can be measured in terms of the ability of the United States to maintain a consistently high level of agricultural exports in poor as well as good crop years, meeting an appropriate share of the import demand of the rest of the world. The argument for government financed reserves is based on the goals of farm and food price stability, a stable export capacity with some potential to meet unusually large export demands, and considerations of national security. From the mid-1950s to the mid-1960s, the grain stocks carried in the United States were generally adequate for these purposes.

Although some studies have linked low grain prices from the mid-1950s to the late 1960s with large stocks in storage, this study suggests that under an alternate model without such storage, the average grain prices might have been even lower. From 1961 through 1972, grain sales were augmented by the reduction in government held stocks. Prices were not necessarily depressed by holding stocks, but by their release, especially in good crop years, and by insufficient withdrawals of stocks from the market in years of large crops.

Alternative price bands and prices for wheat, maize, and soybeans under a specified multi-year reserve-stock model.

Conclusion

The results of the current study are compatible with the idea that the magnitude of stocks in a government financed grain reserve and the rules for their management must be related to the policy goals that are established. Reserve stocks provide a means of softening the effects of periodic fluctuations in grain supplies by leveling off the peaks of surplus production and filling in the troughs of short crops or large export demands. Limited stocks of grain rise or fall as needed, in lieu of a no-stock policy. The model for stock management must take account of very short run, year to year injections and withdrawals as well as some of the long cyclical swings in crop production. At the present stage of development of science in general and the art of projections in particular, however, making accurate projections covering a long period is hardly possible. Even within the framework of the projection models, the future weather and other economic conditions especially affecting the supply of grains and oilseeds are subject to uncertainty.

A scenario approach is one way of dealing with the future, and this approach is more convincing if the scenario information can be generated on the basis of a consensus by the experts in each specialized field. In order to avoid unnecessary discrepancy between the projections and the evolving market conditions, the projections must be continually updated on the basis of new information. Price ranges and carryover guidelines should also be reviewed and revised at the early stage of each cropyear, to reflect any new situation in the world food economy. If this is done properly, other forms of government interventions, such as acreage set-aside programmes and export controls can be more generally avoided, or at least given less emphasis in national policy. The general benefit can be measured in terms of price stability at a high production level, which also means stability in food consumption in the United States and the rest of the world.

OPENER'S REMARKS--Walton J. Anderson

Further explanation of the concept of structural instability used in the paper would be helpful. What is meant by clearing the market? Does it mean that at some point in the year all that has been produced has been consumed? If so, the appearance of negative prices in certain yield scenarios is understandable. However, clearing the market does not provide a satisfactory basis against which to compare the storage operations resulting from using the selected price bands.

I was not able to find anywhere in the paper how the results of the imposition of the price bands on the acquisition and release of stocks compared with what actually happened during 1977 and 1978. The paper speaks of an optimum price band. How were the bands actually selected and why is the smallest sum of withdrawals and injections into storage a significant criterion for selecting a plan? I am also puzzled as to how the widest price band can result in the largest sum of withdrawals and injections.

Prices in the world grain market are indeed unstable. The chain reaction leads into the livestock industry through changes in the grain-livestock price ratios. The transmittal of grain prices has been exprienced time and again, the most dramatic being the grain price increase in the early 1970s which played havoc with the livestock industry. Grain price instability originates primarily from unstable crop yield from one year to another, mainly in the USSR, Canada, and Australia. The United States contributes much less to unstable yields because the large area over which grain is produced has a dampening effect on changes in average yields.

A study of the possibility of one country undertaking to stabilize its own GOL economy with the expectation of spillover effects on world grain stability presumes that an international stabilization agreement is unlikely to be achieved. Otherwise it would seem that an international agreement would be both cheaper and more likely to be successful than stabilization by one country, even a very large grain producer. Is it possible that the United States could effectively stabilize prices when the real source of instability is outside the country? Can it really be envisioned that the United States would be willing and able to assume an even greater role in price stability than it did in the 1960s? Moreover, would the implementation of such a supply management plan need to be reinforced with a strong set of import restrictions (quotas, tariffs, or both) which would run counter to the U.S. position of greater liberalization of world agricultural trade?

I would like to see some discussion on how trade policy might enter into the achievement of stabilization under the unilateral approach examined in this paper. Would changes to a more liberal trade policy in agricultural commodities by the two giants, the European Community and Japan, lessen the instability of the world grain economy? Can one reasonably expect that exporting countries will cooperate and forego opportunitites to benefit from the known policy of the United States of setting price bands and backing it up with a storage programme? Might not the USSR, with its pattern of yield variability, and acting in its own interest, be in and out of the international market in a manner that would introduce an element of uncertainty and cost which the study has not taken into account, and thereby force a much larger acquisition and release of stocks than that shown in the study?

I suggest that there remains a big question of how the private sector would react. Would the introduction of such a plan change the expectations on which production decisions are based and thereby alter the supply response function from the one on which the plan has been based?

The private trade is engaged in storage operations and will presumably continue these operations. Would the price bands under some circumstances not provide an incentive to private traders to speculate against the price bands in the expectation that the government would be forced to allow a breakthrough? In the foreign exchange markets, for example, speculation against the government has made it difficult to maintain an exchange rate within a price band. How would the private sector respond if the firms simply had the information that a study such as this generates? Would their buying and selling be any different than it is under the present circumstances?

RAPPORTEUR'S REPORT--Graham E. Dalton

The results of this study were interesting, although confidence in the conclusions was reduced when it was pointed out that the basic structure of the model seemed to result in explosive behaviour in the GOL markets. Defending this point, the authors referred to the fact that normal behaviour had been simulated when real data were used for the values of the input variables.

The U.S. model treats the variation in world prices caused by climatic changes in the USSR, Canada, and Australia as an exogenous variable. This excludes study in a direct way of the effects of interactions between U.S. policy and that of other countries.

The degree of generalization necessary in these types of models precludes a consideration of the reactions of private traders, including speculators, to the types of price control investigated. The authors do, however, believe that aggregate market behaviour is satisfactorily represented.

Two interesting suggestions for further investigations were that price control might be more effective within asymmetric price bands, and that the effects of autocorrelation between the yields of various crops, if such exist, be tested.

POLITICOECONOMIC FACTORS AFFECTING
PUBLIC AGRICULTURAL RESEARCH INVESTMENT
IN DEVELOPING COUNTRIES

Kym Anderson

It is now well established that agricultural research is an important contributor to technological change and hence economic growth (Arndt, Dalrymple, and Ruttan). It is equally well established that public support for many types of agricultural (especially biological) research is necessary because of the public good nature of these research findings. An important question for developing countries, then--especially those in which agriculture dominates the economy and where public funds are difficult to raise--is whether the optimal amounts and types of public research investments are being undertaken. This paper addresses this question by drawing on the emerging economic theory of politics. This theory shows that on a priori grounds one should not expect an optimal allocation of public resources to agricultural research. Rather, one should expect both underinvestment in agricultural research and an excessively labour saving bias in the types of technologies produced by that research. If this were supported by empirical evidence, it would have a number of important policy implications, as discussed in the final section of the paper.

Certainly the available evidence is not inconsistent with the paper's findings. As table 1 shows, virtually all studies on social rates of return to research have found average internal rates of return well above those of many other investments--typically more than 25 percent. True, they are not marginal rates of return, and inherent in them are numerous problems of measurement (Arndt, Dalrymple, and Ruttan, chapter 6). Nonetheless, the informed consensus seems to be that even if allowances are made for measurement biases, marginal rates of return are still extremely high, implying considerable underinvestment (to varying degrees between countries and commodities) in this important source of economic growth (Arndt, Dalrymple, and Ruttan, chapter 1). In addition, numerous scholars are concerned that there is an excessively labour saving bias embodied in new agricultural technologies in developing countries. They feel that perhaps lower yielding crop varieties which make less use of purchased inputs relative to labour would be more profitable for societies with relatively high labour to capital ratios, and in particular would be more profitable for the mass of small farmers with access only to expensive credit. If this is in fact so, the production of such technology would not only boost economic growth more but would tend to produce a more equitable income distribution than currently produced technologies.

It is not the purpose of this paper to evaluate the empirical validity of these alleged phenomena of underinvestment in, and excessive labour saving biases in the technologies produced by, public agricultural research in developing countries. Instead, it is to ask whether there are any a priori reasons as to why one might expect such phenomena. Government leaders are continually confronted with demands from various groups and individuals for policies of assistance and expenditure of public funds. Their job, in part, is to decide how to raise and then allocate the public funds to meet these demands. Following Downs, one might assume that government leaders are motivated by self-interest as much as any consumer or business person, and that this manifests itself in their seeking to remain in office by providing policies which favour their most supportive groups. Thus, any policy decision can be thought of as depending largely on factors affecting the incentives for various groups of individuals to seek that policy and for the government to provide that particular policy rather than, or in addition to, other policies. In the case of agricultural research expenditures, both the total amount of public funds allocated for research in agriculture as a whole and in individual industries, and the research projects on

Table 1--Agricultural Research Productivity in Developing Countries

	Country	Commodity	Time period	Internal rate of return Percent per annum

Sources of Growth Studies

	Country	Commodity	Time period	Internal rate of return
Barletta	Mexico	Crops	1943-63	45-93
Bal and Kahlon	India	Aggregate	1960-64	14
		Aggregate	1967-72	72
Evenson	India	Sugar Cane	1945-58	60
Evenson and Jha	India	Aggregate	1953-70	50
Arndt, Dalrymple, and Ruttan, chapter 5	India	Aggregate	1960-72	63
Tang	Japan	Aggregate	1880-1938	35

Cost-Benefit Studies

	Country	Commodity	Time period	Internal rate of return
Akino and Hayami	Japan	Rice	1915-50	26
		Rice	1930-61	74
Barletta	Mexico	Wheat	1943-63	90
		Maize	1943-63	35
Ayer and Schuh	Brazil	Cotton	1924-67	77+
Flores-Moya, Evenson, and Hayami	Philippines	Rice	1966-75	27+
Arndt, Dalrymple, and Ruttan, chapter 6	Colombia	Rice	1957-72	60-82
		Soybeans	1960-71	79-96
		Wheat	1953-73	12
		Cotton	1953-72	None
Hines	Peru	Maize	1954-67	35+
Kumar, Maji, and Patel	India	Dairy Cattle	1963-75	29
Pee	Malaysia	Rubber	1932-73	25
Scobie and Posada	Colombia	Rice	1957-74	79-96

which those funds are spent, depend on these factors in a direct as well as an indirect way. They depend indirectly on them in the sense that groups also demand and governments supply market intervention policies which have the side effect of influencing the eventual allocation of funds to research via the induced innovations mechanism.

Possible Causes of Underinvestment in Public Agricultural Research

Direct Factors

Agricultural research investment involves large government outlays which have an uncertain (even if high) payoff sometime in the distant future and which do not provide as obvious a monument to development as, say, steel mills or roads. Public research expenditures are therefore likely to appeal relatively less to government leaders than many other public investment projects, especially in countries that are politically unstable, where politicians' planning horizons are short, and where government revenue is difficult to raise.

In addition, there is little effective demand for public agricultural research from most of the groups who would benefit from new technologies: urban businessmen and consumers seeking lower food prices, farmers seeking lower production costs, farm input suppliers seeking expanding markets, research administrators seeking bigger budgets, and research scientists seeking more publications. Urban consumers, for example, are unlikely to press the government for more agricultural research expenditures, given that any payoff to them individually from such investment is likely to be small and not forthcoming for many years (or not forthcoming at all if the commodity's export demand or import supply is very elastic).

Among those on the land, it is landowners who are likely to reap most of the producer gains from research, via higher land values (Herdt and Cochrane). Landless tenants and labourers are therefore likely to add little to the demand for agricultural research. This is especially so since they constitute probably the least educated, least politically articulate, and least organized group in any developing country, and partly because of the free rider problem of collective action among such a large geographically spread group of people. There is is little incentive for an individual to contribute toward his interest group's seeking of a policy which, if adopted, would benefit him regardless of whether he contributes (Olson).

The strength of demand from land owning producers depends on the numbers involved and the distribution of holding sizes. In some industries, such as rubber, there are two clearly defined groups of landholdings: a large number of small family farms capable of employing little nonfamily labour, and a much smaller number of large plantation estates capable of employing many labourers. The former group is unlikely to be actively demanding research funds, again because of the free rider problem of collective action. The latter group, on the other hand, would have much less of a free rider problem, both because fewer individuals are involved and because each has much more to gain in absolute terms from new cost reducing technologies. So one would expect more effective demand for public agricultural research from industries with a few large firms than from those with many small firms; and, where there is a dualistic industry structure, one would expect the demand to come mainly from large firms.

Indirect Factors

Perhaps more import than direct factors leading to underinvestment in agricultural research are factors affecting the price mechanism and hence the profitability of agricultural research investment as measured by domestic prices. The conclusion that emerges from the induced innovations literature is that the higher price of a commodity relative to input and factor prices faced by farmers, the more researchers direct their research toward the production of new technologies for that commodity (Hayami and Ruttan; and Binswanger, Ruttan, and others). The well documented bias in trade policies of developing countries towards protecting the import competing industrial sector and often taxing the export of primary products ensures that agricultural production is discouraged relative to industrial production (Little, Scitovsky, and Scott). The reasons for this bias are no doubt complex, but they might include the following. First, there may be a need to raise government revenue via trade taxes, possibly for want of a politically or economically lower cost tax instrument. Second, the incentive for a minor manufacturing industry with a small number of geographically concentrated firms to lobby for import barriers is much stronger than is the incentive for a dominant rural export industry with a large number of geographically spread farms to seek government assistance or less taxation. The free rider problem is much greater in the latter case, and while import competing assistance can raise government revenue via tariffs, say, assisting agriculture would generally require massive explicit government handouts or reduced government revenue in the case of lowering export taxes. Third, assistance to any one small manufacturing industry has little effect on factor or input prices in other industries, whereas higher prices for rice, say, may have a marked effect on wage rates in the cities of low income countries where rice absorbs a large part of an urban worker's income. Indeed, this effect on wages gives urban industrialists an incentive to lobby for low food prices and to encourage wage earners to do likewise via the threat or practice of street riots. For all these reasons, one might expect agriculture in developing countries to face a less favourable set of prices than the industrial sector, vis-a-vis the free trade situation. This in turn, would induce less agricultural research than would be the case in the absence of government intervention in the market.

Possible Reasons for Excessively Labour Saving Technologies

Direct Factors

Perhaps the most obvious reason one might observe a labour saving bias is that many new technologies are simply adaptations of technologies transferred from higher wage countries. Inappropriate though they are from an equity point of view, it may still be worthwhile adapting and promoting them from an efficiency viewpoint; that is, if the net return from doing so is greater than that from domestically producing more appropriate technologies. Similarly, if an industry's structure changes from mainly large to mainly small farms or plantations (due, for example, to land reform), it is conceivable that it still pays to continue at least some research begun earlier if a great deal of relevant human capital and knowledge is already available in the country's research institutes, even though such research may produce technologies less appropriate for the present than the past industry structure.

A further reason for biased new technologies may be that scientists and perhaps government planners and the ruling elite tend to be interested more in technical than in economic productivity indices, and, in particular, often look to increase output per unit of land or labour without considering the farmer's credit constraints. Their fallacious line of reasoning may simply be that given the amount of land and labour in the rural sector, the obvious way to increase food output is to inject capital into the sector both directly and via new capital using technology.

It is important to note at this point that technologies appropriate for large farm circumstances may well be unsuitable for small farm circumstances. This is because large farms may face different factor prices than small family farms. Hired labour for the former is more expensive than family labour for the latter because large farms have to cover the costs of recruiting and supervising labour and have to pay sufficient wages to cover the labourers' job search and commuting costs, which could be considerable if permanent employment were not offered. Capital for large farms, on the other hand, is generally cheaper than for small farms because there is often a fixed cost component to borrowing and a greater risk in lending to small farms with little or no collateral. For these reasons, large farms face a higher wage-rental ratio than small farms and so are encouraged to demand land augmenting technologies that are more labour saving and capital using than would be appropriate for small farms.

This difference in relative factor prices as between large and small farmers is important because large farmers have relatively more influence on research resource allocation, for a number of reasons. First, because they tend to be more educated, they are likely to adopt new technologies better and faster than average (Chaudhri). They therefore have a greater incentive to demand agricultural research expenditures than smaller, less educated farmers because by adopting early they may reap quasirents from, say, increased yields prior to wide adoption and a consequent fall in product prices. Second, they tend to be far less numerous than small farmers and so suffer less of a free rider problem in acting collectively. Third, being more educated, they are more politically articulate and socially mobile and thus come in more contact with research scientists, both directly and indirectly via extension officers. Thus, researchers and extension officers tend to become more familiar with the constraints facing larger farmers and may well be unaware of any differences between these and the constraints of small farmers.

In addition, given that job promotion for research scientists depends heavily on their published research output, one would not be surprised to find scientists seeking funds for projects which make full use of their knowledge and skills and maximize their chances of obtaining publishable results quickly. This may well lead to a bias in research proposals toward projects which build on an existing body of literature, especially one with which the researchers are familiar. If that literature is related to more capital abundant countries or to a more capital intensive industry structure of earlier colonial times (as with plantation crops), this bias would lead to the production of more labour saving, purchased input using technologies than may be appropriate for the mass of farmers in today's developing countries. And, one would expect input suppliers such as the agrochemical industries to encourage such a bias.

Indirect Factors

The bias mentioned above would tend to be reinforced by the factor price distortions often present in developing countries. In particular, when credit is subsidized and then has to be rationed, it is usually the larger farmers with more collateral, lower transactions costs per dollar borrowed, and better abilities to bribe loan officers who are served first, leaving small farmers to borrow on the more expensive informal money market (Gonzales-Vega). Indeed, it is possible that subsidized credit policies are sought by the politically more influential large farmers because the distributional effects of such policies are so much in their favour. This is especially so when credit is restricted to investment purposes and excludes working capital needs, because large farmers have less need to borrow for short periods than do small farmers, and small farmers have relatively less use for capital to invest in tractors, pumpsets, or whatever. The resulting factor market distortion further induces the development of more capital using technologies than would be the case with free markets.

Some Policy Implications

The above theoretical discussion suggests that there may well be reasons to expect systematic underinvestment in, and excessively labour saving biases in the technologies produced by, agricultural research in developing countries. If this is so, a number of important policy implications follow. First, economists have a role to play as a pressure group in informing other pressure gorups and governments of any inefficiencies and inequities of present research resource allocation and pricing policies. Second, extension workers need to be encouraged to find out and pass on to scientists more details of the constraints facing the whole range of farmers, not just the larger ones. Third, given the economic and political realities which tend to exclude small farmers from formal (and especially subsidized) credit, it is particularly important from their point of view--and from the eocnomy's as a whole, given their significant contribution to production--that technologies be produced that are less dependent on purchased inputs. Since for political reasons such technologies may not be forthcoming from national or state agricultural experiment stations, it is even more important that the international research institutes not only make up for any underinvestment in national research but also help to offset the biases against research for small farm conditions.

References

Akino, M.; Hayami, Y. (1975) Efficiency and equity in public research: Rice breeding in Japan's economic development. American Journal of Agricultural Economics, 57 (1) 1-10.

Arndt, T.; Dalrymple, D.; Ruttan, V. (1977) Resource Allocation and Productivity in National and International Agricultural Research. Minneapolis, Minnesota, USA; University of Minnesota Press.

Ayer, H.; Schuh, E. (1972) Social rates of return and other aspects of agricultural research: The case of cotton research in Sao Paulo, Brazil. American Journal of Agricultural Economics, 54 (4) 557-569.

Bal, H.; Kahlon, A. (1977) Methodological issues on measurement of returns to investment in agricultural research. Indian Journal of Agricultural Economics, 32 (3) 181-192.

Barletta, N. A. (1970) Costs of social benefits of agricultural research in Mexico. Ph.D. dissertation. Chicago, Illinois, USA; University of Chicago.

Binswanger, H.; Ruttan, V.; and others (1978) Induced Innovation Technology, Institutions, and Development. Baltimore, Maryland, USA; Johns Hopkins University Press.

Chaudhri, D. P. (1978) Education, Innovations, and Agricultural Development. London; Croom Helm.

Downs, A. (1957) An Economic Theory of Democracy. New York; Harper and Row.

Evenson, R. E. (1969) International transmission of technology in sugarcane production. New Haven, Connecticut, USA; Yale University.

Evenson, R. E.; Jha, D. (1973) The contribution of agricultural research systems to agricultural production in India. Indian Journal of Agricultural Economics, 28 (4) 212-230.

Flores-Moya, P.; Evenson, R. E.; Hayami, Y. (1979) Social returns to rice research in the Philippines: Domestic benefits and foreign spillovers. Economic Development and Cultural Change, 26 (3) 591-607.

Gonzales-Vega, C. (1977) Interest rate restrictions and income distribution. American Journal of Agricultural Economics, 59 (5) 973-976.

Hayami, Y.; Ruttan, V. (1971) Agricultural Development: An International Perspective. Baltimore, Maryland, USA; Johns Hopkins University Press.

Herdt, R.; Cochrane, W. (1966) Farm land prices and farm technological advance. Journal of Farm Economics, 48 (2) 243-263.

Hines, J. (1972) The utilization of research for development: Two case studies in rural modernization and agriculture in Peru. Ph.D. dissertation. Princeton, New Jersey, USA; Princeton, University.

Kumar, P.; Maji, C.; Patel, R. (1977) Returns on investment in research and extension: A study on Indo-Swiss Cattle Improvement Project, Kerela. Indian Journal of Agricultural Economics, 32 (3) 207-216.

Little, I.; Scitovsky, I.; Scott, M. (1970) Industry and Trade in Some Developing Countries: A Comparative Study. London; Oxford University Press.

Olson, M. (1965) The Logic of Collective Action. Cambridge, Massachusetts, USA; Harvard University Press.

Pee, T. (1977) Social returns from rubber research in peninsula Malaysia. Ph.D. dissertation. East Lansing, Michigan, USA; Michigan State University.

Scobie, G.; Posada, R. (1978) The impact of technical change on income distribution: The case of rice in Colombia. American Journal of Agricultural

Economics, 60 (1) 85-92.
Tang, A. (1963) Research and education in Japanese agricultural development. Economic Studies Quarterly, 13, 27-41, 91-99.

OPENER'S REMARKS—E. Dettwiler

It is vital that people know about the discrepancy which exists between the goals in the developing countries and the goals of research activities undertaken in the developed countries to serve the needs of the developing countries. Anderson's paper is not very clear about this discrepancy.

To what extent do agricultural projects also benefit from research in private industry? Does Anderson's paper refer to basic research, applied research, and research projects that are financed through both the public sector and the private institutions?

I fully agree with Anderson when he talks about unilaterally directed research which benefits some large farms, with a view to labour saving technologies. However, this problem not only exists in the developing countries, but is a real problem in the disadvantaged areas of many developed countries. For example, when developing new agricultural machines, private industry often ignores the problems of these disadvantaged regions.

Khan gave us some interesting insights into small scale machinery development for labour surplus economies. What he said with respect to the needs of developing countries can be applied in some sense to disadvantaged areas in developed countries.

Some more general questions also arise out of Anderson's paper. To what extent can we allow the research to be autonomous? Are not many scientists seeking to illuminate their own scientific halos without regard to the public good?

One should be able to foresee the success of the research and know how to present it to the authorities concerned who should then support the project financially. This again raises the problem of estimating costs on the one hand and the specific returns on the other. Anderson identifies various measures and methods for assessing the success of research, but he does not evaluate them. I would be very interested to hear more about this, particularly with reference to the specific circumstances in the developing countries. It is well known that the procurement of information necessary for the development of a research project is sometimes very difficult and varies from one country to another.

Anderson supports the idea that research administrators need to be convinced about the potential contribution of economists to advance evaluation of research proposals. The agricultural economist has a very central position; the need is great but he cannot solve all the problems with mathematical models. His professional skill must be very broad, and he must be able to quantify the benefits of research. it is also important that he know his own limits and is prepared to collaborate with specialists in other disciplines.

Reference

Khan, A. U. (1981) Small scale machinery development for labour surplus economics, in Rural Change: The Challenge for Agricultural Economists (edited by G. L. Johnson and A. H. Maunder). Farnborough; Gower Publishing Co.

RAPPORTEUR'S REPORT—Bernard H. Sonntag

A similar analysis of international institutions would be useful. The approach is applicable to both developed and developing countries, but the empirical efforts on the topic have been directed to the latter. International institutions face different political constraints than do national institutions and thus have some capacity to remedy defects in research programmes within countries.

Failure of researchers to sell their product to administrators is one factor in limiting research funding. Return to the whole research package may not be as high as some of the published estimates suggest--usually only the successes are reported.

There are varying time periods and high risks associated with agricultural research. There has been a lack of success to date on utilization of atmospheric nitrogen, despite considerable efforts. There is a tendency toward underinvestment in research with a long gestation period; for example, development of perennial versus annual crop varieties. High rates of return in nonagricultural research might explain underinvestment in agricultural research.

Contributing to the discussion were Judith Heyer, Howard A. Osborn, Ulf Renborg, Chandrahas H. Shah, and Juan Pablo Torrealba.

ON-FARM RESEARCH TO DEVELOP
TECHNOLOGIES APPROPRIATE TO FARMERS

Derek Byerlee, Stephen Biggs, Michael Collinson,
Larry Harrington, Juan Carlos Martinez,
Edgardo Moscardi, and Donald Winkelmann

It is now widely accepted that technological change is a necessary although by no means sufficient condition for agricultural development. It is clear that despite the widespread diffusion of new wheat and rice varieties, many new technologies are not being widely used by farmers because they do not fit the particular circumstances of farmers for whom they are intended. This is despite the fact that considerable public expenditures are often made to provide the infrastructure such as credit and markets to enable the farmer to adopt these technologies.

This paper attempts to synthesize our experiences with national research programmes and with the International Wheat and Maize Improvement Center's (CIMMYT) wheat and maize programmes in deveolping research methodologies to ensure that agricultural technologies generated by scarce research resources are consistent with the circumstances of target farmers. It emphasizes collaboration of technical and social scientists in on-farm research--both in diagnosing farmers' problems and demands for technology and in developing and testing in farmers' fields those technologies which appear to meet these problems.

Traditional Approaches to Agricultural Research

Agricultural research is generally characterized by the gap between the researcher and the farmer. That assertion arises from our experience in many countries. There are many exceptions to that and the other generalizations in this section. On the one hand, much research has been guided by disciplinary interests. Although the importance of the problem to the farmer is sometimes advocated in determining research priorities, no explicit means of identifying priorities is employed. On the other hand, even research aimed at farmer problems has traditionally used a top down approach; that is, it is conducted on research stations under conditions quite different from those of farmers and then passed to extension for promotion to farmers. Although the problems of extrapolating these results to farmers have been recognized (see for example, Swanson), the movement of research to farmers' fields has been slow. An exception is experimentation on fertilizers which has long been conducted on farmers' fields in many countries, but practices under which these experiments are conducted (for example, weed control and land preparation) are often quite different from those of local farmers.

The economist in this process has usually been a late actor. Large scale involvement began with production function analysis of agronomic (usually fertilizer) experiments. In some cases this led to the collaboration of agronomists and agricultural economists in the design of fertilizer experiments (see, for example, Hoffnar and Johnson). More recently, in developing countries, economists and other social scientists have been even later participants through studies, after the fact, of technology adoption. Increasingly these studies reflect the fact that recommended technologies are not appropriate to particular farmer circumstances. (See, for example, the Perrin and Winkelmann review of several such adoption studies.) However, these adoption studies have largely been conducted by economists outside of agricultural research institutions, and, as a result, there has been little immediate feedback to decisionmaking on research priorities for developing improved tehnologies.

There is now increasing emphasis on collaboration of technical and social scientists in on-farm research to bridge the gap between researchers and farmers. The general approach embraced in various degrees by various institutions (see, for example, Norman; CIMMYT; Dillon and others; Hildebrand; and Navarro) has three important components:

1. The approach emphasizes solving farmer problems which are specific in time and location. It begins with an identification of current farmer problems and possible technological solutions to these problems that are feasible under the natural and socioeconomic circumstances faced by farmers and that are consistent with national policy goals.

2. Technologies appropriate to farmers are then developed and evaluated by experimentation in farmers' fields under farmers' conditions.

3. Farmers' experiences with the new technology are monitored and this information fed back to research decisionmaking.

There is now growing support for the central role of on-farm research in national agricultural research programmes. However, the actual methodologies for implementing this type of research vary quite widely. In searching for such a methodology, we have been conscious of the need for several basic criteria:

1. The research should be well focused to enable quick payoffs to relatively limited research resources. This means research should be highly location specific and should focus on technology for an important or potentially important crop or crop mixture (in our case wheat or maize) rather than considering all crops and crop technologies in the system as variables. However, the identification and evaluation of potential technologies for a single crop must be made in the context of the farming system. Often small farmers operating in imperfect factor markets in an uncertain environment will use highly complex systems to meet an overriding food security objective. While yield increasing technologies are important, technologies for the target crop which have total system benefits are also necessary (for example, an earlier variety to allow two crops per season).

2. The farmer's decisionmaking with respect to technology is conditioned by natural circumstances, such as soils and climate, and by economic circumstances such as resource endowments and access to markets. To understand this complex of factors, a multidisciplinary research team usually consisting of an agronomist and an economist is needed to plan research with farmers.

3. Technological adoption by farmers is a learning-by-doing process that proceeds in small steps. The on-farm research should therefore set as an objective the generation of a few best-bet technological components. Furthermore, it is not possible to provide precise recommendations to each farmer, but recommendations can be made which are generally relevant to representative groups of farmers.

4. On-farm research should be part of a broader programme to improve crop production and farmers' incomes, and must therefore be closely linked to experiment station research, policymaking, and extension.

5. The methodology of on-farm research should be practical and replicable in

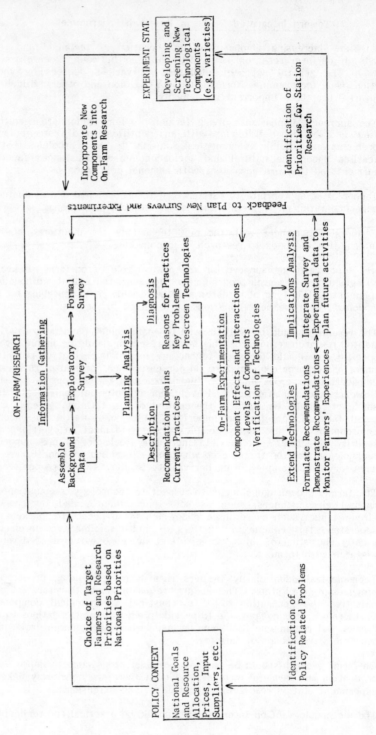

FIGURE 1. OVERVIEW OF AN INTEGRATED RESEARCH PROGRAMME

the context of scarce research resources of developing countries. It should be relatively cheap in implementation and make possible a fast turnaround in results.

The remainder of this paper summarizes the methodology we have found to meet these criteria. Figure 1 shows the specific steps in the methodology, which is described in detail in CIMMYT.

Choice of Target Region and Crop

Initially, the choice of the crop and region for an on-farm research programme must be justified in relation to the objectives of national policy and the resources and logistics available for the research. If national policy dictates that low income farmers should be priority beneficiaries of research expenditures, then the on-farm research will focus on a region where low income farmers are concentrated and where technologies are available with potential to increase production of a crop which is important in the farming system of these low income farmers. In this process, researchers will want also to consider the future perspective as well as the present; for example, whether there will be an adequate market for the increased production. This initial matching of the likely outcome of the research with national development priorities helps in the allocation of scarce research resources.

Collecting Information on Farmer Circumstances

The research then focuses on an understanding of farmer circumstances in the target region. This phase has both diagnostic and descriptive objectives. The primary objective is to diagnose the problems and constraints to crop production in the area in order to prescreen from a wide range of possible technological components a few best-bet components for experimentation in farmers' fields. Information from this diagnostic stage can also be used to guide experiment station research such as the development of new technological components, particularly varieties. The diagnostic effort also uncovers particular constraints at the farm level which are the result of policy decisions or problems in policy implementation (for example, problems of input availability, product marketing, and credit). Second, a description of farmer circumstances enables farmers in the target region to be tentatively classified into relatively homogeneous groups or recommendation domains for which the same recommended technology will be generally applicable. Also, this description of current farmers' practices and fields is important to establish representative farmers' practices and sites for on-farm experiments.

In the context of this paper, farmer circumstances are all those factors which bear on farmers' decisions with respect to technology for the target crop. These include natural factors such as climate, soils, and pests, and socioeconomic factors including marketing institutions, infrastructure, land tenure, and the farmers' own goals and resource constraints. Often these factors influence the farmers' choice of a crop technology through interactions within the farming system; that is, resource competition, crop rotations and multiple cropping, risk management, and food preferences. To the extent that these interactions are important, information must be obtained on other activities of the farming system.

Three sources of information on farmer circumstances are used: (1) background information on the farmers' environment, usually from secondary sources; (2) interviews with farmers; and (3) observations in farmers' fields. Typically available background agroclimatic and socioeconomic data are the first collected and analyzed. For example, in dryland areas, rainfall data from several sites are checked for important differences across the region and for periods of major rainfall uncertainty. A team--usually an agronomist and economist--will then spend one to four weeks touring the region in an exploratory survey of farmers and other persons linked to the farming community such as merchants, input suppliers, and extension agents. At this stage, information interviews of farmers and visits to farmers' fields are conducted. A questionnaire is not used, although the data are collected in a systematic manner against a mental checklist of issues and problems. Efforts are made to talk to traditional leaders who can often explain traditional practices, to innovative farmers who may or may not be working closely with the extension service, and to farmers encountered by chance on the tour. The researchers begin by trying to obtain a broad perspective on the farming system. As the exploratory survey proceeds, the interviews become more focused on specific problems and hypotheses to explain farmers' practices for the target crop within the context of the larger farming system. Also, at this stage, tentative definitions of recommendation domains are formulated and potential technological components are identified.

The primary role of this exploratory survey is to place the researcher in the farmers' fields in direct communication with the farmer and to help design a sharply focused, formal, and one-contact survey of farmers in the region in order to quantify and verify what has been learned in the exploratory survey and investigate some critical problems in more depth. Because a random sample of farmers is interviewed, the use of certain practices can be quantified and hypotheses on the reasons for these practices formally tested. Furthermore, relatively little emphasis is placed on quantifying farmers' resource use and allocation in order to infer technological needs. Rather, the questions aim to exploit the farmers' own intimate knowledge and experience of their environment in order to identify these needs. As a result, many questions (again based on exploratory survey information) elicit subjective types of information such as preferences about specific varietal characteristics.

The implementation of the formal survey--the training of enumerators, sampling, and field work--generally follows standard procedures for this type of work (see, for example, Collinson, 1972). Farmers are stratified as far as possible by the tentatively defined recommendation domain, and about 30-60 farmers are interviewed in each recommendation domain. The questionnaire is designed to be completed in 45 to 90 minutes.

Data Analysis and Prescreening Technologies

Data are analyzed quickly after the survey (within a maximum of 3 months), usually using hand tabulation sometimes supplemented by computer analysis. Descriptive tabulations of farming systems and cultural practices with respect to factors such as rainfall and farm size are used to refine boundaries of recommendation domains. These recommendation domains are only broad classifications of farmers and much heterogeneity still remains within each domain. The descriptive tabulations also provide a profile of representative farmers' practices and fields in each domain for the design of on-farm experiments.

The diagnosis of research priorities is made in the following steps: (1) important reasons for farmers using current technologies are listed; (2) priority problems and constraints in the target crop are identified on the basis of these reasons, results of field observations, and farmers' opinions and perceptions; (3) possible solutions to these problems and constraints are noted on the basis of practices of innovative farmers, on-station research results, and agroeconomic expertise; (4) all changes in the farming system implied by each solution, including associated costs, labour needs, and risks are listed, and based on researchers' understanding of the current farming system, those changes which are subjectively felt to be inconsistent with farmers' circumstances are

174

eliminated (for example, cash costs too high, unacceptable risks, or conflicts with present multiple cropping system); (5) partial budgets following Perrin and others are constructed assuming a priori best guestimates of yield responses for these technological components; and (6) in each recommendation domain, a few best-bet components arising from this prescreening exercise are chosen for on-farm experiments.

This prescreening process emphasizes identifying technologies which use resources and inputs available to farmers and have short run payoffs. However, experiments may be included with a longer run horizon. For example, such experiments may provide information on the desirability of making a new input available.

On-Farm Experimentation

On-farm experimentation serves three purposes. First, it enables technology to be developed and tested under farmers' conditions. Most experiment stations are managed in such a way that, over time, soil structure, fertility, weeds, pests, and diseases are quite different from those in farmers' fields. Second, the technology can be developed and tested over a variety of environments and cultural practices. Finally, the farmer and the extension agent can be actively involved in the process of developing and demonstrating technological components.

Several types of on-farm experiments are implemented by the same multidisciplinary team responsible for the surveys in order to test the three to four priority technological components arising out of the diagnostic studies (Violic and others; and Winkelmann and Moscardi). Exploratory experiments are 2^n factorials with levels of each factor set at the farmers' level and at substantially higher levels to look at the main effects and the first order interactions of each factor. On the basis of these experiments, experiments with one or two factors (depending on interactions noted in the exploratory experiments) are designed to find recommended levels of these factors in terms of income and risks. (Procedures for analyzing experimental data and making recommendations are described in Perrin and others.) Finally, factors are combined to verify tentatively recommended technologies in comparison to the farmers' technology. These verification experiments often serve as the basic design for extension demonstrations. To ensure relevance, all of these experiments are conducted under conditions determined by the formal survey to be representative of local farmers.

Dynamics of On-Farm Research

On-farm research is a continuous learning process. After each cycle of on-farm research, information from surveys and experiments are integrated and analyzed, and strategies for the following cycle formulated. Special purpose surveys may be organized, particularly to monitor how farmers use the recommended technologies when they themselves must pay all costs and accept the risks. This provides important feedback to the research programme. If cooperating farmers are accepting the technology, then it can be promoted through extension and demonstrations, and new technological components, previously of lower priority, can be incorporated into the research programme. On the other hand, where farmers reject or significantly change the recommended technology, an understanding of why this is so could influence the design of future experiments. Likewise, experimental results may help modify recommendation domains or identify new technological components not previously considered important.

Effectiveness of on-farm research can be greatly strengthened by maintaining close linkages with research at experiment stations. Experiment station research focuses on developing and screening new technological components; that is, research that usually requires greater control (for example, development of new varieties) or would be risky when done on farmers' fields (for example, screening new herbicides). Promising new technological components arising from station research are then submitted to experimental evaluation in farmers' fields. The results of on-farm research also help establish priorities for station research. For example, a knowledge of farmer circumstances can guide plant breeders in deciding between yield, earliness, specific disease resistance, grain type, and storability in varietal development.

On-farm research is also conducted in a specific policy context that might guide the selection of target farmers and technologies consistent with national goals. In addition, in most countries there is a shortage of micro level information for policy analysis. The detailed information on farmers' circumstances and technological responses under farmers' conditions generated by on-farm research can be important for identifying changes in policy and policy implementation that would complement the introduction of improved technologies (for example, increasing the availability of specific inputs).

Finally, the impact of on-farm research is increased if researchers responsible for on-farm research are institutionalized within the agricultural research establishments with appropriate incentives and logistics to work in a multidisciplinary team on priority problems. This will require agricultural research programmes to include economists as an integral part of the research staff. Our work initially focused on demonstrating to research administrators the value of these on-farm research procedures and the potential contribution of economists (for example, see Collinson, 1978). The emphasis has now shifted to assisting national research programmes to develop their own capacity for on-farm research. It has been shown that well trained four year agricultural graduates are capable of implementing these on-farm research procedures in a target region.

References

CIMMYT (forthcoming) Planning technologies appropriate to farmer circumstances: Concepts and procedures. Mexico; CIMMYT Economics Programme.

Collinson, M. P. (1972) Farm Management in Peasant Agriculture. New York; Praeger.

Collinson, M. P. (1978) Demonstration of an interdisciplinary approach to planning adaptive agricultural research programmes: Serenje District, Zambia. Report No. 3. Nairobi, Kenya; CIMMYT Eastern African Economics Programme.

Dillon, J. L.; and others (1978) Farming Systems Research at the International Agricultural Research Centres. Washington, D.C.; World Bank CGIAR Technical Advisory Group.

Hildebrand, P. E. (1976) Generando technologia para agricultores tradicionales: Una metodologia multidisciplinaria. Guatemala; ICTA.

Hoffnar, G. R.; Johnson, G. L. (1966) Summary and Evaluation of the Cooperative Agronomic-Economic Experimentation at Michigan State University. Research Bulletin No. 11. East Lansing, Michigan, USA; Michigan State Experiment Station.

Navarro, L. A. (1977) Dealing with risk and uncertainty in crop production: A lesson for small farmers. Turrialba, Costa Rica; CATIE.

Norman, D. W. (1978) Farming systems research to improve the livelihood of small farmers. American Journal of Agricultural Economics, 60 (5) 813-818.

Perrin, R.; Winkelmann, D. (1976) Impediments to technical progress on small versus large farms. American Journal of Agricultural Economics, 58 (5) 888-894.

Perrin, R.; and others (1976) From Agronomic Data to Farmer Recommendations. Mexico; CIMMYT.

Swanson, E. R. (1957) Problems of applying experiment results to commercial practice. Journal of Farm Economics, 39 (2) 382-389.

Violic, A.; and others (1976) Maize Training in the International Maize and Wheat Improvement Center. Mexico; CIMMYT.

Winkelmann, D.; Moscardi, E. (1979) Aiming agricultural research at the needs of farmers. Information Bulletin. Mexico; CIMMYT.

RAPPORTEUR'S REPORT--Bernard H. Sonntag

Introduction of new farming systems requires a transitional or learning period in addition to resource base changes. Irrigation and new high yielding varieties were cited as examples. Agronomists are generally willing to participate in informal surveys. Problems in establishing multidisciplinary teams should not be attributed solely to physical scientists--economists should share the blame.

The proposed approach would supplant the traditional experiment station. Neither the links between on-farm research and the experiment station nor those between the proposed approach and the farm management work of other institutions appear to be very strong.

Similar work is under way in outreach programmes in some developing countries. This approach is also useful in developed countries; for example, the recent efforts toward establishment of a farm management field laboratory in Alberta, Canada. Physical scientists have been invited to participate in that programme.

How can the programme be made operational in areas where the available staff is not trained beyond the secondary school level?

There is a need for more research on adaptive behaviour of farmers before economists will be able satisfactorily to explain their diagnosis of farm problems. The authors expressed a need for more applied field work in undergraduate training programmes. They also reemphasized the iterative nature of the approach and the need to adapt it as further experience is obtained. There has been little emphasis to date on monitoring and followup efforts. Some recent results in Africa and Latin America are reported in the literature.

Contributing to the discussion were Kym Anderson, Deryke G. R. Belshaw, John H. Cleave, David A. G. Green, T. Alf Peterson, Michel Petit, Refugio I. Rochin, and Chandrahas H. Shah.

CAUSALITY BETWEEN PHYSICAL AND SOCIAL TECHNOLOGIES IN THE PROCESS OF RURAL CHANGE

W. H. Furtan and G. G. Storey

Abstract

The process of rural change can be explained by examining the compatibility of the existing physical and social technologies. These two technologies comprise the basic environment in which we must live. If the physical technology developed and adopted is not compatible with the existing social institutions, which are based on society's norms, then stress and tensions arise within society. The link between physical and social technologies is in part economic in such things as the distribution of income. When tensions arise, an induced change occurs in social technology, physical technology, or both. In Canadian prairie agriculture and in some developing countries, the process of rural change can be explained by examining the interactions between the existing physical and social technologies.

OPENER'S REMARKS--Larry J. Connor

It is not clear which technology the authors consider to be the driving force, or what factors influence the relative importance and relationships between physical and social technologies in various development settings.

More attention should have been given to (1) the nature of the time lags involved in rural development and (2) the externalities involved in the adjustment process. For example, considerable time lags are often involved in putting physical or social technology in place, and there are often different time periods associated with physical and social technological adjustments. Hence, the adjustment problem may not always be one of incompatibility between physical and social technologies, but rather of insufficient time to put both in place. Similarly, unforeseen externalities and resulting impacts on other social groups are exceedingly important. Often these external effects on other farm groups, consumers, government officials, and so forth, are difficult to foresee.

There appears to be some confusion in the paper as to what physical and social technologies actually are. In the Saskatchewan example cited, the authors stated that one group advocates controlling physical technology (placing limits on the number of acres one farmer can operate), and changing the social contract (through possible nationalization of the land base). Placing limits on farm area or nationalization of the land are both methods of altering the system of property rights. Hence, both are social technological approaches.

RAPPORTEUR'S REPORT--Geoff W. Edwards

The authors see a two way relationship between physical and social technologies: changes in social technology could induce changes in physical technology and vice versa.

The system for distributing income (a part of social technology) could be relevant in making decisions about physical technology that may cause unemployment.

Contributing to the discussion were Joseph von Ah and Clark Edwards.

FIFTY YEARS OF TECHNICAL CHANGE IN AGRICULTURE

Fred C. White, Joseph Havlicek, Jr., and Daniel Otto

Abstract

The tremendous increase in productivity in agriculture over the past half century can be attributed largely to public investments in agricultural research and extension. This paper quantifies the effect of research and extension on productivity in the United States, with particular emphasis on measuring how these effects have changed over time. The approach taken in this study is to explain productivity changes by examining the activities which produce quality changes in inputs. A production function including conventional as well as nonconventional inputs was estimated for the average farm situation in the United States. The period of analysis was divided into three periods to test for changes in the effect of research and extension expenditures over time. The internal rate of return to agricultural research and extension investment was 55 percent in the 1919-41 period, 48 percent in the 1942-57 period, and 42 percent in the 1958-77 period.

These results have important implications for developing countries as their economies experience similar stages of development. There was a substantial delay before the increased commitment to improving productivity actually resulted in significant growth in productivity. Increased educational attainment of farmers contributed to the increased productivity. The returns to research and extension investment were highest when there was the greatest potential to substitute improved capital for labour. Although the results indicate that there are diminishing marginal returns, the rate of return in the most recent period (42 percent) indicates that agricultural research and extension are still profitable investments.

OPENER'S REMARKS--Harold C. Love

Can we ignore large investments by the private sector? Certainly part of the incentive for development by the private sector of new capital inputs such as improved fertilizer, new machinery, and pesticides was their low relative price or cost of capital relative to effective demand for the new products. The incentive for farmers to use these new products and technologies was their low capital costs. It was these relationships, along with public investment in research and extension, which brought about rapid change--not public investment alone.

The results are not useful to developing countries. The big return prospect for most developing countries is in the discovery and development of new capital substitutes for land. Many developing countries are burdened with too many people attempting to earn a living from too small a plot of land, a situation made worse by lack of off-farm employment opportunities. These countries want to know which research to invest their scarce funds in to obtain the highest return and what kind of extension is most effective.

The study simply proves again what has already been proved for different developed countries. What new does it really add? What we need to know are the returns on investment in research and extension for different commodities such as wheat, maize, soybeans, sunflowers, rapeseed, grasses, pigs, poultry, and so forth, 'and for practices such as planting date, seeding rate, timing and placement of irrigation water, fertilizer, pesticides, and so forth. With such information, research directors will know to which departments, commodities, and practices to allocate investment funds.

Whether the lag between research and extension expenditures and the peak in the flow of benefits from the expenditures changed over the 49 year period could not be determined without adopting a more disaggregated and very data demanding approach.

The cultural reaction of the utilizing audience governs rates of change in response to research findings. Results for the United States may not apply elsewhere.

The dependent variable (production per farm) may be divided into three components: production per acre of crops, production per head of animals, and production per person. If one looks separately at the relationships between research and extension expenditures and each of the three mentioned variables, one may obtain results that are easier to relate to the situations of other countries.

The study looks at transfers of research findings between ten regions in the United States. To do this on a disaggregated basis (for example, for animals and crops) requires that inputs of land, labour, and capital, as well as research and extension outlays, be separated for different enterprises. Misuse of the results of analyses of this type by those with particular views on the desired pattern of research is possible.

Contributing to the discussion were Joseph von Ah, Larry J. Connor, Vance W. Edmondson, Stewart H. Lane, Ardron B. Lewis, and Donald McClatchy.

PUBLIC CROP INSURANCE FOR DEVELOPING COUNTRIES: THE LESSONS FROM THE JAPANESE EXPERIMENT

Syed M. Ahsan

Crop Insurance as A Public Policy

In view of the overwhelming impact of agricultural risks on peasant economies, many governments have traditionally adopted various measures, often in an ad hoc manner, to help farmers partially meet the losses due to natural hazards. These measures often take the form of reduction of land rent and taxes, cancellation or postponement of loan repayments, and direct subsidies. There are several disadvantages with this practice. An important one is that farmers cannot expect assistance as a right, but only as a privilege, and as a consequence cannot take these possibilities fully into consideration in determining their courses of action (for example, choice of farming techniques or use of agricultural credit). Certainly, in the case of Japan, tenancy disputes over the rent reduction on the part of landlords during the depression years brought the final pressure on the government leading to the introduction of public crop insurance in 1939 (Yamauchi, p. 14-15). The advantages of all-risk crop insurance over these ad hoc measures on various aspects of the farm economy (innovative cultivating methods, credit, and overall stability) have been discussed in the literature (Bardhan; and Wharton).

An Outline of the Japanese Crop Insurance Scheme

The broad reasons why the Japanese agricultural insurance policies are of major interest are: (1) the comprehensive nature of the operation (all major crops, livestock, fruits and fruit trees, and silkworms and cocoons); (2) the public and compulsory nature of the policies; and (3) the small size of farms (the average size being less than one hectare). These considerations suggest that the Japanese experience may have important implications for crop insurance in developing countries.

The basic organizational units are the Agricultural Mutual Relief Associations, most of which coincide with the administrative area of the local communities (city, town, or village). Once an association is formed, all farmers with a certain minimum size holding are required to be members. Next come the Federations of Agricultural Mutual Relief Associations which have jurisdictions coinciding with the political boundaries of prefectures. All associations within a given prefecture are members of its federation. There are two other organizations, the Agricultural Mutual Relief Reinsurance Special Account and the Agricultural Mutual Relief Fund, both of which operate at national level and deal only with federations and, of course, the national treasury.

The sharing of responsibilities is as follows: the Ministry of Agriculture, using the preceding 20 years of data, calculates the standard premium rate, or, simply, the total premium for each prefecture. Each federation (prefecture) then applies this total premium to the associations on the basis of a risk index facing the association. These risk indices are calculated such that the premiums for high risk areas are scaled down by increasing premiums for low risk areas. For details, see Yamauchi. Notice that the actual rate of premium facing an association is expressed as a certain percentage of the total amount of insurance. It is the association's task to assess the total amount of premium due from each farmer, which requires estimating the total amount of insurance and the maximum amount of indemnity payable. Since 1972, for paddy rice, the insurance value on the crop of the whole farm has been set at 0.9 times the fixed price per koku (150 kilograms) times 80 percent of the normal yield on the farm, less the actual yield on the farm. Thus, the maximum indemnity payable is 72 percent of the value of the normal yield on the farm. The marketing of rice is government regulated, with the price being fixed each year by the government. Normal yields are set at the prefecture, association, and farm (or plot) levels by the relevant authorities.

The disbursement of indemnities to farmers is also handled by the association. However, the association, being rather limited in its scope to spread risk over space, is only responsible for 10 percent of the total indemnity. The standard premium rate actually consists of three components: a normal rate corresponding to normal damages; an abnormal rate for abnormal damages; and a superabnormal rate for superdamages. The federation attempts to spread the remaining 90 percent of normal damage within the prefecture and any damage in excess of normal is dispersed nationally by the reinsurance account. Of the premium raised in an association, 10 percent is retained and the remainder handed over to the federation, which, in turn, splits it with reinsurance account in the proportion of normal to nonnormal premium rates. Table 1 provides an illustration.

Table 1--Total Paddy Rice Premium Collected and Its Allocation

Year	Standard Premium Rate[1]	Amount Collected	Association Share[2]	Federation Share[2]	Reinsurance Premium[2]
	--million yen----------------------------				
1948	4.928 (42.4)	1,641	164 (10.0)	671 (40.9)	806 (49.1)
1949	4.928 (42.4)	4,131	413 (10.0)	1,687 (40.8)	2,031 (49.2)
1950	5.058 (43.0)	4,635	464 (10.0)	1,922 (41.5)	2,249 (48.5)

Sources: Yamauchi, p. 24; and Rowe, p. 43.
[1] The figures in parentheses denote the percentage of the normal premium rate in the standard rate.
[2] The figures in parentheses are percentages of the amount collected.

Thus, the federations reinsure damages in excess of normal damages with the reinsurance account, thereby attaining the maximum possible dispersion of risks. The associations, if damages are widespread, may find it difficult to pay 10 percent of the indemnities unless they have reserves carried over from previous years. In the event they are not able to pay, they are allowed to prorate the payments of indemnities. However, the federations are not allowed to default. For this purpose, the Agricultural Mutual Relief Fund was set up to facilitate lending and investment activities. A federation can thus borrow the required amount from the fund when necessary. The fund was initially set up with half the capital coming from the general account of the government and the other half obtained as investments on the part of the federations. The reinsurance account has traditionally received transfers from the general account of the government to write off the deficits, and, likewise, in case of excess funds, it transfers them to the general account.

Performance of the Plan

A review of the loss ratios is a useful starting point formalizing the financial soundness of the plan. Loss ratios are the total amount of indemnity paid divided by the total amount of the premium times 100.

Table 2--Average Premium Rates and Loss Ratios

| | Paddy Rice | | Upland Rice | | Wheat and barley | |
Year	Standard Premium	Loss Ratio	Standard Premium	Loss Ratio	Standard Premium	Loss Ratio
1947-54	5.34	142	16.49	171	3.10	279
1955-63	5.94	59	15.15	105	5.13	225
1964-70	5.14	73	15.79	142	9.15	135
1947-70	5.51	91	15.75	104	5.63	217

Source: Constructed from data in Yamauchi, tables 3 and 11.

It is generally agreed that the actuarial basis for insurance was rather poor until about 1954; since then it has become more sound. However, for wheat and barley (except for the 1964-70 period), it appears that the premium rate was too low. It was raised to 12.13 percent during 1968-70, and to 13.75 percent effective 1972.

We also note from table 2 that the premium for paddy rice insurance seems rather high. This has been taken into consideration since 1972, and the rate since has been set at 3.5 percent for the farm unit calculation (3.9 percent on a plot basis). The recent record (especially post-1964) provides evidence for the contention that the Japanese crop insurance programme, after a somewhat long period of experimentation, is following a stable pattern. It still remains to be determined whether the costs are shared fairly by all parties concerned (farmers and government and whether they are too high for other developing countries to implement similar programmes.

Allocation of Costs

The default risk on the part of associations (due to the very limited nature of their liability) is not a major problem. Federations are, however, not allowed to default, and, as a result, their financial solvency depends crucially on the soundness of the actuarial basis of the premium rate determination. Deficits on the part of the reinsurance account are directly borne by the general account of the government, and, at least in the short run, these shortfalls are not a major problem. Over the long run, however, reinsurance premiums must cover indemnities payable by the reinsurance account for smooth functioning of the programme.

In the early days of the plan, all the agencies (associations, federations, and the reinsurance account) were steadily incurring losses. For example, during 1948-50, the average loss ratios were as shown in table 3.

Table 3--Average Loss Ratios, 1948-50

	Paddy	Upland Rice	Wheat and Rice
Associations	129	65	579
Federations	123	80	221
Reinsurance Accounting	135	60	1,003

Source: Rowe, tables 1 and 2; and Goodwin and Kunimi, Table B.

Clearly such a trend (except for upland rice) could not have continued without disrupting the scheme badly. The actuarial basis has changed over time so that overall loss ratios have declined considerably.

Even though the premium rates are actuarially sound, the farmers do not pay the entire amount. As of 1972, the actual rates and the treasury's share were as shown in table 4.

Table 4--Actual Rates and Treasury's Share, 1972

	Total Premium Rate	Treasury's Contribution
	-----------Percent------------	
Paddy Rice [1]	3.911	59.1
	(3.533)	(58.5)
Upland Rice	18.62	67.8
Wheat and Barley	13.75	67.2

Source: Government of Japan.

[1] The figures in parentheses are the rates applicable on a farm unit calculation. All other figures are on a plot basis.

In 1975, on account of paddy rice, the premium subsidy amounted to 32.5 billion yen.

Another major aspect of the government's contribution is the transfer of funds to cover the deficits in the reinsurance account, shown in table 5.

Table 5--Deficits (-) and Surpluses in the Reinsurance Account

	Cumulative Total for 1948-58	Cumulative Total for 1959-74	Cumulative Total for 1947-74
	-----------------------------million yen ------------------------		
Paddy Rice	(-)5,265	42,875	37,610
Upland Rice	496	(-)2,972	(-)2,476
Wheat and Barley	(-)7,526	(-)18,508	(-)26,034
All Crops	(-)12,295	21,395	9,100

Source: Constructed from data in Government of Japan.

Clearly, the positive balance accumulated over 1959-74 has more than made up for the negative balances accumulated over 1947-58. More accurately, it is the strong performance of paddy rice insurance that has kept the reinsurance account solvent. Over the 15 year period (1959-74), in only 4 years were there deficits on the paddy rice account, while 11 occurred for upland rice and 9 for wheat and barley. It is also evident that unless some such risk spreading across crops is attainable, comprehensive agricultural insurance is unlikely to be successful. Finally, the table suggests that direct public responsibility is indispensable, for there ought to be some agency to absorb the initial losses (perhaps for as long as a decade) in the reinsurance account.

Policy Implications for Developing Countries

1. The Japanese scheme shows that a coverage rate of 60 to 70 percent of the value of the normal yield provides a meaningful insurance for the farmer. A somewhat lower figure of 50 percent should perhaps be the starting point, gradually raised to the eventual target.

2. For the major crops in the country, a total premium rate at least as high as in Japan (say 5 to 6 percent of the indemnification-based insurance value, say, every 4 years or so) will be necessary for the long term viability of the plan. This suggests that some mechanism for premium assistance will have to be devised.

3. Taking 1975 figures, the premium subsidy (for paddy rice) of 32.5 billion yen is approximately 1 percent of the value of the average yield. Using an average yield of 90 million koku per year, at 1975 prices, the average value comes to 3,150 billion yen. If the premium subsidy is earmarked as a percentage of agricultural income taxes, the required subsidy comes to approximately 5 percent of the likely tax base. Using one-fifth as a guide for the amount of the tax base (that is, one-fifth of agricultural income is taxable), 3,150 billion yen gives rise to about 630 billion yen of taxable income. Pechman and Kaizuka (p. 340) report a tax base of 32.7 percent for the Japanese individual income tax.

4. One can conclude that for other countries with similar damage rates and implementing similar crop insurance coverages for a crop such as paddy rice in Japan, the required premium subsidy can be roughly taken to require an additional tax of 5 to 6 percent of taxable agricultural income generated by the crop.

5. Even if this additional taxation is considered feasible, two other major aspects remain to be looked into. The first is the problem of obtaining funds to set up organizations similar to the fund and the reinsurance account. The difficulty likely to be faced by the countries like Bangladesh, Pakistan, and India (with much lower growth rather than Japan in the 1950s and 1960s) may prove insurmountable, unless help is forthcoming from organizations such as FAO, ESCAP, and the World Bank.

6. Finally, although risks can usefully be spread at different levels in appropriate proportions (from village to prefecture to nation, as in Japan), the Japanese experience suggests that eventually risks will also have to be spread across crops. This suggests that simultaneous insurance of all major crops is the only viable alternative for meaningful protection of all farmers. The Japanese case indicates that crops like wheat and barley (even with premiums up to 4 times higher than for paddy rice) would have been extremely difficult to insure without cross-subsidization with paddy rice.

References

Bardhan, P. K. (1974) On life and death questions. Economic and Political Weekly, Special No. 9, 1293-1304.

Godwin, D. C.; Kunimi, S. (1952) Japan's Agricultural Insurance System: A Statistical Description. Tokyo, Japan; Natural Resources Division, General Headquarters.

Government of Japan (1976) Outline of the Agricultural Loss Compensation System. Tokyo, Japan; Ministry of Agriculture and Forestry.

Pechman, J.; Kaizuka, K. (1976) Taxation, in Asia's New Giant (edited by H. Patrick and H. Rosovsky). Washington, D.C.; The Brookings Institution.

Rowe, W. H. (1951) Crop Insurance in Japan. Tokyo, Japan; Natural Resource Division, General Headquarters.

Wharton, C. R. (1969) The green revolution, cornucopia or Pandora's box? Foreign Affairs, 464-476.

Yamauchi, T. (1974) Actuarial structure of crop insurance in Japan and appraisal of its benefits. Bulletin of the University of Osaka Prefecture, Series D, 11-42.

OPENER'S REMARKS--William M. Braithwaite

It might prove useful to examine the four main characteristics of the Japanese scheme to see how they might apply to similar plans in developing countries. The first is the establishment of local community associations to administer the plan. Members of each association are given the right to choose the level of insurance coverage that they want. In this way, they feel that they are involved in the decisionmaking process and thus are more likely to be committed to the plan.

The second is the compulsory nature of the scheme. All farmers above a minimum size must join. This avoids the problem of only very risky farmers taking out insurance, and it permits the government to spread the risk over a broad base to keep premiums at reasonable levels.

The third is the principle of spreading the risk across all major crops. This means that in Japan the more stable paddy rice is used to subsidize the less stable crops like upland rice, wheat, and barley. Without this subsidy, it is doubtful if most farmers could afford to insure high risk crops like wheat and barley.

The fourth is the substantial support from the public purse. The national treasury picked up the deficit during the first decade of the scheme before it became actuarially sound, and the government subsidized insurance premiums by as much as 50 percent. The paper estimates this subsidy alone is equivalent to an additional tax on agricultural income of 3 to 4 percentage points.

I suspect that the Japanese plan could not be transferred to other developing countries without some modifications of these characteristics to take into account the local cultural, social, and economic conditions. The above four characteristics are necessary in some form, but they are perhaps not sufficient conditions for a development plan where the government is trying to introduce a package of new technology to farmers which includes some minimum income guarantee to encourage adoption.

RAPPORTEUR'S REPORT--Wolfgang Wolf

The adaptation of Japan's crop insurance system to developing countries was the main point of the discussion. The financial capacity is still insufficient in many developing countries. This necessitates care in the introduction of a crop insurance programme.

The differences in crop production practices and education of farmers add to the above difficulties, as well as problems of nominating and appointing capable managerial staff, the uniqueness of the Japanese culture, and the costs of managing such an insurance system. Aspects of welfare and productivity were also discussed. The most efficient way to implement a crop insurance system has yet to be found.

AGRICULTURAL PRICING POLICIES IN
DEVELOPED AND DEVELOPING COUNTRIES:
THEIR EFFECTS ON EFFICIENCY, DISTRIBUTION, AND RURAL CHANGE

Malcolm D. Bale and Ernst Lutz

Introduction

Agriculture is the main source of food for the world, and food is the basic input in the daily sustenance of humans. Yet, in many parts of the world there is insufficient food, which in turn implies inadequate agricultural output. The reasons for inadequate agricultural production are many and varied, ranging from poor distribution and poor production techniques to political intervention at various levels in the global agricultural complex. The most important reason for deficient agricultural output is difficult to ascertain, but Schultz (1977) left no doubt as to his ranking of the causes. He suggested that the level of agricultural production depends not so much on technical considerations, but in large measure "on what governments do to agriculture." Schultz has long been the most ardent and eloquent spokesman of this position. See, for example, Schultz, 1964, 1977, and 1978. Export taxes on agricultural products provide government revenue and keep domestic prices low, product price supports in developed countries maintain farm incomes and provide surpluses which in turn find their way to developing country markets to further depress domestic farm prices, and agricultural inputs are frequently either taxed or subsidized. Yet, the magnitude of these effects on agricultural output, income distribution between producers and consumers, efficiency, and on rural-urban migration is often not fully appreciated.

This paper discusses government intervention in agricultural price determination, drawing on welfare theory to quantify the economic impacts on the previously mentioned variables. In this study, we examine France, Federal Republic of Germany, United Kingdom, Japan, Yugoslavia, Argentina, Egypt, Pakistan, and Thailand. The general theme of the paper is that the agricultural policies pursued by developing countries produce effects which are diametrically opposite to those produced by the policies of many developed countries, and that the policies of both are costly in terms of global welfare. Peterson addresses the developing country side of this question in a somewhat different manner.

Method and Theoretical Basis

The results of the paper are derived using standard partial equilibrium analysis. The method is well known both for its usefulness and the limitations. Details are not presented here but the reader is referred to Currie and others for an excellent review of the concept, to Bale and Greenshields for an application of the method, and to Lutz and Scandizzo for a review of other studies and a more detailed mathematical description.

Data Sources

The data used in this analysis are displayed in Bale and Lutz, table 1. The FAO Production Yearbook was used as a source of production levels, and imports, exports, and border prices were derived from the FAO Trade Yearbook. Supply and demand elasticities were taken from Rojko and others. All nominal protection coefficients for the developing countries (including Yugoslavia) are based on coefficients from detailed country case studies by Bertrand (Thailand), Cuddihy (Egypt), Gotsch and Brown (Pakistan), Reca (Argentina), and ULG Consultants Limited (Yugoslavia). The nominal protection coefficients for developed countries are derived from publications of the Commission of the European Communities and from Bale and Greenshields, while rural employment figures are derived from labour-output coefficients obtained from numerous sources described in Bale and Lutz.

Results and Conclusions

Agricultural pricing policies in developed and developing countries show significant differences. While agricultural commodity prices in developed countries generally have positive rates of protection, the agricultural sector in developing countries is being taxed through price intervention measures. As a result, the levels of agricultural production in industrialized nations are higher than without intervention, whereas agricultural output in developing countries is often significantly smaller than what it would be in the absence of distortion. With consumption, the picture is reversed: developing countries consume more and developed countries less than what they would without price intervention measures. The impacts on migration are substantial. In developing countries, agricultural pricing policies result in large numbers of displaced workers who add to urban unemployment, whereas in the industrialized nations a significant number of workers are kept in agriculture by price protection. (See Bale and Lutz, table 2.)

The analysis of monetary effects shows what important consequences result from government price intervention in agriculture. Total net social losses (the sum of net social losses in production and consumption) range from $26 million to $4.1 billion for the countries and the sample of commodities considered. (See Bale and Lutz, table 3.) As our results indicate, the most sizeable effects of the different agricultural policies are the welfare transfers between consumers and producers. While the farm sector of the developing economies studied was taxed by up to $2.2 billion per year, producers in developed countries receive large transfers due to protection. Government revenues are increased as a result of positive and negative protection in all but one country. The effects on foreign exchange earnings are clearly divided along different levels of development. While industrialized nations gain foreign exchange through protectionist policies, developing countries lose foreign exchange. This is particularly serious since foreign exchange availabilities represent a major bottleneck for developing nations. (See Bale and Lutz, table 5.)

What emerges from this paper is the vital role that farm product prices play in achieving optimum output and productivity growth. Because the wrong price signals are being given to farmers, allocative, production, and consumption potentials are not being realized. In many cases the estimated changes in production greatly alter trade patterns, in some cases causing importing countries to become self-sufficient. Another notable feature is the size of the rural employment effects of price distortions. As we explained, these numbers are conservative. The magnitude of the income transfers and efficiency losses (net social losses) is also impressive. (See Bale and Lutz, table 4.)

The ultimate question about agricultural pricing policies is their dynamic effects. Here we have seen the size of the static effects, but our model (and the state of technology of our profession) does not allow us to accurately estimate price distorting effects on income and industrial growth, adoption of technology, investment in agriculture, social consequences, and so forth. While decisions at the public level are made not by agricultural economists but by politicians, our profession plays a vital role in defining and quantifying the issues involved, and in extending these findings to appropriate officials. Our hope is that this paper is in that tradition.

References

Bale, M. D.; Greenshields, B. L. (1978) Japanese agricultural distortions and their welfare value. American Journal of Agricultural Economics, 60 (1) 59-64.

Bale, M. D.; Lutz, E. (1981) Price distortions in agriculture and their effects: An international comparison. American Journal of Agricultural Economics, 63 (1) 8-22.

Bertrand, T. J. (1980) Thailand: Case study of agricultural input and output pricing. Staff Working Paper No. 385. Washington, D.C.; The World Bank.

Cuddihy, B. (1980) Agricultural price management in Egypt. Staff Working Paper No. 388. Washington, D.C.; World Bank.

Currie, J. M.; Martin, J. A.; Schmitz, A. (1971) The concept of economic surplus and its use in economic analysis. Economic Journal, 81, 741-799.

Gotsch, C. H.; Brown, G. T. (1980) Prices, taxes, and subsidies in Pakistani agriculture. Staff Working Paper No. 387. Washington, D.C.; World Bank.

Lutz, E.; Scandizzo, P. L. (forthcoming) Price distortions in developing countries: A bias against agriculture. European Review of Agricultural Economics.

Peterson, W. L. (1979) International farm prices and the social cost of cheap food policies. American Journal of Agricultural Economics, 61 (1) 12-21.

Reca, L. G. (1980) Argentina: Country case study of agricultural prices and subsidies. Staff Working Paper No. 386. Washington, D.C.; World Bank.

Rojko, A.; and others (1978) Alternative Futures for World Food in 1985. Foreign Agricultural Economics Report No. 146. Washington, D.C.; U.S. Department of Agriculture.

Schultz, T. W. (1964) Transforming Traditional Agriculture. New Haven, Connecticut, USA; Yale University Press.

Schultz, T. W. (1977) On economics, agriculture, and the political economy, in Decision-Making and Agriculture (edited by T. Dams and K. E. Hunt). Oxford; Alden Press.

Schultz, T. W. (1978) Constraints on agricultural production, in Distortions of Agricultural Incentives (edited by T. W. Schultz). Bloomington, Indiana, USA; Indiana University Press.

ULG Consultants Limited, in association with Economic Consultants Limited (1977) Yugoslavia: Agricultural prices and subsidies case study. Washington, D.C.; World Bank.

OPENER'S REMARKS--Alois Basler

The authors presume in their model that pricing policies are the main determinants of agricultural output. In the case of developed countries, this assumption is plausible and proved by observations and analyses. In developing countries, however, we find various constraints to the producers' abilities to adjust production programmes to changing market conditions. Increasing producer prices can only stimulate food production and induce income transfers from consumers to producers (as indicated in the model) under certain conditions. Therefore, pricing policies should form a part of a package of measures.

It is plausible to assume that rising producer prices reduce the labour migration from agriculture to other economic sectors in developed countries. In developing countries, however, intersectorial labour migration seems to depend more on real or supposed employment opportunities than on agricultural pricing policies.

For developing countries, the benefits resulting from export taxes largely depend on how these funds are utilized. Evaluation of benefits and costs should therefore include an overall analysis of policies pursued in the countries concerned.

We can draw two lessons for pricing policies from this analysis. First, taking into account that developed countries consume less than they would without protectionism, they should renounce price intervention measures and let price levels fall. This would be desirable for many reasons. However, we are not sure that consumption of agricultural products would rise in a significant way. Here I have in mind that with an average daily consumption of more than 3,000 calories per person, the population of the majority of the developed countries is already overfed.

Second, developing countries, in contrast, consume more than they would without low price policies. Consequently, they should abandon negative protectionism in order to reduce consumption. This result is exactly the opposite of what the respective governments and international organizations concerned are trying to achieve.

I think these controversial findings show the limits of a partial analysis which neglects all problems of income levels and redistribution of both land resources and revenues.

FOOD POLICY ISSUES FOR INDONESIA'S THIRD FIVE YEAR PLAN

Soetatwo Hadiwigeno and Douglas D. Hedley

Abstract

The goals driving food policy in Indonesia have grown out of the experience of the last decade. The predominance of stability in previous plans has shifted to an interest in the equity and distribution concerns in agricultural and food policy. This shift places in very different perspective the opportunities and issues to be faced in the third five year plan. With less rigidity in holding real prices of cereals constant during the next few years, rice prices can be utilized as an instrument for widespread changes in income distribution in Indonesia. Our analysis suggests, however, that considerable caution is needed since large proportions of the population can be made worse off with rises in cereal prices. Furthermore, while it is tempting to pursue outer island crop development opportunities, the soils and the climate dictate that outer island development is fundamentally different than in the case of Java. Different crops, more extensive use of land, and alternative management practices will be needed. The possibility exists of some greater ASEAN cooperation in solving regional food issues in combination with other trade, production, and foreign exchange issues. Programmes to shift consumption from rice to other domestically produced foods may also be desirable. The instruments to achieve such changes may, however, carry certain impacts quite unpalatable for policymakers. Finally, even with the predominance of rice issues in Indonesia's food policy, the impression is gained that while rice related instruments may create massive effects, other instruments may be preferred. Changes in rice related instruments are likely to continue to be small and cautious.

OPENER'S REMARKS--Hisayoshi Mitsuda

Hadiwigeno and Hedley point out the necessity of food policy programmes for the maintenance of social and political stability in Indonesia. Although I fully admit the importance of this point, I would like to suggest that we consider in what ways this programme goal can be achieved; that is, what is the optimum combination of the domestic price and quantity of cereals imported for sociopolitical stability, or, what are the concrete measures needed to shift productive resources and production opportunities to the poorer group of the society? What is the role of policymakers in Indonesia in establishing practical development programmes; in particular, how are they going to get consensus among and support from the poorer groups? It seems difficult to solve the food problems in one country alone. Cooperation among neighbouring countries as well as between developed and developing countries is certainly desirable. As the authors point out, we look for the possibility of ASEAN cooperation in solving regional food issues in combination with trade, production, and foreign exchange issues.

EFFECTS OF INTERSECTORAL TERMS OF TRADE ON AGRICULTURAL OUTPUT

Susumu Hondai

Abstract

Intersectorial terms of trade are regarded as a policy variable which shifts income away from agriculture at an early stage of development. Developing countries had policies which discouraged agriculture, but the results differed widely. This paper hypothesizes that the effectiveness of terms of trade as a policy variable depends on the agricultural employment structure. If the labour force in agriculture is composed of daily contract workers, terms of trade will not work to transfer income.

Japanese data between 1896 and 1939 were uses to investigate the effect of terms of trade on the ratio of nonagricultural to agricultural wages.

The effect is stronger when annual contract wages are used as agricultural wages than when daily contract wages are used. The results imply that the favourable terms to nonagriculture induce labour movement toward nonagriculture and reduce agricultural output when the agricultural labour force consists of daily contract workers. On the other hand, the favourable terms do not induce labour movement very much and do not lower agricultural output when the labour force consists of family and annual contract workers.

From these findings, it can be concluded that if the agricultural labour force consists mainly of daily contract workers, an adjustment of terms of trade in favour of the nonagricultural sector cannot transfer much income to that sector, but it reduces agricultural output. In that case, policymakers have to identify other policy instruments to stimulate the nonagricultural sector without having a disincentive effect on agriculture.

OPENER'S REMARKS--Joseph J. Richter

Hondai did not pursue the consequences of government interference. Manipulation of intersectorial terms of trade can be done only where family farms prevail. Without such an agricultural structure, labour leaves the disadvantaged sector and seeks employment in an industry with higher wages. This reduces the supply of labour (and thus agricultural production) to a level where wages equalize across the economy. In an economy with enhanced labour mobility, a farmer or farm labourer cannot be exploited.

I could not find any explanation for the apparent arbitrariness of the time periods used to estimate the regression coefficients in support of the findings. Nor could I detect how or why the employment structure changed between 1896 and 1939. I expect that the proof of the thesis would be more credible and more generally applicable if a cross section analysis based on studies of comparative economic systems were used.

RAPPORTEUR'S REPORT--Richard F. Bates

The question of how Hondai defined terms of trade was raised. It was stated that if the terms of trade were based on income (the daily contract rates of farm labourers) and not on agricultural prices, then the explanatory strength of his conclusion may be questionable. In the case of India, it was found that over a 20 year period commencing in 1951-52 (using a method similar to Hondai's) the terms of trade between the agricultural and nonagricultural sectors improved in favour of agriculture by approximately 1.4 percent per year. During this same period, the rate of growth of agricultural output averaged approximately 3 percent per year. When output was calculated as a function of the terms of trade (t-1) and technological change, the relationship between output and the terms of trade was negative and not statistically significant. It was argued that technological factors explained the increase in agricultural output. In an economy where there is a relative shortage of agricultural products, the terms of trade may not be construed solely as a determinant of production changes at the aggregate level. For a single crop (sugarcane in India), an improvement in the terms of trade has, however, led to an increase in the area planted to sugarcane and consequently to an increase in the output of sugarcane.

Hondai replied that in calculating the terms of trade he used the average of the nonagricultural commodity output and the weighted average of the agricultural output. He stated that the function represented a reasonable fit and that it gave a good enough indication of how important variables affected the terms of trade and hence the wage rate.

Adjusting the terms of trade may not be the only way of adjusting the wage rates between the two sectors, as the Japanese government has shown by adopting a quota system in the early 1900s. There are many methods which can be used to transfer resources from one sector to another; for instance, the negative pricing policies used during the 1960s in many developing countries. The terms of trade did, however, offer an explanation for resource transfer, although there may be other factors which require further investigation.

Contributing to the discussion was R. Thamarajakshi.

THE MOBILIZATION OF RESOURCES FROM AGRICULTURE:
A POLICY ANALYSIS FOR BRAZIL

Mauro de Rezende Lopes and G. Edward Schuh

Brazil, like many other developing countries, has discriminated rather heavily against its agricultural sector. The chronic overvaluation of the Brazilian currency has constituted an implicit export tax on the agricultural sector. In addition, there have been explicit export taxes, quotas, and embargoes on agricultural products, and complicated export licensing schemes. This discriminatory trade policy has been complemented by various domestic food policies which also attempted to restrain the domestic prices of food.

In contrast, the industrial sector has benefited from high levels of protective tariffs and export subsidies. Moreover, the overvalued exchange rate constituted something of a subsidy to the industrial sector since it was dependent on imports of certain raw materials and critical capital goods.

This combination of policies is clearly designed to capture and transfer the well-known agricultural surplus as a basis for furthering the development process. The research on which this paper is based was designed to make a partial analysis of the impact of these policies on the agricultural sector (see Lopes for the larger study). The analysis compared an overvalued exchange rate and a tax on land as alternative means of extracting the surplus from agriculture. The analytical model was developed along the lines of a model used by Floyd for an analysis of U.S. agricultural policy. It is based on a one sector model of the agricultural sector consisting of six equations: an aggregate production function, equilibrium conditions for the use of labour and capital (input demand equations), supply functions for those two factors of production, and an equation which describes the demand for farm output.

Background

Contemporary policymaking in developing nations has been strongly dominated by the idea that the agricultural sector has abundant resources in terms of both agricultural output and factors of production which can be removed from the sector. According to this perspective, the major source of funds for financing economic development, especially when it starts from a predominantly agricultural base, has to be a net resource flow out of agriculture. This idea has been a key element in shaping economic policy in developing nations.

The policy question has been how best to accomplish this transfer. Historically, many different approaches have been used. In the case of Japan, a land tax played a very important role. In the United States, a great deal of both the capital and labour moved through regular market mechanisms. Countries such as Brazil, on the other hand, have used policies that focused prinarily on product markets. These policies have, in effect, been designed to shift the internal terms of trade against agriculture, and, by this means, have drained resources from agriculture.

This study was an attempt to understand the role of economic policy in the intersectorial transfer of resources between the farm and nonfarm sectors. Its hypothesis is that development policies which focus on extracting the surplus from agriculture primarily through the product markets have had deleterious consequences for agriculture, and have influenced in an important way the general character of development.

The Relevant Theory

Brazil has used a bewildering array of trade interventions in its agricultural sector. In general, these interventions have been designed to keep agricultural products damned up in domestic markets by limiting export markets. By thus shifting the domestic terms of trade, they transfer both agricultural output and resources from the farm to the nonfarm sector.

To simplify the discussion, we can focus on the overvalued exchange rate as a trade intervention. This distortion in the foreign exchange market was an important form of taxation in its own right. Moreover, export quotas and explicit export taxes can be converted to an equivalent form of tax.

An overvalued exchange rate, of course, is an implicit export tax. Under certain conditions, this tax can be shifted to the foreign consumer, as Brazil so effectively did when it was dominant in the international market for coffee. If the small country assumption applies, however, such shifting does not occur, and the incidence of the tax is on the domestic producers, with income being shifted from domestic producers to domestic consumers.

A number of important effects of such a tax can be identified. The domestic price will decline, which in general will cause consumption to increase. There will also be a decline in output, with the amount of the decline dependent on the elasticity of supply. Gross income to the sector will decline, and exports will be reduced. Resources will be released from the export sector to the rest of the economy. Although lost to the export sector, these resources have productive value to other sectors of the economy.

There are also various income transfers, the most notable of which from this study's perspective is a transfer of income from producers to consumers. Producers, in effect, pay a subsidy to consumers, with the amount of the subsidy determined in part by post-tax domestic consumption. An important point about this subsidy is that the government has zero disbursement costs. Moreover, there are no explicit budget costs, with their attendant political difficulties. This subsidy to the wage good sector can be an important stimulus to the nonfarm sector.

Other effects of the tax can be identified, such as a subsidy to domestic importers, and so on. But those already identified illustrate how resources are transferred, both directly and indirectly, from the farm to the nonfarm sector. They also indicate how exchange rate policy can be a means of transferring the surplus from agriculture.

Land taxes can also be an effective means of mobilizing resources from agriculture, as illustrated by the Japanese experience. A tax on the price (Ricardian economic rent) of land will always be borne by the landowner, provided that the tax does not exceed that eocnomic rent. The effect of the tax will be to lower the price of the land. In the Ricardian world, the price of agricultural output will not be affected by the imposition of a land tax. Similarly, there will be no resource allocation effects.

If the assumptions of the Ricardian world are relaxed, there will be some shifting of the tax to workers and owners of capital. There will also be some effect on the price of output. If the tax is greater than the eocnomic rent, the land may be permitted to deteriorate. Under these conditions, the tax will be shifted to the consumer in the long run. Relaxation of the Ricardian assumption of a perfectly inelastic supply of land will also permit shifting—both forward to consumers through higher prices and backward to workers and other supply sectors. Relaxing this assumption seems especially pertinent in land rich Brazil.

Despite these caveats, the presumption is that a land tax will have only limited effects on output, will tend not to be passed on to labour or other resources, and may be at least roughly proportional to asset ownership, depending on how effectively the tax is administered. On the other hand, it is likely to raise the price of agricultural products somewhat, in contrast to the implicit export tax, which tends to lower the price of agricultural output.

Empirical Analysis

The empirical analysis was implemented by means of the reduced form transformation of the six equation structural model. Estimates of the parameters for the underlying model were taken from other studies, or estimated directly. Micro data from a rather large national farm survey were used to estimate the parameters of the production functions and factor shares.

Two main sets of analyses were performed. To evaluate the effect of exchange rate and trade policies designed to shift the internal terms of trade against agriculture, we replaced the demand equation in the model with parametric shifts in the price of agricultural output. The effect of a 10 percent decline in the relative price of agricultural output on resource use and factor returns was then evaluated. This analysis was performed by size of farm, on the assumption that conditions in the factor market differed by size of farm and that therefore there would be a differential effect. The assumption of a 10 percent shift in relative prices due to trade interventions seems quite conservative in the light of the degree of overvaluation over the years and the magnitude of the other interventions. In any case, this assumption is designed to show the relative effect of the export taxes, and does not reflect a judgment about the absolute size of the distortion caused by trade interventions.

To evaluate the effect of the land tax, an estimate was made of what effect the tax would have on the use of land, assuming that in Brazil the supply of land is not perfectly inelastic. This estimate was then introduced into a somewhat different transformation of the structural equations to evaluate the effect on agricultural prices, resource use, and factor returns.

The Empirical Results

Some of the empirical results are summarized in table 1. The results when all farms are pooled together (an aggregate or sectorial result) indicate a differential impact from a shift in the terms of trade on both the level of resource use and on factor returns. The use of capital declines the most, followed by a reduction in employment of labour, and then by a relatively small reduction in the use of land. The effect of factor returns is just the obverse, with the return to land declining the most, followed by a smaller reduction in the wage rate, and a relatively small decline in the return to capital.

TABLE 1. EFFECTS OF A 10 PERCENT SHIFT IN RELATIVE AGRICULTURE
PRICES ON RESOURCE USE AND FACTOR RETURNS, BY FARM
SIZE, BRAZIL

| | R E S U L T I N G | | | C H A N G E | | (P E R C E N T) |
FARM SIZE	EMPLOY-MENT	WAGE RATE	LAND USE	RETURN TO LAND	CAPITAL USE	RETURN TO CAPITAL
ALL FARMS	-18.19	-13.83	- 6.23	-15.77	-26.64	- 3.71
UP TO 4.9 ha.	- 3.25	- 7.23	- 1.66	- 9.08	- 1.01	- 9.59
FROM 5 to 9.9 ha.	- 3.75	- 7.25	- 2.44	-10.56	- 1.05	-11.09
FROM 10 to 49.9 ha.	-24.62	-13.39	- 6.79	-19.01	-25.94	- 2.55
FROM 50 to 99.9 ha.	-22.43	-14.78	- 6.53	-19.74	-23.42	- 3.04
FROM 100 to 499.9 ha.	-25.55	-12.01	-11.09	-21.08	-24.61	- 1.58
FROM 500 to 999.9 ha.	-32.01	-16.36	-14.50	- 6.70	-42.72	- 4.35
OVER 1,000 ha.	-33.62	-17.56	-16.02	- 7.19	-36.42	- 4.88

196

When the results are compared by size of farm, there tend to be relatively strong size relationships. Interestingly enough, for the small farms, the adjustment in capital and land use are relatively small, while the adjustment in employment is relatively larger. The wage rate for labour shows the smallest decline in factor returns of the three input categories, with the decline in the return to land and capital being larger and of about the same order of magnitude.

For the larger farms, the change in employment is larger, and tends to increase with size. The same applies to capital. Land use experiences a small increase, but the adjustment is larger as farm size increases. Once one moves beyond the first two groups by farm size, the relative change in the wage rate is approximately the same. Moreover, it is less than the change in employment.

The decline in the return to land is the largest for the middle size farms. It is smaller for the larger farms, but this is because the elasticity of supply of land is assumed to be relatively large for these two groups. The return to capital declines the least of any of the input categories. Moreover, there is not much of a relationship by sizes of farms.

These results suggest that taxing agriculture by means of an overvalued exchange rate and other trade interventions can have a sizable effect on both the level of resource use and on the returns to factors of production employed in agriculture. Put somewhat differently, the results indicate that such trade interventions can be an effective means to transfer resources from the farm to the nonfarm sector.

The consequences of such resource transfers are far reaching. With a labour transfer of the order of 20 percent of the farm labour force, strong pressures are put on the labour market. A labour transfer of this magnitude requires efficient labour markets. If there are barriers to labour mobility, this may have significant consequences to both wages and the distribution of income. The marginal value product of labour declines by about 15 percent as a direct result of the policy. Labour is in effect undervalued relative to its international opportunity costs. When this effect is combined with the overvaluation of labour in the industrial sector due to the protection of that sector, one begins to understand the large income differential that has emerged between the industrial and agricultural sectors in Brazil.

Land is withdrawn from production up to about 7-11 percent among the middle size farms and between 15-16 percent among the large farms. The implication of this is that in the absence of the policies, Brazil would have been cultivating an area some 10-15 percent larger than it has been. This finding helps explain the underutilization of land common in Brazil. It also explains why land on large holdings tends to be more underutilized relative to land on small farms. In effect, the data suggest that large owners are more able to escape the tax by appropriate resource adjustment. Since they tend to be more dependent on hired labour, they can release the labour, thereby causing the workers to bear the burden of the adjustment. Similarly, they reduce their purchases of modern inputs, thereby passing part of the adjustment on to the nonfarm sector.

To evaluate the effects of the land tax, alternative rates were considered, ranging from 3.45 percent to 15 percent, together with alternative assumptions about the price elasticity of demand for farm output. The results suggest that even with a tax rate as high as 15 percent there would be little increase in the price of agricultural output (1.4 percent when elasticity is -.16). A proper comparison, however, would be with the alternative tax implemented by means of trade policy. Hence, the disparities may be of the order of 10-11 percent of the relative price of agricultural products, a differential that has important income distribution consequences.

The effect of the land tax on returns to capital and labour and on the use of these inputs is quite small. Even assuming a fairly elastic product demand, a land tax of up to 15 percent would lower the returns to capital and labour by only 0.2 and 0.4 percent, respectively. The effect on employment and capital use, although slightly higher, is still negligible.

Concluding Comments

The empirical results show that mobilizing resources from agriculture by means of trade policy has a substantial effect on resource use and factor returns. Mobilizing them by means of a land tax has a much smaller effect on the use and returns to other inputs, even though the total values of the surpluses mobilized were roughly the same.

An important fringe benefit of the results is the insight it offers into why the agricultural development process in Brazil has taken the particular form that it has. The analysis helps explain why labour has migrated from rural areas at such a rapid rate and piled up in the cities. It also helps explain why the farm-nonfarm per capita income differential is so large. And, it also helps explain why land holdings are cultivated so extensively, with the level of utilization so low. Clearly, had Brazil pursued different trade and exchange rate policies, the character of its overall development process would have been quite different, with less concentration of labour in urban centres, a larger agricultural sector, higher relative incomes in agriculture, and more intensively cultivated agriculture.

References

Floyd, J. E. (1965) The effects of farm price supports on the returns to land and labour in agriculture. Journal of Political Economy, 23 (2) 148-158.

Lopes, M. de R. (1977) The mobilization of resources from agriculture: A policy analysis for Brazil. Ph.D. thesis. West Lafayette, Indiana, USA; Purdue University.

OPENER'S REMARKS—Fernando de Faria Estacio

Only the relative effect of export taxes is analyzed, with no judgment about the absolute size of the distortions caused by trade interventions. Also, I have some difficulty in comparing the conclusion in the paper about the adjustment in the use of capital in small farms with the corresponding numbers in table 1. Anyway, the results in table 1 clearly suggest that overvaluation of exchange rates can have important effects on both the level of use and the returns to factors of production in agriculture, and can be an effective way to transfer resources from the farm sector to the nonfarm sector. A land tax, on the other hand, has only a small effect on the use and returns to labour and capital, even though the value of the surplus transferred from agriculture is roughly the same as that mobilized by means of trade policy.

The combination of trade interventions in the Brazilian agricultural sector has been designed, in general, to limit exports of raw agricultural commodities. Brazilian exports of processed agricultural products have increased, however. This suggests the existence of important comparative advantages in Brazilian agriculture. The effects of government intervention on resource use and factor returns identified in the paper make it difficult to introduce technical innovations needed to modernize agriculture and thus cause a misallocation of resources.

RAPPORTEUR'S REPORT—Richard F. Bates

When attempts are made to mobilize labour in developing countries, the number of rural workers diminishes. Before a transfer of people from the agricultural sector to the nonagricultural sector can take place, there should be an increase in productivity of the agricultural sector. The methods of obtaining the increased productivity from agriculture are not accepted by farmers and hence the question arises of appropriate policy measures to obtain the required increase in productivity.

Lopes and Schuh stated that a shift of resources of the magnitude indicated in the paper would not have any impact at all, nor would a shift in the terms of trade unless there were some degree of technical change. There was an implicit assumption of inelasticity of supply of agricultural output. In empirical research, it was found that this assumption was not absolutely correct in Brazil. In the long run, there is a response, and agricultural prices begin to increase, so without technical change there would be an impact on prices and output. There is, however, a necessity for technical change to facilitate a more rapid transfer of resources.

It was agreed that land taxes are an efficient way of transferring resources from the agricultural sector. However, the elasticity of capital was questioned and was thought to be too high. It was assumed that the factor demand was implicit in the function, based on the Floyd model, and that this was a Cobb-Douglas type function. The Cobb-Douglas production function has an extremely high elasticity of substitution which leads to extremely high responses to prices on the demand side of the factor market. The relevance of this fact and of the implied assumption was questioned. Lopes stated that the absolute magnitude of change must be looked at with caution. The importance of the results is the direction and relative magnitude of the change.

The response of large scale farms in Brazil represents a phenomenal shift in the supply of labour. On small farms, a negligible shift was noted. Although the price difference (a 10 percent decline) should have caused the agricultural sector to restrict its supply of goods, it did not.

Contributing to the discussion were M. S. Igben and Samar R. Sen.

ISSUES IN THE EVOLUTION OF FERTILIZER PRICE POLICY

Mohinder S. Mudahar

Abstract

This paper discusses key issues in the evolution of fertilizer price policy and analyzes its role in accelerating the process of agricultural growth, with particular reference to rice in Asia. Rice is the world's most important food crop, and fertilizer is one of the most important inputs to expand rice production. According to preliminary estimates of growth, 37 percent increases in rice output and 62 percent increases in rice yields in Asia from 1965-75 are attributed to fertilizer use.

The empirical evidence from rice growing Asian countries indicates that there exists a strong inverse relationship between the fertilizer-rice price ratio and fertilizer use. Raising prices received by rice farmers and lowering retail fertilizer price can accelereate growth in rice production. However, required incentives must be accompanied by ensured supplies of fertilizer and complementary inputs at the farm level, agricultural research and extension to facilitate a shift in the fertilizer response function, and adequate marketing facilities.

Small farmers, the intended target group, benefit relatively little from existing fertilizer subsidy programmes. Sometimes expenditures on fertilizer subsidies exceed the expenditures on agricultural research. However, relatively little is known about the returns from expenditures on fertilizer subsidies.

Efficiency improvements in fertilizer production, marketing, and use can result in lower retail fertilizer prices without really reducing the incentives for fertilizer producers and dealers, leading to substantial national benefits. For example, doubling nitrogen efficiency for rice in Asia is estimated to have generated additional rice output valued at approximately U.S.\$4 billion during 1965-75.

OPENER'S REMARKS--C. Kenneth Laurent

That the rice price seems to be much more powerful in influencing fertilizer use than the price of fertilizer seems logical since product price encompasses all of the factors a farmer must consider, whereas fertilizer price affects only one.

Mudahar states that fertilizer subsidies can play only a limited role in raising the productivity of small farmers. Since raising the productivity of small farmers is about the only hope for small farmers to improve their level of living, there should be some discussion of ways small farmers can obtain fertilizer.

Mudahar says little is known about the returns to expenditures on fertilizer subsidies. I find this difficult to understand in view of the existing knowledge about yield increases, fertilizer prices, and product prices.

Mudahar has pointed out that the crucial constraint on fertilizer use is its nonavailability at the farm level. Obviously, no matter how much farmers want fertilizer (subsidized or nonsubsidized), they cannot use it if it is not available when they need it. This is a problem that must be considered in developing a fertilizer policy.

Finally, I fully agree that if fertilizer subsidies are established in order to induce fertilizer use generally or for specific crops, these subsidies must be withdrawn gradually to prevent them from becoming built into the system.

RAPPORTEUR'S REPORT--Richard F. Bates

There are difficulties in identifying who should be eligible for fertilizer subsidies, but it is worthwhile to make inputs available to small farmers so that they may have an opportunity to increase their productivity. A price support programme is only relevant to small farmers who have marketable surpluses, however.

There are many factors which determine the production response to fertilizer and these are listed in the paper. Price policy plays a rather limited role if the fertilizer response function tends to be flat. Efforts should therefore be devoted to pushing the response function up so that all the factors alluded to would be included.

With regard to fertilizer subsidies, the author did not state whether he agreed or disagreed with the conclusions reached by other writers, but merely posed a problem which may require further investigation. There are many aspects of both agricultural price policies and fertilizer subsidies which must be carefully considered, especially with regard to their social cost and the distribution of benefits from such policies among producers and consumers. Also, small farmers often do not benefit from fertilizer subsidies because they are frequently not in a favourable position to obtain fertilizer.

Contributing to the discussion was R. Thamarajakshi.

GRAIN SECTOR

R. H. D. Phillips

Introduction

Canada is a very large country, second in land mass to the Soviet Union. Canada covers an area just short of 10 million square kilometres, but only one-third of the land is developed, and occupied farmland represents less than eight percent of the total. The western provinces, where most Canadian grains are produced, are landlocked and most of the area is far from the coast. There is only sufficient growing season for one crop, and the winters are long and severe. Rainfall in the summer is limited and not predictable.

Canada is divided into 10 provinces and two northern territories. The provinces have jurisdiction over their own resources and responsibility for much economic activity and matters such as property rights and education. But, jurisdiction over some economic actvity is divided between the provinces and the national government; for example, agriculture and transportation. The federal government controls external and interprovincial trade.

There is crop and animal production in each of the provinces and territories, but, as might be expected, there is regional concentration of some agricultural activity. The three prairie provinces, for example, account for three-quarters of all agricultural land, and about half of all farmers who grow most of the crops which Canada exports and who generate about half of total farm cash income.

The Importance of Grains to The Canadian Economy

By federal statute, Canada defines grain in terms of six specific crops: wheat, oats, barley, rye, flax, and rapeseed. Maize is increasing in importance and is included along with some other oilseed crops. Grain receives the greatest attention in the three western provinces of Alberta, Manitoba, and Saskatchewan.

Wheat is by far Canada's most important crop, and its production and marketing is one of the major agricultural activities. In recent years, wheat production has exceeded 18 million tonnes, of which more than 17 million tonnes are spring wheat. The spring wheats are produced mainly in the three prairie provinces and the winter wheat in Ontario. Wheat accounts for half of Canadian farm income from all grains and about 20 percent of total farm income. Three-quarters of the wheat crop is exported.

Barley has been traditionally the second most important crop, and although it remains important, rapeseed production now accounts for more revenue in total and is increasing in importance as an export crop. In recent years, Canada has produced 10 million tonnes of barley per year on the average and exported about one-quarter of it.

Rapeseed was introduced into Canada during the Second World War to provide an oil source for marine engine lubrication. In the years since, new varieties and husbandry practices have been introduced which have made rapeseed increasingly important as a source of food and feed food. Rapeseed production averages 1.3 million tonnes. The other oilseed crops (flax, soybeans, sunflower seed, and mustard) together account for about one million tonnes of production. More than half of the total oilseed production is exported.

Coarse grains, including barley, oats, rye, maize, and the mixed grains average 20 million tonnes (slightly more than half is barley), and about 20 percent of the total is exported (barley is the most significant coarse grain export).

Forage crops in recent years have involved about six million hectares of tame hay and annual forage crop production, and another 18 million hectares of pasture lands. Forage production averages 24 million tonnes of tame hay and about 13 million tonnes of fodder maize, all of which is utilized domestically by the

202

livestock industry.

Within Canada, grain and indeed agriculture account for a declining percentage of domestic production, and the number of persons engaged in farming and related industries is declining. Despite the relative decline, the grain sector remains significantly important in terms of the trade balance and in the demands it makes in one form and another on other sectors of the Canadian economy.

Canada's exports have produced an annual average value of $34 billion in recent years. The export value of farm and fish products together accounts for about 12 percent of the total, and wheat and wheat flour account for 45 percent of the farm and fish exports and average six percent of total exports. Barley, oats, and rye account for 10 percent of all farm and fish exports and a bit more than one percent of the total.

Wheat and wheat flour were once Canada's major export commodities, but in more recent years have been exceeded in importance by lumber, newsprint, wood pulp, and more recently by automobiles and auto parts. The exports of most of the alternatives have been mainly to the United States, while exports of wheat, wheat flour, and some of the other grains remain mainly to the rest of the world.

In recent years, Canada has exported about 70 percent of total wheat production and about 20 percent of coarse grain production. In both instances, Canada exports a higher percentage of total production than does the world considered in total. In the last five years, for example, world trade in wheat accounted for 18 percent of world production and world trade in the coarse grains accounted for 11.5 percent of total production.

While Canadian wheat production now accounts for only five percent of world production, trade in wheat and wheat flour accounts for about 20 percent of total world trade in these commodities. Coarse grain production accounts for about three percent of world production and Canadian trade in these grains for about five percent of world trade.

In comparison with most other countries, Canada's grain exports are high. In the last four years, for example, western Europe exported 16 percent of total wheat production, Argentina 44 percent, and the United States 53 percent. Only Australia, among the major exporters, had an export record comparable to Canada's, exporting on average 81 percent of the total.

The Canadian Grain Commission supervises Canada's grain sector, licensing and regulating facilities and quality standards for all grains sold domestically or for export.

In 1935, the federal government established the Canadian Wheat Board as a crown corporation. The Wheat Board is a government directed marketing board, but is financed totally by the grain producers whose crops it markets. Originally it operated only a voluntary pool for wheat, but in 1943, during the Second World War, was given full control over the pricing and marketing of all prairie wheat, an authority it still has. Later the Board took jurisdiction to a lesser degree over oats and barley.

To demonstrate the importance of the role of the Canadian Wheat Board, a brief review of how the Board is involved in the marketing of Canadian wheat will help:

1. The Board establishes price for all Canadian wheat sold for export.

2. It operates pools for the various grains. Under this system, producers receive an initial payment on delivery of their grain and an additional payment or payments based on the average returns realized by the Wheat Board for particular grades.

3. It administers a grain delivery quota system which regulates farmer deliveries to country and mill elevators of wheat and each of the other

major grains (oats, barley, rye, flax, and rapeseed) grown in the prairie area. Every farmer must have a grain delivery permit to deliver grain to the Board.

The Board owns neither grain handling facilities nor sales agencies, but operates through contractual arrangements with Canadian and foreign companies. In the handling of grain within Canada, the agents are four major farmer companies and a number of joint stock companies. These and several others are agents for the Board for export sales.

Conclusions

1. The Canadian system of variety licensing centred on a statutory milling standard has served Canada well through the years and is admired by many exporting countries.

2. The control of the Canadian grading system and of the grain handling industry by the Canadian Grain Commission and its predecessors has provided a guarantee of honesty and quality for Canadian grain producers and assurance of both for grain importers around the world.

3. The central selling agency operated through the Canadian Wheat Board provides a marketing institution which has served Canadian farmers and the world's importers well for more than four decades.

4. Farmer participation through the cooperative associations they have built over the years has given grain producers assurance that they can influence directly the marketing of their grain; support from these cooperatives has strengthened the Canadian Wheat Board and has provided Canadian government negotiators around the world's bargaining tables with home support that few countries can equal.

LIVESTOCK AND POULTRY SECTOR

S. L. Medland

In 1978, farm receipts from the sale of livestock and livestock products, including dairy products, poultry, and eggs were $6.6 billion or 55 percent of total cash receipts from farming operations. The other major contributor was total crops at $4.9 billion or 41.5 percent.

In 1976, a total of 1,045 establishments engaged in one or more of slaughter, meat processing, or processing of poultry or dairy products. They employed a total of 68,318 people and paid wages and salaries of $85 million. The total value of shipments of goods of their own manufacture was $7.4 billion.

Consumption, Imports, and Exports

Most of the output of Canada's livestock and poultry sector goes into domestic consumption. In 1978, per capita consumption of beef was 45.8 kiograms, veal 1.8, pork 26.2, mutton and lamb 0.8, poultry 21.7, butter 4.5, and eggs 18.2 dozen. During the 1970s, per capita consumption of beef has increased while consumption of eggs and butter has declined.

Expenditures for food account for about 15 percent of all personal expenditures on consumer good and services. About 48 percent of the expenditures for food to be prepared at home is on products of the livestock and poultry sector.

In recent years, there has been a very substantial increase in meals eaten away from home. By 1976, the eating place share of total personal food expenditures was 26.6 percent, and some industry sources estimate that it is now 33 percent.

Distribution

Except for the Montreal market for beef where wholesalers have a significant role, most of the food produced by the livestock and poultry sector goes direct from processor to retailer or food service outlet.

Retail stores are the principal source of food for Canadian consumers. Their key function is to make the food available to the consumer in small quantities. Fresh meat is cut and packaged in appropriate sizes and weights and eggs are packed in dozens. Foods already in consumer type packages such as bacon, sliced meats, and dairy products are removed from the shipping cartons or containers, priced, and placed on the shelves for selection by consumers. Some retailers also have their own warehousing, and a number have integrated back into processing of meat and dairy products.

About 60 percent of the food retail business is done by chain stores, including convenience stores. About 26 percent of the business is done by voluntary groups of independents, and the remainder by unaffiliated independents.

The trends in retailing in recent years have been to larger stores, concentration of business in the chains and voluntary groups, and vertical and horizontal integration. The major merchandising tool used by food stores is newspaper advertising of specials to draw customers into the store. No brand name grocery products at lower prices have recently proved to be popular with consumers, but this tool has not been used extensively with products of the livestock and poultry sector.

The food service industry, commonly known as HRI (hotels, restaurants, and institutions), is enjoying remarkable growth. Increased mobility, higher discretionary income, greater leisure, and modern life styles have caused this change. In the fast food outlets, the main livestock and poultry sector products sold are hamburger, steak, and chicken. Supplying the food service industry is a conundrum for Canadian cattle producers. The bulk of fed cattle marketed now carries a moderate but adequate finish for the eat-at-home consumer. The same consumer eating out at a fancy restaurant expects beef with much more finish, which may be imported form the United States. The next day that same person eats at a fast food outlet. The best sources of meat for that market are dairy cow beef, grass fed cattle, or imported boneless beef.

Slaughter and Processing

Operations at the slaughter and processing level for products of the livestock and poultry sector vary considerably in complexity and magnitude. Processing and distribution of milk and other dairy products is complicated. Beef is simple, but volume is very large. Pork is somewhat more complicated than beef, with much processing. Most poultry involves mainly slaughter, and eggs require only selection and packaging.

Dairy products are processed by specialized firms, some owned by large retailers. The highly perishable items such as fluid milk, cream, yougurt, and cottage cheese must be produced and marketed within a matter of days. Butter and cheese are less perishable and can be stored under refrigeration. Milk powder and evaporated milk are shelf stable.

Cattle and calves, pigs, and sheep and lambs are slaughtered in meat packing plants. The slaughtering and processing of red meats is Canada's largest food industry, and in 1976 it ranked fourth among major manufacturing industries in value of shipments. In that year, there were 467 separate establishments, and 33,237 employees. Total wages and salaries were $439 million, and the value of shipments of own manufacture $4.0 billion. In the same year, the value of shipments of own manufacture by each of the three leading industries was: motor vehicles $7.2 billion, petroleum $6.7 billion, and pulp and paper $6.0 billion.

All red meats and poultry meat for interprovincial or international transit must be federally inspected at the place of slaughter and point of origin. Also, the major retailers require that all the meat they buy come from federally inspected operations. Meat inspection is carried out by trained government lay and veterinary inspectors. Meat destined for intraprovincial transit may be inspected under authority of provincial governments.

The evaluation of quality of meat and poultry is routinely done through a grading system administered by the federal government. Additional selection to meet brand specifications is done by the processors.

Cooperatives have an important role in processing of dairy products. In 1977, a total of 113 establishments owned by 52 cooperatives had sales of over $2.2 billion, which represented 60.7 percent of total industry sales of milk and milk products in Canada. In the same year, 11 poultry cooperatives had sales of poultry and eggs of $113 million—22.9 percent of total industry sales. The activities of 21 livestock marketing cooperatives with sales of $8.7 million were confined mainly to the assembly and sale of livestock.

Farmer's Marketing

Except for the marketing of cattle, calves, sheep, and lambs, farmer's marketing in the livestock and poultry sector is largely through marketing boards and agencies under authority of provincial or federal legislation. The primary purpose of such boards and agencies is to improve income and stabilize prices for agricultural producers. Critics of the boards and agencies argue that by their actions some boards tend to reduce supply, cause waste and inefficiencies, and raise prices to consumers.

There is considerable difference in the powers of the various boards and agencies in the livestock and poultry sector. Milk marketing boards determine prices to producers for all milk delivered to market. This directly affects consumer prices. Poultry product marketing boards can set minimum sales prices for producers and establish marketing quotas. The Canadian Egg Marketing Agency sets a national production quota which is shared out to provinces and thence to producers. Pricing is based on a cost of production formula. Pig boards organize pig marketing through teletype or other selling arrangements.

Cattle producers have resisted the trend to marketing boards, and maintain an open system. Canadian beef competes with the United States in the North American market, and price is determined by the larger United States market. Three main channels are used—direct to packers, through public stockyards, and country auctions. Sales direct to packers may be made either on a live weight or rail grade basis using sealed bids or private treaty. Sales thorough public stockyards and country markets are generally by auction, on a live weight basis.

Production

Dairying

Dairying is a major part of Canada's livestock and poultry sector. About 13 percent of all farm receipts are from the sale of dairy products. In the East, they account for over 21 percent. In addition, the dairy herd provides an estimated 25 percent of the beef produced in Canada. As of January 1, 1979, there were 1,870,500 milk cows on Canadian farms.

About 7.7 million tonnes of milk are produced each year. Production is divided into two main types, fluid and manufacturing. Fluid is characterized by high production in large, efficient herds, the latter by generally smaller herds and more seasonal production.

Dairy production is based primarily on forage grown largely on land not generally suited to other crops. Such feed provides for maintenance, replacement, and a modest output of milk. For higher levels of production, grain and supplements of protein, vitamins, and minerals are fed. It has been estimated that each dairy cow uses the output of 0.4 hectares of land for grain crops, 0.8 hectares for pasture, and 1.2 hectares of forage for hay and silage, on the average. The total dairy industry land base is estimated at 5.2 million hectares.

Cattle and Calves

Beef is the largest segment of the Canadian livestock and poultry sector. Farm cash income from sale of cattle and calves in 1978 amounted to $3.0 billion or 24.9 percent of total farm cash receipts. As of January 1, 1979, there were 12,328,000 cattle and calves on Canadian farms.

Canada has a major resource base of rangeland, some 20 million hectares in the West and two million in the East. Seventy to eighty percent of the beef cow herd is maintained in the West. Forage accounts for 80 percent or more of the total feed required for beef cattle. Beef production is an efficient means of converting these forage resources and some agricultural wastes into high quality food products. In addition to the rangelands, an estimated 2.4 million hectares of hay, grass silage, and maize silage, and about 1.6 million hectares of land for cereal production are utilized for producing feed for beef cattle.

Though a significant number of producers have both cow-calf and growing-finishing operations, many tend to specialize. The output of the cow-calf operators is weaned calves of 180-230 kilograms which may be sold as feeders or maintained on a forage programme to go into the feedlot at a later date. The cow-calf segment depends upon inexpensive grazing land and low cost feed.

The bulk of the feeder cattle is produced in western Canada. About 80 percent are finished to market weight in the West. The remainder are either shipped to Ontario for finishing or exported to the Untied States.

Pigs

Pigs provide Canadian farmers with about 9.6 percent of their receipts from the sale of farm products. As of January 1, 1979, there were 7,495,000 pigs on Canadian farms. Historically, a large proportion was produced on relatively small mixed farms, providing an efficient market for home produced grains and a source of income. A growing percentage are now produced by large, specialized operations which buy the bulk of their feed requirements.

The three to four year production and price cycle is a major feature of the industry. As in beef, the cycle is related to lags between price and production changes, but is shorter due to the relative ease of expanding or contracting proudction. The cycles tend to be more erratic because in addition to the North American market influence, pig production is strongly affected by the market for barley in western Canada.

Feed grain is the major input used to produce pigs. Barley is the main feedgrain used, except in Ontario where it is maize. In 1978, pigs consumed the equivalent of about 3.3 million tonnes of barley from 1.4 million of hectares of land, and protein equivalent of 0.6 million tonnes of soybeans from another 0.4 million hectares. A large proportion of the protein supplement used is imported from the United States.

There are three main types of pig enterprises in Canada. Weaner pig producers specialize in selling weaned pigs (at about 18 kilograms and 2 months of age) to producers who specialize in feeding market pigs (about 95 kilograms and 5-6 months old). The third group, a large number of smaller and some large operators are farrow-finish operators.

During the early 1970s, western Canada enjoyed a boom in pig production due primarily to the abundant supplies of low cost feedgrain. In recent years, there has been a sharp reduction in the West, and increases in the East. The factors favouring increases in the East appear to be lack of alternative opportunities for intensive agriculture, proximity to major markets, availability of maize as feed, and, in Quebec, the absence of a marketing board. The latter permits feed manufacturers and packers to contract for pigs and gives them an incentive to make inputs of capital and management expertise.

Poultry

Poultry and eggs are an important source of farm income, accounting for about 7 percent of cash receipts from the sale of farm products. Poultry is almost completely dependent on cereals and protein for feed. The annual feed requirement is about 1.5 million tonnes of barley and 450,000 tonnes of soybean meal, equivalent to the production of one million hectares of land. About three-quarters of this is produced in Canada, the remainder (mostly soybean meal) is imported from the United States.

Poultry production is highly specialized with primary breeders, hatcheries, flock suppliers, and producers of started pullets, chicken broilers, turkeys, and waterfowl. The trend for some years has been to fewer producers with those remaining becoming larger and much more efficient. Entry into the business is becoming more difficult due to high investment costs for land and buildings, environmental laws, and difficulty in getting production quotas from marketing boards.

Sheep and Lambs

Sheep production in Canada has suffered a marked decline since 1950. It contributes only about 0.1 percent of cash receipts from the sale of farm products. As of January 1, 1979, there were 420,800 sheep and lambs on Canadian farms.

Sheep and lamb production uses about 282,500 tonnes of hay or equivalent in feed or pasture. Sheep compete with beef cattle for feedstuffs and grazing land, and are considered to be competitive in initial investment and potential return. Approximatley 60 percent of Canadian sheep production is in the West due primarily to the availability of feed at reasonable cost.

Observations

Canada's livestock and poultry sector enjoys the advantage of large land areas suitable only for pasture, particularly in the West, and large supplies of barley in the West and maize in Ontario. Production technology and knowhow compare favourably with those of other major producing countries. Disadvantages include price and income instability due to cycles and fluctuations in feed supply and costs, the relatively small domestic market of under 24 million people, a long expensive haul to market for much of the product, and a relatively harsh climate which adds to costs of production and distribution. The net result is that the sector, providing it remains competitive with the United States, will continue to grow and prosper with the general economy, but, except in times of feedgrain surplus, Canada is unlikely to be a major exporter of livestock and poultry products.

HORTICULTURAL AND SPECIAL CROPS SECTOR

Robert W. Anderson

Introduction

Canada's horticultural and special crop production is limited to a few areas of the country which enjoy favourable micro climates. These include the Okanagan Valley of Southern British Columbia, parts of Southern Ontario, especially the Niagara Peninsula, and small areas in Quebec and the Atlantic Provinces (New Brunswick, Nova Scotia, and Prince Edward Island). Approximately 302,000 hectares—about 1.2 percent of Canada's improved land area—are in fruit and vegetable crops. In terms of farm receipts, these crops generate about $600 million annually. In addition, special crops such as tobacco, sugarbeets, dry beans and peas, buckwheat, mustard, maple products, and honey annually contribute about $265 million from approximately 242,000 hectares. In total, horticultural and special crops contribute about 11 percent of total Canadian farm receipts, as well as providing considerable employment in processing, distribution, and retailing. The industry produces almost one-half of the fruits and two-thirds of the vegetables consumed in Canada. It also produces two-thirds of Canadian sales of ornamentals. Tobacco production is more than sufficient to meet domestic consumption.

Production

About 37,000 Canadian farms (10 percent of the total) are involved in horticultural products. Of these, 40 percent produce fruit and 60 percent vegetables. Approximately 93,000 persons are employed in the primary sector including 5,500 temporary workers largely from the Caribbean and Mexico. Tobacco production provides an additional 30,000-35,000 seasonal jobs during the harvesting period in August and September.

Canada is self-sufficient in the production of applies and potatoes. An annual average apple production of 400,000 tonnes places Canada among the top ten major producing countries. Annual potato production of 2.4 million tonnes place Canada among the major potato producing countries of the world.

Although perhaps surprising to many visitors, Canada produces such crops as peaches, cherrries, apricots, and grapes in quantity. These crops are confined to the Niagara Peninsula and Essex County in Ontario and to the Okanagan Valley in British Columbia. While not able to supply all of Canada's requirements for these commodities, the domestic industry is an important source of freshly harvested produce. Canada also has developed a substantial seed potato export industry based in New Brunswick and Prince Edward Island. With the continued introduction of new varieties and improved production and marketing practices, Canada's seed potato industry anticipates an expanded export market.

Over 48 percent of the value of Canada's horticultural production originates in Ontario. Quebec and British Columbia, while much smaller producing regions, also have substantial horticultural activity. Apples, raspberries, and tender fruits (peaches, pears, plums, and cherries) are major crops in British Columbia, while potatoes, apples, and blueberries are major eastern Canadian crops. Canada produces two-thirds of the limited world supply of maple products, mostly in Quebec. Canada's tobacco industry (over 113,000 tonnes in 1978, green weight) is concentrated in Ontario, with Quebec and the Maritimes producing small amounts. Many Canadian visitors are surprised to learn that Canada is a net exporter of tobacco.

In western Canada, honey is an important crop with rising production (30,000 tonnes in 1978) and exports. Mustard is also becoming an important crop in the prairie provinces with approximately 100,000 hectares planted annually. Buckwheat at one time was grown principally in eastern Canada, but production is now concentrated in Manitoba.

Market Structure and Marketing

Most primary production units in horticulture are family farms. There are, however, a number of individual, large corporate farms and large farms operated by processing firms. Both private and corporate producers have associations to represent their interests with the government and the public.

The Canadian fruit and vegetable marketing system includes direct to consumer farm sales, open wholesale markets, negotiated prices, contracted prices, and commission sales. All are used to varying degrees for most commodities. Florist products are marketed directly by producers to retailers, wholesale commission houses, chain store operators, auctions, or directly to the public. At the retail level, mass merchandising of flowers in traditional and chain stores has become a new marketing system with its full potential yet to be realized.

Intermediaries in the market structure for fruit and vegetables are 35 provincial marketing boards, 860 wholesalers, 51 food brokers, 140 farmer's markets, 3 auctions, 62 cooperatives, 26,216 food stores, 3,221 chain stores, and 19,140 independent stores.

Cooperative producer marketing is a major factor in both the horticultural and special crops industries. Annual sales of fruit and vegetable cooperatives are close to 12.5 percent of total Canadian sales with 17 British Columbia cooperatives accounting for two-thirds of the total. Cooperative sales of honey and maple syrup are also important.

The producer marketing boards involved in marketing horticultural and special crops have a variety of powers which range from negotiation only to full agency powers under which boards take title to the product and handle all sales. Some boards can set prices while others only promote the product. Every province has legislation and a controlling body to regulate the operation of marketing boards.

Producer marketing boards have been widely adopted in Canada under provincial legislation, beginning as far back as 1929. When a provincial marketing board is established, all producers of a certain minimum size are bound by the regulations established by the board. Major objectives include maintaining or increasing incomes, stabilizing production, and standardizing the terms of sale. The British Columbia Tree Fruit Marketing Board and the Ontario Flue-Cured Tobacco Growers' Marketing Board are two of the better known full agency boards. Of the 35 horticultural and special crops marketing boards functioning in Canada, 9 are for fruit, 14 for vegetables, 6 for tobacco, 1 for dry beans, and 1 for honey.

Technology and Research

Technologically, Canada's horticultural and special crops industry has benefited from new varieties, better insect, disease, and weed control, improved equipment, and mechanical harvesting. Canadian plant breeders have produced a productive variety of strawberry for Canadian growers (Redcoat), a new variety of apple which is suitable to Canadian conditions (Spartan), and new peach varieties adapted to Canadian climatic conditions. Better grading equipment, storage facilities, and qualitative instruments have assisted in improving product quality. Improved storage techniques, notably controlled atmosphere storage for apples and jacketed storage for carrots, have allowed producers to extend their marketing season considerably.

The greenhouse industry, especially the floriculture segment, practices a high level of technology. Controlled growing environments, wide use of chemical growth regulators, tissue culture for virus control and plant propagation, and precise maintenance of soil fertility levels are the key technological factors. Canada's virus free programmes have also assisted in propagating crops such as berries, grapes, and cherries.

Canada's horticultural industry has become increasingly mechanized in recent years as a replacement for more costly or unavailable seasonal labour. Harvesting, weeding, thinning, grading, and packaging have all been assisted by mechancial or chemical technology.

Government Assistance Programmes

There are few government programmes specifically designed for horticultural and special crops. The federal government has had a fruit and vegetable storage construction financial assistance programme since December 1973. This programme assists producer groups in constructing or modifying specialized storage facilities for fruits and vegetables. Modest tariff and anti-dumping regulations protect domestic producers of fruits, vegetables, and honey from low priced imports during the marketing season for the domestic product.

Other more general programmes which apply to the horiticultural sector include a federal market development programme to expand or improve markets for Canadian products. This programme has assisted in determining consumer requirements for apples, and in promotion of raspberry, fresh fruit, and vegetable consumption. The Agricultural Stabilization Act provides price stabilization for agricultural commodities during periods of market stress. Under this programme, price supports for horticultural products are generally provided at 90 percent of the previous five-year average return, with an adjutment for increased production costs.

Considerable government assistance in the form of research and advisory services is provided to the fruit and vegetable industry by the federal and provincial governments. The areas of research include the development of virus free fruit and vegetable stocks by federal research stations, while provincial extension services provide producers with information on husbandry practices. General market outlook information is provided by both levels of government.

Competitiveness

Canada is competitive in season for most cool climate fruits and vegetables, particularly in the fresh market. Total product disappearance, however, is increasing more rapidly than domestic production, and, as a result, imports are taking a large share of most expanding markets. Canada continues to retain a large share of some of the storage vegetable market, especially for onions, carrots, and cabbage. Despite a certain degree of inefficiency resulting from small production units, Canada's best production areas have costs comparable to those of the United States. Crop yields are also generally equal, except tender fruits which generally do not yield as well in Canada as in California, Australia, or South Africa. Some apple producing areas (for example, the Okanagan Valley of British Columbia) are also at a disadvantage because of higher labour and land costs and lower crop yields than in the northwestern United States. In recent years, Canadian imports of apples have surpassed exports.

Mushrooms and greenhouse tomatoes are relatively expensive to produce in Canada and consequently face stiff import competition. Since canned mushroom imports are very competitive, Canada's mushroom industry now concentrates entirely on the fresh market. Greenhouse vegetable production experiences stiff competition from both field grown imports and early domestic production. Cut flower imports have increased in recent years, forcing a shift in domestic production to potted plants.

Raw cane sugar is Canada's largest import item in the horticultural and special crops product line, supplying about 90 percent of the country's annual sugar disappearance. Production of sugarbeets is concentrated in Manitoba and Alberta, which benefit from the high transportation cost of the competing product.

Canada's horticulture and special crop exports, while usually priced above those of most competitors, have a very good reputation for quality on world markets. Canada's northern climate, which limits the number of commodities produced, can result in a high quality for those commodities which can be produced. Tobacco is the most important export item. Blueberry exports have increased in both volume and value as Canadian production increases and world markets have expanded. Fresh apple exports are a major factor in marketing the domestic crop each year. A north-south trade in potatoes between Canada and the United States results in a significant volume of trade although the net result in terms of exports is relatively minor. Canada sells into the eastern United States while the United States sells to all of Canada when Canadian stocks are down.

Industry Structure

There are about 500 plants, employing about 38,000 persons, processing horticultural food products in Canada. In 1978, approximately 300 of these plants were registered for interprovincial and international trade and about 100 of them pack only for local or regional distribution within their own provinces. Another 100 plants produce partially processed products, such as chilled fruits and fresh cut potatoes for restaurants and institutions. There are 14 plants making Saratoga style potato chips, two major distilleries making fruit liqueurs, 31 wineries, and several cideries.

The majority of registered fruit and vegetable processing plants are located in Ontario (148) and Quebec (71), followed by British Columbia (53), the maritimes (48), and the prairie provinces (11). Ontario and Quebec supply approximately 65 percent of the Canadian processed food products market.

The processors obtain raw products in a number of ways including the open market, contracting, and producing some of the raw product themselves. Most vegetables are purchased on a contract basis either through marketing boards or individual growers. Imported raw products are usually purchased by processors on the open market.

Over one-quarter of Canadian fresh fruit and vegetable production is processed to some degree before sale to the consumer. The processing includes canning, freezing, dehydrating, and producing of a variety of products using fruits and vegetables as major ingredients. Basic fruit and vegetable products (canned and frozen fruits, vegetables, and juices) comprise about 40 percent of industry shipments, while formulated and other products (soups, baked beans, and frozen specialities) make up the balance.

Canada imports a large quantity of processed fruit products, especially canned juice and juice concentrate. Even so, domestic fruit processing is not expanding, except for blueberries and apple products. Fruit exports are mainly frozen blueberies, raspberries, and apple products.

Vegetable products imported are mainly canned tomato products, canned mushrooms, dried vegetables, and preserved vegetables for reprocessing. Vegetable processing continues to expand slowly in products other than these. Fresh asparagus is imported in substantial volume for processing. Exports include frozen vegetables (mainly potatoes and sweet corn), canned sweet corn, peas, and asparagus, dried potato products, infant foods, and frozen prepared dinners.

Many imported products continue to gain an ever larger share of the domestic market, as shown by the following data:

Imported Commodity (Canned)	1963-67	Percent of Market 1974-75	1977
Carrots	2.8	27.4	33.3
Mushrooms	12.4	59.0	84.1
Tomato paste	72.0	95.3	93.5
Apricots	45.6	73.0	80.1
Peaches	52.7	79.5	82.7
Pears	17.0	31.9	40.2

Imports of these six products, all producible in Canada, have sharply increased their share of the Canadian market since 1963-67.

Technology

In recent years, the introduction of new machines for washing, peeling, blanching, and other preparation functions have reduced the volume of waste water, improved the quality of the product, and increased labour productivity. Water consumption has been reduced by reusing water and by replacing flume transfer with mechancial transfer. New blanchers and precook or partial cook machines have economized both energy and water use. Continuous pressure cooking and freezing facilities for fruits and vegetables allow for storage and initial handling in bulk lots. Yearround packaging activity is also scheduled in order to optimize the use of warehouse space, labour, and marketing. New types of containers such as polyethylene cans, two piece cans, drawn steel cans, and laminated pouches are under development. The industry is receptive to technolgoical changes and has introduced many improvements in recent years.

Government Programmes

The principal legislation supportive of the processing sector is the protection provided under the anti-dumping tariff measures. These measures provide that duties may be levied when imports have been found to be causing or threatening to cause serious injury to Canadian industry. While few cases occur, one example is that dumping of foreign apple juice concentrate was found by the Anti-Dumping Tribunal in January 1972 to be causing serious injury to Canadian apple producers and processors. Imports of canned mushrooms, cherries, and canned tomatoes have also been controlled by this legislation.

The federal Agricultural Products Board Act empowers the Agricultural Proudcts Board under Cabinet direction to assist in the marketing of processed food products of domestic origin which are in oversupply by buying, storing, selling, and distributing agricultural products. While not active every year, this programme has assisted in marketing such processed products as sour cherries, grape juice, canned solid pack apples, and Kieffer pears.

Trends and Prospects in the Industry

Consolidation, vertical integration, and contract processing are all increasing. There has been a decrease in the number of Canadian processing plants in recent years but the average capacity has increased. While the multinational firms continue to purchase plants in Canada, there is a trend toward other Canadian firms processing under contract for major retail chains.

A major review of Canada's fruit and vegetable tariff structure has been completed with a number of major recommendations implemented. Before this review, the existence of many parts of the industry was threatened, but now producers and processors look forward to growth and expansion.

Transportation facilities for perishable commodities are inadequate and expensive because of the long distances and thin population distribution in Canada. Increased energy and equipment costs will necessitate a reappraisal of present marketing strategies by the industry. More consideration will have to be given to choosing specific markets and forms of packaging to meet these new constraints. While improved transportation often results in more competition from other countries, the rising costs of energy will make domestic products, especially local products, more price competitive.

Canada's horticultural and special crops industry will devote more time and effort in the near future to expanding exports and replacing imports where profitable to do so, especially for such commodities as blueberries, raspberries, tobacco, honey, dried beans, and seed potatoes.

STABILIZATION POLICIES

A. W. Wood

Agriculture is one of the least stable Canadian industries with respect to product prices, the volume of production of many products, and the net incomes received by farmers. Each of these aspects of instability has negative impacts on the income and financial security of farmers as well as on the rest of the economy. Price instability irritates many consumers. Variation in volume of output affects employment levels and unit costs in those industries handling agricultural products. Variation in farm income has similar effects on farm supply firms and consumer goods and service industries in predominantly agricultural regions.

Sources of Instability

Instability in agriculture is not peculiar to Canada, but three elements in the Canadian environment help to make it a more serious problem than in many countries. A large part of the production base is located in a region where the annual rainfall is low and the growing season short. Crop yields over large areas are subject to wide variations even with small variations in the amount, geographical distribution, and timing of seasonal rainfall. Delays in seeding due to excessive moisture lead to risk of crop damage from early frost, and, in some cases, to diversion of land to shorter season crops or to noncrop uses for the entire year.

Dependence on export markets for a large part of its wheat production exposes the Canadian industry to the instabilities inherent in being a marginal or supplemental supplier to countries seeking to shield their own producers from the impact of demand-supply imbalances in world markets. The effect on Canada is a great degree of variability in wheat prices, volume of sales, or both.

Much of Canada's agricultural industry is located at great distances from ultimate markets for its products. Relatively heavy transportation charges leave relatively small margins per unit of output to producers. Large scale production and controlled domestic transportation rates have kept the wheat industry viable but subject to highly variable net returns with even moderate swings in world wheat prices.

A fourth cause of instability is the commodity cycle, particularly for cattle and pigs and, until recently, the poultry industry. Unlike the first three causes, cycles are not an unavoidable consequence of the physical environment and are therefore more subject to control through government measures.

Measures to Protect Producers from Instability

Canadian governments have attempted to cope with problems of depressed or unstable farm incomes arising from each of these major causes. The main thrust of the attack on crop yield variability has been the provision of heavily subsidized crop insurance programmes. A number of measures have been aimed at helping the wheat industry to cope with the vagaries of the export market. The establishment of the Canadian Wheat Board was central among these. The Board has attempted to moderate swings in price by utilizing buffer stocks and restricted delivery mechanisms. One of the effects was to exchange variation in sales volume for variation in price at a probable loss in aggregate income and possibly an actual decrease in the stability of net farm incomes. Several supplementary programmes involving substantial subsidies, including public funding of the storage of excess grain stocks, were found to be necessary to help producers cope with the delayed income effects of the delivery quota restrictions. All programmes combined did not significantly increase the stability of wheat producer incomes.

216

The major policy measure designed to shield wheat producers from the possible crippling effect of an increase in transportation charges on the narrow producer margins was the establishment of statutory freight rates on wheat destined for export. Rates were frozen at levels set in 1897, and with minor exceptions have been maintained at that level ever since. The rates currently cover less than 30 percent of the total cost of transporting wheat to ocean ports. A new policy is now being urgently sought because the railway system is losing its capacity to provide an efficient and effective service. During the years these rates have been in effect, producers of wheat (and other grains) have received substantially higher net incomes from the sale of grain than they would have received otherwise, but the policy has not contributed directly to the stabilization of producer incomes.

Measures to cope with cyclical as well as seasonal and episodic price fluctuations have included a series of price support and price stabilization programmes beginning after World War II. A brief review of these programmes will illustrate the gradual evolution of policy measures specifically designed to stabilize prices, incomes, or both.

Though producers and policymakers have long recognized the problems of instability, they have never managed to clarify their objectives when formulating policies for the assistance of agriculture. The causes of instability have not been clearly understood and measures adopted have not always been the appropriate means to increase stability.

Producers, in fact, have always focused their attention on the price level. Most policy measures have been directed at price even when maintaining a certain price level resulted in lower sales, less stable incomes, and uneconomic shifts of resources which extended instability to other commodities. Continued emphasis on price reflects the fact that producers have apparently not considered stabilization as a primary goal. Their prime objective has always been to raise prices, and they have never been interested in redistributing income over time. They deplore instability only as evidenced by low yields or price declines; they welcome it in the form of bumper crops and price increases.

Price stability has frequently been specified as a producer goal by farm organizations and as an objective in agricultural policy measures. It has, however, seldom been reflected in the policy instruments chosen or in the way policies hve been administered. Until recently, all price policies have been of the support type with no tie to costs or income. They have contributed little to stability and then only incidentally. Producer criticisms of these policies have been directed mainly at the inadequate level of support, not at the failure to achieve stability.

Pricing policies adopted by producer cooperatives and producer marketing boards have usually been directed at the objective of raising prices or maximizing it at all times, rather than stabilizing it. Efforts made to maintain price levels by storing products or restricting output may have succeeded in achieving higher prices at the expense of lower incomes in the long run, and perhaps even in the short run. The only instrument directly affecting stability has been the pooling device which eliminates the short term fluctuations in prices received by producers. But, pooling has been adopted only in cases where it proved to be a necessary adjunct to the operation of a centralized selling system. It has permitted agencies to adopt selling strategies, including multiple pricing, without risking the alienation of individual producers whose products do not receive the highest price.

Canada has attempted to influence the price of wheat by giving very strong support to the efforts to establish and renew international agreements and by withholding part of the Canadian supply to avoid putting downward pressure on prices. Stocks have been allowed to accumulate to very high levels while some competitors increased their sales. Though some price stability may have resulted, it was sometimes at the cost of greater income instability. The

Canadian government has guaranteed a floor price for wheat each year for 45 years but has seldom had to implement the guarantee. That policy has reduced uncertainty in some degree but has not contributed directly to income stability.

Federal Price Support Programmes

Government support of prices of products other than wheat began under the Agricultural Prices Support Act of 1944. The objective was to protect farmers from possible price collapse during the post-war transition period and to compensate them for price ceilings imposed on farm products during the war. Prices were supported by means of deficiency payments at the discretion of an appointed Board which did not apply a known formula in its decisons. Stabilization was not an objective. Expenditures were moderate--$100 million in 12 years, mostly related to the closing of the U.S. market during a brief outbreak of food and mouth disease in 1952.

Stabilization was the first listed objective of the Agricultural Stabilization Act (ASA) of 1958 which superseded the Prices Support Act. No provisions were made for moderating price peaks, but deficiency payments were provided which did moderate the depths of price troughs. This contributed indirectly to stability of price, while a purchase, storage, and resale programme had a more direct impact on seasonal instability. A 12 month advance commitment of support levels gave some assurance relative to minimum gross returns and may have had some effect on the stability of production. If any, it would have been largely limited to the dairy industry to which 88 percent of the $2.3 billion of support was given up to 1977.

The ASA provided for the mandatory support of the prices of nine major commodities at no less than 80 percent of the previous 10 year average price. Other products could be designated for support at discretionary levels. Except for dairy products, support given was minor in degree and contributed almost nothing to price or income stabilization.

The 80 percent support level provided no support until prices dropped to extremely low levels. Even a moderate rate of inflation of 2 percent per year would let the support base lag behind the general price level by 10 percent. With the high rate of inflation betwene 1970 and 1975, the 10 year base price became virtually irrelevant. Rapid escalation of farm costs left many producers exposed to very serious losses for extended periods when price supports for their products lagged behind the increases in costs. The inadequacy of price alone as a basis for protecting farmers from adverse market conditions was finally demonstrated conclusively.

Provincial Stabilization Schemes

Amendments to ASA were clearly needed, but, before they were finally introduced in 1975, most of the provincial governments had entered the price and income support field. Some provinces passed acts which provided for support for a wide range of farm products, while others enacted legislation for the support of a single product. All provincial plans provided for support to cover part or all of the current cash costs of production, and most of them covered part or all noncash costs, including return on investment and an allowance for operator labour and management. Most of the provincial programmes provided for producer contributions to cover part of the actuarial cost, usually between one-third and one-half, and provided for higher levels of support than the federal programme had ever provided, usually between 95 and 100 percent of the support level, based on current costs. Most of the provincial programmes operated on a voluntary basis and involved financial cost sharing by producers and government. Most of them placed a limit on the amount of support given to an individual producer, though the limits varied from province to province. The programmes differed in so many features that it is difficult to compare their cost-benefit ratios, the degree of subsidy involved or the relative effect on price, income, and production stability. They all involved the potential to make production more profitable in one province than in another.

One of the first provincial stabilization and support measures was the British Columbia Farm Income Assurance Act of 1973 under which several commodities are covered by voluntary programmes. Originally, producers contributed one-third of the actuarial cost and payments covered 75 percent of the amount by which the market price failed to cover cost of production. All costs were covered including cash costs, depreciation, interest on capital items, and a return to family labour and management. Cost estimates were developed in consultation with the British Columbia Federation of Agriculture. The program paid out $89 million to 5,600 producers in four years, an average of approximately $15,900, of which producers contributed about $3,400 in premiums. The cost of production figures were reported to be unrealistically high. It was reported that the price of fluid milk quotas had increased from $35 to $97 in three years, indicating that producer earnings were excessive.

The plan was amended in 1978 to place a ceiling of $15,000 on annual payments to an individual producer. Returns on investment in land and the management fees were removed from the cost of production calculations and the final decision on changes in the formula was reserved to the government. Coverage was increased to 100 percent and producer contributions to one-half the actuarial cost.

Quebec enacted the Farm Income Stabilization Insurance Act in 1975. The provisions fo the act were similar to those in the British Columbia Act. Some of the programmes are designed to guaranteee the average producer a return to labour and equity capital equal to 90 percent of the annual income of a skilled worker. It is reported that the government hopes to stimulate an expansion in agricultural production in Quebec, particularly of commodities of which Quebec is a large importer.

The Manitoba Beef Producers Income Assurance Plan, established in 1975, provided support for beef cow-calf producers whose product had never been supported under the federal act. The Plan offered five year voluntary contracts to cow-calf operators, guaranteeing them full cost of production for an efficient producer, including interest on half the invested capital. There was an upper limit of 70 cows on the size of operation covered, and the producer agreed to market an increasing proportion of the output as finished cattle, also at a guaranteed price which would cover production costs. There was to be no producer contribution to cost unless the market price rose above the support price during the five year period of the contract, in which case the excess over cost became payable to the fund up to the point where all payments received under the programme had been repaid with interest.

The Manitoba programme guaranteed a calf price of 57 cents per pound in the first year, approximately double the market price of 29 cents. The government expended $38.8 million in the first three years of the programme and has written off about $10 million paid to 1,400 producers who opted out in order to join the federal plan, and who were then not required to repay the funds received. Since prices have risen well beyond the support level in the last two years, part of the funds advanced will be recovered, although the enforceability of the payback requirement has not yet been fully established.

The federal act was amended in 1975 to provide a formula for support more favourable than 80 percent of the 10 year average. The minimum support level for specific commodities was raised to 90 percent. The averaging period for the support base was reduced to five years and the support level determined by the new formula was adjusted by the amount of increase in production costs in the current year over the average cost in the base period. These three changes raised the pig price support level for 1975-76 from $27.18 per cwt to $46.44, an increase of 70 percent. The new support level was still far below the current market price of $70, so the programme had no immediate effect on the price level or stability.

By 1975, several provincial programmes were in effect which guaranteed higher levels of support than the new federal 90 percent level. The provincial schemes had multiple objectives which included the enhancement of farm incomes, the expansion of provincial output, and, to a lesser degree, the stabilization of prices and incomes. They all involved a substantial amount of subsidy, and, since the degree of subsidization varied between provinces, there was concern that separate provincial programmes would distort regional production incentives and erode the economic unity of the country. Several provinces are now willing to vacate the field, but only if federal programmes provide an adequate level of support.

Federal Income Stabilization Policy

The federal government enacted the Western Grain Stabilization Act (WGSA) in 1976. It was the first programme directed at support and stabilization of income rather than price. It was the first scheme in which prices are not included in calculating the level of support except as a factor in determining income. It was the first scheme to include several commodities in a single support guarantee and thereby avoid the risk that the prospect of future payouts would induce producers to shift resources from one crop to another.

The WGSA involved a new approach to support and stabilization, some features of which may soon be extended to other commodities. New federal programmes may replace most of the provincial programmes. The main features are:

1. The Act is regional in application, covering the area where grain marketing is largely under the jurisdiction of the Canadian Wheat Board. National coverage would probably be feasible, but the western grain industry operates under different conditions than that of other regions and has been treated separately under programmes with different objectives almost from the time it was first established. The new programme is not likely to interfere with location incentives between regions. In any event, the subsidies involved are largely offset by subsidies to producers elsewhere under different types of programmes.

2. The programme covers the aggregate net cash income from seven major crops grown in the western region. No single crop is supported separately, so that the amount of subsidy received does not inhibit market induced shifts from one crop to another.

3. The plan guarantees that the aggregate net cash income received by producers of the seven grains, after all cash costs of production are paid, will not fall below 100 percent of the average margin received during the previous five years. The margin above cash costs, which is thereby stabilized, contains the returns on long run investments, operator labour, and management. That margin varies mainly with the selling price and volume of sales, both of which reflect market conditions rather than variations in supply. The programme is not designed to protect producers from the effects of low yields, but subsidized all risk crop insurance programmes already cover production risks. The plan involves a significant amount of subsidy that will raise the level of long run profitability of producing the crops covered but does not guarantee that the level will be maintained.

4. Participation in the plan is voluntary on an opt-out basis. Participants

contribute 2 percent of gross receipts from the sale of the seven commodities up to a maximum of $25,000 per year. The federal government contributes twice the amount collected from producers and pays all administrative costs. Making the plan voluntary was essential to insure that it would be acceptable to most producers. There would clearly have been strenuous opposition to a compulsory plan, even though the cost-benefit ratio to producers is three to one. One-quarter of all producers have opted out and participation has not increased, though the actual payout in the first three years has been three times as great as producer contributions.

5. Payments are made to participants in proportion to their contributions to the fund during the current and two previous years. The maximum level of contributions allowed automatically limits the benefits received by individual producers. Hence, only a small part of the net income flow of producers with average sales in excess of $100,000 per year is covered. The limit of contributory sales has recently been raised to $45,000 per year, a level necessary to achieve the objective of bringing potential coverage up to 90 percent of total eligible sales. This will raise the maximum annual levy to $900 per year and the actuarial value of the expected payout to $2,700 per year, of which $1,800 would represent a subsidy. The Act might have provided for optional additional coverage for producers with sales above $25,000 with a reduction in the level of subsidy, by stages, to zero at a prescribed level such as $100,000. This would have provided some indication of the willingness of producers to trade an unstable income for a stable income of the same magnitude.

No other commodities have yet been brought under stabilization programmes similar to WGSA. The other federal programmes are still on an individual commodity basis, the minimum support level is 90 percent, and they are noncontributory. Several provincial programmes are contributory and provide support at the 100 percent level, but they include some noncash costs. The inclusion of allowances for returns to labour, management, and invested capital involves arbitrary decisions regarding what the returns to these factors should be, which ones should be included, and what proportion of the standard returns should be guaranteed.

Harmonization of Provincial and Federal Programmes

The array of present programmes does not conform to the principle of a uniform level of support across the country. There is a risk of distorting resource allocation to different commodities within provinces, and between provinces for individual commodities. There is a danger of a competitive escalation of support levels if provinces continue to operate support programmes. Several provinces recognize that federal programmes are essential if support is to be uniform across the country. The main provincial concern is that the levels in most federal programmes have been inadequate, especially in recent years of high rates of inflation.

The federal and provincial governments have been discussing the need for harmonization of stabilization programmes for several years and have reached a considerable measure of agreement on the features that would be desirable in a federal programme. There is general agreement that plans should be voluntary, that producers should contribute one-third of the actuarial cost, and that producers should be guaranteed their cash costs plus 100 percent of the average margin over the previous five years. Most governments would favour a federal programme of this type for nationally produced commodities, including slaughter cattle, beef cow-calf production, sheep, pigs, maize, soybeans, and for oats and barley not included in WGSA. Regional and specialty crops would be left to the provinces.

Major problems remain to be resolved. Some provinces want to retain their own programmes and some wish to retain control of the way plans operate in order to use them as tools for the promotion of agricultural development or to mould industry structure within their own boundaries. Production costs vary considerably among provinces and some high cost provinces, unable to use tariff barriers to protect their farmers from lower cost competition, would like to be free to use subsidies to promote agriculture within their boundaries.

These issues may not be fully resolved, but ASA amendments incorporating provisions on which agreement has already been reached would permit a considerable degree of harmonization. One or two provinces may opt out of an improved federal programme. The operation of a uniform programme for the rest of the country would still be more efficient and less distorting than a minimal federal programme supplemented by nonuniform provinical programmes which could escalate competitively.

Hopefully, reluctant provincial governments will be persuaded that devices other than price supports can be used to favour one sector over another within a province and even to promote the development of a particular industry within the province in competition with producers from other provinces. There is enough danger that national marketing agencies will interfere with regional comparative advantage in production. If price support programmes are used to the same effect, the future prospects for a progressive and efficient agricultural industry will be jeopardized and national economic unity will be further threatened.

EFFICIENCY AND EQUITY CONSIDERATIONS
IN WATER RESOURCES DEVELOPMENT AND MANAGEMENT
IN THE CONTEXT OF AGRICULTURAL DEVELOPMENT

Terrence S. Veeman

Abstract

Improved water availability, control, and management are vital to agricultural development and the expansion of food supplies in most poor nations. The current theory of agricultural development is weak in its treatment of institutional change. Nevertheless, the development of appropriate water institutions is essential for the implementation of water policies which would facilitate agricultural modernization. The existing system of ground water rights in northern India, for example, will prove inefficient, inequitable, and increasingly ill suited to the environmental and economic conditions of that region. It is argued that a system of correlative rights, based on the common property concept, can be helpful in the solution of emerging ground water problems in India and other poor nations. Water organizations such as water users' associations or public districts are also needed for the integrated development and management of surface and ground water in many developing countries.

OPENER'S REMARKS--Raphael S. J. Shen

The decision as to whether to develop institutions to regulate how much ground water can be extracted by whom should be a function of the abundance or scarcity of ground water, the number of agricultural producers per land unit, and the water requirement of diverse crops under cultivation. How can a system of correlative rights be helpful in the solution of ground water problems? More basic and crucial to solving any ground water problems in developing countries is to have the personnel necessary to provide organizational and managerial expertise. With such people, concepts other than common property could be applied which, for a given situation, might be more appropriate and efficient.

While northern India may indeed need enabling legislation to facilitate the development of decentralized water organizations, other low population density or water abundant rural areas in developing countries may not need government assistance. The fact that many poor nations lack suitable water organizations such as local water users' associations is perhaps because there are more pressing problems. Or maybe there is no need or managerial capability for such organizations. Given these circumstances, legislation might not be the appropriate solution to such problems.

RAPPORTEUR'S REPORT--Hiroyuki Nishimura

The discussion was extended to the different types of water resource development problems in Libya, including the requirements of a large amount of investment for getting water to locations far from the densely populated areas, and the problem that pumping ground water results in the flow of salt water from the sea into the ground water.

Further studies are required concerning equity and efficiency problems caused by the current system of canals. Water loss in the distribution and drainage systems is of great concern.

Contributing to the discussion were Puran C. Bansil, Tirath Gupta, and Prafulla K. Mukherjee.

EFFECTIVE MANAGEMENT OF NATURAL RESOURCES FOR SUSTAINED CHANGE IN RURAL INDIA

Tirath Gupta

Abstract

Forest land is one of India's major resources but little conscious effort has been directed to harness it appropriately. Data concerning the labour absorption capacity of forestry and related activities are used to argue the importance of effective management of the existing forests and of bringing barren, un-cultivable and cultivable waste lands, marginal agricultural lands, and lands under shifting cultivation under tree crops. Expected private and societal benefits from and opportunity costs of the proposed steps are discussed in qualitative and quantitative terms. The discussions show that policies aimed at utilization of the land resource according to its inherent capabilities can help in bringing about substantial change in rural India.

Some problems (for example, lack of adequate data and conflicts between individual and societal interests in the use of common property resources) are discussed and solutions suggested. It is concluded that the agricultural economist has enough incentive to accept the challenge to help change rural India.

OPENER'S REMARKS--Peter L. Arcus

That this paper does not offer any suggestions for ameliorating the condition of the rural poor in India is a significant omission. The suggestion to establish a forest grazing regime raises some questions. How long does it take for the various species that might be grown to mature? Will there be any work for the rural poor during this period? With land tied up in forests for several years, if not decades, the opportunity costs of this allocation plus that represented by the growing trees must be evaluated. Further, the capital investment required for establishing a paper manufacturing industry can be very substantial indeed, and no mention of it has been made in paper. Some estimates of discounted benefits and costs are necessary in addition to the observation that planting and harvesting trees would provide work for persons presently (seasonally) un-employed.

Better management of both the agricultural and forest lands in India is already a goal worth pursuing, especially if benefits can accrue directly to the rural poor. This paper has raised a number of questions in this regard. However, it is hard to see how management can be improved without greater specificity in the data and analysis.

RAPPORTEUR'S REPORT--Hiroyuki Nishimura

There was some concern whether efforts to increase the productivity of forest lands would hamper their protective and ecological values. In answer to this, the author pointed out that his paper clearly implied that 20 to 25 percent of forest lands in India were to be left in their natural state. Doubts were expressed with regard to the social and anthropological constraints on using the land under shifting cultivation for trees. In the author's opinion, an integrated development of forests and forest based industries in the hill regions would take care of such constraints, to a large extent. The shifting cultivators appear to be economically rational people like most other farmers. The job opportunities offered by intensive management of forest resources may be insufficient. It was pointed out, however, that forests offer seasonal jobs when no farm work is available. More importantly, regular job opportunities in forestry can be substantially increased, and the paper provided some facts to this effect. Is there sufficient demand for wood products given the competition from synthetic substitutes? The author felt that such limitations were not relevant, at least in India's context. In fact, the country is faced with an acute shortage and rising prices of many forest based products such as fuelwood and paper.

Contributing to the discussion were Joachim von Braun, Kamta Prasad, and Indra Jit Singh.

THE ECONOMIC EFFICIENCY OF
WATER USE IN EGYPTIAN AGRICULTURE:
OPENING ROUND OF A DEBATE

James B. Fitch, Hassan A. Khedr, and Dale Whittington

Introduction

In Egypt, the era of relatively abundant water supplies which followed the completion of the Aswan High Dam is now coming to an end. Plans to expand land cultivation appear to be on a collision course with Nile water availability. Ultimately, consideration will have to be given to where cutbacks can be made and how to reallocate water among existing and future uses. It will thus be necessary to rethink trade policy, cropping patterns, and agricultural regulation.

History records a long series of endeavours to control the Nile flow and increase its use. The Aswan High Dam and the draining of part of the Sudd Swamp, currently underway in the Sudan, are the most recent efforts. Egypt now releases the full 55.5 billion cubic metre allocation under the Nile Water Agreements of 1959. New projects under way in the Sudan will entail the full use of Sudan's quota of 18.5 billion cubic metres. Yet Egyptian policymakers, faced with expanding food import bills, now talk seriously of the need to irrigate two to three million more feddans (1 feddan = 0.42 hectares) by the year 2000, in addition to the six million currently used. Sudanese plans call for reclaiming another 1.5 million feddans in the 1980s, in addition to 4.5 million already irrigated or being developed. Moreover, although agriculture still accounts for more than 95 percent of consumption, both countries are rapidly increasing nonagricultural water uses.

Of all the water used for agriculture in Egypt, the largest quantity goes to irrigating the "old lands" along the Nile and in the Nile Delta. These old lands account for more than 85 percent of all current water use, and more than 95 percent of agricultural production. The average size of the operational unit in these lands is about three feddans (Radwan, p. 17-25). Typically, such units are broken down into smaller parcels where water is lifted by a variety of means, both modern and traditional. There is no metering of this water, nor is there a charge for it. While the farmer who uses greater amounts incurs greater costs from lifting, there is no other incentive for efficient use.

Aside from the issue of water pricing, there have been a number of forces which appear to have distorted resource allocation. The government has set prices substantially below international levels for cotton, basic food grains, and many other commodities, as part of a system of de facto taxation (Hansen and Nashashibi, p. 164). Low prices have been coupled with mandatory delivery quotas for grains and government control of all marketing channels for cotton, plus a system of obligatory acreage requirements. To avoid quota and acreage restrictions, some farmers have shifted to the production of orchard and truck crops. Probably because the government has not had effective means of controlling meat and fodder prices, there has been a marked shift to the growing of clover, which at almost three million feddans is now the country's largest single crop. In spite of mandatory acreage rules, cotton and food grain acreage has declined over the past twenty years, and grain production has fallen far behind consumption needs.

In 1974, Egypt became a net importer of agricultural products for the first time in history. This has naturally caused a debate about the wisdom of prevailing policies, and has raised questions about comparative advantage and efficiency of resource use. Some critics argue that Egypt should abandon its reliance on cotton exports and turn to producing more food for its expanding population. However, this debate has all occurred during the time when the extra water from the High Dam made land the binding constraint on production.

This paper seeks to determine how the picture of resource use efficiency is likely to change as water becomes the binding constraint on production. In particular, we examine the impact of water restrictions on the old land areas.

Measuring the Value of Water in Egyptian Agriculture

Under conditions of efficient resource use, water would be reallocated from lower to higher value uses until the values of the marginal products were equated. One way to estimate marginal values would be to start with prevailing water prices and then adjust these to take account of externalities and other distortions in the pricing system. Since Egypt has no water prices or charges of any significance, this approach is not practical. The alternative chosen in such circumstances frequently has been to use mathematical programming models, especially linear programming. Such procedures are, however, data intensive and usually take a long time.

The approach here is to measure the value of water as a residual--the return from a given crop rotation after charges for all factors except water are counted. Calculations were made at both domestic market and accounting prices. For accounting prices, a variety of adjustments were made, following the procedures for shadow pricing normally used to determine comparative advantage for production of tradeable commodities (Pearson, Akrasanee, and Nelson).

In Egypt, double cropping is the standard practice. It is not possible, however, to compare short term crops like maize and rice with crops like sugarcane due to the different durations they occupy the land and due to the different periods in which they consume water. It was decided to evaluate alternative full year crop rotations, to avoid problems of noncomparability. To account for regional agroclimatic variability, key rotations were chosen for each of the country's three main regions--the Nile Delta and Middle and Upper Egypt. The crops considered account for 79 percent of the cropped area nationwide.

In deriving accounting prices for outputs, international farm gate prices were obtained by adjusting for the various processing and marketing costs incurred between the border and the farm. The farm prices of several crops, such as wheat, where straw and fibres are important farm level byproducts, were increased to reflect their additional domestic market value. The shadow pricing of berseem clover, a nontraded good, was problematic. Here it was decided to use the domestic price as the shadow value, although meat does enjoy substantial effective protection in Egypt, and this undoubtedly augments the price of clover.

Wages, draft animal prices, and organic fertilizer prices were taken at market value in the shadow valuing of the costs of production. Costs of utilizing machinery provided by cooperatives were adjusted upward to reflect the average government subsidy. Pest control and chemical fertilizer costs were adjusted for both direct price subsidies and indirect subsidies, such as from foreign exchange dealings. Seed costs were adjusted upward in proportion to the ratio of the international farm gate price of the commodity to the domestic price.

It is difficult to determine an appropriate accounting price for land. Rights to water are, in effect, attached to land ownership in Egypt, and thus land values and rental charges would normally be expected to reflect the value of the accompanying water. In Egypt, however, land rents are controlled at levels which are probably below the value of the marginal product of land per se. Our approach is to use the estimated cost of reclaiming desert land as a replacement cost for old lands of low quality, and then to index this upward, following the patterns of average domestic rents paid for the various rotations, to reflect the variability in values for lands of different quality.

The returns to land and water are calculated on a unit of land basis. Land costs are then subtracted from these figures, and the remainder is divided by water use coefficients to obtain the returns on a unit of water basis. These returns are estimates of the values of product attributable to water when both land and water are scarce factors. Since the calculations are based on a 1977 cost structure and since water will probably not begin to become scarce until the mid-1980s, the current relative cost structure is assumed to continue into the future. Long run shadow prices are used based on the World Bank's 1985 commodity price projections, but indexed to 1977 prices.

Although it would be preferable to measure the marginal value of water in each crop rotation, we have been forced to rely on regional averages. The analysis assumes a fixed, linear technology and cost structure for crop rotation, including fixed water requirement coefficients. Finally, rotations are characterized by the total water required. System capacity constraints are not included.

Results and Conclusions

The results of the analysis are presented in the table. The returns to land and water (cols. 6-8) reflect the picture of resource use today. Land per se should be assigned the major portion of these residuals since it is currently the binding resource. The returns to the farmer (col. 6) favour devoting land to long term clover production in the Delta, in rotation with maize or rice. This explains why production and acreage of cotton and short term clover have declined in recent years. The soybean rotation predominates in middle Egypt, but the cotton-clover prevails in upper Egypt, where shorter staple cotton is grown and its yields are higher. The current price policy in Egypt is clearly directing the farmer away from the production of the most socially profitable crops. In terms of social profitability (col. 7), cotton was clearly king among the major crops under 1977 conditions. Based on this calculation, Egypt should be devoting more resources to producing cotton as well as to specialty crops like winter onions. Wheat, soybeans, and other grains ranked far behind the cotton-clover rotation. If clover had been shadow priced at a lower level, then wheat may have been somewhat more competitive than these findings indicate.

Surprisingly, with water a scarce factor in the long run (col. 12), the direction of resource reallocation does not change appreciably from when land alone is the limiting factor. Maize appears to be at less of a disadvantage to rice, its competing high water use summer crop. In middle and upper Egypt, sugarcane production should probably be expanded despite its high water requirements. Even if world sugarcane prices do not improve in the long run (as expected), sugar still seems to have an advantage over grains like wheat and sorghum. High valued vegetable crops would also be emphasized.

This analysis indicates that Egypt should deemphasize grain production, even after water becomes scarce, if social profitability is to be pursued. Grain imports will have to be drastically expanded, unless new lands prove to have a comparative advantage in grain. With Egypt currently importing two-thirds of its wheat needs, this raises the issue of food security, and presents a clear picture of the security-efficiency tradeoff which Egypt faces (Goueli).

The residual values of water derived here may serve other useful purposes in planning and project evaluations. For example, the one to two piastre value range for water could be used to evaluate canal linings and other devices for reducing water wastage. Indications are that such investments would be justified if their annual costs are less than 10 to 20 Egyptian pounds per 1,000 cubic metres of water saved.

Currently, new land reclamation projects are evaluated without assigning any cost to the water they consume. However, projects built now will operate in a water scarce future. We thus suggest that the opportunity cost of water should be assessed at approximately 1 to 2 piastres per cubic metre. This would help in sorting out those projects which are truly justifiable.

In the future, Egypt will need more sophisticated means of valuing water. In

228

Table. Cost and Returns to Land and Water for Major Crop Rotations in the Three Agricultural Zones of Egypt.

Zone/Crop Rotation	Production Costs		Gross Returns			Returns to land and water			Water use Per Feddan	Returns to Water		
	Domest. Prices (1)	Shadow Prices (2)	Domest. Prices (3)	Int'l 1977 Prices (4)	L.Run Prices (5)	Domest. Prices (6)	Int'l 1977 Prices (7)	L.Run Prices (8)	(9) M³	Domest. Prices (10)	Int'l 1977 Prices (11)	L.Run Prices (12)
	......	......	...... Egyptian Pounds per Feddan			...... Egyptian Pounds per Feddan				...... Piasters per M³		
Nile Delta (Sharkia)												
Clover[a](2)-Cotton	183	227	356	790	757	173	563	530	8,701	1.3	4.7	4.3
Clover (4)-Rice	153	166	405	542	661	252	376	495	12,422	1.4	1.4	2.4
Clover (4)-Maize	141	152	408	445	510	267	293	358	7,989	2.3	1.1	1.9
Wheat-Maize	156	178	257	351	479	101	173	301	8,362	0.7	0.7	2.2
Middle Egypt (Menia)												
Clover (2)-Cotton	194	246	329	736	705	135	490	459	10,066	0.7	3.2	2.9
Onion-Maize	217	229	402	1,253	1,329	185	1,024	1,100	8,220	1.7	11.1	12.0
Clover (4)-Soybean	120	123	454	466	474	334	343	351	8,312	3.1	1.8	1.9
Sugar Cane	168	190	298	590	1,309	130	400	1,119	11,879	0.7	2.4	8.5
Upper Egypt (Sohag)												
Clover (2)-Cotton	169	219	341	832	794	172	613	575	12,251	0.9	3.8	3.5
Wheat-Sorghum	144	159	257	361	489	113	202	330	11,137	0.6	0.8	2.0
Beans-Sorghum	127	135	253	353	496	126	218	361	9,839	0.9	1.2	2.7
Sugar Cane	169	192	271	534	1,189	102	342	997	14,880	0.4	1.6	6.0

a Clover grown in rotation with cotton yields two (2) cuts compared to four (4) in other rotations.

b International prices converted to pounds at the "parallel" market rate of L.E.0.70 = U.S.$1. There are 100 piasters in the Egyptian Pound.

the meantime, these estimates will hopefully be useful in starting the opening round of the debate on the agricultural implications of Egypt's water limited future.

References

Goueli, A. A. (1978) National food security programme in Egypt. Mexico City; IFPRI-CIMMYT Conference on Food Security, November.

Hansen, B.; Nashashibi, K. (1975) Foreign Trade Regimes and Economic Development: Egypt. New York; National Bureau of Economic Research.

Pearson, S. R.; Akrasanee, N.; Nelson, G. C. (1976) Comparative advantage in rice production: A methodological introduction. Food Research Institute Studies, 15 (2) 127-138.

Radwan, S. (1977) Agrarian Reform and Rural Poverty: Egypt, 1952-75. Geneva; International Labour Organization.

OPENER'S REMARKS--Nigel T. Williams

The Egyptian government is facing a two faceted problem. First, it must decide how to encourage water conservation. Second, it must define the optimal product mix given the available water supply. This paper is useful in that it provides data that will help in the formulation of an answer to the second question.

The derived value measure for water is the net return to the crop after charges for all factors, excluding water, are deducted. The underlying assumption is that, at the margin, the value product of each factor is equated to its cost. How confident are the authors that this is so in reality? For example, if labour is in surplus, to value it at the market price would overstate its value product and therefore understate that of water.

It is unfortunate that the crop rotations were characterized by their total annual water requirements in the analysis. The availability of water and the water requirement of each crop varies from month to month. I feel that a mathematical programming model should have been used to provide monthly water use coefficients for each rotation. In this way, those crops with a high annual water use coefficient but with monthly requirements that do not coincide with periods of water shortage or with the peak requirements of competing crops could be given due weight in the results.

I think that this paper offers an excellent illustration of the dilemma facing many developing countries in having to achieve a balance between maximum social profitability on the one hand and food security on the other. It is a very useful first round in the debate.

RAPPORTEUR'S REPORT--Hiroyuki Nishimura

Water in the Middle East is a crucial factor, and should therefore be used in an efficient way. Sometime in the future, water will become a limiting factor of production in Egypt, and the regional distribution of cropping patterns will be affected.

Khedr agreed, at least theoretically, that mathematical programming techniques could provide better estimates of the shadow prices of water resources. However, there is a master plan for water in Egypt which is applying such a technique. The approach of measuring the value of water as a residual was taken in order to have a quick answer, relatively rough in nature, but one which uses the entire body of available information.

Egypt should set a price on water in order to prevent waste. To prepare for the future scarcity of water resources, new technology, such as drip irrigation, should be studied. Khedr responded that there should be some criteria for allocating water. Moreover, there is a need for a complete change in the technical structure and administrative system of water supply if there is to be less overuse of water. Such a change might be possible in Libya because of the dependence on wells, but is not possible in Egypt.

Khedr indicated that new techniques are not the solution to Egypt's water problems, nor are they the solution to the lack of rationalization of water use in most of the developing countries. Drip irrigation needs a large amount of capital investment. Moreover, it needs a very efficient maintenance system, in addition to highly skilled labour which is often not available in developing countries.

What is the possibility of the micro level rationalization of water use; that is, saving water on the farm? Khedr responded that emphasizing the role of agricultural extension would be a means of doing that.

Contributing to the discussion were Puran C. Bansil, Richard Fraenkel, Robin W. M. Johnson, Heinrich Niederboster, and Robert O. Rogers.

IMPACT OF PER CAPITA INCOME GROWTH ON POPULATION GROWTH:
A CROSS SECTIONAL ANALYSIS

Mudiumbula Futa and Luther Tweeten

A number of writers contend that rising per capita incomes will reduce birth rates and solve problems of high population growth in developing countries (see, for example, Clark and Simon). This contention is attractive because family planning programmes that may conflict with some religious and ethical values need not be implemented. But the contention is dangerous if it is wrong. Even if developing countries temporarily achieve per capita income gains, failure of such gains to retard population growth can eventually offset advances in total income and relegate developing countries to low per capita incomes and undernutrition for years to come.

The purpose of this paper is to test empirically the null hypothesis that the population growth rate is not influenced by the per capita income growth rate. This hypothesis has been addressed in the past on both deductive and empirical grounds. Microeconomic theoretical analysis suggests that higher family income results in higher fertility rates (Becker). Some empirical evidence supports this conclusion (Adelman). However, other empirical studies report negative income elasticities of fertility (Ben-Porath, for example).

Theoretical Model

The Cobb-Douglas production function has been widely used to relate national output to labour and capital resources. Comparisons between developed and developing countries suggest somewhat comparable elasticities of production and of factor shares (Thirlwall), hence providing empirical support for this functional form for a global assessment.

Defining Y as national output, K as human and material capital, L as labour and α, β, and γ as constants, then:

(1) $\quad Y = \alpha K^{\beta} L^{\gamma}$; and

(2) $\quad y = Y/L = \alpha K^{\beta} L^{\gamma -1}$.

Designating proportional rates of growth in neutral technology change (NTC) as $\dot{\alpha}$, in capital as $\dot{K}$, and in labour as $\dot{L}$, the proportional rate of change in output per unit of labour is:

(3) $\quad \dot{y} = \dot{\alpha} + \beta \dot{K} + (\gamma - 1)\dot{L}$.

It is apparent from (3) that, in the absence of induced NTC or induced capital formation, an increase in labour supply will reduce output per unit of labour if $0 < \gamma < 1$ with $\dot{K} = 0$. Estimated values of γ are frequently near 0.75, although values ranging from 0.6 to 0.9 are sometimes found. If $\gamma = 0.75$, a 1 percent increase in labour force (or population if labour is a constant proportion of population) will reduce per capita output by 0.25 percent.

If constant returns to scale prevail, in the absence of labour induced changes in K and NTC, (3) can be expressed as:

(4) $\quad \dot{y} = \beta(\dot{K} - \dot{L})$.

Output per worker grows if labour grows at a slower rate than capital. If $\beta = 0.25$ and labour is constant, then output per labourer will grow at 1 percent per year if capital grows at 4 percent per year.

If growth in y sufficiently reduces $\dot{L}$, it is possible that y can be stabilized or even raised without increases in K. Or the impact of $\dot{K}$ on $\dot{y}$ can be enhanced if an increase in $\dot{y}$ induces a reduction in $\dot{L}$. The parameter central to this analysis is the behavioural response of labour supply to per capita income growth as defined by:

(5) $\delta = (dL/dy)(y/L)$; or

(6) $\dot{L} = \delta\dot{y}$.

With no induced NTC and constant returns to scale, substituting (6) into (3) gives:

(7) $\dot{y} = [\beta/(1 + \beta\delta)]\dot{K}$, or

(8) $\dot{y} = \dot{K}/[(1/\beta) + \delta]$.

If $\beta = 0.25$, then $\dot{y}$ will change at the same rate as $\dot{K}$ if $\delta = -3$. But for rapid economic progress, it is desirable for $\dot{y}$ to be highly responsive to increments in $\dot{K}$. As the denominator $(1/\beta) + \delta$ approaches zero, small increments in $\dot{K}$ induce large changes in growth in per capita income $\dot{y}$. If $\beta = 0.25$, additional capital brings large changes in $\dot{y}$ as δ approaches -4. In the absence of gains in $\dot{K}$ or α induced by L, most rapid rates of growth in income per unit of labour come from values of δ slightly larger than $1/\beta$. Whether δ is consistent with such numbers is an empirical question addressed in the remainder of this paper.

Econometric Models of Population Growth

Table 1 contains two econometric models used to estimate δ. The assumption in the cross sectional model is that the labour force is proportional to population in the long run so that L can be replaced by population. Because population growth rate (PGR) is crude birth rate (CBR) minus crude death rate (CDR), the latter two variables are used to measure PGR in order to obtain information on its components. In model I, CBR is a function of life expectancy and CDR, and is used to account for the social security provided by surviving children as well as the stage in the demographic transition. These variables are determined jointly. Other variables in the CBR equation are per capita income growth rate $\dot{y}$, family planning, literacy rate, religion, and proportion of rural population. In model II, CBR is simultaneously determined only with life expectancy and is exogenously influenced by family planning programmes, rural-urban income differences, and by the interaction of current per capita income and the historical rate of growth in per capita income.

Crude death rate in model I is a function of endogenously determined life expectancy and per capita income, and exogenously determined past growth rates in per capita income and number of persons per physician. In model II, CDR is a function of endogenously determined life expectancy, and of exogenously determined per capita income, family planning programmes, number of persons per physician (a proxy for health care), and the interaction of current per capita income and the historical rate of growth in per capita income.

Empirical Results

Statistical estimates were computed for each equation in table 1 by ordinary least squares (OLS), two stage least squares (2SLS), and three stage least squares (3SLS). Observations are for 64 countries ranging from low income to high income for which complete data were available.

Results of OLS estimates for CBR and CDR equations in model I are shown below:

(9) $CBR = 59.29 - .3097X_3 - .0006443X_4 - .2813X_5 - 9.701X_9$
　　　　(.01) (.03)　　　(.09)　　　　　(.45)　　　(.01)
　　　　　[-.29]　　　[-.12]　　　　　[-.037]　　[-.33]

　　　　$- 7.959X_{10} + 1.912X_{12} + 3.785X_{13}$
　　　　　(.08)　　　　(.09)　　　　(.32)
　　　　　[-.20]　　　[.080]　　　[.073]

$[R^2 = .92]$

(10) $CDR = 40.41 - .5026X_3 + .001062X_4 - .3005X_5 + .07905X_{11}$
　　　　(.01) (.01)　　　(.01)　　　　　(.70)　　　(.01)
　　　　　[-1.04]　　　[.43]　　　　　[-.087]　　[.18]

$[R^2 = .91]$

All coefficients display theoretically admissable signs. Based on the standardized regression coefficients in brackets, life expectancy and presence of family planning programmes most strongly influence CBR. Probabilities of a larger t (in parenthesis) are reported for a two tailed distribution. Given the expected negative sign on the coefficient of the literacy rate and the expected positive sign on the coefficient of the religion variable, these coefficients can be viewed as significant by a one tailed t-test.

Crude death rate is strongly related to life expectancy and, to a lesser extent, to per capita income based on standardized regression coefficients. But better health care as evidenced by fewer persons per physcian significantly reduces CDR.

Although the coefficient of $\dot{y}$ (variable X_5) is not significantly different from zero in equations for either CBR or CDR, we shall use the estimated coefficient $-0.02813 + 0.03005 = 0.00192$ as the most likely value of δ. (Because CBR and CDR are in number per 1,000 persons, the value is converted to percent by moving the decimal one place to the left.) One percentage point increase in per capita income growth increases population growth by only 0.00192 percentage points. Clearly no basis exists to reject the null hypothesis of $\delta = 0$.

It is possible that $\dot{y}$ impacts on PGR through intervening variables such as life expectancy, but the coefficient of $\dot{y}$ in the life expectancy equation was small and significantly different from zero only at the 85 percent level. Statistical results of 2SLS and 3SLS are not shown because they gave even less evidence that δ differed from zero.

In searching for alternate functional forms that would reveal a greater absolute value of δ, model II was estimated by the same three statistical procedures as used to estimate model I. We postulate that the impact of the per capita income growth rate on the population growth rate is a function of the current level of per capita income. Furthermore, fewer variables were specified as endogenous, to simplify the model. (See table 2.)

All coefficients display theoretically admissable signs as can be seen below:

(11) $CBR = 68.34 - .5070X_3 - 9.425X_9 + .0007999X_{14} - .0005169X_{15}$
　　　　(.01) (.01)　　　(.01)　　　(.01)　　　　　(.01)
　　　　　[-.4742]　　　[-.3251]　　[.2139]　　　[-.3823]
　　$[R^2 = .91]$

(12) $CDR = 40.74 - .5229X_3 + .00165X_4 + .08202X_{11} - .0001590X_{15}$
　　　　(.01) (.01)　　　(.01)　　　(.01)　　　　　(.05)
　　　　　[-1.0818]　　　[.6731]　　[.1808]　　　[-.2600]

　　$[R^2 = .91]$

234

Table 1. Econometric models of population growth

Variable, Units and Date	Model	1	2	3	4	5	6	7	8	9	10	11	12	13	14	15 (4x5)
1. Crude birth rate (No./1,000 pop., 1975)	I		E	E	X					X	X		X	X		
	II			E						X					X	X
2. Crude death rate (No./1,000 pop., 1975)	I		E	E	X						X					
	II		E	X							X					X
3. Life expectancy (Years, 1975)	I	E	E		E	X				X	X					
	II	E	E	X						X	X					X
4. Per capita GNP (U. S. dollars, 1976)	I	E	E				E		E					X	X	
5. Growth rate, GNP per capita (%/yr., 1960-76)																
6. Investment per labourer (U.S. $/worker, 1976)	I		E	E			E	E								
7. Proportion of GDP from agriculture (1976)	I					E		E						X	X	
8. Proportion of GNP invested (1976)	I			E		E	E									
9. Family planning (1=programme; zero other, 1976)																
10. Literacy rate (Proportion lit., 1974)																
11. No. of persons per physician (1,000, 1974)																
12. Religion (1=Catholic, zero other, 1975)																
13. Proportion of population rural (1974)																
14. Rural-urban income diff. (U. S. dollars, 1976)																

[a]E = endogenous, X = exogenous.

Source of data: World Bank. World Development Report, 1978. Oxford: Oxford University Press, 1978.

Table 2. Two-stage least squares (2SLS) and three-stage least squares (3SLS) estimated from Model II.

	D. V.	Item	Int.	3	4	9	11	14	15
CBR	2SLS	Reg. Coeff.	70.77	-.5565		-8.651		.00074	-.00048
		Prob. > t	(<.01)	(<.01)		(<.01)		(<.02)	(<.01)
	3SLS	Reg. Coeff.	70.42	-.5481		-9.031		.0072	-.00046
		Prob. > t	(<.01)	(<.01)		(<.01)		(<.02)	(<.01)
CDR	2SLS	Reg. Coeff.	39.80	-.5058	.0015		.0884		-.00015
		Prob. > t	(<.01)	(<.01)	(<.01)		(<.01)		(<.06)
	3SLS	Reg. Coeff.	39.56	-.5020	.0015		.0921		-.00015
		Prob. > t	(<.01)	(<.01)	(<.01)		(<.01)		(<.06)

See Table 1 for definitions of variables, source of data and form of complete model. DV: Dependent variable, Int: intercept.

The coefficient of the income interaction variable $X_{15} = X_4X_5$ is highly significant for each estimation procedure in the CBR equation, and the standardized regression coefficient is -0.4 in the OLS form, above. The coefficient of the income interaction (4 x 5) was highly insignificant in the life expectancy equation of model II, and hence gave no evidence that PGR was influenced by income growth through the intervening life expectancy variable.

Holding per capita income at the sample mean of $1,842, the estimated value of δ is -0.066. With per capita income set is $500, δ is -0.018, and for y set at $100, δ is -0.000344. Results from the 2SLS and 3SLS estimations were consistent with these values. Estimates of δ were also near zero for equations computed separately for high income and low income countries using models I and II.

We chose to measure δ from the 1960-76 growth rate of income per capita (variable X_5) because time is required to adjust birth and death rates to per capita income. However, alternative estimates of δ were computed from current per capita income (variable X_4). These estimates of δ were found to be small and approach zero for low income countries.

Conclusions

Estimated values of δ are too small to justify rejection of the null hypothesis that $\delta = 0$. The results hold out little hope that increasing per capita income alone will reduce the rate of population growth in developing nations or result in large coefficients for K in equation (9). On the other hand, the results suggest that family planning programmes can significantly reduce population growth rates.

Population growth rates in many countries have declined in recent years. The decline characterizes countries with high and low per capita incomes and low growth rates in per capita income. Thus, the decline seems to be associated not with changes in income but with shifting attitudes toward ideal family size.

References

Adelman, I. (1963) An economic analysis of population growth. American Economic Review, 53, 314-39.

Becker, G. S. (1960) An economic analysis of fertility, in Demographic and Economic Change in Developed Countries (National Bureau of Economic Research). Princeton, New Jersey, USA; Princeton University Press.

Ben-Porath, Y. (1973) Economic analysis of fertility in Israel: Point and counterpoint. Journal of Political Economy, 81 (2) 202-233.

Clark, C. (1969) The population explosion myth. Bulletin of the Institute of Development Studies, May.

Simon, A. (1975) Bread for the World. New York; Paulist Press.

Thirlwall, A. P. (1972) A cross section study of population growth. Manchester School, 40, 339-356.

OPENER'S REMARKS--Jesus C. Santa Iglesia

The finding that income growth does not affect population growth is difficult to dispute. The theoretical framework and the econometric models are widely accepted and the statistical analysis is sound. But there are other dimensions which the present analysis may not have considered.

A country by country analysis may bring up different results. A high income level effect in one country may equate to a low income level in another country. Aggregating the two countries will therefore not capture the differential effects. This point may also be expanded within a country. Certain threshold levels of income may have to be reached before the effects of income growth on population growth may be felt.

Intervening factors between income and population growth may have to be examined in more depth. Effects of income growth on population growth may have to come through increased education, which in turn results in different attitudes, including an increased appreciation for (and circumstantial delay of) marriage, increased awareness of ways of obtaining sexual gratification that do not result in conception, and so on. The effects of income growth in a particular period may be seen, then, only at a later period, hence cross sectional analysis may not be an appropriate method of estimating them.

RAPPORTEUR'S REPORT--Kanok Khatikarn

The model should be disaggregated by income level in developing countries. However, the author indicated that the model cannot be used to do country by country analysis because of problems with the low degrees of freedom.

Crude birth rates and death rates should be adjusted for the age structure within each country, but the model was found to exhibit more multicollinearity error by including manipulated data on age structure.

It was suggested that the model should have employed income distribution data such as those available from the World Bank, but the author indicated that the World Bank data are not reliable.

DISTRIBUTIVE BIAS OF NEW FOOD GRAIN TECHNOLOGIES AND INTERSECTORAL FLOWS OF RESOURCES

C. G. Ranade

Abstract

There is ample evidence to show that the gains of new food grain technologies have been distributed unevenly among big and small farms and landless labourers. This paper examines the effect of this distributive bias upon the flow of resources between food grain and nonfood grain sectors within the framework of a two sector model. The simulation exercise for the model relates to the Indian economy.

The net flow of resources is defined as the difference between the savings of landlords who own land and capital and their investment within the food grain sector. The paper shows that if technological change increases per capita food grain output and if the distribution of this increase is skewed against labourers, the terms of trade move in favour of the nonfood grain sector, and the food grain sector experiences net outflow of resources. At the same time, the transfer of food grain labour towards the nonfood grain sector increases and the nonfood grain sector's capital-labour ratio declines. The opposite is the case when the share of labour in food grain production increases. When the share of labour is maintained constant, but the share of capital decreases and that of land increases, then the terms of trade move in favour of the food grain sector, but that sector faces net outflow of resources.

If total capital stock increases faster than population growth while per capita food grain output and income distribution remain unchanged, then the terms of trade move in favour of the food grain sector and that sector enjoys a net inflow of resources.

After examining several scenarios, the paper shows that by simply looking at the terms of trade, one cannot say anything definite about the direction of intersectorial flows of resources, which depend very much upon changes in income distribution in a general equilibrium context.

OPENER'S REMARKS--M. Louis Upchurch

Agricultural economists have generally given far too little attention to the consequences of technological innovations in the agricultural industries. Traditionally, when changes in production practices occur (whether induced or spontaneous), economic appraisal is focused on changes in the net income or net asset position of entrepreneurs or on the relative distribution of resources within the producing unit.

When the mechancial cotton picker and related technology came into widespread use in the U.S. cotton industry following World War II, dozens of economic studies appraised this change. So far as I know, all dealt with the effect on tenants and hired labourers. Yet this change drove many thousands of people from farms to cities--in both the North and South. We were remiss in not directing at least some of our research resources at an innovation that profoundly affected the lives of many thousands of people.

When mechanical refrigeration and bulk tank handling of milk came into the dairy industry, a number of researchers examined the capital requirements for this innovation and the effects it would have on the incomes of dairy farmers. Few bothered to point out that this technology substantially changed the economies of scale in dairy production and would be a contributing factor in driving many small producers out of the business.

The illustrations of our failure to focus on indirect and sometimes profound consequences of technical change could be multiplied many times. Yet the need for agricultural economists to deal directly with the consequences of change is increasingly important. We can be forgiven, perhaps, for our failures when technical change occurs somewhat spontaneously, for we have an innate faith that the unseen hand will somehow make the adjustments to the long run benefit of all. In a rapidly growing economy, migration of resources among sectors tends to be obscured by growth in the total economy. Or when changes occur spontaneously, we feel no responsibility for the consequences.

But technical innovations in agriculture are induced by overt acts of government. When this occurs, it behoves us to anticipate the direct and indirect effects of change. Here we have failed far too frequently. We must know who benefits from change and who suffers as a result of redistribution of flows of income and employment opportunities. Ranade is to be congratulated for his examination of the effects of change in his paper. He has dealt with a topic much neglected by agricultural economists.

I hope this paper will stimulate other agricultural economists to ask themselves with increasing frequency, "What happens when a technical change is injected into agricultural production?" We know from simple observation that a technical change can benefit the early innovators (and likely will) or they would not adopt the change, and we know that changes often make some producers, some labourers, and some sectors of the population either relatively or absolutely worse off. When we promote technical change, especially in the developing countries, we frequently ignore or fail to take these changes into account in planning and operating agricultural programmes.

The fact that some sectors of the population may be worse off as a result of technical change does not mean that we should eschew change. We should strive to anticipate the consequences of change and to mitigate the unfavourable effects of change. Failure to do this may account in part for the unsatisfactory results sometimes observed in agricultural development programmes.

RAPPORTEUR'S REPORT--Kanok Khatikarn

What is the distinction between the food grain and nonfood grain sectors? Do both fall within the agricultural sector? How can we assume that there is no surplus labour in the nonfood grain sector? The author indicated that surplus labour in the nonfood grain sector is relatively small and that many unemployed persons in urban areas are really food grain sector surplus labour looking for first time employment in the nonfood grain sector.

This two sector model should be analyzed in terms of both the commodity flow and the saving-investment flow simultaneously. However, the necessary financial data are only available in Taiwan and Japan.

What is the level of aggregation in the model, and is there variation over regions in India? Small area studies using time series data on farmers may be worthwhile. The author suggested that the model could be strengthened with respect to public finance aspects, regional differences, and distributional characteristics. He contended that the model is more useful than a large complicated model if used to look at subsystems. The model is illustrative and is not necessarily to be used directly for policy decisions.

THE QUEST FOR EQUITY

Lyle P. Schertz

Abstract

Equity issues related to distributions of income and wealth pervade the transformation that has occurred and is occurring in rural America. The profession has over many years given substantial attention to equity between the farm sector and other sectors of the American economy. In contrast, only limited attention has been given to equity within the farm sector and to the distribution problems of those who left agriculture. Recent events portend important income and wealth distribution issues within the farm sector, as well as between the farm and nonfarm sectors. They include increased farm commodity prices and farm income and the related explosion in the wealth of land owners, steps to improve environmental quality, inflation, energy prices, and food aid cutbacks when U.S. commercial exports expanded. In addition, congressional and administrative actions may indicate a political sensitivity to these issues. The Food and Agriculture Act of 1977, the principles and standards for planning water and related resources, and U.S. food aid legislation include provisions indicating interest in income and wealth distribution. There is uncertainty about the eventual follow through by political leaders. Theory is deficient and data grossly inadequate. The problems need first to be defined through discussion and then addressed through data collection and research.

OPENER'S REMARKS--Carl E. Dahlgren

What is the aim of the research? Is it to examine which factors influence distribution, search for solutions to distribution inequities, or both? Determining which factors influence distribution is an appropriate challenge for the agricultural economist. A list of these factors, moreover, must include an estimate of the effects they have had on distribution. Solutions to the distribution inequities, however, must be determined by the politican. The solutions probably depend on which political system is prevailing in the particular country. The task for the agricultural economist is to estimate the consequences of different political alternatives. Which are the target groups--the big farmers, the small farmers, the farm labourers, the farmers who have left farming, or consumers in general? The factors affecting distribution can be external or internal to the country or sector with different consequences for the different target groups. I think that inflation has the largest distribution effects--both positive and negative--but it affects the whole society and not only the agricultural sector. And when we talk about environmental problems, should a price be set on the environment which the consumer must pay as well as the farmer?

RAPPORTEUR'S REPORT--Dinesh K. Marothia

What factors influence distribution, especially within the farm sector in the United States? How do the problems of value judgments influence the equity question, and what groups in the society, particularly in the farm sector, are most affected by distribution inequities? How can distribution effects on the large and small farms be isolated and quantified? There was a general consensus that in the quest for equity it is necessary to measure the impact of farm income on net national product, as this has important implications in forming appropriate policy measures.

REGIONAL PLANNING GOAL: EMPLOYMENT OR INCOME?
A CASE STUDY OF AN ARID REGION IN INDIA

Baldev Singh

Hypothesis

The failure of development strategies adopted during the U.N. development decade (1960s) to reduce differentials across regions and within a region across social and income classes has led to an added emphasis on alternative strategies for the development of rural areas. Accordingly, we find greater emphasis on the redistribution aspect as advocated by the World Bank and its member governments. For instance, growth with equity has been the prime objective of the Indian fifth and sixth five year plan.

The welfare of the poorer sections of society can be enhanced through a number of policy instruments. The redistribution of productive assets, particularly land, is the most obvious policy option during the initial phase of the development process, although it is politically as well as administratively the most difficult. (For a strong theoretical case in favour of fundamental structural reforms during the initial phase of development process see Fox, Sengupta, and Thorbecke, p. 447-467.) It is no wonder that policymakers and planners easily succumb to the politically rewarding soft options. The planning objective of employment maximization with the help of state power appears to be such an option. Indeed, employment maximization is the prime objective of India's sixth five year plan (Government of India, p. 3).

The success of this objective will, however, depend on how far the government succeeds in influencing through its policy instruments (fiscal or monetary) the factor-product price structure in favour of labour intensive rather than capital intensive technologies. The plan fails to suggest any innovative way to achieve this.

However, even when the price structure is successfully changed in favour of labour embodying technologies, there is no a priori evidence that the present capitalistic production structure in the country will increase employment opportunities, particularly for the poorer sections of society. Given that the entrepreneurial behaviour relations flowing from the existing production relations appear to be governed more by income (or profit) than by employment maximization considerations (except in a self-sufficient subsistence agricultural economy where the production decisions are likely to be governed more by household consumption than by market considerations), there is no reason to expect that they will change in the near future. If so, the employment maximization objective, instead of solving the problem, is likely to introduce more distortions in production relations.

Objectives

An empirical validation of these behavioural premises is essential, especially when planning at the region level is the prime objective. The region is likely to adopt the national planning objective as its planning structure. This paper is, accordingly, devoted to verify empirically whether entrepreneurs of the region maximize income or employment. Since the possibilities of the subsistence mode of production exist more in the primary sector than in other sectors of the economy, the verification is confined to the primary sector. Moreover, it is the primary sector which, in India, has historically been forced to play the role of host to the swelling ranks of the unemployed or underemployed. For instance, the primary sector accounted for 73 percent of the Indian work force in 1921 and again in 1961 and 74 percent in 1971. (For details, see Government of India, p. 82.)

Methodology

We propose to accomplish this verification task with the help of a 78 x 83 regional programming model. For details on the specification and estimation of the coefficients of this model, see Singh (1978b), p. 160-197. In 1971, the Surendranagar district had a population of 8.45 lakhs. Of these, 73 percent lived in rural areas. The primary sector was the dominant sector in the district economy; it employed 66.3 percent of the male workforce and contributed 61.9 percent of the district's domestic product. Indeed, farm households are represented by three relatively homogeneous farm size classes: small (up to 12.5 acres), medium (between 12.5 and 25 acres), and large (above 25 acres). On the resource front, 16 of the 78 regional resource constraints represent the macro resource position of the rural economy of the district, while the other 62 resource constraints represent the specific resource position of each of the four rural classes: small, medium, and large farm households, and nonfarm households. On the activity front, 58 of the 83 regional activities represent the productive activities (that is, crop and animal activities engaged in the four groups), and the remanent 25 regional cost activities represent the households' option to supplement their resources from the regional pool at regional market prices.

Results

Presentation and Interpretation

The regional programming model has been developed to achieve employment and income maximizing objectives. The standard simplex technique was employed to obtain the optimum solutions. But as the mode of production becomes relatively capitalistic in nature—as the contribution of capital input to the production process increase and that of labour input declines—the two objective functions are likely to generate divergent optimum solutions.

Regional Scenario: Employment or Income?

It can be seen from table 1 that the employment maximization objective is not only inferior to the income maximization objective, but unrealistic. With the given range of regional technology, it not only yields substantially low regional income estimates (that is, 30.11 crores compared to 82.84 crores generated by the income maximization objective) but even fails to maximize regional employment. In fact, the income maximizing objective yields higher regional employment estimates (380.94 lakh labour days) than those generated by the employment maximizing objective (303.83 lakh labour days).

Interestingly, the two objective functions invoke markedly different responses from rural husehols. While the income objective encourages market dependence of rural households, the employment objective discourages this trend. Of the four factor markets considered, the optimum solution based on the employment maximization objective reveals dependence of rural households on only one factor market (the capital market), whereas the income maximization objective reveals the rural household's dependence on three factor markets—the labour market (with a dependency rate of 27.2 percent), the capital market (2.1) and the animal labour market (1.1). The policy implications of the limited market response generated by the employment maximization objective is that it restricts the ability of policy intervention effectively to influence the behaviour pattern of rural entrepreneurs in the planned direction.

Incidentally, neither of the two optimum solutions given in table 2 suggest any dependence of the regional rural sector on the plant nutrient market; that is, chemical fertilizers. This result highlights the limited success or probably failure of the high yielding crop technology in a typically dry region like

Table 1—Relative Economics of Income and Employment Maximization
Objectives as per Optimum Solutions of the Regional Linear
Programming Model, Surendranagar, 1975/76

Selected Economic Aspects	Optimum Solutions	
	Income	Employment
1. Labour use (lakh labour days)	380.94	303.83
2. Income (rupees crores)	82.84	30.11
3. The degree of dependence on factor markets for farm resources		
(a) Labour services (percent)	27.22	--
(i) Hired labour (lakh labour days)	103.68	--
(ii) Total labour used (lakh labour days)	380.94	nc
(b) Draft power services (percent)	1.74	--
(i) Hired animal draft power (lakh animal pair days)	1.11	--
(ii) Total draft power (lakh animal pair days)	63.70	nc
(c) Plant nutrient input (percent)	--	--
(i) Nitrogen bought (lakh kg.)	--	--
(ii) Total nitrogen input (lakh kg.)	nc	nc
(d) Farm capital input (percent)	2.05	2.09
(i) Borrowed capital (rupees lakhs)	34.45	34.45
(ii) Total farm capital input (rupees lakhs)	1,677.77	1,646.73

nc = Not computed.

Surendranagar. We may note that during the last 45 years that district received an average rainfall of 439 mm with the probability of 0.72 that it will fall between 20 mm and 600 mm.

Given the regional technology spectrum, regional income and employment cannot be increased by injecting fertilizer supplies into a dry region. But this can be done by promoting the use of farmyard manure, which also helps in the absorption, retention, and conservation of the region's limited, highly uneven precipitation.

Overall Regional Scenario: The Historical Test

How do these optimum programming solutions of income and employment maximizing objectives stand the test of historical experience? Since land is the most important resource input of rural India, this test is conducted in terms of the pattern of land use. Historical experience is confined to three periods: the decade of the 1960s, the agricultural census year 1970/71, and the reference year of the programming model, 1975/76. Historically, cultivators of the district have been taking one crop per annum from the cultivable land. This is reflected by the coefficients of cropping intensity which have hovered around 100 (table 2). It is the optimum solution based on the income maximizing objective which yields a cropping intensity of this magnitude (99.70 percent). The optimum

Table 2--Historical and Optimal Land Use Patterns for Income and Employment Maximizing Objectives as per Optimum Solutions of the Regional Linear Programming Model, Surendranagar

Aspects of Land Use	Historical Experience			Optimum Solutions	
	Between 1960/61 1969/70	1970/ 71	1975/ 76	Income	Employment
1. Cropping pattern (percent)	100	100	100	100	100
Bajri					
Nonirrigated	18	22	25	20	16
Irrigated	--	1	3	1	2
Cotton					
Nonirrigated	43	40	32	43	14
Irrigated	--	4	5	3	--
Jowar					
Nonirrigated	19	20	15	1	21
Irrigated					
Kharif	--	1/	2	2	1
Rabi	--	1/	2	1	1/
Wheat					
Nonirrigated	3	3	5	1	3
Irrigated	--	1	4	3	4
Groundnuts					
Nonirrigated	10	4	2	13	--
Irrigated	--	1/	1/	--	--
Til					
Nonirrigated	2/	2/	3	11	--
Pulses					
Nonirrigated	2/	1	2	--	15
Green fodder					
Irrigated	3	1/	1	1/	7
Vegetables					
Irrigated					
Kharif	2/	1/	2	1	13
Rabi	2/	--	--	--	5
Other crops	6	3	--	--	--
2. Gross cropped area (lakh acres)	17	17	3/25	17	7
3. Net sown area (lakh acres)	17	17	3/24	17	17
4. Cropping intensity (percent)	101	102	102	100	43

1/ Less than 0.5 percent.
2/ Included in other crop category.
3/ Unit acres.

solution based on the employment maximizing objective fails miserably, however, with the cropping intensity being 42.9 percent. The decision behaviour of the farmers appears to be governed by the income maximizing objective. On the other hand, forcing the employment maximization objective on farmers is likely to lead to underutilization of tilled land.

A comparative analysis of the cropping pattern brings to light further distortions in the land use pattern introduced by the employment objective. While the cotton crop, which enjoys a specialized market in the district, loses its share from 40 to 14 percent, the vegetable crop, with very poor marketing facilities, improves its share from around 1 percent to 18 percent.

Regional Disaggregated Scenario

Since rural households do not form a homogeneous group, it will be interesting to explore how far different groups of these households support the overall supremacy of the income maximizing objective. An examination by category of optimum solutions of income and employment maximizing objectives, given in table 3, tends to corroborate the overall supremacy of the income over the employment objective.

Table 3—Relative Economics of Income and Employment Maximization Objectives as per Optimum Solutions of the Regional Linear Programming Model, Surendrenagar, 1975/76, by Category

	Optimum Solutions	
Selected Economic Aspects	Income	Employment
A. Cultivator Households		
(i) Labour use (lakh labour days)	359.67	283.54
(ii) Income (rupees crores)	78.69	29.07
(a) Small cultivator households		
(i) Labour use (lakh labour days)	66.10	67.66
(ii) Income (rupees crores)	10.13	8.21
(iii) Gross cropped area (lakh acres)	1.73	1.73
(iv) Net sown area (lakh acres)	1.41	1.41
(v) Cropping intensity (percent)	122.70	122.70
(b) Medium cultivator households		
(i) Labour use (lakh labour days)	106.57	107.79
(ii) Income (rupees crores)	25.04	15.27
(iii) Gross cropped area (lakh acres)	5.04	3.23
(iv) Net sown area (lakh acres)	4.68	4.68
(v) Cropping intensity (percent)	107.69	69.02
(c) Large cultivator households		
(i) Labour use (lakh labour days)	187.00	108.09
(ii) Income (rupees crores)	43.52	5.59
(iii) Gross cropped area (lakh acres)	9.81	2.20
(iv) Net sown area (lakh acres)	10.60	10.60
(v) Cropping intensity (percent)	92.55	20.75
B. Noncultivator rural households		
(i) Labour use (lakh labour days)	21.27	20.29
(ii) Income (rupees crores)	4.15	1.04

However, when assessed in terms of the employment norm, the differentials in the optimal solutions of the objectives are marked in the case of the large cultivator group which is most sensitive to the change in objective functions. Under the employment objective, it puts under plough only one-fifth of its land (and that mainly under irrigated cultivation of vegetables and green fodder), hires no labour, and, thus, causes a steep fall in the income of labour households in the nonfarm category. The small cultivator is not as sensitive to change.

Lastly, both objectives suggest the need for land redistribution, although the need is more vividly brought into focus by the employment objective. Note the marked decline in cropping intensity as we move from the small to the large cultivator category. For a comprehensive treatment of the land distribution aspect of the regional programming framework see Singh (forthcoming), and for its resource development alternative as approximated by irrigation investment, see Singh (1978a).

To sum up, the disaggregated analysis by category reveals that as the mode of production becomes relatively capitalistic in nature (that is, as we move from the small cultivator category to medium and large cultivator categories), the two objectives, income and employment maximization, yield divergent solutions.

Concluding Remarks

In conclusion, it would not be too much to say in the light of our empirical analysis that the employment maximization objective, if rigorously implemented in dry regions, will adversely affect not only regional income but also regional employment. Thus, for drought prone regions, the objective of a growth strategy should be income, not employment maximization.

References

Fox, K. A.; Sengupta, J. K.; and Thorbecke, E. (1966) The Theory of Quantitative Economic Policy with Applications to Economic Growth and Stabilization. Amsterdam; North Holland Publishing Co.

Government of India (1978) Draft Five Year Plan, 1978-83. New Delhi; Planning Commission.

Singh, B. (1978a) Economics of irrigation: A regional perspective. Indian Journal of Agricultural Economics, 33 (4) 231-239.

Singh, B. (1978b) Integrated local level planning: Some empirical explorations. Ahmedabad, Gujarat, India; Sadar Patel Institute of Economic and Social Research.

Singh, B. (forthcoming) Planning for rural development: Economics of land redistribution, in Seminar on the Design of Backward Areas Development (Indian Economic Association). New Delhi; Vikas Publishing House.

OPENER'S REMARKS--Andre H. Brun

To maximize employment and income are two objectives which may diverge. This kind of question is obviously challenging and concerns not only developing countries but developed countries as well, whether or not they have market or centrally planned economies. We must thank Singh for attempting to tackle this problem in a very concrete and closely examined example--the Surendranagar district.

In the income maximization run, the results seem quite logical as tested by the land use pattern in the 1970/71 census. However, one distortion appears: farmers in fact grow jowar (millet), yet the model predicts groundnuts. But by and large, farmers seem to behave in such a manner as to maximize regional

246

income. At this stage one can raise the problem of aggregation. To behave in such a manner as to maximize regional income is not necessarily identical to an individual's income maximizing behaviour, even within the prevailing rules of the game reflected by the market prices and given technology.

What would the model predict if it were disaggregated into four submodels corresponding to maxima for each of the four social groups identified? What are the conflicts existing in the region which are not reflected by market prices and can interfere with individual and collective targets?

In the employment maximization run of the model, nothing has been changed in the matrix--only the objective function has been changed. To maximize employment without any consideration of or constraint on income is easy for the simplex procedure. But it is difficult for our common perception. It means that we must imagine a kind of productivity which would be a ratio between the work done (taken as output) and the costs implied by the labour input. It is equivalent to postulating that labour intensive activities are more productive than activities requiring more capital. In this case, it is clear that it is not always possible to use all the labour available in the regions since each labour day is associated with the consumption of other limited resources.

But, what is more difficult to understand from the very sketchy knowledge that we have of the model is that in maximizing employment the model could give an optimum in which the rate of employment is lower than the employment level obtained when income is maximized. The author agrees that since income is taken as unimportant, the model generates only a small cash flow for large farmers and, as a result, they cannot hire as much labour as when income is maximized. This would imply that the maximization process cannot occur. Something is probably impeding the process and forcing it to stop at some second best solution. It is necessary to identify this obstacle in order to be able to interpret this second best solution. This point is mathematical in nature, not behavioural.

RAPPORTEUR'S REPORT--Dinesh K. Marothia

The inherent deficiencies in the too simplistic linear programming model and the emerging conflicting conclusions were highlighted. The inherent deficiencies in the model include the static nature of input-output coefficients based on the existing factor endowments and market technologies. The policy implications under such a situation with regard to output, income, and employment issues were questioned as being seemingly conflicting (an aggregation problem). To explore the desirability of pursuing employment or income objectives, it is necessary to consider alternative production and marketing technolgies, resource endowments, and policy measures.

ECONOMIC ANALYSIS OF FERTILITY BEHAVIOUR AMONG POOR RURAL HOUSEHOLDS IN BRAZIL

Ram D. Singh

Abstract

The economic value of children to the household provides a strong incentive to low income parents to increase the number of children or to substitute number for quality of children. Infant mortality has a strong positive impact, modern technology has a strong negative impact, and child quality (defined by schooling) has a negative and significant influence on the fertility behaviour of low income households. The mother's time allocation and her schooling has a weak influence. The coefficients of the father's schooling and his outside contacts are negative. Land has little impact, but increases in income have a positive effect on numbers, although this positive effect decreases as income rises. Important policy inferences pertain to: (1) the role of modern agricultural technology and income raising policies for the low income farms as deterrents to having children; (2) the need for reducing infant mortality through the provision of health care, medical facilities, information, and extension centres easily accessible to poor rural households; and (3) the deterrent effect of quality on numbers suggesting an ultimate decline in family size as a result of increase in schooling of children. Policies to deal with high fertility rates, low investment in human capital, and rural development are definitely interlinked and must form an integral part of a country's overall development policies.

OPENER'S REMARKS--Kenneth L. Bachman

Population growth and education should be important policy issues in development programmes in most poor rural areas or countries. This paper sheds some new light on the interrelationships that may exist. The traditional proposition, derived largely from regional and international relationships, is that lower birth rates and higher levels of education are associated with higher incomes. The findings in this paper suggest a somewhat different picture. They are derived from analysis of data obtained from poor rural households in Brazil using a cost-benefit approach. Emphasis is put on policies to raise small farm income to reduce family size, although incomes were found to be positively associated with larger families. Infant mortality was identified as having a strong positive effect on fertility behaviour, but was it sufficient to also affect actual family size and population growth? Further discussion of hypotheses that might be drawn from the interesting relationships suggested by these data would appear desirable in view of the crucial importance to the development of human resources of many poor rural areas of reducing population growth and improving education levels.

RAPPORTEUR'S REPORT--Dinesh K. Marothia

Population growth and education were discussed as being important interdependent variables. A high correlation between the lower birth rates and higher levels of education of children of rural family incomes was highlighted. The effects of production technology and higher income on family size were discussed. Medical and information services influence infant mortality and thereby fertility behaviour. Increased schooling of children and the ultimate decline in family size go hand in hand to increase the economic status of the poor rural households in the developing countries.

The Rural Challenge
at the Supranational Level

THE IMPACT OF MULTIPLE TRADE PREFERENCE GROUPS
ON WORLD TRADE PATTERNS

H. Evan Drummond and Ivarth Palacio

Abstract

The expected Vinerian impacts of economic integration are complicated when several preference groups are formed at approximately the same time. Members of each group hope to benefit at the expense of the members of the other groups. Using a modified form of a trade flow model, it is shown that the European Economic Community has been the only preference group of the four studied that has gained through trade diversion from members of all other groups. As expected, trade creation within each group occurred. The estimated change in the merchandise trade balance of the United States and Canada due to trade diversion by the four preference groups totaled US$4.2 billion in 1969.

RAPPORTEUR'S REPORT--E. David Walker

Although the presentation emphasized methodology rather than results and implications, the discussion centered on more practical issues. Limitations to the study were, among others, that the model did not take into account that the EEC is more than a preference group, the impact of the geographical size of countries on their trading patterns, or the trade diversion effects on excluded countries. Interest was also expressed in the experience since 1969. This period was purposely excluded from the study as it was believed that factors such as the expansion of the EEC, floating exchange rates, domestic issues in certain countries, and oil market developments may have had a larger impact on trade flows than preference group developments. The implications of the results of the study in the context of EFTA and EEC trade objectives were questioned, as well as the author's assessment of these two trade preference groups' trade performance. The interrelationship between the perceived overvaluation of the U.S. dollar and the formation of the preference groups during the study period was also a topic of discussion.

Contributing to the discussion were Charles W. Capstick, Ralph G. Lattimore, and Adolf Weber.

WORLD GRAINS: EVALUATING THE USE OF BUFFER STOCKS FOR REDUCING THE IMPACT OF YIELD VARIABILITY OF FOUR GRAINS

John O. S. Kennedy

Introduction

The issue of buffer stocks has been debated by various world agencies, and has stimulated contributions on the theoretical and empirical benefits of buffer stock schemes. The aim of this paper is to contribute to the current debate by describing the welfare results of simulating world production and consumption of four grains over a 20 year period before and after the introduction of alternative buffer stock schemes. Results from various models of this type have already been published (for example, see Cochrane and Danin; Johnson; Kennedy; Reutlinger; Sharples, Walker, and Slaughter; and Zwart and Meilke). The purpose of developing another model is to complement such results by taking a more disaggregated approach.

The world is divided into three regions: North and Central America (NCA); USSR, Europe, and Oceania (UEO); and China, Asia, Africa, and South America (CAAS). Income levels and consumer preferences may be assumed to be similar within the NCA and UEO regions. The CAAS region, representing the developing world, contains a much more heterogeneous set of countries, which could be subgrouped further in a more refined model.

The four grains selected are wheat, rice, maize, and barley. Wheat and rice represent the staple grains for human consumption, and maize and barley are taken as representative of the coarse grains mainly used for livestock feeding.

Model Description

For simplicity, a stationary process is assumed. Variables simulated in each year of a 20 year run do not take account of any trend changes, but relate to the 1975 base year. Production and trade relationships were estimated using FAO data where available for the years 1955 to 1975.

The simulation components of the model deal with production, consumption, and price determination. A decision component models storage, and an evaluation component records the impact of storage decisions on price variability, social economic benefits, and variability in the availability of energy intake from grains. These components are described in turn. Their interaction is summarized in equations (1) to (17) in figure 1. The following subscript notation is used: i = 1, 2, 3 refers to a particular region, whilst j = 1, 2, 3, 4 refers to a particular grain.

Production [Equations (1) and (2)]

Production (G) equals planted area (L) (which is assumed to be fixed) times yield (Y). Y equals the linear trend yield for 1975 $(\overline{Y})$ plus an error term (E). E is a random variable drawn from multivariate normal distributions of deviations from trend for each grain within the j-th region. Thus, it is assumed that all yields are approximately normally distributed, that the E are independent through time, and that there are no yield correlations between regions. The Kolmogorov-Smirnov test and the Durbin-Watson statistics show that the first two assumptions to be reasonable with few exceptions. About 30 percent of within region yields are significantly positively correlated. As regards between region correlations, about 10 percent are significantly negative and about 10 percent significantly positive.

Yield Production	$$Y_{ij} = \overline{Y}_{ij} + E_{ij} \quad (1)$$ $$G_{ij} = L_{ij} \cdot Y_{ij} \quad (2)$$

Storage
$$\Delta S_{ij} = S\{S_{ij}, G_{ij}, LB_{ij}, UB_{ij}, CL_{ij}\} \quad (3)$$

Availability
$$A_{ij} = G_{ij} - \Delta S_{ij} \quad (4); \qquad A_j = \sum_i A_{ij} \quad (5)$$

$$C'_{ij} = d_{ijo} + \sum_{k=1}^{4} d_{ijk} \cdot A_k \div d_{ij5} \cdot POP_i + D_{ij} \quad (6)$$

Consumption
$$C_{ij} = C'_{ij} (A_j / \sum_i C'_{ij}) \quad (7); \qquad C = \sum_i \sum_j C_{ij} \quad (8)$$

Exports
$$X_{ij} = A_{ij} - C_{ij} \quad (9)$$

Price
$$P = P\{C\} \quad (10)$$

Consumer Surplus
$$CS_{ij} = (\int_o^c P\{Q\} \, dQ - C.P\{C\}) \cdot (C_{ij}/C) \quad (11)$$

Producer Revenue
$$PR_{ij} = P.G_{ij} \quad (12)$$

Intervention Costs
$$IC_{ij} = P.\Delta S_{ij} \quad (13)$$

Storage Costs
$$SC_{ij} = k.S_{ij} \quad (14)$$

Social Benefit
$$SB_{ij} = \Delta CS_{ij} + \Delta PR_{ij} - IC_{ij} - \Delta SC_{ij} \quad (15)$$

Export Revenue
$$ER_{ij} = X_{ij}.P \quad (16)$$

Calorie Availability
$$CA_i = \sum_j C_{ij}.W.(1-ML_j)/(POP_i.365) \quad (17)$$

Figure 1. Flow diagram for the simulation of one year.

253

Consumption [Equations (4) to (9)]

Rather than attempting to simulate trade directly with a supply and demand model, simple linear regression equations for regional consumption are used. Regional consumption of each grain was regressed on world production of all grains and regional population (POP). Regional consumption (C) of each grain estimated from these equations is standardized by multiplying by the ratio of simulated world availability of the grain to estimated world consumption of the grain. This ensures that global exports equal global imports.

The random error term (D) permits variability in the estimates of regional consumption. D is drawn from regional multivariate normal distributions, based on the means and variance-covariance matrices of historical error terms of standardized consumption.

Exports (X) are defined as grain available within a region after any storage (A) less consumption (C).

Price [Equation (10)]

The system for simulating consumption did not permit the simultaneous determination of the regional price for each grain. In the absence of regional own and cross price functions for each grain, a global price indicator (P) is used. Global price is a function of total world consumption of all four grains (C). Such a global price is a very approximate device because its use implies perfect demand substitutability between grains and ignores price differentials which result from trade barriers and transport costs.

The total demand for world production of grains can be expected to be very inelastic in the short run. A constant price elasticity of demand of -0.1 was used in most runs of the model. Price was set equal to U.S.$120 per metric tonne for consumption equal to mean consumption.

Storage Rules [Equation (3)]

The efficacy of storage rules set in terms of production, prices, stocks, or emergency situations has been much debated. To be politically acceptable, storage rules have to be seen as fair and not offering scope for windfall gains. In the model, regional storage is a function of regional production relative to planned production. With the increasing accuracy of estimates of production from satellite observations, such a storage system would be practical. Production determined storage rules are not divorced from market signals to the extent that area planted to grain is responsive to price.

Lower and upper production bounds (LB and UB) are set around the mean production for triggering release and accumulation of stocks so that consumption falls within these bounds to the degree that stock levels (S) and storage capacity limits (CL) permit. For most runs of the model, regional storage capacity limits for each grain were set equal to 20 percent of the mean production.

Opening regional stock levels for wheat, rice, maize, and barley were set to equal 12, 4, 8, and 8 percent of mean regional production respectively. These are historically low levels and therefore represent feasible takeoff levels in practice.

Storage costs (before interest charges but including fixed costs) are $10 per tonne per year. A high value was chosen to cover costs of deterioration of stored grains.

Storage rules can be specified for any combination of region and grain. Further, integrated world storage policies based on trigger levels for world production are allowed. Storage activity and associated costs are shared between regions in proportion to mean regional production. A world storage policy allows greater flexibility because regional storage is no longer restricted by regional stock levels. However, for all policies, world and regional, any opportunities for storing different grains at different times in the same storage facility are ignored.

Evaluation of the Effects of Storage [Equations (11) to (17)]

The model keeps track of welfare variables in each of the simulated years if an active storage policy is followed, compared with what they would have been if stocks had been maintained throughout the 20 year period at their opening values. The social benefit of a storage scheme is defined as the present value of the stream of annual social benefits (see figure 1) in each period t:

$$SB_{ijt} = \Delta CS_{ijt} + \Delta PR_{ijt} - IC_{ijt} - \Delta SC_{ijt}$$

A real rate of interest of 3 percent per year is used for discounting.

If a region pursues a storage policy, costs or benefits follow for consumers and producers in all regions. However, intervention and storage costs are specific to the region. Intervention costs include the discounted value of the difference in the closing levels in year 20 and the opening stock in year 1.

Results for Selected Storage Policies

For each policy, 100 replications of a 20 year period were run. Storage trigger levels were set at 0.1 standard deviations above and below the mean production.

An active policy implemented only for wheat by the NCA region results in an increase in social benefit for each region ($690 million in total). However, the probability of per capita energy intake falling below 1,750 calories per day remains at 23 percent for the CAAS region, the region most at risk. Milling losses (ML) for wheat, rice, maize, and barley are assumed to be 10, 30, 10, and 10 percent respectively. Energy content (W) is taken to be 3,500 calories per kilogram of milled grain. By contrast, an active policy followed only for rice by the CAAS region leads to a substantial reduction in the probability of such a shortfall--to 12 percent. Changes in social benefit for the NCA, UEO, and CAAS regions are -$6,600, +$100 and -$12,000 million respectively. In all regions under both policies, consumers gain and producers lose.

Because most discussion on storage policy centres on wheat, the implications of alternative combinations of regional policies for wheat were tested. The UEO region as both the major producer of world wheat (50 percent) and the major importer of all grains gains most from an increase in the number of regions following a policy for wheat. If all regions follow an independent storage policy for wheat, changes in social benefit for the NCA, UEO, and CAAS regions are -$2,600, +$5,600 and +$1,700 million respectively. A switch to a cooperative world policy for wheat under which storage facilities are shared increases world social benefit from $4,700 million to $5,400 million.

Conclusion

The UEO region stands to benefit from storage policies for wheat and barley, and the CAAS region from a policy for rice. The NCA region, being an exporting region, would lose. However, the loss would not be as great to the extent that rice does not substitute perfectly for wheat in consumption. Also, the scope for policies for rice may be curbed by technical difficulties in storage.

Storage policies could bring benefits without maintaining average stock levels much higher than the low levels of the 1972-74 period, with the exception of rice. An upper capacity limit of 20 percent of the mean production is desirable if price and consumption variability are seen as major problems, otherwise a lower capacity limit would be preferred so that storage costs are reduced and social benefit is increased.

References

Cochrane, W. W.; Danin, Y. (1976) Reserve Stock Grain Models, the World and the United States, 1975-85 (Technical Bulletin No. 305). Minnesota, USA; University of Minnesota Agricultural Experiment Station.

FAO (1954-76) Production Yearbook and Trade Yearbook. Rome; Food and Agriculture Organization of the United Nations.

Johnson, D. G. (1977) Increased stability of grain supplies in developing countries: Optimal carryovers and insurance, in The New International Economic Order: The North-South Debate (edited by J. N. Bhagwati). Cambridge, Massachusetts, USA; MIT Press.

Kennedy, J. O. S. (1979) Optimal buffer stock policies for wheat at the world level. Australian Journal of Agricultural Economics, December.

Reutlinger, S. (1976) A simulation model for evaluating worldwide buffer stocks of wheat. American Journal of Agricultural Economics, 58 (1) 1-12.

Sharples, G. A.; Walker, R. L.; Slaughter, R. W. (1976) Managing Buffer Stocks to Stabilize Wheat Prices (Agricultural Economic Report No. 341). Washington, D.C.; U.S. Department of Agriculture.

Zwart, A. C.; Meilke, K. D. (1976) Economic implications of international wheat reserves. Canadian Journal of Agricultural Economics, July, 62-77.

RAPPORTEUR'S REPORT--E. David Walker

The discussion generally centred on the applicability of the paper due to the limitations of the model and results. The regional division of the world was not considered particularly relevant with regard to actual stockpiling policy development. The author noted that the study could be replicated with different regional selections to provide more relevant guidance in this respect. The constant stock level and free trade assumptions were also believed to limit the validity of the results in a practical context.

The rural social benefits suggested by the study were relatively minor in comparison with the rural value of global grain production. Further, the relatively large social benefits for the CAAS region for rice in comparison with other regions and other grains was related to the scale of rice production in the CAAS region rather than to any fundamental difference in the impact of stock policy.

It was suggested that it would be appropriate for individual countries to utilize a game theory model in conjunction with this model when developing strategies with respect to buffer stock policies.

Contributing to the discussion were Hans G. Hirsch, Donald MacLaren, and Ammar Siamwalla.

TRADE AND DEVELOPMENT: THE POTENTIAL FOR CONFLICT

Kirby Moulton and Patrick Shea

Abstract

The expansion of domestic and international trade opportunities is an important objective of EC agricultural policies. Yet, the investments which facilitate this trade have not been well coordinated with rural development projects. The result is the continuation of regional economic imbalances and trade flows which shift development problems from one region to another. The problem is exacerbated by the preponderance of EC funds used for agricultural purposes and the five to one agricultural investment advantage of the Italian Mezzogiorno over Mediterranean France during 1964-77.

Market oriented development policies have facilitated the economic export of table wine from Italy to France, to the detriment of French development programmes. Efforts by the French to shift the trade impact through expanded wine exports to third countries can lead to development problems in those countries. The results of the imbalance between market oriented programmes and rural development programmes are also evident in Italy where commodity and trade oriented programmes displaced more people than could be absorbed in other activities.

Strong factors militate against a future improvement in programme balance. They include the relative potential strength of agricultural ministries and national and supranational commodity organizations, the protectionist stance being taken by EC members which views regional aid in one country as detrimental to other countries, and the high proportion of agriculturally derived revenues which are used to fund EC investments. This suggests that agricultural development rather than coordinated rural development will continue to dominate the future and that trade flows will create added problems.

RAPPORTEUR'S REPORT--Sylvestre Ndabambalire

There was a general consensus among the participants on the inevitable conflicts between the objectives pursued, the trade partners, the policymakers and the beneficiaries of the measures to be undertaken. To prevent such conflicts, an ex-ante analysis of divergent interests and an ex-post evaluation of the trade and development policies have to be undertaken. Furthermore, active participation of the citizens and coordination at all levels of authority are required.

The regional economic content of the paper (Mezzogiorno Italy and Southern France) elicited some observations concerning the nature, objectives, and operation of the Common Agricultural Policy in the member states of the EC. Within the European Agricultural Guidance and Guarantee Fund, the member countries have set goals to assure farmers an acceptable minimum income level, facilitate structural changes and adjustments in rural areas, and avoid and reduce regional disparities.

Contributing to the discussion were Christa Haebler and Ulrich Koester.

MINIMUM INCOME POLICY: ELEMENTS AND EFFECTS OF AN ALTERNATIVE INSTRUMENT OF FARM POLICY OF THE EUROPEAN COMMUNITY

Gunther Schmitt and Harald von Witzke

Introduction

Price support for farm products through import restrictions still represents the main instrument for raising farm sector incomes within the Common Agricultural Policy (CAP) of the European Community (EC).

The objective of this paper is first to analyze the effects of the traditional price policy of the CAP. Next, an alternative type of farm income policy will be discussed which seems to be more consistent with the general principles of income policy outside agriculture, and which should be able to avoid, or at least reduce, most of the negative effects of the present price policy of the EC.

The Present Agricultural Income Policy of the EC

The Instruments of Agricultural Income Policy

Price support instruments differ to a certain degree according to the specific supply and demand conditions of the product in mind. However, almost all types of price support fall into two basically similar categories; namely, (1) levies on imported goods which refer to the difference between world market prices and fixed minimum import prices; and (2) guaranteed minimum prices for farm products within the Community in order to maintain a minimum level of prices and income if internal supply should exceed internal demand.

Every year the Council of Ministers of the member countries has to make unanimous decisions on the level of common prices for farm products. Due to differing economic conditions among the member countries, these unanimous decisions have become more and more difficult, and these difficulties will increase with the future enlargement of the EC. The national prices for agricultural products differ, however, since changing exchange rates of currencies are compensated by the monetary compensatory amounts (MCAs) (Schmitt, 1977 and 1978; and Heidhues, Josling, Ritson, and Tangermann).

The Effects of the Common Price Policy

It is quite obvious that the CAP results in prices above the world market level and that production in nonmember countries is lower than without such a policy, while production in member countries is higher. For important agricultural products there is even excess supply. Furthermore, the system of variable levies has accentuated the instability of world market prices of the products concerned (Johnson). Potential welfare gains of the Common Market are probably decreasing new trade barriers within the Community via MCAs. Due to the supported prices, the EC suffers welfare losses because of a suboptimal intersectorial factor allocation and a suboptimal structure of consumption (Koester and Tangermann). Finally, it has to be mentioned that in the long run, high income farmers who, strictly speaking, do not need income support measures benefit absolutely and relatively more from price supports than those with low incomes (von Witzke, 1979b).

258

An Alternative Concept of Farm Policy

Various proposals have been put forward in the past in order to substitute the present price support policy with alternative instruments of income policy. The alternative concept to be discussed in this paper is different from those proposals, because it would not only avoid most of the negative effects mentioned above, but could also resolve the existing problem of low incomes in agriculture without inhibiting necessary structural adjustment of the farm sector, and it is also consistent with the general principles of income policy.

The System of Minimum Income Policy

A system of a guaranteed minimum income is characterized by two essential elements: (1) the level of guaranteed minimum income; and (2) the marginal decrease of income transfers in relation to increasing income. Various types of minimum income guarantees (negative income taxes) with respect to these elements have been suggested (Wille). The efficiency of a minimum income policy depends (among other factors) on the level of minimum income. If it is fixed too low, there might be an insufficient income support. If it is fixed relatively high, there might be negative effects on the incentives for structural adjustment which cannot be ignored.

The marginal decrease in income transfers depending on increases in market income should be such that there are sufficient incentives for farmers to increase their market incomes. There will probably be no special income tax rates for farmers. The marginal rate of decrease in transfers, therefore, has to take into account that farmers above a certain market income level have to pay income tax (BMF).

Each member country has already installed a different system of income policy which contains income guarantees in one form or another (Kaim-Caudle). The main objective of these minimum income guarantees is to avoid the standard of living of a household falling below a given minimum level. There is no reason, from the point of view of income policy, why the systems which guarantee a minimum standard of living for the nonagricultural population should not be applied to agriculture and should not enable agricultural households to realize at least this minimum standard of living. Compared with the present agricultural income support via price policy, the income support via minimum incomes guarantees, as proposed here, is relatively low, but it is the same income as that guaranteed for all other households which do not earn a sufficient market income.

It is obvious that the level of minimum income has to be different among member countries not only because there are different systems of minimum income support but also because of different opportunity costs of labour in each country. This is also in conformity with the Treaty of Rome which states that the agricultural policy of the Community has to take into consideration the fact that the agricultural sectors are closely linked with the economy of each of the member countries. For a detailed analysis of this point, see von Witzke (1979a). It cannot be concealed that there might be administrative problems concerning the ascertainment of the true farm income. As far as we can see, rural income maintenance programs in different states of the United States indicate that these problems can be overcome (Palmer and Pechman).

Minimum income payments are normally granted if households have both very low income and no assets which could be sold or used to obtain loans. If the same criteria were applied, farm households would not get income transfer payments unless they sold their farm or could not get any more borrowed money for consumption and investments. As far as we can see, this is consistent with

259

the general principles of income policy, but would be unacceptable to politicians, specially because of the capital losses farmers have to suffer before being eligible for income transfers. Hence, the minimum income policy for farmers should be oriented along the general principles of national income policies of each of the member countries, but it should not be necessary to count all their capital when applying for minimum income grants.

Effects of a Minimum Income Policy on Agriculture

If the present price support policy were replaced by a minimum income policy, restrictions on imports of agricultural products from nonmember countries could be reduced, as well as the minimum price guarantees for such goods within the EC. Farm prices could then be reduced to the world market level or a level which still guarantees regular supplies of farm products according to Article 39 of the Treaty of Rome. Price policy would then only aim at stabilization of world markets prices and at the desired level of self-sufficiency.

It is obvious that a partial substitution of price support policy by minimum income guarantees would (1) reduce the rise of agricultural production within the EC, (2) remove the EC barriers to international trade in agricultural goods, and (3) avoid any excess supply. Most of the negative effects on income distribution in agriculture, factor allocation, and international trade of the present price support policy would thus also be reduced.

Minimum Income Guarantees in the EC

Although the negative effects of the CAP are quite obvious, the member countries of the EC have up to now resisted any basic change in the agricultural price support system. It has to be assumed that they will behave so in future too, so that they will not agree to any sudden and fundamental change in the CAP like the minimum income guarantees proposed in this paper. An abrupt and fundamental change in the present system, however, is not desirable either, because this would not be consistent witht the general principle of a stable economic policy, and would surely cause high private and social costs of adjusting to the new policy. Any alternative measure of income policy would have to be introduced gradually to have any chance of being realized.

On the other hand, continuing the present policy of price supports as a vehicle for increasing farmers' incomes as much as nonfarm incomes within the Community is becoming increasingly difficult. These difficulties are exaggerated by the economic recession since 1973--the process of structural change has slowed down, population and income growth are extremely low, technological progress and thereby growth in farm output is still rather high, and, in the near future, the Community will be enlarged by developing countries, such as Greece, Spain, and Portugal, which will very probably accelerate the surplus situation of the EC. Together with the difficult economic problems, especially as far as the balance of payments levels of most present and future member countries are concerned, the present policy of relatively high producer prices cannot be continued over a long time period in order to support producers' incomes.

A minimum income policy can indeed gradually reset the system of price support. For this, each member country first has to introduce a system of minimum income guarantees which is consistent with its general national income policy and which takes into account the special situation of farmers as discussed above. In this situation, relatively few farmers will be able to apply for an income transfer, because farm incomes are still supported by the price policy. After introduction of such a system, the real level of price support can be gradually reduced to the average long run world market prices, which is a level of price support which guarantees the desired rate of self-sufficiency. Average

260

farm income will probably also decrease but none of the farm households will have less than the income guaranteed to all other households in each of the member countries. The substitution of the price support policy by minimum income guarantees, however, requires politicians to have the courage to cut off the privileges of the present agricultural income policy and to apply the principles of the general income policy to both nonagricultural and agricultural households.

References

BMF-Schriftenreihe (1978) Gutachen zur Einkommensbesteuerung der Land-wirtschaft (Vol. 24). Bonn.

Heidhues, T.; Josling, T. E.; Ritson, C.; Tangermann, S. (1978) Common Prices and Europe's Farm Policy (Thames Essays No. 14). London; Trade Policy Research Centre.

Johnson, D. G. (1973) World Agriculture in Disarray. London; St. Martin's Press.

Kaim-Caudle, P. R. (1973) Comparative Social Policy and Social Security: A Ten Country Study. London.

Koester, U.; Tangermann, S. (1976) Alternativen der Agrarpolitik. Land-wirtschaft--Angewandte Wissenschaft, 182.

Palmer, J. L.; Pechman, J. A. (editors) (1978) Welfare in Rural Areas: The North Carolina-Iowa Income Maintenance Experiment. Washington, D.C.

Schmitt, G. (1977) The relationship between agricultural policy, the economy, and economic policy on the national level in different economic systems, in Decision-Making and Agriculture (edited by T. Dams and K. E. Hunt). Oxford; Alden Press, 208-244.

Schmitt, G. (1978) Grenzen und Moglichkeiten der landwirtschaftlichen Einkommenspolitik unter veranderten gesamtwirtschaftlichen Rahmenbeding-ungen. Agrarwirtschaft, 27, 165-180.

Wille, M. (1974) Formen, Moglichkeiten und Wirkungen direkter Einkommen-subertragungen an die Landwirtschaft. Gottingen.

Witzke, H. von (1979a) Mindesteinkommenspolitik auch fur die Landwirts-chaft.

Witzke, H. von (1979b) Personelle Einkommensverteilungen in der Land-wirtschaft und Agrarpreise. Volkswirtschaftliche Schriften Heft, 281.

OPENER'S REMARKS--Per Lundborg

The authors have identified important problems associated with the current income support policy of the European Community. But the questions are very complex and need more exhaustive treatment. Their proposal is vague and not original. I agree that a guaranteed minimum income is essential for a minimum income policy, but I cannot see that a marginal decrease of income transfers in relation to increasing income is necessary. It is more a question of how progressive the income tax is and how the social transfer system works. Thus, I must conclude that the authors have suggested a minimum income policy combined with a system of other direct income transfers, without explicitly recognizing this point. Direct income payments have for a long time been considered the alternative to the present price policy, and minimum incomes are widely used within the frameworks of the social security systems of the member countries.

There is a large number of aspects that are not discussed or that are commented upon too briefly, such as the effects of the minimum income policy on farmers' incentives. It is claimed that a minimum income policy would not inhibit structural adjustment. There is, however, no extensive discussion of this.

Any minimum income high enough to substantially improve the welfare of farmers may very easily inhibit structural change. It is not very easy to find a minimum income level that has no negative effects.

A totally neglected question is the political implications of exchanging the present system for the one suggested by the authors. We know that farmers tend to regard direct income payments as socially demeaning charity. Therefore, political difficulties of implementation may arise.

The authors stress the need to lower the rate of production increases within the Common Market and to increase the import share of consumption. Assuming that productivity increases at an unchanged rate, this will require that labour leave agriculture even faster than otherwise. There will be political resistance to reducing the rate of production increase, and it is doubtful whether farmers will regard the suggested policy as helpful.

The paper points out several important problems with the present EC price policy, as have several other papers presented during this conference. The purpose of the paper is therefore to be appreciated and commended. However, I am very sceptical about the proposal presented. A minimum income policy can at the most be a complementary tool for the Common Market. But it can hardly be a substitute for the present policy, even in the long run.

RAPPORTEUR'S REPORT--Sylvestre Ndabambalire

The participants agreed on the social character of the direct income payments which are supposed to be an alternative policy instrument. However, almost all rejected the authors' assumption about the supply and cost curves as well as about domestic and world market conditions. The administrative, political, and social problems (eligibility criteria and perception of the direct income payments as socially demeaning) which impede the applicability of the minimum income policy and neutralize its presumed positive effects were repeatedly emphasized. The generally expected but also questionable advantages of the minimum income policy are trade expansion, enhanced social welfare, optimal factor allocation, desired structural changes and adjustments, and equitable income redistribution, among others.

Contributing to the discussion were Harold F. Breimyer, Michael Haines, Ulrich Koester, and John R. Raeburn.

ECONOMIC AND SOCIAL DIMENSIONS OF WEED CONTROL TECHNOLOGY: AN INTERNATIONAL PERSPECTIVE

Stanley F. Miller and Frank S. Conklin

Abstract

Agricultural weed control in the United States in which chemicals are generally applied by aerial or tractor pulled conveyances is labour saving and capital using. Extension of this model to developing countries has typically taken the form of chemical application with backpack sprayers, also labour saving. This meets economic and social efficiency criteria only for developing countries faced with relative labour scarcity and abundant land and capital resources. Many developing countries, however, face relative labour abundance and capital scarcity. This includes El Salvador and two sites in Brazil in which the International Plant Protection Centre has conducted agroeconomic research on weed control. Traditional manual methods are the dominant form of weed control there. Government policies in both countries have reduced the herbicide-labour price ratio some 35-55 percent below what it would have been under open market conditions, which encourages a switch to chemical weed control. If this occurs, an increase in agricultural labour unemployment of some 40-80 percent is expected in those regions, exacerbating an already serious social problem. However, in the North Atlantic zone of Costa Rica, an environment with some seasonal labour scarcity, current research which incorporates chemical weed control treatments into the traditional no-tillage mulching practice appears both privately and socially promising, with some adoption occurring on farms employing hired labour. Diversity of relative factor endowments and ecological conditions, therefore, must be carefully assessed in determining the appropriateness of introducing weed control technologies.

The Rural Challenge
at the Multinational Level

MULTINATIONAL COOPERATIVES: THEIR POTENTIAL ROLE IN THE INTERNATIONAL GRAIN MARKETING SYSTEM

Michael L. Cook, Ronald D. Knutson, and Thomas L. Sporleder

In recent years, concern has arisen about the structure of the international grain trade and its ability to operate in the interest of exporting or importing countries (McCalla and Schmitz). Producers and consumers question whether international market intermediaries' interests or strategies operate in a manner consistent with producers' and consumers' interests.

Efforts to address these issues have emphasized policies where government becomes more directly involved in trade. Examples include state trading, marketing boards, and bilateral trade agreements. While recognizing such alternatives, this paper addresses the potential for producers and consumers to become more directly involved in the international grain trade through cooperative organizations and thus to improve the performance of the international grain marketing system. To accomplish this, it is necessary to review the structure of international grain marketing.

Marketing Structure and Functions in Grain Trade

The services and decisions involved in importing and exporting grain can be performed and made by government agencies acting as state traders, by proprietary corporations, or by cooperatives. The services include assembly, purchase arrangements and hedging, storage, transportation, blending, international shipping, unloading at receiving port, receiving port storage, interior storage, processing, and ultimate sale.

In the exchange process, various forms of risk are encountered. These include the risk of changes in government policies, commodity prices, variable levies, currency exchange rates, ocean freight, inland freight, demurrage charges, and buyer credit risks. While many of these risks can be reduced by forward contracts and hedging in futures or currency markets, the need for substantial sophistication and scale of operation in performing these functions is apparent.

The complexity and risks associated with international grain marketing have led to relatively high levels of concentration in the functions performed by public and private participants. Private participants include proprietary trading companies and cooperatives. Public participants are referred to as state traders.

Continental, Cargill-Tradex, Bunge, Dreyfus, and Garnac are considered to be the largest of the private international market intermediaries (Thurston, Phillips, Haskell, and Volkin). These firms are multinational in scope; that is, they deal in the grains from any source as either exporters, importers, or market intermediaries, and generally have a legal base of business operation in most major importing and exporting countries. A fringe of smaller trading companies exists as rivals to these major companies. Among this fringe are a number of Japanese trading companies which now have growing third country sales, own exporting country elevators, and thus hold the potential for challenging the position of the largest firms. Our studies of the major exporting and importing countries indicate that the proprietary grain trading companies are involved as exporters in 74 percent of the volume of international trade in grain and 47 percent as importers. They are involved in market intermediary functions in an even larger proportion of international trade in grain.

Grain cooperatives play a significant role in most market economies. In first handler functions of grain assembly, storage, and transportation, it is estimated that cooperatives handle 45 percent of the grain produced in exporting nations. Cooperative activity in the international grain trade tends to be limited to trading functions that comprehend less risk. Overall, it is estimated that cooperatives are involved in approximately 9 percent of the world grain trade exports and 10 percent of the imports, at least to the extent of making an f.o.b. sale to or purchase from an international trader. The greatest cooperative participation in grain export trade exists in Argentina, United States, France, and Brazil. The grain importing countries which have substantial cooperative involvement include Japan, Netherlands, the Federal Republic of Germany, and Belgium.

State traders acting as public agencies operate primarily as exporters or importers of grain; that is, they make decisions on the purchase or sale of grain including quantity, quality, price, and timing. They are also involved in making arrangements for shipping which frequently involves the services of market intermediaries. State traders of major centrally planned economies also may perform many or all of the market intermediary functions on at least a portion of their grain purchases. Our study indicates that approximately 17 percent of the world grain trade exports and 43 percent of the imports involve state traders (Knutson, Cook, and Sporleder).

Significant structural differences exist in the international market for food grains, coarse grains, and soybeans (table 1). High levels of country concentration exist in both soybean and coarse grain exports while lower levels of concentration exist in imports. State trading in these commodities is relatively unimportant. International trade in soybeans and coarse grains is thus dominated by the proprietary grain trading companies in exporting, importing, and market intermediary roles. The market shares for cooperative exports of coarse grains and soybeans range from 8 to 11 percent, and their imports from 17 to 22 percent.

Table 1--Comparison of grain importing and exporting
country concentration ratios by commodity and by
proprietary, cooperative, and state trading market shares
for the largest eight exporting and importing countries, 1977-78

	Soybeans and meal	Coarse grain	Wheat
	(Percent)		
Exporting countries			
4 country share	100	88	85
8 country share	100	96	91
State trading share[1]	0	9	31
Proprietary trade share	92	80	61
Cooperative share	8	11	8
Importing countries			
4 country share	46	47	36
8 country share	72	72	51
State trading share[1]	7	10	90
Proprietary trade share	71	73	10
Cooperative share	22	17	0

Source: Knutson, Cook, and Sporleder.

[1] State trading, proprietary, or cooperative share is the estimated percent of the total volume of direct grain exports or imports by state traders, proprietary firms, or cooperatives for the eight largest exporting or importing countries.

In wheat, the structure is significantly different. Exporting country concentration remains high, yet importing country concentration is relatively lower with an eight country concentration ratio of 50 percent. State traders are much more important in wheat. Two of the four largest wheat exporting and seven of the largest eight importing countries are state traders. State traders are estimated to account for one-third of the exports and 90 percent of the imports of wheat. Yet, market intermediaries still perform a significant role since they are frequently called upon by state traders to handle shipping arrangements and other noncommodity price risk functions. Cooperative involvement in wheat trade is very small with less than 8 percent of the exports and no significant volume of imports.

Coordination Arrangements for Cooperatives

Three alternative coordination arrangements for cooperatives are presented which represent means for linking international grain trade activities. These alternative arrangements impact on the pricing and operational efficiency of international coordination between cooperatives.

A previous study of U.S. cooperatives in international grain trade dealt solely with their role as exporters (Thurston, Phillips, Haskell, and Volkin). The alternative arrangements, discussed below, expand the perspective to import and export activities at the international level.

Intercooperative trade agreements establish a system of grain trading practices among cooperatives in two or more countries. Parties to the agreement may be either exporters or importers. Agreements may cover quantities of grain to be bought and sold, quality, timing, pricing methods, and financing.

International marketing agencies in common combine the international marketing efforts of cooperatives located in two or more exporting or importing countries. This involves the formation of a new federated cooperative to handle functions such as sales contacts, market information, ocean shipping, and financial arrangements. The agency does not take title to the grain, thus leaving the final decisions on purchase or sale to the cooperative members.

A multinational cooperative is owned by cooperatives in two or more exporting or importing countries, takes title to the grain, and performs other functions of international grain traders.

Of particular significance to developing countries, a multinational grain cooperative also acts as a catalyst in developing livestock and poultry production systems. While already a significant aspect of proprietary grain company market development activities, cooperative livestock and poultry production systems hold the potential for being more responsive to local producer needs as well as sharing in the economic benefits of cooperative involvement in the world grain trade.

Objectives of Cooperatives and Performance Implications

Which alternative arrangement is chosen by cooperatives to expand their role in the international grain trade depends on the goals they seek to achieve. Three objectives with decidedly different performance implications are suggested.

Improving competition as a means of enhancing pricing and operational efficiency has been the traditional cooperative role and basis for extending special public policy treatment to cooperatives. In international grain trade, the most significant source of benefits appears to accrue from: (1) improved timeliness in the sale or purchase of grain; (2) improved market information; and (3) margins from performing grain marketing functions. The first two sources of benefits may be considerably greater than the latter. To capture these benefits, direct involvement in grain trading through either an international marketing agency in common or a multinational cooperative would appear to be essential.

Certain behavioral patterns are necessary if an international grain marketing cooperative is to have its full impact in terms of improving competition in the grain trade. These conditions were first specified by Helmberger and further adapted here for consideration of an international grain cooperative having both producer and consumer interests. The conditions include: open membership providing freedom of entry and exit from the cooperative for both exporters and importers, no attempts to control members' production or purchases, cooperative operations as efficient and effective as proprietary traders, and net margins distributed in an equitable manner to both importers and exporters.

To compete, an agency or multinational cooperative would need to trade in the grains of two more more countries as exporters with as many importing countries as possible. While the source of grain would likely be limited to cooperative member suppliers in two or more countries, sales could be made to either cooperative or noncooperative firms under either the agency or multinational enterprise structure. These structures could thus become a significant alternative source of supply for state traders or private importers in both developed and developing countries.

Cooperative market shares and facilities already exist in coarse grains and soybeans from which a successful marketing agency in common or multinational cooperative could be formed. Cooperatives in the EC, Argentina, Brazil, United States, and Japan would be logical participants in such ventures. Expansion into wheat is possible with the eventual inclusion of Australian, Canadian, and developing country cooperatives.

The benefits of an international grain cooperative having the objective of increasing competition would be shared by both exporters and importers. One could realistically anticipate that exporter benefits would be mainly in the pricing efficiency arena; that is, in terms of increased speed and accuracy of market signals to producers. Pricing inefficiencies in the grain trade have been particularly apparent during times when substantial grain sales have been consummated but information on their magnitude withheld. Cooperatives operating in the international grain market could be more sensitive to the producer and public interest in more perfect information systems.

Importing country benefits would likely concentrate on opportunities for increased operational efficiency. Such benefits include sharing in cooperative margins, improved grain quality, and providing purchasers of relatively small quantities with the benefits of larger volume shipments to areas such as the EC, Southeast Asia, or Africa.

Improving coordination of international grain movements to assure market supplies and outlets has been recognized as a basic need since 1972. This need has resulted in the establishment of numerous bilateral trade agreements between governments. Trading agreements between exporting and importing cooperatives, exporting cooperatives and state traders, or state traders and importing cooperatives could be at least equally beneficial where direct control over grain supplies exists. Such trade agreements could either be part of or separate from agency or multinational cooperative arrangements. Bilateral cooperative trade agreements have been in effect between U.S., Japanese, European, and South American cooperatives for a number of years.

Benefits of such agreements would be limited to cooperatives and countries involved in agreements. Unless combined with an agency or multinational cooperative arrangement, the dispersion of benefits in a broader market performance context would be limited.

Increasing grain prices through various coordinated export devices has received much attention since OPEC successes have become evident. High country export concentration ratios in the major grains suggest, at first glance, potential for monopolistic exploitation equal to what has been accomplished in oil (table 1). Relatively low cooperative market shares do not, however, hold the same potential. Even if cooperative exporting efforts were to be combined with those of marketing boards, export market shares would in each grain be less than 40 percent.

In the long run, it will be difficult to maintain grain prices above competitive levels. Recent studies of grain supply response indicate a potential for substantially increased production at higher prices (Peterson; and Heady). In addition, since many of the major wheat importers are either centrally planned or developing countries, international economic and political tensions might increase. The main beneficiaries would, of course, be producers in the United States, Argentina, Australia, France, and Canada.

Concluding Remarks

A combination of trade agreements and either a common marketing agency or a multinational cooperative holds the potential for reducing market imperfections in the international grain trade--particularly in coarse grains and soybeans. Of these alternatives, trade agreements are clearly the easiest to implement. Expanding trade agreement activities into a common marketing agency holds substantial potential. Interest in this concept exists on both importer and exporter sides, largely as a basis for spreading high fixed costs of an international sales and market information network. The multinational cooperative concept deserves consideration as a longer run goal. Prerequisites for effective operation include the ability to deal in the grains of several countries as a separate operating entity and commitment of both exporters and importers to utilize the cooperative to the fullest extent. A recent survey of cooperative leaders and government trade policy officials in 20 countries indicates that serious consideration of coordinated cooperative arrangements in the international grain trade is appropriate (Knutson, Cook, and Sporleder).

References

Heady, E. O. (1978) World food production potential and constraint upon it, in World Agricultural Trade: The Potential for Growth. Kansas City, Missouri, USA; Federal Reserve Bank of Kansas City, 18-33.

Helmberger, P. (1964) Cooperative enterprise as a structural dimension of farm markets. American Journal of Agricultural Economics, 46, 603-617.

Knutson, R. D.; Cook, M. L.; Sporleder, T. L. (forthcoming) Assessment of International Cooperative Coordination in World Grain Trade.

McCalla, A. (1977) Strategies in International Agricultural Marketing: Public vs. Private Sectors (Paper No. 466). Berkeley, California, USA; Giannini Foundation, University of California.

Peterson, W. E. (1979) International farms prices and the social cost of cheap food policies. American Journal of Agriculutral Economics, 61 (1) 12-21.

Schmitz, A. (1977) Implications of prospective international commodity trade agreements and changes in marketing strategies for farm income levels and stability, in Farm and Food Policy Symposium (Publication No. 84). Lincoln, Nebraska, USA; Great Plains Agricultural Council, 97-120.

Thurston, S. K.; Phillips, M. J.; Haskell, J. E.; Volkin, D. (1977) Improving the Export Capability of Grain Cooperatives (Research Report No. 34). Washington, D.C.; Farmer Cooperative Service, U.S. Department of Agriculture.

OPENER'S REMARKS--W. E. Hamilton

This paper deals with a subject that deserves attention due to the growing importance of international trade in grains and the leading role played by a few multinational firms in the private portion of this trade. It would be hard to disprove the authors' modest conclusion that a combination of trade agreements and either a common marketing agency or a multinational cooperative holds the potential for reducing market imperfections in the international grain trade-- particularly in coarse grains and soybeans. This potential undoubtedly exists, but the obstacles to achieving significant results are substantial. It is, therefore, unfortunate that space limitations apparently precluded a more detailed discussion of the approaches that may be necessary to develop viable multinational cooperative arrangements.

Two fundamental considerations appear to deserve particular attention. First, international trade in grain is a high risk business for private participants. Second, as middlemen, multinational grain companies can deal with buyers and sellers and trade in grain from different origins without the tensions that are likely to develop in cooperative efforts to serve competing or conflicting interests. The differences between direct cooperative exporters and the major multinational grain exporting firms were summarized by Thurston and others and are well known. If these differences actually reflect the greater freedom of proprietary companies to develop mechanisms for reducing and spreading risks, it would appear that the multinational companies have some rather substantial advantages over cooperatives. Cooperatives, of course, have their own strong points and have been able to develop a modest volume of direct exports in some instances.

The obstacles to the development of mechanisms for reducing and spreading risks may be even greater for a multinational than for a national cooperative. If so, this suggests a need to explore arrangements which require a multinational entity to take title to grain. Direct transactions between cooperatives respresenting producers and cooperatives representing users are clearly possible, but the opposing interests of buyers and sellers suggest that there are likely to be times when buying and selling cooperatives cannot reach agreement. A common buying agency representing importers in two or more countries appears to be a practical possibility and the formation of such an agency should increase opportunities for cooperative to cooperative trade. The use of a common agency to represent both buying and selling cooperatives appears impracticable due to the conflicting interests of buyers and sellers. A common agency representing exporters form two or more countries would need to find ways of convincing its members that sales of grain from different national origins would be made on a completely impartial basis. That could prove to be difficult.

It may be that something other than the typical type of cooperative organization is needed to permit cooperatives to work together on a multi-national basis in competition with the multinational grain companies. One possibility is that cooperatives in two or more countries could set up, invest in, or acquire a multinational grain company. A trading company owned in whole or in part by cooperatives presumably would operate very much like any other multinational grain company. It would have the ability as a separate operating entity to deal in the grain markets of several countries, which the authors cite as a prerequisite for the effective operation of a multinational cooperative. It would need to have the commitment of both exporters and importers to utilize its facilities to the fullest extent, but, as a practical matter, it is to be expected that both exporters and importers would insist on retaining the right to utilize other channels.

Strong national cooperatives which have the ability to compete with multinational companies are probably a prerequisite for the development of effective multinational cooperative arrangements. If multinational arrangements are to retain the support of their sponsors, they will probably have to yield benefits which can be clearly identified by participating cooperatives and their members.

Some of the potential benefits cited by the authors are highly conjectural. Multinational activities should improve the flow of information to the managers of participating cooperatives, but this would not necessarily mean a significant improvement in the speed and accuracy of market signals to producers. The authors say that cooperatives operating in the international grain market could be more sensitive to producer and general public interest in more perfect information systems. Cooperatives could be more sensitive, but it does not necessarily follow that they would be. It is not unusual, at least in the United States, for cooperatives to take essentially the same position as their noncooperative competitors on anything that relates to their business activities.

In my opinion, the basic objective of multinational cooperative grain marketing activities should be to increase competition in the international market. While other benefits, such as better information, may be useful byproducts, the long term survival of any multinational cooperative activity probably requires operating results which convince its sponsors that it is adding directly to farmers' incomes through its impact on grain prices, marketing costs, or both.

RAPPORTEUR'S REPORT--David I. Bateman

The authors' classification of trading organizations in table 1 made the definition of a cooperative an important issue. Some organizations that might call themselves cooperatives would be regarded in most countries as state traders. In reply, Cook said that he and his coauthors had difficulty in agreeing on a definition of cooperative. They decided that insistence on the Rochdale principles is too narrow an approach and that the most satisfactory procedure in their empircial work was to accept self-classification by the organizations concerned.

Some participants thought that in certain cases (for example, exporting and importing cooperatives) conflict was more likely than cooperation. A co-operative would not give up its own objectives for the sake of cooperative philosophy. Others gave examples of instances where such cooperation had occurred or might occur. Long term supply contracts were referred to as offering the possibility of mutual benefit in the future. Cook agreed that "cooperative philosophy isn't worth half a cent" to most cooperatives, but said that his survey had identified many examples of agreements between apparently antagonistic cooperatives. For example, long term supply contracts between cooperatives already exist. The problem of price setting in this context is one where he has some confidential information, but new ideas are required. There was evidence of a move over time towards "more sophisticated" forms of coordination between cooperatives.

Because international grain trading is a high risk industry, it is possible that a form of coordination that was organizationally feasible might not be cost feasible. Cook emphasized that he had deliberately not addressed this issue. It was important to examine case studies of successes and failures as a guide to cost feasibility.

Contributing to the discussion were Harold F. Breimyer, Hans G. Hirsch, Christian Jorgensen, and Allan D. McLeod.

The Rural Challenge
at the Disciplinary Level

A THEORY OF PRODUCTION, INVESTMENT, AND DISINVESTMENT

Alan E. Baquet

Rural change often involves altering the combination of durable assets owned by an economic unit. Rural change may involve the acquisition of additional durables, the disposal of current durables, or using retained durables in a different manner. The current theories of production, investment, and disinvestment in durable assets do not handle accurately the issues relating to using durable assets at varying rates, nor do they specify completely the related issue of the optimal length of life for durable assets. In this paper, we consider a production process which has both durable assets and the flow of services from the durables as inputs. We allow for a varying extraction rate and determine internally both the optimal amount of services to extract from the durable in each production period as well as the optimal life for the durable. We relate the optimal production activities associated with the durable to investments and disinvestments in the durable. The economic theory which guides decisions concerning these changes is important to decisionmakers at micro, regional, national, and supranational levels.

Theoretical Model

Our specification of the production, investment, and disinvestment process conceives the production process to be vertically integrated. The determination of the flow of services from durables will be specified at one level. This service flow is then fed into the production function to determine output. The expected future time pattern of utilization will in part determine the investment or disinvestment decision. A diagrammatic representation of this process for a production process using one durable is presented in figure 1.

Figure 1. Two tiered vertically integrated production process

The mathematical characterization of the physical production process represented in figure 1 is:

(1) $Y_t = F(X_{1t}, Z_t)$, and

(2) $Z_t = G(X_{2t}/D_t)$,

where Y_t = quantity of product Y produced and sold in time period t,

X_{1t} = quantity of nondurable inputs X_1 used in production of Y_t in time period t,

Z_t = quantity of services generated from D_t used in production of Y

277

in time period t, and

D_t = the stock of the durable asset D in time period t.

Equation (1) is a standard representation of a product process with flow variables as inputs. Equation (2) is a production relationship which indicates that service flows from a durable asset are generated or produced according to the function G by using one nondurable input (a flow variable) with a given stock of the durable asset. Thus, at this level of integration we need both stocks and flows in the production of services.

Specification of the production process in this manner allows us to vary the rate of use for durable assets. It also permits us to determine investment and disinvestment in durables simultaneously with the production activities associated with the durable. Finally, the optimal length of life for the durable is also determined internally.

The physical life of a durable asset is related to both the services extracted and the maintenance carried out during each year of its life. In our model, we express this physical relationship as:

(3) $T_D = h(Z_1, ..., Z_t, ..., Z_{TH}, X_{31}, ..., X_{3t}, ..., X_{3TH})$,

where T_D = physical life of durable,

X_{3t} = aggregated maintenance variable in time period t, and

T_H = planning horizon for the firm.

T_H is chosen such that costs and returns beyond T_H would be discounted essentially at zero for any positive discount rate $T_H \geq T_D$.

We assume that the firm operates in each time period to maximize current profits plus the change in the net present value of the durable asset. This objective function is consistent with the gain function used by Edwards and with Boulding's writings.

(4) $G_t = P_{yt}Y_t - P_{x1t}X_{1t} - P_{x2t}X_{2t} - P_{x3t}X_{3t} - TUC_N(Z_t)$

$- FC_t + \propto(D_t - D_t^o)$,

where P_{yt} = price received for Y in time period t,

P_{xjt} = price paid for nondurable X_j in time period t (j = 1, 2, 3),

$TUC_N(Z_t)$ = total user cost of extracting services Z_t in time period t,

FC_t^o = fixed cost associated with the durable in time period t (the "o" notation refers to initial levels while the "*", used below, refers to optimal levels), and

$\propto$ = gain in net present value of a unit of the durable.

For $D_t > D_t^o$, $\propto$ will equal the difference between the durable's value in use, NRD, and its acquisition price, P_{Dt}^a. For $D_t < D_t^o$, $\propto$ will equal the difference between the durable's value in use and its salvage price, P_{DT}^s. For $D_t = D_t^o$, $\propto$ will equal the durable's value in use.

The total user cost variable (TUC_N) in (4) deserves special explanation. The concept of user cost as recognized by Keynes and subsequently modified by Neal and Lewis considers the cost of using the asset as opposed to not using it. Equations (5) and (6) express the Neal and Lewis versions respectively.

(5) $TUC_N(Z_t) = S(t|Z_t = 0) - S(t, Z_t)$,

where $S(t|Z_t = 0)$ = salvage value at time t given no services are extracted, and

$S(t, Z_t)$ = salvage value at time t with Z_t services extracted.

(6) $TUC_L(Z_t) = NPV_{T+dt}$,

where $TUC_L(Z_t)$ = Lewis' formulation of user cost, and

NPV_{T+dt} = net present value of asset in time period T+dt (this is the time period excluded by current use of the asset).

The Neal version is an off-firm opportunity cost while the Lewis version is a within-firm opportunity cost. The former is important for service extraction decisions, while the latter is relevant for investment or disinvestment decisions.

Maximizing (4) subject to (1), (2), and (3) involves determining the optimal production, service generation, and investment or disinvestment activities. We separate the determination of the production and service generation activities from the investment or disinvestment activities for ease of presentation. Determining the optimal production and service generation activities involves maximizing the following Lagrangian expression:

(7) $L = P_{yt}Y_t - P_{x1t}X_{1t} - P_{x2t}X_{2t} - P_{x3t}X_{3t} - TUC_N(Z_t) - FC$

$\qquad - \lambda_{1t}[Y_t - F(X_{1t}, Z_t)] - \lambda_{2t}[Z_t - G(X_{2t}|D_t)]$

$\qquad - \lambda_{3t}[T_D - h(Z_1, ..., Z_{TH}, X_{31}, ..., X_{3TH})]$.

Upon taking the required partial derivatives, equating them with zero, and making appropriate substitutions, the following necessary conditions are derived:

(8) $P_{yt}(\partial Y_t/\partial X_{1t}) = P_{x1t}$,

(9) $P_{yt}(\partial Y_t/\partial Z_t)(\partial Z_t/\partial X_{2t}) = P_{x2t} + MUC_N(Z_t)(\partial Z_t/\partial X_{2t})$

$\qquad - [P_{x3t}/(\partial h/\partial X_{3t})](\partial h/\partial Z_t)(\partial Z_t/\partial X_{2t})$,

(10) $\{[MUC_N(Z_t) + P_{x2t}/(\partial Z_t/\partial X_{2t}) - P_{Yt}(\partial Y_t/\partial Z_t)]/(\partial h/\partial Z_t)\}(\partial h/\partial X_{3t})$

$\qquad = P_{x3t}$, and

(11) $P_{yt}(\partial Y_t/\partial Z_t) = MUC_N(Z_t) + [P_{x2t}/(\partial Z_t/\partial X_{2t})]$

$\qquad - [P_{x3t}/(\partial h/\partial X_{3t})](\partial h/\partial Z_t)$.

Equation (8) indicates that the optimal quantity of X_{1t} to use is determined by equating the value of its marginal product to its price. Equation (9) states that the optimal quantity of X_{2t} to use involves having the instrumental marginal value product equal to the marginal cost of using X_{2t}. The marginal cost of X_{2t} is the price of X_{2t} plus the marginal user cost of the services generated by using

279

X_{2t} plus the increased maintenance costs which must be incurred as a result of using the durable. For X_{3t}, equation (10) indicates that the net marginal value of maintenance should be equated to the marginal factor cost of maintenance. The net value of a unit of maintenance is given in the braces in (10). Equations (8) through (10) state the marginal conditions for the optimal levels of X_{1t}, X_{2t}, and X_{3t}, respectively. For services from the durable, equation (11) indicates that the value of the marginal product of services should be equated with the marginal cost of acquiring services. This marginal cost is composed of the marginal user cost, the weighted cost of acquiring X_{2t} and the weighted cost of increased maintenance.

The simultaneous solution of equations (8) through (11) for each t, t = 1, ..., T_H will yield the optimal production activities for the firm with its initial endowment of D_t. The following section specifies the optimality conditions for acquiring additional durables or disposing of currently held durables.

Investment and Disinvestment Decisions

In making adjustments to its initial quantities, the firm will want to acquire units of a durable when its value in use exceeds its acquisition price. It will want to dispose of units of an existing durable when its value in use is less than its salvage price. A durable's value in use is derived from the services generated over its lifetime. Both the services generated and the lifetime of the durable optimal quantity of services to generate in each time period was specified above. Determining the optimal lifetime for a durable, in essence, determines the point in time when the firm should disinvest in the durable.

The durable's value in use can be represented as:

$$(12) \quad NRD(Z^*, T_D) = PVS(Z^*, T_D) + [1/(1 + r)^{T_D}][S(Z^*, T_D)],$$

where $NRD(Z^*, T_D)$ = the net return to the durable as a function of the optimal services generated in each time period, Z^*, and the length of time the durable is used, T_D,

$PVS(Z^*, T_D)$ = present value of services generated which depends on Z^* and T_D,

r = discount rate, and

$S(Z^*, T_D)$ = salvage value of durable in time period T_D after Z^* services have been extracted.

With Z^* determined according to equations (8) through (11), T_D is determined so as to maximize $NRD(Z^*, T_D)$.

If we treated time as a continuous variable, we would differentiate (12) with respect to t and equate with zero. However, our model treats time as a discrete variable; thus, we cannot take derivatives. We can only state approximate marginal rules for determining T_D^*. Our approximate rule is to equate the additions to $PVS(T_D)$ with the reductions in $S(T_D)$. T_D^* is the point in time when the additions to $PVS(T_D^* + 1)$ are less than the reductions in $S(T_D^* + 1)$. In other words, $PVS(T_D^*) > S(T_D^*)$, but $PVS(T_D^* + 1) < S(T_D^* + 1)$. This procedure determines when to disinvest in a durable. It is based on comparing the durable's value in use with its salvage value.

As indicated above, the firm will acquire units of a durable when $NRD(Z^*, T_D^*)$ exceeds the acquisition price. Note that the investment decision requires the determination of both the optimal production activities and the disinvestment activities. The optimal quantity of a particular durable is determined in an iterative manner, since we consider durables to be available in discrete units only. For each unit the firm considers, the potential value in use is calculated and compared with the acquisition price. If the potential value in use exceeds the acquisition price, the firm acquires that unit and repeats the calculations for another unit. It continues until it finds the unit whose value in use does not cover its acquisition price. A similar process is followed for disinvesting. The firm disinvests in units of durables until either the value in use for a particular unit exceeds it salvage price or the initial endowment of durables is entirely disposed of.

References

Boulding, K. D. (1950) A Reconstruction of Economics. New York; John Wiley and Sons.

Edwards, C. (1959) Resource fixity and farm organization. Journal of Farm Economies, 41, 747-759.

Keynes, J. M. (1936) The General Theory of Employment, Interest, and Money. New York; Harcourt and Brace.

Lewis, W. A. (1949) Overhead Costs. London; Allen and Unwin.

Neal, A. C. (1942) Marginal cost and dynamic equilibrium. Journal of Political Economy, 50, 45-64.

OPENER'S REMARKS--Richard A. King

Baquet has demonstrated that the decision concerning optimum replacement of a durable asset cannot be separated from decisions made in each period concerning the flow of services which the asset makes possible. An illustration may help to clarify the problem. Leontief was fond of using a taxi company to describe the interrelationship between flow of services and asset replacement. Suppose that a taxi has a life of five years. An individual operating a single taxi would provide new taxi services the first year, two year old taxi services the second year, and so on over each successive five year period. Only in the event that five taxis were in operation could the flow of taxi services be uniform form one period to the next. However, it is not necessary to drive a taxi the same distance every year.

A recent example comes from a conversation with the bus driver on our Conference farm tour. Asked the age of the vehicle, he responded that it was 18 years old. Rather than the 100,000 or 200,000 miles we thought it might have logged, he reported that it had traveled well over one million miles to date and was still going strong. Clearly, a sizeable amount of upkeep had been required to achieve such a flow of services.

In the general case, there are two dimensions to the issue of extraction of services: the services available in a given period, and the total units of services remaining to be extracted. Every input has an implicit price at the end of every production period. In the case of nondurables, this price is zero. In the case of durables, this price is larger than or equal to zero.

Baquet has provided a formulation in which a variable input X_2 such as the driver (flow) is added to the vehicle (stock) to provide the intermediate taxi input, Z. Transport services Y are produced when another variable input such as gasoline, X_1 is combined with the intermediate input Z. The cost of extracting a given level of services from a durable good can be thought of as the change in the end of period price (salvage value) from one period to the next or as the value of services in some future period that would be precluded by the planned level of extraction in the present period (opportunity cost).

The problem can be viewed as that of assembling a new bundle of inputs at the beginning of every production period. In making a decision concerning replacement time, a comparison must be made between three values: salvage value of the existing unit, the use value of the existing unit in future production periods, and the market price of new unit. Salvage value is determined by age and deterioration (salt on the road), maintenance (frequency of oil change), and services extracted (miles driven). Use value in future periods is the present value of alternative future streams of services. The price of a new unit must reflect the prices of replacements (new or used) and the cost of rental services as an alternative to ownership.

Each of these three measures must be considered simultaneously in investment or disinvestment decisions. Only the third measure is unaffected by the level of output selected in each production period. For this reason, output and durable asset holding decisions must be made simultaneously.

RAPPORTEUR'S REPORT--S. N. Kulshreshtha

The question of present use value of a durable input from current stock versus replaced stock has not been handled in this paper. Furthermore, optimal use of a durable input may also require variation in the degree of maintenance. Maintenance expenditures could be determined by conditions outside the system. For example, the road conditions affecting maintenance expenditures for a taxi company. The exclusion of risk and uncertainty in decisions regarding durable inputs was also noted.

Baquet replied that replacement and maintenance decisions are not included, but the theory presented would lend itself to these extensions. Risk and uncertainty are also not included, but work is under way in this regard. Empirical work is also under way. The inclusion of changes outside the farming system to make the model deal with a more or less general equilibrium type of situation is somewhat more complex, but Baquet felt that it should be possible.

NEW APPROACHES TO THE THEORY OF RENTAL CONTRACTS IN AGRICULTURE

Clive Bell and Pinhas Zusman

This paper addresses two issues: the relationship between the choice of rental contract in agriculture and the set of conditions or environment under which such contracts are arrived at, and the implications of this relationship for efficiency, equity, and development policy. Both issues have been the subject of much discussion in the theoretical literature of late. In particular, close attention has been paid to the role of imperfections in, or outright failure of, one or more markets. This has led, in turn, to the notion of "market interconnectedness" in the narrow sense that the same two agents will deal with one another in several markets simultaneously, an obvious example being the landlord who also provides credit to tenants. Two main analytical approaches are discernible. The first posits free entry for an indefinitely large set of agents who have access to parametrically given alternative utility levels elsewhere in the economy. The resulting equilibria are normally characterized by utility equivalent contracts, which are the outcome of a Nash noncooperative game. The second assumes barriers to entry in the face of market failure so that, in equilibrium, the set of contracts is the outcome of a system of Nash cooperative games. Taken together they yield a rich taxonomy and a number of interesting results.

Why Does Tenancy Exist?

Suppose, first of all, that there is a complete set of perfect markets. If every agent also has access to the same constant returns to scale production function, it is immaterial whether he buys inputs in order to produce output for eventual sale, or exchanges part or all of his initial endowment for other commodities. Hence, there may be no particular incentive to trade in a specific good or factor. Taking the argument one step further, if land, say, is not tradeable, profit maximization will still ensure that the marginal product of each tradeable input is equated to its price in all uses, so that production will still be efficient. There is no need for land to be leased in or out, as all necessary adjustments can be made by varying the amounts of traded inputs combined with it (Bliss and Stern). The argument applies symmetrically to each case in which there is just one nontraded factor or good.

If there are two or more nontraded factors, then production will not be efficient unless all agents' endowments of them are the same (up to a scalar multiple)—an improbable state of affairs. In many rural settings, there is no separate market in the cultivators' managerial and husbandry skills, and there may also be none for the services of their draft animals. Moreover, even though labour markets are generally active, some family labour is often less than perfectly marketable. Nevertheless, while the leasing of land cannot bring about full efficiency in production under these circumstances, it will still bring about an improvement therein (Bell; and Bliss and Stern). In this connection, it is generally the case that hired workers require closer supervision than family workers. Hence, households which are relatively well endowed with land can save on supervision costs by leasing land to households which are relatively well endowed with labour.

There is nothing in the argument so far which points to one form of lease being preferred over another, but there is a strong suggestion that the choice of least contract is likely to be connected with the structure of markets for other factors and goods. As we will see, this is especially important in the presence of risk and the absence of a full set of insurance markets, because one reason commonly advanced for the existence of sharecropping is that it provides a way of spreading risks.

Equilibria with Free Entry and Utility Equivalent Contracts

Traditional Anglo-Saxon theory emphasized the inefficiency of resource allocation under sharecropping arrangements, in sharp contrast to the allocative efficiency of fixed rents and long leases (the so-called "English" system). This proposition, which has inspired much land tenure legislation in some developing countries, went largely unchallenged until Cheung's seminal contribution which served as the point of departure for further important theoretical work (Newbery, 1975 and 1977; and Stiglitz). The "new school," as it might be called, retained the old assumption of free entry—by would-be tenants at least—but insisted on the propostion that in a competitive equilibrium the only contracts to exist would yield agents exactly the (parametrically given) utilities available to them elsewhere in the economy.

There are two ways of contriving utility equivalent contracts in a timeless world. The first is to assume that there is costless contractual enforcement of all input levels. Before discussing this case, we need the following result: if (1) all inputs are tradeable in perfect markets, except insurance (for which there is no market), and (2) production is stochastic and takes place under constant returns to scale, then a competitive wage-rent equilibrium exists and is a constrained Pareto efficient allocation (Newbery, 1977). This leads to a key proposition: With costless contractual enforcement, sharecropping contracts are at best equivalent to a combination of wage and fixed rent contracts (Newbery, 1977; and Stiglitz) so that the introduction of appropriate sharecropping contracts will have no effect on allocation or equity. Hence, as sharecropping normally involves heavier transaction costs than fixed rent leases, it will not be observed under these particular circumstances. The risk spreading argument for the existence of sharecropping advanced by Cheung is therefore invalid. If, however, the assumption of a perfect labour market is relaxed to admit risky wages, then, with multiplicative risk in production, a competitive equilibrium which is production efficient can be established with agents entering all three forms of contract—wage, fixed rent, and sharecropping. If several input markets are risky, the introduction of share contracts permits increases in output in all states of nature, and, even if production risk is not multiplicative, such contracts enlarge the economy's set of contingent consumption possibilities (Newbery, 1977). On this line of argument, the risk spreading advantages of share leases arise out of uncertainty in input markets, but, if they are to be realized, all three forms of contract must coexist, and at least one agent must enter into all three simultaneously.

In the preceding story, the possibility of mixing contracts, espcially wages with leases, is of the essence. But if, as the traditional theory implicitly assumes, the contractual enforcement of input levels is prohibitively costly, especially where labour "effort" is concerned, then utility equivalent contracts must be of an exclusive kind. In particular, the landlord must have the power to prevent the tenant from working for wages outside his tenancy if the tenant is not to earn intramarginal rents. Otherwise, there will be excess demand for sharecropping leases unless the rental share is unity, in which case tenants would not enter into them at all. With this option closed, the tenant will apply himself more diligently to the landlord's plots, the level of his effort being set by its disutility as well as the income it yields, as against the (given) utility he can obtain by working elsewhere in the economy. If tenants differ in their responsiveness to incentives, there will not be production efficiency unless the production function has unitary elasticity of substitution, although it does not necessarily follow that labour effort would be lower under sharecropping than a wage system with enforceable contracts (Stiglitz).

284

Costly Enforcement and Barriers to Entry

If the contractual enforcement of input levels is out of the question and agents can mix contracts, then an equilibrium in the land market with utility equivalent share contracts will not exist unless the technology demands inputs in fixed proportions, in which case there is no enforcement problem. With this exception, the landlord does not then possess the means to tax away the intramarginal rent that will accrue to the tenant when the latter can choose, without restriction, the levels of variable inputs to be used on his tenancy, whatever its size. Indeed, in this so-called "Marshallian" setting, there are circumstances in which agents will not enter into sharecropping contracts. Bliss and Stern, in a careful and scholarly treatment of Marshall's analysis of sharecropping, show convincingly that Cheung's discussion of Marshall's views is somewhat misleading. For example, if there is no uncertainty and both landlords and tenants have the same constant returns to scale production function and access to a perfect labour market, then landlords will never find it profitable to offer share contracts, whether the land market be competitive, monopolistic, or imperfectly competitive (Bell and Braverman). Here the technology rules out any role for nontraded inputs specific to the firm, such as management or possibly draft power services, so that share contracts do not offer any incentives. On the contrary, as landlords cannot keep their share tenants to their tasks, they must resort to fixed rent leases or self-cultivation with hired labour if they are to maximize their incomes. Moreover, as nontraded inputs are not present, it is implicitly the case that there is free entry for tenants who therefore obtain from wage or fixed rent contracts what they could earn by working elsewhere in the economy.

It is hardly realistic to assume that nontraded factors can be ignored. In particular, some farmers have superior husbandry and managerial skills, and if there is no market for such skills, landlords can get access to them only by leasing out land. If there are also barriers to the entry of new tenants, as may happen, for example, if the ownership of nontraded factors depends on the workings of imperfect capital markets, then both landlords and existing tenants stand to gain from cooperation through lease contracts, and the division of these gains depends on their respective bargaining strengths. Hence, the set of equilibrium contracts will be the outcome of a system of cooperative games. As long as the marginal product of nontraded factors remains positive, the landlord always stands to gain from the entry of new tenants if the only contracts available to him are "Marshallian" share contracts. In this case, free entry remains compatible with bargaining within the framework of a cooperative game.

Assuming that the conditions for utility equivalent contracts exist is certainly one way of dividing up the gains from cooperation in a constrained Pareto efficient way. In many circumstances, it may be the most plausible way, given the dominance of landlords over their tenantry, which is shored up by a whole apparatus of extraeconomic coercion. However, it cannot lay sole claim to the role of solution concept. Indeed, once it is conceded that there are gains from cooperation, then it is proper to seek solution concepts from cooperative game theory. This is the tack taken by Bell and Zusman (1976 and 1977) who use Nash's solution to the bargaining problem as the basis for deriving the set of bilateral lease contracts in a universal cooperative equilibrium without co-alitions.

The foundations are provided by the following simple model of a system featuring only sharecropping leases (Bell and Zusman, 1976). A single landlord who does not personally cultivate can deal with a fixed and sufficiently large number of identical tenants who grow one crop under perfect certainty and have access to a perfect labour market, the wage in which is their disagreement payoff. The tenant decides on the labour input, the landlord on the size of each tenancy, and the rental share is the outcome of a series of bilateral bargains which underpin a universal cooperative equilibrium. All land is cultivated and resource allocation is inefficient (unless the elasticity of substitution between workers' labour and land is zero) when there is costless enforcement brought about by the technical conditions of production. The rental share depends on the exogenous wage rate, the size of each tenancy, and the form of the production function. (In certain cases, it is possible to derive closed form solutions for the rental share in terms of these parameters.) If the assumption that tenants are identical is relaxed to allow them to have differing abilities as farmers (though not as workers), then it can be shown that the distribution of land is identical with the distribution of abilities (up to a scalar) if the latter appear as Hicks neutral efficiency parameters in the production function. The rental share is the same across the board, and the distribution of tenants' incomes will usually be more equally distributed than would be the case under a system of competitively determined fixed rents (Bell and Zusman, 1977).

Screening

So far it has been assumed that landlords are fully informed about the abilities of the tenants with whom they are dealing, even if they are not always able to tax away the rents associated with those abilities. However, if landlords are not thus well informed, then the worker's choice of contract will reveal something of his abilities. The most productive of them will choose fixed rent contracts, those of middling ability will opt for share contracts, and those who are least productive will work for wages. In effect, the spectrum of contracts operates as a screening device (Hallagan; and Newbery and Stiglitz).

If landlords are risk neutral and workers match their abilities with contracts in the manner just indicated, there is one form of screening equilibrium in which the expected return per acre is the same on all plots of land (Newbery and Stiglitz). In general, the values taken by the contractual parameters when they are performing their screening function will afford the middling and superior workers a rent over and above their alternative utility levels as unscreened, least able workers. This is to be contrasted with the cooperative game approach which does the same thing but on the basis of full information. Naturally, allocation and distribution will not be the same in the two systems even if everything else is identical.

Conclusions

Throughout this paper, we have placed great emphaiss on the role played by incomplete or imperfect market structures in the broad sense. And, the discussion suggests that it is natural to look at contractual arrangements as the outcome of attempts, however faltering, to achieve fair levels of efficiency in the face of the constraints imposed on agents by market structure, uncertainty, imperfect information, and the workings of institutions. It follows that any changes in these features of the economic environment will alter contractual arrangements and, hence, in general, both equity and allocative efficiency. In particular, movements toward a more complete market structure will probably make for greater allocative efficiency, although there can be no presumption that equity will also change for the better.

References

Bell, C. (1976) Production conditions, innovation, and the choice of lease in agriculture. Sankya, Series C (38) 165-190.

Bell, C.; Braverman, A. (1979) On the nonexistence of Marshallian share-cropping contracts under constant returns to scale. Washington, D.C.; World

Bank.

Bell, C.; Zusman, P. (1976) A bargaining theoretic approach to cropsharing contracts. American Economic Review, 66 (4) 578-588.

Bell, C.; Zusman, P. (1977) Sharecropping equilibria with diverse tenants. Economie Appliquee, 30, 391-411.

Bliss, C. J.; Stern, N. H. (1980) Palanpur: Studies in the Economy of a North Indian Village. London; OUP.

Cheung, S. N. S. (1969) The Theory of Share Tenancy. Chicago.

Hallagan, W. (1978) Self-selection by contractual choice and the theory of sharecropping. Bell Journal, 9, 344-354.

Newbery, D. M. G. (1975) The choice of rental contract in peasant agriculture, in Agriculture in Development Theory (edited by L. Reynolds). New Haven, Connecticut, USA; Yale University Press.

Newbery, D. M. G. (1977) Risk sharing, sharecropping, and uncertain labour markets. Review of Economic Studies, 44.

Newbery, D. M. G.; Stiglitz, J. E. (1978) Sharecropping, risk sharing, and the importance of imperfect information (Discussion Paper No. 8). Cambridge.

Stiglitz, J. E. (1974) Incentives and risk sharing in sharecropping. Review of Economic Studies, 41, 219-255.

OPENER'S REMARKS—Norman Rask

Recent changes in the land market have raised some very interesting questions about equity in the minds of landlords operating with fixed cash rent contracts. Inflation has increasingly caused land to be viewed as both a hedge against inflation and a factor input to production. This additional demand has pushed land values well above their income generating capacity. Many landlords do not clearly recognize the dual valuations of the land resource. Hence, as land values rise, they feel that land rents should continue to hold a fixed relationship to market value of land even though productivity may not have increased. Thus, general inflation and overvaluing of land for production purposes leads to demands by landlords for relatively higher cash rents and shorter term leases. Under these conditions, tenants could not be expected to maintain soil fertility or to make capital improvements. It may also drive the final negotiated leases more toward share leases. Depending on how share leases are written, this may result in lower overall investment in production inputs. In either situation, allocation efficiency could decline. Equity changes are unclear.

What are some of the shortcomings of the theoretical literature dealing with rental contracts, and does it deal at all with the issue of inflation and inflated land values, which are real problems for those advising landlords and tenants on current leasing arrangements?

RAPPORTEUR'S REPORT—S. N. Kulshreshtha

How does the inflation in land prices affect the tenancy arrangements? How do the risk aversion tendencies on the part of the landlord and tenants determine the rental contracts, particularly with respect to the crop insurance practices? Input sharing between tenant and landlords also poses another complication in the rental contracts.

Bell responded that in the situations which he was talking about the landlords were more powerful than the tenants. However, this may not apply in the U.S. situation where both may be working more or less as partners trying to optimize their returns. Landlords select tenants based on their ability to farm.

In situations where land prices are increasing, Bell suggested two approaches: indexing of rental contracts or sharing of a part of the profits. Similar arrangements can be made where inputs are shared between the tenant and landlord. However, there is the possibility that the landlord may implicitly change the conditions of rental contracts by sharing the inputs. For example, more fertilizer used by the landlord and shared by the tenant would lead to more labour input by the tenant.

RESOURCE ALLOCATION BY RICE FARMERS IN SRI LANKA:
A DECISION THEORETIC APPROACH

H. M. Gamini Herath

[Read by Paul G. Webster.]

Too often, tests of economic rationality of agricultural producers are based on the assumption of profit maximization and certainty of outcomes of production decisions (Hopper; and Yotopoulos). However, multiple goals and uncertainties may be relevant to the decisionmaker. Consequently, single goal models under certainty are not always a realistic approach to the decision process and may not provide a farmer with an acceptable solution.

Progress in using multiple goals and uncertainties in decision models has been slowed by the difficulty of incorporating multiple goals and uncertainties into analytical models. However, with the development of decision theory, procedures became available that permit explicit incorporation of uncertainties and multiple goals. Decision theory describes how a rational decisonmaker ought to behave given his beliefs and preferences. Whether or not the model explains the behaviour of peasant farmers can only be answered by empirical tests.

The objectives of this study are: (1) to compare alternative theories of choice (single attribute utility maximization, multiattribute utility maximization, and expected profit maximization in terms of their abilities to explain and predict actual resource allocation decisions of producers, and (2) to explore implications for policy decisionmakers of the impact of and uncertainty on farmers' choices. The present research was conducted on a sample of rice farmers in Sri Lanka.

Approach

If $x = (x_1, x_2, ..., x_n)$ is the vector of resource allocations, then the decision problem is to select the best value of x. If the axioms of rational choice (Keeney and Raiffa) are to be met, then the decisonmaker should select that value of x which maximizes his expected utility:

(1) $\int_y u(y)f(y|x)dy,$

where $y = (y_1, y_2, ..., y_n)$ represents a vector of attributes, f is the decisionmaker's probability density function over y given the value of x, and u is his utility function.

Feasible Land Allocation

After discussions with farmers, it was felt useful to concentrate on the allocation of scarce land resources under uncertainty. Preliminary observations indicated that many farmers allocated land to mixtures of two varieties of rice. The most important observation made was that these two varietal mixtures contained one high yielding (HYV) and one traditional variety (TV). Thus, for examining this decision to allocate land between the HYV and the TV, the allocation was specified by $x = (x_1, x_2)$, where x_1 is the proportion of land of the HYV and x_2 is the proportion of land of the TV. The problem can now be stated as:

(2)   maximize $\int_y u(y)f(y|x)dy,$

(3)   subject to $x_1 + x_2 = 1.$

Attributes

Discussions with farmers indicated that subsistence consumption y_1 and net cash income y_2 are the main goals in rice production. To analyze the above decision problem using multiattribute utility theory, a set of measures of effectiveness for y_1 and y_2 need to be developed. Net cash income could be measured in Sri Lankan rupees. For y_1, however, the volume of farm produced rice consumed by the farm family was used as a simple measure because of the need to make probability and utility judgments.

Probability Distributions: Performance-Allocation Relationships

To evaluate all feasible allocation plans, a large number of probability distributions need to be derived. However, to simplify data acquisition and subsequent analysis, this optimization was represented as a one period, two investment portfolio model as follows:

$$(4) \quad \text{Max EU} = \text{Max} \iint u[x_1 q_1 + (1 - x_1)q_2] L df(q_1, q_2),$$

where q_1 is the yield of HYV, q_2 is the yield of TV, L is the total land allocated to HYV and TV, and f is the joint probability distribution of yields per acre between the two varieties.

To simplify the analysis, the joint distribution of yields was assumed to be bivariate normal. The assumption of normality permits the specification of the joint distirbution of n variables using the means and the standard deviations together with the values of the $n(n - 1)/2$ conditional means and the standard deviations (Anderson and others). If q_1 and q_2 are jointly normally distributed with means $E(q_1)$ and $E(q_2)$, standard deviations s_1 and s_2 respectively, and correlation p_{12}, then the conditional distribution of q_1 given $q_2 = q_2^*$, is characterized by mean and variance, as follows:

$$(5) \quad E(q_1 | q_2 = q_2^*) = E(q_1) + p_{12}(s_1/s_2)[q_2^* - E(q_2)], \text{ and}$$

$$(6) \quad \text{Var}(q_1 | q_2 = q_2^*) = s_1^2(1 - p_{12}^2),$$

respectively. Equations (5) and (6) provided a method of estimating the parameters of the bivariate yield distributions in this study.

Utility Function Structure

Keeney has developed two main assumptions, namely preferential and utility independence, which simplify the assessment of multiattribute utility functions. In the case of only two attributes, it has been shown by Keeney that if these two attributes are mutually utility independent (that is, if y_1 is utility independent of y_2 and vice versa) then either:

$$(7) \quad u(y_1, y_2) = \sum_{i=1}^{n} k_i u_i y_i, \text{ or}$$

$$(8) \quad u(y_1, y_2) = \prod_{i=1}^{n} [(1 + K k_i u_i y_i) - 1]/K$$

where u and u_i are utility functions scaled from zero to one, the k_i are the scaling constants with $0 < k_i < 1$, and $K > -1$ is a nonzero scaling constant.

Data Assessment

Probability Distributions

Two samples of rice farmers--one from the wet zone and the other from the dry zone--were selected for this study. Two marginal distributions and one conditional distribution were assessed for each farmer using the visual impact method (Anderson and others) in order to specify the bivariate distribution of yields using (5) or (6). These distributions were checked for normality using the Kolmagarov test. Most of the distributions approximated the normal distribution very well. The distributions which were not normal were symmetrized using a generalized power transformation of the form:

$$(9) \quad z = (q^w - 1)/w, \ w \neq 0,$$

where w is the transformation parameter and z is the transformed value of the variable. The value of w was varied over a reasonable range in order to obtain the value which best symmetrizes the distribution.

A test of symmetry was made by computing the value of T where

$$(10) \quad T = [z_{(\alpha)} + z_{(1 - \alpha)}]/2z_{(0.5)}, \ 0 \leq \alpha \leq 1,$$

where α is a given fractile value. The best w gives a value of 1 to equation (10).

For single attribute utility maximization, the joint yield distributions were transformed into distributions of net income (defined as gross income less variable costs) by the use of a linear transformation (Herath).

Utility Functions

The utility independence assumption was not tested rigorously in this study. It was considered a reasonable assumption (Herath). The multiattribute utility function was specified using the individual utility functions for y_1 and y_2 derived using the equally likely certainty equivalent method (Anderson and others) and the scaling constants k_1 and k_2 for y_1 and y_2 respectively. Most of the utility functions showed risk aversion. Several different functional forms such as the cubic, the spliced cubic, and the negative exponential were fitted to the elicited data. The negative exponential function was found to approximate the shape of most of the curves. This function also shows constant absolute risk aversion and has found favour in many multiattribute situations (Keeney and Raiffa). Consequently, the negative exponential function was fitted for all farmers for both y_1 and y_2 using procedures developed by Buccola and French.

Scaling Constants

The scaling constants k_1 and k_2 were assessed using a lottery technique (Keeney and Raiffa). In all cases, the sum of the k_i for i = 1 to i = n was not equal to one, and hence the multiattribute utility functions were multiplicative. The value of K in (8) was determined from the elicited value of k_1 and k_2 (Keeney and Raiffa). In a majority of the cases, k was found to be negative, indicating multivariate risk aversion (Richard).

Optimization Procedure

The optimal solutions under the three criteria were computed using a Monte Carlo approach. Here, x_1 was varied between zero and one in increments of 0.1, and the value among these that maximized the objective function was chosen as the optimal solution.

For single attribute utility maximization, a level of net income for each variety was generated randomly from the bivariate normal distribution of net income, truncated at plus and minus three standard deviations from the expected value, for a given value of x_1. The output variables were calculated according to the following sequence:

$$(11) \quad y_2' = [x_1 r_1 + (1 - x_1)r_2]L,$$

where y_2' is total net income, $(1 - x_1)$ is the proportion of land allocated to TV, r_1 is the random net income from HYV, and r_2 is the random net income from TV.

Then, y_2' was substituted in the utility function derived for net cash income to compute the total utility. The above sequence was repeated 1,500 times. Finally, the mean (expected) utility was calculated for a given value of x_1 for the total number of iterations. The adequacy of 1,500 iterations was determined by trial and error. The use of the utility function for y_2 as a proxy for the utility function for net income is only approximate. However, the use of a negative exponential assumption provides some justification for the approximation (Herath). The computation was repeated for each successive value of x_1. The output obtained in the simulation is the expected utility for different allocations of land to the HYV for proportions varying from zero to one. The proportion giving the highest expected utility was approximated as the theoretically optimal solution.

The structure of the simulation was slightly modified for multiattribute utility maximization, as follows. A random yield from each variety was generated from the bivariate normal distribution of yields. The output variables were then calculated according to the following expressions:

$$(12) \quad Q = [x_1 q_1 + (1 - x_1)q_2]L,$$

where Q is total random yield, q_1 is the random yield from HYV, and q_2 is the random yield from TV.

The Q obtained from the two varieties was allocated between y_1 and y_2 to maximize the utility according to:

$$(13) \quad u = [(1 + Kk_1 u_1 y_1)(1 + Kk_2 u_2 y_2) - 1]/K.$$

Making use of the fact that:

$$(14) \quad y_2 = (Q - y_1)p - t,$$

where p is the price of a bushel of rice and t is the total cost of production, equation (13) can be written as:

$$(15) \quad \{(1 + Kk_1 u_1 y_1)(1 + Kk_2 u_2[(Q - y_1)p - t] - 1\}/K.$$

The allocation of Q between y_1 and y_2 can be determined by maximizing (15) with respect to y_1. The associated optimal value of y_2 can be found from (14). The utility maximizing solution in terms of y_1 was established using the Newton-Rhapson technique (Hartree). This procedure was repeated 1,500 times and expected utility was computed by averaging the total over the number of iterations.

For expected profit maximization, a formal optimization procedure was not required. Here the choice for each farmer is to grow either the HYV or the TV depending upon which of the two varieties has the highest (subjective) mean yield.

292

Comparison of Optimal Solutions with Actual Allocation

The main aim of this study was to determine which is the best predictor of farmers' behaviour: (1) expected profit maximization, (2) expected utility maximization (single attribute), or (3) expected utility maximization (multi-attribute).

An evaluation of the closeness of prediction was made by computing the mean absolute deviation of the predicted area of HYV form the actual grown. The mean absolute deviation was computed using the following:

$$(16) \quad (\sum_{i=1}^{n} |PA - AA|)/n$$

where PA is predicted area, AA is actual area, and n is the number of farmers in the sample.

The mean absolute deviation so computed is then expressed as a percentage of the mean actual area under the HYV. This indicates the percentage deviation of predicted area from the actual area.

The percentage deviations for single attribute utility maximization were about 10 to 7.7 for the wet and dry zone samples respectively. For multiattribute utility maximization, the corresponding deviations were 34 and 15. For expected profit maximization, the deviations were very high, of the order of 49 and 29 percent for the wet and dry zones respectively. These figures indicate that the deviations in the prediction were smallest for single attribute utility maximization, which performed better than either of the other two. It can thus be concluded, at least in this study, that single attribute utility maximiation is the more appropriate model to explain the behaviour of peasant farmers over the conventional profit maximization hypothesis.

Policy Implications and Concluding Remarks

This study suggests that risk is an important factor in the adoption of new technology by peasant producers. An obvious implication is to introduce policy measures, to reduce the subjective uncertainties felt by farmers by improving communciations and making local demonstration plots, both of which could reduce the perceived risks of new technology. The development of infrastructure such as irrigation could also minimize the variability of yields, thereby reducing risk in adoption of innovations.

In addition to reducing risks, farmers must be helped to bear risks. Programmes to reduce price variability and schemes of crop insurance against undue losses help bear some of the risks in agricultural production. Another important implication is that plant breeders must focus not only on yield potential in breeding but also on those features which help reduce the yield variability. These policies could encourage adoption of new technology by small farmers, thereby reducing the disparity of incomes between the rural and the urban sector--a primary aim of rural development.

In conclusion, the usefulness of studying the decisionmaking process with explicit consideration of risk and uncertainty has been illustrated in this study. There appears to be greater merit in a decision analysis approach to study allocation decisions of peasant producers. Such decisions, in the aggregate, impinge in a substantial way on the well-being of large numbers of people and have a crucial impact on the success or failure of important aspects of rural development planning.

References

Anderson; and others (1977) Agricultural Decision Analysis. Ames, Iowa, USA; Iowa State University Press.

Buccola, S. T.; French, B. C. (1978) Estimating exponential utility functions. Agricultural Economics Research, 30 (1) 37-43.

Hartree, B. R. (1958) Numerical Analysis (2nd Edition). Oxford; Oxford University Press.

Herath, H. M. G. (1970) Resource allocation by rice farmers in Sri Lanka: A decision theoretic approach. Ph.D. thesis. Armidale, Australia; University of New England.

Hopper, D. W. (1965) Allocation efficiency in a traditional agriculture. Journal of Farm Economics, 47 (3) 611-624.

Keeney, K. L. (1974) Multiplicative utility functions. Operations Research, 22, 22-34.

Keeney, K. L.; Raiffa, H. (1976) Decisions with Multiple Objectives: Preferences and Value Tradeoffs. New York; Wiley.

Richard, S. F. (1975) Multivariate risk aversion, utility independence, and separable utility functions. Management Science, 22 (1) 12-21.

Yotopoulos, P. A. (1968) On the efficiency of resource utilization in subsistence agriculture. Food Research Institute Studies, 13 (2) 125-135.

OPENER'S REMARKS--Deryke G. R. Belshaw

Richardson, Hardaker, and Anderson foresaw that the use of decision modeling techniques would be confined to developed agriculture where their application would depend on the number of very large farms with computers or computer terminals in their offices. Heady took the view that the work on decision theory represented a large leap forward for understanding farm decisions in developed countries, but nevertheless believed that "we have a considerable distance to go in (a) meaningfully measuring risk reference, utility curves, subjective probability distributions and related phenomena, and (b) using them either to better understand decisionmaking under uncertainty or applying them in manners useful to farmers in the actual decisionmaking process" (p. 39).

Decision modeling has not been generally envisaged in the profession as a useful tool for application to small scale or peasant agriculture. In the light of the quoted discussion, it is clear that the research undertaken by Herath--applying decision theory to illuminate peasant farmer decisionmaking processes--is an imaginative and pioneering extension of previous work.

How well has the author succeeded in this attempt? In this case, we are probably close to the technique in search of a problem situation. Although subject to denigration, such research can be justified in the early phases of development of a new methodology as long as a critical assessment is made by the researcher of the wider social utility of the approach. In practice in the research "industry," the tendency is usually to advocate further applications of the new methodology irrespective of its utility or potential demand by decisionmakers for the information it generates.

It will be clear from these remarks that the evaluative criteria adopted here concern the value of the insights and data for advisors and planners responsible for formulating agricultural development strategies in developing countries. Indeed, in the final section of his paper, the author claims that precisely such benefits follow from his research. Are the claims soundly based? Does much wider use of decision theory in the investigation of peasant agriculture appear justified? Should decision theory be inserted in standard curricula for training agricultural economists in developing countries?

There are several difficulties in understanding the precise methodology employed from the description supplied in the paper. This is not necessarily the author's fault, as he is summarizing the contents of a Ph.D. thesis within the very severe paper length constraints imposed by the Confernece organizers. Nevertheless, there are important aspects of the data collection procedures about which we should be informed. How was the farmer sample chosen? How representative is it? What is meant by farmers?--Heads of households, accessible informants, key decisionmakers, or members of the family labour force? The opportunity was apparently not taken to record objective features of the farmer's environment which might account for differneces in risk bearing capacity, nor to suggest additional or alternative objective functions pursued by some, if not all, of the farmers in the sample. Interfarmer variation in risk aversion is now recognized as an important variable accounting for differential adoption of HYV technology and the associated weak equity impacts in terms of raising labour productivity of poorer farm families. Additional objective functions which in general might improve the explanatory power of multi-attribute utility maximization functions include reduction of normal labour inputs, improvement of social standing, and reduction of social risk. A potentially powerful explanation of differential decisionmaking by peasant farmers appears to be offered by Chayanov's model of the developmental cycle of domestic groups. This framework suggests that farmers will switch from one utility maximization function to another at different points in the cycle of family growth and decline--a feature which would have important implications in terms of the identification of target groups and the design of appropriate technological and institutional packages.

The particular decision problem selected for study--the areas planted to high yielding and traditional varieties of the dominant food crop--is an important aspect of the Green Revolution situation. But other types of decisions are also presented and may be more fundamental--the combination of variable inputs, changes in product risk, and long run investment decisions, for example. What light can decision theory throw on these areas?

An important consideration which is glossed over in the paper is the assumption of utility independence. This was not tested rigorously, and it seems likely that the savings potential of increased cash income would reduce the utility of a given level of self-sufficiency in staple food supply. The absence of utility independence, of course, would weaken the explanatory power of the multiattribute utility function.

Finally, the policy insights of the research results presented in the final section of the paper appear unremarkable. The general significance of risk as a factor affecting technology adoption in peasant agriculture has long been appreciated by agricultural economists. Qualitative analyses by Raeburn and by Lipton--the latter a powerful critique of Schultz's "efficient but poor" hypothesis central to his seminal book on transforming traditional agriculture--come to mind. The ingenuity of the quantitative decision theory techniques applied in this study have added nothing to our knowledge at this level, although perhaps they would have done so had they been concentrated on the search for significant variation in objectives and attributes between farmers operating in the same development environment. It is, therefore, too early to conclude from this study that decision theory has no potential social utility when applied to peasant agriculture; only that the claimed insights of the particular application carried out by the author would not seem to justify the replication of similar work in other farmer populations. The case for including decision theory in training curricula is certainly a long way form being convincingly demonstrated.

References

Heady, E. O. (1981) Micro-level accomplishments and challenges for the developed world, in Rural Change: The Challenge for Agricultural Economists (edited by G. L. Johnson and A. H. Maunder). Farnborough; Gower Publishing Co., 29-42.

Richardson, R. A.; Hardaker, J. B.; Anderson, J. R. (1977) Farm-level decision models for developed agriculture, in Decision-Making and Agriculture (edited by T. Dams and K. E. Hunt). Oxford; Alden Press, 105-115.

RAPPORTEUR'S REPORT--Lorraine C. Bassett

The assumption of utility independence between attributes was discussed. It was posited that the incorporation of this assumption could possibly explain why the multiattribute utility maximization approach to predicting the actual behaviour of Sri Lankan rice farmers was poorer than the single attribute utility maximization approach. Further discussion on the assumption of utility independence between attributes was recommended. It was noted that the utility functions derived in the study were based on a hypothetical gambling procedure. Because past studies have indicated that utility functions derived from hypothetical gambling or lottery games are not indicative of an individual's real utilities, it was suggested that the utility functions derived for subsistence consumption and net cash income could be biased.

The point was raised that the use of different data sets in studies which introduce small variations to the main body of utility theory makes it difficult to evaluate models, such as the model presented by Herath. In response to this point, it was stressed that an alternative approach to utility analysis such as employing one set of data and testing different theories is a viable alternative and had been undertaken by the author.

Contributing to the discussion were Allen N. Rae and Inderjit Singh.

A BEHAVIOURAL FRAMEWORK FOR EVALUATING
THE PROCESS OF ECONOMIC DEVELOPMENT

Mervin J. Yetley and Brady J. Deaton

The need for more comprehensive development models to capture the behavioural dynamics of peasants in subsistence economies was emphaiszed at the 1976 IAAE Conference (Deaton; Mbithi; and Shapiro). This emphasis is consistent with Polanyi's claim that as a social being, man acts to "safeguard his social standing, his social claims, [and] his social assets" (p. 46). From this perspective, Deaton posited a general model of satisfaction maximization and illustrated the policy significance of the hypothesized behavioural relationships. The purpose of this paper is to extend the above thinking by: (1) presenting a conceptual framework of essential relationships for a satisfaction maximization model by drawing on three bodies of thought—economic anthropology, adoption-diffusion (sociology), and production economics; (2) analyzing selected inter-relationships; and (3) discussing the significance and implications of the model for economic development.

A Conceptual Framework

The economic anthropology perspective argues that status and prestige in peasant societies are obtained through expenditures for (1) ritualistic ceremonies and future reciprocal labour obligations, and (2) conspicuous consumption. The first category may be viewed as socially mandatory. This expenditure represents the social equivalent of capital depreciation expenses, in that failure to make adequate expenditures in these categories is to risk loss of social standing and the cooperation of peers and kin. The terms social standing, status, prestige, and esteem are all seen as being synonomous with personal satisfaction. This is based on the assumption of a socially rational individual, the direct counterpart of the assumption of an economically rational individual. Thus, just as an economically rational individual maximizes profit for maximum utility, so a socially rational individual maximizes social standing to maximize personal satisfaction.

The second category of expenditures, labeled personal discretionary, includes conspicuous consumption and productive investment above that needed to cover depreciation. However, productive investment is not usually viewed as contributing significantly to social standing and may in some developing country cultures even detract from it (Foster).

Expenditures aimed at increasing personal satisfaction are largely determined by social norms. Consequently, maximization of personal satisfaction will include profit maximizing behaviour only if this behaviour contributes more to satisfaction than does alternative behaviour. Thus, a rational peasant must satisfy competing claims for capital surplus within the framework of his social system. In more traditional economic terms, the objective function of the peasant requires evaluation of the relative elasticity of unallocated surplus between socially mandatory and personal discretionary expenditures. Within each of these categories, allocation must be made between ritualistic ceremonies versus reciprocal obligations on the one hand and conspicuous consumption versus productive investment on the other.

Additional increments of surplus capital will aid the development process only if used for productive investments. However, unless the cultural norms favour expenditures for productive investment over other areas, the development process will not be enhanced. Indeed, the potential for expenditures on conspicuous consumption items is virtually unlimited. Also, ritualistic expenditures to gain social prestige are dependent on the relative level of expenditure of others in the community since the search for prestige and status is a competitive process. Each participant is forced to spend relatively greater amounts to achieve a desirable level of status as more unallocated surplus becomes available. Hence, we have a social treadmill effect, and any accumulated surplus can quickly be reduced to zero with no expenditures made for production investment.

The production economics approach to development focuses on increasing agricultural production through the efficent use of inputs, especially capital. Whether the marginal profit over traditional practices from using the inputs is large or small, the assumption is that profit maximization is sufficient motivation to assure adoption. Assuming the primacy of profits, the marketing aspect of production then becomes a critical influence on the peasants' perceived economic risk. Accumulating surplus capital depends on the belief that profits can be achieved through commercial product markets.

The adoption-diffusion approach investigates the influence of social values, beliefs, and attitudes on adoption of new practices and capital inputs. Since the individual's beliefs are perceived truths, this approach provides the interface with the economic marketing discussion above. Review of the adoption-diffusion literature reveals that the effect of many variables on the use of capital inputs has been analyzed. However, it is suggested that only perceived technical risk is involved in the dynamics of the system. Therefore, only this variable is discussed here. The reader is referred to Yetley and Deaton for detailed discussion of these variables and the overall model.

Use of any new capital input is perceived by peasants as increasing the level of technical risk (Nietschmann; and IRRI). The importance of this variable lies in its intervening effect between accumulated surplus capital and the use of capital inputs. Omitting this variable would assume that the use of capital inputs is risk free. Perceived technical risk is the peasant's subjective estimate of the probability of obtaining an adequate harvest given a set of technical inputs. It is suggested that peasants view traditional farming practices and inputs as having the lowest possible risk. Therefore any new inputs will, at least initially, be viewed as increasing the risk of obtaining an adequate harvest.

The concepts discussed above have been organized into a systems model (figure 1). The arrows in the model are hypothesized sequences of cause and effect. The nature of the relationships among variables is given by the algebraic sign (+ or -). The system becomes dynamic with the inclusion of feedback loops, labeled socially mandatory and personal discretionary.

Following Schultz, we assume peasant societies are highly stable; that is, development has not progressed rapidly and peasants are allocating their limited resources efficiently, given social mores. New inputs are necessary if development is to proceed. The implication of this position, combined with the above discussion on unallocated capital, is that significant economic development will occur only with continued massive infusions of new capital inputs from outside the system. It is, therefore, instructive to analyze the proposed model to gain insights into strategies that might reduce the magnitude of these capital infusions and simultaneously allow development to become self-sustaining.

By representing figure 1 symbolically, a system of simultaneous equations was specified. This system is amenable to mathematical manipulation, and conditions for stability of the proposed model can be evaluated. Each relationship (arrow) in figure 1 is represented by a b_{ij} term, where b is the strength of the relationship between the two variables x_i and x_j (b is a regression coefficient). That is, $-b_{11,4}$ represents the negative influence of surplus capital (x_4) on the perceived technical risk (x_{11}) of harvesting a crop, meaning that greater levels of capital reduce the perceived (subjective) risk of loss. The b_{ij} representing the feedback loops are lagged, thus connecting the successive time periods.

Blalock gives two necessary mathematical conditions for system stability. Condition I states that $\Sigma b_{ii} < 0$. Condition II states that the determinant $|D|$ of

Figure 1: The Dynamic Model with term "c", [$(b_6, 6^b 7, 7^b 8, 8^b 11, 11)$ $(b_5, 4^b 9, 5^b 12, 9^b 19, 12^b 20, 19^b 23, 20^b 24, 23^b 4, 24)$], and term "f", [$(b_4, 4^b 5, 5^b 7, 7^b 8, 8^b 11, 11)$ $(b_9, 6^b 12, 9^b 19, 12^b 20, 19^b 23, 20^b 24, 23^b 6, 24)$], where "c" is shown as ⇝ and "f" as →

the matrix representing the system must be $|D| > 0$ for K = even, or $|D| < 0$ for K = odd, where K is the number of variables. From Schultz's argument, we can infer that both necessary and sufficient stability conditions are met in most peasant economies.

From the model in figure 1, we find that for mathematical stability, the determinant $|D| = K[a + b - c - d - e + f + g - h] > 0$ since K = an even number.

$$|D| = K[+ \ (b_{4,4}b_{5,5}b_{6,6}b_{7,7}b_{8,8}b_{9,9}b_{11,11}b_{12,12}b_{19,19}b_{20,20}b_{23,23}b_{24,24}) \quad \xleftarrow{\text{Symbol}} a$$

$$+((b_{5,5}b_{6,6}b_{7,7}b_{8,8}b_{9,9}) \cdot (b_{11,4}b_{12,11}b_{19,12}b_{20,19}b_{23,20}b_{24,23}b_{4,24})) \quad \leftarrow b$$

$$-((b_{6,6}b_{7,7}b_{8,8}b_{11,11}) \ (b_{5,4}b_{9,5}b_{12,9}b_{19,12}b_{20,19}b_{23,20}b_{24,23}b_{4,24})) \quad \leftarrow c$$

$$-((b_{5,5}b_{6,6}b_{8,8}b_{11,11}) \ (b_{7,4}b_{9,7}b_{12,9}b_{19,12}b_{20,19}b_{23,20}b_{24,23}b_{4,24})) \quad \leftarrow d$$

$$-((b_{5,5}b_{6,6}b_{7,7}b_{8,8}b_{9,9}b_{12,12}) \ (b_{11,4}b_{19,11}b_{20,19}b_{23,20}b_{24,23}b_{4,24})) \quad \leftarrow e$$

$$+((b_{4,4}b_{5,5}b_{7,7}b_{8,8}b_{11,11}) \ (b_{9,6}b_{12,9}b_{19,12}b_{20,19}b_{23,20}b_{24,23}b_{6,24})) \quad \leftarrow f$$

$$+((b_{4,4}b_{5,5}b_{6,6}b_{7,7}b_{11,11}) \ (b_{9,8}b_{12,9}b_{19,12}b_{20,19}b_{23,20}b_{24,23}b_{8,24}) \quad \leftarrow g$$

$$-((b_{4,4}b_{5,5}b_{6,6}b_{7,7}b_{9,9}b_{11,11}) \ (b_{8,12}b_{19,12}b_{20,19}b_{23,20}b_{24,23}b_{8,24}))] \quad \leftarrow h$$

where $K = (b_{1,1}b_{2,2}b_{3,3}b_{10,10}b_{13,13}b_{14,14}b_{15,15}b_{16,16}b_{17,17}b_{18,18}b_{21,21}b_{22,22})$.

Letting each term in major parentheses be represented by a letter, the determinant $|D|$ can be written as:

$|D| = K \{a+b-c-d-e+f+g-h\}$, where

$a = (b_{4,4}b_{5,5}b_{6,6}b_{7,7}b_{8,8}b_{9,9}b_{11,11}b_{12,12}b_{20,20}b_{23,23}b_{24,24})$,

$b =((b_{5,5}b_{6,6}b_{7,7}b_{8,8}b_{9,9}) \ (b_{11,4}b_{2,11}b_{19,12}b_{20,19}b_{23,20}b_{24,23}b_{4,24}))$,

etc. as noted in the righthand margin.

This can be rewritten as $|D| = K[(a + b + f + g) - (c + d + e + h)] > 0$, which implies that $(a + b + f + g) > (c + d + e + h)$ since K is a positive constant. The b_{ii} in term K derive from exogenous variables included in the overall model (see Yetley and Deaton). These variables are not included in the stability conditions. Specifically, the b_{ii} terms in K are not involved in condition I, b_{ii} 0. We have carefully examined each b_{ii} in K and have tentatively concluded that each is positive. Since K is the product of these b_{ii}, K is also positive.

Selected Interrelationships

The objective of this analysis is to gain insight into those variables and relationships critical to initiating and sustaining the development process. From the previous discussion and figure 1, examination of the two allocative feedback loops and the impact of expenditures for productive investment and ritualistic ceremonies on social standing would appear fruitful. Accordingly, terms f and c from the determinant have been selected for detailed analysis. Both terms have diagrammatic interpretations (figure 1).

From the determinant $|D|$, assume $(a + b + g) \simeq (d + e + h)$, then for $|D| > 0$, the inequality $f > c$ must hold to satisfy stability condition II. Evaluation of the complete set of b_{ij} terms included in this approximate equality, reduces to:

$$(b_{4,4}b_{7,7})+(b_{19,19}b_{20,20}b_{23,23}b_{24,24}) \simeq (b_{7,4})+(b_{19,11}b_{20,19}b_{23,20}b_{24,23}b_{4,24}).$$

The right hand term is effectively the traditional economic productive relationships which Schultz suggests must be significantly increased to promote economic development. The multiplicative terms to the immediate left of the approximate sign are the b_{ii} terms which indicate leakage from the system due to exogenous forces. While the details for the above approximation cannot be directly supported by evidence found in the literature, two points argue strongly for its tentative acceptance: (1) there is nothing in the configuration that is obviously contrary to the assumption of approximate equality; and (2) recent research by IRRI indicates that lack of control over various environmental factors can negate gains made by use of capital inputs. Thus, while Schultz's argument may be a necessary condition for sustained agricultural growth, it does not appear to be sufficient. The b_{ii} terms common to both f and c, being on both sides of the inequality, mathematically cancel out. This leaves:

$$(b_{4,4}b_{5,5})X(b_{9,6}) > (b_{6,6})X(b_{5,4}b_{9,5}).$$

Since there is little information on the magnitude of the b_{ii} terms, we tentatively assume that $(b_{4,4}b_{5,5}) \approx (b_{6,6})$. The inequality then simplifies to $b_{9,6} > b_{5,4}b_{9,5}$. This means that, given stability, the contribution to social standing from expenditures on ritualistic ceremonies is greater than the contribution of productive investments. Not only does this satisfy the mathematical stability conditions, but it is also consistent with empirical evidence and economic anthropological observations.

Policy Implications

Ritual expenditures clearly reduce the flow of accumulated surplus into regenerative productive investments. The nature of the inequality may be such that virtually all surplus capital is expended on nonregenerative investments within one time period. This implies that external injections of capital are required in each period to sustain the growth process and increase productivity. The need for massive capital investments over extended periods is thus implied. Alternatively, a policy could be designed to change social norms so that product investments contribute more to satisfaction than alternative expenditures. This would encourage expenditures for productive investments from internally generated surplus capital. From the above discussion, such a change would also reverse the inequality of the determinant (that is, $|D| < 0$, because $b_{9,6} < b_{5,4}b_{9,5}$), thus negating the mathematical stability condition II, which may allow the economy to break out of its low level stability trap. Note that increasing productivity by use of capital inputs does not alter the stability conditions. This may explain why development has been so slow in many countries.

In terms of sustained development, it is clearly necessary that a significant portion of accumulated surplus be allocated to personal discretionary expenditures and thence into productive investments. Evidence from economic anthropology suggests this does not now occur in many developing economies. Hence, it is again clear that a change in social norms, specifically those involving allocation of accumulated surpluses, would greatly enhance the development process. Innovative educational approaches are needed to strengthen the relationship between productive investment and satisfaction, such that the same security can be dervied from the new economic order as is now provided by the traditional system.

To summarize, the model meets both intuitive and mathematical stability conditions. Increasing productivity by use of capital inputs will not negate the stability conditions. However, changing social norms to reward productive investments can both negate the stability conditions and direct internally generated surpluses into productive investments, thus allowing sustained development. At present, regenerative investment must compete against both social obligatory and conspicuous consumption for allocation of accumulated surpluses. Hence, these social relationships are suggested as key entry points into the system to initiate and aid development. This seems reasonable since these relationships relate to fundamental survival needs through acceptance by peers and kin (Polanyi). In addition, these relationships are amenable to educational approaches designed to enable peasant societies to modify their reward systems.

The main conclusion is that current lending programmes will not be sufficient to stimulate and sustain development. Such programmes do not provide the necessary condition for peasant societies to escape the stability trap. However, the necessary conditions can be created through innovative adult education and extension programmes designed to increase social reward for productive investments.

References

Blalock, H. M., Jr. (1969) Theory Construction, Englewood Cliffs, New Jersey, USA; Prentice-Hall.

Deaton, B. J. (1977) Capital formation in peasant economies, in Contributed Papers Read at the 16th International Conference of Agricultural Economists. Oxford; Institute of Agricultural Economics, University of Oxford, 259-270.

Foster, G. M. (1967) Tzintzuntzan. Boston; Little, Brown and Co.

IRRI (1977) Constraints to high yields on Asian rice farms. Los Banos, Laguna, Phillipines; International Rice Research Institute.

Mbithi, P. M. (1977) Farm decision-making with respect to social psychological elements and the human factor in agricultural management, in Decision-Making and Agriculture (edited by T. Dams and K. E. Hunt). Oxford; Alden Press, 131-139.

Nietschmann, B. Q. (1970) Between land and water: The subsistence ecology of the Miskito Indians, Eastern Nicaragua. Ph.D. dissertation. Madison, Wisconsin, USA; University of Wisconsin.

Polanyi, K. (1967) The Great Transformation. Boston; Beacon Press.

Schultz, T. H. (1964) Transforming Traditional Agriculture. New Haven, Connecticut, USA; Yale University Press.

Shapiro, K. H. (1977) Efficiency differentials in peasant agriculture and their implications for development polices, in Contributed Papers Read at the 16th International Conference of Agricultural Economists. Oxford; Institute of Agricultural Economics, University of Oxford, 87-98.

Yetley, M. J.; Deaton, B. J. (1978) A consideration of the dynamics of satisfaction maximization in the process of economic development. College Station, Texas, USA; Texas A&M University.

OPENER'S REMARKS--Martin H. Yeh

This paper is welcomed for its comprehensive approach to the process of economic development, based upon the behaviour framework for a satisfactory maximization model. This approach draws together essential relationships among economic anthropology, adoption-diffusion theory (sociology), and production economics. It also analyzes the linkages involved in the dynamic process. The model's policy implication for economic development is also presented.

The paper mainly emphasizes the conceptual framework for evaluating the process of economic development. However, any treatment of development is bound to be misleading when limited to economic and social factors, neglecting political and institutional aspects. To effectively promote social and economic development goals requires a wider conceptual framework of the development process as an integrated system of societal change in which a whole complex of economic, social, political, and institutional forces interact, permitting all human and physical resources of a society full participation in the development process.

The authors suggest that a system of simultaneous equations can be used to gain insights into critical development relationships and to follow social norms governing the allocation of surplus capital and the behaviour resulting in increased satisfaction. Besides a system of simultaneous equations, I would suggest considering a set of specific techniques which can be used in various stages of development; namely, the systems research technique for identification, the program planning and budgeting system for formulation and control, and the performance evaluation and review technique for adjustment and reformulation.

With respect to policy implications, the authors suggest that external injections of capital are required in each period to sustain the growth process and to increase productivity. Their analyses further suggest that current lending programmes will not be sufficient to stimulate and sustain development. Such programmes do not provide the necessary condition for peasant societies to escape the stability trap. However, the necessary conditions, according to the authors, can be created through innovative adult education and extension programmes designed to increase social rewards for productive investment. It would be helpful for the authors to clarify what is involved in the social reward system. What are the basic criteria for assessing alternative capital investments for development? How is control exerted over environmental factors in the economic development process?

The authors have presented a conceptual framework for evaluating the economic development process in a very systematic manner. However, the empirical evidence and testing of such a behaviour framework for stability conditions are lacking. A systems approach to development planning in general, and to agricultural sector development planning and policy analysis in particular, as suggested by the authors, is both feasible and promising. The potential for the future application of the systems approach to development is very great in both developing and developed countries.

RAPPORTEUR'S REPORT--Lorraine C. Bassett

Discussion of the paper was limited to the author's response to the opener's statements. Concerning the need for a broader conceptual economic development framework (which includes both political and institutional aspects in addition to the social and economic aspects presented by the authors), Yetley commented that this approach to the process of economic development is only in an infancy stage. Further criticisms were made concerning the lack of empirical evidence and testing of the behavioural framework for stability conditions. Yetley indicated that they would be proceeding in that area in the future.

FUNDAMENTAL EXPLANATIONS OF FARMER BEHAVIOUR AND AGRICULTURAL CONTRACTS

James A. Roumasset

[Read by Inderjit Singh.]

Abstract

This paper assesses the state of the arts in three areas: measuring risk preferences, the new household economics, and the role of institutions in agricultural development. It is shown in each instance that the conventional models omit the fundamental source of the phenomenon of interest. Alternative models are discussed for each of the three areas. The fundamental explanation of farm household behaviour is that households maximize expected accounting prices, where shadow prices depend on farm household characteristics. This model is used to explain the substitution of hired for operators' labour observed in Laguna, Philippines. The fundamental method for explaining rural institutions is called the new institutional economics. This method is used to explain patterns in Philippine share contracts.

OPENER'S REMARKS--Harald R. Jensen and Wesley B. Sundquist

[Remarks read by Richard Fraenkel.]

A methodological issue raised by Roumasset is that the theory of induced institutional change is not precise enough--that although the theory can generate refutable hypotheses, the process for generating such hypotheses is not replicable, Roumasset's statement that "this is not the case with the new institutional economics" to the contrary. In his further reference to the "new" institutional economics, Roumasset states that "once particular restrictive assumptions have been made, two researchers cannot, using the theory correctly, generate contradictory hypotheses." In the philosophy of science, the argument usually runs as follows: Two researchers beginning with the same set of assumptions and following the rules of logic must reach the same conclusions because the conclusions, though not obvious, are implied in the premises. We do not know whether Roumasset's hypotheses are synonymous with conclusions. However, of greater concern to us is that he seems to be arguing throughout for a theory which is no theory at all, or, if not case specific, of very limited application.

RAPPORTEUR'S REPORT--Lorraine C. Bassett

The need to include both transaction costs and the cost of using markets in household economic theory was indicated, as it helps to explain household behaviour. It was emphasized that the problem with household economic theory is that it considers market prices to be homogeneous. A need was voiced to seek means other than gambling to determine risk aversion and its effect on resource allocation. The application of fundamental explanations is in its infancy and requires further consideration. The need to include transaction costs, imperfect markets, and the role of institutions as fundamental explanations of risk aversion, household behaviour, and agricultural contracts was reiterated.

Contributing to the discussion were Dale W. Adams and Graham E. Dalton.

304

A GUIDE TO TEACHING AGRICULTURAL ECONOMICS
IN NONSPECIALIST COURSES IN A DEVELOPING ECONOMY:
EXPERIENCE OF TEACHING FOR RURAL CHANGE IN MALAWI

D. A. G. Green

Bunda College of the University of Malawi provides all university level agricultural education in Malawi. Currently there are around 240 students, with a planned expansion to about 420. College entrants are largely from rural backgrounds. On qualifying, a wide range of occupations is open to students: after three years of training, diplomates find employment in both public and private sectors; after five years, graduates are employed predominantly in the public sector. There are 40 staff members distributed over a wide range of disciplines constituting the School of Agriculture, which is grouped into four departments: agricultural engineering, crop production, livestock production, and rural development. The latter is multidisciplinary, and during 1976-78 was headed by a professor of agricultural economics. Throughout 1975-78, considerable time was concentrated on restructuring the curricula for the general degree and diploma in agriculture. The present curricula and experience of their development provide bases for discussion and the identification of recurrent themes and guidelines. There is no claim to perfection; curriculum development is a dynamic process. Experience from the microcosm of a single university college can provide insights which pragmatic academic staff may appreciate more readily than generalizations from surveys.

Problems

Common problems exist in institutions of higher rural education throughout the developing countries of Africa: different levels of student streams, students' inadequate pre-college training, crowded teaching schedules, and expatriate staff on short term contracts (FAO). Bunda College's experience appears representative, but the development of "end-on" (sequential) diploma-degree curricula may well be unique. The present curricula emphasize practical application of the rural sciences. The need to maintain an integrated approach to the subject matter of rural change persists (Sangare). These common problems are expanded with reference to Bunda College.

1. Interrelationship of student streams. The College is responsible for diploma and degree training and, increasingly, short term inservice training. Despite their ultimate professional involvement in indigenous problems associated with rural development, the diploma and degree streams tended to separate. This problem has been resolved to some extent by sequential curricula: degree candidates are selected from the diploma class on the basis of achievement and demonstrated potential.

2. Students' abilities in agricultural economics. Student's training prior to university selection is hardly adequate to begin conventional social subjects or the applied agricultural sciences. Thus, the first year concentrates on basic subjects (63 percent of total teaching). The rural social sciences, conceptually so different from the technical sciences, are introduced in the second year. Introductory agricultural economics develops decisionmaking concepts in practical areas of farm production and marketing in the context of rural development.

3. Balance of agricultural economics with other rural development subjects. Larger classes and heavy staff commitments are the result of larger student intake and the necessity to teach basic sciences in the first years

of both diploma and degree training (63 percent and 30 percent of total teaching respectively). Moreover, agricultural economics (including farm management) is only one of the rural development subjects (others are extension, communications, rural sociology, home economics, nutrition, and public health) being crowded into a quarter of total teaching time (36 percent in the home economics option).

4.   Relevance of professional material.   Agricultural economics draws on empiricism and the application of analytical concepts. Short term expatriate staff members frequently lack both facts on the economy in which they find temporary employment and relevant practical analytical experience. Thus, there is a tendency to resort to conventional materials with origins in the advanced economies, a situation which lacks satisfaction for both teacher and student. Improvements could occur as appointments are increasingly filled by indigenous staff. However, a pragmatic philosophy will still be necessary in selecting appropriate course materials.

Role of Agricultural Economics in Subject Matter Selection

In drawing from a body of professional knowledge, selection of appropriate subject matter must consider quality and quantity of students and staff, professional expectations of both, employers' expectations, and the country's future professional needs (Mather, Davis, Brannon, and Bordeaux, and Beck). Objectives of university education must also be incorporated (Lewis; and Williams).

The subject matter of the rural social sciences borders on the humanities, dealing substantially with values, judgment, and humanistic concepts, in sharp contrast to subjects based in the natural sciences. Discussion on the role of agricultural economics in general agricultural education reiterate the integrative quality of the discipline and the pragmatism of the majority of its practitioners. Agricultural economics is generally accorded first priority.

The responsibility for course material which trains the young professional in an integrative approach to rural change and the development of reasoning skills and judgment as essential tools for continued learning lies with the rural social sciences, and with agricultural economists in particular (Manderscheid).

This philosophical position is also responsible for containing the various social science disciplines within the rural development department. Thus, within the college there exists a cohesive influential unit which can encourage the development of linkages among the rural sciences. With increasing emphasis on integrated rural development, the socioeconomic subjects will continue to gain in importance (Hoffman).

The Curricula

Currently, teaching is directed toward undergraduate and diploma training, although the future possibility of postgraduate training must be kept in perspective (Green, 1976a and 1976b). The incumbents of four established posts are responsible for teaching agricultural economics: two posts in farm management, one in marketing and development, and the departmental head. Table 1 presents the essential details of the curricula for the diploma and degree courses which are now arranged sequentially, in contrast to the time up to 1975 when both courses existed in separate streams. The sequential ordering of courses creates new problems for upgrading mature students, but these are not fundamental, as was the previous segregation of student levels and duplication of classes.

Emphasizing undergraduate and diploma training in general agriculture, the curricula permit no specialization, except for the choice of a final year degree

TABLE 1.   Analysis and distribution among subjects of teaching time by year of course for the General Degree and Diploma in Agriculture, Bunda College of Agriculture, University of Malawi, 1978

Analysis of teaching time

Analysis and Distribution by year of course	General Diploma in Agriculture by year of course				General Degree in Agriculture by year of course		
	Year 1	Year 2	Year 3	Total	Year 4	Year 5	Total (5 years)
Total hours per academic session[a]	900	840	750	2,490	750	640	3,880
Average hours per week	30	28	25	28	25	21	25
Ratio of lectures: practicals[b]	37:63	53:47	45:55	45:55	53:47	39:61	45:55

Distribution of teaching time

a. Among all subjects (exl HE / incl HE[c])

Subject	Y1 exl HE	Y1 incl HE	Y2 exl HE	Y2 incl HE	Y3 exl HE	Y3 incl HE	Total exl HE	Total incl HE	Y4 exl HE	Y5 With RD[d] exl HE	Y5 With RD incl HE	Y5 Without RD[d] exl HE	Y5 Without RD incl HE	Total 5yr With RD[d] exl HE	Total 5yr With RD incl HE	Total 5yr Without RD[d] exl HE	Total 5yr Without RD incl HE
	%	%	%	%	%	%	%	%	%	%	%	%	%	%	%	%	%
Basic subjects[e]	63	63	58	46.5	63	53	50	39	51	63	39	77	53	52	41	54	44
Technical agriculture[f]	30	20	7	7	–	–	25	25	30	–	–	–	–	26	22	27	22
Rural development subjects[g]	7	17	35	46.5	37	47	25	36	19	37	61	23	47	22	37	19	34
Total	100	100	100	100	100	100	100	100	100	100	100	100	100	100	100	100	100

b. Among components of rural subjects

Component	Y1	Y2	Y3	Total	Y4	Y5 With RD	Y5 Without RD	Total (5 yr) %
								%
Economic theory	–	5	–	2	3	–	–	1.6
Farm management	–	6	17	8	–	19	–	7.7
Marketing economics	–	3	–	<1	4	–	–	1.3
Development economics	–	2	–	<1	5	–	–	1.4
Total: Agricultural Economics	–	16	17	11	12	19	19	12.0
Agric systems & rural development	–	–	8	2	–	4	–	3.0
Total: Economics related subjects	–	16	25	13	12	23	19	15.0
Other rural development subjects	7 / 17	19 / 30.5	12 / 22	12 / 23	7 / 19	14 / 38	24	11 / 22 (With) · 9 / 24 (Without)
Total: Rural development subjects	7 / 17	35 / 46.5	37 / 47	25 / 36	19	37 / 61	23 / 47	22 / 37 (With) · 19 / 34 (Without)

a. Based on three 10 week terms.
b. Equal weighting of lectures and practical time.
c. Excluding/Including Home Economics. Agricultural Engineering is included in "Technical agriculture" taken, usually by men students, Home Economics included in "Rural development subjects" usually taken, as a substitute for Agricultural Engineering by women students.
d. Degree Projects taken in the final year with some freedom of choice among four departments. Project selected in the Rural Development Department adds 9 practical hours (14%) to the "Rural development subjects".
e. Mathematics, Agricultural Statistics, Biology, Physical Science, Use of English/Communications (50% of first year is basic English).
f. Agricultural Chemistry, Crop Production, Livestock Production, Farm Practice, Farm Project, Agricultural Tour.
g. Use of English/Communications (50% of first year and all second year is technical writing and communications). Home Economics, Agricultural Economics, Farm Management, Agricultural Systems and Rural Development, Extension and Rural Sociology, Human Nutrition and Public Health.

Source: "Syllabus for the Diploma/Degree in Agriculture". Paper submitted to the University of Malawi Senate by the School of Agriculture, May, 1978.

project and the possibility of substituting home economics for agricultural engineering. The curricula reflect fairly well the relative importance of essential major subject areas. Students receive scientific explanations in adequate breadth and depth; they are able to think about farming, and to observe and develop reasonable arguments. There are opportunities also to work with smallholder farmers, but time allocation appears to be relatively limited. For students who subsequently work in extension or rural development planning, this could result in an inadequate understanding of rural change at the "grass roots" of the community.

Agricultural professionals concerned with rural change must be conversant with the problems of rural village communities. The analysis in table 1 shows the strong practical bias persisting throughout the diploma and degree courses (45:55, lectures:practicals). However, the analysis cannot differentiate between students' practical learning of scientifically based skills (taught in the laboratory or on the modern college farm) and practical observations and socioeconomic analysis of rural change (which may necessitate more contact with local rural communities than the present curricula permit despite substantial amounts of time being spent in local villages during practical extension classes). Education for rural change implies an integrated approach to the socioeconomic problems, and where this objective conflicts with the practical mastery of technical skills (also important in the total perspective of rural change), there may well be good reason to introduce a greater degree of specialization according to this dichotomy of needed skills.

Analysis of the curricula for the diploma and degree courses leads to the following observations:

1. Among the four departments, time allocation is reasonable. A quarter of total time is made available to rural development subjects for students following the diploma, and, for those following the home economics route, an average of 9 percent is made available.

2. Substantial time is devoted to basic subjects in the first year of both diploma and degree curricula; this is necessary and not unusual. The degree, 12 percent agricultural economics or 15 percent for all economics related subjects, appears to fall a little below an average of 18 percent in a range from 9 percent (Khartoum) to 29 percent (Tanzania) (Thimm). In the first degree year (year 4), basic subjects shift to a higher level of scientific understanding, but the applied, practical emphasis persists.

3. Total agricultural economics content is not very high at either diploma (11 percent) or degree (12 percent) levels. Of this, almost two-thirds (8 out of 13 percent) of the diplomas and slightly over half (8 out of 15 percent) of the degrees are farm management, giving a practical bias to applied economics. The scope for developing reasoning and critical abilities in relation to change in the rural socioeconomic system is limited in some 125 hours of the diploma and an additional 174 hours of the degree.

Contributions of agricultural economics in the limited available time must obviously concentrate on the development of basic analytical concepts and thought processes, and on an integrated approach to rural change. The approach is not easy in the face of, on the one hand, students' unfamiliarity with elementary economics, and, on the other hand, some professional antipathy toward disciplines concerned with values, attitudes, and reasoned arguments in a physical environment with an obvious potential for increasing agricultural productivity.

The following are considered to be areas on which agricultural economists might concentrate:

1. Concept of the economy. An elementary conception of the economy is essential to understanding sectorial interrelationships. Thus, early in the student's career, an unsophisticated description of the economy is necessary to provide a basis for developing a more functional knowledge as elements of macroeconomics and economic development are introduced. However, there is little scope to teach more than the rudiments of development in only 1.4 percent of total course time.

2. Basic concepts of economic analysis and management. Concepts of marginal analysis are more readily accommodated at the micro level because of the emphasis on agricultural production and management. The importance of good teaching of management as a discipline cannot be overemphasized in solving problems of economic development. Basic concepts of economic efficiency and optimization and their interpretation and application can be examined by developing case studies.

3. Agricultural systems and rural development. The introduction of new technology and institutions into different socioeconomic systems of rural life requires a conceptualization of economic activity as a series of interrelated systems. For this reason, a special type of seminar has been introduced to provide the opportunity for integrating technical and socioeconomic training. The pivotal and integrative functions of agricultural marketing tend to be neglected.

4. Indigenous interpretations of economic concepts (Chipeta). More attention could be devoted to indigenous interpretations of basic concepts of economic analysis. Conceptually, the same processes occur in all socioeconomic systems, but students often fail to perceive the application to their own environment when instructed in conventional terms, thereby missing the relevance of much economic analysis. Explorations into indigenous economics demand of the teacher considerable professional maturity and experience in the local economy.

Recurring Themes: Hypotheses

Although generalizations from a single case can be misleading, a similarity exists in rural economies throughout Africa and in many of their teaching institutions (Modebe). The situation in Bunda College appears representative. A number of recurring themes emerge which can be succinctly presented as hypotheses. Guidelines then become apparent.

1. Different levels of professional agriculturalists tend to become professionally separated. Separation of diploma and degree students was evident in past experience at Bunda College and is more likely to be resolved in the sequential design of current curricula. Upgrading and inservice training courses can also be accommodated in this system. The possibility of cooperation with other agricultural training institutions could well be explored in greater depth, however.

2. Curriculum development tends to be "teaching objective" rather than "learning objective" oriented. Curriculum development is a continuous process tending to be the preserve of professional teachers. Increasingly, the curriculum development committee will feel the need to seek the guidance of all interested parties: teachers, students, employers, development planners, and scientists with a contemporary knowledge of the applied sciences.

3. Students are ill prepared to handle university level agricultural economics. Functional manifestations of basic economic concepts merit greater emphasis in order to develop an integrated understanding of the economy. Indigenous case study material, a painstaking occupation at which African university teachers are likely to do better than short term expatriates, will provide needed support.

4. The social sciences provide appropriate integrative preparation to handle problems of rural change. These subjects are maintained under the umbrella of the rural development department in which exists a unifying philosophy of developing critical skills and judgment based on values. The department as a whole provides the means of developing students' integrative perception of rural change which include a systems approach to problems of rural development. In future, some greater specialization in these study areas may be desirable to meet Malawi's increasing needs for planners and managers of the National Rural Development Programme.

5. Monitoring of appropriate technological and sociological changes requires sophisticated analytical techniques. At present, Malawian students showing an aptitude for postgraduate training in agricultural economics go abroad. However, the strength of the teaching institution and the skills of its agricultural economists will be more rapidly enhanced as specialist training and research programmes can be developed within the college and associated social science departments of the university.

6. Indigenous research is a necessary function of university agricultural economists. The research function not only provides a basis for postgraduate training but also the infusion of relevant subject material into courses. Cooperative resarch with related government departments can be a vehicle for pursuing relevant research topics and building up both the teaching and research capabilities of the college (Green, forthcoming).

Conclusions: Guidelines

In conclusion, the guidelines are summarized beginning with two referring generally to curriculum development.

1. Sequential professional training, upgrading, inservice courses, and inter-institutional cooperation all ameliorate tendencies for professional separation.

2. Curriculum development committees need the guidance of all parties interested in training young professional agriculturalists. Keeping the general objectives of univeristy education in perspective requires considerable professional maturity among rural scientists.

3. More emphasis on developing an understanding of analytical concepts in terms of the indigenous environment is needed in agricultural economics.

4. Linkages between the rural sciences and an integrative approach to rural change may be fostered by the rural sciences giving more attention to marketing and a systems approach.

5. Some specialization of undergraduates' training may be justifiable because of the qualitatively different skills required to handle technical changes in contrast to socioeconomic changes.

6. Research in cooperation with government departments (and other organizations) can lead to improvements in the relevance of the curricula.

References

Chipeta, W. (1974) Indigenous economics. Blantyre, Malawi; University of Malawi, Chancellor College, Department of Economics.

FAO (1976) Training in Agriculture and Food Marketing at the University Level in Africa. Report on the FAO/AFAA consultations. Rome; Food and Agriculture Organization of the United Nations.

Green, D. A. G. (1976a) Toward a postgraduate training programme in agricultural economics in the University of Malawi. Paper presented at the African Seminar on Postgraduate Training in Agricultural Economics in Nairobi, Kenya. Lilongwe, Malawi; Bunda College.

Green, D. A. G. (1976b) Toward a strategy for postgraduate research in agricultural economics at Bunda College. Paper presented at the African Seminar on Postgraduate Training in Agricultural Economics in Nairobi, Kenya. Lilongwe, Malawi; Bunda College.

Green, D. A. G. (forthcoming) The role and function of social science research in higher agricultural education in Malawi: A search for relevance. Journal of Social Science.

Hoffman, H. K. F. (1977) The organization of degree structures and course content in institutions of higher agricultural education, and relation to the need for the improvement of agricultural production in Africa, in Proceedings of the Second General Conference of the Association of Faculties of Agriculture in Africa, Cairo, 1975. Nairobi, Kenya; Association of Faculties of Agriculture in Africa, University of Nairobi, 37-40.

Lewis, W. A. (1966) Education and economic development, in Selected Readings to Accompany Getting Agriculture Moving (edited by R. E. Borton). New York; Agricultural Development Council, Vol. 1, 363-377.

Manderscheid, L. G. (1973) Guidelines for curriculum development in agricultural economics. American Journal of Agricultural Economics, 55 (4, Part II) 740-748.

Mather, L. L.; Davis, J. T.; Brannon, R. H.; Bordeaux, A. F., Jr.; Beck, R. L. (1977) Developing a competency-based curriculum in agricultural economics. American Journal of Agriculutral Economics, 59 (4) 760-765.

Modebe, A. N. A. (1977) The need for participation of institutions of higher agricultural education in the rural development of Africa, in Proceedings of the Second General Conference of the Association of Faculties of Agriculture in Africa, Cairo, 1975. Nairobi, Kenya; Association of Faculties of Agriculture in Africa, University of Nairobi, 49-51.

Sangare, S. (1977) The need for a functional relationship between higher, middle, and lower levels of agricultural education, in Proceedings of the Second General Conference of the Association of Faculties of Agriculture in Africa, Cairo, 1975. Nairobi, Kenya; Association of Faculties of Agriculture in Africa, University of Nairobi.

Thimm, H. U. (editor) (1977) Proceedings of the African Seminar on Postgraduate Training in Agricultural Economics in Nairobi, Kenya, July 22-August 4, 1976. Bonn; Germany Foundation for International Development, Division of Education, Science, and Documentation.

Williams, H. T. (1971) An approach to university teaching in agricultural economics. Journal of Agricultural Economics, 22 (3) 223-229.

OPENER'S REMARKS—Juma A. Lugogo

Green's paper presents a case study of Bunda College in Lilongwe, Malawi, within which numerous serious issues involved teaching of agricultural economics for rural change in developing economies are raised. The paper confirms the problems that were identified in a seminar in Nairobi in 1976 during the last IAAE Conference. The problems identified in Nairobi for post-graduate training in African universities are similiar, even at lower levels of training.

Granted that transfer of proven technologies from developed to developing economies is the order of the day, one question that is begged by professionals working in developing countries is how suitable, adaptable, or appropriate the technologies are. They are developed and derived from experience and observations in environments completely different in endowments and socio-political settings from those prevalent in most developing economies. In this context, agricultural economics concepts and principles--particularly at the applied level--are no exception. The paper rightly calls for indigenization not only the presentation of the subject matter but, more importantly, of the discipline itself.

The more pertinent issues raised by the paper include: (1) sequential diploma-degree training, (2) inadequate pre-college training, (3) student crowded teaching schedules, (4) dependence on expatriate staff members and their high turnover, (5) inadequate case studies from local economies, (6) limited research activities, (7) problem oriented presentation and exercises, (8) inadequate textbooks and teaching materials, (9) staff loading, and (10) lack of retention of local staff in academic institutions.

Green analyzes these problems well and suggests courses of action for Bunda College in order to improve the curriculum and therefore provide Malawi with the agents for rural change for development.

Governments in developing economies are in a hurry (Nyaoism in Kenya). They have to deliver the goods of independence and growth. Hence, the political considerations dictate that experiments in agricultural training can have very adverse effects. At issue is the sequential diploma-degree training. Diploma training is terminal and serves purposes different from degree training. The diploma graduate needs to be equipped with practical skills that will be of immediate use to the farmer or rural person.

Government intervention in curriculum development is becoming increasingly prominent. Academic freedom to choose what to teach at what level is fast being phased out. As the greatest employer and main agent influencing the economy, the government dictates on a short term basis and encourages problem solving training programmes; that is, it will go more for applied areas such as farm management, marketing, cooperatives, project planning and evaluation, farming systems, and agricultural finance, rather than the basic concepts of micro and macro economics. Where should the onus lie for the final curriculum? What is the tradeoff between basic principles and applied areas? How much indigenization, as stated earlier, should be allowed to creep into the traditional economic theories?

Job identification for graduates is very important for curriculum development. Experience shows, however, that government assignments in developing economies are very dynamic in content and character. How much flexibility, therefore, particularly in time allocation, should be built into university programmes?

Finally, I cannot help but underline the importance of research by both faculty and students. Case study assignments, even for diploma trainees, are very useful in getting home conceptual messages. The question worth noting, however, is who should decide on the subject areas--those who have funds such as private firms and parastatals? They have specific objectives mind. Should we ignore the conflicting public and private interests for the training opportunities these funds offer? As Green states in another paper to be published soon, let us "search for relevance" in agricultural training for rural change in the developing countries.

RAPPORTEUR'S REPORT--R. Thamarajakshi

Sequential training is a solution to the problems of professional separation, although, in the process, students undergoing graduate training have to take several courses which are not quite necessary. While research is important for both the faculty and the student and case study assignments could be made even to diploma students, there are questions as to who should determine the areas of research when there are conflicts between public needs and individual interests, and whether specialization might not tend to overproduce degree holders in the face of the immediate needs of the government for diploma holders to work as extension staff at the field level. Agricultural problems in these economies are specific, and while the basic concepts of economic theory need to be understood by the students, they also have to be trained to comprehend the processes of decisionmaking and investment changes in these labour surplus rural communites. For this purpose, it is important to ensure that the students have a real feeling of the rural life so that they develop a flexible approach to the problems of rural change. The process of indigenization of training could be made possible by enabling the students to be in constant touch with the villages and by engaging them during vacations in survey work in villages for the collection of requisite material for such indigenization. Also, textbooks need to be written by indigenous staff. There is also the problem of job identification for graduates as a guide to the type of training and the extent of flexibility that is available in the basic allocation between various disciplines and between basic preferences and applied areas in order to be able to accommodate the requirements of the government and parastatal organizations.

Contributing to the discussion were Ardron B. Lewis, John S. Nix, Kenneth H. Parsons, and Morag C. Simpson.

AGRICULTURAL MARKETING TRAINING IN DEVELOPING COUNTRIES

Michael Haines

Abstract

This paper argues that the expenditure of scarce resources on agricultural marketing training is justifiable only if it brings a real improvement in the efficiency of the marketing system, and that this will depend less in the short term on the extension of undergraduate and graduate teaching than on a concentrated effort to develop marketing appreciation at all levels of public administration and business. Since graduates take many years to reach positions of authority from which to implement their specialist knowledge (and may even then not be able to use it to best effect) and since they often do not go into business because of social constraints, reliance on graduate training alone cannot bring any improvement in real terms. Although, therefore, every effort should be made to consolidate and improve existing degree schemes in order to make a basic core of agricultural marketing a compulsory component of all agriculture related studies and to develop specialist courses in marketing at the graduate level at one or two national centres, this should be accompanied by short term and ongoing measures to increase marketing awareness and collaboration between specialists and practical marketing personnel already in employment. This should aim to convince administrators and employers of the long term need for properly trained specialists to be employed in the marketing system, which will produce a far sounder basis for the long term training of specialists and their optimal deployment than any preconceived employment plan.

OPENER'S REMARKS--Jean-Francois Soufflet

The author is to be commended for providing us with a few definite aims in teaching marketing, and for focusing on those who today make marketing decisions and tomorrow, perhaps, provide graduates with employment. In many countries, there are many small producers and traders who often represent a large part of the market and know how to produce, handle, and trade livestock, for instance, or fresh fruits and vegetables. They generally have no time to study marketing, and the bulk of them do no want to. But they are necessary actors in the marketing systems of many products. How can we train only some of the marketing actors, but expect all of them to work together? If we first choose to train those who already have a large amount of decisionmaking power, and those in administration and business who have enough time and money to be trained, I wonder whether we are not going to reinforce the economic power of those who already have power and further weaken the others. This problem is important, especially in many countries where the government, parastatal institutions, or supranational firms hold a big part of the economic information, data, and economic power. There are struggles and strikes in any production and marketing system--the struggle for the life of certain types of enterprises, the struggle to catch a part of the consumer's expenditures, and so on. How do we manage to teach when there are clashes between opposite interests? Must we teach the same things to everyone, or can we train each one in light of his own struggle?

RAPPORTEUR'S REPORT--R. Thamarajakshi

There are innumerable small traders operating in most of the developing countries. The problem of market performance and efficiency could perhaps be tackled by a preference for training the teenagers in business methods given that small traders might not have the necessary time for such training. There is also the problem that if training is directed to the larger units with greater economic power, it would tend to perpetuate the present skewed economic power structure. There are a number of actors operating in the marketing system and all of them have to be trained. The needs of agricultural marketing actors are diverse and stress may need to be laid on training executives and middle level managers. There are limited job opportunities for trained marketing personnel in developing economies at the present stage of development. This is particularly so since business firms in these economies are foreign firms, although this tendency has declined in recent times with the increasing trend towards cooperative marketing structures.

Contributing to the discussion were Morgan A. M. Rees and Morag C. Simpson.

CONTRIBUTION OF MARXIST ANALYSIS TO THE STUDY OF RURAL ECONOMY: THE FRENCH EXAMPLE

Michel Blanc

Abstract

The basic concept of the Marxist analysis is undoubtedly that of class struggle. The classes of society are defined in terms of the relationships they form with one another. The analysis of labour exploitation relationships does not apply to the reality of French rural society today. The approach might, however, be relevant to the study of other societies. In French rural society, the classes are mainly defined in terms of competition: wealthy farmers, an intermediate class of farmers, and poor farmers. The conflicts between these three social groups are described in this paper. Nevertheless, this analysis in terms of classes is not sufficient to understand the struggles within the rural society and to analyze the evolution of production. A new concept needs to be introduced: that of a "social production system" which describes the relationships between farmers and various economic agents involved in the same production activity in a given area. The analysis of these different social production systems existing in an area leads to the acknowledgement of different subgroups within each class. In the final analysis, the struggle and alliance of these different subgroups determine the evolution of production in each area.

OPENER'S REMARKS--G. Edward Schuh

Blanc makes the point that his analysis is not cast in terms of the orthodox dogma of Marx, Engels, and Lenin, even though he believes it to be consistent with the Marxist tradition. This move away from dogmatism is consistent with the current emergence of pluralism in Marxist thought around the world. The Marxist and neoclassical interpretations of reality can be complementary rather than competing versions of the "truth." Two gaps in Blanc's interpretation--lack of allowance for economic forces leading to change that might provide the basis for social and political conflict, and arbitrary specification of classes--can be filled by neoclassical economics.

RAPPORTEUR'S REPORT--Dorothy F. Miller

The analysis includes agribusiness capital, and that social stratification could be analyzed in terms of competition and the social relation with capital. In developing countries, large farms are not always in the hands of the most capable farmers. Agrarian reform may be where the two schools of thought, Marxist and neoclassical, merge. It is difficult to agree on classification of economic versus social and political forces. In the last resort, the rate of development is determined by the society's wage rate. This wage rate depends on the relationship between capitalists and labourers. Market imperfections such as labour unions and entrepreneur or capitalist associations exist. In a perfect labour market in a capitalistic society, it is impossible for the "atoms" of society to be individuals rather than classes. If the method of land appropriation is such that the most skillful get the land, why in the United States, as in France, has agrarian capitalism not developed? Analysis of nonagrarian capitalism in France leads to the group of intermediate farmers.

Contributing to the discussion were Jacques Brossier, Andre H. Brun, Clark Edwards, Ferenc Fekete, Ali Mohammad, and Claude Viau.

316

TOWARD A PHILOSOPHICAL FOUNDATION OF
THE SCIENCE OF AGRICULTURAL POLICY

Yang-Boo Choe

[Read by R. J. Hildreth.]

Abstract

In dealing with value laden policy questions on agriculture and the farmer, modern applied agricultural economists are often committed to disguised value judgments under the influences of positivism and conditional normativism. In social inquiry into agricultural policy, the problem of identifying policy problems and proposing policy proposals unavoidably raises the problem of the value judgment and its criterion. Popper's idea of critical dualism of fact and standard may help agricultural economists to decide upon humanitarian agrarianism as a philosophical foundation for the science of agricultural policy. The existing agricultural dilemma and economic unfairness working against the farmers calls for such a decision. A challenge for new agricultural economists is not to interpret the agricultural dilemma but to help to change it by applying the impartial and scientific attitude of critical rationalism.

OPENER'S REMARKS--R. J. Hildreth

Choe holds that the major task of policy analysis is to contribute to the solution of real world problems. Contributions can be made on different levels. An economist can leave the university or government and become a political actor to solve policy problems. At another level, the economist may wish merely to explain and predict policy problems, which much more indirectly, but still usefully, contributes to their solution. In both cases, he must think through his moral and value positions in relation to his acts, but the social consequences of his acts are different. Does the role chosen by the economist make a difference? Can or should I be more of a positivist or a conditional normativist in the prediction and explanation role than in the political actor role?

Choe's list of unsettled questions is a good start for continued discussion. Does distributive unfairness exist equally in most economies? Does it change over time with shifts in demand and supply elasticities? For example, farm landowners' wealth position is growing rapidly in the United States at present, but was not during the time of publication of Choe's list of citations from the 1950s and 1960s. These are questions on which empirical analysis can shed illumination.

It appears clear that, in developed economies, farmers are not a homogeneous group. Witness the short run conflicts between feed grain and livestock producers. It is difficult to identify the relatively depressed group of farmers as they change over time. Many people in the United States feel that the most depressed group in farming is farm workers who are oppressed by the farmers.

I have found a paradigm given to me by Glenn Johnson useful in policy analysis. The answer to "What ought to be?" (policy), is dependent on answers to two prior sets of questions--value questions (What is good? What is bad?) and nonvalue questions (What is? What will be? What could be?).

Both kinds of questions are subject to analysis, and both are needed to answer the question, "What ought to be?" Choe's paper helps us think through value questions for our actions as economists.

The philosophers have had much difficulty with classifying values. But it still seems useful to consider the split into goodness, beauty, and truth. We should be careful to emphasize truth values in our work as economists and not let them be obscured.

As a country develops, agriculture becomes part of the industrial system. Farmers are not receptive to economists' views except with respect to equity. Because of the farmers' work ethic, they feel they should be compensated if prices fall too low.

Over time we have (as a profession and as farmers) justified many things we have done to improve welfare within the farm sector. People tend to question the advisability of transfers from the public sector to private individuals.

There seems to be an assumption that there is something immoral about inequality.

People in natural sciences will ask what is good and what is bad. Policymaking should be a science as well, since many economists want to be scientists. Distributional unfairness exists and is a real dilemma for parts of the world. In the paper, Choe discusses differences in income distribution, but does not necessarily advocate equality.

To arrive at a truth, none of us can be totally objective, as truth values differ. The idea of using public dollars to support lower income people is wrong--the degree of support in the United States, for example, is too large. With regard to the immorality of inequality, Choe actually said that the questions of income distribution are of an equity nature.

Contributing to the discussion were Denis K. Britton, William E. Hamilton, George T. Jones, Lyle P. Schertz, and Adolf A. Weber.

ETHICAL ISSUES AND INTERNATIONAL DEVELOPMENT: NEW CHALLENGES FOR THE AGRICULTURAL ECONOMIST

James R. Simpson

"Analytic effort is of necessity preceded by a preanalytic cognitive act that supplies the raw material for the analytic effort... This preanalytic cognitive act will be called vision" (Schumpeter). "But as soon as truly 'ultimate' problems are at stake, the ends are not given. With this, we come to the final service that science can render" (Weber). The 1980s will witness serious questions about distribution of income, cost-benefit relationships of development programmes, and ethical relationships in the use of scarce resources due to the energy crisis, a drastic cut in the world food balance, the accelerated depletion of many scarce resources, and rapid population growth (Survey; and Meadows and others). Parallel with the surfacing of these development issues has been a natural concern by planners about the effect their efforts have on individuals, communities, regions, and countries. This concern has brought about renewed interest in explaining the terms "development," "being developed," and "the good life" (Simpson). In effect, there is a growing interest in ethical aspects as they relate to goals, means, and economic theory in national and international development (Heilbroner). The conservation movement of the early 1900s, socialism in the 1930s, and the ecological movement of the 1960s are earlier manifestations of concerns about ethics and economics.

Support for the contention that we need to concentrate to a greater extent on theories relating economics and equity are available from many sources. A recent example is Carter and Johnston. In their words, "The recent concerns expressed about the 'global reach' of multinationals, conglomerates, and other actions that transcend markets and countries lead one to believe that our traditional kit of tools comes up short. Furthermore, efficiency measures judged against a competitive model say little about external effects on equity and quality of life considerations with alternative structural/organizational/control figurations" (pp. 738-739).

The depletion of many of the world's resources, in juxtaposition with an expressed desire to improve the well-being of the world's poor and along with a questioning about whether economic growth leads to "the good life," has important implications for agricultural economists (Adelman and Morris). Now, more than ever, there is a substantial and growing demand for economists to do research on topics which have major ethical components. An example of economists' recognition about the need to work on issues with major ethical considerations is the 160 acre limitation problem in California (Ip and Stahl; and Stanton).

This paper deals with some considerations which economists might find useful in deriving personal and collective philosophies about ethically related issues found in international development. The objective is to demonstrate that economists have a whole new area open to them, and that they are well equipped to objectively meet the task.

Ethical Issues in International Development

The following are 22 issues with major ethical components. The list is not exhaustive; rather, attention is focused on the variety of problems which have relevance to agricultural economists concerned with international development.

Issues Between Developed and Developing Countries

1. The rise of ever greater affluence (along with the failure to eliminate poverty) in the developed countries while massive poverty exists in most

319

developing countries.

2. Imminent scarcity of many natural resources, focusing on the flow of resources from developing to developed countries.

3. The right of one person or country to influence another country's norms and values.

4. The question of whether multinational development aid should be given primarily to those countries best prepared to use it (in terms of a benefit-cost ratio) or whether other criteria should be employed.

5. The amount of technical and financial resource flows to developing countries.

6. The role and obligation of multinational corporations.

7. Periodic shortages of food at the world level.

8. The trade-not-aid concept in trade concessions.

Issues Fundamentally Related to Developing Countries

1. The extent to and rate at which special efforts should be made to achieve income redistribution.

2. The right to form cartels for export products.

3. The proper mixture of popular participation in decisionmaking.

4. The form of political and economic systems to adopt.

Issues Mainly Relating to a Worldwide Development Strategy

1. Worldwide austerity as a development philosophy.

2. Brain drain to the more advanced countries.

3. Creation of a world technological expertise pool.

4. Dissolution of international borders.

5. A worldwide concern with ecology and use of certain resources such as the sea.

7. Creation of a "no growth" society or "steady state" economy.

8. Population control.

9. Use of labour intensive techniques versus introduction of greater mechanization.

10. Quality of food and life versus efficiency. A related issue is the extent to which public policy leads to a deviation from the "social optimum" in the use of capital or labour.

Economists and Ethical Considerations

The first thesis in the paper is that many, if not most, key international development issues are ethical and political as well as economic in nature. The apparently simple decision to increase the economic well-being of a certain group means that an ethical decision has been made. But what are ethics?

Moral philosophy (ethics) is a branch of philosophy which critically examines, clarifies, and reframes the basic concepts and presuppositions of morality. Philosophers devoting themselves to ethical relationships reflect on questions of good or bad and right or wrong within human conduct. Care must be taken not to confuse ethics with morality. Whereas ethics is a branch of philosophy which examines concepts in its inquiry for truth about morality, the term morality refers to a system of morals or rules for moral conduct. Close examination of the definition of ethics clearly indicates the desire for objectivity, which is exactly the methodological goal of agricultural economists.

The specific problems of ethics can be divided into three classes (McGreal). First are problems of duty which treat questions like rights or duties of developed nations vis-a-vis developing nations. The second class of problems deals with the highest good. For example, is anything good for its own sake, quite apart from any value it might have as a means to something else? Defining "development" or "progress" and relating them to means fit in this area. The third topic relates to value. An example is defining whether value is a matter of opinion, interest, attitude, custom, or law.

A second thesis is that ethical factors are best handled by economists involved with development projects by viewing the factors as constraints in studies. It cannot be overstressed that agricultural economists are well equipped to work on issues which have major ethical overtones, as the economist's training is oriented toward objectivity (Johnson and Zerby). Many of the discipline's forefathers had strong ties to ethics as a branch of philosophy. Some examples are Adam Smith who was a professor of moral philosophy, and John Stuart Mill who wrote widely on economics and ethics. Other major figures who explicitly acknowledged the need to relate economics and ethics are Alfred Marshall, John Maynard Keynes, and Frank Knight.

Perhaps most important, economists think in terms of evaluating alternatives-- an orientation which is generally not stressed in other social science disciplines such as philosophy and anthropology. Furthermore, it is asserted that economists should not be concerned about working on normative issues, for this class of problems can be treated as objectively as can questions dealing with positive data (Moore). Economists have a long history of dialogue on this point. The problem is avoiding the advocation of prescriptions even though the delineation of prescriptions is encouraged.

Visions versus Goals

A third thesis presented is that a vision (of the preanalytic type described by Schumpeter) of the terms "development" and "being developed" is necessary; that is, the "ends" of the economic and social processes must be envisioned before the means can be discussed. If agricultural economists are to collaborate effectively on development efforts or individual projects, they need to have an overall vision of what is to be accomplished in terms of improving society. A vision is very different from goals, as the latter are used in setting targets for specific projects or certain efforts. For example, one component of a development vision is that people should be able to have equal opportunities to achieve the life style they desire (within reasonable bounds, of course). Another part of the vision might be that it is good to have farms as family enterprises (and limited in size), or that large corporations are bad. These are ethical problems.

Once a vision is developed, shorter term goals can then be adapted to it. For

321

example, current measurements such as increases in total income generated in a town may be completely inconsistent with a larger vision of a quiet, peaceful life. Then, we have conflicts in goals which require measuring tradeoffs. Certainly, setting forth the ethical bases of different types of economic systems (capitalism and economic liberalism, or socialism and communism) can be very fruitful for the agricultural economist who is truly interested in international development. In other words, in order to get at the real issues, we must pause and ask why the issue is good or bad. In this way we can carefully examine the basic premises of visions, goals, and policies. Premises are the starting point in any deductive reasoning.

If the concept is accepted that a vision is useful prior to setting forth goals, then it also follows that an ethic of international development is greatly needed as a first step in setting forth a vision of development. Agricultural economists are in a unique position to work with philosophers, political scientists and others on such an ethic, as economists are well versed in the cold realities of real world constraints. Setting forth an ethic is fine, but it must be practical. As some futurists seek a world without borders, and others advocate a steady state economy (Boulding), the economist is constantly being asked to work on new and challenging issues (Knight). The question is: Will the demand be met, or will the time worn cliche, "Oh, I don't work on those issues," be heard?

Economics and Building for a Better Life

Our changing world is characterized by unparalleled improvement in some peoples' purchasing power. Nevertheless, the conundrum of defining progress still confronts the analyst. Increasingly, our attention fouces on noneconomic criteria impelled by predictions about imminent deficits of many goods that we have come to regard as necessary for an adequate life style. Concomitantly, there is a desire of socially conscious people in both the developed and developing countries rapidly to improve the living standards for countless millions left behind in the mad dash for economic growth. The result is an impending moral controversy about the desirability of economic forces as a major determinant of resource allocation, for many people are becoming convinced that there should be greater political intervention to achieve proper levels of living.

Scarcity of some natural resources also enters as a major factor in relations between industrialized nations (which are the principal consumers of the world's resources) and the developing countries (which in many cases are net exporters of raw materials). Consequently, there is an urgency about obtaining a certain level of economic development in which industrial or agricultural production supplements the export of raw materials as a major sources of foreign exchange. More than simple international tariff regulations are involved, for this problem is also interwoven with moral overtones. In the few decades since World War II, the approach to development has changed from determining how much capital was required and where to invest it for economic development of the country as a whole to improving the quality of life for the lowest income groups given the newly recognized and generally accepted constraints. As a consequence, there is a shift toward tempering economic questions with a strong component of moral philosophy in the search for indepth solutions.

The changing emphasis from concentrating only on maximizing growth to concerns about how growth relates to the quality of life has left the Third World leaders in a quandary as they seek a development model. A feeling of vulnerability is natural in determining where they fit in vis-a-vis the industrialized countries. It can be persuasively argued that economic and political goals have taken precedence over the objective of improving peoples' happiness and that while a steady increase in per capita GNP is undoubtedly desirable it should not be the outstanding goal but rather only one measurement of progress.

The key is to help people achieve their own goals, with the state and society assisting when appropriate. The emphasis in this philosophy thus changes from economic development at any cost (that is, growth in GNP) to a focus on people.

A caveat is in order. The philosophy expounded does not mean that development programmes should be reduced. Indeed, each one should be evaluated according to its benefit-cost ratio. Rather, what is meant is that we need to ask what the programmes' effects are on the overall vision and whether they push or steer people. It is recognized that most countries' development plans explicitly mention social goals such as improving health. Economists also usually mention in passing that social and ethical aspects must be considered. But this is not enough, for I am prepared to argue that this is simply lip service being paid because it is the right thing to do.

Conclusion

Moral philosophy is of greater relevance today than ever before as the world becomes increasingly technologically oriented. Ethics is not an abstruse academic study far removed from everyday life. On the contrary, it is precisely the philosopher who is needed to help chart a course out of labyrinth of social tensions and international confusion about mankind's future. The message in this paper is that moral philosophy can be taught and its principles incorporated by agricultural economists in the solution of real world problems. Relevance means understanding the issues which, in turn, requires careful examination of premises and constraints. Many of these issues relate to problems of values and how they fit in the higher social purpose. In recent years, it has been fashionable to argue for greater interdisciplinary research. I agree, but strongly add that moral philosophy has too long been neglected by too many agricultural economists.

An appropriate manner to close this paper is an example of the need for a vision. One example is a paper by Gardner. He observed, "Consider finally the larger purpose of policy. What is it that the Administration wants to attain in farm food programs? For both Ford and Carter, I believe that there is no well defined goal, no ideal that policy is striving toward." We could inquire that if the richest country in the world is operating in a rudderless fashion, reacting to political exigencies of the moment, how is it possible to expect the developing countries to have a vision? Nevertheless, it is rather obvious that some feeling is required about where the ship of development is headed. Assisting in determining the destination as well as charting altenrative courses is a challenge which agricultural economists would do well to consider accepting. Philosophy is everybody's business.

References

Adelman, I.: Morris, C. T. (1973) Economic Growth and Social Equity in Developing Countries. Stanford, California, USA; Stanford University Press.

Boulding, K. E. (1973) The economics of the coming spaceship earth, in Toward A Steady-State Economy (edited by H. E. Daly). San Francisco, California, USA; W. H. Freeman and Co.

Carter, H. O.; Johnston, W. E. (1978) Some forces affecting the changing structure, organization, and control of American agriculture. American Journal of Agricultural Economics, 60 (5) 738-748.

Gardner, B. (1978) Comments on emerging agricultural policies of the Carter administration. Southern Journal of Agricultural Economics, 10 (1) 50.

Heilbroner, R. (editor) (1969) Economic Means and Social Ends. Englewood Cliffs, New Jersey, USA; Prentice Hall.

Ip, P. C.; Stahl, C. W. (1978) Systems of land tenure, allocative efficiency, and economic development. American Journal of Agricultural Economics, 60 (1) 19-28.

Johnson, G. L.; Zerby, L. K. (1973) What Economists Do About Values. East Lansing, Michigan, USA; Department of Agricultural Economics, Michigan State University.

Knight, F. (1922) Ethics and the economic interpretation. Quarterly Journal of Economics, 36, 458.

McGreal, I. P. (1970) Problems of Ethics. Scranton, Pennsylvania, USA; Chandler Publishing Co.

Meadows, D. H.; and others (1972) The Limits to Growth. New York; New American Signet.

Moore, G. E. (1903) Principia Ethica. Cambridge; Cambridge University Press, 1956 edition.

Schumpeter, J. (1954) History of Economic Analysis. Oxford; Oxford University Press.

Simpson, J. R. (forthcoming) Toward a Third Alternative: Ethics and International Development.

Stanton, B. F. (1978) Perspective on farm size. American Journal of Agricultural Economics, 60 (5) 727-737.

Survey of International Development (1975) 12 (1) 1.

Weber, M. The Methodology of the Social Sciences.

OPENER'S REMARKS--Norman J. Beaton

The topic of Simpson's paper certainly coincides with the general theme of this conference, but his paper is more abstract, in a positive sense, than many of the other papers in a number of ways. It is futuristic, it has a global perspective, and it challenges the thought processes of agricultural economists as it stresses the viewpoint that we may be too pedestrian in our approach to the scientific method if we do not further integrate the precepts of moral philosophy into our work.

Simpson points out that, in the forthcoming decade, the issue of allocating scarce resources among the people of the world will become increasingly significant. In essence, he attributes this situation to the energy crisis and an ever expanding world population. He stresses that ethical issues will become much more prominent in achieving the goals of both national and international development.

The central theme of the paper is that agricultural economists can and should incorporate ethics into their problem solving tasks. Simpson feels that economists' training in objectivity will enable them to deal adequately with problems that have some ethical constraints. I would question whether the leap from training in objectivity to actually dealing with ethical constraints is that simple. This difficulty has been recognized in part by Simpson and others who have expressed the viewpoint that the tools of economists are not adequate to deal properly with ethical issues. By what process do agricultural economists acquire a formal knowledge of moral philosophy, or is such a knowledge necessary? How are they to learn to integrate this knowledge of moral philosophy into the basket of tools that they already posses? Does this integration have implications for the discipline of agricultural economics as a whole and the teaching of courses in research methodology in particular?

The apparent change in emphasis from maximizing growth rates to improving the quality of life has caused a great deal of concern in many developing countries. In the past, economic and political goals were of prime importance. Simpson states that the key is helping people to achieve their own goals with the state and society assisting when appropriate. What happens in countries where the objectives of the state are foremost? Other than perhaps being given lip service, how compatible would the concept of helping people to achieve their goals be in those countries? For example, what implications does the imposition of martial law have? The goals of the state may be different than the views of a large segment of the population. This poses a particular problem to the agricultural economist working in the field of international development.

I somewhat question the central theme of this paper which implies that we agricultural economists do not utilize moral philosophy (or at least not enough of it) in our work. A strict positivist might take this viewpoint. I would argue that we implicitly utilize ethics (maybe in a very informal way) in all of our work. This is especially apparent in earlier writings as Simpson acknowledges in his paper. On most applied problems, especially in international development, it would be very difficult to separate the normative from the positive aspects.

RAPPORTEUR'S REPORT--Philip J. Thair

Everyone is involved with moral questions. But why deny the title of agricultural economist to someone who works in the area of "what is, will be, or could be"? Value judgments are often concealed in constraints, and constraints may be used as a means of avoiding value judgments.

In earlier days we had many normative schools, but a heterogeneity of value bases. What you know, and how you know what you know, were major questions. Now we must establish such a dialectic toward truth. Today, education of agricultural economists is very homogeneous, and we must struggle with problems of values and moral philosophy. Whose vision are we to address, that of people as a whole, or that of the policymaker? How many are for the vision, and how many against it?

Simpson responded that philosophy is everybody's business. We must recognize that we must become more aware that many questions involve a philosophical basis. As we go through time, more and more issues will have a philosophical overtone. He did not look at vision in particular. He argued that we talk about goals or targets. These are part of one's vision of how society should be organized. More specifically, we must recognize that the people are the state, and the state is for the good of the people.

Contributing to the discussion were Rufus O. Adegboye, James T. Bonnen, Denis K. Britton, John D. M. Hardie, and George T. Jones.

NAME INDEX

Abalu, G.O.I., 15
Abkin, M.H., 124, 127
Adamowicz, M., 97
Adams, D.W., 46, 304
Adams, R.I., 104
Adegboye, R.O., 325
Agrawal, R.C., 22, 144
Ah, J. von, 178, 180
Ahn, C., 131
Ahsan, S.M., 181
Akinwumi, J.A., 20, 77
Al-Zand, O.A., 8
Anderson, K., 162, 177
Anderson, R.W., 210
Anderson, W.J., 160
Antrobus, G.G., 22
Arcus, P.L., 224
Ashton, J., v

Bachman, K.L., viii, 248
Baker, C.B., x, 124
Bale, M.D., 187
Bansil, P.C., 21, 223, 231
Baquet, A.E., 277
Barichello, R.R., v
Basler, A., 189
Bassett, L.C., 296, 303, 304
Bateman, D.I., 144, 273
Bates, R.F., 192, 198, 200
Bauer, S., 143
Beaton, N.J., 324
Bell, C., 283
Belshaw, D.G.R., 177, 294
Beusmann, V., viii
Biggs, S., 170
Bird, A.R., 74
Blanc, M., 316
Bollman, R.D., 57
Bonnen, J.T., 149, 325
Bourne, C., iv
Braithwaite, W.M., 186
Braun, J. von, 77, 225
Breimyer, H.F., 262, 273
Britton, D.K., 142, 143, 318, 325
Brossier, J., 33, 316
Brun, A.H., 142, 143, 247, 316
Byerlee, D., 170

Capstick, C.W., 251
Chase, L., 64, 69
Cherene, L.J., 124
Chirapanda, S., 113
Choe, Y., 317
Cleave, J.H., 177
Collinson, M., 170

Colwell, M.T., 93, 94, 96
Conklin, F.S., 263
Connor, L.J., 178, 180
Cook, M.L., 267

Dahlgren, C.E., 240
Dalton, G.E., 155, 161, 304
Daly, R.F., 144, 149
Day, R., 125
Deaton, B.J., 297
Dettwiler, E., 168
Donaldson, G.F., 108
Drummond, H.E., 251
D'Silva, B., 15
Due, J.M., 47
Duncan-Watt, J., 94

Edmondson, V.W., 180
Edwards, C., 178, 316
Edwards, G.W., 103, 178, 180
Elterich, G.J., ix
Estacio, F. de F., 198

Fan, Y., 124
Farrell, K.R., vi
Fekete, F., 316
Fendru, I., 8
Ferguson, D.S., 23
Ferro, O., ix
Fitch, J.B., 26, 108, 226
Fox, R.W., 3
Fraenkel, R., 231, 304
Freshwater, D., 116
Furtan, W.H., 178
Futa, M., 232

Gilshon, A., iii
Goncalves, A.S., 118
Gonzales, L.A., 93
Goueli, A.A., 26
Green, D.A.G., 177, 305
Gupta, T.R., 23, 223, 224

Hadiwigeno, S. 191
Haebler, C., 257
Haines, M., 8, 262, 314
Halcrow, H.G., 156
Hamilton, W.E., 271, 318
Hardie, J.D.M., 74, 76, 325
Harrington, L., 170
Harsh, S.B., iv
Havlicek Jr., J., 179
Hedley, D.D., 191
Henrichsmeyer, W., 142, 143
Herath, H.M.G., 289

328